ECOLOGICAL URBANISM

ECOLOGICAL URBANISM

Edited by Mohsen Mostafavi
with Gareth Doherty

Harvard University
Graduate School of Design

Lars Müller Publishers

Contents

12   **Why Ecological Urbanism? Why Now?**
Mohsen Mostafavi

ANTICIPATE

56   **Advancement versus Apocalypse**
Rem Koolhaas

72   **Zeekracht**
OMA

78   **Mumbai on My Mind:
Some Thoughts on Sustainability**
Homi K. Bhabha

84   **Urban Earth: Mumbai**
Daniel Raven-Ellison and Kye Askins

94   **Notes on the Third Ecology**
Sanford Kwinter

106   **Social Inequality and Climate Change**
Ulrich Beck

110   **For a Post-Environmentalism:
Seven Suggestions for a New Athens
Charter *and* The Weak Metropolis**
Andrea Branzi

114   **Weak Work:
Andrea Branzi's "Weak Metropolis"
and the Projective Potential of an
"Ecological Urbanism"**
Charles Waldheim

122   **From "Sustain" to "Ability"**
JDS Architects

124   **Forty Years Later–
Back to a Sub-lunar Earth**
Bruno Latour

COLLABORATE

130   **Art Fieldwork**
Giuliana Bruno

132   **Ecological Urbanism
and/as Urban Metaphor**
Lawrence Buell

134   **Black and White in Green Cities**
Lizabeth Cohen

136   **The Return of Nature**
Preston Scott Cohen and Erika Naginski

138   **Urban Ecological Practices:
Félix Guattari's *Three Ecologies***
Verena Andermatt Conley

140   **Retrofitting the City**
Leland D. Cott

142   **Productive Urban Environments**
Margaret Crawford

SENSE

146   **The City from the Perspective of the Nose**
Sissel Tolaas

156   **Urban Earth: Mexico City**
Daniel Raven-Ellison

164   **CitySense: An Urban-Scale Sensor Network**
Matt Welsh and Josh Bers

166   **Eat Love**
Marije Vogelzang

168   **Self-Engineering Ecologies**
Christine Outram, Assaf Biderman, and Carlo Ratti

174   **There's More to Green than Meets the Eye:
Green Urbanism in Bahrain**
Gareth Doherty

184   **Play Me, I'm Yours**
Luke Jerram

186   **Mapping Main Street**
Jesse Shapins, Kara Oehler, Ann Heppermann,
and James Burns

CURATE

190 **Curating Resources**
Niall Kirkwood

194 **The Sea and Monsoon Within:
A Mumbai Manifesto**
Anuradha Mathur and Dilip da Cunha

208 **Transcendent Eco-cities
or Urban Ecological Security?**
Mike Hodson and Simon Marvin

218 **New Waterscapes for Singapore**
Herbert Dreiseitl

222 **To Raise the Water Level in a Fishpond**
Zhang Huan

224 **Envisioning Ecological Cities**
Mitchell Joachim

230 **Return to Nature**
Sandi Hilal, Alessandro Petti, and Eyal Weizman

236 **Harmonia 57**
Triptyque

238 **Grounding a Sustainable Urban Strategy**
Michael Van Valkenburgh Associates

240 **Center Street Plaza**
Hood Design

PRODUCE

244 **Energy Sub-structure,
Supra-structure, Infra-structure**
D. Michelle Addington

252 **Wave Farm**
Pelamis Wave Power Ltd.

254 **CR Land Guanganmen Green
Technology Showroom**
Vector Architects

256 **Aux Fermes, Citoyens!**
Dorothée Imbert

268 **Local River: Home Storage Unit
for Fish and Greens**
Mathieu Lehanneur with Anthony van den Bossche

270 **Soft Cities**
KVA MATx

274 **The ZEDfactory**
Bill Dunster

280 **Logroño Eco-city**
MVRDV

282 **The Big-Foot Revolution**
Kongjian Yu

292 *La Tour Vivante,* **Eco-tower**
soa architectes

COLLABORATE

296 **Management Challenges in Urban
Transformation: Organizing to Learn**
Amy C. Edmondson

298 **Air Purification in Cities**
David Edwards

300 **Social Justice and Ecological Urbanism**
Susan S. Fainstein

302 **Governing the Ecological City**
Gerald E. Frug

304 **Underground Future**
Peter Galison

306 **Temperate and Bounded**
Edward Glaeser

308 **Bioinspired Adaptive Architecture
and Sustainability**
Donald E. Ingber

INTERACT

312 **Urban Ecology and the Arrangement of Nature in Urban Regions**
Richard T. T. Forman

324 **The Agency of Ecology**
Chris Reed

330 **New York City Infrastructure**
Christoph Niemann

332 **Redefining Infrastructure**
Pierre Bélanger

350 **User-Generated Urbanism**
Rebar

356 **Situating Urban Ecological Experiments in Public Space**
Alexander J. Felson and Linda Pollak

364 **A Holistic View of the Urban Phenomenon**
Barcelona Urban Ecology Agency

370 **Gwanggyo New City Park System**
Yoonjin Park and Jungyoon Kim (PARKKIM)

372 **A Methodology for Urban Innovation**
Alfonso Vegara, Mark Dwyer, and Aaron Kelley

374 **Greenmetropolis**
Henri Bava, Erik Behrens, Steven Craig, and Alex Wall

MOBILIZE

380 **Mobility, Infrastructure, and Society**
Richard Sommer

382 **Sustainable Urban Mobility through Light Electric Vehicles**
William J. Mitchell

398 **Sustainable Mobility in Action**
Federico Parolotto

402 **Sustaining the City in the Face of Advanced Marginality**
Loïc Wacquant

406 **A General Theory of Sustainable Urbanism**
Andrés Duany

412 **The Political Ecology of Ecological Urbanism**
Paul Robbins

416 **The SynCity Urban Energy System Model**
Niels Schulz, Nilay Shah, David Fisk, James Keirstead, Nouri Samsatli, Aruna Sivakumar, Celine Weber, and Ellin Saunders

420 **Oil City: Petro-landscapes and Sustainable Futures**
Michael Watts

425 **Niger Delta Oil Fields**
Ed Kashi

428 **The Upway**
Rafael Viñoly

430 **GSD RESEARCH**
Nairobi Studio
Jacques Herzog and Pierre de Meuron

MEASURE

444 **Five Ecological Challenges for the Contemporary City**
Stefano Boeri

454 **Revolutionizing Architecture**
Jeremy Rifkin

456 **The Canary Project**
Susannah Sayler

458 **"Performalism": Environmental Metrics and Urban Design**
Susannah Hagan

468 **Nature Culture**
Kathryn Moore

472 **Investigating the Importance of Customized Energy Model Inputs: A Case Study of Gund Hall**
Holly A. Wasilowski and Christoph F. Reinhart

476 **Perception of Urban Density**
Vicky Cheng and Koen Steemers

482 **London's Estuary Region**
Sir Terry Farrell

488 **Urban Earth: London**
Daniel Raven-Ellison

496 **Sustainability Initiatives in London**
Camilla Ween

500 **Moving beyond LEED:**
Evaluating Green at the Urban Scale
Thomas Schroepfer

502 **Landscapes of Specialization**
Bill Rankin

504 **GSD RESEARCH**
Half a Million Trees: Prototyping Sites
and Systems for Sustainable Cities
Kristin Frederickson and Gary Hilderbrand

506 **SlaveCity**
Atelier Van Lieshout

510 **EcoBox/Self-Managed Eco-urban Network**
atelier d'architecture autogérée

512 **Temporary Urban Scene:**
Beach on the Moon
Ecosistema Urbano

COLLABORATE

516 **Comfort and Carbon Footprint**
Alex Krieger

518 **Ecological Urbanism and Health Equity:**
An Ecosocial Perspective
Nancy Krieger

520 **Nature, Infrastructures,**
and the Urban Condition
Antoine Picon

522 **Sustainability and Lifestyle**
Spiro Pollalis

524 **Ecological Urbanism and the Landscape**
Martha Schwartz

526 **Old Dark**
John Stilgoe

528 **Religious Studies and Ecological Urbanism**
Donald K. Swearer

530 **Ecological Urbanism**
and East Asian Literatures
Karen Thornber

ADAPT

536 **Insurgent Ecologies:**
(Re)Claiming Ground in Landscape
and Urbanism
Nina-Marie Lister

548 **Performative Wood:**
Integral Computational Design for
a Climate-Responsive Timber Surface
Structure
Achim Menges

554 **Shrinking Gotham's Footprint**
Laurie Kerr

560 **Adaptivity in Architecture**
Hoberman Associates, Ziggy Drozdowski
and Shawn Gupta

568 **GSD RESEARCH**
Climate Change, Water, Land Development,
and Adaptation: Planning with Uncertainty
(Almere, the Netherlands)
Armando Carbonell, Martin Zogran, and Dirk Sijmons

INCUBATE

572 **Balances and Challenges**
of Integrated Practice
Toshiko Mori

578 **The Luxury of Reduction:**
On the Role of Architecture
in Ecological Urbanism
Matthias Sauerbruch

584 **Bank of America**
     Cook+Fox Architects

588 **GSD RESEARCH**
     A Place in Heaven, A Place in Hell:
     Tactical Operations in São Paulo
     Christian Werthmann, Fernando de Mello Franco,
     and Byron Stigge

590 **In Situ: Site Specificity**
     in Sustainable Architecture
     Anja Thierfelder and Matthias Schuler

598 **Progetto Bioclimatico**
     Mario Cucinella

600 **Wangzhuang Eco-city of Agriculture**
     Arup

606 **Ecosystemic Master Planning,**
     DISEZ Region, Senegal
     ecoLogicStudio

608 **Vegetal City: Dreaming the Green Utopia**
     Luc Schuiten

610 **Verticalism (The Future of the Skyscraper)**
     Iñaki Ábalos

616 **Urban Prototypes**
     Raoul Bunschoten

622 **Taiwan Strait Climate Change Incubator**
     Chora Architecture and Urbanism

629 **THE CITY**
     Ian McHarg

630 **ECOLOGICAL URBANISM**
     CONFERENCE BLOG

APPENDIX

642 **Contributors**

648 **Acknowledgments**

650 **Index**

654 **Illustration Credits**

Why Ecological Urbanism?
Why Now?

Mohsen Mostafavi

Preamble—The world's population continues to grow, resulting
in a steady migration from rural to urban areas. Increased numbers
of people and cities go hand in hand with a greater exploitation of
the world's limited resources. Every year, more cities are feeling the
devastating impacts of this situation. What are we to do? What
means do we have as designers to address this challenging reality?

For decades now, reminders have come from many sources about
the difficulties that face us and our environment. The Brundtland Report
of 1987, scientific studies on the impact of global warming, and former
U.S. Vice President Al Gore's passionate pleas have all made their
mark. But a growing concern for the environment is matched by a great
deal of skepticism and resistance. The United States has not only failed
to ratify the Kyoto Protocol, it is also, along with Canada and many of
the Gulf States, among the largest per capita users of energy resources.
The failure of the Copenhagen Summit to produce a legally binding
agreement further confirms the scale of the challenges that lie ahead.
The concept of "one planet living" can only be a distant dream—and
not just for the worst offenders, but for everyone else as well.

Architects have been aware of the issues for some time, of course,
but the proportion of those committed to sustainable and ecological
practices has remained small. And until recently, much of the work
produced as sustainable architecture has been of poor quality. Early
examples were focused mainly around the capacities of simple
technologies to produce energy and recycle waste. Sustainable architecture, itself rudimentary, often also meant an alternative lifestyle

of renunciation, stripped of much pleasure. This has changed, and is changing still. Sustainable design practices are entering the mainstream of the profession. In the United States, LEED certification—the national standard for the evaluation of sustainable buildings—is being more widely applied. But there remains the problem that the moral imperative of sustainability and, by implication, of sustainable design, tends to supplant disciplinary contribution. Thus sustainable design is not always seen as representing design excellence or design innovation. This situation will continue to provoke skepticism and cause tension between those who promote disciplinary knowledge and those who push for sustainability, unless we are able to develop novel ways of design thinking that can contribute to both domains.

The second issue concerns scale. Much of the work undertaken by sustainable architects has been relatively limited in scope. LEED certification, for example, deals primarily with the architectural object, and not with the larger infrastructure of the territory of our cities and towns. Because the challenges of rapid urbanization and limited global resources have become much more pressing, there is a need to find alternative design approaches that will enable us to consider the large scale differently than we have done in the past. The urban, as the site of complex relations (economic, political, social, and cultural), requires an equally complex range of perspectives and responses that can address both current conditions and future possibilities. The aim of this book is to provide that framework—a framework that through the conjoining of ecology and urbanism can provide the knowledge, methods, and clues of what the urban can be in the years to come.

Why Ecological Urbanism?

The city is so vast and we have so much to say to each other.

–François Périer to Giulietta Masina in Federico Fellini's *Nights of Cabiria* [1] (1957)

Ecological Urbanism—is that not an oxymoron in the same way that a hybrid SUV is an oxymoron? How can the city, with all its mechanisms of consumption—its devouring of energy, its insatiable demand for food—ever be ecological? In one sense the "project of urbanism," if we can call it such, runs counter to that of ecology, with its emphasis on the interrelationship of organisms and the environment—an emphasis that invariably excludes human intervention. And yet it is relatively easy to imagine a city that is more careful in its use of resources than is currently the norm, more energy-efficient in its daily operations—like a hybrid car. But is that enough? Is it enough for architects, landscape architects, and urbanists to simply conceive of the future of their various disciplines in terms of engineering and constructing a more energy-efficient environment? As important as the question of energy is today, the emphasis on quantity—on energy reduction—obscures its relationship with the qualitative value of things.

In other words, we need to view the fragility of the planet and its resources as an opportunity for speculative design innovations rather than as a form of technical legitimation for promoting conventional solutions. By extension, the problems confronting our cities and regions would then become opportunities to define a new approach. Imagining an urbanism that is other than the status quo requires a new sensibility—one that has the capacity to incorporate and accommodate the inherent conflictual conditions between ecology and urbanism. This is the territory of ecological urbanism.

Three Narratives—There is ample evidence all around us of the scope of the challenge we face. A while ago, a single issue of *The Guardian* newspaper in the United Kingdom by chance carried three articles that addressed fundamental questions of sustainability.[2] Such stories are now typical of what one reads on a daily basis and constitute the norm rather than an exception.

The first, by Canadian political journalist Naomi Klein, explored the connections between the invasion of Iraq and the oil boom in Alberta. "For four years now, Alberta and Iraq have been connected to each other through a kind of invisible see-saw," says Klein. "As Baghdad burns, destabilizing the entire region and sending oil prices soaring, Calgary booms." Klein's article gives a glimpse of a large territory being laid to waste in the search for oil. Alberta has "vast deposits of bitumen—black, tarlike goo that is mixed up with sand, clay, water and oil ... approximately 2.5 trillion barrels of the stuff, the largest hydrocarbon deposits in the world." The processes involved in turning these tar sands into crude are both complex and costly. One method involves open-cast mining. For this, great forests have to be leveled and the topsoil removed before huge, specially designed machines dig out the bitumen and place it in the world's largest two-story dump trucks. The tar is then chemically diluted and spun around until the oil rises to the top. The waste products, the tailings, are dumped in ponds that according to Klein are larger than the region's natural lakes. A second method involves the drilling of large pipes that push steam deep underground to melt the tar before a second pipe transfers it through various stages of refining.

Both of these processes are much more expensive than conventional oil drilling; they also produce three to four times the amount of greenhouse gases. Despite this, they became financially viable after the invasion of Iraq, and resulted in Canada overtaking Saudi Arabia as the leading supplier of oil to the United States. The "success" of this enterprise has led the Pembina Institute, a nonprofit think-tank that advances sustainable energy solutions, to warn of the threat to an area of boreal forest as large as the state of Florida. More recently the Institute, together with Ecojustice, has presented evidence documenting the damaging effects of oil-sands development on Alberta's fresh-water resources. The extent of this environmental devastation, encompassing land, air, and water—all in aid of relatively cheap oil for the consumer and hefty profits for the oil companies—is a vivid reminder of the urgent need for future conurbations to discover and design alternative and efficient ways of using energy resources.

The second story involved the construction of a high-rise residence in Mumbai for one of India's richest tycoons, Mukesh Ambani, chairman of the country's largest private-sector company, the Reliance Group. The building, called Antilla after a mythical island, is equivalent in height to a sixty-story tower block. Besides providing accommodation for Ambani, his mother, his wife, three children, and 600 full-time staff, it comes with its own helipad, health club, and six floors of parking. The family's proposed move from its current residence, a mere fourteen stories high, has been given additional impetus by the rapid growth of the Indian economy and the simmering rivalry between Mukesh Ambani and his brother. According to Praful Bidwai, a local newspaper columnist quoted in the article, "there is growing anger about such absurd spending," as the divide between rich and poor is becoming obscene. Even the name of this "house" suggests the idea of separation and the desire for autonomy from the rest of Mumbai. But is there such a thing as our "individual share" of the resources that our cities have to offer? What are the guidelines for evaluating the impact of a building on the city, not just in terms of its aesthetic appearance but also in relation to its ethical performance?

The third story was about the making of a film, *Grow Your Own*, which chronicles the progress of a group of traumatized asylum-seekers as they work their inner-city allotment gardens in Liverpool. The film was inspired by the research of a psychotherapist, Margrit Ruegg, who runs a refugee support center. Her experience had shown the therapeutic as well as the physical benefits of gardening. "Many [refugees] had left such places as Somalia, Angola and the Balkans in horrific circumstances," says Carl Hunter, one of the producers of the film. "War had robbed them of their homes, their families and, in many cases, their identities. Margrit's experience was that, in the confinement of a room with a desk and a chair, the refugees clammed up. But once she'd had the idea of giving them each a little plot of land, they were able, over time, to open up to her." The story of these allotments is not simply limited to the lives of the refugees but is in turn entangled with the local community—with the tensions and conflicts between people of diverse cultural and ethnic backgrounds. In tending to their vegetables on the plots, alongside their neighbors, the participants are able, in a modest and unsentimental way, to construct a collaborative and productive ground for communication and integration.

These three stories are all facets of the multiple realities that our individual and group actions shape in the context of the contemporary urban domain. Taken together, they illuminate Gregory Bateson's argument that, in contradistinction to the Darwinian theory of natural selection, "the unit of survival is organism plus the environment."[3] A broader articulation of Bateson's ideas can be found in Félix Guattari's *The Three Ecologies*, a profound yet concise manifestation of a relational and holistic approach to our understanding of ecological issues. Guattari's ethico-political concept of "ecosophy" is developed in the form of three ecological "registers" (environment, social relations, and human subjectivity). Like Bateson, Guattari places emphasis on the role that humans play in relation to ecological practices. And according to him, the appropriate response to the ecological crisis can only be achieved on a global scale, "provided that it brings about an authentic political, social and cultural revolution, reshaping the objectives of the production of both material and immaterial assets."[4]

One of the most important aspects of Guattari's argument concerns the interrelations between individual responsibilities and group actions. An emphasis on the role of the "ecosophic problematic," as a way to shape human existence within new historical contexts, leads to a proposed reformulation of the "subject." In place of the Cartesian subject, whose being is solely defined by its thinking, Guattari has "components of subjectification" who engage with real "territories of existence," that is, with the everyday domains of their lives and actions. These alternative processes of subjectification are not rooted in science but instead embrace a new "ethico-aesthetic" paradigm as their primary source of inspiration.

Guattari's position, developed at the end of the 1980s, is as much a criticism of a depoliticized structuralism/postmodernism that "has accustomed us to a vision of the world drained of the significance of human intervention" as it is an ethical and aesthetic project that promotes the "reshaping of the objectives of the production of both material and immaterial assets." Such a radical approach, if applied to the urban domain, would result in a form of ecological design practice that does not simply take account of the fragility

The city historically constructed is no longer
lived and is no longer understood practically. It
is only an object of cultural consumption for
tourists, for aestheticism, avid for spectacles and
the picturesque. Even for those who seek to
understand it with warmth, it is gone. Yet, the
urban remains in a state of dispersed and
alienated actuality, as kernel and virtuality. What
the eyes and analysis perceive on the ground
can at best pass for the shadow of the future
object in the light of a rising sun. It is impossible
to envisage the reconstitution of the old city,
only the construction of a new one on new foundations, on another scale and in other conditions,
in another society. The prescription is: there
cannot be a going back (towards the traditional
city), nor a headlong flight, towards a colossal
and shapeless agglomeration. In other words, for
what concerns the city the object of science
is not given. The past, the present, the possible
cannot be separated. What is being studied
is a *virtual object*, which thought studies, which
calls for new approaches.

–Henri Lefebvre[5] (1968)

of the ecosystem and the limits on resources but considers such conditions the essential basis for a new form of creative imagining.

Extending Guattari's suggestion that the "ecosophic problematic" has the capacity to define a new form of human existence, we might consider the impact of the ecological paradigm not only on ourselves and our social actions in relation to the environment, but also on the very methods of thinking that we apply to the development of the disciplines that provide the frameworks for shaping those environments. Every discipline has the responsibility to constantly create its own conditions of progress—its own instabilities—and today it is valuable to recognize that we have a unique opportunity to reconsider the core of the disciplines that help us think about the phenomenon of the urban: urban planning and design.

The prevailing conventions of design practice have demonstrated a limited capacity both to respond to the scale of the ecological crisis and to adapt their established ways of thinking. In this context, ecological urbanism can be seen as a means of providing a set of sensibilities and practices that can help enhance our approaches to urban development. This is not to imply that ecological urbanism is a totally new and singular mode of design practice. Rather, it utilizes a multiplicity of old and new methods, tools, and techniques in a cross-disciplinary and collaborative approach toward urbanism developed through the lens of ecology. These practices must address the retrofitting of existing urban conditions as well as our plans for the cities of the future.

In recognizing the productive values of the relationships between reality and this project, the methods of ecological urbanism include the feedback reciprocities that Henri Lefebvre described as "transduction."[6] Take the case of the Promenade Plantée in Paris, the precursor of the High Line in New York City, where a disused railway line, part of which is on top of a viaduct, has been transformed—reused—as an urban park that traverses a variety of conditions and prospects. Given the undulating topography of the city, the promenade affords an ever-changing sectional relationship to its surroundings. As a result, the park produces a different experience of the city

compared, for example, to that of a Parisian boulevard. This is achieved through the discovery and construction of stark juxtapositions and contrasts that include the experience of the city from different horizon lines.

This type of urban recycling of the remnants of the industrial city benefits from the unexpected and given context of the site that needs to be remade, a context far from a tabula rasa. In these examples, the site acts as a mnemonic device for the making of the new. The result is a type of relational approach between the terrain, the built, and the viewer's participatory experiences. Other examples of this type of development include the Downsview competition in Toronto, and the Forum area of the North East Coastal Park project in Barcelona, designed by Ábalos and Herreros, which combines infrastructure and public space by juxtaposing a municipal waste-management complex with a new waterfront beach on the site of an artificial landfill.

A reference point for many such contemporary projects is the unbuilt competition entry for the Parc de la Villette by OMA. The architects claim that their 1982 proposal was not for a definitive park but for a "method" that combined "programmatic instability with architectural specificity,"[7] a condition that would eventually generate a park. In essence, the design involved the conceptual and metaphorical turning on its side of the section of Manhattan's high-rise Athletic Club, with its variegated program spread horizontally rather than vertically. This process also included a rethinking of the relationship between architecture and landscape, through a suppression of the three-dimensionality of architecture.[8]

It is also no coincidence that OMA's La Villette scheme in turn pays homage to another theoretical project, Frank Lloyd Wright's Broadacre City; but whereas Wright proposes to cultivate the surface of the country to provide the individual with a dispersed and equitable portion of land, OMA's emphasis on congestion demands a gathering together—interaction—rather than separation. Broadacre City is a manifestation of anti-urbanity, while OMA's "park" superimposes urbanism on the artifice of landscape. The operative design procedures undertaken by OMA—or for that matter by Bernard Tschumi in the selected and subsequently built version of La Villette—are suggestive of the potentials of an ethico-aesthetic design practice that brings together architecture, landscape architecture, and urbanism.

Despite these examples, one could argue that the traditional divisions between architecture, landscape architecture, planning, and urban design are still necessary for the formation and accumulation of specific disciplinary knowledge. But each individual discipline is of limited value in responding to the range and diversity of contemporary urban issues. The pitfalls of acting in isolation become especially evident in the extreme conditions of the most densely populated conurbations around the globe, where it is much harder to identify disciplinary boundaries. While a collaborative mode of working among various areas of design expertise is mandatory in thinking about the contemporary and future city, the transdisciplinary approach of ecological urbanism gives designers a potentially more fertile means of addressing the challenges facing the urban environment.

Yet another key characteristic of ecological urbanism is its recognition of the scale and scope of the impact of ecology, which extends beyond the urban territory. The city, for all its importance, can no longer be thought of only as a physical artifact; instead, we must be aware of the dynamic relationships, both visible and invisible, that exist among the various domains of a larger terrain of urban as well as rural ecologies. Distinctions between rural and urban contingencies can lead to uncertainties and contradictions—calling for unconventional solutions. This regional, holistic approach, with its consequent national and global considerations, demonstrates the multi-scalar quality of ecological urbanism. Much of the knowledge necessary for this mode of design practice can be gained from disciplines such as environmental planning and landscape ecology, with an emphasis on biodiversity. But this must be supplemented with advances from a host of other fields, from economics to history, from public health to cultural studies and (despite Guattari's warnings) the sciences. The insights found at the interface of these disciplines will ultimately provide the most synthetic and valuable material for alternative multi-scalar design strategies.

The visionary Italian architect and urbanist Andrea Branzi has for many years espoused the advantages of a different approach toward the city—one that is not reliant on a compositional or typological approach. Rather, for Branzi it is the fluidity of the city, its capacity to be diffuse and enzymatic in character, that merits acknowledgment. In a series of projects that deliberately blur the boundaries between the disciplines (and are as much indebted to art practice as they are to agriculture and network culture), Branzi has proposed an adaptive urbanism based on their symbiotic relationship. A key feature of this type of urbanism—like the agricultural territory—is its capacity to be reversible, evolving, and provisory. These qualities are necessary in response to the changing needs of a society in a state of constant reorganization. In particular, the open areas that are no longer in use in many cities, such as New Orleans, could become productive domains where residences, workplaces, and spaces of leisure could be intertwined. Branzi's curating of the urban territory is in some sense a form of art practice, where the parallelism with agriculture is presented in a highly conscious manner that is fully aware of its aesthetic and visual qualities. It is a form of nature that resists naturalism and uses its references to the agricultural territory in an operative and temporal way.

More specifically, the blurring of boundaries—real and virtual, as well as urban and rural—implies a greater connection and complementarity between the various parts of a given territory. Conceptually akin to acupuncture, the interventions in and transformations of an area often have a significant impact beyond perceived physical limits. Thinking simultaneously at small and large scales calls for an awareness that is currently unimaginable in many existing patterns of legal, political, and economic activity. One of the major challenges of ecological urbanism is therefore to define the conditions of governance under which it could operate that would result in a more cohesive regional planning model.

The network of relations among multiple localities at different scales provides a window onto the ways in which we could reconsider the implications of developments such as sprawl. According to a recent study, "New York City has 47,500 vacant land parcels totalling more than 17,000 acres, New York City faces an acute housing shortage, and the fastest growing part of the New York area is in the Pocono Mountains of north-eastern Pennsylvania. There, far from the city core, forests are being cleared for big box stores, high-speed roadways, and low-density subdivisions for long-distance commuters."[9] What is the impact of this form of automobile-based living on the health of the community? One effect can be seen in the alarming rate of increase in the proportion of Americans who are overweight, from 24 percent in 1960, to 47 percent in 1980, to no less than 63 percent today. Surely the problem of obesity is fueled by the ongoing development of residential communities with so much emphasis on the automobile and so little encouragement of walking. Other factors include the general lack of investment in public transport in the United States compared to most European countries, where urban and regional infrastructures are seen as necessary provisions for the citizens.

These figures show the importance of density as a determining criterion of ecological urbanism. The importance of long-range planning, together with the potential benefits as well as challenges of denser, more compact cities, necessitates a much closer collaboration between the public and private sectors. Although an increasing number of private development companies, for ethical as well as financial reasons, are now espousing the values of sustainability, their concerns are often focused on the technical performance of individual buildings rather than on the larger territory. The articulation of long-range public policies defined by an ethico-aesthetic principle—on topics such as density, use, infrastructure, and biodiversity—will therefore require a greater imaginative involvement than has been the norm in the past.

Because the public sector deals with the operations and maintenance of existing cities, it bears primary responsibility for considering alternative ways of addressing these issues.

Many progressive cities already have active sustainability policies and procedures for the greening of the urban environment. But most of these plans are largely pragmatic, with a focus on energy reduction or the addition of green spaces. The question is: Could such efforts be transformed by the approach of ecological urbanism? Couldn't the everyday elements, needs, and functions of the city be creatively imagined in new and unconventional ways that are not simply subjugated to the imperatives of the ecological?

British architectural historian and critic Reyner Banham, for example, argued that the form of a city matters little as long as it works. This for him was especially the case with Los Angeles, which he believed broke all the rules. Banham wrote and spoke brilliantly about the city, with the enthusiasm of a serious tourist. His *Los Angeles: The Architecture of Four Ecologies* discovers the logic and the spectacle of this horizontally expanding metropolis.[10] It is hard to imagine many other examples of urban sprawl today that match the sense of impermanence, mobility, and fantasy that LA presented in the late 1960s and early 1970s (and to some degree today). But Banham's contextualization of the evolution of Los Angeles is itself a call for our openness to unexpected models of urban development—ones that are opportunistic in their modes of practice and use of available resources.

During the sixteenth century, the city of Rome had an ambitious plan linking the private initiative of watering the extensive gardens of the wealthy with the provision of external wall fountains for the mass of the people: water was both a necessity and a source of pleasure—as exemplified in later manifestations such as the fountains at San Carlo alle Quattro Fontane or in Piazza Navona. This is of course still the case today, but we have become more disconnected from the pleasures of water in our cities, oblivious to either its sources or its distribution. And this invisibility, this stealth quality, applies to most other resources and services as well. One can point to some contemporary parallels with the Roman example, such as the formation of pocket parks in the city of New York, or a range of major waterfront developments such as those in Baltimore, San Francisco, Monaco, Dubai,

Why Ecological Urbanism?

Singapore, and Sydney, but on the whole we underutilize the unexpected opportunities afforded by ecological practices as well as the location, functions, and daily operations of maintaining our cities. Our approach to the city has become more anesthetized, lacking the sense of wonder and achievement that characterized many urban projects in the past. We still cling to the inheritance of an Enlightenment philosophy that, for example, regarded cemeteries in the midst of the city as unhealthy and unhygienic, something be banished to the outskirts at the first possible opportunity.

Given the limitations of space, perhaps it is not unreasonable that we do the same today, not just with the bodies of the dead but also with the waste of our own consumption. Who really has a sense of the mountains of garbage that are produced by most cities (unless you happen to have been in Naples during one of the frequent strikes by city workers): out of sight, out of mind. If we don't see the garbage of our culture, both literally and metaphorically, then we are not confronting the reality of what that garbage actually says about us. One can only imagine that in New York City, with its enormous appetite for fast food and takeout, the relation between consumption and waste would produce some frightening statistics. But this interrelation can also be seen as an ethico-aesthetic, cultural, and environmental project, an opportunity based on viewing the garbage as a measure of who we are, rather than as yet another difficulty, a hindrance to be overcome technically. We must find new ways not only of dealing with the problems of waste management and recycling but also of addressing garbage more forensically, for traces, clues of what we are doing to ourselves. What kind of foods are we consuming, for example, and in what manner?

We have already witnessed an increasing interest in new ways of producing food closer to and within cities. The global transportation and distribution of food is being supplemented by more local growers, whose farmers' markets create temporal events in many cities. But in some places, such as Havana, urban allotments and other forms of productive urban landscapes are being cultivated in a more large-scale and commercial manner than ever before. These developments

provide the possibility of designing such terrains as the continuation of the urban territory—in part, as new forms of public space. Detroit, an example of a shrinking city, has been the site of various experiments in urban farming on the ever-expanding terrain between the remnants of its residential fabric. One can also imagine that a city like New Orleans, devastated by Hurricane Katrina and with little likelihood of major reconstruction any time soon, is ripe for such a project—for an urbanism that can address the vast areas of sparsely populated territory with productive and other forms of biologically diverse urban landscapes just as effectively as it can those areas still populated by a resilient community. These spaces also carry a potential for social interaction and healing that is presumably not dissimilar to the example of the allotment gardens in Liverpool.

Yet much more common than decreases in the urban population are examples of sharp rises, particularly in Asian cities, in line with the tripling of the world's population during the last century alone. The rate of population growth in many cities is so dramatic that conventional methods of planning are unable to respond to their rapid rates of transformation. The challenge of ecological urbanism is to find ways of effectively responding to these conditions. While in some instances, such as the *favelas* of Rio de Janeiro or the markets of Lagos, these cities can construct their own informal productive logics, they can nevertheless benefit from large-scale strategies that not only take account of the ecological impact of rapid urbanization but also provide the necessary resources and restorative actions for the well-being and recreation of the citizens.[11] These strategies have a long tradition, dating back to the early part of the last century and the work of Patrick Geddes, who argued for an ecological approach toward the planning of large cities. Similarly, ecological urbanism has the potential to respond to and transform other criteria that affect and shape cities, such as geography, orientation, weather, pollution, sound, and smell.

Just as geographical orientation often determines the prosperity of cities, so it can, together with other factors, produce a large degree of variability in the definition of ecological or urban practices. For example, in the case of African cities, according to AbdouMaliq Simone:

> while it is clear that the pursuit of structured plans, development agendas, and rational decision-making require economic supports and political will often lacking in impoverished societies, the apparent provisionality of African urban life also masks the degree to which residents capitalize on some of the most elemental facets of "cityness" itself… whereas planning discourses center largely on defining, consolidating, and articulating a given position in relation to others, the urban game for many Africans is to become nodes of gravity that draw attention not by standing still and defending niches, but by an ability to "show up," make oneself present, no matter the circumstances, in a kind of social promiscuity. [12]

The "informality" of many African cities points to the importance and value of participatory and activist planning by citizens. This type of bottom-up, "extraterritorial" urbanism, developed outside conventional legal and regulatory frameworks, often produces novel and ingenious solutions to urban life. It invariably also produces major problems, such as poor standards of health and hygiene. Can we not incorporate the lessons learned from the informal and provisional character of these cities into our future plans? Ecological urbanism must provide the necessary and emancipatory infrastructures for an alternative form of urbanism, one that brings together the benefits of both bottom-up and top-down approaches to urban planning.

What is a standard norm or value in parts of Africa may be unacceptable or uncommon elsewhere. The traditions, for example, of the growth of Islamic cities did not result in a singular and identifiable pattern of urban development. Rather, they were highly dependent on variable local contingencies such as climate and materials. The pitfalls of nostalgia notwithstanding, the uneven development of much of the Gulf region today, with its fetishism of the object, compares unfavorably to the principles and sensibilities of earlier traditions. The need for differentiation demands that ecological urbanism not take the form of fixed rules but promote a series of flexible principles that can be adapted to the circumstances and conditions of a particular location. Instead of

Why Ecological Urbanism?   41

the wholehearted use of an imposed, imported form of planning, non-Western nations would benefit from a more careful reexamination of the conditions, rites, and progressive social relations that are more or less specific, but not limited to their region. Today we face a situation where there is an erasure of differentiation and a surprising degree of apparent sameness of conditions and circumstances connected to urban development in various parts of the world.

Gregory Bateson, writing some forty years ago, spoke of both the need for flexibility and the difficulties in achieving it.[13] For Bateson, maintaining flexibility—of ideas, systems, and actions—was like being a tightrope-walker: to remain on the wire, you have to continually shift from one condition of instability to another, adjusting certain variables along the way (in the case of the tightrope-walker, the position of the arms and the rate of movement). But the skill of the acrobat also grows through practice and repetition—what Bateson calls the "economy of flexibility." This describes a set of practices that have survived through repeated use and come to mind spontaneously, without much introspection. And it is the dynamic interrelationship between flexibility and formed habits—habits that must be open to their own conditions of instability and change—that produces the ecology of ideas as an evolutionary process. The production of these ecologies and of ecological urbanism depends on both certain traditions of practical knowledge and the flexibility to respond to a host of networked physical and nonphysical variables.

Some designers have already shown how this might work in practice. French architect Jean Renaudie, for example, developed an architecture of social housing in the 1960s and 1970s that instead of the typical, anonymous high-rise block was based on a dense, organic arrangement of building clusters. These buildings both in the south of Paris as well as the south of France present a radical, visionary departure from the modernist idea of "existence minimum," which over time had become debased and pedantic. Renaudie designed his buildings according to a complex geometric pattern that placed as much emphasis on the outdoor areas—the terraces and gardens between the apartments—as it did on the apartments

Today it is not the city but rather the camp that is the fundamental biopolitical paradigm of the West.

–Giorgio Agamben [14] (1998)

themselves. At first, such novel care and attention to the design of low-income housing was criticized by potential inhabitants, who argued that Renaudie's design was not in keeping with the ethos of the working class. Today, of course, the buildings represent a desirable community of mixed-income residences. The buildings themselves are also one of the best examples of the use of nature in a high-rise context. Their organizational structure demonstrates the benefits of the flexibility and diversity of relations between the inside and the outside as well as their inseparability from politics.

More recently, French President Nicolas Sarkozy announced a plan for the creation of a new sustainable Greater Paris, a domain that according to Sarkozy does not belong to a single party or group, but to everyone. Despite the political subtexts of his intentions, the idea of Paris as an environmentally sensitive and integrated economic region that can merge the city with its blighted suburbs and beyond is one of the most ambitious urban planning projects of recent years. To explore this agenda, a number of architects, landscape architects, and urbanists were asked to consider Paris as the sustainable city for the post-Kyoto era. Regardless of their individual merits, the projects presented by these teams, which were exhibited at l'Institut français d'architecture, provide concrete examples of what could be done. The early emphasis on projects rather than policies is a recognition of the value of projective possibilities for the physical development of the region. This type of speculative design is a necessary precondition for making radical policies that are embedded in imaginative and anticipatory forms of spatial practice.

A key feature of the overall plan is its focus on the pragmatic necessities and liberating potentials of mobility and infrastructure by proposing the creation of a 90-mile (145-kilometer) automated rail system that would circle Paris, connecting its business centers and suburbs as well as providing additional links to the heart of the city. Given the context of the riots in 2005, creating better connections between the suburbs and the city will be a step toward greater social mobility. It is in part the lack of connectivity of social housing slums that renders them as isolated "camps" whose inhabitants are "imprisoned" within a larger territory. Whether this project will be able to survive its economic and political realities (who will finance it? who will rule the new metropolis?) has yet to be seen.

The ethico-aesthetic dimension of ecological urbanism—defined through the registers of mental, social, and environmental ecology—is directly concerned with the articulation of the interface, the liminal space, between the urban and the political. Unlike some other forms of revitalization, such as the City Beautiful movement in the past or New Urbanism today, this approach does not rely on the image, nor on social homogeneity and nostalgia, as its primary sources of inspiration, but rather recognizes the importance of the urban as the necessary site of conflictual relations. Political philosopher Chantal Mouffe makes a valuable distinction between "the political" and "politics." She says that by "the political, I refer to the dimension of antagonism which I take to be constitutive of human societies; while by politics, I refer to the set of practices and institutions through which an order is created, organizing human coexistence in the context of confliction provided by the political." Consequently, it is only when we recognize the political in relation to its agonistic dimension—the potential benefits of certain forms of conflict—that we can begin to address the central question for democratic politics.[15]

This also implies that we have to pay greater attention to the role of the urban as the provider of spaces of difference and disagreement. Disagreement, though, is not about arguing, but what is being argued—the presence or absence of a common object or idea between the participants. According to this point of view, it is rather naive, overly optimistic, and ultimately confining to expect a society of total consensus and agreement. The satisfactions of urban life are in part the pleasures of participation in the diversity of the spaces of the other. And it is physical space that provides the necessary infrastructure for alternative and democratic forms of social interaction. As Mouffe insists, "Instead of trying to design institutions which, through supposedly impartial procedures, would reconcile all interests and values, the aim of all who are interested in defending and radicalizing democracy should be to contribute to the creation of vibrant, agonistic public

Politics revolves around what is seen and what can be said about it, around who has the ability to see and the talent to speak, around the properties of spaces and the possibilities of time.

–Jacques Rancière [16] (2000)

spaces where different hegemonic political projects could be confronted."[17]

Similarly, the intention behind engaging new subjectivities and collectives through the frameworks of ecological urbanism is to engender greater opportunities for social and spatial democracy. While recognizing the significance of agonistic pluralism, the urban will also need to go beyond the purely political by acknowledging the ethical and the just. For Slavoj Žižek, "In this precise sense, ethics is a *supplement* of the political: there is no political 'taking sides' without minimal reference to some ethical normativity which transcends the sphere of the purely Political."[18] Still others have warned us about the consequences of undue emphasis on the ethical over law and politics. Jacques Rancière has argued this in the case of Guantanamo—another example of a contemporary camp— as "the paradoxical constitution of an individual's absolute right whose rights have, in fact, been absolutely negated."[19]

Guattari's conception of an ethics of the ecological is an inherently political project with a commitment to countering the global dominance of capitalism. The recent financial crisis, with all its ramifications, suggests the ongoing need for a methodological reconceptualization of our contemporary cosmopolitan condition.[20] In this context, it is now up to us to develop the aesthetic means—the projects—that propose alternative, inspiring, and ductile sensibilities for our ethico-political interactions with the environment.[21] These projects will also provide the stage for the messiness, the unpredictability, and the instability of the urban, and in turn, for more just as well as more pleasurable futures. This is both the challenge and the promise of ecological urbanism.

1 Influenced in part by his collaboration with Roberto Rossellini on *Rome, Open City* (1945), Fellini's film exposes the harsh realities of postwar Rome, its inhabitants, and their mutual entanglements.

2 *The Guardian,* June 1, 2007.

3 Gregory Bateson, *Steps to an Ecology of Mind* (New York: Ballantine, 1972; reprint Chicago: University of Chicago Press, 2000), 491. Bateson goes on to say, "Formerly we thought of a hierarchy of taxa – individual, family line, subspecies, species, etc. – as units of survival. We now see a different hierarchy of units – gene-in-organism, organism-in-environment, eco-system, etc. Ecology, in the widest sense, turns out to be the study of the interaction and survival of ideas and programs (i.e. differences, complexes of differences, etc.) in circuits."

4 Félix Guattari, *The Three Ecologies* (London and New Brunswick, NJ: Athlone Press, 2000), 28.

5 Henri Lefebvre, *Writings on Cities* (Oxford and Malden, MA: Blackwell, 1996), 148 (originally published in French in 1968 as *Le Droit à la ville*).

6 Ibid., 151. "Transduction elaborates and constructs a theoretical object, a possible object from information related to reality and a problematic posed by this reality. Transduction assumes an incessant feedback between the conceptual framework used and empirical observations. Its theory (methodology) gives shape to certain spontaneous mental operations of the planner, the architect, the sociologist, the politician and the philosopher. It introduces rigour in invention and knowledge in utopia."

7 http://www.oma.eu/ Parc de la Villette, France, Paris, 1982.

8 Ibid. Furthermore, the competition "seemed to offer the ingredients for a complete investigation of the potential for a European Culture of Congestion. Here was the par excellence metropolitan condition of Europe: a terrain vague between the historical city – itself raped by the greedy needs of the 20th century – and the plankton of the banlieue … what La Villette finally suggested was the pure exploitation of the metropolitan condition: density without architecture, a culture of 'invisible' congestion."

9 Howard Frumpkin, Lawrence Frank, and Richard Jackson, *Urban Sprawl and Public Health: Designing, Planning, and Building for Healthy Communities* (Washington, DC: Island Press, 2004), xi.

10 Reyner Banham, *Los Angeles: The Architecture of Four Ecologies,* 2d ed. (Berkeley: University of California Press, 2009; originally published in 1971).

11 The concept of "informality" is not limited to the cities of the developing world but is also at the heart of most industrial nations. This condition is often rendered more explicit through the impacts of urban migration. The Dardenne brothers filmmakers have recently dealt with this topic in *Lorna's Silence,* a film shot in the grim and gritty context of the Belgian city of Liége.

12 AbdouMaliq Simone, "The Last Shall Be First: African Urbanities and the Larger Urban World," in *Other Cities, Other Worlds: Urban Imaginaries in a Globalizing Age,* edited by Andreas Huyssen (Durham and London: Duke University Press, 2008), 104–106.

13 Bateson, *Steps to an Ecology of Mind,* 505.

14 According to Agamben, this thesis "throws a sinister light on the models by which social sciences, sociology, urban studies, and architecture today are trying to conceive and organize the public space of the world's cities without any clear awareness that at their very center lies the same bare life (even if it has been transformed and rendered apparently more human) that defined the biopolitics of the great totalitarian states of the twentieth century." Giorgio Agamben, *Homo Sacer: Sovereign Power and Bare Life* (Stanford: Stanford University Press, 1998), 181–182.

15 Chantal Mouffe, "Agonistic Public Spaces, Democratic Politics, and the Dynamic of Passions," in *Thinking Worlds: The Moscow Conference on Philosophy, Politics, and Art,* edited by Joseph Backstein, Daniel Birnbaum, and Sven-Olov Wallenstein (Berlin and Moscow: Sternberg Press and Interros Publishing, 2008), 95–96.

16 Jacques Rancière, *The Politics of Aesthetics: The Distribution of the Sensible,* translated by Gabriel Rockhill (London and New York: Continuum, 2004), 13 (originally published in French in 2000 as *Le Partage du sensible: Esthétique et politique*).

17 Mouffe, "Agonistic Public Spaces, Democratic Politics, and the Dynamic of Passions,"104. In this context, it is interesting to consider the work of the contemporary artist/designer Krzysztof Wodiczko, who through a series of interactive instruments and urban projections has given voice to the other.

18 Slavoj Žižek, *The Indivisible Remainder: An Essay on Schelling and Related Matters* (London and New York: Verso, 1996), 213.

19 Jacques Rancière, "Guantanamo, Justice, and Bushspeak: Prisoners of the Infinite," *CounterPunch,* April 30, 2002.

20 In contrast to multiculturalism that is a form of "plural monoculturalism," cosmopolitanism "makes the inclusion of others a reality and/or its maxim." See Ulrich Beck, *World at Risk* (Cambridge: Polity Press, 2007), 56.

21 According to Jacques Rancière, in its broadest sense aesthetics "refers to the distribution of the sensible that determines a mode of articulation between forms of action, production, perception, and thought. This general definition extends aesthetics beyond the strict realm of art to include the conceptual coordinates and modes of visibility operative in the political domain." *The Politics of Aesthetics,* 82.

ANTICIPATE

Advancement versus Apocalypse
Rem Koolhaas

Zeekracht
OMA

Mumbai on My Mind:
Some Thoughts on Sustainability
Homi Bhabha

Urban Earth: Mumbai
Daniel Raven-Ellison and Kye Askins

Notes on the Third Ecology
Sanford Kwinter

Social Inequality and Climate Change
Ulrich Beck

For a Post-Environmentalism:
Seven Suggestions for a New Athens Charter
and **The Weak Metropolis**
Andrea Branzi

Weak Work:
Andrea Branzi's "Weak Metropolis" and the
Projective Potential of an "Ecological Urbanism"
Charles Waldheim

From "Sustain" to "Ability"
JDS Architects

Forty Years Later–Back to a Sub-lunar Earth
Bruno Latour

Advancement versus Apocalypse

Rem Koolhaas

I'm interested in the coexistence of modernity and endlessly improvised, spontaneous conditions that don't consume much energy or material. For me, a hybrid condition is the condition of the day. Therefore, I don't think that I need to repudiate modernity or announce its end. Both conditions will continue to coexist. I think that we are only becoming more sensitive to their coexistence and less gung-ho about modernity, because we all know its flaws and faults, and we are more perceptive about its alternative. We are therefore perhaps more enthusiastic about imagining how the two can coexist.

I did not assume that anyone in the academic world would ask a practicing architect in the twenty-first century, given the architecture that we collectively produce, to participate in a volume on ecological urbanism. So I'm very grateful that you challenge me, but I am also deeply aware that my participation is defined by this doubt and this condition.

Because you invited me, we did some research.
We looked first at antiquity and realized that twenty-five years before Christ, there was already a profound knowledge about ecology and how people should build to be economical, logical, and beautiful.

Vitruvius, for instance, was completely aware that the sun would cast shadows at different degrees and different inclinations depending on the orientation of the site, and that his architecture should address these conditions.

Since the sun was shining from the south, the hottest parts of Roman baths should also be in the south. This knowledge was not limited to individual buildings, but extended to the planning of cities that were effortless and logical, based on engagements with and an understanding of nature.

"For fortified towns the following general principles are to be observed. First comes the choice of a very healthy site. Such a site will be high, neither misty nor frosty, and in a climate neither hot nor cold, but temperate; further, without marshes in the neighborhood. For when the morning breezes blow toward the town at sunrise, if they bring with them mists from marshes and, mingled with the mist, the poisonous breath of the creatures of the marshes to be wafted into the bodies of the inhabitants, they will make the site unhealthy. Again, if the town is on the coast with a southern or western exposure, it will not be healthy, because in summer the southern sky grows hot at sunrise and is fiery at noon, while a western exposure grows warm after sunrise, is hot at noon, and at evening all aglow." Chapter IV, "The Site of a City", Vitruvius, *De Architectura*

During the Renaissance, this knowledge was cultivated and further amplified.

A century later, the so-called Enlightenment broke out, and with Enlightenment came a formal launch of modernity.

The red line here is 1750.

What we see is that the Enlightenment had a phenomenal effect on reason, in terms of triggering the apparatus of modernity in a surprisingly short time.

ZIPPER 1910
COMBUSTION ENGINE 1876
OIL 1859 MOVING PICTURES 1877
RAYON 1855 **DEISEL ENGINE** 1892
MICROPHONE 1827 NEON LIGHT 1901
TIN CAN 1810 PASTEURISATION 1856 TRACTOR 1904
GAS LIGHTING 1804 PLASTIC 1862 **ZEPPELIN** 1900 TANK 1912
LITHOGRAPHY 1798 **ELECTROMAGNET** 1825 MODEL T 1908
SMALLPOX VACCINATION 1796 MACHINE GUN 1862 **ROBOT** 1921
BICYCLE 1791 RAILROAD 1830 TYPEWRITER 1867 HELICOPTER 1907
STEEL ROLLER 1783 **BLUEPRINT** 1840 TELEPHONE 1876 **SONAR** 1906
BIFOCAL EYEGLASSES 1780 **MORSE CODE** 1838 ESCALATOR 1900
SPINNING JENNY 1764 STETHOSCOPE 1819 LIGHT BULB 1879 **PYREX** 1915
POWER LOOM 1764 SPECTROSCOPE 1814 DYNAMITE 1866 VACUUM 1899
THERMOMETER 1724 HOT-AIR BALLOON 1783 **ANASTHESIA** 1846 RADAR 1887 INSULIN 1922
STEAM ENGINE 1712 **SPINNING FRAME** 1768 PORTLAND CEMENT 1824 MAIL ORDER 1872
LIGHTNING ROD 1701 CHROMATIC LENS 1758 **PHOTOGRAPH** 1814 GLIDER 1853 AC MOTOR 1888
SLIDE RULE 1614 **TELESCOPE** 1668 TUNING FORK 1711 SEXTANT 1758 COTTON GIN 1793 **REFRIGERATOR** 1834 FLIGHT 1903

1600   1650   1700   1750   1800   1850   1900

Also inscribed in Enlightenment were people like Goethe, who effortlessly combined art and science.

And people like Caspar David Friedrich. I like this painting because it shows highly sophisticated and cultivated people in search of and interacting with nature in a way that doesn't show any tension or alienation; the interaction actually seems to work for both sides.

Perhaps the final outcome of this highly reasonable streak of our civilization is the nuclear power plant.

There is also an entirely different streak in our culture. It is a not a narrative of linear and reasonable progress, but one of disasters and fundamental tensions between nature and mankind.

It depicts nature as a kind of punishment of mankind and, occasionally, mankind as a punisher of nature. That narrative, however we look at it—religiously or otherwise—is fundamentally anti-modern, insisting on apocalyptic expectations.

Friedrich also symbolizes this feeling in this painting, which has generated a series of prophets. Perhaps Malthus was the first one, with his belief that a premature death must visit the human race.

"The Power of Population is so superior to the power of the earth to produce subsistence for man that premature death must in some shape or other visit the human race". Thomas Malthus, *An Essay on the Principle of Population* (1798)

Others were Paul Ehrlich in 1968 and James Lovelock.

"The battle to feed all of humanity is over. In the 1970s and 1980s hundreds of millions of people will starve to death in spite of any cash programs embarked upon now. At this late date nothing can prevent a substantial increase in the world death rate". Paul R. Ehrlich, *The Population Bomb* (1968)

"By 2040, parts of the Sahara desert will have moved into middle Europe. We are talking about Paris—as far north as Berlin. In Britain we will escape because of our oceanic position." James Lovelock, *The Revenge of Gaia* (2006)

What we have is two completely opposite strains, both with very eloquent and impressive practitioners. Both ideologies read the same phenomena in completely contradictory terms: one as a line of reasonableness and the other as a line of disastrous manipulation and wrongness. The confusion at the current moment is generated by the tension between these two lines. We are not able to disentangle them or understand when one of the traditions speaks and when the other speaks. This polarity is still operating and has been for an incredibly long time.

To introduce a slightly more autobiographical moment, when I studied in London in 1968, I was taught in a school where tropical architecture was still on the curriculum. Although I didn't take it entirely seriously, I was fascinated by its teachers, who taught us an incredible respect for the landscape.

They taught us to look at other cities to see how they work, and to look at seemingly nonarchitectural environments. For them, no issue was too humble or lowly.

This is Jane Drew and Maxwell Fry, drawing open sewers and ways to clean them. That kind of humility in architectural education has practically disappeared.

But it's not only about humility. They were also interested in the tropics as a special domain, which is now the front line of the tensions and impossibilities that we are confronted with.

They looked at these areas in great depth and were able to analyze to what extent this climate required specific architectures and planning.

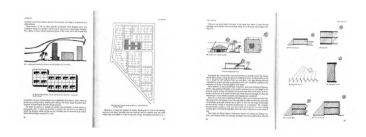

The studies also examined how an architecture could emerge that would actually persist in this climate without the degree of artificiality that we now take for granted.

What I find touching in retrospect is not only the earnestness of this discourse, but also the conviction that they had relevant knowledge worth teaching. The equivalent of this kind of knowledge today is rather tenuous in our academies.

They developed a repertoire of measures, avoiding air conditioning and the trappings of typical Western architecture, and created strange prisons of avoidance.

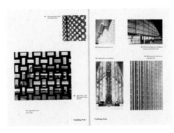

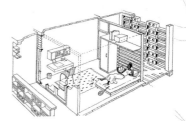

They also created an aesthetic that was able to renew modern architecture, which at the same time was running into issues of puritanism and unpopularity.

They not only worked on architecture but also on cities or villages.

I am impressed by the perhaps condescending but still highly efficient didactic intensity of this kind of effort. Even the simplest words were explained in plausible language. As a student, I cannot say that I embraced this knowledge. But in retrospect, I was being confronted with knowledge that was on the way out because it stood in the way of development. That is one of the tragedies.

I have since become increasingly involved in researching Africa and the tropics, and have found examples of engineering like this one for Lagos by an East German firm.

They seemed to ruthlessly turn Lagos into a modern metropolis, making everything local disappear.

But upon closer inspection, the project coexisted plausibly with expressions of poverty and of social improvisation. Though it appeared completely chaotic, things actually worked extremely well in a process of mutual interdependence. There is a subtlety to this kind of engineering that is not visible at first sight. But if you look over time as the infrastructure decays, you see that it has a certain depth.

That depth came not from the capitalist West but from the communist world, which influenced Africa in the 1960s and 1970s.

It was so frugal, so efficient, so methodical, and so coherent that it could actually realize complex and subtle entities.

In the period between 1965 and 1975, there was an incredible ability to take difficult conditions seriously, to take different climates seriously, to take the question of energy use seriously, and to try and combine the words "design" and "science." Unfortunately, thirty years later, these words are further apart than ever before.

This joint entity, design and science, was stimulated and sponsored not only by designers and scientists, but also by free-form intellectuals like Marshal MacLuhan and Ian McHarg, a sociologist who, in *Design with Nature*, wrote one of the most subtle manifestos on how culture and nature could coexist.

At a meeting on a boat in the Mediterranean, the anthropologist Margaret Mead and other intellectuals discussed in 1965, at a high level of intelligence, the issues that we are discussing now.

They produced sketches like this one, where, almost as a matter of course, human energy, solar energy, and commercial forms of energy are intertwined and mixed in ways we barely know how to do now.

What I find particularly impressive in the handwriting of these sketches is how enforced and urgent they are compared to our current, more smooth and perfect renderings.

These sketches show the inevitability of nature and networks together.

"Almost 40 years ago, Ian McHarg proposed a bold theory and a set of ecologically related planning methods in *Design with Nature* (1969). While the proatical measures he proposed have been incorporated into subsequent design and planning practices, the theoretical implications have not yet been fuly-realized. Present-date forms of the model include the amalgam "landscape urbanism," with its focus on infrastructure and urban ecology, a hybrid discipline arguably indebted to McHarg while distinct in its avoidance of the more strenuous effects of his project". Fredrick R. Steiner, "The Ghost of Ian McHarg", *Log*, 2009

Perhaps Buckminster Fuller's contribution to the field was the apotheosis of this combination of nature and network.

He did the most with the least, producing on the one hand diagrams of ponderous simplicity, like this one.

On the other hand, he worked on radical inventories of the world, both of cultural and natural elements, documenting the neck-and-neck race between them in a very forward-looking way.

ANTICIPATE

"Doing the most with the least"

For instance, this group was appalled by the predominance of American consumption. In each of these grids, the blue part represents specific sources taken by America, and the red is what is available to the rest of the world. This is a stunning indictment of the American way of life, produced for a main-stream publication.

Also, these people were not political lightweights, but actually political players.

This grid represents the total military budget of the world. Each of these squares represents $1 billion. Fuller is showing how the problems of the world could be resolved by switching military resources into these domains. This kind of clarity doesn't exist at this moment. It is the absence of this kind of clarity that makes us so desperate for a degree of coherence.

This is a drawing of making energy in the world run in certain kinds of streaks or vents, therefore enhancing the entire effi-ciency of the system. There's more about it later.

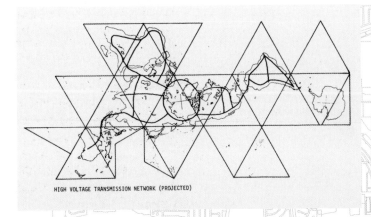

HIGH VOLTAGE TRANSMISSION NETWORK (PROJECTED)

Now, if you put everything that's happening in the late 1960s and early 1970s in a cloud or cluster, it seems that there is a very confusing mixture of good and bad.

But if you put the events into different zones or categories, a pattern emerges. There are of course many crises, but an explosion of green consciousness as a response to those crises. At the same time, a highly developed and imaginative form of engineering, theorized by Fuller and others, was put into practice:
the bridge across the Bosporus,
the reversal of a river current to irrigate entire parts of Siberia,
the spread of computers,
the Concorde,
the World Trade Center,
and the first international conference about international environmental issues.

Bosporus Bridge, Istanbul 1972

A POTOMAC ASSOCIATES BOOK

THE LIMITS TO

growth

A REPORT FOR
THE CLUB OF ROME'S PROJECT ON
THE PREDICAMENT OF MANKIND

Donella H. Meadows
Dennis L. Meadows
Jørgen Randers
William W. Behrens III

Universe Books
NEW YORK

Perhaps part of the meeting was also the first Club of Rome, which talked about the limits of growth. It's interesting to see that there were a number of iterations of the Club of Rome's reports in 1972.

"If the present growth trends in world population, industrialization, pollution, food, production, and resource depletion continue unchanged, the limits to growth on this planet will be reached sometime in the next one hundred years". The Club of Rome, *The Limits of Growth* (1972)

It was a reasonable and dramatically illustrated argument about the limits of resources and showed how in the next hundred years we have to be more careful and more restrained in our consumption.

But then the market economy was unleashed in the mid-1970s. The market economy had a devastating effect on the knowledge that had been accumulated at this point. Here we have forced the apocalyptic streak of the polarity that I defined at the beginning.
Twenty years later, the Club of Rome is completely open about the fact that "global warming, water shortages, famine and the like, would fit the bill ... In searching for a new enemy to unite us." You could say that in the same year, they even suggested that "democracy is no longer well suited for the task ahead." You see a perverse amplification and intensification of the arguments: seemingly rational, but actually on the apocalyptic side.

"In searching for a new enemy to unite us we came up with the idea that pollution, the threat of global warming, water shortages, famine and the like would fit the bill." The Club of Rome, *The First Global Revolution* (1994)

"It would seem that humans need a common motivation, namely a common adversary, to organize and act together in the vacuum ... the common enemy of humanity is man ... democracy is no longer well suited for the tasks ahead. The Club of Rome, *The First Global Revolution* (1994)

So, these two tendencies almost merge, or the evidence that they use is the same. But one continues to use *the evidence* for a rational and reasonable future, such as the application of atomic power.

This map represents relative reliance on atomic power.

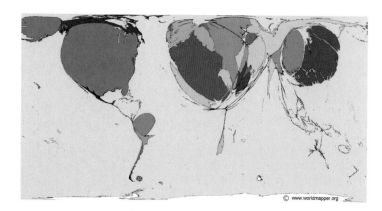

In France, about 80 percent of electricity is generated from nuclear energy.

The country in which the Enlightenment began is still the most enlightened nation, in a way, with its energy policy.

Scientists such as Freeman Dyson are relativizing the disaster of CO_2 levels, saying that actually they could also, in certain areas, have a positive effect.

"Dyson had proposed that whatever inflammations the climate was experiencing might be a good thing because carbon dioxide helps plants of all kinds to grow. Then he added the caveat that if CO_2 levels soared too high, they could be soothed by the mass cultivation of specially bred "carbon-eating trees" ..." *New York Times,* March 29, 2009

He is, of course, completely vilified for these statements.

"Chat rooms, Web threads, editors' boxes and Dyson's own e-mail queue resonate with a thermal current of invective in which Dyson has discovered himself variously described as a "pompous twit," "a blowhard," "a cesspool of misinformation," "an old coot riding into the sunset" and, perhaps inevitably, "a mad scientist." *New York Times,* March 29, 2009

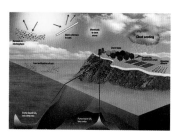

But this kind of thinking leads perhaps to a school of thought that engineering can finally offer a number of strategies that could help us.

Then there is the apocalyptic streak, which portrays trains powered by coal as a holocaust, and which develops more and more extreme scenarios.

"The trains carrying coal to power plants are death trains. Coal-fired power plants are factories of death ... Clearly, if we burn all fossil fuels, we will destroy the planet we know." Dr. James Hansen, NASA, *The Guardian*, February 15, 2009

For example, the deadline on intervention that the Club of Rome envisioned in its first report has been revised to four years, confronting all of us with a desperate time limit.

"We have only four years left to act on climate change" Dr. James Hansen, NASA, *The Guardian*, January 18, 2009

Here, nothing is predicted beyond a certain date. So science is an exacerbation of the crisis, no longer talking about responses.

These are all the stock markets. We all know what happened there. We know that the market economy is not the only possible model of our existence. We realized that 9/11 was not only a disaster, but also created a fundamental rift between America and the rest of the world.

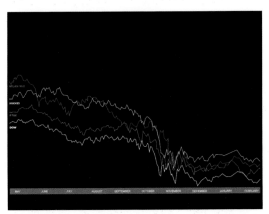

We have an energetic crew of people working on the problem, but we doubt their seriousness and whether they have the necessary information at their disposal.
Interesting accusations emerge: "White people with blue eyes have caused it."

"This crisis was caused by the irrational behavior of white people with blue eyes, who before the crisis appeared to know everything and now deminstrate that they know nothing." Luiz Ignacio Lula da Silva, President of Brazil, BBC, March 27, 2009.

"America can no longer dictate"

"There is a direct challenge under way to the paradigms that America has been trying to sell to the rest of the world. Emerging markets now think they can do what they want without hectoring from the United States." Eswar S. Prasad, IMF, *International Herald Tribune,* March 29, 2009

1940   2009

Comparisons of US economy with rest of the world

RESPECTIVE SHARES

RESOURCES

PRODUCTION

PRODUCTS IN USE

"Western consumption is no longer necessary."

"Many developing countries look to the west as a model but that cannot be the model. These [western] buildings use too much power and would not be affordable to us. In India the population has gone beyond all control and it is wrong to expect western development to help us." Jockin Arputhan, Founder of the National Slum Dwellers Federation of India

"The dollar has to be abandoned."

"The outbreak of the crisis and its spillover to the entire world relected the inherent vulnerabilities and systemic risks in the existing international monetary system … [What is needed is a new reserve currency] that is disconnected from individual nations …" Zhou Xiaochuan, Governor of the Peoples' Bank of China

What you see is a pushback of the American position.

Now, what about architecture? I think what the crisis will mean for us is an end to the ¥ € $ regime.

For those who didn't recognize it, this is a collection of masterpieces by architects in the last ten years. It's a skyline of icons showing, mercilessly, that an icon may be individually plausible, but that collectively they form an ultimately counterproductive and self-canceling kind of landscape.

So that is out.

Unfortunately, the sum of current architectural knowledge hasn't grown beyond this opposition. That is where the market economy and the evolution of architectural culture have been extremely irresponsible in letting knowledge simply disappear between the different preoccupations.

I still think that architectural dialectics are between this building and this building—and are therefore not deep enough.

We have all of these images of buildings that do not perform correctly, but our answers are not necessarily very deep. I don't exclude myself from any of these comments, as I hope you realize.

Embarrassingly, we have been equating responsibility with literal greening. This is the boutique of Ann Demeulemeester in Seoul, covered entirely in green.

Greenwash, n. disinformation disseminated by an organization so as to present an environmentally responsible public image. *Concise Oxford English Dictionary*, 11th Edition (2008)

Editt Tower, Singapore (TR Hamzah & Yeang)
Currently pending construction in Singapore, the EDITT Tower will be a paragon of "Ecological Design In The Tropics". The 26-story high-rise will boast photovoltaic panels, natural ventilation, and a biogas generation plant all wrapped within an insulating living wall that covers half of its surface area. The verdant skyscraper was designed to increase its location's bio-diversity a rehabilitate the local eco-system in Singapore's 'zeroculture' metropolis. TR Hamzah & Yeang

Even significant buildings by serious architects, such as the California Academy of Sciences in San Francisco, for me almost falls into the same category.

What is very difficult about architecture today is that architects themselves are the main commentators.

California Academy of Sciences, San Francisco (Renzo Piano)
"You can say that the building is made of shadows," says Renzo Piano. "Being inside is like being under a tree in summer. The green roof with its bubbles is like foliage wrapping itself over branches. And Pacific breezes make sure you don't feel trapped inside some heavy institutional building." *The Guardian*, November 11, 2008

This is a language that is either outrageously innocent or deeply calculated—probably both—but in a shocking way. If you read the criticism in the *New York Times* by Nicolai Ouroussoff, the architect's commentary seems to work very well, because Ouroussoff is extremely happy with this building.

"… If you want reaffirmation that human history is an upward spiral rather than a descent into darkness, head to the new California Academy of Sciences, in Golden Gate Park … This building's greatness as architecture, however, is rooted in a cultural history that stretches right through modernism to classical Greece. It is a comforting reminder of the civilizing function of great art in a barbaric age." Nicolai Ouroussoff, *New York Times*, September 23, 2008

Here is an interior view. A question that doesn't seem to be asked is: is it all so necessary? And, do we need more aquariums?

"... Mr. Piano's building is also a blazingly uncynical embrace of the Enlightenment values of truth and reason ..."

Ouroussoff continues in more complex language...
This is the section. We still haven't moved on from the harmless arrows of Buckminster Fuller. That is, in an embarrassing way, still the way we prove our correctness.

We have a kind of Parthenon with a planetarium, a piazza, and a rainforest. I would politely submit that it is not a Parthenon. In Abu Dhabi, Norman Foster makes a much more serious effort with his zero-carbon city, Masdar, which will have no cars and will be carbon-neutral by using technologies that are still to be revealed.

"... a new 6 million square meter sustainable development that uses traditional planning principals (sic.) of a walled city, together with existing technologies, to achieve a zero carbon and zero waste community ... the city itself is car free. With a maximum distance of 200 m to the nearest transport link and amenities." Foster and Partners

I didn't really want to talk about our own work, but there is one project that I will show because it resonates with the material here. It also indicates the direction in which I think we need to move: we need to step out of this amalgamation of good intentions and branding in a political direction and a direction of engineering.
We are working on an analysis of what Europe could do with power harvested from the North Sea. You can recognize Norway and Sweden, Denmark, Holland, Belgium, and England. All of these countries have large territories on the North Sea.
We have divided them into sections, which means that Holland is not this shape, but this shape.
The project imagines that wind energy could be combined and that supply and demand could be regulated.
A single ring of integrated wind turbines would not only generate energy but would also have additional benefits like the reuse of some of the redundant oil-extraction apparatus, and potentially even generate its own tourism.
A single ring could generate more energy than the Middle East currently produces each year.

WIND FARMS
HYDRO DAM
SOLAR PANELS
CONCENTRATED SOLAR POWER
BIOMASS PLANT
GEOTHERMAL PLANT
WAVE
TIDAL

Looking even further, there would be a potential North-South connection to try to exploit the specific potentials in each area: wind, tidal, and solar. All these sources of energy can be mobilized into a single European grid. It's simply through the combination of politics and engineering that this needs to be addressed.

In working on this material, I discovered that what we are doing is inadvertently exactly what Fuller proposed when he looked at the map forty years ago.

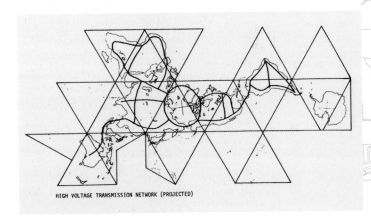

HIGH VOLTAGE TRANSMISSION NETWORK (PROJECTED)

Zeekracht

OMA

Given its high and consistent wind speeds and shallow waters, the North Sea is arguably the world's most suitable area for large-scale wind farming. The potential magnitude of renewable energy in the North Sea in fact approaches that of fossil-fuel production in the Persian Gulf states today. In the changing landscape of twenty-first-century energy demand, the North Sea could become a major player in global energy production and trade through wind power alone.

The North Sea master plan is envisioned as the result of cooperative international offshore development. Rather than a fixed spatial plan, it proposes a system of catalytic elements that, although intended for the present, are optimized for long-term sustainability. Primary components of the plan include: the *Energy Super-Ring*–the primary infrastructure for energy distribution and supply; the *Production Belt*–the industrial and institutional infrastructure supporting research and

manufacturing; the *Reefs*–stimulated marine ecologies reinforcing the natural ecosystems (and eco-productivity) of the sea; and the *International Research Center*–promoting international cooperation, research, innovation, and development.

The Dutch Sea master plan proposes an operative development strategy for immediate national implementation that simultaneously takes into account long-term development and coordination of national and supranational interests. Unlike the usual technocratic planning methods based on least-conflict zoning, the master plan suggests a proactive and multidimensional approach based on enabling possibility.

The proposed circular wind farms provide destinations at sea through their explicit connection with the parties they are supplying (e.g., communities, companies, cities, etc.). The farms are also designed

to be sited, programmed, and phased to meet the evolving demands and plans of North Sea regional development. Locally, the wind farms perform a series of hybrid functions according to their location and performance mandate: depleted subsea natural gas reservoirs are used for energy storage, untapped gas fields support hybrid energy production, farms adjacent to shipping lanes act as offshore power stations, etc. Farms developed along ecological zones and around existing decommissioned platforms create marine remediation areas, new recreational parks, and recreational sea routes. At a mature stage of offshore development, wind farms are clustered along the length of the Super-Ring, distributing national surpluses and supplying regional energy needs efficiently and profitably.

North Sea master plan

Int. Ocean Energy
Research Station
Existing Marine Ecological Zon
Artificial Reef/ Marine Remedia
Super-Ring Offshore High Volti
Onshore High Voltage Power L
Superring Energy Export Cable
Wind Farm
Wind Turbine Manufacturing/
R&O Center
Converted Oil/Gas Production
Shipping Port

500km

**Components of the
North Sea plan**

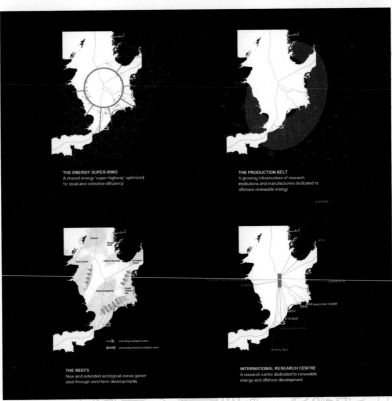

THE ENERGY SUPER-RING
A shared energy 'super-highway' optimized
for local and collective efficiency

THE PRODUCTION BELT
A growing infrastructure of research
institutions and manufacturers dedicated to
offshore renewable energy

THE REEFS
New and extended ecological zones generated through wind farm developments

INTERNATIONAL RESEARCH CENTRE
A research centre dedicated to renewable
energy and offshore development

**The Netherlands'
master plan**

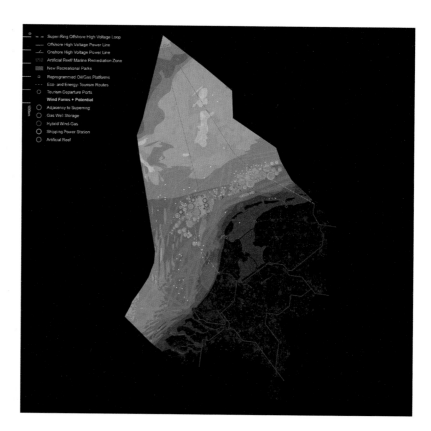

**Built-up components of
the Netherlands' plan**

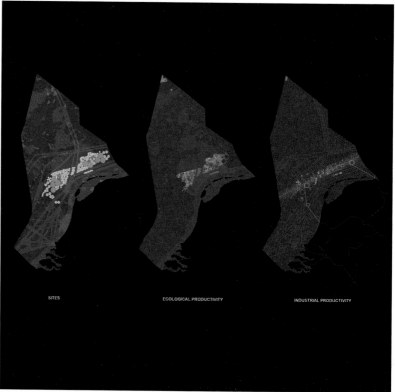

SITES   ECOLOGICAL PRODUCTIVITY   INDUSTRIAL PRODUCTIVITY

Detail of the plan

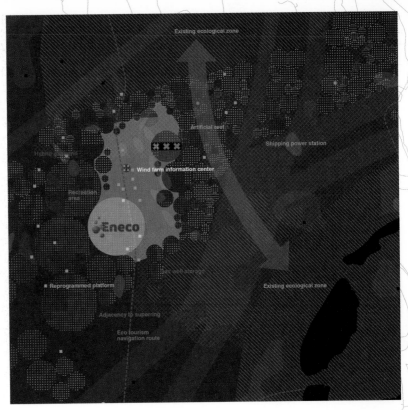

The Zeekracht system

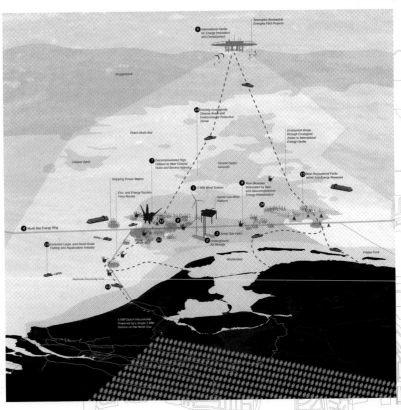

Zeekracht

International Center for Ocean Energy | Ecological Preserve | Artificial Reefs | Energy Storage Cavern | High Power 5MW Windturbine | New Recreational Parks | Innovative Fishing and Aquaculture | Windfarm Sights

NO
DK
UK
NL
DE
BE
FR

13.400TWh
Theoretic Production Capacity (See Atlas p IV)

4TWh
2008 Worldlife Production

1.300TWh
2020 ECN projection

11.300TWh
2008 Gulf Production

ll Gas Cavern | Decommissioned Oil rig | Ecotourism | Diving and Wildlife Watching | Historic Shipwreck | Energy Super-Ring | Marine Recreation | Dutch Town

Mumbai on My Mind:
Some Thoughts on Sustainability

Homi K. Bhabha

It is always too early, or too late, to talk of the "cities of the future." The "Just City" or the "Generic City" floats before our tired eyes in the half-light of dusk and returns to our expectant gazes in the dawn of a new day. The futurity of the city, as the Office for Metropolitan Architecture once proposed, "is the post-city being prepared on the site of the ex-city." It is in those anomic hours in-between dusk and dawn—when we experience the wakeful "present" of our predicament—that we build the city of the future, the "new city," precariously and proleptically—prophetically. Any claim to newness, any proposal that we are "at the turning point" of history, urbanity, or ecology, is at once a historical commitment and a tendentious and transitional proposition. Tendentious not because of a lack of intelligence or imagination in our thinking, nor a failure of integrity or technology in our planning, but because of the "transitional" temporality that mediates both the conception and the construction of the projects of the future. Transitional, in the sense in which Antonio Gramsci conceives of the "turning point in history" as a constelled reality—an archive of the contemporary balanced on the knife-edge of the emergent and the residual. The historically "new" is always a moment of incubation, Gramsci writes: "What exists at any given time [in the name of the new] is a variable combination of old and new, ... a momentary equilibrium of cultural relations..."[1]

It is, indeed, the "momentary equilibrium of cultural relations" that I want to address, anxiously aware as I am of my deep ignorance in matters of "ecological urbanism." My ignorance—or let's call it my innocence—leads me, however, to suggest that sustainability as a mode of "relational" thinking is profoundly implicated in the "momentary equilibrium" of cultural, social, and geopolitical relations. Certain environmental and ecological discourses seem to suggest that "sustainability" is an ethical or architectural practice for the *longue durée*—an intervention into the given ground of an immanent Environment in order to protect its integrity and propagate its productivity for the ages. Such perspectives yield considerable benefits in historicizing a political "moment" and mobilizing a movement. I would like to suggest, however, that circulating within the *longue durée* are incubational presences of *petits récits* that support the environmentalist project, but conceive somewhat differently of the narrative plot of ecology. I take courage from texts that seem to stress the crucial importance of "momentary equilibrium" in ecological thinking. In Félix Guattari's *The Three Ecologies*, "eco-logic" is defined as a "process, which I here oppose to system or to structure, [and which] strives to capture existence in the very act of its constitution, definition and deterritorialisation. This process of 'fixing-into-being' relates only to expressive subsets that have that have broken out of their totalising frame and have begun to work on their own account.... Ecological praxes strive to scout out the potential vectors of subjectification and singularisation at each partial existential locus."[2] Just as I was trying to morph my mind around this verbal tsunami—deeply attracted, nonetheless, by "eco-logic" as a capturing of existence "in the very act of its consitution... a fixing-into-being"—I was comforted by Mohsen Mostafavi's ringing endorsement of Guattari's concept of effective social agency—the "singularisation of existence"—as a transformative force in the discourse of ecological urbanism. "Such a practice requires a new mindset," Mostafavi writes, "what Guattari called a process of the re-singularisation of existence... [which] depends on the collective production of unpredictable and untamed 'dissident subjectivities'.... An ecological urbanism needs to incorporate an ethics of size, of social mix, of density and of public space." What is more significant, I believe, than an essential but discrete itemization of "ecological public goods"—size, mix, density, etc.—is the relational value that eco-logical thinking establishes as the conditions for an ethics of sustainability.

The most prosaic, dictionary definition of sustainability suggests that it is a city designed or landscaped in such a way as to ensure the continued conservation of natural resources and the surrounding built environment while providing the cultural, social, and economic base needed to support its inhabitants. It seems natural that the normative "measures" of the discourses of ecology or sustainablity are spatial. However, in that innocent-sounding phrase "to ensure the continued conservation," we move from territoriality or "ground"—landscape, city, forest, industrial park—to an ecological temporality—*the continued conservation*—that supports or "houses" the agency and ethical activity of the ecologist. (Let us not forget that the root of "eco" in ecology comes from the ancient Greek *oikos*: house or dwelling.) Sustainability is the moral injunction to put your house in order so as to enhance and empower the dwelling of both selves and others. What does it mean to ensure continued conservation? What is the time frame of such intervention? Is sustainability an evolutionary process, a teleological task, or a strategic, interstitial intervention into fragile and fractal reality that we call the urban environment? If, like me, you want to say "all of the above," then you cannot rest easy in some form of pragmatism because those three layers or tiers of sustainability form an intriguing palimpsest of overlapping intentions, differential time-scales and partial, contradictory aims that overwrite each other and create multiple ecological potentialities. The crucial task of the ecological agent then is to maintain a "momentary equilibrium" between these various practices of sustainability and their diverse definitions of what constitutes the "future." And this brings us back to the capacity of the agent or the capability of the activist—and agency might be individual, collective, or institutional—to intervene in the urban existence in the present tense: in the very act of its constitution, its being fixed-into-being. Is this merely a theoretical problem with no practical application? Is all this just a fireside chat between Guattari, Mostafavi, and, belatedly, Bhabha, generating much smoke of a distinctly narcotic variety? Is this agency for the angels, if not the birds?

It became both conspicuous and clear to me as I read through the illuminating proceedings of the Urban Age India Conference[3] that one of the major issue for urban planners is indeed how to calculate the "time" of environmental intervention. Now "time" is not as abstract a quantity, as discussions of temporality sometimes suggest. When time becomes the medium of agency or the vehicle of urban ecological intervention, then, as Rahul Mehrotra suggests, temporality becomes intimately connected to governmental policy and bureaucratic decree—code, site, and practice. Time is politics and policy; time is geopolitical locality and its situation in the archive of memory, record, and regulation. Mehrotra's complaint against the "mistiming" of the ecological intervention in Mumbai/Bombay makes my point about the need to act at the point of a "fixing-into-being" rather well. There is of course no "ideal" time of intervention, but there are good times and worse ones. Mehrotra writes:

> Over the last three decades in Mumbai, planning has been largely concerned with rearguard actions versus the avant-garde approaches that traditionally led planning. Thus today most infrastructure follows city growth rather than facilitating and opening up new growth centres within and outside the city's core. In con-temporary Mumbai, planning happens systematically "posterior," as a recuperative and securing action.
>
> Thus, the profession is chiefly engaged in recuperative action, intervening post-facto to clean up the mess! It is therefore no coinicidence

that in Mumbai there is an increased celebration of projects involving "cleaning up"—whether that is the restoration of historic buildings, precincts or districts, waterfronts and pavements, or the relocation of slums to make way for infrastructure.[4]

Sustainability represents an ecological and ethical commitment to what Ludwig Wittgenstein, in his scattered notes on architecture, describes as "not constructing a building, as much as in having a perspicuous view of the foundations of possible buildings."[5] More than a master plan, I think Wittgenstein is suggesting that we think deeply about what I will call the "unbuilt." If I might put it another way, in keeping with my interest in ecological time-space as "a momentary equilibrium of cultural relations," then I would say that ecological urbanism should reflect deeply on the unbuilt. Let me end with a few proposals about the place of the unbuilt in the time of ecological reflection. A perspicuous view of possible buildings is a counterfactual interest in what could have been built if economic, cultural, and ecological conditions were otherwise; it is an aspirational commitment to what might have been better built or not built at all; and, finally, the unbuilt is a spectral, virtual perspective on the ghost of open ground that haunts the history and the conscience of every construction. The unbuilt is a gesture of ethical and architectural vigilance that makes it possible for ecological agency to capture human existence in the very act of its constitution of an emergent world within the representational and historical realms of both being and meaning.

Nothing conveys this process of "building and unbuilding," of capturing the urban experience of Mumbai in the very act of its constitution, its "fixing into meaning," than Salman Rushdie's *Midnight's Children*. In postcolonial Mumbai, the past hope of the Indian nation for a free and equal cosmopolitan city will not surrender itself to a shuttered sectarian future of communal strife and ethno-religious violence. Civilization and barbarism—the enlightened ideals of Indian independence on the one hand, and the various attempts to divide and destroy its kinetic sense of partial and diverse communities on the other—are the ambivalent tensions that create the narrative energy of Rushdie's *Midnight's Children*, Mumbai's *Buddenbrooks*. *Midnight's Children* is built on a scale of energetic movement across the landscape of the city, and the *paysage moralisé* of the country's political history. Never forget that the last paragraph of the novel has Saleem Sinai, the author's double, being trampled underfoot. But before that happens there is so much traveling to do:

Drive! On Chowpatty sands! Past the great houses on Malabar Hill, round Kemp's Corner, giddily along the sea to Scandal Point! And yes, why not, on and on and on, down my very own Warden Road, right along the segregated swimming pools at Breadh Candy, right up to the huge Mahalaxmi temple and the old Willingdon Club…. Throughout my childhood, whenever bad times came to Bombay, some insomniac night-walker would report that he had seen Shivaji's statue moving; disasters in the city of my youth, danced to the occult music of a horse's gray, stone hooves.[6]

Saleem has a nose for the energy of Mumbai, just as it is Mumbai's *energeia* that brings the narrative to life. *Midnight's Children* survives because it lives on, and off, this remarkable "energy" to move across the city, and the country, like an insomniac street-walker—profligate and promiscuous, vulnerable and venereal—hungrily in search of language in which to picture the movement of the city. The narrative moves in a single page from the coconuts of Juhu Beach to the ritual of rice eating in the city and then to the Ganesh Chaturti festival of the Elephant god at Chowpatty Beach, where both rice and coconuts are cast into the sea as ritual offerings. The narrative "energy" builds up list by list, word by word, name by name, place by place, in that palimpsestical style of the layered descriptions of places, peoples, and things. Saleem's olfactory explorations of the city also reveal an underlying anxiety, an ongoing awareness that Independence comes at the cost of Partition, and the dream of pluralism may be threatened by the nightmare of provincialism, regionalism, and communalism. The nightwalker is kept awake by the sound of the hobnail boots on the cobbles.

The fetish of profuse and desperate linguistic description of urban landscapes represents a desire to preserve in minute and persistent detail the elements of a larger pluralism associated with Mumbai, which feels itself under threat. The larger idea of India was, regrettably, achieved only by disavowing and destroying the "constitutive" difference of the way of life of the subcontinent's majority populations, Hindus and Muslims, by cracking the country at Partition and dividing its peoples. Division is not the "independence" of difference; it is the disappearance of difference.

Attacks of terror—the first in 1993, the most recent in November 2008—as well as incidents of communal rioting have tragically left their mark on a city that seems, on the surface, to work busily against and across such ethnic and religious boundaries. Rushdie most often takes the coastal road Marine Drive as he makes his way from south to north. The north is the world of Bollywood with its left-leaning Muslim Communist, Qasim the Red, who hangs out at the Pioneer Café with Amina Sinai. But if you turn away just before Chowpatty Beach

1 Antonio Gramsci, "The Philosophy of Praxis and 'Intellectual and Moral Reformation,'" from *A Gramsci Reader: Selected Writings 1916–1935*, edited by David Forgacs (London: Lawrence and Wishart, 1988), 353.

2 Félix Guattari, *The Three Ecologies* (New Brunswick, NJ: Athlone Press, 2000), 44–45.

3 Entitled *Urban India: Understanding the Maximum City.* Accessed from http://www.urban-age.net/03_conferences/conf_mumbai.html. The conference was held in Mumbai, November 2007 and organized by the Cities Programme at the London School of Economics and Political Science and the Alfred Herrhausen Society, the International Forum of the Deutsche Bank.

4 Rahul Mehrotra, "Remaking Mumbai," in *Urban India: Understanding the Maximum City*, 46.

5 Ludwig Wittgenstein, *Culture and Value*, edited by G. H. von Wright with Heikki Hyman, translated by Peter Winch (Chicago: University of Chicago Press, 1980), 7e.

6 Salman Rushdie, *Midnight's Children* (London, Picador, 1982).

7 Prakash Jadhav, "Under Dadar Bridge," in *Poisoned Bread: Translations from Modern Marathi Dalit Literature*, edited by Arjun Dangle (London: Sangam, 1992), 56–57.

into the city's old interior, you enter a different world. You drive past Azad Maidan, just the other side of Cathedral School, past the Goan-Roman Catholic communities around Girgaum, then around the Parsee settlements in Grant Road and toward the Muslim areas in Mohamedalli Road. If you turned a sharp left before getting to the poorer Anglo-Indian communities of Byculla, you would enter the once-Jewish quarters of Nagpada with wraith-like women selling string-cheese and flat Iraqi-Jewish sesame breads. The teeming hinterland of the city is where the communal riots have left their most lasting memories.

But this multistoried world of Mumbai exists beyond the inspired *métier* of Rushdie's middle-class world. It develops a very different kind of *energeia* in the interior landscape of Mumbai's northwest suburbs, part of the hinterland I just sketched out for you. Here the old closed-down cloth mills decay, and the unemployed settle in slums around their former place of work as if to suck on a dried-out teat. There, in a poem titled "Under Dadar Bridge," named after a Mumbai landmark that connects the central city with the nearest of its once industrialized and now mall-ified suburbs, a Marathi Dalit (Untouchable) poet Prakash Jadhav tells a different Hindu-Muslim story:

> Hey, Ma, tell me my religion. Who am I?
> What am I?
> You are not a Hindu or a Muslim!
> You are an abandoned spark of the
> World's lusty fires.
> Religion? This is where I stuff religion!
> Whores have only one religion, my son.
> If you want a hole to fuck in, keep
> Your cock in your pocket![7]

The place of "ecological" ethics lies somewhere in-between memory and the present; it dwells in that transitional movement, the to-and-fro, between a past whose ghosts refuse to die and a future whose gods refuse to await the moment of their destined birth. The enraged god of *Eco-Oikos-Dwelling* screams to be properly housed, made to feel at home in the realms of alterity and proximity. "Language is hospitality," Emmanuel Levinas attests. And in the tension through which we move hither and thither, in-between the built and the unbuilt—there will emerge a currency of creative communication—language, landscape, the vocabulary of everyday life—that may not save us for all time, but will at least help us to survive the history of our own existence.

an Earth

Raven-Ellison and Kye Askins

To mark Earth's shift to majority urban dwelling, the Urban Earth project was started in 2008 with the aim of (re)presenting our habitat by walking across some of Earth's biggest urban areas, to explore their spatial realities for the people who live there and challenge dominant media discourses regarding the places in which most of us now live. The idea is to walk a transect across an urban area, taking a photograph every ten steps, and then stitch the images together to make a speeded-up film of the journey and the place. Urban Earth walks always start and finish on the rural fringe. The urban footprint of the town or city is used to calculate the length of the walk, while a map revealing a pattern of deprivation is used to plot the route. Where the most deprived fifth of a population occupy 10 percent of an urban footprint, 10 percent of the distance walked will go through areas that fit that profile. In practice, this means overlaying an Index of Multiple Deprivation map onto a route map and then measuring out a route that mirrors the distribution of deprivation within the urban area. Although this technique is possible for cities with good socioeconomic data, in Mumbai a lack of accurate low-level data led to a consultation with the Geography Department at the University of Mumbai, which assisted in designing the "most representative" route.

The photographs shown here were selected at regular intervals from the fully documented Urban Earth walks in Mumbai, Mexico City, and London.

Mumbai

Just over 24 kilometers were covered in this two-day walk across Mumbai in August 2008. More than fifteen people took part at various stages, walking through a city in which 55 percent of the population live outside of the normal public or private housing market on around 6 percent of the city's land.

Mexico City

More than 6,400 photographs were taken in the walk across Mexico City. Taking three days, seven people took part in various stages of the 65-kilometer urban adventure. Seventeen percent of the walk went through the city's least deprived areas, while 21 percent of the images were taken in the most deprived places.

London

This walk covered around 58 kilometers and took place in August 2008 over two days. Thirty percent of the walk is through London's least deprived areas, while just 12 percent of images are in the most deprived parts of the city, reflecting the distribution of deprivation. A total of 5,789 images were taken over the walk, and at various stages four people joined this walk.

ANTICIPATE

ANTICIPATE

Urban Earth Mumbai

89

ANTICIPATE

ANTICIPATE

Notes on the Third Ecology

Sanford Kwinter

"Ecological Urbanism" might refer to Cities and Nature, but it also might mean something larger than this. The habitual way we understand the relationship between these two entities was imprinted on us largely by the Anglo-Saxon culture of the Industrial Revolution, when immense upheavals in social, economic, and political life transformed the very landscape around us and our relationship to it irreversibly and in depth. The dyad of City and Country was the imaginary axis within which progress and modernization were conceived, not only then, but perhaps implicitly forever thereafter.

The modern transformations of territory—of which even today's most recent economic and biospheric crises are direct results—are rooted in this archaic and false opposition. To speak of transformations of territory today, especially if we are to take seriously our historical task to begin to "think ecologically," we cannot exclude the "existential" territories, that is, the existential ecologies, that define our ways of inhabiting the worlds we have made. For if there is an ecological crisis at hand, it is one that as much concerns the deterioration and deformation of human experience (and the infinite improvisations that make up its history) as it does that of the physical habitat on which we rely to provide the overabundant wealth that we too often use to hide from ourselves this uncomfortable fact.[1] It is here that some new thinking about cities, or better, about the culture of cities, comes to the fore.

Cities arose as direct products of the (once) new means of concentrating wealth, a development that exploded once wealth was able to be detached or abstracted from its moorings within the natural (or should we say "empirical" so as not unduly to dilute the term "nature") world. Once motive force or power, for example, could be detached from its fixed mooring "at the river" where it is extracted in situ by means of a waterwheel, and transposed, say, to an upper-story manufactory site in the heart of a densely populated urban environment like London—a process made possible by the invention of the detachable heat or expansion engine—there immediately arrived to meet it the administrative and banking innovations that permitted accumulations of both wealth and population that both simply came to forget that this is what they were: abstractions only, and not true emancipations, from the obdurate, finite facts of nature.

The heat engine's "emancipation" from nature—both temporal-spatially and in terms of the balance sheet of energy, matter, and order—was of course no more than a willful illusion, despite the formally stated principles of the thermodynamic science that gave rise to the heat engine in the first place. This was a lesson that occupants of cities ironically began to relearn in the 1960s with respects to fossil fuel limits, acid rain, famine, and the effects of phosphate, pesticide, and industrial chemistry use on a wide range of causally networked systems. Then, a neo-agrarianism began to flourish, sometimes taking the tenor of neo-Malthusianism. The publication of the Club of Rome's "Limits to Growth" (1972) became the linchpin by which most of us still recall this period. But the once-famous work of Yale Law professor Charles A. Reich, *The Greening of America* (1970), provided the most comprehensive popular synthesis of how the concept of human liberty (and the "good life") came to be conceived within this framework. It is the stunning popularity of this work and not its depth or accuracy that earns its mention here. At any rate, several dozen works, from Norman O. Brown and Alan Watts to Kurt Vonnegut and Herbert Marcuse, could be cited to fill out the claim that a transformed view of the human relationship to nature provided the sinews of a total refashioning of the existential territories of the period, ones with profound roots in the period's political, musical, and literary culture. At the very least—and even a cursory survey of American or French popular cinema of the time would dramatically confirm this—the very concept of "life" during this period was saturated with a sense of open-endedness and an experimentalist ethos at every level. Clearly even the predominant psychedelic culture of the period had at its core the concept of a fluidity and relativism of consciousness, not the static and universalist notion that came to replace it during the ensuing yuppie revolution. Drugs, particularly with their roots in botanical (and ethnobotanical) cultures, were seen as means by which the human nervous system's possibilities could be relearned and reexperienced as a profound return to natur(e)(al) states. Pathological formations, to wit schizophrenia and other florid psychic "refusals" to conform to models of State obedience, were frequently presented as new forms of "sanity" and instances of an embrace of natural states, or at least of natural resistance (R.D. Laing, Timothy Leary, David Cooper, Felix Guattari, etc.) Nature's abundance and creativity was often presented as a form of invention not greatly different from psychic and social "pathology." While

> The garden in the machine: Mumbai's Sanjay Gandhi National Park is a natural wildlife–and especially panther–habitat situated in the heart of what will soon be the world's largest metropolis. In addition to dozens of resident panthers, tiger spoor were found there in 2003. Mumbai is also home to hundreds of vultures whose feeding behaviors are still relied on to dispose of the deceased bodies of the city's large and prosperous Parsi population.

ANTICIPATE

a great deal of this particular existential formation has over time been shown to have been based in errors, a considerable portion that was profound and fertile and especially liberatory was lodged permanently into history and represents an asset—albeit buried today—to which a future moment might yet return to profitably reclaim. The aim of the foregoing reflection is to demonstrate the centrality of the human/nature dyad in the production of actual reality, of the actual territories in which social and natural processes are experienced and expressed.

Three billion of earth's citizens today live in cities, and virtually all of the exponential growth in population anticipated over the next fifty years will be urban. A significant number of those who do not live in physical urban environments increasing live in psychic ones, however, as even the proliferation of communal mobile telephones in the remotest rural environments connect local artisans not only to global markets but to

Corridors of waste:
In Dharavi disposal gives way
whenever possible to circulation
and transformation.

the rhetorics and representations through which their logics and operations are expressed; the imagery and associated effects of global cinema have also penetrated the remotest societies on earth, making the arrival of "output" communications within a society (phones, internet, or even market-price-adjusted goods) into an immediate completion of a circuit of exchange. Current ameliorative development in cities targets the archaic physical structures and the archaic social life-forms that adhere to them. Two examples among hundreds are the destruction of Beijing's Hutongs and the proposed redevelopment of the Dharavi slum quarter in Mumbai. It is an unexamined and possibly dangerous supposition that the solution to the new demographic and economic pressures is to fully rationalize and modernize our existing urban habitats; indeed the opposite may be the case. Take for example the proposed Dharavi redevelopment (as a model for very rapid capital-intensive development taking place in India, China, Brazil, and other giant economic territories). Among the great singularities of India is the intensity of its local commerce, the vastness and ubiquity of its social markets, which are virtually coextensive with its metropolitan fabrics. Within this fascinating urban tapestry there exist myriad networks of social processing of social goods. One example is the astoundingly exhaustive system of recycling that takes place in Indian cities, in which newsprint, copper wire, rubber, plastics, metals, rags, and even dung gets gathered, sorted, sold, resold, and recovered for reuse. (One resident in a hundred in Delhi is engaged in recycling, and up to 15 percent of all solid waste generated in Indian cities is recovered. Some materials will gain up to 700 percent in value as they move through the recycling chain, even before reprocessing.) Another well-stud-

Woman sorting plastic in resupply chain

ied but ill-understood network phenomenon, particularly in Mumbai but now virtually anywhere in the world where there is an Indian community, is the system of midday meal delivery known as the Dabba or "tiffin" system. Tens or even hundreds of thousands of meals are accurately gathered up at Mumbai households and delivered to remote locations of work within hours, with a precision and efficiency unmatched in perhaps any reticulated distribution network in the world. (The tiffins are also recovered after use and returned to their household of origin with similar efficiency and accuracy.) The networks of tiffin walas, their agents, brokers, relays, and physical and administrative infrastructures (from the community kitchens in which the meals are prepared to the cart, bicycle, and rail connections that take place repeatedly across the urban web, to the system of color coding that specifies from where the lunches come and to where they are to be delivered) are old and rooted in archaic networks. To separate these networks of distribution and recovery from the more classical ones of food production and distribution, or the markets in which pharmaceuticals, jewelry, textiles, or stone, wood, metal, or electronic goods are manufactured and sold, would be impossible. The Dharavi quarter is but one such site where these activities are part of an ancient ecological and urban web. Over a million

Just-in-time economics: More than 100,000 lunches are delivered (and recovered) daily in Mumbai through a largely informal system of distribution and tracking. It is said that perhaps twenty meals a year are even delivered late, let alone misplaced along their complex multi-segmented routes, displaying a level of efficiency that knows no rivals in the developed industrial world.

people live in Dharavi's two-thirds of a square mile of territory and operate more than 15,000 one-room factories, often as small as 100 square feet. Though it may be the world's largest slum, it has 100 percent employment. But Dharavi is also a city in itself, and its streets and alleys know no distinction between work and social space or even domestic or residential functions. It is said that no manufactured object in Mumbai does not spend at least one phase of its production chain in Dharavi. Although sanitation, water, and sewerage represent acutely serious problems in Dharavi, it nonetheless represents the veritable lungs, liver, and kidneys of greater Mumbai, as it cleans, reprocesses, removes, and transforms materials—and adds value—that are endemic to the economic and material functioning of greater Mumbai and beyond. Initial projects aimed at relieving the ground congestion by relocating residents to residential towers have clearly disrupted the web of Dharavi's magical "immanence" of social market functioning. The vertical dimension simply cannot bear the density of interactions upon which its multiple economies—and synergies—are based (families and workers typically live in or just above, in lofted granges, the shops and workshops in which they spend their days). Dharavi's contribution to the local economy is currently approaching

Low overhead is itself an engine of abundance.

Notes on the Third Ecology   101

$1 billion annually, and fortunes are made within its confines. The informal nature of what takes place within it, the mind-boggling compression and mutual proximities of skills and knowledge, and the novel ways of conducting business there represent an efficiency for many sectors of the economy that could be achieved in no other way or place (I refer to efficiencies that are not simply based on low wages and lack of social benefits, etc.). Dharavi, although certainly the site of the large-scale crime of social inequity, is also a place of visible and palpable civic pride (indeed most of the fortunes made there, remain there). The social and the economic may well be spatially and modally coextensive, but they are not identical, and the fit between the two is something often referred to in historical literatures of economics, but it has by no means been explained or understood. It presents an extraordinary challenge and exercise to the imagination simply to reflect on the implications and impacts that the destruction of this social-economic habitat will have on all parts of the larger urban ecology.[2] Although such urban transformations are always done in the name of remediation and modernization and presented as a way to transfer prosperity to ever greater numbers of inhabitants, it is clear that the effects in this case will not only be cultural and political but will have profound ecological impacts, both existentially and in terms of the efficient means—currently at risk of being lost—by which raw materials have traditionally cycled over and over through the system. The issues presented by these examples are not new. What is new, however, is that we have effectuated a major turn in thinking; we now have the conceptual tools, the intellectual models, and increasingly the predilection to understand the role of the palimpsest of archaic and modern, formal and informal, systems of organization to the economies they support as an asset and feature of urban ecologies and hence as a bona fide form of (free) equity that could, if desired, be preserved, extended, or even reproduced as we begin to imagine and plan our future worlds.

Among the basic issues of which we must not lose sight over the next decades is that what is required to give birth to a true ecological "praxis" for our cities and our civilization cannot be found or resolved within the scope of sustainability workshops, environmentalisms, policy reforms, and technological and scientific research and their applications. The ecological question is, by its very definition, much larger and more comprehensive. As it is, the relationship between nature and economic life—for long shunned as a habit of primitive and passéist thinking—is one that is beginning to appear in the foreground again. One popular example of this recrudescence was Thomas Friedman's op-ed pieces in the *New York Times* regarding what he calls "'Market to Mother Nature' accounting."[3]

There can be no "ecological thinking" that does not place human *social* destiny at the heart of our posture toward our environmental context. We may well learn over the next years that cities, even megacities, actually represent dramatically efficient ecological solutions, but this fact alone does not make them sustainable, especially if the forces of social invention remain trapped in tyrannies that only ecological thinking on an ecumenical scale can free us from. For ecological thinking too has its counterfeit and debased forms, and many "sustainability" discourses remain more oppressive than liberatory, more stifling than inventive, and it would be at great peril if we were to continue to assume that these two areas of approach, and especially their methods and presuppositions, are necessarily complementary.

We especially must not make the mistake of believing that one can detach the "human" and the "natural" from the aesthetic and still maintain that we have met the challenge of ecological thinking and ecological praxis. Similarly, it must not be assumed that by "human" we are referring to same set of qualities and potentials that are traditionally associated with these terms. For example, among the most radical and potentially fruitful conceptions of nature that have arisen in ecological circles in recent times are those from the Deep Ecology movement in the 1970s (coined 1973), whose foundational mandate was to think human being within and as part of the larger ecosphere, and not simply as an independent entity that inhabits it. This movement of thought sought to displace utilitarian approaches to the environment by refusing

Rooftops warehouse recycled goods so they can achieve the scale needed for the next transaction in the redistribution pyramid.

to see "nature" or the environment as a mere set of resources to be placed at the service of human purposes. Without a doubt, this conception of nature and environment opens the way to juridical, moral, and even cosmological arguments that are both controversial and profoundly suggestive. The same years in which the Deep Ecology movement was forming saw the emergence into the public imagination of James Lovelock's and Lynn Margulis's work on the Gaia Hypothesis (1972). Interestingly, one of the Gaia Hypothesis's most controversial features was to present the "natural" system of the self-managing biosphere as an autonomous entity, morally and theologically distinct from the interests and received purposes of the human species. Critics of the theory largely missed the deeper principles and opportunities provided by Lovelock's (and later, Lynn Margulis's) wager, that ecological thinking is at once scientifically sound and potentially far more "egalitarian" and accurate than much presupposition-infused orthodox science of the postwar period. Both of these developments (Deep Ecology and Gaian theory) have suggested that ethical and philosophical thought cannot be divorced from scientific creativity. This latter development defines another significant front that future design thinking will need to acknowledge and address.

Cities, on the other hand, have become the quintessential human habitat, confederacies as natural to us as were those of hunter-gatherer bands in the stone age whose optimum size of 150 members is said to have been ideal for both the easy and efficient exploitation of the resources of savannah biomes and the maintenance of the social and cultural equilibrium of these societies in all their overlapping dimensions— sexual, religious, and otherwise.

The role of what I am calling the "existential ecologies" of cities (in deference and homage to Felix Guattari), a concept intended to comprise everything that is required for the creative and dynamic inhabitation and utilization of the contemporary environment or, in a word, the cultural and social dimensions of our environment as rooted in the natural— are poorly theorized and understood, and at any rate insufficiently acknowledged. Yet they are key components of our ecology, without which none of the other parts could fit.

The challenges of ecological thinking are found principally in the deepest arenas of our imaginative and intellectual life. For example, as much promising and creative work is being made public today with respects to ultra-efficient and low-emission automobiles and novel proposals for large-scale transport, there is still relatively little evidence of a culture in which entirely new concepts and visions of "mobility" are

1 The title of former Vice President Al Gore's recent film and campaign, "An Inconvenient Truth" alludes to this problem.
2 My thanks to Noorie Sadarangani, whose work and interest with respect to Dharavi were critical to my acquaintance with this remarkable urban phenomenon, both as an object of study and as an extraordinary world to experience.
3 Ideas preliminarily developed in Thomas L. Friedman, *Hot, Flat, and Crowded: Why We Need a Green Revolution–and How It Can Renew America* (New York: Farrar, Straus and Giroux, 2008).

emerging to challenge the received ideas, and romance, of individualism and freedom long represented by the libertarian automobilist encounter with "the open road" that decades of especially American cinema and literature from the John Ford Western to the Wim Wenders Road Movie have methodically cultivated. The supposition that there are no possible alternative myths of modern mobility is an embarrassing aspect of contemporary lack of faith in human invention. The existential components of modern mobility are inseparably connected to the "pragmatic" dimensions that will continue to emerge as our society democratizes travel, distributes wealth, and intensifies, rather than discourages and inhibits, broad and genuine interest among all peoples and classes in the marvels of a diverse multicultural world and the natural assets and places that endow it. Although these twin interests—the need to manage the increasing ecological cost of travel and the need to encourage acquaintance with and curiosity about the environment—may seem contradictory, they are not. The forms of their future marriage are simply what must be invented.

Further still, the issue of mobility itself must be seen as embedded within the system of social communication and interaction as it currently exists—despite the extraordinary transformations that have already taken place in the last two decades of computer-driven networks. A broader ecological approach will see these as intimately linked, and the need to find genuinely new forms of social connection and organization—tantamount to new mores, myths, and habits—and the implicit belief that these are evolvable, is mandatory. Likewise our relationship to objects generally, to accumulation and consumption, must change; whether this happens before or after the 2- to 6-degree increase in global temperatures, and the demographic, geographical, and economic cataclysms that will accompany anything beyond the very lowest end of this already unavoidable spectrum, is up to history itself. At every level our historical cultural relationship to our environment is poised to transform significantly over the next very short period of time, and despite the incontrovertible testimony of the hard data, we are still unable to imagine most of the changes required of us, nor even to imagine the scale of required change as possible. It is not millenarian to speak this way, but it does pose an unprecedented challenge to the design community to serve as an organizing center for the variety of disciplines and systems of knowledge whose integration is a precondition for connecting them to clear political and imaginative and, most important, formal ends.

Social Inequality and Climate Change

Ulrich Beck

Thesis: *Climate change, which is held to be man-made and catastrophic, occurs in the shape of a new kind of synthesis of nature and society. While the inequality of life-chances arises from the ability to dispose of income, educational qualifications, passports, etc., their social character being very evident, the radical inequality of the consequences of climate change takes material form in the increasing frequency or exacerbation of natural events—floods, tornadoes, etc.—which are in principle familiar natural occurrences and are* not *self-evidently the product of societal decisions. The expression "force of nature" takes on a new meaning: The natural law evidence of "natural" catastrophes produces a naturalization of social relations of inequality and power. The political consequence: The conception of the natural equality of human beings tips over into the conception of a natural inequality of human beings produced by natural catastrophes.*

The facts are well known: Global warming, melting polar ice caps, rising sea levels, desertification, increase in the number of tornadoes. All of it usually treated as a natural catastrophe. But nature is not in itself catastrophic. The catastrophic character is only revealed within the field of reference of the society affected. The catastrophic potentials cannot be deduced from nature or from scientific analyses, but reflect the social vulnerability of certain countries and population groups to the consequences of climate change.

Social Vulnerability

Without the concept of social vulnerability, it is impossible to understand the catastrophic content of climate change. The idea that natural catastrophe and social vulnerability are two sides of the same coin is familiar wisdom to a way of thinking that sees the consequences of climate change as a co-product. In recent years, however, social vulnerability has become a key dimension in the social structural analysis of world risk society: Social processes and conditions produce an unequal exposure to hardly definable risks, and the resulting inequalities must largely be seen as an expression and product of power relations in the national and global context. *Social vulnerability* is a sum concept, encompassing means and possibilities, which individuals, communities, or whole populations have at their disposal, in order to cope—or not—with the threats of climate change (or financial crises).

A sociological understanding of vulnerability certainly has a crucial relationship to the future, but also has historical depth. The "cultural wounds" that, for example, result from the colonial past, constitute an important part of the background to understanding border-transcending climate conflicts. The more marginal the available economic and political options are, the more vulnerable a particular group or population. The question that allows the unit of investigation to be determined is this: What constitutes vulnerability in a particular context, and how did it become what it is?

In southern Mali, for example, the increasing vulnerability of villagers to catastrophic fires is a consequence of the implementation of state-prescribed fire policies, which in turn were a response to international pressure to deal with deforestation and desertification; to this end, links with various international organizations have to be officially established and, finally, the conditions for international indebtedness burdening the country in question addressed. For many countries in this have-not situation, these relations, which are now being reoriented and expanded under conditions of "globalization," can be traced back to colonialism.[1] Climate change can dramatically exacerbate regional vulnerability—or reduce it. Russia today already sees itself as benefiting from the future ecological crises, because it has large reserves of fossil fuels, while warmer temperatures also permit an expansion of agriculture in Siberia. If the ecological imperative asserts itself, then human beings will have to radically alter their behavior in a wide variety of spheres—from health to politics, business and education, and questions of justice. The ecological imperative is not about something that might be "out there." Our whole way of life is attuned to industrial society modernity—with its extravagant use of resources and indifference to nature—which is disappearing thanks to the triumph of industrialism. The more we are driven out of the paradise of climate innocence, the more do the forms of thinking, living, and acting that we had previously taken for granted give rise to conflicts, and are even considered criminal.

The Side-Effects Principle

I have argued that the nation-state principle is no longer in a position to describe the inequalities resulting from climate change. What can take its place? My suggestion is the *side-effects principle*. It states: The basic unit of natural-social inequality is constituted by persons, populations, regions that are existentially affected across nation-state frontiers by the side-effects of decisions of national others. Methodological nationalism can be defined once more from this perspective: Within its horizon the nation-state principle coincides with the side-effects principle. This identity becomes increasingly false as environmental problems become worldwide world-internal problems. Often, however, it is also the case that climate threats are exported, either spatially (to countries whose elites see a chance to make a profit) or temporally (into the future of generations not yet born). National frontiers do not need to be removed for this flourishing export of dangers; on the contrary, their existence is a precondition of it. What is deliberately done remains "latent" and a "side-effect" only because these walls (whether actual or discursive) continue to exist in people's heads and in law. Not wanting to accept environmental dangers as internal world dangers is most frequently encountered where people have no possibility of escape. Accordingly the risks are dumped in places where they are not perceived as such. The acceptance of dangers in these countries is not to be equated with the agreement of the people living there, rather with silence and speechlessness fed by need. The ignoring of climate-related threats in countries in which poverty and the illiteracy rate are particularly high does not at all mean that these societies are not integrated in world risk society. Rather, the opposite is true: They offer as their "wealth" the otherwise limited resource of silence and so are the worst affected. This is exactly what global environmental dangers presume and set in motion. The production of risk and being subject to risk are spatially and temporally uncoupled. The catastrophe potential one population creates affects "others": people in other societies and future generations. It is accordingly true that whoever takes a decision that exposes others to danger can no longer be held accountable. There arises—worldwide—an organized irresponsibility. The construction of climate change as "latent side-effect" is also made possible because the actions required for the management of transnational environmental problems collide with the national perspective and the national logic of political institutions. In this sense global climate risks are both latent and a threat to humanity; and the nation-state institutions whose responsibility it is to deal with them are blind both to their global character and their natural society character. It is climate researchers, in particular, ignoring scientific doubts out of a sense of responsibility and acting as cosmopolitan citizens, who have pointed this out.

There is no longer any question that climate change globalizes and radicalizes social inequalities. To research them more thoroughly, it is necessary to break up the misleadingly narrow framework, restricted to "gross social product" or "income per head," into which the problem of inequality is usually forced. Accordingly research must concentrate on the fatal conjunction of poverty, social vulnerability, corruption, accumulation of dangers, and loss of dignity.[2] The region worst affected by all of that—apart, that is, from island states, which are disappearing under the waves—is the Sahel zone south of the Sahara. It is already impoverished and torn apart by religious and ethnic tensions, and the decline in rainfall could lead to an explosion of violence and to wars. In the Sahel the poorest of the poor live on the edge of the abyss, and climate change threatens to push them—those who have done least to cause it—over the edge. By every existing standard, that is a crying injustice. Yet at the same time it appears as a "natural catastrophe": No rain. What does it mean?

This text is an excerpt from a paper entitled "Remapping Social Inequalities in an Age of Climate Change: For a Cosmopolitan Renewal of Sociology," delivered at the Harvard Graduate School of Design on October 6, 2009.

1 See J. X. Kasperson and R. F. Kasperson, *The Social Contours of Risk*, 2 vols. (London: Earthscan, 2005).

2 In this context, Amartya Sen has proposed and elaborated mortality as a key indicator: "The epidemiological atmosphere in which someone lives can have a substantial influence on morbidity and mortality." See "Mortality as an Indicator of Economic Success and Failure," *Economic Journal*, vol. 108 (1998).

For a Post-Environmentalism: Seven Suggestions for a New Athens Charter

Andrea Branzi

There is the environmental problem, but there is also the problem of environmentalism and environmentalists.

Post-environmentalism is a cultureless monologic that doesn't promote the government of the scientists and allies itself with the cultural vanguards (of which it has been a daughter, and of which today it's an orphan). A culture that together with the environment saves the mythical and epic roots of the cosmic environment.

When we talk about a "New Athens Charter," we mean to describe a cityscape in the age of the Third Industrial Revolution, of globalization and of diffuse work, of the environmental crisis and of the environmentalism crisis.

The aim of the "New Athens Charter" is not the city of the Future but rather the city of the Present, with all of its faults and contradictions. A city that has always to be reformed, reshaped, and replanned, in search of temporary balances that need an ongoing setting. A city that corresponds to our "self-reformist" society, that every day has to produce new laws and rules to manage its permanent crisis in a positive way.

First suggestion:
Urban refunctionalization.

Foster the reuse of the existing estates, to fit the present city to the new need of diffuse work, of mass enterprise, of creative economy, and of cultural production and consumption.

Second suggestion:
Great transformations through microstructures.

The quality of the city is made by the quality of its domestic objects, tools, facilities, products shown in the shop windows, people, flowers in their vases. As with the microcredits of Muhammad Yunus, we have to enter in the home economies and the interstices of daily life.

Third suggestion:
The city as a high-tech favela.

Avoid rigid and definitive solutions and foster reversible facilities that can be dismantled and transformed, allowing the interior space to accommodate new activities that are unforeseen and not programmed. Thus, a city that considers as a value the integral liberalization of the urban system.

Fourth suggestion:
The city as a personal computer every 20 square meters.

Avoid specialized typologies, rigid facilities, and identification between form and function; create interior spaces similar to functionoids, that can host any kind of activity in any place, changing their function in real time.

Fifth suggestion:
Cosmic hospitality.

Realize (as in the Indian metropolis) the conditions for a cohabitation between man and the animal kingdom, technologies and divinity, alive and dead people.

A metropolis less anthropocentric and more open to biodiversities, to the sacred and to human beauty.

Sixth suggestion:
Weak urbanization models.

Create threshold areas between city and countryside, through hybrid territories, half urban and half agricultural; productive territories, horizontal, hospitable (but without cathedrals), following seasons and weather, allowing conditions of flexible and discontinuous housing.

Seventh suggestion:
Shade borders and fundaments.

Realize architectural facilities with crossable perimeters, to create an urban texture where the difference between interior and exterior, public and private, is intended to disappear, creating an integrated territory without specializations.

The Weak Metropolis

Andrea Branzi

The models of weak urbanization consist in the cohabitation of half-agricultural and half-urban territories.

The weak metropolis is not a system of architectural boxes, but an always changing enzymatic territory, consisting in a personal computer every 20 square meters.

It's not the metropolis of the future, but the metropolis of the present.

A metropolis must always change its functions from inside;

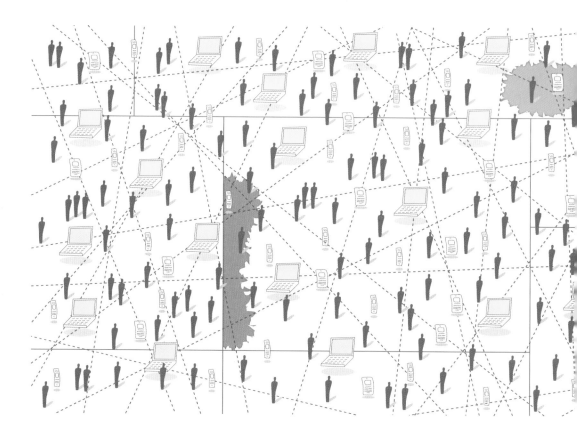

without permanent solutions, but based on reversibility;

on functional un-definition;

on fluid perimeters;

on cohabitation between living and dead beings, humans, and animals.

It's a territory of experience;

a concave space;

a high-tech favela;

an air-conditioned area.

It's the space of a civilization of goods;

the uncertain site of a self-reforming society.

The quality of the weak metropolis is in the quality of its objects.

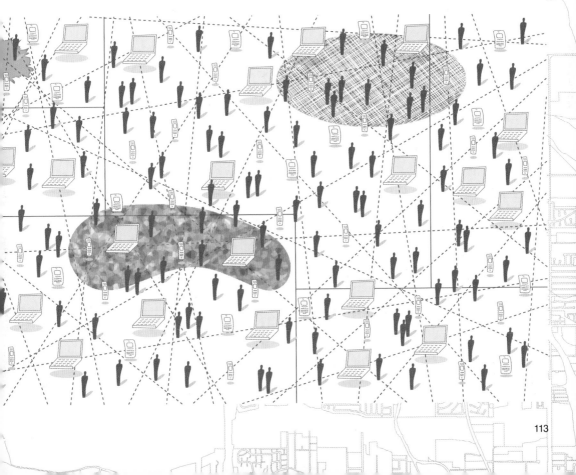

Weak Work:
Andrea Branzi's "Weak Metropolis" and the Projective Potential of an "Ecological Urbanism"

Charles Waldheim

In his introduction to the Ecological Urbanism conference, Mohsen Mostafavi described ecological urbanism as both a critique of and a continuation by other terms of the discourse of landscape urbanism. Ecological urbanism proposes (just as landscape urbanism proposed over a decade ago) to multiply the available lines of thought on the contemporary city to include environmental and ecological concepts, while expanding traditional disciplinary and professional frameworks for describing those urban conditions. As a critique of the landscape urbanist agenda, ecological urbanism promises to render that dated discourse more specific to ecological, economic, and social conditions of the contemporary city.

Mostafavi's introduction suggested that ecological urbanism implied the projective potential of the design disciplines to render alternative future scenarios. He further indicated that those alternative futures may place us across various "spaces of disagreement." These spaces of disagreement span the range of disciplinary and professional borders comprising the study of the city. Any contemporary examination of those disciplinary frameworks would acknowledge that the challenges of the contemporary city rarely respect traditional disciplinary boundaries. This realization recalls Roland Barthes' formulation on the various roles of language and fashion in the production of interdisciplinary knowledge:

> Interdisciplinarity is not the calm of an easy security; it begins *effectively* when the solidarity of old disciplines breaks down—perhaps even violently, through the jolts of fashion—in the interests of a new object and a new language.[1]

In reading the new language proposed by the ecological urbanism initiative, the subtitle of the recent Harvard conference on the subject, "Alternative and Sustainable Cities of the Future," is equally telling. This construction indicates the linguistic cul-de-sac that confronts much of contemporary urbanism, constructed around a false choice between critical cultural relevance and environmental survival. The conference title and subtitle further signify disciplinary fault lines between the well-established discourse on sustainability and the long tradition of using urban projections as descriptions of the contemporary conditions for urban culture.

This reading suggests that ecological urbanism might re-animate discussions of sustainability with the political, social, cultural, and critical potentials that have been drained from them. This shift would be particularly apt as the design fields presently experience a profound disjunction of realms in which environmental health and design culture are opposed. This historical opposition has produced a contemporary condition in which ecological function, social justice, and cultural literacy are perceived by many as mutually exclusive. This disjunction of concerns has led to a situation in which design culture has been depoliticized, distanced from the empirical and objective conditions of urban life. At the same moment, increased calls for environmental remediation, ecological health, and biodiversity suggest the potential for reimagining urban futures. Among the results of this disjunction of intellectual and practical commitments has been that we are collectively coerced into choosing between alternate urban paradigms, each espousing exclusive access to environmental health, social justice, or cultural relevance.

Homi Bhabha used his keynote address at the conference to frame the ecological urbanism project in temporal terms, arguing that "it is always too early, or too late, to talk about cities of the future." In so doing, Bhabha locates the ecological

Andrea Branzi, et al., "Masterplan Strijp Philips, Eindhoven," model view (1999–2000)

urbanism project in a complex intertwined dialectic between the ecologies of the informal and the relentless reach of modernization. Bhabha maintains that one is in effect always working with the problems of the past, but these problems appear differently in new emergent contemporary conditions. Thus the project of ecological urbanism, Bhabha insists, is a "work of projective imagination."[2]

It is in those terms, as work of projective imagination, that the urban projects of Andrea Branzi might be found relevant to the emergent discourse on ecological urbanism. Branzi's work reanimates a long tradition of using urban projects as social and cultural critique. This form of urban projection deploys a project not simply as an illustration or "vision" but rather as a demystified distillation and description of our present urban predicaments. In this sense, one might read Branzi's urban projects as less a utopian future possible world than a critically engaged and politically literate delineation of the power structures, forces, and flows shaping the contemporary urban condition. Over the past four decades, Branzi's work has articulated a remarkably consistent critique of the social, cultural, and intellectual poverty of much laissez-faire urban development and the realpolitik assumptions of much urban design and planning. As an alternative, Branzi's projects propose urbanism in the form of an environmental, economic, and aesthetic critique of the failings of the contemporary city.

Born and educated in Florence, Branzi studied architecture in a cultural milieu of the Operaists and a scholarly tradition of Marxist critique, as evidenced through speculative urban proposals as a form of cultural criticism. Branzi first came to international visibility as a member of the collective

Archizoom Associati, "No-Stop City" (1968–71)

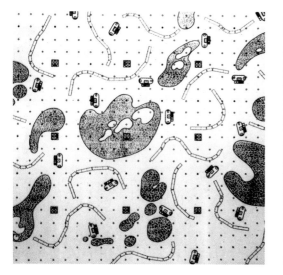
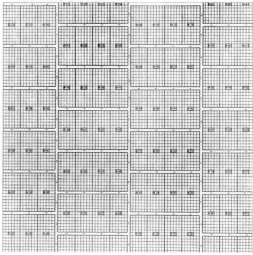

P.V. Aureli and M. Tattara/Dogma, "Stop City," aerial view (2008)

Typical plan, forest canopy (2008)

Archizoom (mid-1960s), based in Milan but associated with the Florentine Architettura Radicale movement. Archizoom's project and texts for "No-Stop City" (1968–71) illustrate an urbanism of continuous mobility, fluidity, and flux. While "No-Stop City" was received on one level as a satire of the British technophilia of Archigram, it was also viewed as an illustration of an urbanism without qualities, a representation of the "degree-zero" conditions for urbanization.[3]

Archizoom's use of typewriter keystrokes on A4 paper to represent a nonfigural planning study for "No-Stop City" anticipated contemporary interest in indexical and parametric representations of the city. Their work prefigured current attention to describing the relentlessly horizontal field conditions of the modern metropolis as a surface shaped by the strong forces of economic and ecological flows. Equally, these drawings and their texts pointed toward today's investigations of infrastructure and ecology as nonfigurative drivers of urban form. As such, a generation of contemporary urbanists have drawn from Branzi's intellectual commitments. This diverse list of influence ranges from Stan Allen and James Corner's interest in field conditions to Alex Wall and Alejandro Zaera Polo's concern with logistics.[4] More recently, Pier Vittorio Aureli and Martino Tattara's project "Stop-City" directly references Branzi's use of nonfigurative urban projection as a form of social and political critique.[5] Branzi's urban projects are equally available to inform contemporary interests within architectural culture and urbanism on an array of topics as diverse as animalia, indeterminacy, and genericity, among others.

As a deliberately "nonfigurative" urbanism, "No-Stop City" renewed and disrupted a longstanding traditional nonfigu-

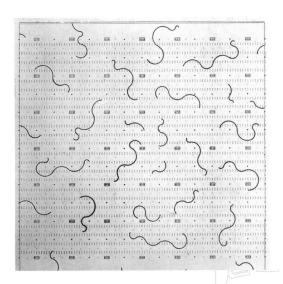

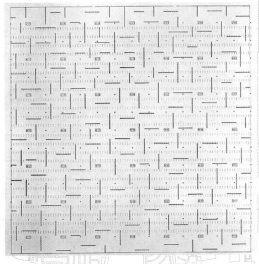

rative urban projection as socialist critique. In this regard, Branzi's "No-Stop City" draws on the urban planning projects and theories of Ludwig Hilberseimer, particularly Hilberseimer's "New Regional Pattern" and that project's illustration of a proto-ecological urbanism.[6]

Not coincidentally, both Branzi and Hilberseimer chose to illustrate the city as a continuous system of relational forces and flows, as opposed to a collection of objects. In this sense, the ongoing recuperation of Hilberseimer, and Branzi's renewed relevance for discussions of contemporary urbanism, renders their work particularly meaningful to discussions of ecological urbanism. Andrea Branzi occupies a singular historical position as a hinge figure between the social and environmental aspirations of modernist planning of the postwar era and the politics of 1968 in which his work first emerged for English-language audiences. As such, his work is particularly well suited to shed light on the emergent discussion around ecological urbanism.

Branzi's 1993/94 project Agronica returns to his interest in the relentlessly horizontal spread of capital across thin tissues of territory, and the resultant "weak urbanization" that the neoliberal economic paradigm affords. Agronica represents the potential parallelism between agricultural and energy production, new modalities of post-Fordist industrial economy, and the cultures of consumption that they construct.[7] More recently in 2000/01, Branzi (with the Domus Academy, a postgraduate research institute founded in 1980s) executed a project for Philips in Eindhoven. These projects returned to the recurring themes in Branzi's oeuvre with typical wit and pith, illustrating a "Territory for the New Economy."[8]

Ludwig Hilberseimer (with Alfred Caldwell), bird's-eye view of commercial area and settlement unit (c. 1943)

Ludwig Hilberseimer, "The City in the Landscape" (1949)

Andrea Branzi's intervention in the ecological urbanism conference was timely in that it followed a presentation by Andrés Duany. That the ecological urbanism agenda could be found relevant to a cultural and professional breadth of urban

thought spanning from Andrea to Andrés is accomplishment enough, considering the relatively narrow confines within which debates in contemporary urbanism are often described. Branzi's primary contribution to the proceedings consisted of a keynote lecture featuring a surreal video anthology of his greatest hits of "weak urbanism," accompanied by a Patti Smith soundtrack. This montage of four decades of urban projection offered a visual manifesto of sorts, proclaiming "weak urbanization" as a medium of environmental and cultural relevance. Branzi prefaced his prepackaged multimedia mashup with a brief introductory text prepared for the event (read in Italian with simultaneous translation by Nicoletta Morozzi) proposing seven suggestions toward a "post-environmentalism."[9] These points succinctly framed Branzi's longstanding call for a conception of contemporary urbanism as a field of potentials, shaped by weak forces and spontaneous programmatic eruptions. Branzi's seven "suggestions" (reprinted in this volume as a "New Athens Charter") offer a surreal and nonlinear set of propositions simultaneously accounting for and celebrating the failings of the contemporary city.

Branzi's "weak work" maintains its relevance for generations of urbanists. His longstanding call for the development of weak urban forms and nonfigural fields has already influenced the thinking of those who articulated landscape urbanism over a decade ago. Equally, Branzi's projective and polemical urban propositions promise to shed light on the evolving understanding of ecological urbanism and its potential for reconfiguring the disciplines and professions responsible for describing the contemporary city.

Andrea Branzi, et al., "Agronica," model view (1993–94)

> **Archizoom Associati, "No-Stop City" (1968–71)**

1 Roland Barthes, "From Work to Text," *Image Music Text*, translated by Stephen Heath (New York: Hill and Wang, 1977), 155.

2 Homi Bhabha, "Keynote (Footnote)," with Rem Koolhaas and Sanford Kwinter, Ecological Urbanism Conference, Harvard Graduate School of Design, April 3, 2009.

3 Archizoom Associates, "No-Stop City. Residential Parkings. Climatic Universal Sistem," *Domus* 496 (March 1971): 49–55. For Branzi's reflections on the project, see Andrea Branzi, "Notes on No-Stop City: Archizoom Associates 1969–1972," *Exit Utopia: Architectural Provocations 1956–1976,* edited by Martin van Schaik and Otakar Macel (Munich: Prestel, 2005), 177–182. For more recent scholarship on the project and its relation to contemporary architectural culture and urban theory, see Kazys Varnelis, "Programming after Program: Archizoom's No-Stop City," *Praxis,* no. 8 (May 2006): 82–91.

4 On field conditions and contemporary urbanism, see James Corner, "The Agency of Mapping: Speculation, Critique and Invention," *Mappings,* edited by Denis Cosgrove (London: Reaktion Books, 1999), 213–300; and Stan Allen, *"Mat Urbanism: The Thick 2-D," CASE: Le Corbusier's Venice Hospital and the Mat Building*

Revival, edited by Hashim Sarkis (Munich: Prestel, 2001), 118–126. On logistics and contemporary urbanism, see Susan Nigra Snyder and Alex Wall, "Emerging Landscape of Movement and Logistics," *Architectural Design Profile*, no. 134 (1998): 16–21; and Alejandro Zaera Polo, "Order Out of Chaos: The Material Organization of Advanced Capitalism," *Architectural Design Profile*, no. 108 (1994): 24–29.

5 See Pier Vittorio Aureli and Martino Tattara, "Architecture as Framework: The Project of the City and the Crisis of Neoliberalism," *New Geographies*, vol. 1 (2009): 38–51.

6 Ludwig Hilberseimer, *The New Regional Pattern: Industries and Gardens, Workshops and Farms* (Chicago: Paul Theobald, 1949).

7 Andrea Branzi, D. Donegani, A. Petrillo, and C. Raimondo, "Symbiotic Metropolis: Agronica," *The Solid Side,* edited by Ezio Manzini and Marco Susani (Netherlands: V+K Publishing/Philips, 1995), 101–120.

8 Andrea Branzi, "Preliminary Notes for a Master Plan," and "Master Plan Strijp Philips, Eindhoven 1999," *Lotus*, no. 107 (2000): 110–123.

9 Andrea Branzi, "The Weak Metropolis," Ecological Urbanism Conference, Harvard Graduate School of Design, April 4, 2009.

Andrea Branzi, et al., "Masterplan Strijp Philips, Eindhoven," model view (1999–2000)

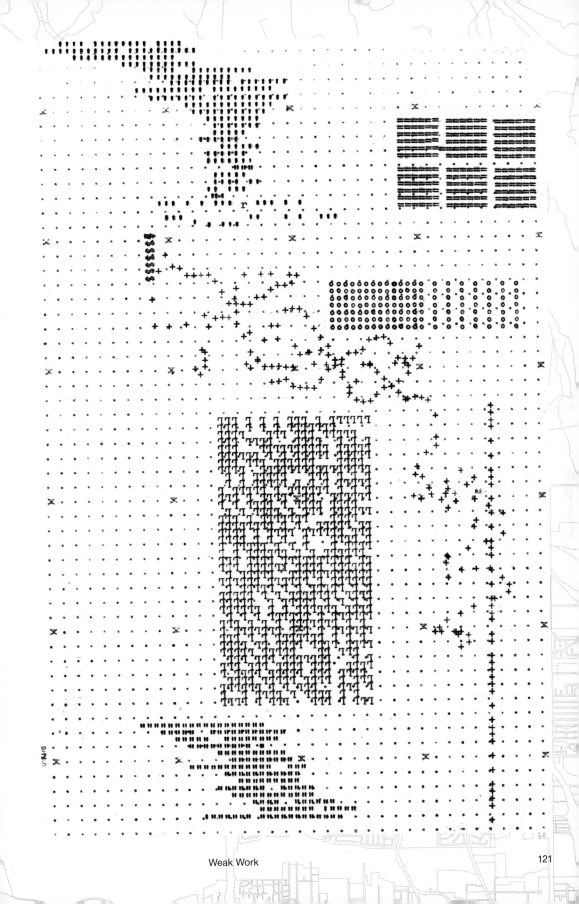

From "Sustain" to "Ability"

JDS Architects

There's a definition problem: "Green" and "sustainable," the terms used to name the answer to the most pressing problem of our time, have become dangerously afloat in ambiguity and indeterminacy. Sustainable architecture is everywhere and nowhere.

There's a coolness problem: "Green" and "sustainable," in their current form, have made architecture a task rather than a desire. Sustainability as a proliferation of green Photoshopped pixels is considered cool, but articulate, intentional, enthusiastic positions on sustainability aren't.

There's an ambition problem: "Green" and "sustainable" have become codified, commodified, and certified. Prescribed checklists masquerade as design philosophy. Inherited truths appear stale, and piecemeal solutions provide only temporary fixes.

As young architects, our generation must enthusiastically embrace new ideas about sustainability, questioning inherited doctrine and forging new trajectories. We are no longer impressed by the latest one-off LEED Platinum building. We integrate sustainable principles fundamentally and combine historically verified practices with youthful creativity and eager ingenuity to discover new pathways to a more ecological architecture. We are the first generation of architects for whom sustainability was embedded in our education— what could in the near future come to be known as the "post-sustainability" generation. We believe that architecture must shift its focus from "sustain" to "ability," abandoning the ambiguity, guilt, and compromise characteristic of too much "sustainable" design today, and demanding instead precise, beautiful, and systematic instigations for change.

Shenzhen Logistic City is a 1,111-meter tower that instigates a dense and diverse vertical urbanism. Unlike most skyscraper towers that are merely tall, the JDS proposal is tall and thick, interior and exterior, urban and rural, public and private, gritty and green. Its monumentality is achieved both from a distance and from within.

Forty Years Later–
Back to a Sub-lunar Earth

Bruno Latour

Space shuttle *Columbia* hurtles toward space on mission STS-107. Following a flawless countdown, liftoff occurred on time at 10:39 a.m. EST. Landing was scheduled for about 8:53 a.m. EST on Saturday, February 1, 2003.

How odd they look, the so-called spaceships of forty years ago! Makeshift assemblages of what in retrospect resemble cans of corned beef wrapped in reused sheets of aluminum foil from some improvised picnic. And indeed, what a picnic it was when it happened. How moved I was as a young man glued at night to the black-and-white TV, this glorious summer of 1969. And yet we don't look at them with the same consideration as we do, for instance, the Blériot number XI now hanging from the ceiling of the Romanesque church that houses, oddly enough, the Museum of Technology in Paris. Exactly a century after Louis Blériot crossed the Channel (July 25, 1909), many of us travel safely inside the huge whalelike hull of Boeings and Airbuses—wondering how this tiny seed bloomed into this magnificent institution of air travel.

And yet nothing of the sort has happened with the makeshift spacecrafts of forty years ago. While the Blériot XI is clearly the precursor of planes of today, the Apollo missions are no longer seen as the precursors of any sort of travel. They look rather the odd but somewhat baroque remnants of some daring adventures that led nowhere. An impasse. The men on the moon remind me less of Blériot than of some of Werner Herzog's heroes, as if Neil Amstrong were closer to Aguirre or Fitzcarraldo, lost in the jungle of dreams that never added up to much. Why are they called "the first pioneers of the conquest of space"? Can you call pioneers those who are followed by no one? Where is the New Frontier if it has reverted to the limit of a desolated desert that will never be fit for any inhabitant?

Could I have imagined, forty years ago, that the Apollo missions were not leading toward outer space, but, on the contrary, would soon backfire and lead our attention to inner space? I mean the space of the Blue Planet that astronauts were filming with such rapt precision. We have learned in the meantime that space is a contested territory. It is hard to imagine that in such a short span of life the "arrow of time" too has so thoroughly changed its shape and direction. It is not an arrow anymore, targeting some well-accepted goal. It is rather like a plate of spaghetti, zigzagging around without leading in one direction, to one climax—even if you cook them *al dente.* So much for the macho imagination of space adventure: Forward! Forward! Back to Earth, rather. And to discover what? That the Earth is about as fragile as this tiny model of the Earth that was called a space station. Billions of dollars spent by NASA to give some weight to a sheer metaphor: the Blue Planet as a spaceship—and a makeshift one at that.

To discover what? That the metaphor is not a good one, because even the crew inside Apollo 13 could at least call back to Earth. But who will answer if earthlings begin to panic and report: "Houston, we have a problem." As far as I know, we on this Earth have no backup staff to calmly and competently advise us on how to handle our little problems and tell us how to purge carbon dioxide from the spacecraft atmosphere, as NASA engineers did with the lost crew of Apollo 13, who had rehearsed every gesture down on Earth. Even if gods, angels, and cherubs were picking up the phone, I doubt that they would know how to handle our carbon dioxide problem. And if they did, how would we understand their gentle spiritual advice, anyway? If we could hear their voices, they would probably suggest other solutions, other problems, other missions. "Mission aborted; sorry, we suggest you go back home." The sixty-year space-time between Louis Blériot and Neil Armstrong has probably been more stable than the forty years

Kennedy Space Center, Florida: The Columbia Reconstruction Project Team is attempting to reconstruct the orbiter as part of the investigation into the accident that caused the destruction of *Columbia* and loss of its crew as it returned to Earth.

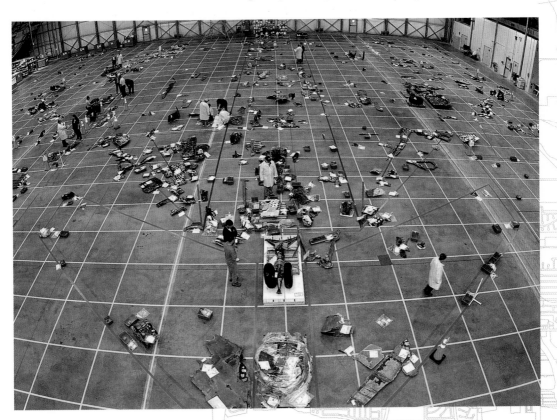

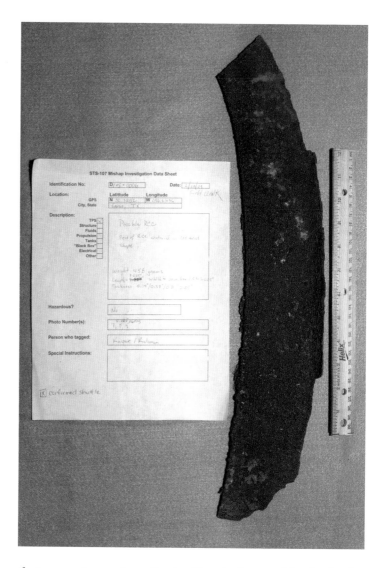

that separates us from the Apollo mission. Nothing looks the same. Space is different, and so is time. Space is now that of a fully urbanized planet Earth, the fragility of which we begin to fathom and the complete design—or rather redesign—of which we have to take up. As for time, it is no longer an arrow that will thrust forward and allow us to unequivocally tell progress from regress, conservatives from revolutionaries. This dream of sorting things out has become an impasse as well.

It is not only that time has passed. It has changed thoroughly from the way it used to pass. We need to do a little bit of cosmopolitics history here. When they left Cape Canaveral, the spacecrafts left an Earth for a moon that was taken to be roughly the same type of heavenly body. Remember that back then, we used to reside in the Galilean cosmos. Remember (we have to make an effort because it is so close in time and so far in spirit) Galileo showing to his astonished colleagues that there was no difference between sub-lunar and supra-lunar bodies. What a shock it was. But today, forty years later, when we watch the rockets leaving Cape Canaveral, it is no longer from a Galilean soil aiming at a Galilean Mars or a Galilean moon. They leave from Gaia! What a shock it is: between Gaia and a Galilean Earth, there is probably as much difference as between Galileo, Descartes, or Newton and the Aristotelian cosmos that they had destroyed (or so the official story goes). We have learned the hard way that there is now not much relationship between, on the one hand, the imaginary world of Cape Canaveral, of the spacecrafts, of the Galilean moon and planets, and, on the other hand, Gaia. Both are real, for sure, but not woven in the same sort of hard and harsh realities. This very Earth that for centuries had been a sub-lunar sphere wholly different from the supra-lunar one has again become a sub-lunar sphere of existence wholly different from the lunar and supra-lunar spheres. What a paradox! What a twist in history! Welcome to the sixteenth century.

And yet of course everything is different from that age as well. Gaia is not the mere return of a pre-Galilean cosmos. Nothing much is left of modernism, and yet everything is new. To reengineer the imagination of architects, of urban planners (of Earth planners), of designers, of social scientists, of activists, and of citizens now unwittingly in charge of this planet, there is no way to turn to the past—there is no past to which to direct our queries, no help desk, no competent staff ready in Houston, and no gods or cherubs either. Those who have left the Cape Canaveral of modernism have to renew everything without the benefit of the modernist cosmos. They have to inhabit a wholly new place, a place as different from a holy cosmos as it is from the cosmos of forty years ago. Where will they learn their new skills?

COLLABORAT

Art Fieldwork
Giuliana Bruno

Ecological Urbanism and/as Urban Metaphor
Lawrence Buell

Black and White in Green Cities
Lizabeth Cohen

The Return of Nature
Preston Scott Cohen and Erika Naginski

Urban Ecological Practices: Félix Guattari's *Three Ecologies*
Verena Andermatt Conley

Retrofitting the City
Leland D. Cott

Productive Urban Environments
Margaret Crawford

Art Fieldwork

Giuliana Bruno

A wide-ranging cultural phenomenon, ecological urbanism extends far beyond architecture, landscape architecture, and urban planning and design, and especially engages the visual arts. Its visions, methods, and imaginary models can be powerfully generated in the form of an artwork.

Icelandic artist Katrin Sigurdardóttir creates inventive architectural models whose inner construction speaks of such active fieldwork. She makes haptic environmental installations animated by spectatorial movement that, in turn, activates the space imaginatively. *Untitled* (2004), for example, consists of a long jagged wall that, in formal terms, resembles a Nordic coastline, which museum-goers can imaginarily visit by wandering through the installation. Appearing to fold in on itself, this large architectural structure unfolds for us the image of a distant landscape. Nature and culture become connected here, as they do in *Island* (2003), which resembles a miniature island and produces the same effect at a different sculptural scale. In both works this form of imaginary architectural traversal enables different experiences of habitation to unfold as a creative geography.

Sigurdardóttir's work reminds us that, as a production of space, ecological urbanism is a complex phenomenon, in which perceptual and representational aspects cannot be separated from function or use. She works with a representational space that is conceptually used and perceptually lived. Her space shows the marks of living, as in *Odd Lots* (2005),

whose seven transport crates imaginarily contain segments of a New York neighborhood. These discrete units of urban dwelling are able to travel: the individual crates can be shipped separately, find their homes in disparate locations, and display proof of their journeys in transit documents. When seen together, the crates make up an urban landscape, with all the potential journeys of dwelling it contains, thus rendering the composite image that makes up the very composition of the architectural imaginary of ecological urbanism.

Sigurdardóttir shows that the image of a city is a truly moving internal assemblage: it is that mental map we carry within us of the place in which we live. This kind of urban fabric, materialized in *Odd Lots,* becomes earthy in *Haul* (2005), whose eleven transport crates form the composite image of a natural landscape. Displacements and condensations take place on this artist's map as her imaginary traversal of sites weaves unconscious material into it and envelops mnemonic fabrication. The work of recollection shows in *Green Grass of Home* (1997, above), a suitcase/toolbox with multiple compartments that fold out. As we open this particular suitcase, the baggage of memories unfolds. Each compartment contains a model of a park or

a landscape that, at one time or another, was near the artist's home in the different cities she inhabited. This composite memory landscape takes us from Reykjavik to New York, San Francisco, and Berkeley. The mnemonic suitcase was made by an artist in transit and functioned as a mobile studio, traveling as luggage with her, and carrying with it the journey of dwelling.

The inside of this suitcase is an exterior landscape that in turn contains the traces of an interior world. And thus the internal map of a lived space becomes fabricated as a foldout—a structure that turns things inside out. In this female artist's work, interior and exterior show as two sides of the same architecture, and we experience the type of reversal that exists in reversible fabrics, where inside and outside are not distinct but rather made to be exchangeable. Sigurdardóttir's installations are fashioned as if architecture could be textile, a space dressed with reversible fabric so that everything that is inward can turn outward, and vice versa. This manner of turning space inside out recurs in *2nd Floor* (2003), a version of the large foldable landscape of *Untitled* that also recalls the miniature *Island*. The same logic of reversal is used here as the shape of the hallway of the artist's New York apartment is twisted to suit the map of an

Icelandic riverbed, thus connecting the landscape of the place of origin to the urbanism of the elected home.

As migrant memories of lived spaces are held together in the textural construction of the architectural imaginary of ecological urbanism, the generative fabric of architecture unfolds its own reversible fabrication. This cultural landscape shows its inner wear, for it is in many ways a trace of the memories, the attention, and the imagination of those inhabitant-passengers who have traversed it at different times. These artistic environments can contain us, the viewers, in their geopsychic design and navigate our own stories, for they also carry our emotional response to space, as Sigurdardóttir shows in *Fyrirmynd/ Model* (1998–2000). In yet another inner-outer reversal, a miniature highway is mapped out from a diagram of the neuronal pathways activated inside our brains when we have an emotional response to perception. As she makes the fabric of lived space perceivable in foldable, reversible pathways, the artist exposes the neurological texture of the architectural fabrication, proving that, as an architectural imaginary, ecological urbanism is a product of mental life, propelled by the movement of mental energy and the empathic motion of emotion.

Ecological Urbanism and/as Urban Metaphor

Lawrence Buell

For an environmental humanist to discuss "ecological urbanism" is sure to convey the impression of beginning from the extreme margins of the subject proper. I approach the topic as a keenly interested outlier, curious as to what this luminous, suggestive, but previously unfamiliar rubric might mean. As an "ecocritic"—one who specializes in literary and artistic discourses and representations—I immediately think in terms of metaphor. A number of master tropes suggest themselves as possible lenses through which to envisage the particular kind of community that ecological urbanism is or might become. Is it to be thought of an an agenda? A school? a nexus? a dialogue? a marketplace? Perhaps all of these, and others as well, might to some extent apply. But however the fomenters may prefer to define their project, metaphor will certainly play a constitutive part, however unobtrusive, in the shaping, communication, and reception of what is thought to count as ecological urbanism.

My confidence here arises in part from awareness of the longstanding practice within urbanism more generally of relying upon metaphor for schematic encapsulation of the relation between the built and the natural in cityspace. Surveying the history of literary and other modes of imaging urban space, we find a cornucopia of "defining" metaphors variously used for this purpose, some of recent coinage, some in circulation for millennia. These include—not that this exhausts the list of possibilities—city/nature as *binary*, as *holistic macro-organism*, as *palimpsest*, as *fragment* (either in the sense of fissured

districts or as spatial frames through which one navigates serially), as *network*, as *sprawl*, as *apocalypse* (city as ultimate utopic or dystopic mode of inhabitance). All arguably have both heuristic advantages and shortcomings for understanding environmental materiality and the lived experience of urbanism.

The specific case I want to take up here is organismal metaphor. This is a longstanding way of poetic imagining. The romantic poet William Wordsworth pictures himself standing on London's Westminster Bridge at dawn, imagining London's "mighty heart" "lying still" underneath the scene of pastoral tranquility ("Earth hath not anything to show more fair"). His American successor Walt Whitman personifies "million-footed Manhattan." James Joyce's *Finnegans Wake* mythicizes Dublin as a configuration of primal land and river deities, Humphry Chimpden Earwicker and Anna Livia Plurabelle. These urban personifications, however, have a longer continuity in the history and theory of urban design itself. Cultural historian Richard Sennett argues that city "spaces take form largely from the ways people experience their own bodies," tracing this supposed linkage in his book *Flesh and Stone* from the theory of the polis in classical Athens to the fragmented multi-cultural metropolises of today, contending that at each stage architectural practice is inflected by predominant strategies of bodily display or concealment. Cultural theorist Elizabeth Grosz subjects this model, for good reason I think, to feminist critique as overly intentionalist and teleological, contending that environment and body "produce each other" in ways that are mutually transformative. Yet this counterargument only reaffirms the underlying idea of the body-city analogy.

Even more striking for present purposes is the frequency with which the language of corporeal holism seeps into the idioms of urban planning, as when landscape architects and planners recycle the Olmstedian cliché that parks are "the lungs of the city" and metaphorize major roadways as "arteries"; when urban engineers and environmental analysts discuss "urban metabolism" and a city's "ecological footprint" not as figures of speech but as actualities subject to quantitative measurement. Neither creative writers nor academic humanists, in other words, have anything like a monopoly on urban organismal metaphor. On the contrary, it seems to have a much more pervasive and durable vitality within both vernacular culture and (for that reason?) across an astonishingly wide range of professional vocabularies.

That said, now for the "So what?" question. What good—or harm—is done by reliance on urban organismal metaphor in these various contexts? Some obvious advantages would be these. First, that it affords a catchy, accessible way of considering the urban scene as a unitary gestalt that presents itself as vital rather than static, not as unmanageably or unfathomably alien but potentially intimate, symbiotic with its human denizens. City-as-body also potentially evokes and fortifies a shared sense of collective identity. Beyond that, at least in a rudimentary way it telegraphs an environmental ethics, an ethics of environmental salubrity: the assumption that city should function like healthy body.

All this isn't to say that urban organismal metaphor doesn't have its downside. Its holism conduces for example toward a certain giganticism, merging individual people into masses. To fixate on what is healthy for the city-body as a whole is to slacken your mental grip on the integral part. (When one starts to think of central arteries, for instance, poor people and neighborhoods in particular can easily get lost sight of.) A related, but more subtle problem is the ease with which the two main components of organismal metaphor pull apart and get taken to extremes—body/city as mind game, environmental hygiene as fetish—as when

architectural theorist Donatella Mazzolini writes of metropolis as the "concretization of the great oneiric structures of our collective body" or when city-as-body is felt to be under attack by some alien pathology that must be combatted by expunging objectionable human presences through a regime of "urban cleansing," as anthropologist Arjun Appadurai calls it.

A minimalist defense of the instructive value of holistic urban organismal metaphor, notwithstanding its possible abuses, would be that when deployed in a spirit of critical self-consciousness it offers an instructive *via negativa* for citizens, planners, thinking people of all kinds, dramatizing how actual city falls short of what city should be, or maybe once was. That is the spirit of much "ecological footprint" analysis, for instance.

But I don't want to come out sounding mainly like a defender of urban organismal metaphor—or any other species of metaphor. Yes, metaphor can have both an affective power and a helpfully focalizing clarity to enable perception of and rivet attention to what otherwise might escape notice. But metaphors are also slippery, ductile, subject to abuse or to naive (or willful) misconstruction. My point is rather that it behooves us to be prepared for both because we can't avoid them. Whether or not we are card-carrying humanists, we live by metaphor much more than we tend to realize, as George Lakoff and Mark Johnson (among many others) point out in their illuminating little book, *Metaphors We Live By*. The discourses of my fellow authors implicitly confirm this. I am fascinated to see most if not all of the other metaphors I ticked off at the outset embedded therein at different points—particularly city/nature as binary, as network, as apocalypse. The same will surely hold for the project of ecological urbanism now unfolding at Harvard's Graduate School of Design. It is bound to find metaphor a necessary resort.

Black and White in Green Cities

Lizabeth Cohen

When I, as a historian, consider the ecological sustainability of cities, I start by asking how fundamentally sustainable cities have been since World War II as places where people want to live, work, and play. I will focus here on the extent to which Americans have viewed cities as an appealing residential environment during the second half of the twentieth century.

We can learn a great deal about the popularity of cities broadly and certain cities in particular by examining some simple population statistics from 1950 to 2000. These numbers create a crucial historical context for any discussion of contemporary ecological urbanism.

If we look at my chart, "U.S. City Population, 1950 versus 2000, by Size, Rank, and Degree Racially Segregated for 2000," we first note the rank order of cities by size in 1950. Listed are the ten largest U.S. cities in 1950, followed by five cities that will appear among the top ten in 2000 but were much smaller in 1950. All five additions to the top ten are in the south or southwest. Seven of the fifteen cities listed are in red, indicating that they increased in size between 1950 and 2000. With the exception of New York City, all these sites of urban growth were in the south or southwest. Whereas the top ten cities in 1950, with the exception of Los Angeles, were northern industrial and commercial centers, by 2000 urban population had shifted to the south and west. Midwestern cities such as Chicago, Cleveland, and St. Louis lost population, while southwestern cities like Houston, San Diego, and Phoenix gained.

But this chart tells us more than about how American cities redistributed population among themselves over the second half of the twentieth century. It also reveals that cities in general declined in size. Over the half century, when the total U.S. population almost doubled from 150.7 million to 281.4 million, New York City barely expanded in population, and the other six cities to increase—all in the south and southwest—lagged far behind New York and were not as large as one might have expected. What becomes clear from these figures as well as other historical evidence is that from 1950 to 2000, suburbs and exurbs exploded in population while cities declined precipitously. The availability of cheap energy and a lack of concern about environmental degradation fueled the preference for suburban sprawl over urban density.

Today, however, the United States faces a new opportunity. Americans are finally becoming more aware of how their choices over the last half century have depleted resources, skyrocketed energy costs, and damaged the environment. At the same time, the current economic crisis has made it harder for people to afford these high costs. This convergence of ecological consciousness and financial constraint makes it possible to argue in new ways for the superiority of cities—in particular the advantages of density for the environment, economic opportunity, sociability, efficiency, convenience, and historical connection. Suddenly we have a unique opportunity to reverse the trends of the last half century.

U.S. City Population, 1950 versus 2000, by Size, Rank, and Degree Racially Segregated for 2000

Total U.S. population: 1950 = 150.7 million; 2000 = 281.4 million

RED = cities that increased population from 1950 to 2000
*0 = complete integration; 100 = complete segregation

Sources: U.S. Bureau of the Census, Table 18, "Population of the 100 Largest Urban Places: 1950," http://www.census.gov/population/www/documentation/twps00027/tab13.txt; "2000 Census: U.S. Municipalities Over 50,000: Ranked by 2000 Population," http://www.demorgraphia.com/db-uscity98.htm; "Racial Segregation Statistics for Cities and Metropolitan Areas," Censusscope, http://www.censusscope.org/segregation.html.

City	1950 rank	1950 population (millions)	2000 rank	2000 population (millions)	2000 white-black Dissimilarity Index*
New York	1	7.9	1	8.0	85.3
Chicago	2	3.6	3	2.9	87.3
Philadelphia	3	2.1	5	1.5	80.6
Los Angeles	4	2.0	2	3.7	74.0
Detroit	5	1.8	10	1.0	63.3
Baltimore	6	.9	17	.7	75.2
Cleveland	7	.9	33	.5	79.4
St. Louis	8	.9	48	.3	72.4
Washington, D.C.	9	.8	21	.6	81.5
Boston	10	.8	20	.6	75.8
Houston	14	.6	4	2.0	75.5
Dallas	22	.4	8	1.2	71.5
San Antonio	25	.4	9	1.1	53.5
San Diego	31	.3	7	1.2	63.6
Phoenix	99	.1	6	1.3	54.4

We could stop here, content that cities will likely have a new appeal, but I think we have to go further and ask, "What kind of cities, with what kind of social character, do we want to revive through greater ecological consciousness?" Of course there are many measures of a successful city. I will just mention one that I consider critically important: American cities of the future will be more socioeconomically, particularly racially, integrated than most are today. I would argue that social sustainability cannot be separated from ecological sustainability.

The last column on the right in the chart is something called the "Dissimilarity Index." It is a way of measuring how similar or different people are who live in the same census tract. According to this calculation, 0 represents complete racial integration, 100 complete racial segregation. Granted, the United States is a complex, multiracial society, divided along more than white-black racial lines. But given that white-black segregation is more extreme than other racial divides, I have used it as a measure of social segregation, which often implies inequality of income, wealth, and other kinds of opportunity as well.

Almost all of these cities had very high dissimilarity indices in 2000, which was typical of most cities. In general, a score of 60 or above is considered very high, 40–50 moderate, and 30 or below fairly low. Low scores, indicating more integration, are common in college towns such as Cambridge, Massachusetts, where the dissimilarity index is 49.6. Note in the chart that the southern and southwestern cities generally had lower dissimilarity scores than the old midwestern cities—though none were very low. And these cities were often cities in name only, with their sprawling, suburbanized, and ecologically offending sites.

Thus, as we fantasize about how we might use a greater embrace of ecological consciousness to revive American cities, let us not forget the all-important social dimension. I would not want to promote cities that claim more LEED buildings, have greener infrastructure, and operate better mass transit without also thinking about how we can use these new tools to make cities more racially and economically integrated as places to live, work, and play. On the simplest level that means including in definitions of sustainability—and investing money in—infrastructure improvement that includes not just mass transit but also quality public education to make cities attractive places for a variety of Americans to raise families.

To put it bluntly, sustainable urbanism cannot mean green cities for the white wealthy.

The Return of Nature

Preston Scott Cohen and Erika Naginski

Our oaks no longer proffer oracles, and we no longer ask of them the sacred mistletoe; we must replace this cult by care…
–Charles-Georges Le Roy [1]

American biopolitics sees in nature its same condition of existence: not only the genetic origin and the first material, but also the sole controlling reference. Politics is anything but able to dominate nature or "conform" [formare] to its ends so itself emerges "informed" in such a way that it leaves no space for other constructive possibilities.
–Roberto Esposito [2]

That Nature has returned with a vengeance in architectural theory and practice goes far beyond the transmutation of the Vitruvian qualities of *firmitas, utilitas,* and *venustas* into sustainability's motto of equity, biodiversity, and wise development. The relation of architecture and nature found in the abundant literature on sustainability rests on a moral imperative provided by the current environmental crisis, which sets, as in a Greek tragedy, the finitude of natural resources against the dismal and infinite cycle of human production and consumption. From this agon emerges the quest for a responsible architecture. The apocalyptic drama is rehearsed in such movements as natural architecture, which reifies the presumed mysteriousness and fragility of natural materials by disposing and exposing leaves, branches, and rocks in ephemeral interventions. By the same token, hope is made to reside, resolutely and problematically, in the promise of technology (this despite the specter of historical modalities such as pollution and obsolescence); thus there is biomimicry, to give but one example, in which the emulation of natural forms and processes undergirds the creation of such materials as adhesives replicating the bonding materials found in mussels, ceramic tiles with the strength of abalone shells, or glass with the air-purifying capacities of certain plants.

Yet to what degree such bioethical platforms potentially negate the project of architecture remains a fundamental question. At present, the trend to "naturalize" architectural form in the digital regime has made manifest two tendencies that, each in its own way, reject the cultural, social, and symbolic life of forms: the first involves a direct calculus attempting to translate the perceived conduct of natural systems, thereby imbuing form with a sort of naturalized behavioralism; the second, tied to a classical tradition aligning mathematics and nature, replaces the compositional authority of the designer with the computational generation of pattern. The result is all too often the production of a devitalized ornament, of rhetorical forms that, in the end, re-present nature and so return to mimicry as principle (the copy newly moralized). If modernist formalism veered too far toward the utopian purity of the autonomy of art, then sustainability has radically tilted the scales the other way—that is, toward the ontological primacy of bio-environment, all the while finding refuge in an ethical agenda and so eschewing critique and denying that it, too, belongs to a formal and formalized system. Such tilting of the scales has not come without costs: namely it risks endorsing a critical terrain marked by neo-empiricism and ahistoricism. As Andrew Payne has recently remarked, the ostensive "priority of the natural system over its social and political correlatives can have the effect of precipitously foreclosing the question of how these various regimes interact with one another within the dynamics linking natural and cultural history, and further, of what degree and sort of autonomy those interactions make possible." [3]

Precisely because sustainability introduces new and complex constraints, it becomes necessary to shift gears—this to prevent subsuming the social, political, and cultural dimensions of the built environment under nature's primary status. We would need, first, to say something about the role of those constraints in modern interpretations of nature as they are related to matters of function and codes. Then we would need to provide real comparison between the environmental limiting condition and other moments of "functional interference" with architectural form (such as the introduction of the elevator, which transformed the relationship of buildings to the city and thus the city itself; fire safety, which radically altered the social arrangements of interiors; and the adoption through ADA rules of access ramps, which fundamentally altered the conception of thresholds and sequences). In all of those instances in which constraints did, in fact, operate on the corpus of architecture, spatial and institutional mutations of profound consequence occurred; there is, after all, a long tradition of architects pushing back against that which intervenes to grant themselves experimental license.

More important, there is no one-way street here; architecture is just as likely to provoke change (transformative architecture) as it is to respond to it (responsive architecture). We could argue that despite the maelstrom of claims to newness and the moralistic rhetoric now swirling around the sustainable what-have-yous or what-have-you-nots, the problem may be capable of contributing to a legacy of how externalities have imposed themselves on architecture—and vice versa—in both recent and distant pasts, in both concrete and symbolic ways. Put another way: to demystify the ecological and the sustainable is to reveal the possibility of architecture.

Indeed, sustainability's call to arms belongs to a complex historical arc with crucial junctures ranging from Giambattista Vico's primordial forest, antipode to human civilization, to twentieth-century analogies between ecological systems and political economies, to more recent demonstration of the ways in which fundamental forces and resonances accumulate into shapes and figures—all of which reveals that the problem of form in design is vital, not ancillary, and above all, need not be deemed simply

subservient to (or the passive recipient of) the claims of an ethical horizon as it is delimited by current environmental modalities. How do we weigh the legacy of a posthuman(ist) framework in architecture against the value ascribed to nature in bioethical ideologies? How might form demarcate the shifting crossroads between ecology, society, and aesthetic philosophy? How might we clear the (ideological) air?

This text stems from the program description for the *Harvard Symposia on Architecture*, a lecture series in 2009–2010 focusing on the question of architecture's autonomy in the face of the sustainability imperative.

1 Charles-Georges Le Roy, "Forêt," in Denis Diderot, Jean Le Rond d'Alembert, eds., *Encyclopédie ou Dictionnaire raisonné des sciences, des arts et des métiers, par une Société de Gens de lettres* (1751–1772), vol. 7, 129: "Nos chênes ne rendent plus d'oracles, et nous ne leur demandons plus le gui sacré; il faut remplacer ce culte par l'attention…" A profound discussion of Le Roy's entry appears in Robert Pogue Harrison, *Forests: The Shadow of Civilization* (Chicago: University of Chicago Press, 1993), 113–124.
2 Roberto Esposito, *Bios: Biopolitics and Philosophy*, translated by Timothy Campbell (Minneapolis and London: University of Minnesota Press, 2008), 22.
3 Andrew Payne, "Sustainability and Pleasure: An Untimely Meditation," *Harvard Design Magazine* 30 (Spring/Summer 2009), 78.

Urban Ecological Practices:
Félix Guattari's *Three Ecologies*

Verena Andermatt Conley

Several decades ago, in his *Urban Revolution*, Henri Lefebvre announced the erasure of the time-held distinction between the country and the city. He staked his hopes for the future of the planet on a process of urbanization that would remedy the ills induced by modernism based on the mastery of man over nature.[1] Less utopian about the intrinsic benefits of urbanization, Gilles Deleuze and Félix Guattari, recognizing their debt to the cultural theorist Paul Virilio, who has been chronicling the impact of the techno-sciences since World War II, declare repeatedly that any ecological thinking has to be done from today's condition, that is, in view of the genetic revolution, the globalization of markets, the acceleration of transportation and communication, as well as the interdependence of large urban centers. Guattari, who ran—unsuccessfully—for public office on an environmental ticket, writes in his brilliant and concise essay *The Three Ecologies,* published in French in 1989 at the time of the fall of the Berlin Wall, that we must make do "with" these conditions in order soon to rectify them by recomposing the objectives and methods of the social movements in their entirety.[2] It is not a question of going back to former ways of life. Ecology is not the prerogative of a slightly folkloristic and archaic bunch of nature lovers at a time when, more than ever, nature and culture cannot be separated. Unlike most French thinkers (with the notable exception of Bruno Latour) who lost themselves on Heideggerian *Holzwege*, Guattari argues that the techno-sciences are crucial for the survival of the planet with its current demographic density and ecological problems.

Reorienting the techno-sciences, however, cannot come about without recomposing subjectivity and the formation of capitalist powers. Technocratic adjustments alone will not suffice. Guattari devises an *ecosophy* that would work simultaneously on three registers: social, mental, and environmental. It would produce new—and more pleasurable—ways of living in common. In its present state, the world is under the sway of the media and the market. Infantilized, people live in death-laden aggregates. Guattari claims that in today's capitalism, the former distinction between infra- and superstructures has been relayed by several interchangeable regimes of signs: economic, juridical, scientific, and those dealing with subjectivation.

Denouncing the preeminence of the economic regime and hoping to introduce time and space into the sciences, Guattari focuses especially on subjectivation. In an effort to devise an ethico-political articulation and with recourse to a neo-Sartrean vocabulary, Guattari declares that all those engaged in fields pertaining to the pro-cesses of subjectivation have the responsibility to open a deadly "in itself," *en-soi*, of current existential territories into a precarious and processual "for itself," *pour-soi*, that is open to the world. Those who, individually or collectively, are in a position to intervene on people's psyches include not only psychoanalysts but educators, artists, architects, urban planners, fashion designers, musicians, sports and media people, and others, none of whom can hide behind a so-called transferential neutrality. They must

Reorienting the techno-sciences, however, cannot come about without recomposing subjectivity and the formation of capitalist powers. Technocratic adjustments alone will not suffice.

help bring about change by introducing a wedge, producing an interruption or making openings that can be inhabited by human projects leading to other ways of feeling, perceiving, and conceiving. An ethical paradigm has to be complemented with an aesthetic paradigm that will prevent processes from getting fixated in deadly repetitions. In the case of the latter, each concrete performance introduces openings that cannot be assured by theoretical foundations or an authority but that are always "work in progress" (*TTE*, 40; in English in the French text).

Rejecting former paradigms of social struggle organized around unified ideologies, Guattari calls for diverse ecological recompositions in various domains. While not entirely discounting unifying objectives that deal, for example, with urban ecology, he underlines that we cannot have recourse to slogans or stereotypical order-words that promote charismatic leaders in the place of singular inventions. To make the city habitable, micropolitics and not only macropolitics are necessary. Of importance too is not to replace one term with its opposite. The question is not one of establishing universal rules, of marking things simply as "in" or "out"—as is being done in the current economic crisis—but of disengaging binary oppositions between different *ecosophical* levels and of helping produce changes in sensibility and intelligence in a gradual, sliding, and nonviolent manner.

Guattari advises practitioners not simply to replace a discredited modernism with a single new vision but to engage in an ongoing process of transformation. The latter can include building a porous city with more ecological materials, collecting rainwater, harnessing solar and wind power, but also other ways of relating to one's body, of interacting in a group, and of undoing the current equation between natural, material, and cultural goods that is based solely on profit.

Though Guattari makes it clear that we need constantly to renew our theoretical paradigms, his slim essay and its urgent message to be analytically militant, to think and act, to theorize and practice simultaneously, remains valid for an ecological urbanism today. In a global world with large megacities, those dealing with subjectivities, from architects to urban planners and others, have the responsibility of helping to produce openings that can be made habitable by human projects through the interchangeable lenses of the three ecologies.

1 Henri Lefebvre, *La révolution urbaine* (Paris: Gallimard, 1970); *The Urban Revolution*, translated by Robert Bononno (Minneapolis: University of Minnesota Press, 2003).
2 Félix Guattari, *Les trois ecologies* (Paris: Galilé, 1989); *The Three Ecologies*, translated by Ian Pindar and Paul Sutton (London: Athlone Press, 2000).

Retrofitting the City

Leland D. Cott

How might we work to make our cities sustainable? The problems are already well documented; proposed solutions range from familiar concepts such as localized urban farming and water conservation measures to more advanced notions of net-zero energy enclaves in suburbs and in deserts. There appeared to be a sense that, in spite of the enormity of the task ahead, we do have the collective wisdom to confront and solve the problems brought about by our global insensitivity to the environment and therefore might just have a chance to create an alternative future to the one toward which we are headed.

To do so will necessitate effective action at all scales of effort. Long-range, energy-efficient solutions will be needed if we are to leave a smaller carbon footprint, but there is also a great deal that can be done now to ameliorate the current situation. Our cities contain millions of residential, commercial, and institutional structures, nearly all of which we now recognize as inefficient and wasteful of energy. By any standard of measure, almost all of our existing buildings are the antithesis of "sustainable." They were conceived and constructed long before the later part of the twentieth century, during the era when energy costs were considered negligible and energy supplies were thought to be endless. So what measures can be taken by the building design and real estate industry to ensure that we substantially improve what we already have?

To begin, we must set out in an effort to reuse as many of our existing buildings as possible. It is within our reach to save as much as 40 percent of the energy we currently use—and limit carbon emissions—by effectively retrofitting the entire U.S. building stock. This argument is made even stronger if one considers the amount of embodied energy in an existing building, thus making the case for demolition, waste disposal, and the construction of a new building more difficult to justify. Municipal, state, and federal governments have begun to offer assistance to the real estate community by providing property tax abatements and income tax credits similar to those created to encourage historic preservation and building reuse thirty-five years ago.

Greater subsidies of this sort will be needed to encourage for-profit real estate developers and property managers to participate in a comprehensive nationwide energy retrofitting program. From the real estate perspective, value is traditionally measured by return on investment; given the present-day cost of improvements and energy, very few retrofits currently meet the criteria of five- to seven-year paybacks. Subsidy assistance will likely be necessary to offset perceived high up-front costs versus long-term savings. Presumably as building tenants become more savvy, they will understand that excessive energy use negatively affects their bottom line and will choose not to lease space in obsolete buildings. A building that has been retrofitted will use less energy, can have lower rents, and is likely to have greater street appeal.

It is within our reach to save as much as 40 percent of the energy we currently use–and limit carbon emissions–by effectively retrofitting the entire U. S. building stock.

A future with an entirely reformatted, sustainable, energy-efficient stock of existing buildings in our cities should be achievable in the next decade or two. The successful result will provide us with the basic collection of efficient buildings, enabling us to move toward a more ecologically sustainable urbanism for distant futures beyond our own.

Productive Urban Environments

Margaret Crawford

Currently cities possess a heavy carbon footprint. To become sustainable, future cities must aspire to be carbon negative. We need to find new ways to offset the city's embodied energy and increase the production of sustainable energy, food, transport, and dwellings, while advancing public health and the quality of life. To do this, we first need to question the conventional wisdom of environmentalism and many of the existing definitions of cities.

Pointing out the significant fact that most energy loss occurs during the delivery stages from power plants to distribution systems, Michelle Addington's essay in this volume suggests a new focus and scale for saving energy, challenging the current architectural obsession with producing energy-saving buildings. This shifts emphasis away from individual buildings to regional and national power grids distant from urban areas. This enlarged framework suggests that it may be more useful to think about cities as one element in larger systems rather than as bounded entities, an idea also represented through Richard T. T. Forman's "Urban Regions" maps.

Although rural and urban have been historically polarized, with the former supplying food for the latter, contemporary agricultural practices are becoming increasingly diverse. Changing definitions of farms and farmers have encouraged farming in almost any location. Across metropolitan regions, derelict and underused urban land, agricultural land held in trust, community gardens, school and university campuses, and even suburban back and front yards are now producing food. New channels of distribution have also emerged. Farmers markets, CSAs (community-supported agriculture), restaurants and markets specializing in local produce, and even gleaners who distribute fallen fruit all contribute to making local food widely available. Although these forms of agriculture cannot compete with the giant agribusinesses of the Midwest and California's Central Valley, as Dorothée Imbert argues, their benefits go far beyond the merely economic. In addition to providing jobs and augmenting incomes, urban agriculture can foster civic and community engagement, bring people closer to the rhythms of nature, maintain ethnic and cultural traditions, educate children about food and eating, provide high-quality produce, and, not least, offer the pleasure and beauty that are part of growing and eating delicious food.

Imagining what the future might bring, Mitchell Joachim's images of sustainability offer a range of possible if highly speculative proposals for urban environments based on fitting people into natural environments. Envisioning a "city" that produces its own necessities, he offers designs based on manipulating organic forms using new technologies. The Fab Tree Hab, for example, takes the metaphor of a living house literally, using a shaped tree as the basis for a new type of ecological living. Joachim also proposes new technologies of mobility ranging from underground transport systems to redesigning automobiles to be soft and slow, propelled by individual electric motors in the wheels. In this way, he designs the vehicles to fit the city, not the other way around.

What kind of urban environment would these ideas produce? Certainly not the compact city many proponents of sustainable urbanism are currently promoting. Instead, taken together, they suggest an expansive form of urbanism, with dwellings and workplaces far more integrated with nature and agriculture than current cities. Combining the various ideas that are united around the idea of a productive urban environment, it is possible to imagine a variety of new landscapes that might emerge. Supported by a sustainable energy grid that can accommodate and distribute both large- and small-scale energy sources, this would be a green environment, with energy and transportation infrastructure, dwellings and workplaces, agricultural and natural spaces interwoven in new and still to be imagined combinations. Rather than reimposing past models of urbanism based on density and boundedness, in the name of sustainability, perhaps we should keep our options open. Instead of a normative urban ideal, we should move toward multiple yet highly focused directions that have the ability to produce completely different outcomes.

SENSE

The City from the Perspective of the Nose
Sissel Tolaas

Urban Earth: Mexico City
Daniel Raven-Ellison

CitySense: An Urban-Scale Sensor Network
Matt Welsh and Josh Bers

Eat Love Marije Vogelzang

Self-Engineering Ecologies
Christine Outram, Assaf Biderman, and Carlo Ratti

**There's More to Green than Meets the Eye:
Green Urbanism in Bahrain**
Gareth Doherty

Play Me, I'm Yours
Luke Jerram

Mapping Main Street
Jesse Shapins, Kara Oehler, Ann Heppermann,
and James Burns

The City from the Perspective of the Nose

Sissel Tolaas
2009 Rouse Visiting Artist, Harvard Graduate School of Design

Smells—Bad and Good, or Just Interesting

I believe that tolerance is the key word for a new approach to the city and our surroundings. I believe we have to learn to be tolerant so that we can live together in a different way. This process starts with the NOSE!

Intolerance for the nose and for smell per se has had a lasting serious effect on the status of smell in our societies. In general, smell tends to be communicated in terms of clichéd associations with ethical, moral, and mental decline. So-called bad smells remain bad even when there are chances to communicate them in a new way, be it in films, novels, or other media.

The ideal world is presented to us as clean and deodorized; it is primarily perceived through the visual and auditory senses. The shiny white surface, be it the deodorized body or the white wall or the clean street, is the clear and obvious visualization of the status of smell—an instance where smells and images are confounded in the convergence of their semantic fields. This hygienic rhetoric dominates the collective imagination; it is widely believed that to be clean and shiny is to represent or present.

Our sanitized cities are depriving us of the chance to use our noses for navigation and information.[1] What are we missing out on here? The 5 percent of our genes that are related to smell are not called into play. What would happen if the nose started to play a role equal to those of the eyes and ears in the process of perception, navigation, and communication?

Human beings, along with rats and cockroaches, are the world's most successful generalists. We can live in any ecological habitat on the planet and survive by eating the available foods. For generalists, the function of smell is to learn how to respond appropriately to a particular smell source when it is encountered, and not hold a predetermined set of responses to particular smells. Animals that are specialists have innate smell responses to prey and predators, whereas animals that are generalists do not.[2]

Our responses to smells are based on associative learning; they are not innate, not hardwired into us. We associate a smell with the circumstances under which we first experienced it, and it remains so until we want to change it. Cultural adaptation, insideness, and understanding are very important here.

Smell is the first sense through which we interact with the world and react to it—we smell before we see. Smells are very closely associated with personal and group identity. What separates two people most markedly is their individual smells. Humans manipulate their smell identity to keep to or create a "new" personal identity or to display connection to a group. No feeling of like or dislike is quite so fundamental as a physical feeling. Race hatred, religious hatred, difference of education, of temperament, of intellect, even differences of moral code, can be gotten over, but physical repulsion cannot.[3]

Smell repulsions and preferences are deeply rooted; to manipulate these is a very efficient way to get effects and results, be they political, social, or individual. Nothing is more successful then manipulation of people's feelings—this is what is happening in the commercial world of smells. There is a strong relationship among smells, power, and society.[4]

We have to overcome all the prejudices concerning smells and get beyond the notion that "they can't stand each other's smell." We need to change it so that they can stand each other's smell. This will change the world!

What to Do, and How to Do It?

I believe that smells are a crucial component in the definition of and orientation to an environment, be it the body or the city. Smell settings may be taken for granted in an unreflective way, but they are nonetheless cues to particular methods of involvement and engagement within a situation. Places may be characterized individually, or even typed, by smells, and unforgettably so. Smells surround us all the time, wherever we are. The nose never sleeps! During every breath we take, we inhale smell molecules that give us important information about micro levels in our surroundings.

In cities we operate in three zones: the industrial, the public, and the private. Each zone has its own infrastructures and laws as far as smell acceptance is concerned. We normally operate with a high tolerance for bad smells when we move around in industrial areas, whether they are factories, garbage dumps, etc. Why is this? In public areas, we have a different discussion. Our relationship to these areas is normally "neutral," but in reality we operate with a lot of boundaries and prejudices. These can be provoked by the smell of "unfamiliar" cooking or a person in the subway smelling "different."

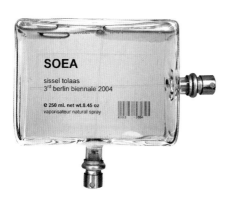

without borders – *NOSOEAWE*
Berlin Biennale, 2004

The research project consisted
of eleven bottles slowly fusing
the smells of four neighborhoods
in Berlin: North = NO, West = WE,
East = EA, South = SO.

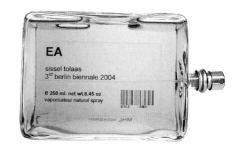

SENSE

1 Jim Drobnick, ed., *The Smell Culture Reader* (Oxford and New York: Berg Publishers, 2006).
2 Ibid.
3 George Orwell discusses smell and class differences in *The Road to Wigan Pier* (New York: Mariner Books, 1972).
4 Constance Classen, David Howes, and Anthony Synnott, *Aroma: The Cultural History of Smell* (New York: Routledge, 1994).

In the private zone, nearly all smells are accepted, but if any of these happens to cross the border of privacy, it can easily be perceived as problematic. Can this be changed? Can we train ourselves to go beyond acceptance? What would this do to the notion of tolerance in general?

If we learn to train our noses to navigate in the urban setting, we can make progress in tolerating each other. We should redefine the notion of cleanliness and the terms "bad" and "good." This is important because cleaning things up has different meanings in different cultures.

There is a playful aspect about discovering the world through smells and discovering more about ourselves and our potential to interact with our environment. A more comfortable relationship with smells brings about a more optimistic attitude toward environmental issues. It changes the mood. Challenging people to use their noses gives them new methods to approach their reality, different from those they learn from watching disasters on TV. I think we need more optimism and positive attitudes to be able to understand the seriousness of what we face: New challenges, new methods, new methodologies, new tools…. The nose is the key here.

My experience is that people all over the planet really get challenged when they are seriously asked to use their noses for purposes other than breathing in and out. And it doesn't matter whether they smell a so-called bad or good smell. What counts is that they rediscover their own surroundings in that very moment—be it other human beings, places, the city—and start to approach them differently. If people get the message through the nose, they really get the message.

We need a new and different discussion on how we can use the hidden smell codes for the purpose of unity instead of separation. We have to get rid of the notion that smell concerns only the personal, private, and intrinsic aspects of our lives. We have to get out there and challenge the conventional perception of smells as private and not to be discussed. Only this way can we make progress; I think a new intellectual approach to the nose and smells is on the way.

The most crucial question is what constitutes an acceptable smell environment. Who make those rules? What justifies the existing rules and their definitions of bad and good? Is it not time to redefine these rules, and relearn our own approach to them?

Nothing stinks, but thinking makes it so.

TALKING NOSE_Mexico City

TALKING NOSE is a site-specific research project about the smells of Mexico City.

TALKING NOSE is a project on smell as information and as a system of communication.

THE SMELLS = 200 smells from 200 neighborhoods

Two hundred neighborhoods were identified through their smell molecules—the DNA of a site. Smells are (chemical) signals from our environment, from animate and inanimate things around us. I picked up and interpreted parts of their escaping substance using advanced collection and analysis tools, the smell effects repertory, and a smell-adapted method. The smell phenomena in each area were understood and collected during several visits. I used, in each case, a phenomenological approach to on-site smells.

The advanced Headspace technology was used to collect molecules from the sites. If a smell source is localized enough in space and time, its position can be fixed (localization). However, air movements can lead to spatial localization mistakes (dislocation). Air inertia can delay smell detection.

THE FILM = silent movie showing only noses when they smell the city air

Two thousand people were asked to describe the smell of their city and its pollution in their mother tongues. Participants were chosen because they know their areas very well. Using what I call the city-walk method, what they perceived and felt during a walk through a familiar area was filmed and recorded. Walkers were asked to focus on their smell sensations, using their noses with full gestures. These descriptions were analyzed, using the smell effects to develop hypotheses on the specific smell phenomena of the site. This analysis was then matched and compared with the electronic analysis. The film

TALKING NOSE_Mexico City
2001–2009
A research project on smell as
a tool for navigating through the
city while gaining awareness
of the surrounding air–in the case
of Mexico City, polluted air–and
reacting to it

is screened without voice, showing only the movements and gestures of the nose and face.

THE LANGUAGE = audio track of the city walk

The audio portion of the project presents the walkers' words and narration while they are smelling in their neighborhoods. It is interesting that when people were asked to use their noses to perceive their city, they suddenly became aware that they themselves were causing pollution. Another aspect of the spoken track was the discovery that several of the indigenous languages (i.e., pre-Columbian) include precise nonmetaphorical terms and terminologies to describe smells. Some of these expressions were documented so that they can be presented together with the audio track.

The study of urban smells provides an additional dimension to our understanding of cities. It enriches our sensual experience and provides input for urban design and architecture. The invisible city can communicate and be understood.

AFIISH

➲ AFRICAN FISH SHOPS

CHEPDU

➲ CHEAP FURNITURE STORAGE

DUSBI

➲ DUSTY BRICK

HIIN

➲ MAGIC

TARR

➲ ASPHALT

TALKING NOSE—the language
Mexico City, 2001–2009
Nasalo is a language invented by Sissel Tolaas,
consisting of words to be used to communicate
smells and smell impressions. The language is
only partly connected to actual languages spoken
in areas included in her research into smells,
from which fragments of words are drawn; the
rest has its own logic and linguistic rules.

BEETEE

➲ CONCRETE

CIKAN

➲ SOAPS THAT SMELL OK BUT
ARE SOMEHOW DISPLACED

FRE

➲ WET AND RAINY STREET
AFTER A SUNNY DAY

ISJ

➲ GRASS

ORANJ

➲ HOT BODY MIXED
WITH HOT ENGINES

UNDEGRA

➲ SUBWAY PLATFORM: METAL,
TIRES AND BURNED PLASTIC

BEETWE

➡ WET CONCRETE

CAA

➡ TRAFFIC

CASSPO

➡ SWEAT IN CONNECTION
WITH SPORT

CASSLET

➡ LEATHER AND SWEAT

FREE

➡ WET AND RAINY STREET

GOOWHA

➡ WET DOG

ISJFE

➡ FRESH CUT GRASS

JACSA

➡ FINE, BUT SO PENETRATING
THAT IT DISTURBS, LIKE THE JUICE
OF ORANGE PEEL

SHIIZA

➡ CANALIZATION

TARNEK

➡ AIRPORT TAKE-OFF STRIPES,
BURNED RUBBER AND KEROSENE

VLOO

➡ BAWDY, GROSS, VULGAR

XC'UTA

➡ SOUR, SPICY, DAZZLING

Urban Earth Mexico City

SENSE

SENSE

CitySense: An Urban-Scale Sensor Network

Matt Welsh and Josh Bers

Understanding the dynamics and health of a city can be enabled through high-density instrumentation. Sensors deployed throughout a city can capture data on weather conditions, air quality, noise pollution, road traffic, and more. A key challenge is linking those sensors into a cohesive infrastructure that provides real-time access to the data via the internet. Stand-alone data loggers require regular maintenance to collect the data, and one cannot expect to find a physical connection to the internet everywhere a sensor can be placed. One solution is to leverage wireless networking to link the sensors to form a mesh network.

CitySense is a National Science Foundation-funded project to build a wireless sensor network that spans an entire city. CitySense nodes are mounted on streetlights and rooftops, and are interfaced to a wide range of sensors. The data is relayed via a wireless mesh network to a central server, connected to the internet, which archives and presents the data via the web. Remote users can query the sensor database and visualize the data in real time.

CitySense is being developed by a research team at Harvard's School of Engineering and Applied Sciences and BBN Technologies.[1] The current prototype consists of 25 sensor nodes deployed around Cambridge, Massachusetts, and the plan is to scale up the test bed to 100 nodes or more over the coming months. We are working closely with domain experts in environmental monitoring and public health to drive the design of the network.

A critical aspect of CitySense is that it will be open and programmable by the research community, allowing external users to upload and execute their own experiments on the CitySense network via a web-based interface. CitySense nodes are based on the ALIX 2d2 single-board computer, a stripped-down PC contained in a weatherproof enclosure, which can be mounted on a streetlight or rooftop. The node provides connectivity to various sensors via serial, Ethernet, and USB interfaces. Power is provided through the streetlight or from an external AC power supply.

Nodes are connected to the internet via wireless networking. Each node is equipped with two separate radios based on the popular 802.11 standard. The nodes form a mesh network in which they relay data for each other over the radio: a message originating at one CitySense node may travel over multiple hops before it reaches its destination. A small number of CitySense nodes have a physical internet connection and act as gateways. The advantage of wireless mesh routing is that it allows us to scale up the network to potentially thousands of nodes without incurring the high cost of wiring each node physically to the network. Essentially there is a fixed per-node cost for the radios on each node. However, this approach is not without its challenges. New nodes must be deployed in locations that are within radio range of at least one other node; this is appropriate in a dense urban setting such as Cambridge, perhaps less so in other cities. Also, the mesh network exhibits a high degree of performance variation, primarily due to radio interference from other sources. This requires the software that collects the sensor data to be robust to intermittent network dropouts.

Two servers (one at Harvard and one at BBN) act as data aggregation and control points for the network. Sensor data collected by the nodes is relayed via the wireless network to one of the servers, where it is archived in a database. A web-based front-end provides access to the sensor data, which can be visualized directly in a web browser, downloaded as a file, or queried directly using an SQL database client. The control server allows us to remotely reprogram the sensor nodes, upgrading their software, and monitor their health to detect failed nodes.

A key aspect of CitySense is that it is an open test bed, available to the research community at large. All of the data collected by CitySense is publicly available on our web site and may be used without restriction. In addition, researchers wishing to conduct more advanced experiments—for example, running custom software on the CitySense nodes themselves—are able to do so. This allows CitySense to support research into sensor networking at urban scales, new distributed algorithms for in-network data processing and aggregation, novel programming abstractions, and complete applications leveraging the emplacement of the CitySense nodes and attached sensors throughout a city.

A CitySense node mounted on a streetlight in Cambridge, Massachusetts. The node is powered by the streetlight and has an attached Vaisala weather sensor.

The interior of a CitySense node containing single-board computer, radios, and power supply

1 For more information, see http://www.citysense.net.

Eat Love

Marije Vogelzang

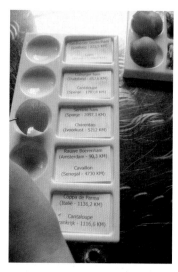

Urban Eco Project
The awareness of "food miles" (how far food has to travel before it lands on our plates) is growing. Some people call themselves "locavores" and eat only food produced within cycling distance of their home. Maybe we can go a step further and be "urbatarians." If you walk consciously around our urban jungle, you might find more edibles than you would have thought possible. Edible weeds are growing everywhere. Pigeons fly on every square. Many parks, graveyards, and flowerbeds reveal edible nuts, berries, or mushrooms. There are ducks in the pond, and they also lay eggs. All of this is not "produced." It's just there: you might even tramp on it while walking to your office or workplace.

Sustainability Dinner
Does food from afar taste better? This project communicated the distance and origin of the ham and melon classic. Other food was prepared using an old energy-saving technique: hay-box cookers.

Roots
Exploring the shared culinary history of British and Dutch root vegetables, I rediscoverd clay cooking. Clay cooking enables one to build sculptures, bake seasoned root vegetables, and create a sensory landscape. In ancient times, whole animals were baked in clay on an open fire, and after being removed from the hot coals, the clay was smashed open. The cooked contents, in this case root vege-tables, were revealed only when the clay shell was broken, creating a dilemma: break the sculpture to sample the warm root inside or leave the form intact?

Self-Engineering Ecologies

Christine Outram, Assaf Biderman, and Carlo Ratti

Nobody wonders where, each day, they carry their load of refuse. Outside the city, surely: but each year the city expands, and the street cleaners have to fall farther back. The bulk of the outflow increases and the piles rise higher, become stratified, extend over a wider perimeter.

—Italo Calvino, *Invisible Cities*

Imagine a future where immense amounts of trash didn't pile up on the peripheries of our cities. A future where we understand just as much about the "removal chain" as we do the "supply chain," and where we can use this knowledge to not only build more efficient and sustainable infrastructures but to promote behavior change. In this future city, the invisible infrastructures of refuse removal (that Italo Calvino so eloquently writes about) will become visible and the final journey of our trash will no longer be "out of sight, out of mind."

In many ways this is contrary to the post-human waste city that is captured in Disney's *Wall-E* animation. In the film, advances in technology have produced robots that automate the removal of garbage without the need for human intervention. In the future city that we imagine, technology is not simply used to replace human action but is harnessed to provide clarity about the operation of existing systems. Through processing this information and making it publicly accessible

A digital layer of information now blankets our cities. MIT's SENSEable City Lab explores the relationship between people, the city, and this blanket of bits.

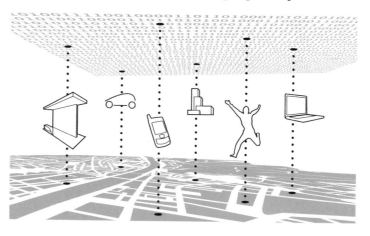

in real-time, the true nature of a hidden infrastructure such as waste removal can be highlighted, and a "feedback loop" of information created that highlights inefficiencies in systems while also promoting awareness of the results of our actions.

At the SENSEeable City Laboratory, we are currently working on such a future.[1] In a project named Trash|Track, inspired by the NYC Green Initiative that aims to increase the rate of waste recycling in the city to almost 100 percent by 2030, we ask how pervasive technologies can help expose the challenges of waste management and sustainability. How can we suggest a future scenario where the same pervasive technologies can make 100 percent recycling a reality, thereby freeing urban land currently used for landfills?

The project is being achieved through developing small, smart, location-aware tags—a first step toward the deployment of "smart dust," networks of tiny locatable and addressable microeletromechanical systems (MEMS) that can be easily distributed in objects to provide useful information. These tags, which conform to the solid waste disposal standards in the United States and abroad, are attached to different types of trash so that these items can be followed through the city's waste management system, revealing the final journey of our everyday objects.

The Trash|Track project is an initial investigation into understanding the removal chain in urban areas, and it has generated

In 2009, the Trash|Track project will tag more than 500 pieces of trash in New York, Seattle, London, and Boston. Through this, the final journey of our everyday objects will be revealed.

a vast amount of interest from municipalities and eco-conscious citizens. It also, however, is representative of another type of change taking place in cities—a bottom-up approach to managing resources and promoting behavior change through the use of distributed and pervasive technologies.

Looking back at the past fifteen years, we see a rise of a new type of infrastructure in cities: networked digital elements have blanketed our environment, and this is lending our urban zones a new layer of functionality. For instance, sensors, cameras, and microcontrollers are used ever more extensively by cities to optimize transportation, monitor the environment, and run security applications. Similarly, however, through hand-held devices, computers, and ambient sensors embedded in the environment, citizens can extract, insert, and recombine information of use to them, in real-time, almost anywhere. For example, in the Trash|Track project, this information can communicate to citizens their impact on the environment. Citizens can also quickly compare and share this information with other people, in their neighborhood or city, adjust habits accordingly, and lobby for changes in the system.

As a result of this new type of distributed infrastructure, our experience of urban spaces is transformed. This is an era of self-engineering our own ecologies, where it is no longer predominantly city designers, developers, and government instigators who give shape to our urban spaces; almost anyone can participate in forming the digital layer of our environment. In short, the physical design and experience of our near-future cities will be intimately bound to the harnessing and transmission of digital information.

The power of distributed computing to support behavior change can be found in other research currently being con-

The project tags and follows pieces of trash as diverse as television sets, jeans, and porcelain soup bowls.

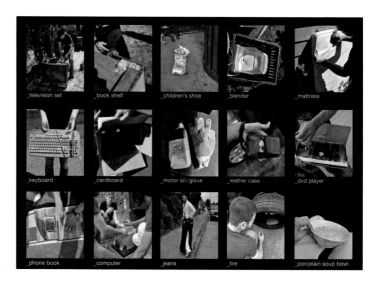

ducted at the SENSEable City Lab. In the Copencycle project, to be showcased at the COP15 United Nations Climate Change Conference in Copenhagen in December 2009, bicycles become smart mobile-sensing devices that monitor the rider's physical performance, exposure to pollution, and mobility throughout the city. This is achieved through strategically placing a small location device and environmental sensors into a bicycle wheel to gather information as people cycle. The sensors are powered using hybrid technology that allows collecting energy while braking.

Collected on the bike, location and air quality information is transmitted to a central server and is then processed and returned to cyclists as well as being displayed through a web interface.

Developed for the 2009 Copen-Cycle project, SENSEable City Lab's "aware" bikes allow cyclists to choose the least polluted and congested routes; connect with friends on the go; and keep track of their personal health goals. When aggregated and anonymized, this data can be used by municipalities to aid planning and development decisions.

These new "aware" bikes become a personal companion, letting cyclists know via an internet application how well they are riding, whether they are reaching their personal health goals, or if they appear to be having trouble at particular points along their ride. It can help a rider identify the least

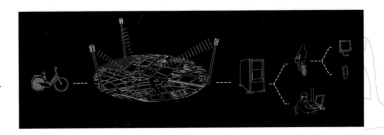

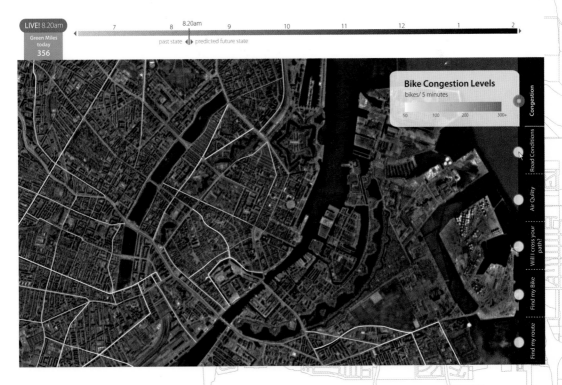

Every day, 175,000 bikes enter the center of Copenhagen.

Thirty-six percent of people commute to work by bike in Copenhagen, a number the city wishes to increase.

polluted route he or she could take to work, and it also alert riders (through an application developed for Facebook) if friends are close by so that they can meet up on the go. Beyond their value in providing personal information to the rider, the new bikes also allow city cyclists to exchange the information gathered by their bicycles with each other and with the city administration, anonymously. The bikes can be used in a crowd-sourcing manner for sensing real-time pollution levels and congestion throughout the city, harnessing the density and number of multiple cyclists to increase the value of the data collected. This information is made accessible on a centralized web site that helps other cyclists make better route choices and municipalities make more informed decisions about the allocation of resources with regard to maintaining infrastructure and improving livability in cities. The bike allows cyclists to take part in citywide initiatives. The "green mileage" scheme, which rewards riders for accruing miles traveled by bike, could ultimately allow the city to obtain funding for their efforts to cut carbon dioxide emissions.

Both the Trash|Track and Copencycle projects show how small technological augmentations of our everyday environments and objects can lead to a new experience of cities. Rich sets of real-time data about environmental conditions and flows of objects or people can provide an improved understanding of city dynamics and support decision-making for individuals as well as large organizations. When collected and displayed, this information creates a "feedback loop" of digital sensing and processing that can begin to influence various complex and dynamic aspects on a wider level, ultimately improving the economic, social, and environmental sustainability of the places we inhabit. At the same time, the very act of sharing this information is powerful enough to promote a personal assessment of our impact on cities. In this sense in today's world, where data about our actions is pervasive, we are all engineers of our future ecologies.

1 Directed by Professor Carlo Ratti and Associate Director Assaf Biderman, the SENSEable City Laboratory at MIT focuses on developing technologies that can mediate between physical urban space and the layers of digital flows produced by everyday urban functions, and on analyzing the changes our cities undergo due to this new coupling with digital technologies. It is a multidisciplinary group of more than twenty people that aims to integrate aspects of urban studies, architecture, engineering, interaction design, computer science, and social science. For more information about the lab, please refer to http://senseable.mit.edu.

There's More to Green
than Meets the Eye:
Green Urbanism in Bahrain

Gareth Doherty

As a color, green does not exist by itself: it is a mix of blue and yellow. Colors, though, have subjective boundaries, and the point at which what we consider blue becomes green, or green becomes yellow, depends to a large extent on the culture and language of the perceiver, as well as the context. Anthropologists Brent Berlin and Paul Kay, writing in 1969, speak of the relativity of color across cultures; still, they found that a word for green almost always exists, even when a word for blue does not.[1]

Philosophers grapple with color, and there is no consensus as to whether an object is actually colored or not. Alex Byrne and David Hilbert outline four main positions on color in philosophy: eliminativists say color is not part of an object and see color as a sort of illusion; for dispositionalists "the property green (for example) is a disposition to produce certain perceptual states: roughly the disposition to *look green*"; physicalists, such as Byrne and Hilbert, regard green as a physical property of an object; and meanwhile, primitivists agree that objects have colors, but do not agree that the color is identical to the physical property of the object that is colored.[2]

But green is more than color; it is vegetation, open space, a type of building or urbanism, an environmental cause, a political movement, "the new black." The color of photosynthesis and chlorophyll, green is mostly regarded as life-giving, bountiful, and healthy (except when referring to the tone of human skin). Talk-show hosts relax in "green rooms" and doctors' scrubs are often green (to contrast with red). As an adjective, green can mean naiveté, or something not yet ripe.

The Bahrain islands are the smallest, densest, and proportionately the greenest of the Arab states of the Persian Gulf. Ten miles wide by thirty miles long, the kingdom is smaller than London or New York and just about the same size as Singapore. As the city-state transitions to an intensely urban landscape driven by the demands of a growing population and limited land mass, the hues of Bahrain's greenery are changing and with them the ecologies of society, politics, and infrastructure with which green is inherently intertwined. The gray-greens of the native date-palm plantations are being replaced with bright grass greens of roadside shoulders, roundabouts, and the lawns of new residential and leisure developments. To have greenery in such a markedly urban environment is not very green from an environmental perspective, given the resources often required to sustain it. Bahrain represents an extreme example of the impulse for urban greenery, an impulse that is both global and local to Bahrain.

Bahrain literally means "Two Seas" in Arabic. One sea, the Gulf, separates Bahrain from Iran on the east and Saudi Arabia on the west (to which it is linked by a 20-mile causeway). The other freshwater "sea" springs up from the Damman aquifer, which originates aboveground in Saudi Arabia and flows eastward, running under the sea and perforating the seabed around the Bahraini archipelago, as well as the land, with a plethora of springs.[3] As a result, Bahrain gained its regional importance disproportionate to its land area largely due to these sweetwater springs that sustained its greenery and its urbanism.

The rich greens of gardens and orchards contrast with the whites and browns of the desert.

Though often considered an antidote to the urban, in arid environments green, through cultivated areas, often indicates the presence of human settlements. The villages that punctuated Bahrain's greenery were sustained for millennia by the freshwater springs and orchards and vegetable gardens that existed between and within the gray-green date-palm groves, until the pressures of increasing population and development of the latter part of the twentieth century upset that relationship. Today Bahrain uses much of its water reserves on irrigating its remaining agricultural areas, which produce only 11 percent of the country's food and less than 0.05 percent of the national income. This agriculture is a remnant of a time when the country was self-sufficient, albeit with a much smaller population; Bahrain has grown from 70,000 in the 1920s to more than 1 million residents today.

A complex system of irrigation channels, *qanats*, were fed by the freshwater springs and water distributed according to detailed customary irrigation laws that ensured fair access to water by farmers.[4] "The Adhari Pond starves the nearby and feeds the far beyond" goes a Bahraini proverb referring to the irrigation system that because of topography and the pull of gravity supplied distant gardens rather than those close by.[5] The proximity of the springs to the greenery was further disrupted by the artesian wells drilled during the 1920s and 1930s (leading indirectly to the discovery of oil), which led to a rapid increase in greenery in Bahrain—by some accounts almost doubling green areas between the 1930s and the early 1970s[6]—but eventually contributed to the overextraction and subsequent depletion and salination

Map of Bahrain, 1901–1902, showing the date-palm groves of the north coast

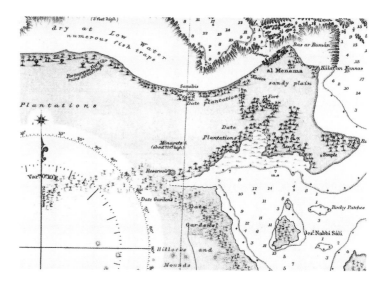

of the underground water reserves. Some of the gardens that are still irrigated from the depleted and saline springs bear exceptionally pungent fruit.

Groves of date palms are the most iconic and distinctive, yet rapidly diminishing, green spaces of Bahrain. Planning laws allow for the development of only 30 percent of agricultural areas (as opposed to all of nonagricultural areas), so many landowners seek to have land declassified as agricultural to be able to develop it. If the land is no longer green, it is no longer considered agricultural, so green must become as white as the desert sands through active neglect.

One property developer told me that it is easy to reconstruct the greenery of the palm groves—that even though date palms are cut down for villas, green areas can be replanted with trees and greenery to regain the same effect. I wish it were that easy. There is something very green about these spaces that is an indispensible part of their appeal: the richness of the hues of green, the range of textures, and the variety and intensity of the shadows. The allure of green is more than the pull of nostalgia, much more than the resonance of a bygone era that can never be recovered. Many of these spaces, whether maintained or neglected, feel timeless and dignified. They take much of their value from their history gathered over millennia of farming and gardening, as well as the microclimates that the plantations produce. The urbanity of that greenness cannot be recovered; it can be imitated, but not regained.

Writing about the social life of the Bahraini date palms, Fuad Khuri states that the culture of palms in Bahrain used to be as elaborate as the culture of camels among the pastoral nomads in central Arabia.[7] There are more than 1,000 words

> Some of the many hues of green in Bahrain

for a camel in Arabic; I am not sure how many words there are for date palms or for greenery, but one Bahraini farmer told me that he gave the date palms close to his house names, like his children, and in this way they are treated like family members. It is considered a great honor for a visitor to be served dates from these trees. It was common for farmers to plant trees to commemorate their child's birth. Shaikh Isa, the previous ruler, is credited with the saying, "The Palm tree is our mother, we can live under it."[8]

Date palms provided building materials for traditional summer housing called *barasti*. Indeed every part of the palm had a use: the leaves, the trunk, and the dates all had particular roles. A diet of dates allegedly provides the basic nutrients the human body needs. The date season starts in May and extends to October or November, depending on the variety. The date palms offered just one layer in gardens with multiple levels of produce including pomegranates, bananas, mangoes, and alfalfa, all sheltered from the blazing sun by the trees. The date palms have the capacity to be urban in that they penetrate so many aspects of Bahraini life, providing food, shelter, building materials, social spaces, and social status as well as facilitating ancillary industries and produce, while serving as a focus for poetry and folklore.

While the date-palm groves offered sources of food and employment, they were also recreation grounds for the elite. With the shade they give from the scorching sun, the palm groves create attractive spaces for social gatherings, especially during the summer months. Owning greenery in Bahrain had, and still has, complex social meanings. Large date-palm plantations were owned by city merchants, who invested in them not for income but for the status of ownership. Farmers were contracted to look after the gardens, supplying a couple of baskets of dates a week to the owners. Wealthy merchants from Manama, the capital, would bring their families to the palm groves on Friday afternoons and issue invitations to relatives and friends to join them there until the *maghrib* prayers at sundown. Sometimes visiting cards would be distributed, granting friends of the merchant permission to visit in their absence.[9]

It is important to note that the date-palm gardens of the past were not very profitable, as is the case today. One large property just outside Manama near Ain Adhari (a formerly important spring that has since dried up, to be replaced in 2008 with an artificial pool) was sold in 1943 for 40,000 rupees (about $1.2 million), while a shop in the souq in the center of Manama at that time cost 4,000 rupees. This land was then rented out at a rate of 27.5 rupees a month, thereby netting

SENSE

There's More to Green than Meets the Eye

an annual rent of 330 rupees, or approximately 1 percent of the value of the property. This was not a good financial investment, and thus it seems fair to deduce that the purchase must have been made for the social prestige that ownership of the greenery would confer.[10]

While the owners of the gardens historically belonged to an elite group of ruling family members and merchants, the farmers who worked in them invariably belonged to the Baharna, the local Arab Shi'i community, who by and large lived in nearby villages. Green is also finely ingrained in Shi'i identity. During the commemoration of the martyrdom of Imam Hussein, on the first ten days of the month of Muharram, the center of Manama is clothed in green banners and flags and the streets strewn with sweet basil, *mashmoom*, since green is considered the color of Hussein, and Islam. Every Thursday evening it is still common to bring green shoots of *mashmoom* to graves in Shi'i cemeteries.

Those Bahrainis old enough to remember the mosaic of date-palm groves often lament their destruction. It is important, however, not to overly romanticize the past and to recognize that the destruction of the date-palm gardens is not just a recent phenomenon, although the scale and pace of destruction has certainly accelerated. Curtis Larsen, in *Life and*

The date-palm groves were in the past punctuated with villages where farmers and fishermen lived—note the shallow green waters of the sea. Now villas replace the date-palm groves with other less varied greens.

Land Use on the Bahrain Islands: The Geoarchaeology of an Ancient Society, cites E.L. Durand, the British Political Resident in Bushire, who made the following observation when visiting Bahrain in 1879: "Foremost amongst the trees is of course the date, and some of the date gardens are extremely fine. Many, however, are going to ruin, the result of bad Government, and indeed in some places that were once flourishing gardens, not a bearing tree remains."[11]

Although the villages were intertwined with greenery, the center of Manama was not very green. Walking though the souq there today, one will not find much greenery apart from the odd tree or weed pushing its way through cracks in the pavement. There are many green shutters and occasional green doors, in partial compensation perhaps for the lack of soft greenery in the city. It was in the urbanization period of the early 1970s, right after full independence from the British, that greenery and city really started to mesh in Bahrain. Nelida Fuccaro links this to the oil crisis triggered by the Arab-Israeli war of 1973.[12] It was during this period, when the green countryside with its villages and the gray and white city subsequently become one in the popular imagination, that city people stopped going out to the gardens at weekends. The garden was no longer "the other" and instead became "corrupted"

and considered part of the city. The special greenness of the gardens was disrupted by the extensive development that has taken place over the past thirty years. Bahrain's limited land mass makes the demand for land and the continuance of the past uses of greenery untenable. At the same time, the extensive distribution infrastructures for water and treated sewage effluent bring the possibility of greenery to much of Bahrain today.

Contemporary green residential compounds in Bahrain, with names such as Green Oasis, are partial compensation for the lost date-palm groves. Together with the date palms of roundabouts, roadside shoulders, and median strips of VIP roads (roads designed for extra-verdant greenery but also with security in mind), they signify the green of contemporary Bahrain. Such residential and transportation infrastructural spaces are important because they are the greenery that most people encounter in everyday life. These green roadsides represent not so much the past—although the palms do symbolize this past—but speak more about Bahrain's present, its place in the world, and its aspirations for the future. Typical ads for new developments, often on billboards positioned beside highways, will show most of an image as green rather than featuring the buildings they advertise.

At weekends and in the evenings, it is not unusual to see expatriates picnicking on the roadside shoulders despite the passing traffic. (I am told that Bahrainis would never do this.) The roadside palms, although of typically different species and hues of green than traditional plantings, still retain some of their social and agricultural value. The date palms at the Bahrain Financial Harbour, built on reclaimed land on the site of the former port in the center of Manama, are pollinated in the spring and the dates harvested in the fall by low-income expatriate workers for their personal use.

The date-palm gardens and the roadside shoulders and roundabouts have similar social values. Roadside greenery can be seen as the date-palm groves of the present era. Both have a certain type of production, although those productive qualities are obviously different: the palm groves are agricultural, whereas the green roadsides indicate economic productivity, a production of development, a landscape of transformation. The plethora of green roundabouts and median strips lined with petunias of the national colors of red and white celebrate the power and benevolence of the state. As seen in the multitude of roadside billboards with pictures of the king, the prime minister, and the crown prince, invariably situated beside greenery, the rulers are happy to be associated with green.

"Together let us make Bahrain Green," urged the organizers of the 2008 Riffa Views Bahrain International Garden Show, who also sponsored a garden design competition among Bahraini schools called "The Riffa Views Eden Challenge." The International Garden Show, which runs for three days every year, is one of just three organizations in Bahrain under the direct patronage of the king, Hamad bin Isa Al-Khalifa. Green retains its position as a social catalyst, with the Gardening Club reflecting increased interest in things green and beautiful and, by association, royal.

The transformative power of turning desert to green is extraordinary. To convert desert into luscious green is to prove that dreams do become reality, to achieve the impossible, to show that paradise can be constructed on earth. Writing in *The Social Life of Trees*, Maurice Bloch, invoking Claude Lévi-Strauss, maintains that to be effective, a transformation needs to be of a certain magnitude.[13] For instance, turning arid desert into gravel or concrete is not as potent a transformation as changing desert into green. The presence of the desert, however, is not easily forgotten.

This text is adapted from my doctoral research at Harvard Graduate School of Design.

1 Brent Berlin and Paul Kay, *Basic Color Terms: Their Universality and Evolution* (Berkeley: University of California Press, 1969), 2–4.

2 Alex Byrne and David Hilbert, *Readings on Color: The Philosophy of Color, Vol. 1* (Cambridge: MIT Press, 1997), xi–xxv.

3 The sea-based springs induced a particular coloration of the green waters of the sea, as well as a particular luster on pearls, a mainstay of Bahrain's economy until the 1930s.

4 See R. B. Serjeant, "Customary Irrigation Law among the Baharnah of Bahrain," *Bahrain Through the Ages: The History*, edited by Shaikh Abdullah bin Khalid Al-Khalifa and Michael Rice (London and New York: Keegan Paul International, 1993), 471–496.

5 Ali Akbar Bushehri, personal communication, April 21, 2008. See also Nelida Fuccaro, *Histories of City and State in the Persian Gulf* (Cambridge: Cambridge University Press, 2009), 23. As Fuccaro suggests, the saying also cynically refers to the appropriation of Bahrain's resources by foreigners.

6 See Mustapha Ben Hamouche, "Land-Use Change and Its Impact on Urban Planning in Bahrain: A GIS Approach," *Proceedings of the Middle East Spatial Technology Conference*, Bahrain, December 2007. Retrieved on June 26, 2009, from: http://www.gisdevelopment.net/proceedings/mest/2007/RemoteSensing-ApplicationsLanduse.htm

7 Fuad Khuri, *Tribe and State in Bahrain: The Transformation of Social and Political Authority in an Arab State* (Chicago: University of Chicago Press, 1980), 39.

8 Fareeda Mohammed Saleh Khunji, *The Story of the Palm Tree* (Bahrain: 2003), 45.

9 Ali Akbar Bushehri, personal communication, April 25, 2008.

10 From the archive of Ali Akbar Bushehri.

11 Curtis Larsen, *Life and Land Use on the Bahrain Islands: The Geoarchaeology of an Ancient Society* (Chicago: University of Chicago Press, 1983), 22.

12 Fuccaro, *Histories of City and State in the Persian Gulf*, 229.

13 Maurice Bloch, "Why Trees, Too, Are Good to Think With: Towards an Anthropology of the Meaning of Life," *The Social Life of Trees*, edited by Laura Rival (New York: Berg Publishers, 1998), 39–40. Bloch cites the example of the transformation of wine to blood in the Catholic mass; the transformation would not be so intense if it were wine to whiskey.

Play Me, I'm Yours

Luke Jerram

Why is it that when I go to the laundrette, I see the same people each week and yet nobody talks to one another? Why don't I know the names of the people who live opposite my house? *Play Me, I'm Yours* is an artwork designed to act as a catalyst for strangers who regularly occupy the same space to connect.

The project places pianos in various spaces within the city. Disrupting people's negotiation of their city, the pianos are intended to provoke people into engaging, activating, and claiming ownership of their urban landscape. The project is also a reaction against the deluge of bad permanent public artwork and architectural clutter in U.K. cities that neither connects with nor empowers a local community.

The pianos have lured many hidden musicians from out of the wood-work. It has become apparent that there are hundreds of pianists who don't have a piano to play. *Play Me, I'm Yours* offers access to musical instruments and gives musicians an opportunity to share their creativity by performing in public. Like Facebook, *Play Me, I'm Yours* provides an interconnected resource, an empty blank canvas, for people to express themselves.

A project web site (www.streetpianos.com) was created for people to post their comments about the pianos and describe their use. The site has helped document each piano's journey while connecting the street pianos and their communities across each city. To date, *Play Me, I'm Yours* has been presented in London, São Paulo, Sydney, Birmingham, and Bristol.

The pianos have had a significant impact. Over the course of three weeks, it was estimated that more than 140,000 people across Birmingham played with or listened to music from the pianos. Statistics like these add weight to the argument that regional art galleries, with much lower attendance figures, are failing to reach potentially large and diverse audiences and engage with communities they have an obligation to reach.

With the support of a special Streetpianos charitable fund, thirteen pianos were distributed across the city of São Paulo (2008). Many people had never seen a real piano before, let alone been given permission to play one. The pianos were ultimately donated to schools and community groups in the area.

Yet the realization of *Play Me, I'm Yours* was not without obstacles. In Birmingham (2008), the city council financially supported the project, yet we were banned (for the usual health and safety reasons) from placing any piano on council-owned "public" land. To enable the artwork to happen in London (2009), organizers had to apply for individual music licenses, for each piano location. The absurdity of licensing the pianos for *Play Me, I'm Yours* was discussed in the House of Lords on June 16, 2009.

Play Me, I'm Yours! In Bury St. Edmunds, London, and São Paulo (where it is known as Toque-me, Sou Teu!)

Mapping
Main Street

Jesse Shapins, Kara Oehler,
Ann Heppermann, and James Burns

When politicians and the media mention Main Street, they evoke one people and one place. But there are more than 10,466 streets named Main in the United States.

Mapping Main Street is a collaborative documentary media project that creates a new map of the country through stories, photos, and videos recorded on actual Main Streets. Once you start looking, you'll notice that Main Streets are everywhere—not just in the downtown areas of small midwestern towns. There's a Main Street in San Luis, Arizona, that dead-ends right into the Mexican border. New York City has five Main Streets, one in each borough. Los Angeles has the longest Main Street in the country. The Main Street in Melvindale, Michigan, runs through a trailer park in the shadow of Ford's River Rouge plant, once the largest factory in the world.

Some Main Streets have only a few buildings, if any. In Dayton, Washington, Main Street passes through rolling wheat fields. In Mobile, Alabama, Main Street is an open green inhabited by a lone fire hydrant. From suburban tracts to overgrown edges, manicured lawns to horse pastures, junkyards to cornfields, Main Street is also a window onto the spaces where ecology and urbanism intersect.

Mapping Main Street is created through MQ2, an initiative of the Association of Independents in Radio with the CPB and NPR. Additional support from Harvard's Berkman Center for Internet and Society.

SENSE

CURATE

Curating Resources
Niall Kirkwood

The Sea and Monsoon Within: A Mumbai Manifesto
Anuradha Mathur and Dilip da Cunha

Transcendent Eco-cities or Urban Ecological Security?
Mike Hodson and Simon Marvin

New Waterscapes for Singapore
Herbert Dreiseitl

To Raise the Water Level in a Fishpond
Zhang Huan

Envisioning Ecological Cities
Mitchell Joachim

Return to Nature
Sandi Hilal, Alessandro Petti, and Eyal Weizman

Harmonia 57
Triptyque

Grounding a Sustainable Urban Strategy
Michael Van Valkenburgh Associates

Center Street Plaza
Hood Design

Curating Resources

Niall Kirkwood

Landscape architecture as a discipline has, from its inception, engaged in a critical way with society, ameliorating the environment and proposing courses of action that reconcile the interests of profit with the public good. Yet although the history of the landscape field has been luminous in many respects, it cannot take leadership in the planning and design of the natural and built environment for granted. What is critical to acknowledge about this moment is the degree to which the field has moved in the last three decades. Three strands of thinking have accompanied this evolution.

First, landscape architecture has moved far beyond the stylistic and often rigid approaches of landscape modernism. Current thinking makes design itself a kind of research and uses models that are as much scientific as artistic, focusing on the metrics of a site, ecological factors, and the interaction with natural and man-made systems. As modern cities grow up and out, what sustainable systems will deliver food, energy, and water? How will cities deal with noise, light, and odor? To reduce the urban carbon footprint, how should new open spaces and buildings be built and old ones fixed?

Second, the idea of nature and the scientific conception of the natural world, to which the profession of landscape architecture is often aligned, underwent dramatic changes in the

Gated entrance to the Maidan, Mumbai, 2008

1970s. Dynamic ecology, characterized by constant change and resilience, is the paradigm today. Third, the capacity of landscape architects to work at multiple scales, to solve environmental problems, and to collaborate with or lead teams of urban planners, engineers, and architects are increasingly the skills that the planning and design challenges of our century require. These skills wielded so effectively by Olmsted and Eliot must be developed and taught if landscape architecture is to make unique contributions. Yet the ongoing global upheaval in economic markets makes the urban landscape today subject to forces of change that are distinctly of our own time. Landscape architects must address and synthesize complex environmental and social issues in their work

In this context, it is worth noting that some of our urban megacenters, particularly in Asia, are scrupulously tidy, controlled, and guarded with their resources, while others are more restless, turning up new uses and old interpretations with each new generation. Still others have left their physical and cultural resources in their original condition: a vast mess of unsorted material across which multinational corporations and pavement scavengers alike wander, uncovering and pulling up interesting fragments that can be sold or recycled for a price, or that may come in handy someday. The lack of any

Above the Dhobi Ghats, Mumbai, 2008

commanding story that dictates how resources should be understood and ultimately used allows space for imagination, pleasure, and originality. Many of these resources have set up their own independent myths. For example (referring to the writings of Ivan Illich), the lakewaters become H_2O, trash shifts from waste to energy, and so forth.

Paradoxically, a set of continuities appear. One is the enduring importance of the larger landscape—the region and the watershed. A second is the opportunity for bridging the traumatic chasm dividing the confident ruling minority and the mistrustful yet hard-working majority. A third is the persistence of the idea of informal intelligence about the pragmatic nature of daily human life (usually collective rather than individual) and the replicability of it at an urban scale. A fourth is the way in which the human experience of resources is built so intimately into the geology and ecology of a place to form a single cultural landscape we call city.

Piped water infrastructure crossing the Mithi River, Mumbai, 2008

Hut community on seaboard,
Mumbai, 2008

Drying clothes outside BDD chawl,
Mumbai, 2008

Spent cotton reels, Textile Mill
No. 2, Mumbai, 2006

The Sea and Monsoon Within: A Mumbai Manifesto

Anuradha Mathur and Dilip da Cunha

The monsoon: "A crash—and the Monsoon's on us, in torrents everywhere," is how one author in 1938 described a phenomenon that begins life anew each June in Mumbai, as elsewhere on the West Coast of India. This phenomenon calls attention to Mumbai as a "monsoon surface" rather than a place where water flows within rivers that begin in point sources.

Mumbai's history, in most accounts, pivots on its European occupation—the Portuguese from 1534 to 1665, but more significantly the English from 1665 to 1947. Little is said in these narratives about an attitude to and vocabulary of terrain that was constructed through this occupation, a vocabulary that rests on a fundamental belief not necessarily shared by previous occupants of Mumbai, namely, that land and sea should be divided. This division was instituted by European seafarers, but more concertedly by English marine and land surveyors in the late 1700s with the drawing of a line on a map. This line traverses rocks, swamps, and beaches of an aqueous terrain. It asserted a divide with a clarity that preceded land-reclamation schemes, which besides claiming land from the sea also sought to remove any ambiguity in the meeting ground of land and sea.

The articulation of a line between land and sea has largely gone unnoticed, and the view from above that facilitated its drawing in maps has become the taken-for-granted visualization of Mumbai's terrain. It is a view by which land can and has been embellished with fine detail of property lines, land uses, and contours, as well as marked with entities such as water bodies, trees, roads, and buildings drawn as islands within the "Island City" that the English sought to cultivate. Indeed, the divide between land and sea was only a beginning of divides that crept across the surface of land in a spirit of separation before connection, land uses before "mixed" uses, inside and outside before thresholds. All the while, however, the sea in this view has had little to say, presenting itself as an undifferentiated surface beyond land's edge, a blank in maps.

Today this view, cultivated in a milieu of colonial power and landed property, is deeply embedded in everyday language and an intrinsic part of imaging Mumbai and imagining its future. Questions are raised from time to time regarding the form of the line between land and sea that this view facilitates, and the purpose and enterprise of its drawing. But little is said about its presence, about the battlefront that it sets up between land and sea, and between land and water in general, which in Mumbai includes the monsoon.

CURATE

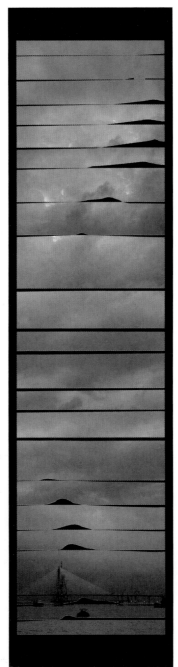

1827 Survey of Mumbai: In his landmark 1827 map—the first professional survey of South and North Mumbai—Lt. William Tate separated fields, terraces, and tanks from channels that he especially assigned for water flows. These "rivers" were drawn with lines that extended inland from the coastline and were colored blue in the same manner as the sea. He provided Mumbai with a vocabulary of "land uses." Today his rivers are the drains of the city, essential to the city administration's resolution of flood. William A. Tate, *Plan of the Islands of Bombay and Salsette, Reduced from the Revenue Survey completed in the year 1827*, December 1831 (detail).

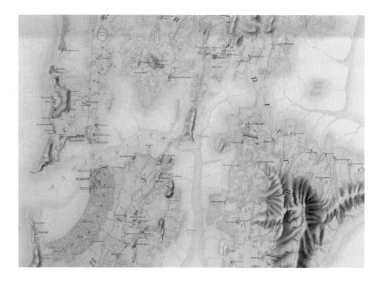

The southwest monsoon was seen by British administrators of Mumbai as a "foul-weather season." It came in from the sea in the beginning of June and lasted until September. It made the surveyors' fieldwork difficult—confounding, even erasing, the lines that they wanted to see with clarity on the ground, such as the edge between water and land. They therefore pursued their task in "fair weather," when edges between land and water were more visible.

For more than two centuries, this "fair-weather" terrain in which the monsoon is made an externality has provided the basis for administrative decisions that not only assumed the course of flows and the edge between land and water but also enforced them with property lines, embankments, and other constructions. It comes as a shock, as it did in July 2005, when the monsoon and sea refused to follow the lines of maps.

1700

1800

1850

1900

Making the Mithi: The Mithi has two ancestors. Its upper portion was the Gopar Nullah, a cultivated swale that gathered the monsoon waters from the Vehar, Powai, and Aarey valleys. Its lower portion is the Mahim Creek, a labyrinth of flows that reached from Mahim Bay to Thane and Mumbai Harbor, touching the sea at more than one place. The Gopar Nullah would become an outlet of the Vehar and Powai reservoirs built in the 1850s and 1890s, and the Mahim Creek would become an inlet for the sea, disconnected from the east by the Sion Causeway, built in 1800. The Mithi today is a combination of nullah and creek. It is seen as a single flow from Vehar Reservoir to Mahim Bay. It largely stays this assigned course. But upon occasion it cannot accommodate the duality of its inheritance, typically when high tide in its lower creek side coincides with a heavy monsoon downpour on its upper nullah side, as it did on July 26, 2005.

Indeed, uncritical acceptance of the line between land and sea brought Mumbai the flood of 2005, when hundreds died and much property was lost as parts of Mumbai went under many feet of water. Those rains were unusual. The average for the whole season (944 millimeters) fell in a day. But more than being improbable and merely a failure of a drainage system or of planning and administration, as portrayed by the media and most analyses, this disaster is a failure to visualize a terrain. This terrain, just beneath the surface, is today as it was in the 1600s, when John Fryer, a medical officer in the service of the English East India Company, described Mumbai as "Spots of Ground, still disputable to which side to incline: For at Low Water most of them are fordable to the Main, or from one to the other; and at Spring-Tides again a great part of them overflowed."[1]

Mumbai, more than an island, is in an estuary, a place where fresh-water environments of rivers transition to the saline environment of the sea. On the west coast of India where Mumbai is located, however, an estuary is far from restricted to the mouths of rivers, especially during the monsoon, when there is too little time and too much water to make an orderly exit through courses delineated on maps. At times like this, when the coast is a continuum of flows too numerous to count and to name, the meeting ground of land and sea is less a north-south line that divides and more an east-west filter that accommodates movement both ways. The material of these movements is diverse. Besides water, it includes deposits coming off an eroding land and those coming in with the tide of the sea. It is a world of stuff that cannot be held to a simple gradient, whether of slope or salinity.

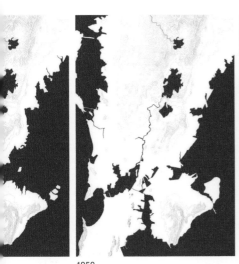

1950

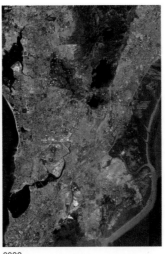

2000

Mithi River

Sections of Mumbai: While the
plan view of the map celebrates the
islands of Mumbai and situates
the sea beyond land's edge, sections
reveal a sea that is beneath,
within–permeating land through
aquifers well known to offer
Mumbai citizens "brackish" water
far inland. Here landfills, cause-
ways, and walls do not keep the sea
out; they merely prevent it from
surfacing in a game of pressure,
saturation, and porosity that
is played in depth. In this estuary,
the flood of 2005 did not come
from just rains from above and flows
on the surface; it came as much
from a saturated and permeated
ground beneath.

This fluid and dynamic world demands to be seen in cross-sectional depth, a representation that was and is appreciated by seafarers, who do not embrace the measure of geographic space that maps celebrate. When out of sight of land, they turn to a world of time operating within a celestial sphere rich in distinguishable moments rather than measurable distances; and they turn to a world of depth, which they read in sectional terms rather than in plan. Here, where space has no presence (perhaps because it is omnipresent), and surface is not read-able except in depth—through rises, waves, soundings, and creatures—terrain is felt more than it is seen. To approach land is to feel depth rising above the horizon. But for a long while in their approach, seafarers inhabit a transition from sectional-depth to plan-surface, from time to space, and from a world marked by a horizon that can only be approached to one of boundaries that by definition assume an "other" side.

The transition from sea to land is not a logical one. There is little if any common ground between time and space, depth and surface, horizon and boundary. These are qualitatively different measures that sit uncomfortably with each other. Instead of a common ground, there is a negotiated unease, an analogical tension that keeps land and sea alive through practices that respect their difference.

These practices are visible in Mumbai today beneath the surface of maps and beyond the eye of those who rely on maps, in ordinary everyday landscapes that elude visual clar-ity while exercising the tenacity and negotiating sensibility of the estuary. These landscapes, which include *maidans, talaos* (tanks that use the pressure of monsoon waters on the sur-face and ground waters from wells to keep salt water at bay), bazaars, and *oarts* (coconut groves), are looked upon in the world of the coastline as either informal or lacking urbanity. In an estuary, however, the appreciation for divergence and accommodation of ambiguity that these landscapes cultivate is an opportunity to rethink the measures and possibilities of design in Mumbai.

Anthropologist Clifford Geertz recounts an "Indian story" that could very well be situated in this new visualization of Mumbai. It is about "an Englishman who, having been told that the world rested on a platform which rested on the back of an elephant which rested in turn on the back of a turtle, asked what did the turtle rest on? Another turtle. And that turtle? 'Ah, Sahib, after that it is turtles all the way down.'"[2] For Geertz the story captures the incomplete nature of under-standing, "in which to get somewhere with the matter at hand is to intensify the suspicion, both your own and that of others, that you are not quite getting it right." Others have not taken

as kindly to the endlessness of the turtle chain in the story. To Stephen Hawking, the idea of an infinite tower of turtles is a denial that the underlying order of the universe is within human grasp: "our goal is nothing less than a complete description of the universe we live in."[3]

What is missed in the appreciation and depreciation of this "Indian story," which is retold in many different ways in Europe and America by those in the business of discussing things like first cause and truth, are the animals in the story and the sectional world they inhabit: the turtle beneath the elephant; a reptilian world beneath a mammalian one; and perhaps the marine-coastal world of the five species of turtles known to inhabit the seas around India (four off Maharashtra) supporting the terrestrial one of the Asian elephant. In India, particularly in the monsoon world of the west coast, it affords another reading of the terrain of settlement. This terrain is not land divided from water, but an ambiguous and mysterious depth that reaches from monsoon clouds above through the labyrinthine world of creeks, to the web of aquifers beneath. It is not a spatial ground as much as a temporal one. Here building concrete walls to channel monsoon waters and barriers to keep out the sea—both practices geared to preventing waters from crossing a line—are out of place. Waters in a sectional world do not flow on a surface as much as they rise and fall, evaporate and condense. They do not flood; they soak.

If Geertz is right in calling the turtle tale an "Indian story," then imaging a sectional world stems perhaps from an Indian imagination that paralleled an English administration, and today parallels a cultivated Indian administration preoccupied with making Mumbai in the image of a map. Indeed Mumbai in an estuary dislodges the image of the map, an image produced by men who avoided "seeing" during the monsoon because in this "foul-weather season," the "truth" of the lines that they wanted to see was lost to an unknown depth of turtles.

While people on coasts everywhere look to the practice of flood and the construction of a battlefront to protect land from the threat of a rising sea, Mumbai can take a route that is intrinsically peaceful and accommodating. The sea is within the measure of landscapes that exist here outside the language of the map. These landscapes encourage practices that do not enforce clear and distinct separations in plan but accommodate fluidities in section. They are absorbent and resilient, making a place that does not assume uncertainty as much as makes room for possibilities. It recognizes that Mumbai is not just in an estuary, but an estuary in the monsoon. It is turtles all the way down.

Design in Mumbai then must begin with a new visualization of its situation in an estuary where the sea and monsoon are insiders rather than outsiders, making a place where ambiguity and possibility, rather than clarity and certainty, are the norm. This terrain does not lend itself to master planning, a way of designing the future that takes the plan-view of maps for granted and as such is predisposed toward the firmness of land and the controlling devices that come with it, such as land-use divisions, zoning regulations, and enforced boundaries. These devices not only demand a clear articulation of geographic space, they also call for a simplified view of everyday life that compartmentalies it into residential, commercial, recreational, industrial, drainage, and transportation, or "mixes" of two or more. Landscapes of the estuary elude this visualization predisposed to control, which is why they were the "other" in a colonial era and why they survive contentiously as the "informal" sector of planning and administration today. It is also why these landscapes are both threatened and threatening.

Presented here are drawings from two of a range of design proposals for the terrain of the Mithi River, which extends from Sanjay Gandhi National Park in the hills of North Mumbai, across a surface consumed by settlement that is more defiant than obedient, to the realm of historic forts that once commanded the flows of Mahim Creek. These three staging grounds of the Mithi are each a place for a distinct set of design interventions—Creek Forts, Nullah Crossings, and Monsoon Surface. Rather than end scenarios, these proposals are conceived as seeds that evolve by a visual, political, and technological fluidity and agility that befits the temporality, uncertainty, and complexity of a terrain between land and sea. They work with an appreciation of the fact that design in an estuary, particularly an estuary in the monsoon, solves the problem of flood not by flood-control measures but by making a place that is absorbent and resilient.

This text is adapted from the exhibition and book *SOAK: Mumbai in an Estuary* (New Delhi: Rupa and Company, 2009).

1 John Fryer, *A New Account of East India and Persia Being Nine Years' Travels, 1672–1681*, vol. 1 (Hakluyt Society, 1909), 160.

2 Clifford Geertz, "Thick Description: Towards an Interpretive Theory of Culture," in *The Interpretation of Cultures* (New York: Basic Books, 1973), 28–29.

3 Stephen W. Hawking, *A Brief History of Time* (New York: Bantam Books, 1998).

Project 2: Mahim Fort: The Mahim Fort Project intervenes in the trajectory of a moving corner where the east-west flows of Mahim Creek, with its finer-grained content of silt and clay, meet the north-south edge of a bay, with its larger-grained content of sand. This corner, once held by the fort, has moved north with depositions against the causeway built across the creek in the 1840s, making land that has been appropriated for a maidan/beach, a fishing village, and a sewage pumping station. The project deflects this northward force that has pinched the creek with interventions that extend in the east-west direction. A new creek cuts opportunistically through the sand bank and settlement toward the east. It links Mahim Bay with the Mithi beyond the causeway, providing the Mithi with another link to the bay while also serving as an axis for docks and a market. Cultivations of coconut palms *(oarts)* that support recreational and economic activities within their grove extend and protect the shore from further erosion at the fort and farther north along the bay. At the fort and possibly elsewhere, these *oarts* provide docking facilities for bio-treating barges that anchor here for periods of time, with amenities assigned to particular families living in the fort. Paid to use these barges for the energy and the manure that can be harvested from refuse, these families are invited to associate with a system that circulates between these *oarts* and anchoring grounds offshore, where the material gathered is given time to process aerobically and anaerobically into energy, manure, and gray waters.

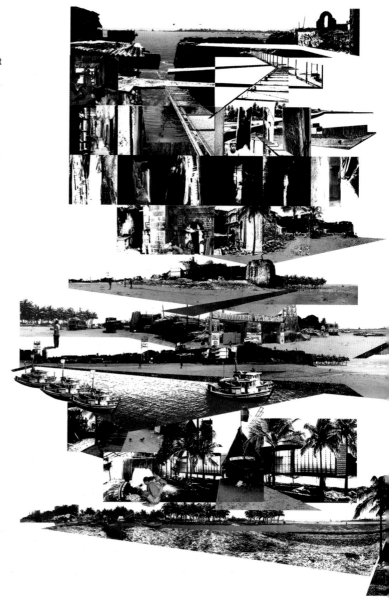

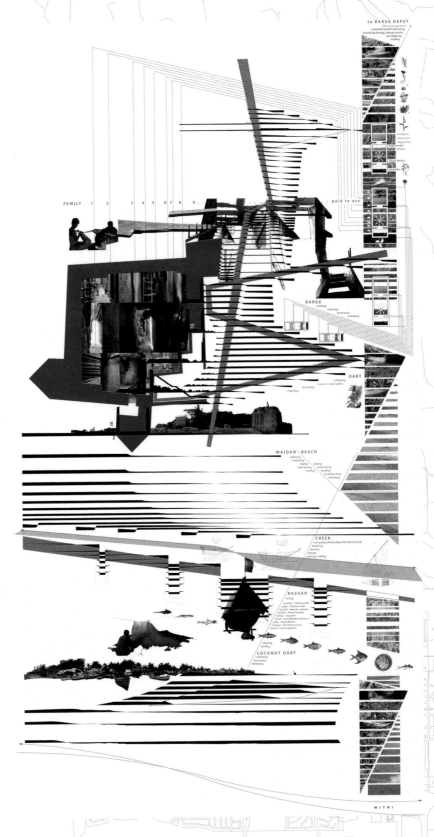

The Sea and Monsoon Within: A Mumbai Manifesto

Project 9: Airport Crossing:
The Airport Crossing Project turns the Mithi into a treatment field—a corrugated surface of holdings planted with biotic material that filter, absorb, and transform effluent, linked by overflows across sills. This surface extends from the Mithi up swales, which likewise are made to operate as processing grounds, reaching out where possible to appropriate available land within their operation. It is also extended through walls along the airport boundary that gather monsoon waters at an upper level while serving the needs of community and the airport on a lower level; and through maidans that hold and absorb excess waters during the monsoon, when these nomadic grounds are less used for other functions. The vectors of sills that hold and modulate overflows of this corrugated surface can serve as thoroughfares, with all the other uses that make thoroughfares in Mumbai operate more as bazaars and maidans than merely service connections between origins and destinations. Most important, however, the surface of the Mithi is extended via carefully calibrated fields across the airport to Vakola Nullah, giving the Mithi an auxiliary route to the sea if necessary.

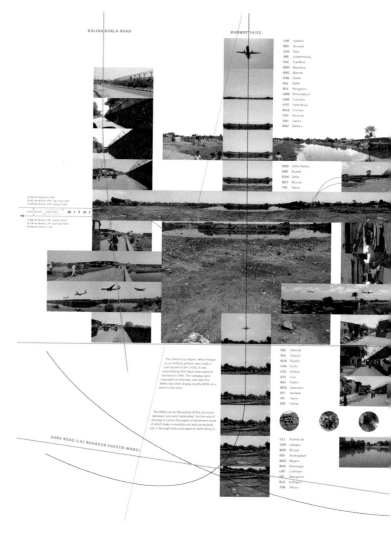

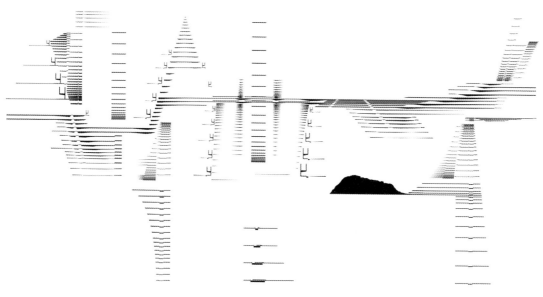

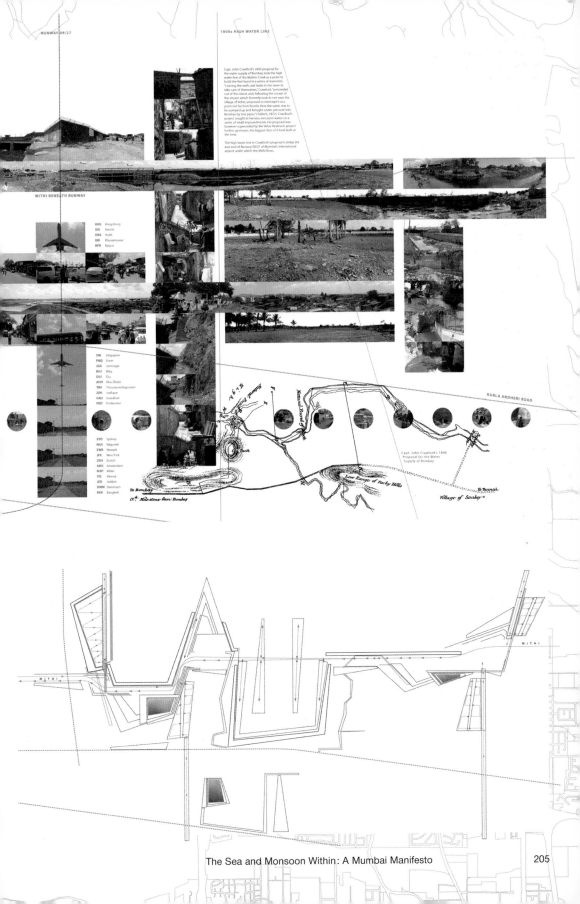

The Sea and Monsoon Within: A Mumbai Manifesto

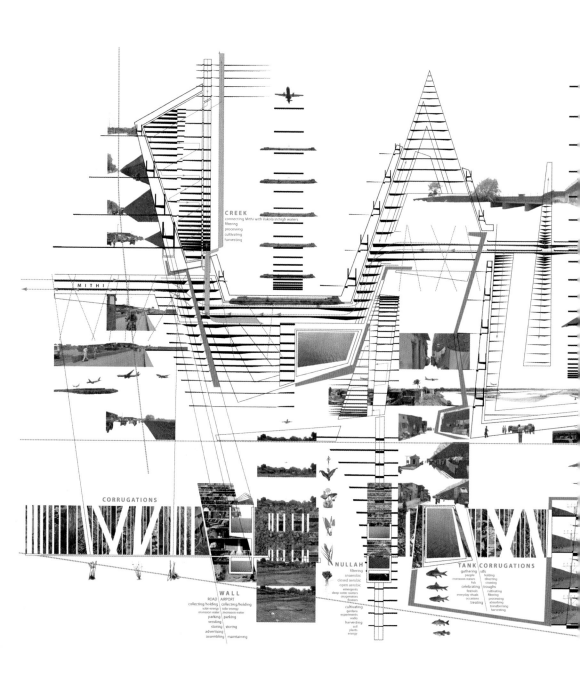

CREEK
connecting Mithi with Vakola in high waters
filtering
processing
cultivating
harvesting

MITHI

CORRUGATIONS

NULLAH
filtering
anaerobic
closed aerobic
open aerobic
emergeds
festivals
deep water visitors
oxygenators
floaters
cultivating
gardens
experiments
walls
harvesting
soil
plants
energy

TANK CORRUGATIONS
gathering   stilts
monsoon waters   holding
fish   diverting
celebrating   crossing
festivals   cultivating
everyday rituals   filtering
occasions   processing
treating   absorbing
                   transforming
                   harvesting

WALL
ROAD   AIRPORT
collecting/holding collecting/holding
solar energy   solar energy
monsoon water   monsoon water
parking   parking
vending
storing   storing
advertising
assembling   maintaining

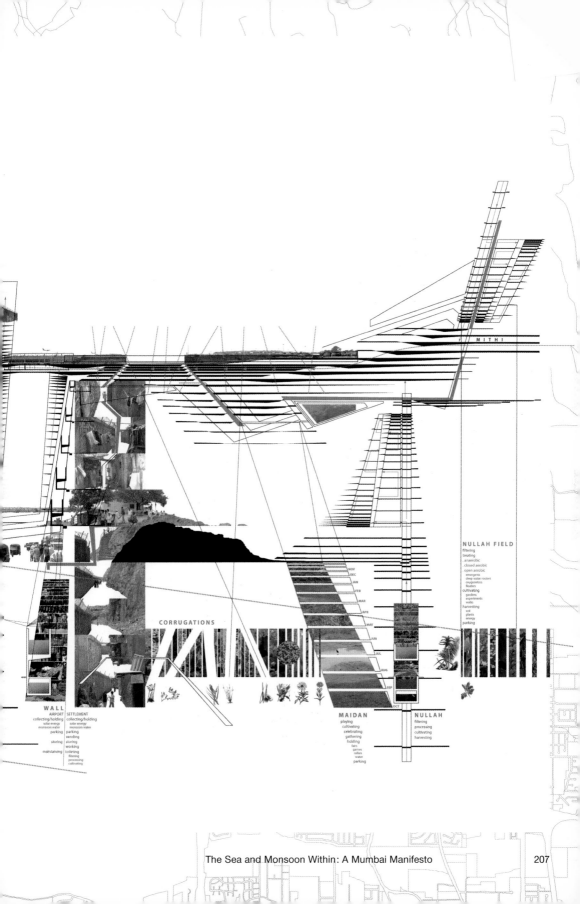

MITHI

NULLAH FIELD
filtering
treating
anaerobic
closed aerobic
open aerobic
emergents
deep-water rooters
oxygenators
floaters
cultivating
gardens
experiments
walls
harvesting
soil
plants
energy
parking

CORRUGATIONS

NOV
DEC
JAN
FEB
MAR
APR
MAY
JUN
JUL
AUG
SEP
OCT

WALL
AIRPORT | SETTLEMENT
collecting/holding | collecting/holding
solar energy | solar energy
monsoon water | monsoon water
parking | parking
| vending
storing | storing
| working
maintaining | toileting
| filtering
| processing
| cultivating

MAIDAN
playing
cultivating
celebrating
gathering
holding
fairs
games
rallies
water
parking

NULLAH
filtering
processing
cultivating
harvesting

Transcendent Eco-cities or Urban Ecological Security?

Mike Hodson and Simon Marvin

Ecological urbanism provides an opportunity to ask important questions about the environmental movement's wider societal implications and potential long-term consequences for our understanding of cities. As urbanists, our primary interest in this study is in looking behind the interests promoting a narrower definition of what we'll call eco-urbanism as a specific temporal and spatial response to the challenges of climate change and resource limits. What most concerns us is the questionable assumption that eco-urbanism is a transformative style of development that will allow cities to continue to grow economically while quite literally transcending environmental constraints, obviating the need for wider societal change. Does eco-urbanism represent merely an attempt to create ecologically secure gated communities, or can it contribute to the development of more collective notions of planetary security in the face of multiple eco-emergencies?

Normalizing Replicant Eco-urbanism

In contrast to the countercultural and alternative movements that responded to the 1973 energy crisis,[1] the new eco-urbanism has gone mainstream, developing it own lexicon of scales through which new projects are implemented around the globe; there are eco-villages, eco-towns, eco-blocks, eco-islands, eco-cities, and even eco-regions. Although many developments have not left the drawing board, there is enormous enthusiasm for replicating eco-city developments, represented as visionary—and exemplary—experiments.[2] The *IEEE Spectrum* sees eco-cities as "a city-scale test bed" for reengineering technologies to maximize efficiency and reduce environmental waste, while Herbert Girardet, the ecologist urbanist and advisor to Arup, argues that Dongtan is intended to set an example. It will be a pioneering eco-city that could become a blueprint for sustainable urban development, in China itself and elsewhere in the world. It holds a promise of a high-efficiency, small-footprint urban design. By 2010, Dongtan will be a compelling model for how to build sustainable cities worldwide that may well be too persuasive to ignore.[3]

Although there is relatively little experience of actually building eco-cities and assessing whether the social visions and technological aspirations are achievable, there are already intergovernmental agreements (for instance, between China and the United Kingdom) to accelerate eco-city development in both contexts.

Integrated (Quasi) Autonomous Ecotectonics

The new ecotectonics of eco-urbanism seeks to integrate environment and infrastructure by rebundling architecture, ecology, and technology in an attempt to internalize energy, water, food, waste, and material flows within the development. Engineers, systems modelers, material flow analysts, and designers are involved in integrating local production technologies, circular metabolisms, and closed-loop systems to reduce reliance on external centralized infrastructure networks. This places a particular premium on low-water-use systems, water recycling, reuse of waste water, local energy production systems, reuse of waste, and local food production systems. These responses strongly echo the early integrated system models of the 1970s; what is different this time is the extension of these systems to consider carbon flows and the impact of climate change, along with aspirations to explore new concepts such as carbon neutrality, waste neutrality, and water neutrality. Significantly, there seems to be much less debate in this current period about wider questions of social and institutional control of these technologies, which, it is largely assumed, will be provided by the market.

Eco-urbanism as Transcendent Urbanism

Linked to the aspiration of greater ecological and infrastructural self-reliance is the claim that eco-urbanism can develop cities in almost any urban context, overcoming both local environmental limits and the consequences of global climate change and resource constraints. So, for example, we have Masdar being developed in the desert of the UAE; Dongtan being built adjacent to an internationally significant wildlife site in Shanghai; and the water-stressed, polluted brownfield, and flood-risk sites of the Thames Gateway being designed to accommodate an additional 160,000 houses through a combination of water, waste, and carbon neutrality, along with unprecedented levels of flood protection. Cities, according to some visions, will even be constructed in the oceans. Eco-urbanism is a new style of urbanism that provides the technological solutions and market frameworks to overcome what we would have conventionally understood as limits while anticipating a period of climate change and ensuring continued reproduction under a period of resource constraint. Given impending eco-emergencies, eco-urbanism will attempt

Eco-cities have received significant coverage in popular science and technology magazines, focusing on their "autonomous" infrastructures.

to provide a guarantee that it can transcend any ecological circumstance.

Corporate and Governmental Leadership of Eco-urbanism
Leadership of the eco-urbanism movement is strongly focused around particular corporate and governmental interests. This is in stark contrast to the 1970s, when at least part of the response by radical and environmental groups was a critique of such interests. For example, General Electric is the strategic partner in Masdar, which is designed to place the UAE in a global leadership role with respect to renewable and environmental technologies. The British engineering firm Arup, which is developing Dongtan, has signed agreements with the Chinese and U.K. governments to establish a series of linked Institutes for Sustainability—the first being developed in the Thames Gateway in London—to develop the expertise and institutional frameworks to roll out eco-urbanism. Environmental and green groups, such as Greenpeace and the World Wildlife Fund, are now supporters or partners with commercial and governmental actors involved in accelerating the construction of eco-urbanism.

How do we understand eco-urbanism as the artificial reconstructions of nature and ecology through design and technology? Are they specific responses to a set of specific historic-geographic pressures, a new means of political-economic reproduction, or a cultural representation of a more ethical urbanism? Our point is that they represent a specific spatial and temporal project in which ecology and economy merge around technoscientific design. To understand why this is the case, we need to locate eco-urbanism within a wider understanding of what is happening to global urbanism.

Dongtan's architectural vision is often celebrated as a potential blueprint for sustainable urban development.

Contemporary Global Cities in the "Anthropocene"

We need to develop an understanding of how the present crisis is constituted before asking whether eco-urbanism is part of the solution—or still part of the problem. The key context is the massive increase in urbanization and the proliferation of cities globally. In 1900, 10 percent of the world's population lived in cities; 100 years later, 50 percent of the world's 6 billion people live in cities; by 2050, it is projected that nearly 70 percent of the world's 10 billion will do so. Consequently the social, technical, and ecological organization of supporting such massive concentrations of people has become more challenging. For political scientist Tim Luke, this means that we must think more carefully about how we conceptualize cities:

> Global cities now are entirely new environments tied to several complex layers of technological systems whose logistical grids knit into other networks for the production, consumption, circulation and accumulation of commodities. In addition to sewer, water, and street systems, cities are embedded in electricity, coal, natural gas, and petroleum and metals markets, in addition to timber, livestock, fish, crops and land markets. All of this is needed simply to supply food, water, energy products and services to residents. Global cities leave very destructive environmental footprints as their inhabitants reach out into markets around the world for material inputs to survive, but these transactions are also the root causes of global ecological decline.[4]

Luke develops the concept of cities as "metalogistical" spaces to capture this sense of contemporary urbanism as formulated through, and constituted by, dense concretions of infrastructural logistics. The prefix "meta" helps to view the city as an active intermediary, which sits as a site of material transformation that anticipates, modifies, and excretes the movement of resources, materials, and people. Any understanding

of urban ecosystems as constituted through material flows also has to take seriously the analysis of urbanized international and inter-environmental relations of critical resource flows.

Although cities exist within a highly unified and integrated global space of capital flows, particular cities vary widely in their access to ecological resources. Highly energy-intensive urban environments in the United States contrast with the cities of the global south, where millions do not have access to clean water, energy, and telephones. The United States has almost 5 percent of the world's population, but generates about 25 percent of greenhouse gases. Americans' ability to control global ecosystems of fossil fuel means that U.S. cities are able to be far more spatially expansive (and destructive) than if they had to survive solely on the resources available in their national space.

Contemporary urbanism is then best understood as a hybrid of economic processes and artificial ecologies that for Simon Dalby are "now changing the biosphere in significant ways."[5] It is no longer tenable to see the environment as separate or external from urbanization. Cities are changing many physical processes in the biosphere to such an extent that earth scientists are now talking about a new geological era, the "anthropocene," during which the "whole planet is being remade by our contemporary urban industrial systems."[6] Central to the emergence of this perspective is the view that the earth is a single system in which contemporary life is a critical player in the production of global ecological change. Human activities are so pervasive and profound in their consequences that they have the potential to alter the systems in ways that threaten the processes on which life depends. Global ecological change is leading to the emergence of an "urbanatura" that is a "more unpredictable, uninviting... hybrid of urbanism and nature."[7] Impending urbanaturalized environments have to contend with a new atmosphere, changing oceans, different biodiversity, constrained resources, and remade land masses to which future generations will have to adapt existing cities, but with few obvious adaptive solutions.

Global Cities Constructing Urban Ecological Security
The term "ecological security" is usually used in relation to attempts to safeguard flows of ecological resources, infrastructure, and services at the national scale. But increasing concerns over "urban ecological security" are giving rise to strategies to reconfigure cities and their infrastructures in ways that help to secure their ecological and material reproduction—that is, their capacity to secure the resources (such

as water and energy, but also including waste disposal and protection from flooding) required to assure their continued economic and social development. Yet cities have differing capabilities to develop strategic responses to the opportunities and challenges of key urban ecological security concerns such as resource constraint and climate change, and consequently these emerging strategies may selectively privilege particular urban areas over others.[8]

A series of new socioeconomic and political problems are placing issues of ecological security higher on the agenda of national governments. For example, climate change poses problems such as constraints on water resources, uncertainties over energy security, and the geographic spread of disease. Concerns over the security of ecological resources have become intertwined with national states' priorities and responsibilities for social welfare and economic competitiveness.[9]

Yet such concerns are also increasingly becoming issues at an urban scale, for three interrelated reasons. First, increasing economic globalization and the changing relationships between national and subnational territories and economic activity have led to new state spaces of governance and intervention.[10] Second, the development of these new state spaces has not received the same attention in relation to environmental concerns as it has with regard to economic activity. What would an "ecological state," with ecological protection as one of its foremost regulatory functions, look like? Finally, there is the issue of how the economic and ecological reproduction of cities can be secured in a context of rapidly growing population, high demand for resources amid increasing resource constraints, and intense competition for economic activity and jobs.

Floating cities have been portrayed as cities for future climate refugees.

The cover of the publication of the Geological Society of America reflects the critical role of cities in contemporary anthropogenic change.

> Global cities are increasingly concerned with understanding the scale and future security of their ecological resource flows.

A Strategic Orientation toward Urban Ecological Security

Increasingly, cities are developing more strategic approaches to meeting future resource requirements, to enhance their standing in the inevitable competition between places, but more profoundly, to provide the conditions that can assure their continuing social, economic, and material reproduction. This reflects a shift from the post-9/11 agenda of critical infrastructure protection from terrorism or the consequences of environmental damage to a focus on safeguarding a city's material resources. A new dimension of cities' competitive positioning is their ability to internalize and control both the resources with which they are endowed and subsequent supply, consumption, and production. The knowledge, expertise, social organization, and socio-technologies required to maintain cities' economic and social roles are thus likely to be defining features of twenty-first-century urbanism. But what actual strategies will places adopt?

New Styles of Urban Infrastructure

The strategic response to resource constraint is leading to the development of new styles of infrastructure development that privilege particular places—or rather particular spatial and sociotechnical configurations of infrastructure. The world's largest cities are beginning to reshape themselves and their relationships with resources and other spaces in three ways: protection, autarky, and global agglomeration of new infrastructure systems.

First: protecting cities from the impacts and effects of climate change and resource constraints. Central to such strategies are investments in understanding the city-specific and long-term effects of climate change, especially in relation to flood risk and temperature rise, and the development of strategic flood-protection systems, green infrastructure, and retrofitting to deal with increased temperatures. The Greater London Authority's assertion that central government should take responsibility for the potential investment required to protect London post-2030 from climate-change-induced flooding typifies such responses.

Second: building autarky into the supply of water and energy, the mobility of people and goods, and the disposal of wastes. Traditionally cities have prospered by seeking out resources and waste sinks from ever more distant locations. Yet this approach is now being reversed, as cities seek to become more self-sufficient by reducing their reliance on international, national, and regional infrastructures and reinternalizing their own resources and recirculating wastes. Understanding the urban metabolism of the city and the potential for its

Acknowledgments: We are grateful to our colleagues in SURF (the Centre for Sustainable Urban and Regional Futures at the University of Salford), Tim May and Beth Perry, for their support in developing the ideas in this essay, and to Vivian Liang for help in securing reprint permissions for figures and photographs. We would also like to express our thanks to the editors for providing constructive feedback on the text.

1 For an excellent review of architectural and urban responses, see Giovanna Borasi and Mirko Zardini, *Sorry, Out of Gas: Architecture's Response to the 1973 Oil Crisis* (Montreal: Edizioni Corraini/ Canadian Center for Architecture, 2008).
2 For example: a "bright green metropolis" (*Wired*) and a possible "blueprint for green cities worldwide" (*New Scientist*).
3 See Herbert Girardet, "Which Way China?" http://www.built-environment.uwe. ac.uk/research/pdf/girardet2.pdf, p. 3 (accessed 15 September 2009).
4 Timothy W. Luke, "Codes, Collectivities, and Commodities: Rethinking Global Cities as Megalogistical Spaces," in *Global Cities: Cinema, Architecture, and Urbanism in a Digital Age,* edited by L. Krause and P. Petro (New Brunswick: Rutgers University Press, 2003), 158–159.
5 Simon Dalby, "Anthropocene Geopolitics: Globalisation, Empire, Environment and Critique," *Geography Compass* 1:1 (2007), 103–118; 111.
6 Ibid., 114.
7 Timothy W. Luke, "Climatologies as Social Critique: The Social Construction/ Creation of Global Warming, Global Dimming, and Global Cooling," in *Political Theory and Global Climate Change,* edited by S. Vanderheiden (Cambridge, MA: MIT Press, 2008), 128.
8 For a longer discussion of urban ecological security, see Mike Hodson and Simon Marvin, "'Urban Ecological Security'– A New Urban Paradigm?" *International Journal of Urban and Regional Research,* vol. 33, issue 1 (March 2009), 193–215.
9 See J. Meadowcroft, "From Welfare State to Ecostate," in *The Global Ecological Crisis and the State,* edited by J. Barry and R. Eckersley (Cambridge, MA: MIT Press, 2005).
10 N. Brenner, *New State Spaces: Urban Governance and the Rescaling of Statehood* (Oxford: Oxford University Press, 2004).

reconfiguration becomes of strategic significance. Key examples are New York's strategy of energy independence, the recent doubling of decentralized energy targets in London, and Melbourne's development of renewably powered desalination. Cities are attempting to reduce reliance on external resources through water and energy conservation and waste minimization schemes, and by developing pricing mechanisms for car-based mobility.

Third: collectively building agglomerations of new urban mobility systems. While focusing on local enclosed resources, cities are also seeking to guarantee intra-city and inter-world-city mobility through the development of new mobility technologies such as pricing, transport informatics, and new fuel systems based on hydrogen, biofuels, or complex hybrids.

Implications and New Research and Policy Agendas

Eco-urbanism's relationships with urban ecological security constitutes a research and policy agenda that must be critically tested. Five key questions emerge: First, are we talking about new forms of autarky based on bypassing national and regional infrastructure, leading to the development of new archipelagos of connected world cities? Second, what will this mean for the places thus bypassed—the new peripheries constructed by enclosure, and the ordinary cities of the developed and major cities of the developing worlds? Third, who will benefit from these configurations, who will be overlooked or disadvantaged, and what material consequences will be produced? Fourth, who will provide material linkages between world cities and the new peripheries—national states or corporate capital? Fifth, what are the alternatives; and where do we look for other forms of innovation driven by approaches more concerned with fair shares and equality of access? These, we argue, are the critical questions of the urban agenda of the twenty-first century.

City Limits

A resource flow and ecological footprint analysis of Greater London

Bottled water
Londoners consume about 94 million litres of mineral water each year. Assuming all the bottles were 2 litres, this would create 2,260 tonnes of plastic waste. Today's top-selling brand of bottled water travels around 760 km from the French Alps to the UK.

In the year 2000 London consumed

49 million tonnes of materials and 154,407 GigaWatt hours (GWh) of energy (or 13,276,000 tonnes of oil equivalent). This produced 41 million tonnes of carbon dioxide. Less than 1% of London's energy came from renewable sources.

The population of Greater London in 2000 was 7,400,000

Imports
25,029,000 tonnes

- Construction & demolition materials 33%
- Food 22%
- Misc. manufactures 16%
- Misc. articles 12%
- Wood 10%
- Metals 2%
- Chemicals 3%
- Crude materials 2%

Miscellaneous manufactures includes paper, card, textiles, leather and clothing.

Con (Imports plus 49,05...

- Food 14...
- Misc. articles 8%
- Misc. manufactures 10%
- Chemicals 2%
- Metals 2%
- Wood 5%
- Crude materials 2%

Energy inputs
(tonnes of oil equivalent)
13,276,000 tonnes

- Renewable energy <1%
- Solid Fuels <1%
- Liquid fuels 23%
- Electricity 21%
- Gas 55%

6.9 million tonnes of food was consumed in London in 2000, of which **81%** was imported from outside the UK.

Water consumption reached 866,000,000,000 litres of which **28%** was leakage.

Production
(including reused materials)
38,100,000 tonnes

- Construction & demolition materials 63%
- Misc. articles 17%
- Misc. Manufactures 9%
- Food 5%
- Chems <1%
- Metals 2%
- Wood <1%
- Crude materials 2%

Miscellaneous articles includes arms, ammunition and other unknown commodities.

Download or order the full report from the City Limits website:

www.citylimitslondon.com

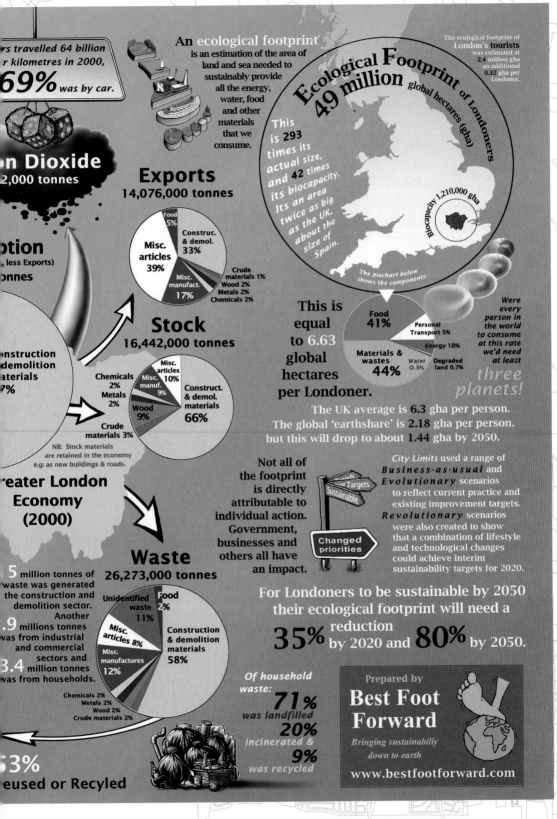

New Waterscapes for Singapore

Herbert Dreiseitl

It should be a way of life to keep the water clean, to keep every stream, every culvert, every rivulet, free from unnecessary pollution. In ten years let us have fishing in the Singapore River and fishing in the Kallang River. It can be done.

—Prime Minister Lee Kuan Yew, February 27, 1977

City regions today face the increasingly difficult challenges of urban water management. It is foreseeable that the impacts of climate change, demands of increasing population, pollution, and lack of available drinking water will endanger the fundamental basis of life, or at least affect it significantly.

Singapore is addressing the challenges of urban water management through comprehensive and complex initiatives that combine water collection measures with recreation and ecological programs. With 3.8 million inhabitants, the city has a highly developed urban water system; 100 percent of all households are connected to the sewage network, the city has extensive wastewater treatment plants, and most of the city has separate sewer and storm-water systems. Singapore has overtaken many American and European cities in terms of urban water management.

Singapore has integrated a water system, called "NEWater," which provides treated wastewater in bottles and pipes for reuse. This hygienically faultless water is supplied in parallel to drinking water. However, even with these water-use reduction measures, it is still not enough given Singapore's enormous water demand. The island city imports 40 percent of its water needs from a river in neighboring Malaysia.

This lack of water is in no way due to a shortage of precipitation. Until recently, the annual precipitation of 2,400 millimeters simply flowed to the ocean in the quickest, most direct way. Given to the enormous water volume in a tropical downpour, the dimensions of the drainage channels and canals are appropriately large. Empty for most of the year, the concrete-lined channels seem lost and ugly, forming barriers, surmountable only by bridges, and dividing residents into defined sectors.

The smooth and hard surfaces in the channels, together with the absence of flora and fauna, create poor characteristics for urban water, and the biological self-cleaning potential is drastically reduced in comparison to a healthy river. Unobstructed dirt from the streets, paths, and plazas is washed directly into the channels, and it is no surprise that the canals are considered dangerous places.

Dams constructed at the river mouths will hold fresh rainwater separately from the ocean and store it for recycling. Over the coming years, one dam will be built across the Marina Channel and four dams will be built across the estuaries of the Punggol and Serangoon rivers. By 2009, Singapore will have seventeen freshwater reservoirs.

With the storage and reuse of runoff rainwater from the densely built city, the catchment area takes on particular importance. The delivery of clean and hydraulically slowed rainwater to the rivers will be a necessity. This can only mean the step-by-step rebuilding of storm-water management to become an integrated, decentral-

ized urban system. In principle, the task is to manage (infiltrate, evaporate, cleanse, reuse) rainwater where it falls and to ease the pressure on the rivers during peak storm events. At the same time, the run-off water should arrive clean at the river banks, which means managing the "first flush" through the likes of green roofs, rain gardens, cleansing biotopes, and trash filters.

Singapore already has a pervasive network of fourteen reservoirs, thirty-two major rivers, and more than 7,000 kilometers of canals and drains. The restoration of several rivers, including the Singapore and Kallang rivers, is propelled by the upcoming completion of the Marina Bay 2008 project. Since the launch of the ABC ("Active, Beautiful, and Clean") Waters Programme in April 2006, three projects at Bedok Reservoir, MacRitchie Reservoir, and a stretch of Kallang River at Kolam Ayer have been under way. The aim also is to increase Singapore's water catchment areas from covering half of the island to two-thirds within five years. Starting first with three sections, projects will be carried out throughout the rest of the island.

The Public Utilities Board (PUB) recently revealed further ABC Waters signature projects, including two new reservoirs to be created in the northeast of Singapore, the rejuvenation of Kallang River, and improving the Alexandra Canal and its water. The two new reservoirs will be created when Sungei Punggol and Sungei Serangoon are dammed, to create Singapore's sixteenth and seventeenth reservoirs. The Punggol Reservoir will include a floating wetland the size of half a football field, which the public will be able to access via a suspended bridge on one side and a floating boardwalk on the other.

One of the pilot projects will be the conversion of the Kallang Canal into a river integrated into the Bishan Park, a public neighborhood park where crowds of people can be seen every morning doing tai chi. This local park has the same number of daily visitors as the famous Botanical Gardens of Singapore. A concrete waterway, located behind fences on one side of the park, has until recently been disconnected both physically and functionally from park activities. Starting with a workshop in April 2007 with PUB, National Parks, and Atelier Dreiseitl on location in Bishan Park, the basis of an integrated strategy was born. With the transformation of the canal into a vital river and its integration into the park, there is the chance to give new life to the park.

This river restoration is complex. With the extreme storms of Singapore's tropical climate, this stream—located downstream of the overflow of two large reservoirs—can grow from a tiny creek to a powerful and dangerous torrent within half an hour. Erosion, sedimentation, and safety have to be considered and solutions carefully worked out. Experience with bio-engineering overseas, such as the case of the Isar River in Munich, can be helpful.

One restoration project within the park will involve the transformation of formal lakes currently used for fishing into a biofiltration water-treatment network and combined water playground. Side canals will be improved and drainage swales with sustainable vegetation added.

The change of this canal into a dynamic meandering river in the context of dense suburbia will be challenging for local people, for whom a concrete canal has somehow become "natural." To this end, carefully planned community liaison with information and temporary environmental art projects involving both children and adults will aim to engage people in envisaging their park anew.

The active participation of private investors and developers will be a deciding factor for each development project. Legislation is not enough: targeted symposiums, professional events, lectures, and individual consultations will be offered by the city.

New Waterscapes in Singapore is more than the restoration of channels, rivers, and reservoirs. Through the integration of city planning with the collaboration of the Urban Redevelopment Authority and green planning with the collaboration of National Parks, a vital network will be brought to life, securing the future. The water systems will become new places of encounter and will connect the diverse societies and ethnic groups who live in Singapore. If successful in making paradigm shifts in attitudes to water, the ABC Programme in Singapore will be a model for many other cities and for ecological urbanism across the world.

The canal is mostly dry at present with short, extreme peaks of flooding. In the future, water flow will be regulated with lower peaks.

219

What happens to the rain today?

Every drop flows into the drains and straight into the canal.

The water level in the canal rises rapidly.

In the future, storm water will be treated on site and slowly released into the river.

New Waterscapes for Singapore

To Raise the Water Level in a Fishpond

Zhang Huan

I invited about forty participants, recent migrants to the city who had come to work in Beijing from other parts of China. They were construction workers, fishermen, and laborers, all from the bottom of society. They stood around in the pond, and then I walked in it. At first, they stood in a line in the middle, to separate the pond into two parts. Then they all walked freely, until the point of the performance arrived, which was to raise the water level. Then they stood still. In the Chinese tradition, fish is the symbol of sex, while water is the source of life. This work expresses, in fact, one kind of understanding and explanation of water. That the water in the pond was raised one meter higher is an action of no avail.

Performance, Beijing, China, 1997

Envisioning Ecological Cities

Mitchell Joachim

Bell Aerosystems Rocket Belt, 1960–61: an untethered two-man test flight

How should urban design foresee new instrumentalist technologies for cities? For 150 years, the innovation of the elevator has done more to influence urban design than most urban designers. Elevator systems had incredible success in the creation of compact and greener cities. Imagine what the advent of the jet pack will do for cities. Urban design is greatly altered by such devices. For instance, automobiles have defined limits in cities for almost a century. Unlike the elevator, however, the car has arguably caused more problems than it has solved. Perhaps it is time for urban design to rethink technologies to fit cities, not constrain them. As a wide-ranging discipline, it can effortlessly illuminate the technological potentials for cities. Urban design will successfully situate itself through the production of future macro-scaled scenarios predicated on innovative devices.

Physicist and polymath Freeman Dyson has said that the best way to comprehend our near urban future is to examine science fiction, not economic forecasts. In his experience, sci-fi is good for decades of technological fulfillment. Unfortunately, economic forecasts are only accurate within five to ten years. Most of these predictive economic models are quantity based and find it difficult to extrapolate the qualifiers associated with creativity. Sci-fi is a phenomenal way to chronicle our plausible urban future that should not be dismissed by urban designers.

Dyson is certain that the urban era of information will soon transition into "the age of domesticated biotechnology." In his novel *Infinite in All Directions,* he states: "Bio-tech offers us the chance to imitate nature's speed and flexibility."[1] He envisions a realm of functional objects and art that humans will "grow" for personal use. According to a *New York Times* article on Dyson, "The Civil Heretic," he also believes that climate change is profoundly misstated: "He added the caveat that if CO_2 levels soared too high, they could be soothed by the mass cultivation of specially bred 'carbon-eating trees.'"[2] He is not concerned with predicting the future but rather with expressing the possibilities. These expressions are founded along societal desire lines as a kind of relevant optimism. Therefore Dyson measures the wants of civilization and advances our expectations.

At some level, urban design engages this position that promises a better tomorrow. Numerous practitioners and urbanists mildly suffer from this invariable search for direction and clairvoyance. Alex Krieger strongly asserts that the broadly defined vocation is more of a scrupulous sensibility than an exclusive authority.[3] The profession is torn between many incompatible agendas, weighty theories and oversimplified applications, ivory towers and new urbanism, developer brands and radical ecologies, and vernacular forms and futurology. One of my research group's chief directives is about shrewdly locating the intersection of technology and urbanism, especially under the rubric of ecology. Our projects range from highlighting the possible effects of self-sufficient cities to studying flocks of jet packs. These ideations keep us thriving as urban design researchers. It is our supposition that the prospective ecological city is about extreme solutions to an extreme predicament. Our future fundamentally depends on the immensity our solutions envision.

Jetpack packing: This flexible body jetpack moves in flocks that bump and glide. Tugged along in groups for longer distances, these devices run on catalyzed hydrogen peroxide. The intention is to have multiple units air-towed to conserve power until a specific destination is reached. Individual jetpacks may decouple from the flock and head to a more localized point.

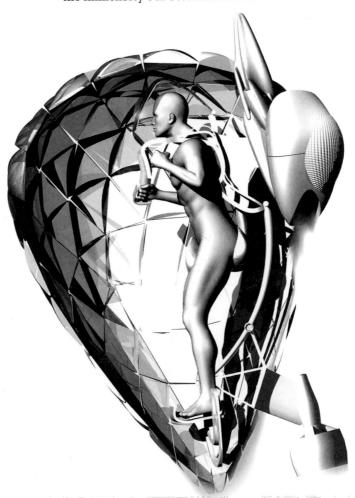

In Vitro Meat Habitat: Plan of geometry to form printed pig cells into a specific shape

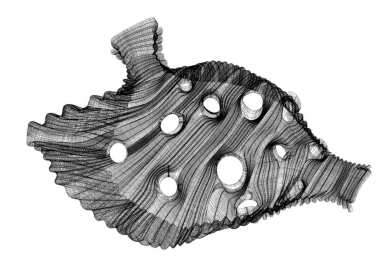

This is a proposal for the fabrication of 3D printed extruded pig cells to form real organic dwellings. It is intended to be a "victimless shelter," because no sentient being was harmed in the laboratory growth of the skin.

Plastic PET scaffold model of meat house located in Prague. We used sodium benzoate as a preservative to kill yeasts, bacteria, and fungi. Other materials in the model matrix are collagen powder, xanthan gum, mannitol, cochineal, and sodium pyrophosphate.

CURATE

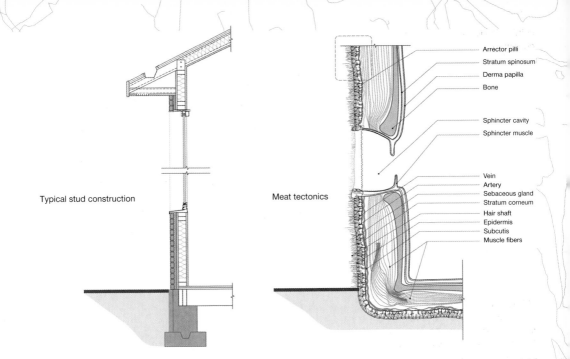

Typical stud construction

Meat tectonics

Arrector pilli
Stratum spinosum
Derma papilla
Bone

Sphincter cavity
Sphincter muscle

Vein
Artery
Sebaceous gland
Stratum corneum
Hair shaft
Epidermis
Subcutis
Muscle fibers

Building wall sections that compare a typical home to a structure prepared from meat cells. The meat-based home provides cilia for shading and sphincter muscles for aperture zones/window.

Envisioning is by definition a view or concept that evolves beyond existing boundaries. This notion of foresight may be interpreted in many different ways, each foregrounding particular ideations and processes describing the next event. Here in America, we need these radical new visions to assist in solving our current global calamity. As of now, the earth's climate endures an unremitting state of trauma. We seek precise prescriptions that cover a wide scope to alter this massive dilemma. To paraphrase, John F. Kennedy said: "If man created problems, man can solve them." This future vision unfolds a truly breathing, interconnected metabolic urbanism. How does it reify from statistics to architectural form? What does the future look like for America's cities? How do technological devices affect these functions?

For a popular audience, the recent Disney sci-fi film *Wall-E* enabled society to anticipate one conceivable future. The film is set in a generic city that is completely buried in trash. Humans have abandoned life on earth for off-world dwelling, leaving being one lone solar-powered robot to clear the rubbish. Part of the message of the film is that technology alone can't solve humanity's "affluenza," yet the film's powerful computer-generated visuals encourage us to confront our colossal wastefulness and rethink the city.

We foresee strategies for people to fit symbiotically into their natural surrounds. To achieve this, all things possible are considered. We design the scooters, cars, trains, and blimps, as well as the streets, parks, open spaces, cultural districts,

Fab Tree Hab: We propose a method to grow homes from native trees. A living structure is grafted into shape with prefabricated CNC reusable scaffolds. We thereby enable dwellings to be fully integrated into an ecological community.

This living home is designed to be nearly entirely edible so as to provide food to some organism at each stage of its life cycle. Imagine a society based on slow farming trees for housing instead of the industrial manufacture of felled timber.

civic centers, and business hubs that comprise the future metropolis. For centuries cities have been designed to accommodate the theater of our human desire. We have joined the ranks of those delivering a new sense of the city, one that privileges the play of nature over anthropocentric whims. We are constantly vying for a profound clairvoyant perspective. We desire to preview a likeness of our collective future yet untold.

Our foresight of ecological design is not only a philosophy that inspires visions of sustainability but also a focused scientific endeavor. The mission is to ascertain the consequences of fitting a project within our natural environment. Solutions are derived from numerous examples: living material habitats, climatic tall building clusters, and mobility technologies. These design iterations succeed as having activated ecology both as a productive symbol and an evolved artifact. Current research attempts to establish new forms of design knowledge and new processes of practice at the interface of design, computer science, structural engineering, and biology.

1 Freeman Dyson, *Infinite in All Directions* (New York: Harpercollins, 1988).
2 Nicholas Dawidoff, "The Civil Heretic," *New York Times* (March 25, 2009).

3 Alex Krieger and William S. Saunders, eds., *Urban Design* (Minneapolis: University of Minnesota Press, 2009).

Return to Nature

Sandi Hilal, Alessandro Petti, and Eyal Weizman

On May 2006, the Israeli army evacuated a military fortress strategically located on one the highest hills at the southern edge of the Palestinian city of Beit Sahour in the Bethlehem region. The fortress, located on the line that separates the arable lands of Bethlehem from the desert of the Dead Sea, has functioned to stop the city's expansion eastward and control the travel of its inhabitants toward the desert. Most houses near the camp were destroyed throughout the last years of the intifada by tank shells and gunfire. Floodlit at night, with searchlights constantly scanning the area, the base was caught in an "endless day," confusing diurnal rhythms.

The evacuation, made unexpectedly and with no stated reason—perhaps because of a change in the military's tactical disposition—was itself a violent operation: at night dozens of tanks rolled into town, raising a curtain of steel and dust that was meant to mask the evacuation, but in fact awoke and alerted the inhabitants of Beit Sahour. In the morning the fortress was empty. A few hours later, Palestinians stormed the buildings and took whatever could be recycled.

The military history of the hill precedes the occupation. It was initially set up as a base built by the British Mandatory army during the Arab revolt. After 1948 it became a military base for the Jordan Legion, and after 1967 an Israeli military base. As part of the 1993 Oslo Accords, an agreement was signed between the municipality of Beit Sahour and the central government of Yasser Arafat, guaranteeing that in case of Israeli evacuation, the fortress would not be used by the Palestinian police but instead be handed over to the municipality for public use. Upon gaining control of the site, the municipality developed a master plan that marked the hill with a set of public functions: a hospital, a park, a restaurant, and a garden. The park has already been constructed on one of the hill slopes.

But although evacuated, the summit itself was still designated by the military as off-limits for Palestinians. It was the summit's view of the surroundings that was denied, as it was the only place from which one could see a new settlers' approach road, leading to the settlement where Israel's foreign minister resides.

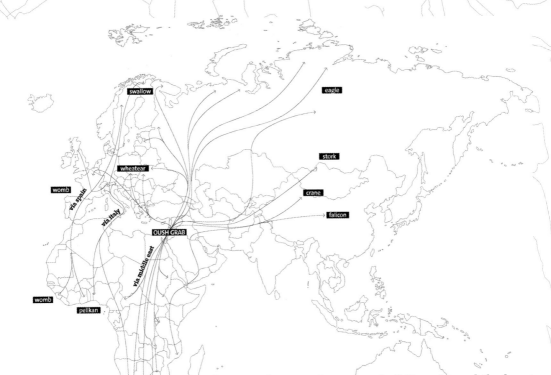

Bird migration routes converge over Palestine.

On the summit, several concrete buildings formed the heart of the fortress. Throughout the intifada, the Israeli military continuously piled earth and rubble in a giant circle around the buildings. The earth rampart grew higher than the buildings, making the hill look like a crater of an artificial volcano, and the buildings, now damaged and evacuated, seem as though they belong to a ghost town, emptied after some natural disaster.

The hilltop is also a point of singularity within the natural environment. More than 500 million birds migrate annually between northeastern Europe and East Africa, and the flocks tend to stop in the same places along the way, usually at high points. The hilltop of Oush Grab is on a "bottleneck" of the routes of starlings, storks, and raptors that use the Jordan Valley Jerusalem Mountains navigation path. For a few days each autumn and spring, tens of thousands of these birds land on the hilltop and its surroundings. Around them a rich micro-ecology of small predators and other wildlife is gathered. It is a breathtaking and terrifying scene, and the inhabitants of Beit Sahour now joke that these birds are the true reason for the military evacuation.

Revolving Door Occupations

Since its evacuation, the remains of the fortress are at the center of confrontations, in which members of our office have been directly engaged, between Jewish settlers, the Israeli

military, and Palestinian organizations. In May 2008, hardline religious settlers sought to use the emptied buildings as the basis for a new outpost. Outposts, which are nuclei for suburbs/cities, are usually built around knots of existing infrastructure. The fortress and earth rampart surrounding it would lend themselves, the settlers believed, to constructing an environment well suited to their regimented and securitized way of life. Although the military declared the summit a closed zone, nearly every week settlers come back to occupy the fortress, hold meetings within the buildings, make repairs, and raise the Israeli flag. Palestinian and international activists, including members of our office, also occupy the site and confront the settlers. Israeli soldiers arrive to protect the settlers. Competing graffiti, written by one side and then obliterated by the other, testifies to a "revolving door" occupation. Our proposal for the reuse of this site becomes an intervention into the contentious political struggle for this hilltop.

Return to Nature
Given the competing claims for the site, and the controversial militancy around it, our intention is not to renovate and convert the base into another function but rather to control and accelerate its process of degradation, disintegration, and

The buildings of Oush Grab will be partially buried.

This text is a part of the project Decolonizing Architecture (www.decolonizing.ps) by the London/Bethlehem Architectural Studio of Sandi Hilal, Alessandro Petti, and Eyal Weizman.

overgrowth—its gradual "return to nature." We seek to employ the first stages of our proposal as forms of partial subtraction/destruction, perforating the external walls in buildings that inhabit the "crater" with a series of equally spaced holes. The holes would create a pattern that visually unites all of the buildings. The environmentalists and zoologists of the Palestine Wildlife Society expect that these holes will be inhabited by some of the smaller birds during migration and local species the rest of the year. We also intend to transform the landscape around the fortress by rerouting the fortified rampart enclosure. This transformation of the earth rampart will partially bury the buildings in the rubble of their own fortifications, reorganizing the relationship between the buildings and the landscape.

The scheme is also a tool in a legal battle. We are posing a legal claim for this site against the military's civil administration and the settler organizations. Together with a legal aid group, we articulate this claim not on behalf of people—perhaps already a futile task in the context of the occupation—but rather on behalf of nature, for the rights of the birds. The models and scheme thereby double as legal documents. Criminal proceedings involving animals were handled with the utmost seriousness by medieval legal authorities (hundreds of animals found guilty were executed by hanging). The legal department of the Israeli military is presently undecided about how to deal with such legal challenges.

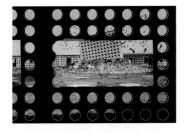

Looking out from the holes

The military base is located in the region of Bethlehem.

Bethlehem // Beit Sahour

Case study south: **Oush-Grab military base**

Harmonia 57

Triptyque

The project on Harmonia Street is located in a neighborhood on the west side of São Paulo, where artistic life and creativity penetrate easily, with galleries and outside walls both functioning as a stage for new forms of expression. The alley in front of the building is an example: its graffiti present a concept of experimentation that flows from the street into the construction.

Like a living creature, the building breathes, sweats, and modifies itself. The outside walls are covered by a vegetal layer that works like skin. This dense wall is made of an organic concrete that has pores from which several plant species grow.

Rain water is drained, treated, and reused, enabling the development of a complex ecosystem. The structure's water-treatment system and other pipelines, like the veins and arteries in the body, are exposed in the façades, while the interior spaces are well finished, with clear and luminous surfaces, as if the construction were inside-out.

The building has a neutral, gray base. The structure is rough and has a primitive elegance, a reflection of concern with environmental issues and an investigation of possibilities for intervention. Its volume is simple but remarkable: two grand vegetal blocks are connected by a metal foot-bridge and punctuated by concrete and glass windows and terraces. The terraces create a visual game between volumes, lighting, and transparency in the internal spaces. The front block is completely suspended, levitating over pilotis, while the back block is solid, complemented by a birdhouse-like volume above it. Between the blocks, an internal plaza serves as a space of encounter.

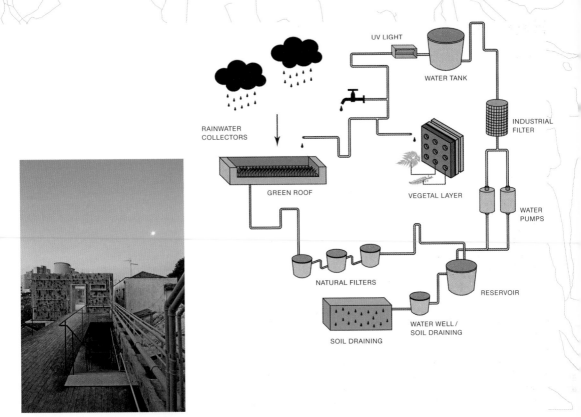

RAINWATER COLLECTORS

UV LIGHT

WATER TANK

INDUSTRIAL FILTER

GREEN ROOF

VEGETAL LAYER

WATER PUMPS

NATURAL FILTERS

WATER WELL / SOIL DRAINING

SOIL DRAINING

RESERVOIR

Grounding a Sustainable Urban Strategy

Michael Van Valkenburgh Associates

The Low2No competition presents the challenge of developing strategies for the creation of urban communities that produce low, and ultimately no, carbon emissions, leaving a sustainable environmental footprint. With global warming occurring at a significantly faster rate than was anticipated only a few years ago, this mandate has become extremely urgent.

With relatively low density, reliance on heavy municipal infrastructure and car usage, and building orientations and configurations not optimized for Helsinki's latitude, the existing master plan for Jätkäsaari has been revised in this proposal to posit a strategy for sustainable urbanism. Nine- teenth- and twentieth-century cities maximized profit at the expense of the environment, resulting in unsustainable economies and ecologies. Today, sustainability can exist only if it undergirds all aspects of city-making.

This competition proposal is the result of a collaborative effort by an interdisciplinary team represent- ing climate engineering, mobility, landscape, ecology, cultural history, economics, structural engineering, and architecture. The Low2No proposal presents a series of sus- tainable urban strategies to guide the future of development at Jätkäsaari toward long-term eco- logical self-sufficiency and fiscal success.

Set within a bedrock archipelago, the Baltic Coast encounters a particularly interesting landscape condition with a paucity of naturally occurring subsoils and associated living systems. In this proposal, these systems are fabricated from the waste products of municipal infrastructure construction and reclaimed historic fill to help neutral- ize the environmental footprint of this waterfront development. The biological functions of each eco- system and plant, of soil and water, are used to work toward specific environmental goals. In the twenty- first century, land cannot simply be the pedestal for the city; it is the medium with which one builds the city.

This work represents largely the landscape scope of the larger team's proposal, led by Peter Rose Architects. MVVA team mem- bers include: Gullivar Shepard, Christopher Donohue, Richard Hindle, Scott Street, and Michael Wilson.

SOIL CANAL

4.5m

8.5m

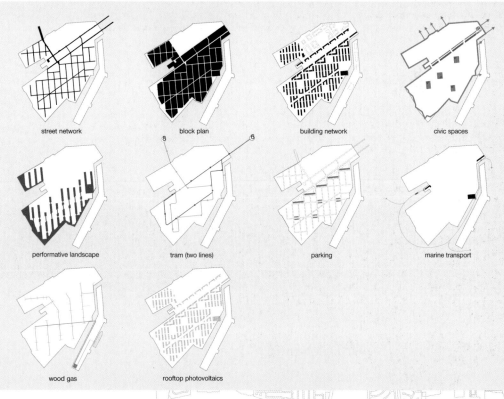

street network

block plan

building network

civic spaces

performative landscape

tram (two lines)

parking

marine transport

wood gas

rooftop photovoltaics

Center Street Plaza

Hood Design

The design strategies for Center Street Plaza in Berkeley, California, explore the enormous potential for Strawberry Creek at Center Street, between Shattuck Avenue and Oxford Street. All schemes were designed with the intent of allowing vehicular access for emergency and commercial transport, and they therefore accommodate planning and dimensional codes. Surface patterns refer to different methods and types of paving, from conventional paving to pervious and other organic pavers. Twenty-eight schemes were prepared and sorted into a matrix according to their fundamental design concept and geometric framework. From this matrix, fourteen design concepts were chosen from the twenty-eight and closely studied for their potential of development within the space. The schemes that proved promising were selected and further detailed to evaluate their capacity for development. Of those fourteen, six were chosen and hybridized to become three possible strategies for celebrating the creek. Each strategy uses water in a revelatory way:

The Open Hybrid is designed as a low-flow channel that daylights water through big openings along the entire corridor. Water is pumped from the creek, channeled through Center Street, and returned back to its original flow path to the Bay. The water and planting areas are maximized, while still allowing spaces for pedestrians as well as emergency vehicular and commercial delivery access.

The Ramblas Hybrid is a series of fountains and rain gardens. The fountain recirculates water, while the rain garden collects surface runoff and successively cleans it as it travels westward. The creek is emulated rather than physically channeled and daylighted through the site, celebrating the water.

The Terraced Hybrid functions as a series of alternating pools marching westward toward the bay. As in the Open Hybrid, water is channeled from Strawberry Creek and day-lighted at specific locations through the site. Once the water reaches Shattuck, it rejoins its original path toward the Bay.

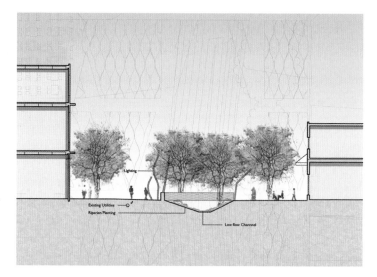

ADDISON STREET

SHATTUCK AVENUE

OXFORD STREET

THEATRE

SUB ENTRANCE AND
THEATRE LOBBY

Meyer Lemon Orchard

GALLERY

YOUNG ARTIST
GALLERY

PUBLIC
GALLERY

LOBBY

MAIN
ENTRANCE

CAFE

BART STATION

Riparian
Planting

Low Flow
Water Channel

Lighting

Outdoor Cafe

Existing Trees

FRANK SCHLESSINGER WAY

Open Hybrid
Scale 1:60

241

PRODUCE

Energy Sub-structure, Supra-structure, Infra-structure
D. Michelle Addington

Wave Farm
Pelamis Wave Power Ltd.

CR Land Guanganmen Green Technology Showroom
Vector Architects

Aux Fermes, Citoyens!
Dorothée Imbert

Local River: Home Storage Unit for Fish and Greens
Mathieu Lehanneur with Anthony van den Bossche

Soft Cities
KVA MATx

The ZEDfactory
Bill Dunster

Logroño Eco-city
MVRDV

The Big-Foot Revolution
Kongjian Yu

La Tour Vivante, **Eco-tower**
soa architectes

Energy Sub-structure, Supra-structure, Infra-structure

D. Michelle Addington

If "zero-energy building" was the rallying cry of the late-twentieth-century approach to green design, then "carbon-neutral development" is the mantra of the current generation of sustainable designers. From the City of London's sustainability plan championed by former mayor Ken Livingston to the Masdar initiative currently under construction in Abu Dhabi, today's large-scale "sustainable" master planning recognizes that the environmental stressors of ecological, sociological, political, and economic systems are not readily evaluated, much less resolved, at the scale of a building. Nevertheless, many of the same weaknesses that result from examining the systems at that small scale are still manifest at the scale of a city. Systems, and in particular, energy based-systems, do not scale geometrically, nor do they have distinct boundaries. Indeed, even if one system is isolated from the others, multiple scales and boundaries come into play. Here I look at just one system—energy generation and supply—and suggest the types of "functional" boundaries that would lead to more effective urban ecological planning.

Master planning of large new developments is typically done as a "parcel." The parcel contains all allocated land and buildings and can either tap into a larger energy infrastructure or produce its own energy. Many of the major new master plans use the latter strategy, and these developments will often include new electrical power generation, typically produced by renewable sources, that can be sold back to the larger regional grid. This is a plug-in approach, and it is premised on the assumption that electrical distribution can be divisible into discrete packets that operate independently as self-contained systems while maintaining the ability to be added onto other systems in the region. Parcelization of power generation does enable the incremental installation of new and renewable sources, but it does so with large energy penalties. Systems connected to the grid are governed by the larger grid operation, particularly with regard to system balancing, and not by the local power requirements of their respective parcel.

Effective planning of new developments requires a comprehensive plan for energy generation, distribution, and consumption at multiple spatial scales and across multiple systems.

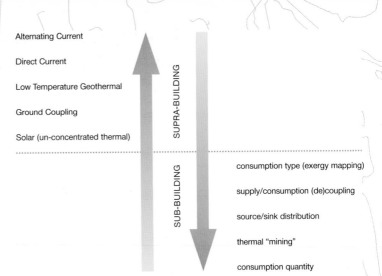

Alternating Current

Direct Current

Low Temperature Geothermal

Ground Coupling

Solar (un-concentrated thermal)

SUPRA-BUILDING

SUB-BUILDING

consumption type (exergy mapping)

supply/consumption (de)coupling

source/sink distribution

thermal "mining"

consumption quantity

Energy generation and consumption cannot be balanced or examined at the boundary of a building. Generation systems operate and optimize at scales much larger than a building, with alternating current operating at the largest scale. Points of consumption have a hierarchy of interrelationships that requires reconciliation at each level.

Most parcel-planning strategies treat energy systems as if they could be collapsed into a single spatial system of alternating current electricity. But many renewable sources, particularly those that can be easily divided into smaller installations such as photovoltaics and fuel cells, produce direct current. By tying these systems back into the alternating current grid, we are cutting their efficiencies by as much as 25 percent. Furthermore, many applications in buildings run much more efficiently on direct current, but because alternating current is all that is available, these applications also lose efficiency in their operation. Efficiency losses at both of these levels are extremely detrimental to the balancing of small systems, and result in the need to install more generating equipment. Besides the obvious issues with the purchase, installation and operation of the additional equipment, increasing the size and concentration of low-efficiency generation has a large impact not only on local microclimate but also on regional albedo. The resultant lowering of albedo exacerbates the greenhouse gas effect on climate change even insofar as the renewable sources themselves may be carbon free.

The master planning of large new developments offers the unique opportunity to investigate the following five salient themes:

1. Exergy Mapping of Energy Generation

The largest consumption of fossil fuels occurs in the generation of alternating current electricity, and the largest consumer of electricity is the building sector. Alternating current is the supply standard, as it can be considered the "universal donor" for all energy needs. Different energy forms may be equivalent in quantity but not in quality; 100 watt-hours of electricity is the same quantity of energy as 100 watt-hours of heat—but the electricity is higher-quality energy and therefore not only available for more uses but able to undergo more conversions before reaching its final form as heat. But since electricity is not naturally available, concentrating low-grade energy to produce it will incur large penalties, so 100 watt-hours of electricity carries a large energy debt even before it is consumed, whereas naturally available heat carries no debt. We have three types of energy needs in buildings: (1) electrical for plug loads and lighting, (2) mechanical for motors, compressors, and rotating equipment, and (3) thermal for space conditioning and water heating. As we have no easily reproducible means for producing mechanical energy directly at the small scale, all of the energy supplied to meet mechanical needs must be degraded from electricity, leaving us with two supplies, electrical and thermal. The principles of exergy would lead us to match the forms of energy supplies with the types of energy needed, and we would particularly avoid using electricity to serve any thermal need. Furthermore, electrical generation has several exergy levels depending on the method of generation: hydroelectric results in the lowest penalty, photovoltaics the largest penalty. By taking into account the true penalties incurred by mismatched energy forms and qualities, we will have a clearer accounting of the full consequences of our buildings' energy debt.

2. Direct Current Systems and Consumers

As noted earlier, any of the small-scale renewables, including fuel cells and photovoltaics, produce direct current, and tying them into the alternating current grid results in as much as a 25 percent energy loss. Yet all digital equipment operates on direct current. In addition, the fastest-growing area in light-

Correlated thermal and land-use data for Atlanta as measured by the Landsat satelite.

ing technology—light-emitting diodes—also operates on direct current. Converting alternating current back into direct current can bring another 10 percent loss. As a result, there is not only a significant energy penalty when digital equipment must be reconfigured to work within the standard electrical infrastructure of a building, but the additional inefficiency of the conversion further increases the already quite internal high heat gain produced by electrical equipment (which brings other consequences: semiconductor-based electronics drop in efficiency as ambient temperatures rise, producing a vicious cycle in which they dump even more waste heat to their surroundings, further pushing down efficiencies and increasing air-conditioning loads). As we build and expand infrastructures, decoupled electrical systems would allow the most efficient matching of generation to use. Truly distributed

Average outgoing thermal radiation along the eastern seaboard of the United States as predicted by NASA's Land Information System for June 11, 2001

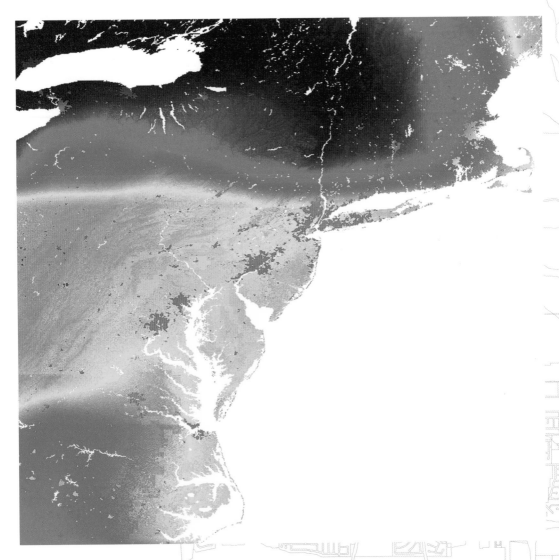

systems would allow for autonomous alternating current and direct current supply systems. The direct current system would not only be much more efficient due to better exergy matching, but much more reliable due to its smaller scale.

3. Optimum Scaling of Energy Systems

The spatial scales of the different systems for supplying energy determine the operational efficiencies of the systems. As a general rule, the higher the quality of energy, the more efficient it is to concentrate (centralize) its production to eliminate repetitive steps, each of which releases excess heat. Alternating current electricity, as the highest-quality source, is produced more efficiently in larger installations than in distributed smaller ones. As technologies improve, we have seen the optimum scale of a new system begin to shrink, but it nevertheless remains at a scale that is regional. Direct current electricity, as produced from fuel cells and photovoltaics, and not from downgraded AC, optimizes at much smaller scales. Nevertheless, both systems operate at scales that have no relationship to building scale even insofar as individual units of generating equipment might happen to be placed within the property extents of a building or group of buildings.

Unlike electrical systems that have no requisite relationship to a site, both geothermal and low-temperature solar thermal are inextricably linked to a site. These are sites, however, determined by natural processes and not necessarily by the bounds of private property. Low-temperature geothermal traps are not infinite sources, and as such, their use must be carefully weighed in terms of replenishment rates and the impact upon subterranean structures. Solar thermal is the only source that can be addressed within the bounds of a building project. And while effectiveness, efficiencies, and economies might improve slightly if we cluster collection systems and share pumps and storage among multiple buildings, this is still a supply type that can be easily optimized at the scale of most building projects. It comes closest to being an ideal solution—using a low-grade supply to meet a low-grade need, particularly for hot water. This is also a type of system that has direct architectural implications for the design process.

4. Heat Sinking

As electrical and lighting loads have become the largest source of internal heat gain in buildings, we need to reconsider the appropriate method for dumping this excess heat. Conventional HVAC systems depend on the enthalpic sponge of circulating air to provide the sink, thereby distributing and diluting heat gains throughout the entire volume of the building.

Rather than thinking of the building as a homogeneous volume that either is losing heat to the surrounding environment in winter or gaining heat in summer, we should imagine it as an assembly of heat sinks and sources. Heat sources abound in buildings—consider every piece of electrical equipment, including lighting, every human body, the combustion processes for cooking and heating, the release of hot water into a building, the solar energy that is transmitted through transparent surfaces, and the thermal masses that have absorbed heat from multiple sources. Heat sinks are less prevalent, but include cooler external areas that a building "sees"—such as the night sky—or that a building "touches"—such as water and earth. Furthermore, there are no natural heat sinks in a building. Chilled air and chilled water become our sinks of choice, but they bring an energy penalty as they generally require high-grade electricity to move low-grade heat.

Because sources abound and are relatively small, sinks become the elements that bring architectural consequences. The key design features for the thermal management of a sink are its exposed surface area and its height relative to the source. To quickly dissipate heat away from a temperature-sensitive source, the sink should be positioned above the source. To slow the rate at which a source dissipates its heat, the positions would be reversed. This is counter to conventional air-conditioning design, which generally delivers the sink from the ceiling—an approach that is excellent for flattening the temperature profile around sources, but does so at the expense of raising the temperature in the occupied zone,

Flow diagram accounting for all input fuels used in energy generation. Unlike many other diagrams that prorate consumption to account for system losses, this diagram illustrates the enormous losses that take place in the generation of electricity, for which buildings are the major consumer.

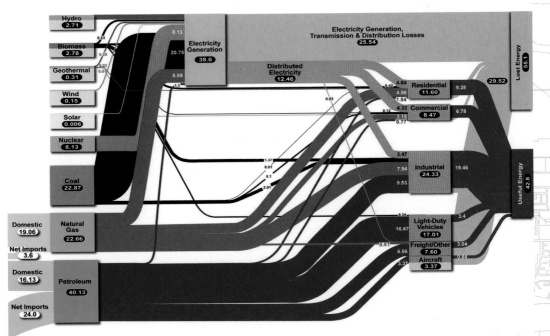

thereby requiring additional air conditioning. This approach is also counter to the conventional wisdom of passive solar that uses a thermal mass, such as a Trombe wall, as a source. Large thermal masses are highly effective as sinks, but are difficult to control as sources. Once we understand the relationship between sinks and sources, we can reconsider their placement in a building to either minimize their impact or maximize their usefulness.

5. Discrete Consumption

Decoupling of generation systems could lead to a decoupling of consumption from the building. HVAC systems and lighting systems serve the building volume. The primary need for heat in a building is ultimately not for the building at all, but for the body. The body always generates heat and thus always

Buildings served by Harvard University's chilled water distribution system, illustrating that the operational boundary of a district system is determined by functional efficiencies rather than by geometric partitioning

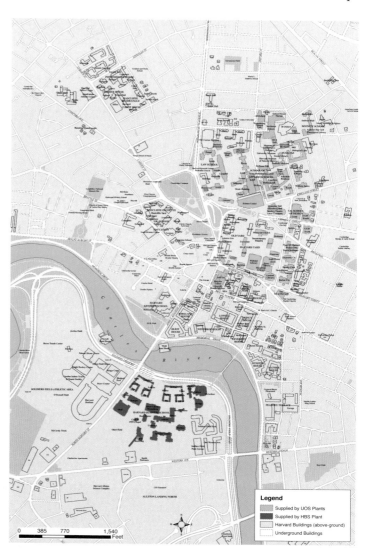

must be able to dissipate its heat into the surroundings. If the rate at which this dissipation takes place does not match the rate at which the body is producing heat, then the body's core temperature will rise (heat dissipation too slow) or it will lower (heat dissipation too fast). Building environmental systems, whether mechanical (HVAC) or passive (natural ventilation), are intended to provide a large homogeneous heat sink that blankets the body in constant thermal conditions such that the up-and-down shifts in the rate of heat dissipation from the body stay within a range that can be mitigated by fluctuating changes in skin temperature. Essentially, current methods for designing building environments subordinate the body to the building, rather than the other way around.

The actual heat exchange of the body takes place within a layer no more than a centimeter thick from the surface of the skin. Our true interest is in that narrow zone, and it is only in that zone that the rate of heat transfer can be controlled. The conditions of the building are irrelevant beyond that one centimeter. There are numerous methods for acting directly on that zone, but the belief that we must heat and cool the entire building prevents us from taking those small actions, and instead we use large and quite energy-intensive systems. Light, as a subset of heat, operates at the smallest scale of heat transfer, the submicron scale. Nevertheless, lighting systems are designed at the scale of the building. We shift the orientation of an entire building to more effectively use daylight, and yet we could provide the same utilization by reorienting the micron-sized features of a material—a tiny and almost invisible change in texture to produce a large change in daylight delivery and direction.

These five "functional" boundaries have subjects that range from regional infrastructures to neurological receptors. Yet all five emanate from the decoupling of systems from the geometries of building scale. By decoupling and remapping, we approach energy generation and consumption at their most efficient and effective levels. Traditional building technologies have changed little from their late-nineteenth-century origins, and it was for these systems that the electrical infrastructure was created. The rapid technological evolution that has occurred in every other industry, with the exception of the automotive industry, has bypassed the built environment. The primary reason for this is our assumption that the building, and not the systems and the consumers, is the appropriate unit by which to evaluate performance. Second is the belief that building systems should be seamlessly integrated. By challenging both of these assumptions, we have an opportunity for an order of magnitude or more of reduction in energy.

Wave Farm

Pelamis Wave Power Ltd.

Simulated wave farm showing
the system to harness wave
energy developed by Edinburgh-
based Pelamis Wave Power Ltd.

CR Land Guanganmen Green Technology Showroom

Vector Architects

The project is a temporary Green Technology Showroom in Beijing, created for three-year use within a residential project. The idea is to develop a meaningful concept of "temporary," to design an installation that could be built, demolished, and recycled in an easy and straight-forward manner, with the least impact to its site. Steel was used to create the main structural system of the building, so that: the structural members can be reused after the building is taken down; the fabrication of structural members can occur simultaneously with site excavation, thus shortening the construction schedule; and the building can be elevated, greatly reducing excavation and foundation work and facilitating easy demolition and site recovery.

A vertical grass panel system and green roof were applied to the building envelope, to reduce heat gain and loss and enhance thermal efficiency. The grass panels will also reduce storm-water runoff. Although the central lawn is taken away to make room for this building, the original planting area was effectively tripled by using grass panels on the roof and two façades. The grass wall panel is planned for relocation onto the fence of the residential compound after the structure's demolition.

Aux Fermes, Citoyens!

Dorothée Imbert

Food has again become overtly political. The Obamas' organic vegetable garden at the White House symbolically returned the quintessential American display landscape—the front lawn—to the production of food. This was but one of many recent mediagenic events concerned with our dietary health and the greening of America. The link between food and environmental responsibility has come to the fore of academic and popular thinking. Writers, politicians, and chefs are fomenting a "delicious revolution," where "real food," "slow food," and "localism" will reduce our carbon footprint and our waistlines. Related to this interest in food is a renewed interest in urban agriculture. Rediscovered as a soft and low-cost equivalent to a technically focused high-end sustainable architecture, urban agriculture is a loosely defined ideology with a long history.

The hybridization of second nature (agriculture) and third nature (the garden) has exerted a long-lasting impact on the landscape imagination, from the rural *ferme ornée*, or ornamented farm, where lawns were for feeding sheep and sowing corn, to the urban garden.[1] In Louis XIV's Versailles, the art of eating was a serious matter: the king was concerned not only with the aesthetics of power but also with the prestige of cuisine. To provide a steady supply of refined produce, Jean-Baptiste La Quintinie created the *Potager du roi*, a 9-hectare ornamental garden with parterres of vegetables and walled orchards.[2] The protective walls, espaliered trees, and greenhouses satisfied the regal appetite for figs, peas, strawberries, and asparagus beyond their typical growing seasons.

Today one can detect two main trends in the current drive for sustainable agriculture and healthy living in the United States: one from above and the other from below. The first is the well-publicized call for food production reform heralded by high-profile advocates such as Alice Waters and Michael Pollan, which even the business world has noticed. This message finds its roots in the nostalgic collective memory of Jeffersonian agricultural ideals and the myth of old Europe, particularly France and Italy. Self-sufficiency and self-satisfaction go hand in hand: if you can't grow your own cardoons and compost the peels, at least take your wicker basket to the local market and buy fresh produce from smiling farmers. At the other end of the social spectrum are many grassroot movements including Milwaukee's Growing Power, Detroit's Urban Farming, and Chicago's City Farm. Reclaiming abandoned lots and underused backyards, they aim at transforming both the urban and the eating experiences. Their goals range from employing inner-city and immigrant populations to educating children and ending world hunger. These organizations use a low-tech method of cultivation suitable to contemporary urban conditions that has parallels with subsistence farming in Latin America, Asia, and Africa.

Self-sufficiency is a typical impulse in uncertain times: kitchen gardens sprung up during both world wars and were popular during the early 1970s. Such a desire also recalls the counterculture environmental politics of the *Whole Earth Catalog*, a compilation of "tools" to help individuals lead their own lives and shape their own environment "off the grid," out of reach of big government and big business. These tools ranged from books on organic gardening to the Dymaxion World of Buckminster Fuller, "doing the most with the least." The *Whole Earth Catalog* also reflected a desire to move environmentalism away from the wilderness and the Sierra Club to embrace a broader view of nature, one reconciled with modernity and technology. The late 1960s' "appropriate technology" aimed at improving living conditions in less-developed nations minus the environmental hazards of industrialization. Today's urban agriculture methods and goals fit the description of appropriate technology: "low investment cost, organizational simplicity, high adaptability to a particular social or cultural environment, sparing use of natural resources, and high potential for employment."[3] What is of particular notice in today's striving for self-sufficiency and a better diet is that it appears to be both off the grid and totally on the grid.

At first sight, urban agriculture presents a paradox: cities are urban and agriculture rural. In the simplistic scenario of city against countryside, development has pushed the farm

First Lady Michelle Obama and White House Horticulturist Dale Haney work with students from Washington's Bancroft Elementary School to break ground for a White House kitchen garden, March 20, 2009.

Espaliered pear tree, *Potager du roi*, Versailles

The Queen's new kitchen garden
at Buckingham Palace, London;
Sunday Times (London), June 14, 2009

Lettuce reign over you: Queen starts allotment

Environment The latest boost for the 'grow your own' campaign is coming from Buckingham Palace, says **Maurice Chittenden**

BRITAIN'S burgeoning army of urban allotment holders have a royal champion — the Queen has ordered part of the Buckingham Palace gardens to be turned into an environmentally friendly vegetable patch.

It is the first time the palace has grown kitchen produce since it took part in the "dig for victory" campaign during the second world war.

The Queen has had the 30ft by 12ft vegetable patch dug at the rear of the 40-acre gardens in an area known as the "yard bed", previously used for growing summer flowers. No chemicals are used and the plot is irrigated from the palace borehole.

The inauguration of the royal vegetable patch follows a similar idea by President Barack Obama and his wife Michelle. In March, they dug up 1,100 sq ft of the White House lawn to plant crops.

The Queen is at the forefront of a national grow-your-own movement as people look for cheap and healthy alternatives to supermarket food.

The National Trust has begun a nationwide campaign to encourage landowners to lend spare plots to the public. Meanwhile, Boris Johnson, the London mayor, has announced a scheme to plant vegetables on rooftops and unused spaces around some of the capital's most famous landmarks.

Some of the first vegetables planted on the Buckingham Palace patch have regal overtones. They include a rare climbing French bean called Blue Queen and a variety of the same vegetable known as Royal Red. Others in the garden include Northern Queen lettuces and tomato varieties such as Golden Queen, Queen of Hearts and White Queen.

Visiting dignitaries might want to try some of the others — Stuttgarter onions might appeal to Angela Merkel, the German leader, and Red Ace beetroot to Vladimir Putin, the Russian prime minister.

The Queen was shown round her new venture last week by Claire Midgley, the deputy gardens manager.

A palace spokeswoman said the Queen was a green gardener. She said: "No chemicals have been used to cultivate the allotment sites. Liquid seaweed has been used to feed the plants and garlic is being used to deter

aphids. Like the rest of the garden, water from the palace borehole is used to irrigate the plants. Everything grown will be eaten within the palace."

To mark the opening of the allotment, the palace has released pictures of the Queen and Princess Margaret harvesting dwarf beans at their allotment at Windsor castle in 1943. The image was used to promote

the wartime campaign for national self-sufficiency.

Christopher Woodward, director of the Museum of Garden History in south London, which is holding an exhibition this autumn called The Good Life: 100 Years of Growing Your Own, said: "It's a good idea for the Queen to start an allotment. The whole thing about urban food is the zeitgeist. It is

**Claire Midgley shows the Queen and Prince Philip the vegetable plot in the palace gardens, ab[...]
The Queen and Princess Margaret helped grow vegetable[...]**

out and, with it, urbanites' connection to the soil and the seasons. In this scenario, food for cities is trucked in from afar at great cost in energy (shipping a head of lettuce from California to New York takes thirty-six times more calories than the lettuce itself contains). City children have to be taught that milk comes from a cow—that is, unless they live on Manhattan's Upper East Side, in which case they are taught how to make buffalo mozzarella from an *artisan fromager*. There are, however, new types of urban-rural exchanges. For one, the land-use collage of European urbanized areas allows for a multifunctional agricultural infrastructure: farming operations on the edge of Paris combine leisure activities and cereal production. Other farms have become productive enclaves within suburban development and cater to their immediate neighbors; others are of a more temporary nature, such as the land leased to immigrant populations in New York through The New Farmer Development Project. Conversely, small plot-intensive farming has become a viable transformer or colonizer of urban vacant land. Cultivating abandoned or underused lots offers ecological, economic, social, and health benefits.

As heirs of both agricultural and urbanism traditions, landscape architects are uniquely situated to articulate a spatial vision for urban agriculture and bring back third-nature aesthetics into our urban second nature. While few will argue against the value of urban agriculture on moral grounds, I would like to explore the role of landscape architecture in helping provide a direction for urban agriculture as a design strategy. I have organized the examples that follow around the themes of Palliative, Recuperative, and Projective. These examples are not intended to be comprehensive but to identify historical and contemporary trends in integrating landscape architecture, agriculture, and urbanism.

Palliative

In the first half of the twentieth century, the garden, and specifically the allotment garden, was frequently presented as an antidote to urbanization as well as a moral and economic stabilizer of modern society. German landscape architect Leberecht Migge, who collaborated with Ernst May, Adolf Loos, and Martin Wagner, was a prolific activist for the productive garden as an integral component of planning *Siedlungen*. In his 1918 and 1919 polemics, "everyone self-sufficient" and "the green manifesto," Migge argued for individual production of foodstuff as a tool for land reform and a counter to overcrowded urban conditions.[4] Planting was the only possible antidote to what he saw as a wasteful contemporary city with hectares of fallow streets and housing tenements.

JOHN STILLWELL

Buckingham Palace

Constitution Hill

Queen's vegetable patch

Lower Grosvenor Place

Grosvenor Place   100 metres

...p.
...or Castle during the war, top left

...t the quantity of food ...
...people feel anxious, ...nt to grow vegetables. ...ate 1970s, the waiting ...lotments increased by ...of 16, but in the 1980s ...eople had money and ...pads they abandoned ...tments."
...ded: "Everybody feels ...vhen they put their

fingers in the earth and nothing tastes better than a strawberry or tomato you have just picked."

Sir Roy Strong, the historian who wrote a book on the royal gardens, said: "The Queen is in line with the times and should be greatly applauded, but the idea of Princess Margaret keeping an allotment would have been laughable."

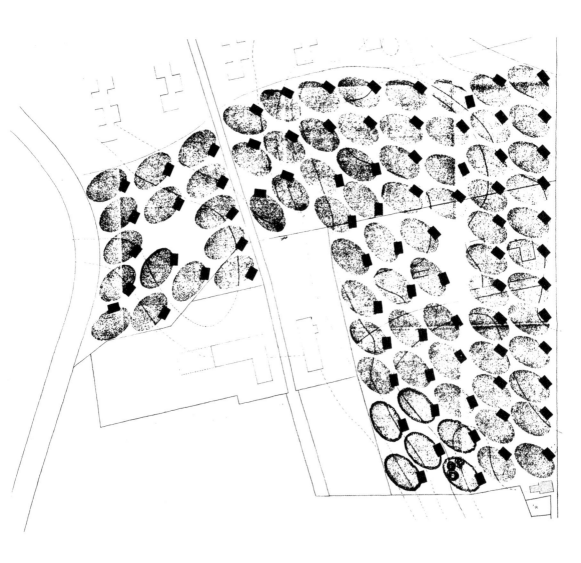

Allotment gardens, Nærum, near Copenhagen; C. Th. Sørensen, 1948. Strict codes govern hedge maintenance.

In contrast to the debilitating and chaotic city, the productive garden was rationally organized according to family needs; it maximized yield with standard dimensions and climate control. Intensive crops such as tomatoes and salads, which required less space and more care, were planted near the house; neighbors shared a composting facility, fish pond, and a lawn. Fruit trees were espaliered along the walls and, if necessary, could be protected at night by lowering screens.

Migge's desire to establish a connection with the soil, both physically and symbolically, was a recurring concern for twentieth-century landscape architects. In Denmark, allotment gardens were part of the open-space system and designed as permanent landscape structures. To C.Th. Sørensen, such gardens offered a cure for modern apartment dwellers who had severed their ties to the ground. In Nærum, outside of Copenhagen, he arranged a series of oval gardens across a slope, with each oval enclosed by a hedge. Like Migge, Sørensen relied on the individual working toward the interest of the group and on standard forms and dimensions, but the spatial effect of Nærum's ovals could not be more different. The sensuous forms and dynamic composition contrasted with the orthogonal order of cities and typical allotment gardens. Sørensen established seven pages of guidelines, mostly concerning the hedges: these could be planted with hawthorn, sweetbriar, crabapple, or lilac; sheared or not, they had to be sufficiently tall for providing privacy. Inside the oval, gardeners could do as they pleased, grow vegetables, currants, or gooseberries. With the ovals running across the slope, the hedges occasionally stack or appear to form a continous curve, the ground in between serving as buffer and playground.

The self-sufficient productive garden unit according to family size; Leberecht Migge, 1919

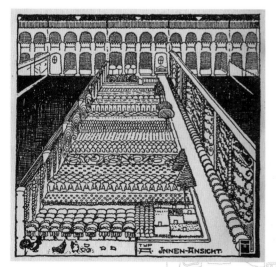
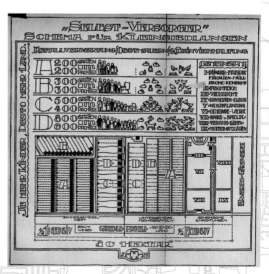

Recuperative

Agricultural practices, including both crops and trees, offer possibilities for making cities sustainable in terms of recuperation—turning vacant or derelict land into a site of public investment. The notion of punctual recuperation to transform the experience of the city is perhaps best exemplified by the playgrounds for postwar Amsterdam, designed by Aldo Van Eyck for the planning department headed by Cornelis Van Eesteren. The hundreds of playgrounds, site-specific and yet assembled with a finite set of standard elements, physically and morally repaired the fabric of the city. They also offered an alternative to the top-down model of CIAM's urbanism, with small interstitial places that responded to local conditions and modified the whole. There are lessons to be learned for urban agriculture here: the modesty of scale and means, the variety of permutations, the understanding of human activity, a systematic approach, and the ability for design to improve living conditions. This was not truly a bottom-up planning process but an iterative one. It transformed the playgrounds from a mosaic of voids into a mosaic of places, where minute and discrete parts formed a new social network within the city.

The notion of urban nature is constantly assessed in contemporary landscape architecture practice. Whether sites are

Agricultural corridor under high-voltage lines, Cantinho do Céu, São Paulo, Brazil; community gardens in Providence, Rhode Island

Self-sustaining colonizing
garden pods, Zug, Switzerland;
Schweingruber Zulauf, 1999

toxic, abandoned, or otherwise compromised, the conflict between vegetation and urban soil is constant. Although several designers have explored the potential of growing food in dense urban conditions in vertical farms, where hydroponics are integral to the structure of buildings, others have looked to low-tech precedents to establish a productive landscape system. Thus the incremental strategy of "Continuous Productive Urban Landscapes"—an open-space network linking inner-city allotment gardens to existing parks and the periphery—builds on the test case of Cuban urban agriculture.[5] In Cuba, the hardship that followed the collapse of the Soviet Union led to an overhaul of the state-based agricultural system with the semiprivate organic cultivation of urban and periurban vacant land. Such a model is heralded as ecologically suitable, economically feasible, and socially redemptive. Its energy consumption is minimal and advantages many, particularly in terms of adaptive reuse.

Often urban agriculture involves an act of defiance, whether it is taking over a street or railway corridor, or appropriating someone else's land as in the "guerrilla gardening" movement.[6] Examples of ornamental landscapes appropriated for other purposes abound, especially when tied to the safeguard of home and nation. In 1940, the parterres of the Luxembourg gardens facing the French senate were turned up for growing food, and sheep grazed on the White House lawn long before the recent seeding of arugula.

Projective

There is also tremendous potential in considering urban agriculture as a means to structure development. In several of his projects, French landscape architect Michel Desvigne has made the case for a landscape infrastructure that precedes architecture. He argues for what could be termed a projective ecology (as opposed to a protectionist ecology)—one in which the landscape not only performs an ecological role in terms of storm-water management and biodiversity but more important, creates a spatial framework for future urban development. On the right bank of Bordeaux, the planting of trees in abandoned parking lots and leftover sites colonizes the waning industrial area. Desvigne insists that his is not a master plan but a spatial system of vegetated solids and circulation voids anticipating the urbanization that will occur in the next seventy years. This banded landscape becomes the generator of the building process rather than its byproduct. Other projects in New York and Paris evoke hybrid landscapes of productivity and leisure. At Governors Island, agricultural practices offer a model for soil management and a strategy for

Lisières project for Paris; Michel Desvigne, Jean Nouvel, 2009

Agricultural gardens: first phase. Île Seguin, Boulogne-sur-Seine; Michel Desvigne, 2009

Lisières project for Paris. Detail of band with greenhouses, allotment gardens, hedgerows, and orchards; Michel Desvigne, Jean Nouvel, 2009

Agricultural gardens: first phase. Île Seguin, Boulogne-sur-Seine; Michel Desvigne, 2009

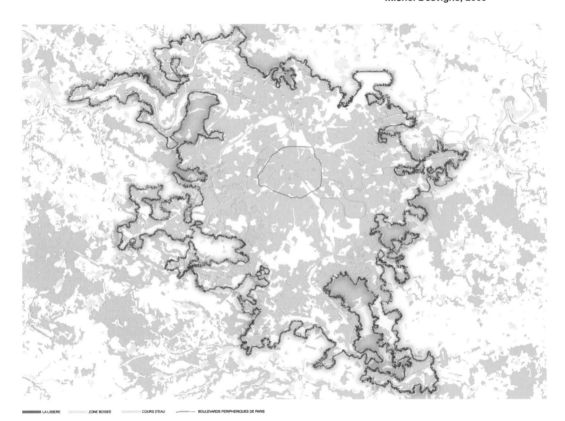

LA LISIERE   ZONE BOISEE   COURS D'EAU   BOULEVARDS PERIPHERIQUES DE PARIS

Aux Fermes, Citoyens!

Five good reasons to have farms
in Allston; Dorothée Imbert
and Scheri Fultineer with Megumi
Aihara, Tzufen Liao, and Takuma
Ono, 2007

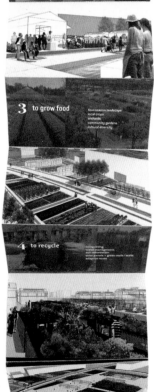

phased development. Similarly, the reclaimed Île Seguin—previously site of a Renault factory—presents a figure-ground diagram without buildings where the fields of garden produce and allotments form the first layer of solids that precede tree planting and architecture. In a sense, agriculture is a trope for both memory and efficiency. The rational layout, fast output, soil improvement, composting, and water management speak to a sustainable urban nature, one that is totally artificial yet triggers a connection to food, the earth, and the rural landscape. At a regional scale, this dual approach is further explored in the 2009 proposal for Grand Paris with Jean Nouvel.[7] In response to Nicolas Sarkozy's call for transportation and ecological visions for greater Paris, Desvigne and the Nouvel team devised an urban-agricultural codification for the periphery's *lisière*—a term describing a forest edge or a seam. The lisière between Paris and the surrounding agricultural zone becomes an 800-kilometer joint of varying width where traces of a long-gone farming landscape articulate a new type of productive open-space system. The hedges, ditches, thickets, and paths reappear within an infrastructure of greenhouses, allotment gardens, recycling, energy production, composting, and sports fields. Strictly codified, this band is not about protection and nostalgia but exchange and experimentation—a means to make the landscape accessible to all users. In this scenario, planned indeterminacy hems the suburbanization of the countryside and allows agriculture to reenter the urban.

For my final example, I will shift gears slightly to suggest how a projective approach to urban agriculture could help to shape development. Harvard's Allston campus presents a unique set of conditions—ecologically, socially, and spatially—to test ideas of urban agriculture.[8] The interconnection of a productive didactic landscape with urban spaces could further demonstrate Harvard's commitment to environmentally conscious development while helping to take landscape architecture and urbanism in a new direction. There is something beautifully matter-of-fact and incongruous about growing food in an urban setting. Considering this new campus as a working landscape would take the concept of urban agriculture beyond the cosmetic, technical, or nostalgic. Such a stance would cause a rethinking of the role of landscape in the planning process, as it would precede building—a proposition not so implausible given the current economic recession and the stalling of the campus plan's implementation.

And if food can be seen as a measure of power, it could also serve as a decoder of academic hierarchy. Although few, if any, university professors still exercise their right to pasture animals on Harvard Yard, they may earn a "produce bonus" from the Allston farms. One could envision an updated version of Louis XIV's *Potager du roi* with Allston's *Potager des présidents*. There, greenhouses would supply Nobel laureates with tasty vine tomatoes throughout the winter. At the onset of spring, senior faculty would receive tender mizuna and white asparagus and, in the fall, a basket of Roxbury Russet—a mid-seventeenth-century local heirloom variety, the first apple developed in America. And perhaps after having turned the compost pile and monitored its worm population, junior faculty could enjoy a refreshing organic tea from the medicinal herbal garden.

1 For a definition of the eighteenth-century *ferme ornée*, see Stephen Switzer, *Ichnographia Rustica or the Nobleman, Gentleman, and Gardener's Recreation* (London, first edition, 1718; second revised edition, 1742), volume 1, xvii; volume III, 10. "Rural and extensive gardening," Switzer asserted, was "not only the most profitable, but [also] the most pleasurable."

2 See Stéphanie de Courtois, *Le Potager du roi* (Versailles: Actes Sud, École Nationale Supérieure du Paysage, 2003).

3 See Andrew Kirk, "Appropriate Technology: The *Whole Earth Catalog* and Counterculture Environmental Politics," *Environmental History*, vol. 6, no. 3 (July 2001), 374–394.

4 Leberecht Migge, *Jedermann Selbstversorger! Eine Lösung der Siedlungsfrage durch neuen Gartenbau* (Jena: Diederichs, 1918), and "Das grüne Manifest," 1919. On Migge's polemics, see David Haney, "Leberecht Migge's 'Green Manifesto': Envisioning a Revolution of Gardens," *Landscape Journal*, vol. 26:2 (2007), 201–218.

5 André Viljoen and Joe Howe, "Cuba: Laboratory for Urban Agriculture," in *CPULs: Continuous Productive Urban Landscapes*, edited by André Viljoen (Oxford: Elsevier, 2005).

6 See Richard Reynolds, *On Guerrilla Gardening: A Handbook for Gardening without Boundaries* (New York: Bloomsbury, 2008).

7 See Michel Desvigne. "Épaissir les lisières," in *Naissances et renaissances de mille et un bonheurs parisiens*, edited by Jean Nouvel, Jean-Marie Duthilleul, and Michel Cantal-Dupart (Paris: Les éditions du Mont-Boron, 2009), 148–175.

8 The scenario for integrating urban agriculture in the Harvard campus plan, "Five Good Reasons to Have Farms in Allston," was the result of a 2007 collaboration with Scheri Fultineer, Megumi Aihara, Tzufen Liao, and Takuma Ono.

Fourth good reason to have farms in Allston: to recycle; perspective by Tzufen Liao, 2007

Local River: Home Storage Unit for Fish and Greens

Mathieu Lehanneur with Anthony van den Bossche

The Locavores appeared in San Francisco in 2005, defining themselves as "a group of culinary adventurers who eat foods produced in a radius of 100 miles (160 kilometers) around their city." By doing so, they aim to reduce the impact on the environment inherent to the transport of foodstuffs, while ensuring their traceability.

Local River anticipates the growing influence of this group (the word "locavore" made its first appearance in an American dictionary in 2007) by proposing a home storage unit for live freshwater fish combined with a mini vegetable patch. This DIY fish-farm-cum-kitchen-garden is based on the principle of aquaponics coupled with the exchange and interdependence of two living organisms–plants and fish. The plants extract nutrients from the nitrate-rich dejecta of the fish, acting as a natural filter that purifies the water and maintains a vital balance for the ecosystem in which the fish live. The same technique is used on large-scale pioneer aquaponics/fish-farms, which raise tilapia (a food fish from the Far East) and lettuce planted in trays floating on the surface of ponds.

This project responds to everyday needs for fresh food that is 100 percent traceable. It bets on a return to favor of farm-raised freshwater fish (trout, eel, perch, carp, etc.), given the dwindling supplies of many saltwater species due to overfishing. It also demonstrates the capacity of fish-farmers to deliver their stock live to consumers as a guarantee of optimum freshness–impossible in the case of saltwater fish that has been netted.

Local River aims to replace the decorative "TV aquarium" with an equally decorative but also functional "refrigerator aquarium." In this scenario, fish and greens cohabit for a short time in a home storage unit before being eaten by their keepers, the end players in an exchange cycle within a controlled ecosystem.

Soft Cities

KVA MATx

This urban initiative explores the design of a distributed clean energy network that operates between the large scale of existing centralized urban energy systems and the multiple small scales and discrete ownership structures of living units in a dense urban building fabric. The SOFT CITIES project creates a new delivery model for clean energy that engages a range of highly adaptable energy-harvesting textile systems using thin-film solar nanomaterials.Working across the fields of urbanism, architecture, engineering, and material science, the SOFT CITIES project explores the technical, spatial, and aesthetic possibilities of organic photovolatics, an emergent class of synthesized photoreactive polymer materials that can be printed or deposited onto flexible substrates in an efficient roll-to-roll manufacturing process. Organic photovoltaics present an intriguing set of material paradoxes for architectural design that challenge building industry assumptions that have developed around glass-based solar technologies.

The SOFT CITIES design strategy is constructed from the paradoxical combination of generous excess and radical inefficiency, and engages the limitations and assets of organic photovolatics in terms of production process, flexible form factor, translucent aesthetics, and energy-harvesting characteristics over time. The conventional form of discrete multifaceted glass solar panel arrays is replaced by pliable solar strands, design to be very long and thin to maximize material flexibility and minimize connecting electric busways. Using contemporary computer-driven textile manufacturing equipment, the solar strands are integrated into a hybrid textile surface—part architecture, part mobile furnishing, and part urban energy-harvesting surface that is ready to work "out of the box."

Organic photovoltaics enjoy a high through-put production process; much surface material can be made in little time, at little cost, with a low carbon footprint. Despite the generosity of roll-to-roll production, organic photovoltaics use significantly less embodied energy than is required to manufacture poly- or monocrystalline glass solar panels. Abundant surfaces are necessary, however, due to the inefficiency of organic photovoltaic materials, which convert only 3 to

271

4 percent of incoming light to electricity. Yet the materials' ability to accept sunlight continuously over time in a broad 120-degree range transforms the conventional solar industry metric of "peak efficiency" across a limited range of hours to one of total accrued energy over the course of a day. Low-cost mass production, a generosity of surface large enough to create space, and the ability to harvest energy throughout the day, in a broad range of solar orientations, creates a clean energy paradigm with the potential for mass adoption in dense urban districts.

Sponsored by the MIT Energy Initiative and the Government of Portugal, prototypes for energy harvesting textiles are being prepared to reduce environmental strain and accelerate the sustainable reoccupation of 25,000 row houses constructed between the seventeenth and nineteenth centuries in the Casa Burguesa district of the City of Porto in Portugal. The aim is to provide daily energy use savings of more than 60 percent per household with textiles of 15 square meters, or about 10 percent of the typical roof area.

The SOFT CITIES pilot project provides households with 6.5kWh/day on average in a new delivery model for clean energy that combines advanced photovoltaic polymer nano-materials with the traditional ventilation and daylighting spaces of the Casa Burguesa row-house typology. Characterized by a narrow and deep plan footprint with tall upper floors, the Casa Burguesa is served by an interior skylit stair well 20 meters or more in height. This vertical interior shaft, perceived only in section from the interior of the domestic space, is reoccupied and enhanced as the vertical interior delivery zone for an efficient direct current (DC to DC) domestic clean energy distribution system that is designed to reduce

Soft House energy-harvesting textile prototype

Illumination of Casa Burguesa pilot project in Porto, Portugal

the overall cost of domestic solar ownership by reducing or eliminating costs of installation, specialized engineering, and inverter equipment.

SOFT CITIES explores the intersection between programmatic uses for clean energy and their aesthetic and political impacts at both domestic and urban scales. The daily experience of harvesting energy with solar textiles creates a new shared infrastructure zone that connects the horizontal urban expanse of rooftop with the vertical domestic circulation system. By day, a horizontal rooftop canopy expands the living space, providing energy with a changing play of striated light and shadow. At night, the lightweight solar textiles can be retracted and rolled into the domestic skylight well for storage. Harvested energy is used to power solid-state interior lighting and digital work tools for home offices, and can be sold as a source of revenue to charge electric motor scooters, expanding the flow of pedestrians necessary to revitalize the economic and cultural life of the Casa Burguesa District and extending the range of urban mobility established by the Porto Metro.

The political urban impacts of this clean energy system include the ability, by the sustainable retrofit of the domestic interior core, to change the demographics of the Casa Burguesa District, enabling co-ownership of a single house and fostering diversity of living and working spaces in the dense urban core of Porto. At night, with exterior illumination, the collective impact of multiple distributed sources extends beyond the boundary of the domestic unit and is leveraged as a defining urban expression of a renewed environmentalism in the historic center of Porto.

SOFT CITIES presents a view where rooftop laundry is accompanied by autonomous energy production: an ephemeral yet transgressive network of performative fabric, drawing from the Portugese aesthetic traditions of the shade arbor and the privacy and porosity of traditional lace curtains. In this active roofscape, new urban reciprocities are discovered as the interior sectional depth of the row house is revealed and turned inside out, allowing the solar textiles to charge. The adaptability and reproducibility of the SOFT CITIES energy delivery model can be extended to meet the need for the sustainable retrofit of dense urban districts in many areas of the world.

Project team:

Sheila Kennedy, Kyle Barker, Eletha Flores, Patricia Gruits, Alexander Hayman, Sloan Kulper, Murat Mutlu, Adnan Zolj

Agencia Arquitectura Thenasie & Valentim, Porto

MIT Energy Initiative

Faculdade de Arquitectura da Universidade do Porto (FAUP)

Faculdade de Engenharia da Universidade do Porto (FEUP)

Agência de Energia do Porto (AdE)

The ZEDfactory

Bill Dunster

The human population of the planet is directly proportional to the availability of cheap fossil fuel.

Climate change is accelerating exponentially, and if the human economy with its urban and agricultural infrastructure continues unchecked, it is likely that a 4- to 5-degree average global temperature rise by the end of this century will result in the loss of two-thirds of the world's productive farmland. This could lead to a massive surge of climate refugees, conflict over fertile land and fresh water, and ultimately billions of deaths. Peak oil, peak gas, and peak nuclear will all occur within the next fifteen to twenty years, leaving us with a cultural imperative to change our human economic infrastructure from a reliance on finite extractive resources to the use of infinite renewable resources, before economic instability precludes any meaningful actions. This is the most important cultural challenge—to build this new lifestyle and workstyle within our contemporary economy, so that the majority of the human population can enjoy democracy and avoid endless conflict for increasingly scarce natural capital.

Avoided carbon becomes the new currency, informing the design of a kettle, a cavity wall, an urban block, or indeed the master plan of an entire city region. The next step is then debating whether this responsibility lies with individuals—planning their personal low-carbon diets within their fair share of the right to pollute the planet's atmosphere—or with the legislative "big brother" state, or some complex combination of the two. Think of it as a choice between voluntary rationing, accompanied by a lifestyle restructuring exercise, or ecofascism that gives key decisions to the nanny state or the vested interests of big business funded by big capital. I know which I prefer.

The big debate today is whether to adopt site-integrated renewable energy systems or export the problem off-site by investing in large-scale renewable engineering projects. This dialogue actually translates into a simple personal response to the climate change problem. Do you reduce your need for energy to the point that it can be met from simple solar panels on your own roof or balcony, or pay someone else to go somewhere else and meet your requirements somehow? The trouble

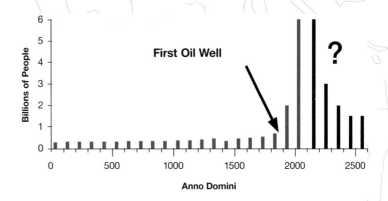

is that everyone wants to take up the limited number of opportunities for off-site solutions, effectively exporting their
problems. Quite quickly it becomes apparent that there is
not enough renewable generating opportunity to ever meet
current demand. National renewable resources have to be
rationed, with each citizen receiving the right to a certain
amount of green-grid electricity, biomass fuel, and transport-
grade vegetable oil. People living or working in inefficient
but culturally important historic buildings are going to need
more of scarce national renewable resources. This is the difference between "Old Greens" and "New Greens": Old Greens
still believe that there are unlimited stocks of renewable energy out there and advocate for big, centralized infrastructure
investment by multinational big business; New Greens understand the importance of minimizing demand on the fragile
national renewable reserves, adding microgeneration funded
by microcredit wherever appropriate.

The credit crunch, moreover, has changed the rules. No
property developer can fund big, low-carbon infrastructure
investment. The cash reserves that could have been used on
large-scale public engineering projects feeding into the green
grid have been spent fighting for fossil fuel outside our national boundaries or shoring up a banking system to avoid
social collapse. There will not be enough offshore turbines,
tidal barrages, or desert power stations built to feed much
more than a small fraction of our current energy demand, and
these resources will be required for basic services such as
agriculture and public transport. The only cash left to invest
is the money that an ordinary household would spend for
basic utilities such as water, drainage, heat, and power each
month. This cash can be diverted from propping up fossil
fuel–addicted utilities to servicing microcredit loans for installing building-integrated renewable energy systems.

The average fuel price increase over the past five years has
been around 15 to 17 percent. As peak oil, peak gas, and peak

nuclear affect limited supplies of finite, nonreplenishable reserves, it is likely that an annual fuel price escalator of 8 percent could be experienced for the next ten years. With this rate of increase, the payback on bulk-purchased monocrystalline photovoltaic panels is around twelve years. It is perfectly possible to redirect the cash previously allocated to your monthly electric bill to meet the monthly payments on the loan required to purchase the panels. With the embodied CO_2 invested in panel production and shipping repaid in around three years, the loan repaid in twelve years, and the panels lasting between twenty-five and forty years, this technology ought to inform the design of new buildings and the renovation of our existing urban fabric. This logic applies to a range of resources:

– Do you pay for expensive water-treatment plants for the city or install water-saving appliances and collect rainwater?
– Do you build a state-of-the-art sewage-treatment plant or design waterless composting toilets in the suburbs?
– Do you invest in expensive district heating mains or super-insulate and install solar thermal collectors so that hardly any additional heat is needed?
– Do you build a nuclear power station or install solar electric panels on your balcony balustrade or roof ?

Each question has a different answer at different city densities, and within different climatic zones.

This is the challenge to the architecture profession. Can we become fluent within the avoided carbon economy quickly enough to transcend mere Darwinian engineering logic and develop a workable zero-carbon built environment?

Fast-forward about twenty years: When budget air travel is folk history, carpools are everywhere, and we visit vegetarian greasy spoons on our lunch hour, the United Kingdom will have to run itself on the limited stocks of renewable energy available within its national boundaries. If every green-grid off-site generation device ever dreamed up by an infrastructure engineer were built—with offshore turbines at minimum spacings over the entire continental shelf—we would still struggle to meet much more than 25 percent of our current energy demand. All of the off-site generating capacity would be needed for our stock of much-loved but inefficient historic buildings. In fact, we have only about 500 dry kilograms of biomass per capita if we harvest woodland sustainably and compress agricultural waste without losing food production, leaving about 250 kilograms per capita to run a household. I call this "the national biomass quota."

BedZED, London: View from skygarden–scheme density 120 homes/hectare

This tiny amount is what is needed for winter domestic hot water in a superinsulated ZED[1] home, with solar thermal providing hot water all summer. Put monocrystalline photovoltaics on the half of the roof facing south, and enough electricity is generated to meet annual electric demand up to densities of fifty homes per hectare, with a summer surplus to cope with reduced outputs from offshore wind. This density band represents 70 percent of all homes in the United Kingdom. This suggests that it is not realistic or sensible to claim limited renewable off-site generation capacity for new buildings, as you are effectively stealing an existing community's rights to a future powered by renewable energy. It is important that we all understand the future shortage of national and international renewable energy supplies today, because we need to apply every renewable harvesting opportunity, both on- and off-site, if we are to achieve an equitable democratic future and workable long-term urban fabric.[2]

The big idea at BedZED[3] was not to indulge in coercive lifestyle changes for residents but to make change to a low-carbon diet attractive and convenient. BedZED also includes low-carbon workspaces and can just as easily produce EdZED (schools) and MedZED (hospitals); current government legislation is pushing for the same environmental performance standards in these public building typologies. Green lifestyles have been adopted slowly by some at BedZED because many residents find social engineering from lifestyle coaches a little patronizing; many people want to adopt these ideas at their own pace.

Cross section of mixed-use BedZED development showing workspaces in shade zone of housing, with gardens above

Critics are correct to emphasize that the carbon footprint of an air-freighted strawberry is larger than the carbon savings from BedZED superinsulated building fabric. Consumer pur-

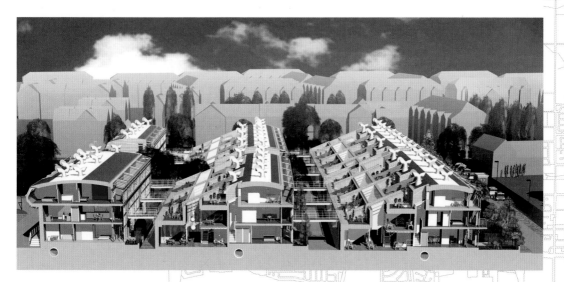

The ZEDfactory

1 Zero Energy Development.
2 For an alternative design strategy that adopts both green lifestyles and maximizes energy efficiency with on-site generation, see Bill Dunster, Craig Simmons, and Bobby Gilbert, *The Zed Book: Solutions for a Shrinking World* (Taylor and Francis, 2008).
3 Beddington Zero Energy Development, a pioneering environmentally friendly housing scheme near Wallington, England, designed by the author and built in 2000–2002.

chasing habits, however, will change quickly as peak oil increases fuel prices and can be considered early quick wins in the campaign to achieve a net-zero-carbon lifestyle. Giving up daft consumption patterns will not help the average family of 2050 get through a cold winter on meager fuel rations, or keep the lights on when the grid becomes increasingly intermittent. It seems that we have forgotten that buildings last a long time, and that in 2050 the cost of fuel will make the occupation of a standard home potentially unaffordable.

The most important lesson from BedZED is the concept of carbon trading in return for planning gain. It has proved that it is possible to increase urban occupation densities while producing measurable increases in overall quality of life compared to that achieved by using standard U.K. developers' templates. The scheme has shown that it is possible to fit all of the government's target of 3.5 million new homes on existing stocks of brownfield land while providing every home with a garden and reducing the demand on scarce national renewable energy reserves. Demonstration projects give politicians confidence to change legislative environmental targets. Slowly, every year, the supply chain reduces in cost, the buildings become more varied and technically more refined, and the potential excuses for not delivering zero-carbon urban regeneration lose their validity.

A low-cost, zero-carbon, off-grid earth-sheltered housing solution specifically aimed at vacant industrial plots

Tongshan urban extension, China.
Undulating linear pedestrian parks
over retail, parking, and office space
provide a townwide network of child-
friendly green open space between
south-facing apartment blocks
optimized for microgeneration.

A self-funding zero-carbon flood-
defense wall with solar-powered
tram on top of the dike

Many cities are built on floodplains.
ZEDfactory are producing a range
of zero-carbon floating apartments
clustered around a communal
solar atrium. The East London suburban street of the future may well
need to rise and fall with the tide.

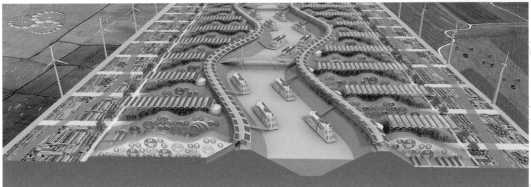

Logroño, the eco-city designed by MVRDV in collaboration with GRAS in the Spanish province of Rioja, encompasses the construction of 3,000 houses and complementary program. The 56-hectare site, just north of Logroño on the two hills of Montecorvo and la Fonsalada, offers views over the city and vast south-facing slopes. The total project cost is 388 million Euro, of which 40 million will be invested in renewable energy technology.

The master plan is designed in a compact way, letting the project occupy only 10 percent of the site. The linear urban development meanders through the landscape, providing every apartment with views of the city. In addition, sports facilities, retail, restaurants, infrastructure, and public and private gardens are part of the plan.

The remaining landscape becomes an eco-park, a mix of park and energy production. One hundred percent of the city's energy demand is generated on site by a combination of solar and wind power: a tapestry of photovoltaic cells clad the south-facing slopes, and on top of the two hills, windmills serve as landmarks for the development. A graywater circuit and on-site natural water purification are part of the plan, which combines dense urban living with ecological improvements. These features will give the new development a CO_2-neutral footprint and earn it the highest Spanish energy-efficiency rating.

By building as compactly as possible (following the height line of the hill), costs are minimized. A further part of the plan is the construction of a funicular accessing a museum and viewing point hidden atop Montecorvo, which will also house a research and promotion center for renewable and energy-efficient technology. The on-site production of clean energies and the quality of construction will result in a savings of more than 6,000 tons of CO_2 emissions annually.

The Big-Foot Revolution

Kongjian Yu

"Little-Foot Urbanism"

For more than a thousand years, young Chinese girls were forced to bind their feet to be able to marry urban elites. Healthy, natural "big" feet were considered rustic and rural. Unhealthy, deformed, and citified small feet, deprived of functionality and malodorous, were considered "beautiful." Foot binding (along with many other cultures' body-deforming practices) was appreciated as a rite of urbanity.

Urbanization therefore began with a highly privileged class that sacrificed function in exchange for ornamental and cosmetic values. This same "Little-Foot" value system has been used for thousands of years by the privileged urban minority to build cities and landscapes. By definition, "Little-Foot Urbanism" is the art of gentrification and cosmetics. Its superficial condition replaces the messy, fertile, and functional landscapes associated with healthy and productive people.

Today we bind natural feet in the city with fashionable tiny high-heeled shoes, and we build a 500-year flood-control dike made of concrete to surround the city and keep it distant from the water. We build a fully controlled storm-water management system that does not allow the reinfiltration of water to the aquifer before being flushed into the ocean; we replace native "messy" and productive shrubs and crops with fancy flowers that bear no fruit, support no other species, and serve no function other than pleasing human beings; and we uproot hardy wild grasses and replace them with smooth ornamental lawns that consume tons of water.

Bound feet

Little shoes

The little-foot girl

The big-foot girl

Shanghai: Little-foot urbanism, a city of cosmetics

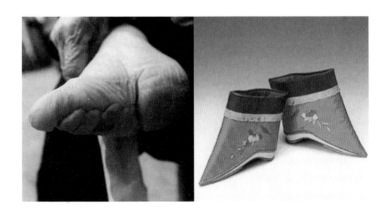

Urbanized landscapes are designed using ornamental criteria, making buildings such as the CCTV Tower and the National Opera House in Beijing the landmarks. Shanghai and Dubai offer other examples—almost all of the landmark buildings there are crowned with ornamental funny hats. Furthermore, the whole city becomes ornamental and cosmetic, with burdens of water shortage, air pollution, global warming, and a massive waste of land and natural resources, along with the loss of cultural identity. The landscapes, cities, and buildings under today's "Little-Foot Urbanism" are like the "Little-Foot" girl: unhealthy, deformed, deprived of functionality, and malodorous. "Little-Foot Urbanism" is a path to death.

The Little-Foot dream used to be limited to an upper-class urban minority of less than 10 percent before the last half of the twentieth century, but now is becoming common throughout the population. In China alone, 18 million people are urbanized each year, migrating to the city from the countryside. These people strive to be "urbane," to be gentrified, to move away from natural functionality and a healthy and productive rural life. When poor developing countries that follow "Little-Foot Urbanism" encounter the "American Jumbo Dream," the scenario gets even worse. Witness China and India, which pursue the American dream of jumbo cars and houses, and whatever jumbo else. Thereafter the land can be seen as a little donkey with a heavy burden: China has only 7 percent of the world's natural resources of arable land and fresh water, with the need to feed 22 percent of the world's population.

It can be imagined where Little-Foot Urbanism with Jumbo Body will lead China: two-thirds of China's 662 cities have a shortage of water; 75 percent of the nation's surface water is polluted; and 64 percent of cities' underground water is polluted; one-third of the national population is in danger of drinking polluted water; 50 percent of wetlands disappeared in the past thirty years. How can we survive in the future?

Urbanity (citified small foot)
The unhealthy, and deprived of productivity, low performance but "beautiful"

vs.   *Rustic* (rural big foot)
Healthy, productive, high performance but "ugly"

The Dream City: bound, deformed, and jumbo, and ornamental.....

Shanghai

You're killing me !

Little feet with jumbo body

How can we survive?

Flood: annual flood damage cost 100 billion US $, 10 million people live in flood plain

Drought: 400 of 662 cities in shortage of water, 20 million people are in shortage of drinking water, in Beijing, underground drops 1.0 meter each year.

Pollution: 75% of the nation's surface water is polluted, 64% of cities' underground water is polluted, 1/3 of the national population are under the threat of drinking water pollution

Habitat loss: 50% wetland disappeared in the past 50 years

Little foot carrying the jumbo body: The crisis of urbanization in China

The crisis of survival: The degraded environment–flood, drought, pollution, and loss of habitat

The "Big-Foot Revolution": Ecological Urbanism

It's time for a change. Ecological urbanism is the art of survival. At this moment, two strategies have to be adopted to provide a guide for sustainable cities in the future.

Urban Development Based on Ecological Infrastructure across Scales

This is the spatial strategy of urban development planning that requires planners to understand the land as a living system, to identify an ecological infrastructure (EI) that will guide urban development. EI is defined as the structural landscape network composed of critical landscape elements and spatial patterns. EI also has strategic significance in safeguarding the integrity and identity of the natural and cultural landscapes, which in turn secure sustainable ecosystem services.

Using a minimum of space, EI will safeguard the following four critical eco-services:

A painting commonly used on the street as propaganda during the Cultural Revolution, demonstrating revolution against Confucianism and little-foot culture

Five projects, five principles

Ecosystem services

Abio-Natural process **Biological Process** **Recreational process**

high SP	high SP	high SP	high SP	high SP
medium SP	medium SP	medium SP	medium SP	medium SP
low SP	low SP	low SP	low SP	low SP

Alternatives of
ecological
infrastructure (EI)

EI at a higher security level

EI at a lower security level

Used to guide and frame urban growth

A framework of urban planning based on ecological infrastructure, where SP means "Security Pattern," the landscape configuration essential for safeguarding ecological or cultural processes

A spatial strategy for ecological urbanism: The building of ecological infrastructure in China across scales

(1) Provide food production and clean water; (2) Regulate climate, disease, flood, and drought; (3) Support nutrient cycles and habitat for native plant and animal species; (4) Sponsor culture, associated with spiritual and recreational benefits.

As an ecological urbanism spatial strategy, ecological infrastructure should be planned across scales. The national and regional EI are to be planned through the identification of strategic landscape patterns (security patterns) to safeguard

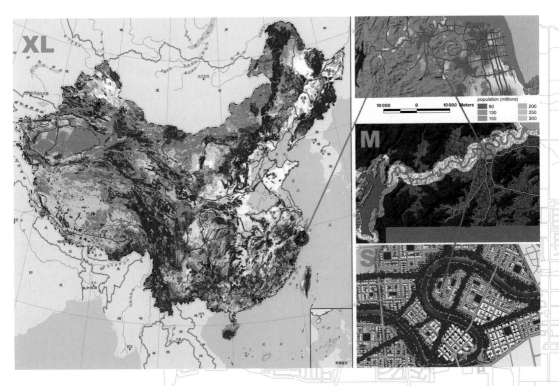

population (millions)
90 130 150 200 250 300

> The Floating Gardens of Yongning River Park: The integration of art with ecology that turns messy nature into beautiful urban green space.

Making friends with floods: The Floating Gardens of Yongning River Park apply the ecological approach to flood control and storm-water management.

The existing site of the Yongning River Park project

Big-foot aesthetics: Hardy native grasses replace concrete bank and are both beautiful and enjoyed by visitors.

the critical ecological processes; this becomes a framework directing regional land-use planning and urban growth patterns. At a medium scale, structural elements of ecological infrastructure such as corridors and patches are clearly identified and drawn to guarantee the integrity of the regional scale. At a small scale, the ecosystem services provided by the regional ecological infrastructure will be extended into the urban fabric and guide urban design for individual sites.

"Big-Foot" Aesthetics: Five Projects, Five Principles

A new aesthetic is required to allow the operation and appreciation of ecological urbanism: the aesthetics of "Big Foot" as an alternative to "Little-Foot" aesthetics. The following five projects were designed and executed by the author and Turenscape over the past ten years, demonstrating some major principles that define "Big-Foot" aesthetics, based on ecological awareness and environmental ethics.

The Floating Gardens of Yongning Park:
Make Friends with Floods

Modern cities that follow "Little-Foot Urbanism" are designed against natural forces, especially water. Nature's services, provided by landscape, are impoverished and replaced with man-made services. As an alternative approach to conventional urban water management and flood-control engineering that uses concrete and pipes, the Yongning Park project demonstrates how we can live and design with the natural "Big Foot" of water. We let loose the bound of concrete on the urban water system and took an ecological approach to flood control and storm-water management, revealing the beauty of native vegetation and the ordinary landscape. The results have been

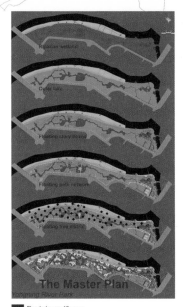

Flooded every 10 years
Flooded every 20 years
Flooded every 50 years
Existing water courses
Location of the park

The ecological approach for storm-water management was proposed by the landscape architect as an alternative to the commonly used concrete embankment and channelization. This proposal was finally accepted. As a result, the former engineering approach was stopped and the concrete-lined river was to be ecologically recovered. The Yonging River Park therefore set up an example for ecological recovery of the whole river.

remarkably successful: flood problems were successfully addressed, and "Big-Foot" native grass has been appreciated by local people as well as tourists.

The Rice Campus of Shenyang Architectural University: Go Productive

For centuries, universities have been places to gentrify the rustic young generation into the urbane, and the landscape as well. Hundreds and thousands of hectares of fertile land have been transformed into campuses of ornamental lawns and flowers in the past three decades in China. As an alternative, the Shenyang Architectural University Campus was designed to be productive. Storm water is collected to make a reflecting pond, which then becomes the reservoir to irrigate the rice paddy in front of the classrooms. Open study rooms are allocated in the middle of the rice fields. Frogs and fish are cultivated in the rice paddy to eat insect larvae, and once grown up, are harvested for the lunch table. This project demonstrates how agricultural landscapes can become part of the urbanized environment yet remain aesthetically enjoyable. This productive landscape is a clear example of the new "Big-Foot" aesthetic: unbounded, functional, and beautiful.

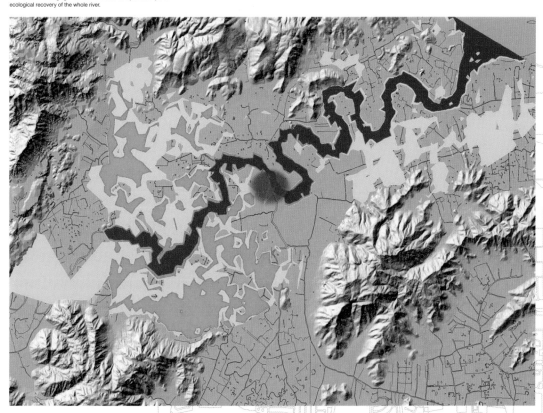

Zhongshan Shipyard Park:
Value the Ordinary and Recycle the Existing

For a long time, we have been proud of ourselves as human beings capable of building, destroying, and rebuilding. Because of this human instinct, both natural and man-made assets have been overused, and we are on the brink of a survival crisis. As an alternative approach, the Zhongshan Shipyard Park demonstrates the principle of preserving, reusing, and recycling natural and man-made materials. The park is built on a brownfield site where an abandoned shipyard was erected in the 1950s. The shipyard went bankrupt in 1999, after a remarkable fifty-year history in socialist China. The original vegetation and natural habitats were preserved, and only native plants were used throughout the landscape design. Machines, docks, and other industrial structures were recycled for educational and functional purposes. This unconventional approach made this park a favorite site for weddings, fashions shows, and daily use by local communities and tourists. It demonstrated how "messy" and "rustic" can be aesthetically attractive, and how environmental ethics and ecological awareness can be built into our urban landscape.

The Adaptation Palettes of Qiaoyuan Park: Let Nature Work

From Versailles and historic Chinese gardens to the contemporary Olympic Park, we have seen great efforts made to create and maintain artificial ornamental landscapes. Instead of providing ecosystem services for the city, public spaces actually become a burden on cities in terms of energy and water consumption. The Qiaoyuan Park in Tianjin City alternatively exemplifies how natural processes originate and lets nature work, providing an environmental service for the city.

The productive campus of Shengyang Architectural University

The site had been a shooting range. It then became a garbage dump and drainage sink for urban storm water, and was heavily polluted and deserted. The soil presented heavy saline and alkaline properties. Inspired by the adaptive vegetation communities that dot the regional flat coastal landscape, the designer developed a solution called the Adaptation Palettes: numerous pond cavities of different depths were dug, storm water retained, diverse habitats created, and seeds of mixed plant species sowed. A regenerative design process were introduced to evolve and adapt in time. The patchiness of the landscape reflects the regional water- and alkaline-sensitive vegetation. The beauty of the native landscape in the ecology-driven and low-maintenance Big-Foot aesthetic has become an attraction that lures thousands of visitors every day.

The Red Ribbon, Tanghe River Park, Qinhuangdao City, Hebei Province: Minimally Intervene

In the process of urbanization, a natural landscape is usually replaced with overly designed and gentrified gardens and parks. The Red Ribbon Park in China's Qinhuangdao City explored an alternative that integrated art with nature and dramatically transformed the landscape with minimal design. Against the background of natural terrain and vegetation, the landscape architect placed a 500-meter "red ribbon" bench integrating lighting, seating, environmental interpretation, and orientation. While preserving as much of the "messy" natural river corridor as possible, this project demonstrates how a minimal design solution can achieve dramatic improvements, turning a natural Big-Foot landscape into a beautiful urban park, while preserving the natural processes and patterns.

Let nature work: The adaptation palettes of Qiaoyuan Park, Tianjin City, that turns native vegetation into attractive landscape

The Big-Foot Revolution

La Tour Vivante, Eco-tower

soa architectes

La Tour Vivante (The Living Tower, 2006) integrates agriculture and energy production with the city through architecture. Such vertical projects raise pertinent questions about agriculture and energy production and their seeming opposition with the city, as something that happens far away. Why should spaces of food and energy production not find their place in the heart of the city?

Integrating windmills, photovoltaic panels, Canadian wells, rainwater, black water, ecological materials, and thermal and hygrometrical regulation, *La Tour Vivante* aims to associate agricultural production, dwelling, and other activities in a single vertical system. This system would, in principle, allow for a denser urban form around it while providing greater autonomy from horizontal plains, reducing the need for transportation between urban and extra-urban territories. The unusual superimposition of these programs makes it possible to consider new relations between agriculture, culture, tertiary spaces, housing, and trade, with significant energy savings and, potentially, gain.

Levels: 30
Height: 112 m (140 m with windmill)
Total area: 50,470 m²
Energy: photovoltaic panels: 4,500 m²;
solar hot water on roof: 900 m²;
a wind factory of two windmills on roof
Cost: € 98,100,000

Mixed program:

Residential	130 apartments in the first fifteen floors: 11,045 m²
Office	Offices on the top fifteen floors: 8,675 m²
Production	Horticultural production up to the top of tower: 7,000 m²
Shopping	Shopping center and hypermarket: 6,750 m²
Amenities	Media library and nursery: 650 m²
Parking	475 underground parking spaces: 12,400 m²

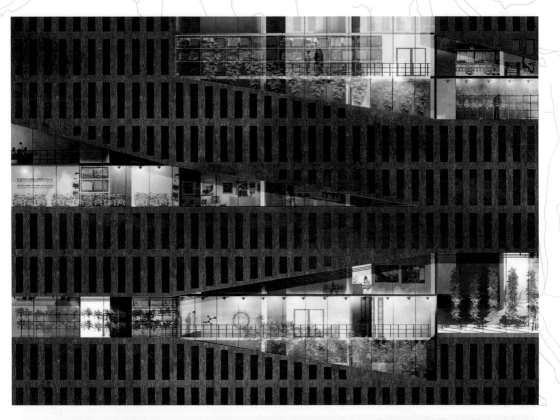

COLLABORAT

Management Challenges in Urban Transformation:
Organizing to Learn
Amy C. Edmondson

Air Purification in Cities
David Edwards

Social Justice and Ecological Urbanism
Susan S. Fainstein

Governing the Ecological City
Gerald E. Frug

Underground Future
Peter Galison

Temperate and Bounded
Edward Glaeser

Bioinspired Adaptive Architecture and Sustainability
Donald E. Ingber

Management Challenges in Urban Transformation: Organizing to Learn

Amy C. Edmondson

My research examines the human interactions through which decisions get made and work gets done to transform complex organizations. Complex organizations are those with many interconnected parts that must coordinate to achieve intended outcomes. Cities surely qualify, introducing the added complexity of multiple interconnected organizations—homes, workplaces, stores, schools, government agencies—that must transform in compatible ways to produce the sustainable urban systems of the future. No one knows how to get this done, but it is clear that it cannot be achieved without both innovation and collaboration. It is also clear that the transformation cannot be centrally planned and controlled.

Elsewhere I have introduced a distinction between *organizing to learn* and *organizing to execute*.[1] Classic management techniques, such as quality control or performance measurement, are designed to facilitate reliable execution of established procedures. These techniques are effective when solutions for getting the job done exist and are well understood. Whether for governing routine operations or for implementing targeted changes, organizing to execute means adhering to plans, eliminating variance, and avoiding diversion from prescribed processes without good cause.

In contrast, situations in which knowledge about how to achieve outcomes is lacking require organizing to learn. Here, managers seek to increase rather than reduce variance—promoting experiments and rewarding learning and innovation over obedience and accuracy. Organizing to learn comprises three essential elements: intense collaboration across disciplines, rapid iteration (small experiments that produce both small failures and small successes), and knowledge sharing (to propagate useful discoveries quickly).

Collaboration. Research on product design and development shows that a collaborative, team-based approach allows gains in quality, efficiency, and customer satisfaction compared to when specialties work separately.[2] Teamwork integrates functional knowledge—engineering, design, marketing, finance—forcing early discussions of trade-offs and allowing better design decisions. At the same time, behavioral research shows that diverse teams—those spanning demographic, status, expertise, or geographic boundaries—frequently underperform when compared with more homogeneous teams. It requires skilled leadership to ensure that the benefits of collaboration are realized.[3]

Iteration. Valuing failure and failure's lessons is essential when organizing to learn. Organizational innovation occurs when teams identify and test novel ideas through trial and error.[4] Yet organizations and professions bring social hierarchy, and experimentation brings uncertainty. Social hierarchy intensifies the interpersonal risks of experimentation (by their nature, experiments often fail) and of the brutally open discussions that follow. When leaders work to build a climate of psychological safety, however, rapid iteration can thrive.[5]

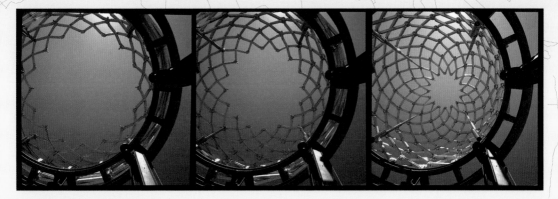

The Iris Dome at Expo 2000, Hannover,
Germany, by Chuck Hoberman. The
retractable roof opens and closes like the
iris of an eye.

Knowledge sharing. **Propagation of knowledge about what works—and what doesn't—allows complex systems to learn faster than through local experimentation alone. In the public realm, problems ranging from malnutrition to infection to crime are benefitting from the sharing of new, potentially better practices.[6] Companies with employees distributed around the world are also finding new ways to spread effective practices—combining the emotional richness of face-to-face interactions with the efficiency of intranet systems.[7] Increasingly, practices that work spread quickly.[8]**

Ecological urbanism, according to this perspective, will take shape through distributed collaborative learning. Cities must transform project-by-project (collaboration-by-collaboration), creating and implementing new technologies and new social contracts through which the promise of ecological urbanism may be realized. Designers must emerge as leaders engaging others' hearts and minds in the uncertain journey ahead.

1 A. Edmondson, "Organizing to Learn," HBS No. 5-604-031 (Boston: Harvard Business School Publishing, 2003), and "The Competitive Imperative to Learning," *Harvard Business Review* 86(7/8) (2008): 60–67.
2 S. Wheelwright and K. Clark, *Revolutionizing Product Development* (New York: Free Press, 1992).
3 I. Nembhard and A. Edmondson, "Making It Safe: The Effects of Leader Inclusiveness and Professional Status on Psychological Safety and Improvement Efforts in Health Care Teams," *Journal of Organizational Behavior* 27(7) (2006): 941–966.
4 A. Edmondson, "The Local and Variegated Nature of Learning in Organizations: A Group-Level Perspective," *Organization Science* 13(2) (2002): 128–146.
5 A. Edmondson, "Psychological Safety and Learning Behavior in Work Teams," *Administrative Science Quarterly* 44(4) (1999): 350–383, and "Managing the Risk of Learning: Psychological Safety in Work Teams," in *International Handbook of Organizational Teamwork and Cooperative Working*, edited by M. West (London: Blackwell, 2003), 255–276.
6 J. Sternin and R. Choo, "The Power of Positive Deviancy," *Harvard Business Review* 78(1) (2000): 14–15; I. Nembhard, "Organizational Learning in Health Care: A Multi-Method Study of Quality Improvement Collaboratives," doctoral dissertation, Harvard University, 2007; J. Seabrook, "Don't Shoot," *New Yorker* (June 22, 2009), 85.
7 A. Edmondson, B. Moingeon, V. Dessain, and A. Damgaard Jensen, "Global Knowledge Management at Danone," HBS No. 9-608-107 (Boston: Harvard Business School Publishing, 2007).
8 C. Shirky, *Here Comes Everybody* (New York: Penguin Press, 2008).

Air Purification in Cities

David Edwards

Toxic volatile substances emitted as gases from many paints, carpets, and fabrics often accumulate in the stagnant circulation zones common to indoor home and office urban environments.[1] Such polluted air can pose short- and long-term exposure dangers of particular concern today because classical HEPA and carbon filtration systems ineffectively remove some of the more notorious airborne gases, such as formaldehyde.[2]

Living plants are a traditional approach to managing indoor air pollution. But the natural air filtration capacity of vegetation, while effective at maintaining air quality within the global environment, proves of limited value in a normally ventilated interior environment without either a very large number of leafy plants–seventy spider plants for a 420-square-meter interior environment, according to one estimate[3]–or the aid of human design and engineering.

Outside, convection and diffusion send pollution past vegetation, where toxic gases absorb onto exposed surfaces, especially leaves, and are degraded by natural metabolic processes.[4] Inside, we sit and stand on, walk past and under, and sometimes even place our faces on the sources of pollution that contaminate the air we breathe. Indoor vegetation, though it may exist, generally has little chance to clean toxic air before we inadvertently sample it.

NASA researchers in the mid-to-late 1980s approached the indoor filtration problem by introducing the idea of blowing dirty air past indoor vegetation.[5] To improve air filtration, researchers redirected dirty air through plant soil, where root systems and associated microorganisms could provide a second degree of metabolic transformation. This combination of ventilation and soil filtration led to a series of early prototype living filters capable of cleaning dirty air.

If previous plant filter designs did not succeed as commercial indoor air filters, it appears at least in part due to the upper speed limit of filtration imposed by the need to avoid drying out plant soil while passing dirty air through it. Plant filters, designed with the basic functionality proposed in the late 1980s, are very efficient at removing toxic gases from the air, but their rate of removal is minor compared to traditional HEPA and carbon filters.[6] This makes plant filters effective when placed within local stagnant zones, though frequently ineffective when placed within robust convection patterns characteristic of most indoor environments.

Mindful of these constraints, we have recently approached the indoor air problem through the design of a living air filter that is both more efficient than the original NASA plant filter design and with aesthetic properties that merit display in many interior environments. The filter is of relatively low cost and has the easy intuitive maintenance traditionally associated

with plant care. Designed by the French designer Mathieu Lehanneur in collaboration with the author for the opening in 2007 of the experimental art and design center Le Laboratoire in central Paris, the filter Bel-Air directs dirty air through the leaves and soil of potted plants, over a water bath and back into the environment with a speed approximately an order of magnitude greater than the original NASA design.

Bel-Air was exhibited at the Museum of Modern Art in New York during the Design and the Elastic Mind exhibition and won a Popular Science Invention of the Year Award in 2008. It is now available commercially as the air filter Andrea. Plant filters such as Andrea are conceivable from small to large scale. Such a living filter strategy might play a role in sustainable urban architecture of the future.

1 L. Mølhave, "Volatile Organic Compounds, Indoor Air Quality and Health," *Indoor Air* 1 (2004): 357–376.
2 W. Chen et al., "Performance Evaluation of Air Cleaning/ Purification Devices for Control of Volatile Organic Compounds in Indoor Air," Syracuse University Report, 2004.
3 B. C. Wolverton, R. C. McDonald, and E. A. Watkins, Jr., "Foliage Plants for Removing Indoor Air Pollution from Energy-Efficient Homes," *Economic Botany* 38 (1984): 224–228.
4 Martina Giese, Ulrike Bauer-Doranth, C. Langebartels, and Henrich Sanderman, Jr., "Detoxification of Formaldehyde by the Spider Plant (*Chlorophytum comosum*)," *Plant Physiology* 104 (1994): 1301.
5 B. Wolverton, "Foliage Plants for Improving Indoor Air Quality," National Foliage Foundation Interiorscape Seminar, Hollywood, Florida, June 19, 1988.
6 Chen et al., "Performance Evaluation."

Social Justice and Ecological Urbanism

Susan S. Fainstein

As a term, ecological urbanism embraces three distinct branches of environmental thought: (1) environmental protection, which focuses on conservation of nature and opposition to pollution; (2) ecology, which views humans as enmeshed within environmental systems and addresses itself to human-natural interactions; and (3) environmental justice, which considers the impact of environmental change on socially disadvantaged groups and analyzes the distributional impacts of environmental policy. Consequently it allows the consolidation of what are rather separate social movements: middle- and upper-class conservationism; and urban-based drives for environmental justice.

Often both of these movements become reduced to forms of NIMBYism. Environmental protectionists use the environment as a rationalization for opposing high-density development and for insisting that undesirable but necessary land uses be placed outside their neighborhoods. Proponents of environmental justice reject these same types of development on the grounds that low-income communities are already overburdened with uses that no one else wants. It is important to reverse this reflexive negativism. The goal of ecological urbanism should be a program that fosters a form of development that people want and that simultaneously improves the environment.

The proposal within the Obama administration's economic stimulus program to create green jobs represents an attempt to bring the political force of the two movements behind a positive effort to create a more sustainable ecology and also promote economic expansion. It is an effort to reconcile what Scott Campbell has labeled the planner's triangle: the tension among property development, equity, and environmental protection.[1] Whether or not the formulation involved in green jobs works in practice, however, is still an open question. Such jobs are not necessarily good jobs, and green technology is not always aesthetically pleasing. For example, trash recycling usually involves immigrant laborers standing over a conveyor belt, sorting people's waste products, and requires garbage trucks trundling through neighborhoods to recycling stations. Wind farms endanger wildlife and result in landscapes that many find extremely unattractive.

On the other hand, initiatives do exist that embody a plus-sum game. For instance, as part of its plan for using federal stimulus money designated for infrastructure, the New York City government is constructing a greenway along the South Bronx waterfront. This part of the city has the highest rate of asthma among children and a severe shortage of open space. The new park will produce immediate jobs in its construction and ongoing ones in its maintenance. At the same time, however, New York has invested much larger sums in the creation of a new Yankee Stadium, also in the Bronx, which has caused the destruction of a popular park, provides extensive garage space for anticipated auto traffic, and will be a heavy energy user. Although the park will eventually to be replaced with a comparable amount of public space, the substitute will be less accessible. Environmental justice demands more than the occasional use of funds for developing greenery in poor neighborhoods. Rather it means the reallocation of spending by city governments so that the overall budget is not tilted to favor developers, sports teams, and wealthy neighborhoods. In the present economic context it calls for the use of funds to acquire foreclosed properties for affordable housing and greater expenditure on service provision rather than highway building.

In the long run, ecological urbanism must be based on the construction of compact cities. This means densification, which tends to be resisted by rich and poor alike. Since limiting peripheral growth raises property values in the center, equity requires that government intervention reduce housing prices for those who cannot afford the increased costs. It also demands ingenuity from architects and planners, who need to find spatial configurations and building designs that cause higher densities to be perceived as attractive; they must find new approaches both for developing commercial and residential structures and for creating inviting and available public open space within the denser urban environment. The windswept plazas of modernism so characteristic of public housing developments need to be filled in, while green spaces that appeal to a diverse mix of users must be created. A rethinking of the urban ecology so that the interaction of people and place is at once intensified, developed equitably, and made appealing constitutes the basis for a better, more interesting, and more just urbanity.

1 Scott Campbell, "Green Cities, Growing Cities, Just Cities? Urban Planning and the Contradictions of Sustainable Development," *Journal of the American Planning Association*, 62 (3), Summer 1996, 296–312.

Governing the Ecological City

Gerald E. Frug

There are many ideas these days about how to change the nature of urban life. These ideas, associated with terms such as ecological urbanism, sustainability, or smart growth, seek to reorient urban policy to limit cities' impact on climate change, reduce spatial segregation, favor density over sprawl, promote mass transit and bicycling rather than cars, and enliven public space. Architects, planners, sociologists, economists, and political scientists differ a great deal about how to accomplish these objectives. But, at least in the academic community, there seems to be a growing consensus that this agenda charts the proper way forward. One basic question, however, is inadequately addressed in the current literature: who is the audience for this menu of ideas? Who has the power to implement any, let alone all, of the items on this agenda?

The answers to these largely unasked questions are found in the legal system. Legal rules organize the way that cities are governed and thereby allocate power (or fail to allocate power) to implement the consensus agenda. The current version of these legal rules is hopelessly inadequate. Much of it is counterproductive. The most critical design problem facing urban transformation therefore is not the design of any particular building or neighborhood. It is the design of the city governance structure. Architects and planners are way ahead of the lawyers and policymakers in thinking about the ecological city.

The current structure of city governance fails for many reasons. I focus here on only one of them: the fragmentation of authority. Some items on the proposed agenda are allocated to state government, and others to city government. Generally, the state can—and often does—limit what cities can do on any particular topic. Other issues (such as clean air standards) are in the hands of the national government, and federal law strictly limits state and local decision making in the area. Others still are allocated to a multitude of state-created public authorities, and the separate authorities that deal with transportation, housing, urban development, and many other matters operate in an uncoordinated fashion. Finally, legal rules empower private decision makers to control important issues, with some issues (such as energy) subject to federal and state regulation, others (such as construction standards for buildings) subject to state and city regulation, and yet others (such as individual decisions about whether to drive or take the bus) under no regulation at all.

Consider the impact of this kind of decision-making structure on simply one ingredient of an environmental agenda. The State of New York has delegated to New York City the power to license taxis and limousines. To limit the impact of these vehicles on climate change (they drive around all day), the City's Taxi and Limousine Commission decided to require an upgrading of the emission standards of both fleets. Most environmentalists would consider such an intervention to be so obvious that it is not even interesting. The fleet owners, however, objected, sued in federal court to invalidate the city action—and won. Federal law, the court reasoned, prevents the city (and, for that matter, the state) from regulating emission standards; only the federal government can do so. Of course, it is quite unlikely that the federal government will adopt a policy that deals specifically with New York City's taxis and limousines. And if they don't, the fleet owners' objections to regulation will prevail—unless, that is, the city can figure out another way to accomplish its objectives.

No one seeking to further the goals of an eco-logical city would design this structure from scratch. The whole governance system requires comprehensive legal reform. Of course, legal change alone is not enough. But it's hard to see why even the best ideas about furthering the consensus agenda matter much unless the governance structure is designed to implement them.

The most critical design problem facing urban transformation is not the design of any particular building or neighborhood. It is the design of the city governance structure.

Underground Future

Peter Galison

Half a mile underground, 25 miles east of Carlsbad, New Mexico, lies a series of high-ceilinged parallel bays cut into a 250-million-year-old dried seabed of rock salt. Fluorescent light illuminates the center corridor-spine that bisects these bays, but that brightness fades quickly into the darkness down corridors to the right and left. Electric carts dart back and forth through a dry wind blown through the mine. In one gallery, a heavy-duty mining truck tears at an off-white salt wall, delivering bits to a parade of dump trucks. Far down a finished "room," an orange lift sits poised, waiting for a canister of dangerous transuranic waste to be lowered down to it, robotically. The machinery rotates the steel case, inserts it into a cylindrical boring in the salt wall, and seals it with a long concrete plug. Elsewhere sit rows of 55-gallon drums piled high and deep. Once each bay is filled, workers seal the gallery with a huge steel barrier, and leave it for all time.

This is the Waste Isolation Pilot Plant (WIPP)—a Department of Energy facility that will be the final resting place for plutonium and other long-lived contaminated materials discarded during the production of nuclear weapons that began at Los Alamos in 1943 and continued for more than half a century. The moment digging stops, the huge geological pressure at this depth squeezes the salt out into the dug-out spaces, surrounding and encapsulating the million or so cubic feet of radioactive detritus. Eventually, the slow creep of the salt walls into the cut-out voids—about 3 inches per year—crushing the waste and, it is

hoped, sealing it from human contact for the very long term.

This is the great waste of our civilization, the remains of the nuclear bomb-making that, at its peak, produced an arsenal of more than 20,000 warheads. Over the years, the planned target for nuclear weapons changed: first, it was to have been Nazi Germany–Los Alamos scientists thought that they were in a deadly race to get the bomb before Werner Heisenberg and his team of physicists and chemists. After the defeat of Germany, the target shifted to Imperial Japan: in Hiroshima and Nagasaki, World War II cascaded into Nuclear War I. Within a year or two of Allied victory, the confrontation shifted toward one of the United States and Western Europe against the Soviet Union and Eastern Europe–until the Soviet Union itself fell apart. Enemies came and went. Plutonium stays. And will remain: its half-life is more than 24,000 years.

By the end of the WIPP Site's first decade (1999–2009), the underground complex was about half full; if plans come to fruition, it will, over the coming few decades, be stacked to its design capacity. Although the vast majority of weapons-related transuranic waste will by then have been removed from production factories all across the United States–from Hanford, Washington, to Savannah River, South Carolina–the waste itself will remain dangerously radioactive for a time long, compared with recorded human history. And so, as mandated

Forbidding Blocks. Left, concept by Michael
Brill, illustration by Safdar Abidi; right,
concept and illustration by Michael Brill.

in the legal action that withdrew land for this
purpose, it is required that this place be marked,
that future humans be warned away from digging
here, for a period of at least 10,000 years.

Ten thousand years: some twice the time since
the beginning of human writing. How could
we warn our future 400 generations hence?
How to imagine our world? The Department of
Energy, through its Sandia National Laboratories,
commissioned a study to assess how this
might be done. Anthropologists, archeologists,
physicists, semioticians—a host of experts
worked to design a monumental marker that
would stand for us, for the legacy of nearly
100 years of nuclear weapons production. One
called for gigantic spikes, another for a black
surface that would become unbearably hot
in the desert sun.

But our attention is drawn to another of these
forever monuments designed for the DOE, one
that is in fact a city that is not a city. Titled
"Forbidding Blocks," the structure represents,
according to its creators, "a massive effort
to deny use," an "exploded landscape, but geo-
metrical … an irregular regularity … ordered but
not respected … too narrow to live in, farm in …"
A mimetic city without any inhabitants—or even
any real possibility of visitors—this was an urban
form of unpassable roads and unlivable blocks.

It is a terrifying monument put in place to
indicate that we were here and no one else ought
to follow, to show an unknowable 10,000-year
future that we have, knowingly, spoiled this
territory to save elsewhere. Perhaps this is the
ultimate ecological urbanism: a city of the
abject. An impossible city. An environmental
megalopolis on the surface warning of an
underground complex composed of the waste
produced in the making of weapons designed
to destroy cities. It is a site for thought—perhaps
the most elaborate, deliberate attempt to
create something that will last as close as we
can come to forever. In a peculiar way, it is
an optimistic monument. If nuclear weapons
are actually used in all-out warfare, there
will be other, bigger, more terrifying monuments
to our failure.

Temperate and Bounded

Edward Glaeser

What makes a city green, or at least low in carbon emissions? Greenness can result from low emissions technologies or more environmentally friendly design, but much of the difference in carbon usage across space comes from more basic forces, such as climate and density. If the world is going to reduce its carbon emissions, it would be wise to consider reducing those regulations that limit building in places with temperate climates, such as coastal California, and in high-density cities.

Matthew Kahn, an environmental economist at UCLA, and I have attempted to estimate the carbon emissions associated with new development in different parts of the United States. Using census data on spending, we estimate the energy used in the home through electricity, fuel oil, and natural gas. Using data on gasoline consumption, we estimate the carbon emissions in every census tract in the United States due to private car usage. We also estimate the energy used, per household, through public transportation. Using these estimates, we were able to calculate the carbon emissions for a large set of metropolitan areas, and for central cities and suburbs within those metropolitan areas.

Across metropolitan areas, we found that the greenest places were all in California. San Francisco, San Jose, Los Angeles, and San Diego had the lowest carbon emissions in the country. These places have mild winters and mild summers and unsurprisingly, as result, they use less energy. The highest levels of carbon

emissions were associated with the growing cities of the south, such as Oklahoma City and Houston. In these places, people drive enormous distances and use huge amounts of electricity to make hot, humid summers bearable. The older cities of the northeast lie between these extremes, with high levels of home heating but moderate driving distances and electricity use.

The odd paradox is that carbon emissions were lowest exactly in those places that restricted building most severely, often for allegedly environmental reasons. If America is to become greener, then there should be more building in San Francisco and less in Houston. If the environmentalists of California really want to help the planet, they need to fight for, not against, new development in their home communities.

Within metropolitan areas, we found that central cities were almost always greener than suburbs. The greenness of cities reflects both lower car usage and less energy use within the home. Typically, urban aeries are smaller than suburban McMansions and, as a result, they use less energy. Building up is greener than building out.

Henry David Thoreau, the patron saint of American environmentalism, was a great fan of living amid the countryside. But his life illustrates the environmental dangers of living surrounded by trees. On a spring day in April 1884, Thoreau had a picnic in the woods outside of Concord. He built a fire to cook a chowder and the flames spread to the dry nearby grass. By the time the fire was finished, more than 300 acres of woods had been burnt. This environmentalist did more damage to the environment than almost anyone who lived clustered in dense, downtown Boston.

The lesson of Thoreau's story, and of my statistical work with Matthew Kahn, is that being good to the environment often means staying away from it. Dense, concrete jungles may not look all that green, but they are, because when we use less space, we do less environmental harm. Cities are engines of economic progress, and places of great cultural innovation. Cities are also among the best tools available to reduce humanity's carbon footprint.

If America is to become greener, then there should be more building in San Francisco and less in Houston.

Bioinspired Adaptive Architecture and Sustainability

Donald E. Ingber

Ecological urbanism means different things to different people, but at its essence it represents the challenge of establishing a new order in architecture in which there is harmony between people, the buildings they inhabit, the cities they construct, and the natural environment in which they live. By contrast, construction approaches used currently are designed to create buildings that function largely in isolation and utilize resources in highly inefficient ways, which can ravage the local environment. We must therefore confront this challenge head-on if we are to sustain the natural resources and quality of life required for fruitful survival of our species. Yet it is unlikely that new applications of existing building materials and construction approaches will satisfy this goal.

One potentially exciting approach to meet this challenge is to learn from living systems. All living creatures–from the simplest single-cell organism to humans–have evolved ways to change their shape and function, and thereby optimize their performance in response to environmental cues, to survive. Humans build with structural materials, and then add separate systems for temperature control, plumbing, electricity, and communications. Nature builds with multifunctional materials that provide all of these functions simultaneously. Cities are filled with buildings that rely primarily on compressive forces for their stability; Nature almost always constructs tensile structures that minimize material requirements. Buildings consume huge amounts of carbon resources,

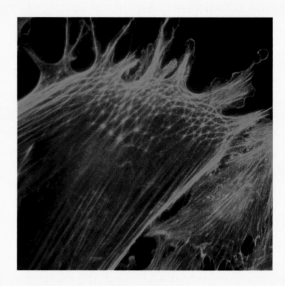

Living cells contain nuclei (blue) surrounded by an internal molecular lattice, known as the "cytoskeleton" (green). The filaments that comprise this lattice exert a tensional pull that stabilizes the cell's structure (here resembling a geodesic dome) using the principles of tensegrity architecture at the nanometer scale. This cytoskeleton is a multifunctional scaffold that gives the cell its shape and allows it to withstand applied mechanical stresses, while also orienting the biochemical machinery that mediates cell metabolism and information processing. Engineering artificial materials that mimic this multifunctionality could transform the construction industry.

and in the rare structures that have automated reconfiguration capabilities (e.g., louvered windows), structural transformations are driven by energy-guzzling motors. In contrast, Nature designs its materials so that they harness energy from their environment and spontaneously change shape through structural rearrangements that manifest themselves across multiple scales. So there is much to be learned here, and to be inspired by.

One can envision a future in which buildings are designed to sense environmental cues and adapt their shape and function to continuously optimize energy efficiency, light transmission, thermal gain, and other behaviors critical for sustainability. Imagine buildings covered with layers of small lenses that mimic how sea creatures concentrate light deep under the sea, but instead these illuminate photovoltaic cells or living bacteria that have been genetically reprogrammed to convert light into energy. Or what about houses trimmed with rain gutters that feed into microscopic capillary systems that work to raise water to a rooftop storage tank without requiring pumps or energy, instead using capillary action and evaporation like leaves in plants. Or perhaps someday we could construct roofs covered with a "fur" that exposes tiny hairs to prevent ice from sticking, collect water from rainfall, or harness energy from wind. At Harvard's Wyss Institute for Biologically Inspired Engineering, we seek to apply lessons learned from Nature, such as these, to design entirely new types of multifunctional building materials.

These bioinspired adaptive materials also can potentially bring a new aesthetic to architecture that combines the beauty of Nature's designs with the efficiency of their performance and adaptability. Chuck Hoberman, winner of the 2009 Wyss Prize for Bioinspired Adaptive Architecture, demonstrated a first step in this direction with his "Adaptive Fritting" installation at the Harvard University Graduate School of Design. His design incorporates a dynamically reconfigurable fritting mechanism to modulate the opacity of glass and thereby control light transmission and thermal gain. He accomplished this by engineering multiple moveable clear sheets layers, each containing opaque circles, that either align to transmit optimal light or move laterally to cover more area and thus fully restrict light

passage. This is reminiscent of the mechanism by which certain living cells found in the skin of amphibians and on the scales of many fish change their color by moving spherical packets containing pigment through the cell. The cell appears clear or light colored when all of the packets are concentrated at one point, where it darkens and restricts light transmission when the thousands of colored spheres are moved laterally and distributed throughout the cell. Although Hoberman's design did not have the richness of color, nor use rail-like microtubule tracks to move around his opaque circles as cells do, it shared the beauty of a living system in the patterns of its transformations. Hence it combined several key features of living systems into a single bioinspired adaptive material.

The problem of sustainability is one that will not go away. A new architecture that incorporates natural designs and biologically inspired materials and mechanisms offers a potential technological solution that brings the beauty of Nature to the fore as well. But making this a reality will require designers to work together with architects, engineers, and biologists in ways they have never worked before.

One can envision a future in which buildings are designed to sense environmental cues and adapt their shape and function to continuously optimize energy efficiency, light transmission, thermal gain, and other behaviors critical for sustainability.

INTERACT

Urban Ecology and the Arrangement of Nature in Urban Regions
Richard T. T. Forman

The Agency of Ecology
Chris Reed

New York City Infrastructure
Christoph Niemann

Redefining Infrastructure
Pierre Bélanger

User-Generated Urbanism
Rebar

Situating Urban Ecological Experiments in Public Space
Alexander J. Felson and Linda Pollak

A Holistic View of the Urban Phenomenon
Barcelona Urban Ecology Agency

Gwanggyo New City Park System
Yoonjin Park and Jungyoon Kim (PARKKIM)

A Methodology for Urban Innovation
Alfonso Vegara, Mark Dwyer, and Aaron Kelley

Greenmetropolis
Henri Bava, Erik Behrens, Steven Craig, and Alex Wall

Urban Ecology and the Arrangement of Nature in Urban Regions

Richard T. T. Forman

Whereas the field of ecology has a storied 140-year history, urban ecology is now emerging just in time for the "urban tsunami," the swift and powerful spread of urbanization across the land. Meanwhile, nearby nature and the natural environmental systems on which we fundamentally and daily depend are in rapid retreat. Thus the goals of this essay are to briefly portray the development of ecology, urban ecology, and environmentalism; outline several useful spatial principles to understand nature around cities; and highlight the distribution of nature and offer insight into its planning in urban regions.

Ecology, Urban Ecology, and Environmentalism

Ecology appeared in the 1860s in Germany, and by the 1890s was a recognized scientific discipline in Europe, tying together animal and plant ecology plus freshwater and marine biology.[1] It emerged in the U.S. Midwest about 1900, with a focus on ecological succession. Professional societies and journals were founded in 1912–15, and modern ecology emerged in the 1940s–1950s, highlighting ecosystem, theoretical, evolutionary, community, and systems ecology. Many subspecialties have evolved since the 1980s, including landscape ecology, conservation biology, and urban ecology. Fortunately, ecologists of diverse ilk have coalesced around a central definition of ecology, as the "study of the interactions of organisms and the environment."

Carrying the concept to the city, I consider urban ecology to be the "study of the interactions of organisms, built structures, and the natural environment, where people are aggregated around city or town." Essentially, organisms are plants/animals/microbes; built structures are buildings/roads; and the natural environment is soil/water/air. Urban ecology is useful for many allied fields, including sociology (people–people interactions), recreation and aesthetics (people–organisms interactions), architecture and transportation (people–built structures interactions), plus engineering and public health (people–natural environment interactions). Since 1990 urban ecology as an embryonic field has added sustained systematic team research to the ongoing insights of perceptive pioneers. Today's major urban-ecology approaches and centers of research include:[2] habitat/biotope mapping (Berlin), species types and richness (Berlin, Melbourne), urban-to-rural gradient (Melbourne, Baltimore), modeling and biogeochemical/material flows (Phoenix, Seattle), coupled biophysical-human systems (Phoenix, Baltimore, Seattle), and urban region structure-function-change (worldwide analyses[3]). Two decades ago environmental urban design had barely any urban ecology to use; today that has changed.

In a two-century history of society's "big ideas"—religion, science/rationalism, nationalism, hard-work-makes-land-productive, communism, and economic growth—the idea of environmentalism barely made a sound.[4] But it hit the headlines and became a household word in the 1960s–1970s, associated with a broad set of issues—wetlands, wolves, foaming rivers, and choking air—and in the wake of Rachel Carson's *Silent Spring*. Environmental organizations, political parties, laws, regulations, and some visible successes rapidly followed in developed and certain developing nations. International conferences and treaties further spurred environmentalism into our consciousness. Then suddenly in the 1990s–2000s, urbanization (especially sprawl) and global climate change pushed environmentalism to the forefront, as one of the big ideas of history. Ecology—with embryonic urban ecology growing rapidly—has emerged as a core field for societal solutions.

Spatial Principles for Nature in Urban Regions

The urban region (typically with a 70–100-kilometer radius for a city of more than 250,000 people) has a central essentially all-built metropolitan area, surrounded by an urban-region ring with inner and outer portions.[5] Is it better for people and nature to coexist in a coarse-grained or a fine-grained region (or landscape)? A coarse-grain area has mainly large patches, whereas a fine-grain landscape is an intermixture of different small land uses.[6] The former supports specialization, such as a city with opera and art museum or a protected area with bear and wild-cat, but requires extensive travel time and cost to access diverse resources. A fine grain eliminates most specialization, but supports generalists that thrive with multiple nearby land uses. To provide the benefits of both landscape types, a coarse-grain region with some fine-grain areas within it is considered to be the optimum design for nature and people.[7] Such a design provides a wide range of land-use resources, limits transportation time and cost, limits the amount of polluted area, and provides for generalists, diversity, and specialization alike.

Nature or natural system (i.e., what humans have not made or strongly altered) is present in certain areas of an urban

Four principles to understand and spatially plan or design for nature in urban regions

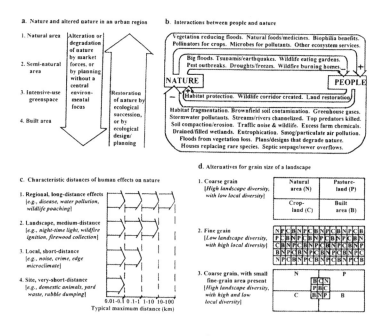

region, but much more commonly it appears in various altered or degraded forms.[8] Four categories, ranging from a natural area (almost "pure" nature) to an area with only bits or shreds of nature present, are easily recognized: natural, semi-natural, intensive-use greenspace, and built areas. A *natural area* is unplanted and without intensive human management or use (e.g., a relatively large forest or desert area with little human usage, usually in the outer urban-region ring). A *semi-natural area* resembles a natural ecosystem but is significantly altered or degraded, sometimes with intensive-use unbuilt spaces intermixed, such as a woodland city park or greenway. An *intensive-use greenspace* is an area mainly covered by plants that is heavily utilized by people or intensively managed or maintained, such as a grass-tree city park, golf course, or farmland. Finally, a *built area* is an area of continuous closely spaced buildings typically with roads and other human structures present, as in various residential and industrial areas. These four categories, from natural to built, represent a broad sequence of ecological alteration or degradation, where human activities decrease natural vertical structure, horizontal pattern, and/or flows and movements. Restoration of the last three types in the direction of a natural condition (which may appear quite different from any previous state) can occur by natural ecological succession when maintenance ceases, by human-accelerated succession, or by ecological planning.[9]

INTERACT

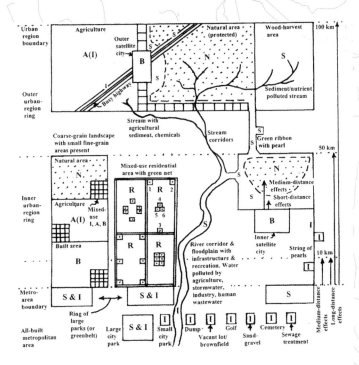

Arrangement of nature, altered nature, and people in the urban region. Many spatial and landscape ecological principles are illustrated. City within a basically all-built metropolitan area is at bottom; inner and outer urban-region rings above. N = Natural area (protected); S = Semi-natural area; I = Intensive-use greenspace; A = Agricultural land (one type of intensive-use greenspace in urban region); B = Built area; R = Residential area; 1 = Semi-natural parkland; 2 = Urban agriculture; 3 = Industry; 4 = Commercial; 5 = Intensive-use parkland; 6 = Government/civic/education/cultural/religious area; dashed line in a natural area differentiates significant edge effects and interior conditions.

The interactions or reciprocal effects of people and nature are central to understanding and planning in urban regions. The relative importance of the four options—people positively or negatively affecting nature, and nature positively or negatively affecting people—is the key.[10] People typically have rather few positive effects on nature, though these can be important particularly where nature is severely degraded. The positive effects of nature on people, and also the negative effects of nature on people, both appear to be intermediate in overall importance. Although some of these effects are highly significant, such as natural disasters and nature's (or ecosystem) services,[11] they seem to engender surprisingly little planning. Nevertheless, the giant among the four interactions is the negative effect of people on nature. The litany of these types of effect is familiar and exceedingly diverse, while the effects are nearly ubiquitous. This predominant negative effect of people on nature means that a fine-grain intermixing of people and nature is the worst design. Natural areas would be eliminated, leaving almost only intensive-use greenspaces and built areas across an urban region, a striking impoverishment of both nature and society.

How far do significant human effects on nature extend? Some, such as greenhouse gases, extend worldwide, but several long-distance "regional" effects typically extending 10 to 100 kilometers are of significance in an urban region.[12] Medium-distance "landscape" effects of 1 to 10 kilometers and

1 D. Worster, *Nature's Economy* (New York: Cambridge University Press, 1977); R. P. McIntosh, *The Background of Ecology* (New York: Cambridge University Press, 1985).

2 H. Sukopp and S. Hejny, eds., *Urban Ecology: Plants and Plant Communities in Urban Environments* (The Hague: SPB Academic Publishing, 1990); S. T. A. Pickett, M. L. Cadenasso, J. M. Grove, et al., "Urban Ecological Systems: Linking Terrestrial Ecological, Physical, and Socio-economic Components of Metropolitan Areas," *Annual Review of Ecology and Systematics* 32 (2001): 127–157; N. B. Grimm, S. H. Faeth, N. E. Golubiewski, et al. "Global Change and the Ecology of Cities," *Science* 319 (2008): 756–760; J. M. Marsluff, E. Schulenberger, W. Endlicher, et al., eds., *Urban Ecology: An International Perspective on the Interaction Between Humans and Nature* (New York: Springer, 2008); M. Alberti, *Advances in Urban Ecology: Integrating Humans and Ecological Processes in Urban Ecosystems* (New York: Springer, 2008); M. J. McDonnell, A. Hahs, and J. Breuste, *Ecology of Cities and Towns: A Comparative Approach* (New York: Cambridge University Press, 2009).

3 R. T. T. Forman, *Urban Regions: Ecology and Planning Beyond the City* (New York: Cambridge University Press, 2008).

4 J. R. McNeill, *Something New Under the Sun* (New York: Norton, 2000); Forman, *Urban Regions*.

5 Forman, *Urban Regions*.

6 R. T. T. Forman, *Land Mosaics: The Ecology of Landscapes and Regions* (New York: Cambridge University Press, 1995).

7 Ibid.

8 Forman, *Urban Regions*.

9 B. R. Johnson and K. Hill, eds., *Ecology and Design: Frameworks for Learning* (Washington, D.C.: Island Press, 2002); M. Hough, *Cities and Natural Process* (New York: Routledge, 2004).

10 Forman, *Urban Regions*.

11 G. C. Daily, *Nature's Services: Societal Dependence on Natural Ecosystems* (Washington, D.C.: Island Press, 1997); *Millennium Ecosystem Assessment: Current State and Trends* (Washington, D.C.: Island Press, 2005); Forman, *Urban Regions*.

12 R. I. McDonald, R. T. T. Forman, P. Kareiva, et al., "Urban Effects, Distance, and Protected Areas in an Urbanizing World," *Landscape and Urban Planning* (in press).

13 G. R. Matlack, "Sociological Edge Effects: Spatial Distribution of Human Impact in Suburban Forest Fragments," *Environmental Management* 17 (1993): 829–835.

short-distance "local" effects of 100 to 1,000 meters are common and especially important for urban region analysis and planning. Very short "site" effects are also quite diverse and important (e.g., at a neighborhood or finer scale).[13] Note that longer-distance effects also operate at shorter distances, so that a huge number and intensity of interactions between people and nature affect adjoining areas. This reinforces the importance of protecting large areas for nature and of avoiding sprawl. Some two-thirds of the human effects on nature extend to about 50 kilometers,[14] which roughly covers the inner urban-region ring of major cities.[15] This distance analysis conservatively assumes that the major city is the source of effects, but of course some sources are dispersed across the urban-region ring, so that the negative effect of humans on nature is much greater. Thus natural areas are most likely to be present in the outer urban-region ring. Also the degraded edge portions[16] of potential natural areas are doubtless wider toward the major city, so that protected areas in the inner urban-region ring must be very large to contain an interior natural area.

Distributions of Nature and Degraded Nature in Urban Regions

Natural, semi-natural, intensive-use greenspace, and built areas are arranged in rather predictable ways in an urban region. Natural areas tend to be scarce, with mainly large ones in the outer urban-region ring, and small ones in the inner ring where built areas are more extensive and edge-effect areas[17] seem to be wide. In contrast, semi-natural areas may be widely dispersed and include large city parks, some river-corridor stretches, green ribbons or greenways, active logging areas, and the edge portions surrounding natural areas. Intensive-use greenspaces characterize small city parks, parts of large city parks, diverse small-patch types (e.g., golf course, dump, sewage treatment area, sand/gravel mining), and agricultural land (including urban agriculture in the metro area, market gardening, and other urban-region-ring farmland). Built areas with bits of nature cover the metro area, as well as surrounding residential, commercial, and industrial areas.

The optimum coarse-grain landscape with small fine-grain areas present[18] is illustrated with natural, agricultural, and built areas. Large patches of the three land-use types maintain their integrity and specialized components. The fine-grain patches are communities of people with their food plots and small intensive-use greenspaces. Four communities surrounded by a green net[19] of corridors illustrate options for a fine-grain mixed-use area, in contrast to zoning for large residential areas. Each community contains frequent-use

14 McDonald et al., "Urban Effects."

15 Forman, *Urban Regions.*

16 Forman, *Land Mosaics.*

17 Ibid.

18 Ibid.

19 R. T. T. Forman, *Mosaico territorial para la region metropolitana de Barcelona* (Barcelona: Editorial Gustavo Gili, 2004); Forman, *Urban Regions.*

20 McDonald et al., "Urban Effects."

21 M. Mugica, J. V. de Lucio, and F. D. Pineda, "The Madrid Ecological Network," in *Perspectives on Ecological Networks*, edited by P. Nowicki et al. (Arnhem, Netherlands: European Centre for Nature Conservation, 1996); B. Babbitt, *Cities in the Wilderness* (Washington, D.C.: Island Press, 2005); Forman, *Mosaico territorial*; Forman, *Urban Regions.*

22 Forman, *Mosaico territorial.*

23 Forman, *Urban Regions.*

resources (e.g., shopping, employment, parkland), which are arranged together with different public transport/walking/biking systems for residents. Long-distance effects of people on nature[20] cover the whole region, medium-distance effects are especially important in the inner urban-region ring, and short-distance effects operate in the immediate vicinity of where people live.

The emerald network concept of large natural and semi-natural patches connected by green corridors is especially useful in most urban regions.[21] The corridors include stream and river (blue-green ribbons), green ribbon, and string (path), all of which are enhanced by having attached small green patches (pearls).[22] These connections are for the movement of people (locals and hikers), wildlife (indeed most animal and plant species), and water (in stream, canal, and river). Three emerald-network components seem most likely to persist in the face of ongoing urbanization (and climate change):[23] (1) large natural areas (because of their size and integrity), (2) river corridors (most rivers are too powerful to cover or permanently divert, and major infrastructure usually parallels a river), and (3) a string of pearls (by being a well-used path attached to neighborhood parks, both providing political support).

In conclusion, urban ecology, as a recent ecology offspring, offers valuable spatial principles in an era of growing urbanization and environmental consciousness. Natural areas are scarce in an urban region, but slightly to highly degraded nature is common and can be enhanced with planning and design. These natural systems are especially important in urban regions where they must serve so many people, providing water supply, one-day recreation, flood control, farmland, wetland benefits, soil erosion/sedimentation protection, biodiversity, waste absorption/breakdown, and aesthetics or inspiration. Proximity is economic value; nearby market gardening provides fresh vegetables and fruits for markets and restaurants, protected aquifers and reservoirs within urban regions provide clean water supply, and attractive greenspaces provide for one-day recreation and tourism. The future of natural systems and these services in urban regions lies in the hands of the designers/planners, or others, who will now step forward for nature and society.

Natural systems and their human uses are of central importance in urban regions where diverse green spaces and built spaces of essentially equal value intertwine. *Urban Regions: Ecology and Planning Beyond the City* combines urban planning and ecological science in examining thirty-eight urban regions around the world. Shown here are a selection of maps from the book. The core aim of the maps is to discover common or distinctive patterns of importance for natural systems and their human uses.

The red in the maps represents built-up metropolitan areas of different size. Dark green signifies forest/woodlands. Notice the proximity of city and major wooded areas, the forest providing context for recreation, streams, slope protection, and clean, cool air. The spigots represent water supply. The owls stand for biodiversity; strawberries, market gardening; and the sound symbols represent the noise of flying aircraft.

Determining the boundaries of urban regions allows us to see the primary zones of flows, movements, and interdependencies between city and surroundings. Alternative patterns of urbanization spread (including sprawl) are evaluated from the perspective of nature and people, using land-use principles extracted from landscape ecology, transportation planning, and hydrology. Spatial patterns for creating sustainable land mosaics are pinpointed, and urban regions are considered in broader contexts, from climate change to biodiversity loss, disasters, and sense of place.

This is an excerpt from Richard T.T. Forman and Taco Iwashima Matthews (graphics), *Urban Regions: Ecology and Planning Beyond the City* (Cambridge: Cambridge University Press, 2008).

Representative findings of the complete set of maps are:
– Only a fifth of the regions have greater than 80 percent natural vegetation cover around rivers and major streams, while another fifth have 40–70 percent natural cover. Cropland is the predominant human land use around rivers and major streams in almost all urban regions.
– More than half of the cities with nearby hill slopes or mountain slopes facing the city have 90–100 percent natural vegetation cover on the slopes, while nearly 30 percent of the cities with nearby city-facing slopes have them only 25–30 percent covered with natural vegetation.
– On average, reservoirs have the best drainage-area protection by natural vegetation, while drainage-area protection for lakes and rivers varies widely.
– A compact metropolitan form in a third of urban regions is the most frequent attribute, suggesting regional planning, and a ring highway in a sixth of the regions is the next most frequent attribute.
– Towns near borders of agricultural and natural areas are widespread, present in more than 75 percent of the regions.

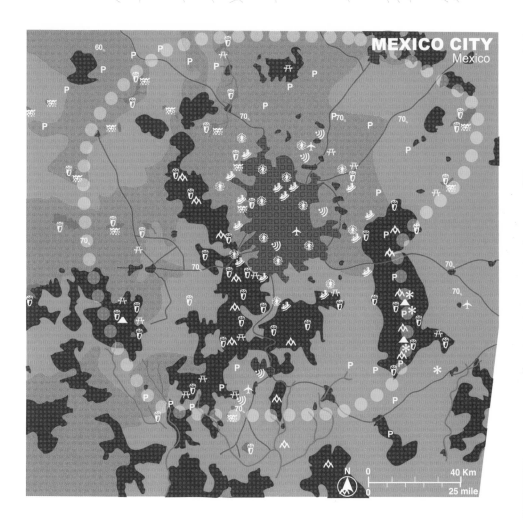

MEXICO CITY
Mexico

N

| 0 | | 40 Km |
| 0 | | 25 mile |

Cover Types

■	Salt water
■	Freshwater
■	Forest/Woodland [1]
■	Small-tree farming [2]
■	Cropland [3]
■	Grassland/Pastureland [4]
■	Desert/Desertified area [5]
■	Metropolitan area [6]
■	Small/Medium built area
—	River/Major stream
—	Multilane highway
- - - -	Paved 2-lane main road
....	Unpaved main road
▩▩▩	Urban region boundary

Site Labels

✈	Airport
☸	Air quality poor
🦉	Biodiversity area
🏘	Commuter residential area
⚓	Docks for shipping or ferry
∪	Drainage basin around water supply
🚋	End of commuter rail
🔥	Fire hazard area
⚓	Flood hazard area
🏭	Industrial area
🍇	Market gardening area for vegetables/fruits near city
⚒	Mining site
⋀⋀	Mountain range
·))	Noise of flying aircraft
P	Political/administrative boundary
⊤⊤	Recreation/tourist area for one-day trip
⚞	Salt flat or intermittent lake
🐚	Sewage treatment

🥾	Slope facing city
♳	Solid waste dump/tip/disposal/recycling
▲	Volcano
▩	Water quality poor
🚰	Water supply
⋅⋅⋅	Wetland
60₁	60% of distance to a smaller, but > 250 000-pop., city
70₁	70% of distance to a < 250 000-pop. city outside region

1 Natural/semi-natural growth or plantation forestry
2 Fruit orchard, coffee, tea, date palm, oil palm, or agroforestry
3 Cultivated/tilled area (e.g., rice, wheat, maize, beans, vegetables)
4 Grass-dominated, with or without livestock (paddocks/ranchland), or wooded savanna
5 Bare earth surface with or without separated shrubs/ other arid plants
6 Major city plus adjoining nearly continuous built area

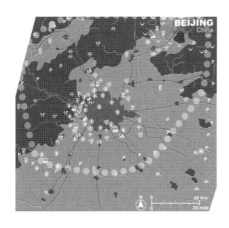

BEIJING
China

40 Km
25 mile

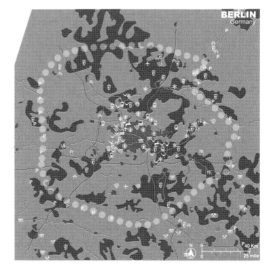

BERLIN
Germany

40 Km
25 mile

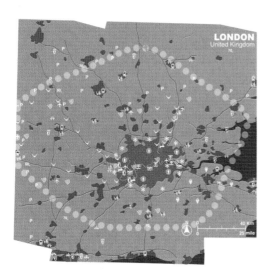

LONDON
United Kingdom

40 Km
25 mile

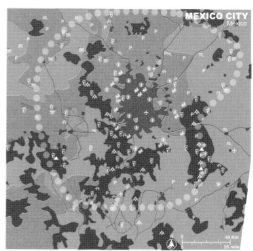

MEXICO CITY
Mexico

40 Km
25 mile

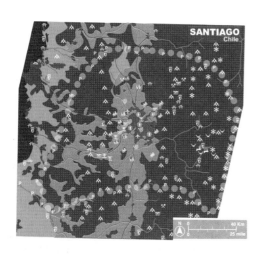

SANTIAGO
Chile

40 Km
25 mile

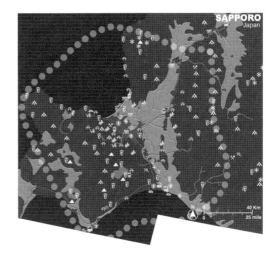

SAPPORO
Japan

40 Km
25 mile

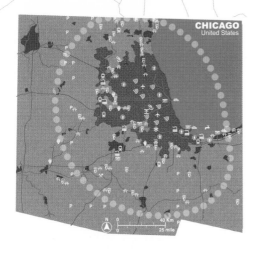

CHICAGO
United States

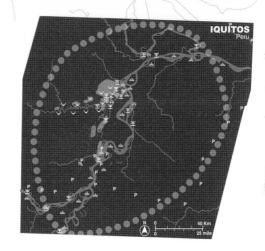

IQUITOS
Peru

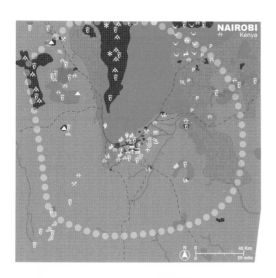

NAIROBI
Kenya

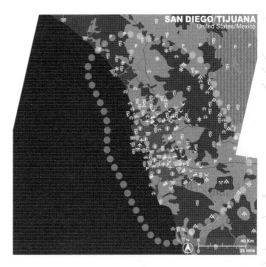

SAN DIEGO/TIJUANA
United States/Mexico

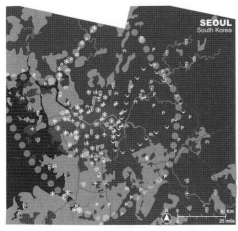

SEOUL
South Korea

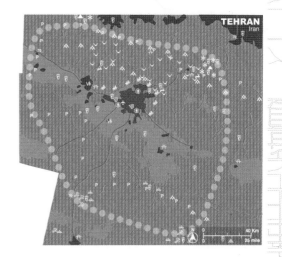

TEHRAN
Iran

Urban Ecology and the Arrangement of Nature in Urban Regions   321

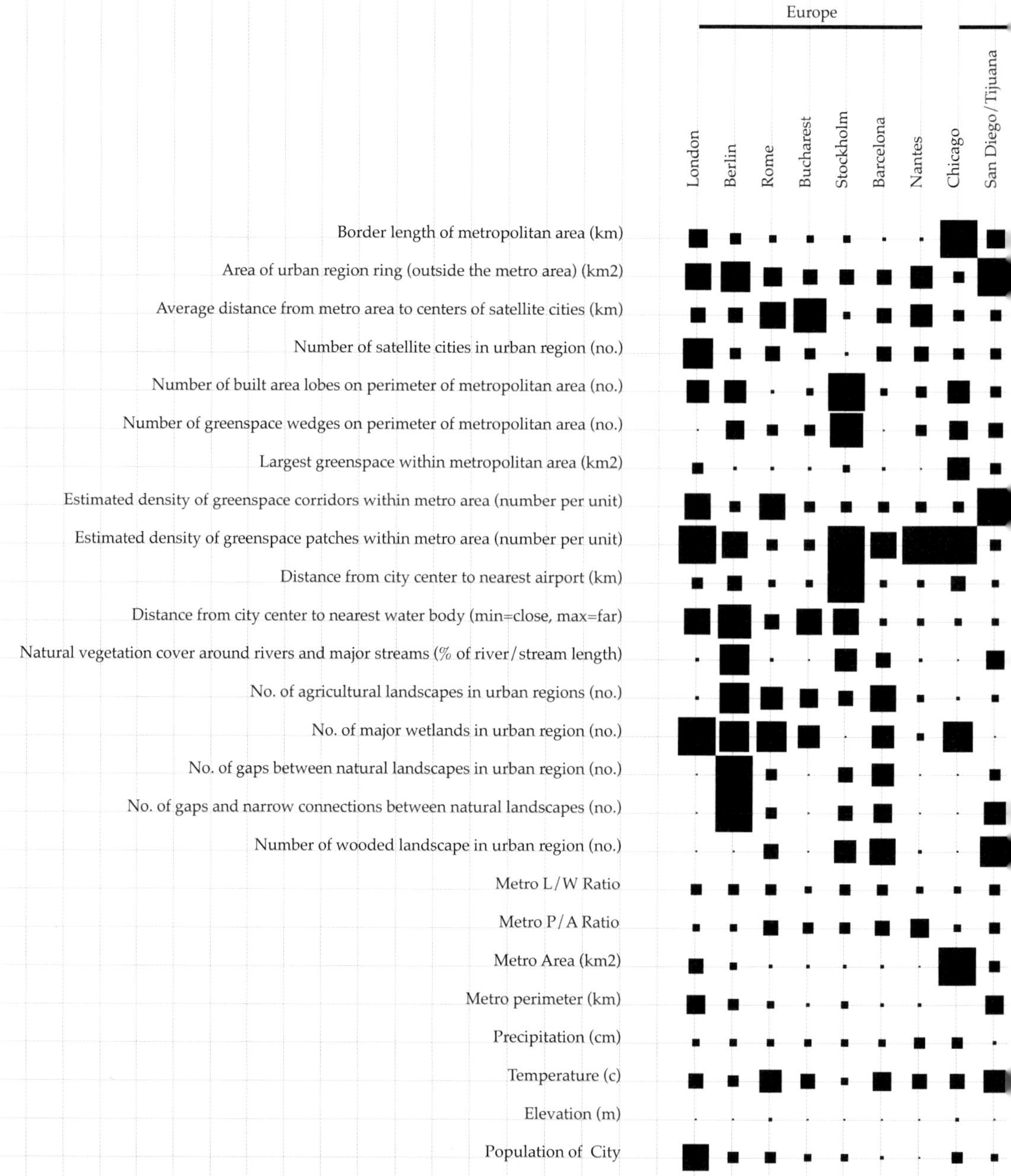

Europe

	London	Berlin	Rome	Bucharest	Stockholm	Barcelona	Nantes	Chicago	San Diego/Tijuana

Border length of metropolitan area (km)

Area of urban region ring (outside the metro area) (km2)

Average distance from metro area to centers of satellite cities (km)

Number of satellite cities in urban region (no.)

Number of built area lobes on perimeter of metropolitan area (no.)

Number of greenspace wedges on perimeter of metropolitan area (no.)

Largest greenspace within metropolitan area (km2)

Estimated density of greenspace corridors within metro area (number per unit)

Estimated density of greenspace patches within metro area (number per unit)

Distance from city center to nearest airport (km)

Distance from city center to nearest water body (min=close, max=far)

Natural vegetation cover around rivers and major streams (% of river/stream length)

No. of agricultural landscapes in urban regions (no.)

No. of major wetlands in urban region (no.)

No. of gaps between natural landscapes in urban region (no.)

No. of gaps and narrow connections between natural landscapes (no.)

Number of wooded landscape in urban region (no.)

Metro L/W Ratio

Metro P/A Ratio

Metro Area (km2)

Metro perimeter (km)

Precipitation (cm)

Temperature (c)

Elevation (m)

Population of City

Richard Forman's *Urban Regions* maps and analyzes thirty-eight urban regions around the world. This diagram, organized according to continent and a selection of characteristics of the urban regions, summarizes some of that information. (Diagram by Adi Assif, M.Arch. II program, Harvard GSD)

	erica				Latin America					Africa					West to East Asia								South Asia to Australia					
Edmonton	Portland	Atlanta	Mexico City	Santiago	Brasilia	Tegucigalpa	Iquitos	Cairo	Nairobi	Bamako	East London	Abeche	Beijing	Moscow	Seoul	Tehran	Sapporo	Ulaanbaatar	Erzurum	Kagoshima	Bangkok	Kuala Lumpur	Cuttack	Samarinda	Canberra	Rahimyar Khan

The table presents values in relation to the highest value in each criteria.
The highest value equals 100% (full square) and the other values are distributed accordingly.

The Agency of Ecology

Chris Reed

I write from the perspective of contemporary landscape, urbanism, and design practices, specifically as they may be informed by ideas of ecology and natural systems. Within this frame, I would like to argue for a fuller, more engaged approach to the ecological aspect of ecological urbanism—but not because I think it is more important than many of the issues that pertain to cities and city systems, and social dynamics and technology, that are involved in the work at hand. Rather, I see the potential of ecology to be a more complex and more provocative informing and formative idea (and force) for how cities are made, and for how cities actively evolve, reshape themselves, and are reshaped through time.

For me, contemporary ideas of ecology and planning can be traced to the work of Ian McHarg in the late 1960s and early 1970s, in which analysis and assessment of natural resources (geology, soils, water, habitat, etc.) could inform the best places and ways to develop land for social occupation.[1] Although the methodology can be easily criticized for its claims with regard to objectivity, and for its objectification of landscape components as things simply to be mapped and quantified, McHarg's methodology and practice opened up planning thought to the idea of the interconnectedness between cities/suburbs and the natural world: Design WITH Nature. Perhaps McHarg's use of the term "propinquity" (nearness, affinity, kinship) best characterizes his sense of this relationship between human and nonhuman worlds.

But even as McHarg's methodology was taking hold, new ideas about ecology were emerging. Richard Forman's research during the 1980s and early 1990s developed new understandings of and new terminologies for ecological systems, which were now described as matrices, webs, and networks, for instance, and which were characterized by adjacencies, overlaps, and juxtapositions.[2] This work importantly recognized the dynamic, living nature of ecological systems—not just the physical stuff McHarg was mapping, but how the stuff of the physical world supports the movement and exchange of ecological matter (water, seeds, wildlife). Others pushed these ideas further—in fact the field was shifting away from an understanding of systems that attempt to achieve a predictable

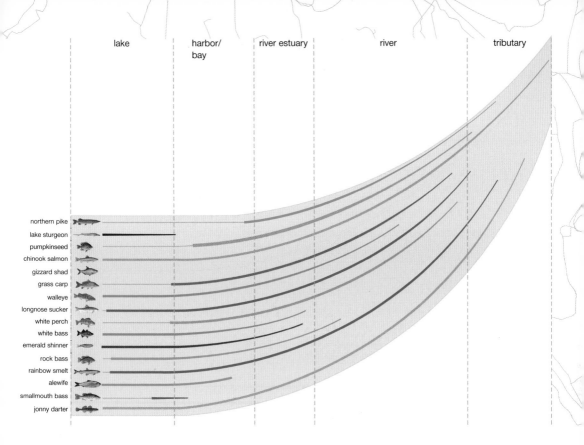

lake | harbor/bay | river estuary | river | tributary

northern pike
lake sturgeon
pumpkinseed
chinook salmon
gizzard shad
grass carp
walleye
longnose sucker
white perch
white bass
emerald shinner
rock bass
rainbow smelt
alewife
smallmouth bass
jonny darter

Fish habitat, Lake Ontario:
mapping of ecological tendencies
(that both river and lake fish breed
in the river-lake interface, or lagoon
marsh) informs the calibration
of design strategies for habitat
generation.

equilibrium or steady-state condition to systems typically in states of change, adapting to subtle or dramatic changes in inputs, resources, and climate. Adaptation, appropriation, and flexibility became the hallmarks of "successful" systems, as it is through ecosystems' ability to respond to changing environmental conditions that they persist.[3]

This shift opened new worlds for critical discourse in design and urbanism: Stan Allen identified the new ecology along with engineering systems as important examples of "material practices," which focused not so much on "what things look like" but more on "what they can do."[4] His work in collaboration with James Corner and the ecologist Nina-Marie Lister in Toronto's Downsview Park Competition of the late 1990s imagined the setting up of physical scaffolds that would sponsor the propagation of emergent ecologies, natural systems that would be seeded initially and then evolve with an increasing level of complexity and adaptability over time. Even the Downsview brief was important here, as it required entries to account for long-term timeframes (and a level of uncertainty) with regard to project evolution.[5]

With this as a backdrop, I would like to offer four trends or tendencies emerging in design practices that have taken on these revised understandings of ecology and natural systems as a basis for design strategy: structured, analog, hybrid, and curated ecologies.

Structured ecologies refers to the strategy of working with or alongside the stuff and processes of dynamic ecologies: the actual mechanics of how plants grow, behave, and adapt; the performance requirements of wildlife habitats; the movement and dynamics of the various waters present in a landscape. Like Corner and Allen and Lister, these strategies construct a set of physical scaffolds with varying conditions (low-high, wet-dry, sheltered-exposed) that can be appropriated over time by different plant communities impregnated on the site, and by different forms of wildlife. Such strategies anticipate a number of possible futures that may emerge specifically in response to a set of potential environmental changes (climate warming, sea-level rise, shifts in wind and moisture patterns,

Management framework, Mt. Tabor Reservoirs: Organization of project inputs, constructions, and feedback mechanisms allows for flexibility and adaptation over the long term.

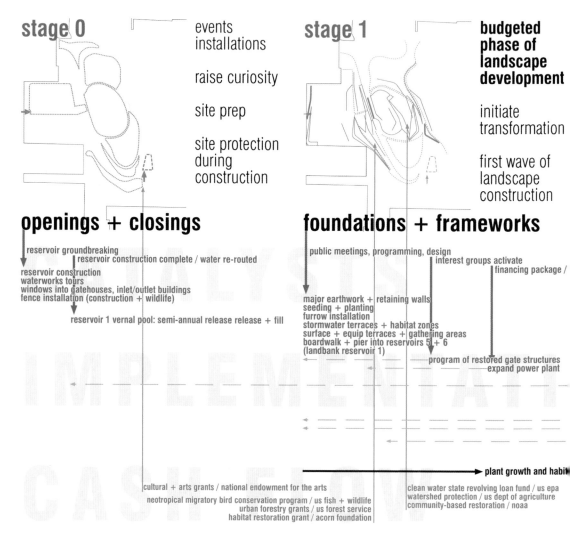

stage 0

events
installations

raise curiosity

site prep

site protection
during
construction

openings + closings

reservoir groundbreaking
reservoir construction complete / water re-routed
reservoir construction
waterworks tours
windows into gatehouses, inlet/outlet buildings
fence installation (construction + wildlife)

reservoir 1 vernal pool: semi-annual release release + fill

stage 1

**budgeted
phase of
landscape
development**

initiate
transformation

first wave of
landscape
construction

foundations + frameworks

public meetings, programming, design
interest groups activate
financing package /

major earthwork + retaining walls
seeding + planting
furrow installation
stormwater terraces + habitat zones
surface + equip terraces + gathering areas
boardwalk + pier into reservoirs 5 + 6
(landbank reservoir 1)

program of restored gate structures
expand power plant

plant growth and habit

cultural + arts grants / national endowment for the arts
neotropical migratory bird conservation program / us fish + wildlife
urban forestry grants / us forest service
habitat restoration grant / acorn foundation

clean water state revolving loan fund / us epa
watershed protection / us dept of agriculture
community-based restoration / noaa

etc.)—in essence, a structuring of natural competition among plant communities in ways that will allow the larger setting and systems to respond, adapt, and be resilient to change.

Analog ecologies includes projects that attempt to model, analogously, the responsive behaviors of living systems in nonliving constructions or processes: the ability of living things—entire ecotones, individual organisms, human skin—to react to changing inputs and to adapt their nature to the new or revised condition at hand. In architecture, we might think of responsive skins such as Chuck Hoberman's "Adaptive Fritting" project, a glass wall with movable fritted panels that changes as inputs fluctuate, creating shifting spaces/environments. In landscape, we might think of the design of flexible social spaces: physical scaffolds for the playing out of open-ended (but not unlimited) social and cultural—as

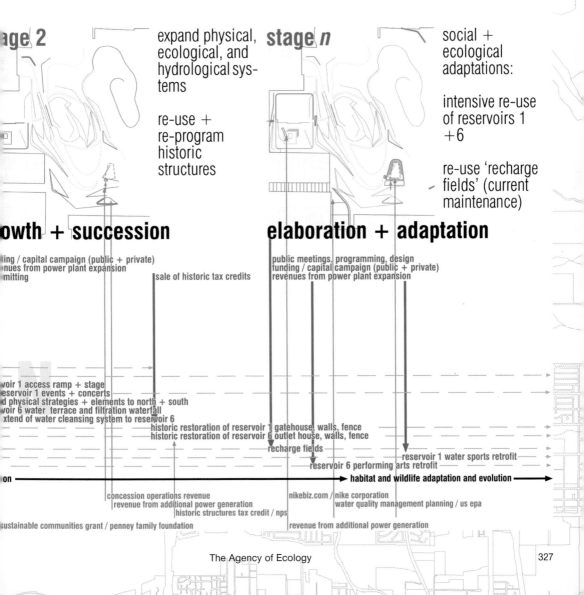

stage 2

expand physical, ecological, and hydrological systems

re-use + re-program historic structures

stage *n*

social + ecological adaptations:

intensive re-use of reservoirs 1 +6

re-use 'recharge fields' (current maintenance)

owth + succession

ling / capital campaign (public + private)
·nues from power plant expansion
·mitting

|sale of historic tax credits

elaboration + adaptation

public meetings, programming, design
funding / capital campaign (public + private)
revenues from power plant expansion

voir 1 access ramp + stage
eservoir 1 events + concerts
d physical strategies + elements to north + south
voir 6 water terrace and filtration waterfall
xtend of water cleansing system to reservoir 6
————historic restoration of reservoir 1 gatehouse, walls, fence
————historic restoration of reservoir 6 outlet house, walls, fence
————————recharge fields—————
————————————————reservoir 1 water sports retrofit————
————————reservoir 6 performing arts retrofit————
on ——————————————————————————→ habitat and wildlife adaptation and evolution ——————→

|concession operations revenue   nikebiz.com / nike corporation
 |revenue from additional power generation   water quality management planning / us epa
  |historic structures tax credit / nps
·ustainable communities grant / penney family foundation   revenue from additional power generation

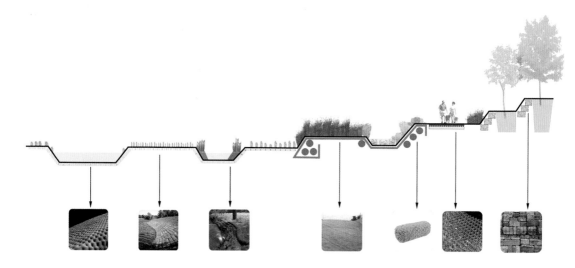

River section, Toronto Lower Don Lands: Hybridization of engineering systems–to maximize a full range of armored to porous surface conditions–inaugurates and supports the open-ended dynamics of river-marsh ecologies.

opposed to ecological—activities. And in large-scale, complex urban projects, we might imagine the setting up of responsive administrative frameworks; "if, then" scenarios; and management strategies that allow for feedback loops, input, and responsiveness over time.

Hybrid ecologies refers to the development of responsive design systems that tap into environmental, engineering, and social dynamics simultaneously—systems that engage both human and nonhuman dynamics and forces. Such systems are open-ended in the multiple ways they remain engaged with large-scale environmental dynamics (rainfall and drought, lake level rise and fall, plant succession, etc.), but they put human and nonhuman systems and elements into dialogue. These are strategies of conflation of social/ecological realms that reveal both their interdependence and their individuality.

Curated ecologies includes projects in which we might take on the role of curator, or producer of a set of dynamics that we structure and interact with over a period of time. The idea here is not simply to frame and set off a collection of plant and animal ecologies that grow untended, apart from direct human interference. Rather, the idea is to structure ways to interact with such dynamics—to curate an evolving set of ecological-urbanistic impulses and interactions not fully under one's control, yet which may be susceptible to productive pokes and prods, or recalibrations, in response to evolving intentions or inputs. Here the role of designer or planner shifts to one of loose but enmeshed project producer, activated intermittently as conditions demand and as these intertwined and engaged systems grow and adapt.

Most broadly, ecology can be a generating force, an active though elusive agent, in the structuring of the city and in the playing out of civic life—an agent that physically, mechanically, and constructively engages the various advanced technologies, public policies, and social and cultural dynamics in play. In all of these, the appropriation of the mechanisms and resiliency and even the language of ecology and ecological systems—in their multiple forms and manifestations, as mechanisms and/or models—forms the basis for a newly charged set of design practices: flexible, responsive, and adaptable as projects evolve and accumulate over time.

1 See Ian McHarg, *Design With Nature* (New York: John Wiley & Sons, 1967/1992).
2 See numerous publications by Richard T.T. Forman, including *Land Mosaics: The Ecology of Landscape and Regions* (Cambridge: Cambridge University Press, 1995).
3 Among the many ecologists and essays that address or articulate this shift are Robert E. Cook, "Do Landscapes Learn? Ecology's 'New Paradigm' and Design in Landscape Architecture," Inaugural Ian L. McHarg Lecture, University of Pennsylvania, March 22, 1999, and Nina-Marie Lister, "Sustainable Large Parks: Ecological Design or Designer Ecology?" in *Large Parks,* edited by Julia Czerniak and George Hargreaves (New York: Princeton Architectural Press, 2007).
4 Stan Allen, "Infrastructural Urbanism," *Points + Lines: Diagrams and Projects for the City* (New York: Princeton Architectural Press, 1999), 46–57.
5 See the full presentation of the scheme by Field Operations/Stan Allen + James Corner in *Case: Downsview Park Toronto,* edited by Julia Czerniak (Munich and Cambridge: Prestel and Harvard University Graduate School of Design, 2001). For a discussion of the competition brief and of the idea of scaffolding, see Kristina Hill's essay "Urban Ecologies: Biodiversity and Urban Design" in the same volume.

New York City Infrastructure

Christoph Niemann

The assignment I received from
the art director of the *New York Times
Magazine* who originally commissioned this piece was to illustrate
the complexities and importance of
infrastructure in our daily lives.
I wanted to use a very technical style,
since most of the elements have
to do with engineering of some sort.
Another important element I wanted
to highlight, though, was that all
of these technical elements end up
forming an almost organic system
that we all depend upon in our
daily lives.

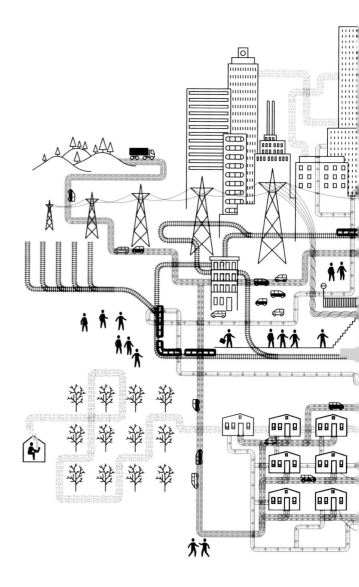

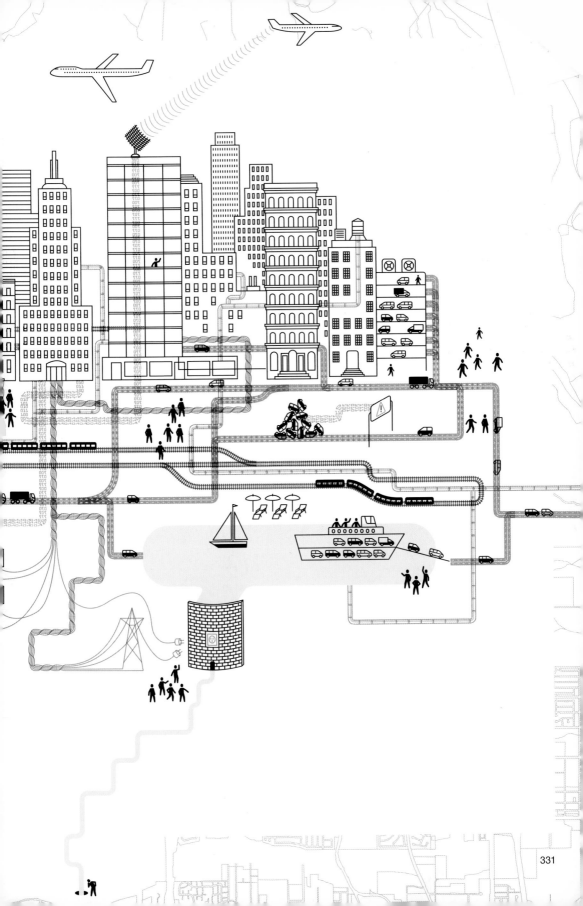

331

Redefining Infrastructure

Pierre Bélanger

Mature technological systems—cars, roads, municipal water supplies, sewers, telephones, railroads, weather forecasting, buildings, even computers in the majority of their uses—reside in a naturalized background, as ordinary and unremarkable to us as trees, daylight, and dirt. Our civilizations fundamentally depend on them, yet we notice them mainly when they fail, which they rarely do. They are the connective tissues and the circulatory systems of modernity. In short, these systems have become infrastructures.

—Paul N. Edwards, *Infrastructure and Modernity*, 2003

Cities are sustained by infrastructure. Highways, airports, power plants, and landfills figure largely among the icons of contemporary urbanism. The sheer size of these elements renders their understanding as a single system practically impossible, yet their smooth functioning depends precisely on their continuity to support urban and industrial economies. Often found underground, or on the periphery of cities, infrastructure remains largely invisible until the precise moment at which it breaks down. Floods, blackouts, and shortages serve as potent reminders of the fragility of this invisible background, which less than a century ago barely existed. Rarely do we stop to interrogate the functioning of this superstructure, but recent events—such as the rise and fall of water levels and the spike in energy and food prices—are instigating a critical review of the basic foundation on which North American cities depend. Reflecting current economic exigencies and ecological imperatives, this essay addresses this technocultural shift by reexamining the precepts of infrastructure—the basic system of essential services that support a city, a region, or a nation—as well as the patterns of urbanization from which it emerged, and how new regional pressures are requiring a thorough rethinking and reinvestment in this vast field of practice.

Crisis and Conflict

Conditional to the redefinition of infrastructure is an understanding of its antecedents. Historically defined as the "collective network of roads, bridges, rail lines and similar public works that are required for an industrial economy to function,"[1] infrastructure in North America emerged in the early twentieth century from crisis and conflict, rather than by design.

Flooding and Federalization. The first recorded usage of the term "infrastructure" occurred in 1927 during the Great Flood, arguably the most destructive flood in the history of the United States, as "the set of systems, works and networks upon which an industrial economy is reliant—in other words, the underpinnings of modern societies and economies."[2] Unprecedented rainfall throughout the Mississippi River Basin started in August 1926 and a year later turned into floodwaters south to the Gulf of Mexico, off the coast of New Orleans. The deluge was devastating: over 120 levees were destroyed, more than 165 million acres of farmland inundated, over 600,000 people displaced, and 246 lives lost. An estimated $230 million in reconstruction and mitigation projects were required, leading to the federal reorganization and reappropriation of levees and tributary lands within the floodplain under the aegis of the U.S. Army Corps of Engineers. Enabled by the 1928 Flood Control Act, the control of levees and waters expanded the operations of the Mississippi River

Urban flooding: Water level of the Mississippi River at 52.8 feet above datum in Arkansas City, Arkansas, on April 27 during the Great Flood of 1927

Public operations: Map of federal flood relief measures and reparation strategies along the Mississippi River in 1927 under the Hoover administration

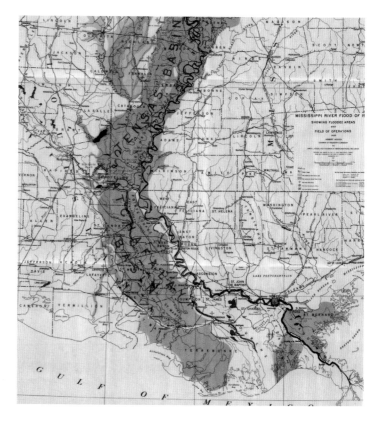

Commission, whose full mandate now included the management and protection of transportation structures (roads and bridges), resource protection (oil and coal), and future energy generation (hydroelectric power). Flood control became a manifold utility and underlying it was the hydrological region of the Mississippi, covering 41 percent of the United States.

Euclidean Zoning and Planning. The inception of zoning is central to the birth of infrastructure in North America. In a landmark U.S. Supreme Court case dating back to 1926, *Village of Euclid, Ohio vs. Ambler Realty Co.* (272 U.S. 365), the Court approved an injunction by a municipality to prevent the development of an industrial cluster next to a residential neighborhood and town center. Symptomatic of not-in-my-backyard arguments, the case led to the first legislated instance of urban land segregation,[3] from which precipitated modern planning by way of single-use, exclusionary zoning. Euclidean planning led to the widespread practice of land-use separation and classification. Its use became so common that, in the absence of regional or national planning authority, Euclidean zoning predisposed peripheral agricultural lands for future urban expansion. With the simultaneous rise of motorization and wider transportation corridors, land-use

INTERACT 334

Euclidean geometry: Spatial effect of exclusionary zoning practices in Euclid, Ohio, the birthplace of modern land planning, with Interstate 90 neatly separating residential land to the north from commercial and industrial land to the south (2008)

subdivision inadvertently enabled the insertion of transportation and utility corridors as buffers between incompatible land uses. Marking the birth of modern land jurisprudence across North America, zoning remains to this day one of the most instrumental mechanisms in the social, spatial, and economic structure of the North American landscape since the Jeffersonian grid.[4]

Urbanization and the Public Imperative for Infrastructure
In the background of flood events and zoning laws, two other major transformations marked the North American landscape: the urbanization of market economies and the regionalization of local resources. With the end of the Great Westward March and the closing of the Western frontier, urbanization established a definitive shift from a rural-agrarian pattern toward an urban-industrial one. The National Census revealed that in 1920, half of the country's population lived in cities and suburbs instead of rural areas.[5] The farming exodus of the nineteenth century marked a turning point: city populations exploded, especially in the Northeast and Midwest. America became urban. From the increasing size of dense agglomerations came a dramatic set of new challenges in the supply of essential services.

Effluents and Engineering. While flooding and land reclamation preoccupied the U.S. Army Corps of Engineers, the effective drainage of cities and towns saw the birth of an entirely new professional specialization: the sanitary engineer. With the Yellow Fever epidemic during the plague decade in the 1790s, the cholera outbreaks in the late 1800s, and the flushing of untreated sewage and dumping of garbage in water courses that served as drinking-water supply, the cities of the East Coast saw considerable cases of waterborne disease.[6] Three types of effluents conditioned the new urban discipline of sanitation engineering: groundwater, surface runoff, and sewage. The most illustrious sanitary engineer of the nineteenth century, Colonel George E. Waring Jr., advocated the separation of effluent conveyance, while acknowledging the inseparability of the planning of these components as a system.[7] From cesspools to illicit dumping, the uncoordinated methods of sewage management posed a clear danger to public health and prompted a reconception of two essential sectors of the urban landscape: sanitation and transportation.[8] With limitations placed on surface capacity, urban density privileged roads and streets for underground pipes (covered canals, buried streams) and subterranean facilities as the principal means of conveyance, doubling

Urbanizing infrastructure:
Integrated plan of sewage, trans-
portation, blocks, and open-space
infrastructure envisioned in 1876
by landscape architect Frederick
Law Olmsted and sanitary engineer
George E. Waring Jr., over Joseph
Ellicott's 1804 street system

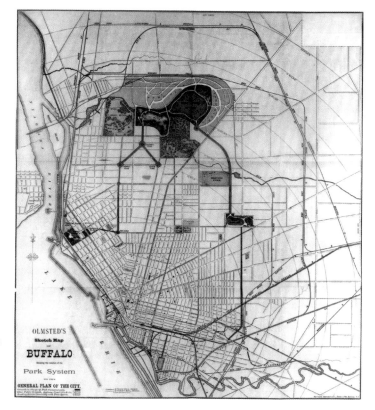

Modern systems of separation:
Engineered profiles of sewers,
drains, and closets for urban sewage
conveyance, from Col. George
E. Waring Jr.'s 1889 treatise, *The
Separate System of Sewerage
and Its Construction*

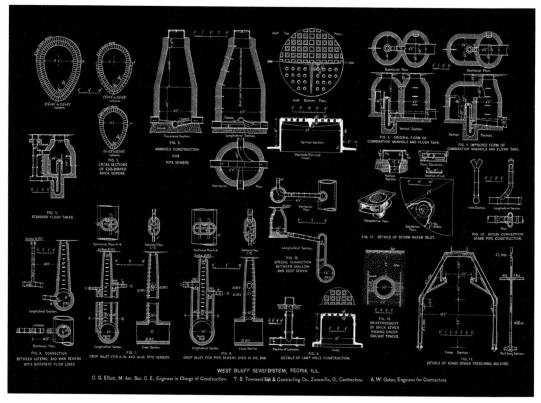

for surface transportation.[9] Simultaneously, the use of comprehensive city plans was fading, largely from the failure of urban planning to control the fragmentary expansion of large industrial metropolises.

Coal and Electricity. No other factor affected the nineteenth-century city more than electricity. Manufacturing towns in the 1800s relied on coal-powered steam for power. Inflexible, dirty, and noxious, heavy industrial activity was better suited to large, compact, central locations with proximity to railheads and harbors for oil and coal. Advances in electrical power enabling long-distance transmission radically opened up larger urban areas. Inexpensive baseload power could also be produced from cheap Middle Eastern oil or abundant Midwestern coal. Since 90 percent of the nation's rural dwellers had no electricity by the late 1920s,[10] electricity provided means for mechanization and automation. The widespread availability of electricity expanded working hours beyond the limits of daylight, and refrigeration of perishables completely urbanized the traditional food chain. By the 1930s, electricity was still far more efficiently produced in one large central location, but transmission over great distances enabled greater urban expansion and regional interconnectivity. Unlike the case for European cities, electrification predated urban development in America, leaving room to grow.[11]

The combination of sewage, transportation,[12] and power infrastructure put civil engineering at the forefront of planning and development. In the absence of federal or state law on land or infrastructure, municipal governments took on the task of development while engineers totalized the design process by embracing the metrics, technology, and construction of new urban systems. The groundwork was laid for the preeminence of a technocratic engineering elite that would soon come to dominate the twentieth century.

Roosevelt, Reform, and Regionalization

Retrospectively, the early twentieth century marked a turning point for urban America. The sudden crash of the stock market in the late 1920s, prolonged droughts in the Midwest throughout the 1930s, and the military buildup to World War II called into question the predominant history of laissez-faire economics and a passive role for government. Responding to the Great Depression, U.S. President Franklin Roosevelt swiftly rolled out the public works era of the New Deal between 1933 and 1935 by creating an alphabet soup of agencies empowered to kick-start the economy and reclaim land.[13] From the AAA (Agricultural Adjustment Act) to the WPA (Work Progress

Administration), the new federal structure addressed the two most pressing issues facing the nation: economic stagnation and imminent decentralization. Influenced by regionalist Howard W. Odum,[14] FDR foresaw the requirement for cooperative planning through the visible hand of government in energy production and soil conservation, housing development and highway construction.

Private Roads to Public Highways. The late 1920s was a turning point for urbanization. The inflexible, centralized structure of industrial cities and heavy manufacturing industrial towns was unlocked by three simultaneous technological shifts: increasing speeds in truck transport, expanding reach of electricity, and the explosion of automobility. Commonly attributed to his second successor, the continental highway

Public roads as public works: The first issue of *Public Roads* magazine was released in 1918, after the inception of the 1916 Federal Road Act and the Bureau of Public Roads authorizing for the first time funds for transportation originally administered by the Department of Agriculture.

The president as planner: Franklin D. Roosevelt and Wally Richards overlooking a comprehensive plan while touring Greenbelt, Maryland, one of three suburbs planned by the Resettlement Administration of the New Deal in the late 1930s

Super-planning: Public exhibition opening of the systemic configuration of National Highways planned under the Federal-Aid Highway Act of 1956 under Dwight D. Eisenhower, the successor to FDR's Interregional System of Toll-Free Highways consisting of seven east-axis and three north-south linkages

Master planner: Pioneer of the relation of forests, streamflow, and flood control, Dr. Raphael Zon with his 1933 proposal for a cross-continental forest shelter belt in the Great Plains following the Rocky Mountain Range

system was the legacy of FDR's New Deal. By the late 1930s, pressure for constructing a network of highways was building. The agony of farm-to-market dirt paths and privately owned toll roads posed significant obstacles to regional mobility and communication. Free roads were synonymous with freedom and democracy.[15] Opposing the private control of roads yet cautious of eminent domain,[16] FDR saw the 41,000-mile interregional urban network that he conceived as the spine of a new urban network for the decentralization of cities and the development of new greenbelt housing settlements. Set back by World War II, FDR's plan for the largest, greatest public works project in the world was resumed by Eisenhower in 1956 as the U.S. Interstate and Defense Highway System.[17]

Crops and Conservation. What motorization did for cities, mechanization did for agriculture. Mowers, reapers, and plows were replaced with the gas-powered tractor, accelerating food production and boosting rural economies. With the use of less manpower, yields skyrocketed but low crop prices and high machinery costs forced farmers to work more land, of lesser quality, to pay off new equipment debts. Meager economic conditions during the Great Depression pushed cost-cutting further. Cash crops of corn, wheat, and oats took precedence, while well-known soil conservation practices were abandoned. From the Canadian Prairies to the Panhandles in the Southern United States, grasslands became vulnerable to the dangers of drought and wind storms—a looming prelude to the decade of the Dust Bowl. Affecting more than 75 percent of the country across twenty-seven states, the farming crisis resulted in a New Deal program to regulate farming practices, diversify

Soil tsunami: Biblical in proportion, the wall of dust and darkness approaching Stratford, Texas, on April 18, 1935, when droughts and tornadoes hit the Dust Bowl after decades of ruthless, unregulated land-farming practices across the U.S. Midwest and Canada during the 1930s

crops, and manage yields. The Soil Conservation Law in 1935 further tackled soil and moisture loss with the Great Shelter Belt Project, involving over 200 million trees to establish a 100-mile-wide, 1,200-mile-long windbreak from Alberta to Texas. Preemptive measures included crop rotation, strip farming, contour plowing, and terracing toward diversifying the crop cover for feedstock, and regional grain cooperatives were formed to help farmers pool their purchasing power. Uncoordinated, ruthless practices of self-guided farmers came to an end by a federally regulated system of soil conservation known today as the Natural Resources Conservation Service.[18]

Private Utilities to Public Power. The late 1920s was a terminus for power speculators. The trust-busting Public Utility Holding Company Act of 1935 burst the bubble on underregulated, overinflated privately held holding companies. Utility giants Wilbur Foshay, Samuel Insull, and George Ohrstrom either went bankrupt or fled the country.[19] In a famous catchphrase, "Power for Defense," FDR saw a major opportunity to combine his agenda of recovery-relief-reform with the production and supply of power in the Tennessee Valley Authority (TVA). Informed by the Connecticut Valley Power Exchange (CONVEX) formed earlier in 1922, the TVA's mandate combined public and private objectives as a model of regional planning never seen before in the United States. Under the guidance of Arthur Morgan and Benton Mackaye, the TVA managed the nation's fifth-largest river system to reduce flood damage, produce power, maintain navigation, provide recreational opportunities, and protect water quality in the 41,000-square-mile watershed.

Region as infrastructure: Display panel of the TVA showing the watershed boundary crossing through seven states as a complex system, whose mandate included flood control, electricity generation, fertilizer manufacturing, and economic development of public resources and private lands throughout the Tennessee Valley

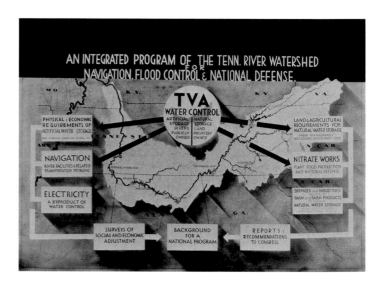

Making planning an imperative, FDR realigned the role of public governance and instituted a decisive shift in the prevailing dynasty of private, localized control of land resources.[20] With the Defense Act in place by 1916, FDR's public plans and programmatic innovations in the 1930s became the blueprint for an interregional infrastructure where farm fields, drainage systems, transportation networks, power plants, and energy grids became matters of national social security.

Deregulation, Divestment, Decline, and Decay

In the context of an overheated postwar economy, the U.S. population doubled from 125 million to 250 million between 1950 and 1990, placing excessive pressure on the demand for public services. A major shift occurred in federal governance and public infrastructure in the early 1980s under the Reagan administration. Mirroring Margaret Thatcher's methods in Great Britain, Ronald Reagan laid the groundwork for deregulation and divestment to kick-start a stagnating economy. To reduce the national deficit, Reagan's strategy relied on corporate tax cutting and privatization of public services.[21] From military manufacturing to energy generation, no public sector was spared. In the footsteps of his predecessor Jimmy Carter, who deregulated the transportation sector, Reagan started with the oil and gas industry in the 1980s. Reversing FDR's legacy, privatization effectively snowballed after Reagan, paving the way for the outsourcing of public services by successive administrations for the next three decades.[22, 23]

Underlying this deregulatory legacy inherited from Reagan's supply-based economics is the decay of urban infrastructure.[24] Privatization of public services extended well into the

Neglect, by design: From faulty design and lack of maintenance, the collapse of Bridge 9340 carrying Interstate 35W across the Mississippi River in Minneapolis, Minnesota, during evening rush hour on August 1, 2007

Learning from failure and disaster:
A timeline identifying the major
urban-regional disasters during the
past century including hurricanes,
droughts, and floods in response
to the occupational hazards of
engineered infrastructure such as
levee breaks, bridge collapses,
and chemical spills

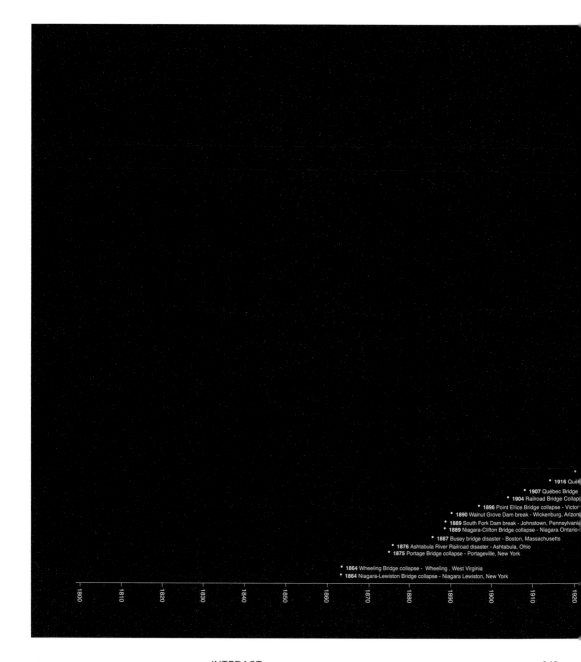

* **1916** Qué
* **1907** Québec Bridge
* **1904** Railroad Bridge Collap
* **1896** Point Ellice Bridge collapse - Victor
* **1890** Walnut Grove Dam break - Wickenburg, Arizon
* **1889** South Fork Dam break - Johnstown, Pennsylvani
* **1889** Niagara-Clifton Bridge collapse - Niagara Ontario-
* **1887** Busey bridge disaster - Boston, Massachusetts
* **1876** Ashtabula River Railroad disaster - Ashtabula, Ohio
* **1875** Portage Bridge collapse - Portageville, New York

* **1864** Wheeling Bridge collapse - Wheeling , West Virginia
* **1864** Niagara-Lewiston Bridge collapse - Niagara Lewiston, New York

1800 1810 1820 1830 1840 1850 1860 1870 1880 1890 1900 1910 1920

- 2008 **TVA Kingston Fossil Plant coal fly ash slurry spill - Roane County,**
  - 2008 Fernley Levee failure - Fernley, Nevada
  - 2008 Little Calumet River levee breach - Munster, Indiana
  - 2008 The Cedar Rapids and Iowa City Railway bridge collapse - Cedar Rapids, Iowa
  - 2007 MacArthur Maze flyover collapse - Oakland, California
  - 2007 Harp Road bridge collapse - Oakville, Washington
  - 2007 I-35W bridge collapse, Minneapolis, Minnesota
  - 2006 Highway 19 overpass (De la Concorde Overpass collapse) - Laval, Québec
- 2005 **CN Rail caustic soda spill - Cheakamus River, British Columbia**
  - 2005 Taum Sauk reservoir break - Lesterville, Missouri
  - 2005 New Orleans Katrina levee failures - New Orleans, Louisiana
  - 2004 Jones Tract levee breach - Sacramento-San Joaquin Delta
  - 2004 Big Nickel Road Bridge collapse - Sudbury, Ontario
  - 2004 Igor I. Sikorsky Memorial Bridge collapse - Stratford, Connecticut
  - 2004 Big Bay Dam breach- Purvis, Mississippi
  - 2003 Sgt. Aubrey Cosens VC Memorial Bridge collapse - Latchford, Ontario
  - 2003 Kinzua Bridge collapse - Kinzua Bridge State Park, Pennsylvania
  - 2003 Interstate 95 Howard Avenue Overpass collapse - Bridgeport, Connecticut
  - 2002 I-40 bridge collapse - Webbers Falls, Oklahoma
  - 2001 Queen Isabella Causeway - South Padre Island, Texas
- 2000 **The Martin County Sludge Spill - Martin County, Kentucky**
  - 2000 Pier No. 34 Collapse - Philadelphia, Pennsylvania
  - 2000 Hoan Bridge Collapse - Milwaukee, Wisconsin
- 1999 **Aamjiwnaang First Nation chemical poisoning - Sarnia, Ontario**
  - 1997 Feather River Levee Collapse - Arboga, California
  - 1993 CSXT Big Bayou Canot rail bridge collapse - Mobile, Alabama
  - 1993 Claiborne Avenue Bridge collapse - New Orleans, Louisiana
- 1992 **Summitville Mine leakage - Rio Grande**
  - 1989 San Francisco – Oakland Bay Bridge Deck Collapse - San Francisco, California
  - 1989 Cypress Street Viaduct collapse - Oakland, California
  - 1989 Tennessee Hatchie River Bridge collapse - Memphis, Tennessee
  - 1987 Schoharie Creek Bridge Thruway collapse - Fort Hunter, New York
  - 1983 Mianus River Bridge Collapse - Greenwich, Connecticut
  - 1982 14th Street Bridge Air Florida Crash - Arlington, Virginia – Washington, DC
  - 1982 Lawn Lake Dam break - Rocky Mountain National Park, Colorado
- 1982 **Berkeley Pit Mine spill groundwater pollution, Butte, Montana**
  - 1981 Hyatt Regency walkway collapse - Kansas City, Missouri
  - 1980 Sunshine Skyway Bridge collapse - St. Petersburg, Florida
- 1979 **Three Mile Island Nuclear Reactor meltdown - Harrisburg, Pennsylvania**
- 1978 **Love Canal Chemical Dump leaking - New York State**
  - 1977 Kelly Barnes Dam break - Toccoa, Georgia.
  - 1976 Teton Dam break - Teton, Idaho
  - 1972 Buffalo Creek breach and flood - Logan County, West Virginia
  - 1972 Sidney Lanier Bridge- Brunswick, Georgia
- 1970 **Ontario Minamata mercury poisoning - Dryden, Ontario**
- 1969 **13th Cuyahoga River Ignition and conflagration, Ohio**
  - 1967 Silver Bridge collapse - Point Pleasant, West Virginia - Kanauga, Ohio
  - 1967 Point Pleasant Bridge collapse, - Pleasent River, Ohio
  - 1966 Heron Road Bridge collapse- Ottawa, Ontario
  - 1963 Baldwin Hills Reservoir breach - Los Angeles, California
  - 1958 Second Narrows Bridge collapse - Vancouver, British Columbia
- 1956 **Basin F Shell Chemical Company spill – Denver. Colorado**
  - 1955 Feather River Levee breach - Yuba City, California
  - 1951 Duplessis bridge collapse - Québec City, Québec
  - 1942 Chesapeake City Bridge collapse - Chesapeake City, Maryland
  - 1940 Tacoma Narrows Bridge (Galloping Gertie) collapse - Tacoma, Washington
  - 1939 Bronx-Whitestone Bridge collapse - Bronx, New York
  - 1938 Thousand Islands Bridge oscillation - Thousand Islands, Ontario
  - 1938 Upper Steel Arch Bridge (Falls View Bridge) collapse - Niagara Falls, NY – Niagara Falls, ON
  - 1937 Golden Gate Bridge oscillation - San Francisco, California
  - 1935 Appomatox River Drawbridge collapse - Hopewell, Virginia

28 St. Francis Dam break - Valencia, California
he Great Mississippi Flood Levee Breaches across 10 states
asses Disaster - Boston, Massachusetts
e - Québec City, Québec
c City, Québec
do
ia

1940 1950 1960 1970 1980 1990 2000 2010 2020 2030 2040

Tipping point: Aerial view of the TVA Kingston Fossil Plant at the confluence of the Emory River and Clinch River in Tennessee, where 4 million cubic meters (1 billion gallons) of coal fly ash slurry were spilled after a dike rupture on Monday, December 22, 2008

ownership of public assets and management of public works, crystallizing the nation's silent crisis today.[25] A major network of postwar infrastructures—airports, harbors, roads, sewers, bridges, dikes, dams, power corridors, terminals, treatment plants—are now suffering from lack of repair and maintenance. Recent bridge collapses in Minnesota and Montreal, and the prolonged effects of Hurricane Katrina, are symptoms of the hidden costs associated with privatization of public infrastructures. Plagued by delayed maintenance and chronic underfunding, crumbling infrastructure will require an investment of $2.2 trillion over the next five years.[26] This represents twice the amount currently invested, prompting urgent questions about the long-term effectiveness of deregulation policies.

How then can we rethink the conventional logic of infrastructure—the background process of essential services that underlies cities and regions—to effectively sustain sprawling populations and diversify urban economies for the future?

Ecology as Economy

The generic, technological apparatus of modern infrastructure has largely overshadowed the preeminence of biophysical systems that underlie it. Whereas in the past, industrialized nations were forced to contaminate or destroy the

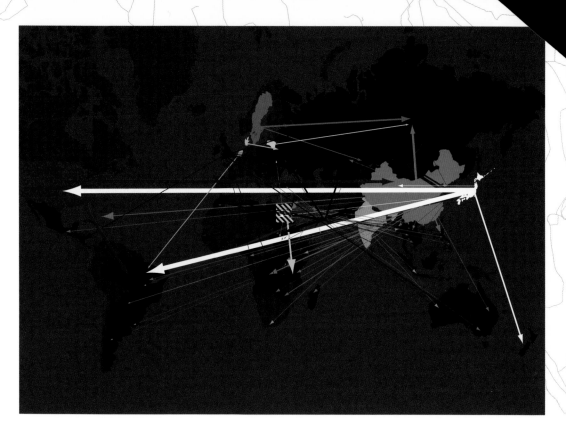

Global land grab: Flows of farm-land sales and purchases for food production between the Middle East, Europe, Africa, Eurasia, and America after the 2005 Atlantic hurricane season and the spike in world food prices

environment in service of the economy, today that equation is being reversed. The economy is now inseparable from the environment.

Responding to the current state of decaying infrastructures and ecological pressures, new models and practices[27] are beginning to challenge the dogma of neoliberal deregulation and the absence of federal planning:

A. Ecological Reengineering: linear, static, monofunctional methods of engineering give way to design flexibilities, circular operabilities, and multidimensional capabilities toward optimization, performance and dynamics.

B. Synergistic Design: through interconnectivity and interdependence, the design of infrastructure relies on strategic synergies to effectively multiply its functionality as a system.[28]

C. Urbanization as Synthesis: rezoning and redeveloping land generates financial mechanisms necessary for the reclamation of decaying infrastructure and contaminated land.

D. Planning for Failure: reliant on a culture of contingency and preparedness, risk forecasts are force generators in the planning of urban regions over successive generations.[29]

E. Regionalization: the watershed region is a hydrophysical infrastructure that provides a strategic, intermediary scale for planning across jurisdictions.

The ecology of urbanization:
Flow diagram of external
and internal processes of a city
as an open system, by Howard
T. Odum

Rolling warehouse: Projected
daily freight volumes by long-haul
truck on the U.S. National Highway System, which will double
their current rates from the rise
of third-party logistics by 2035

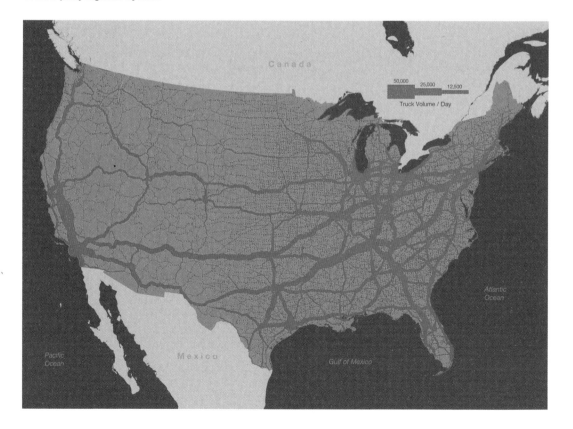

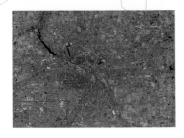

Banking on land: Satellite image of Flint in Michigan, formerly "Vehicle City" and now the seat of the first land-bank authority in the state, reorganizing abandoned, contaminated land with new fiscal and ecological measures associated with the Flint River watershed and Genesee County

The United Regions of America: The pattern of urbanization (Canada, United States, and Mexico) in relationship to the seventeen primary watershed regions of North America

Questioning the prominence of civil engineering as one of the most influential disciplines in the twentieth century, as well as the unnoticed inertia of urban planning, the field of infrastructure is taking on extreme relevance for public practices and public organizations. The merger of biophysical systems with contemporary infrastructure is now rapidly becoming the dominant order for urban regions. Road networks and fresh-water supply can no longer be planned without their watersheds. Sewage treatment and power plants can no longer be engineered without their wastesheds. Buildings and facilities can no longer be designed without their energy systems. From this vantage point, ecology is, in and of itself, an economy.

Infrastructure as Landscape. Demands for more renewable forms of development and flexible forms of infrastructure are sponsoring interdisciplinary cross-over. Sliding between planning and engineering, contemporary landscape practice can propose a sophisticated operating system for urban regions where the complex agency of living systems and dynamic processes can be deployed through long-range, large-scale planning. From the rise of environmental concerns in the 1970s to the crisis of public works in the 1980s, to the

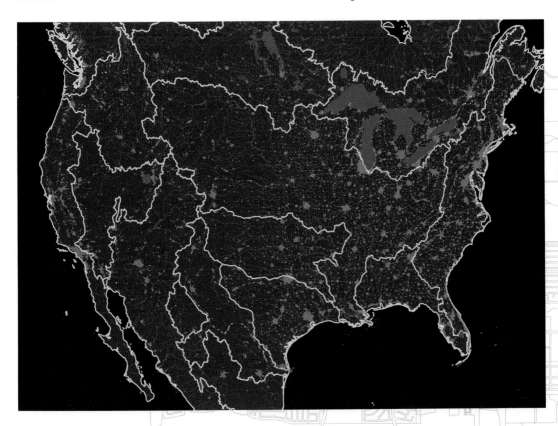

erosion of engineered structures in the 1990s, the ecological restructuring of urban infrastructure must include the management of water resources, waste cycling, energy generation, food production, and mass mobility. Paramount to both practice and pedagogy, infrastructure needs to be reintegrated and redefined as a sophisticated, instrumental landscape of essential resources, processes, and services that collectively underpins and upholds the ongoing, unfinished urbanization of the twenty-first century.

Acknowledgments: Richard F. Weingroff and Senquola Seabron from the Infrastructure Division of the Federal Highway Administration, Kenneth Johnson from the Library of Congress, Jan McDonald from sewerhistory.org, Angela King from Geology.com/NASA Landsat and the Media Information Department at the Tennessee Valley Authority were especially helpful in image procurement for this essay. Daniel Rabin, Fadi Masoud, Anna Kramer and Laura Gosmino deserve acknowledgement for their assistance in the production of diagrams.

This essay is a condensed version of a chapter for a forthcoming book entitled *Landscape Infrastructure,* on the contemporary convergence of landscape and urban infrastructure in the fields of planning, design, and engineering, to be published by the Canadian National Research Council Press in 2010. This essay is also informed by a 2008 symposium held at the University of Toronto, "Landscape Infrastructures: Emerging Practices, Paradigms, and Technologies Reshaping the Urban Landscape," and an earlier essay entitled "Landscape as Infrastructure" in *Landscape Journal* 28 (Spring 2009): 79–95.
Epigraph: Paul N. Edwards, "Infrastructure and Modernity," in *Modernity and Technology,* edited by Thomas J. Misa, Philip Brey, and Andrew Feenberg (Cambridge, MA: MIT Press, 2003), 185–226.

1 According to the *American Heritage Dictionary of the English Language* (4th edition, 2000).
2 Prior to the Civil War, the work of the U.S. Army Corps of Engineers was preceded by the Corps of Topographical Engineers. See Henry P. Beers, "A History of the U.S. Topographical Engineers, 1813–1863," *Military Engineering* (June 1942), 287–291, and (July 1942), 348–352.
3 As an instrument for assigning land-use types, Euclidean zoning should be differentiated from "zoning density," used in inner cities. See M. Christine Boyer, *Dreaming the Rational City: The Myth of American City Planning* (Cambridge, MA: MIT Press, 1983), 139–170. The first case of the use of zoning density was in New York, explains Raphael Fischler in "The Metropolitan Dimension of Early Zoning: Revisiting the 1916 New York City Ordinance," *American Planning Association,* vol. 64, no. 2 (spring 1998), 170–188.
4 Sidney Willhelm's *Urban Zoning and Land-Use Theory* (1962) and Michael J. Pogodzinski and Tim R. Sass's *The Economic Theory of Zoning: A Critical Review* (1990) are two of the most important texts from the planning discipline that have argued for a deeper understanding of the significance of zoning practice.
5 Between 1880 and 1890, almost 40 percent of the townships in the United States lost population to urban migration.
6 See Martin V. Melosi, *The Sanitary City: Urban Infrastructure in America from Colonial Times to the Present* (Baltimore, MD: Johns Hopkins University Press, 2000).
7 See George E. Waring Jr., "The Separate Sewer System," *The Manufacturer and Builder*, vol. 21, no. 9 (September 1889). In an 1889 article entitled "Sanitary Engineering," the *New York Times* reported that lack of attention to this new science was considerable and that architects ignored its developments at their peril (Bottom of Form September 8, 1889).
8 In 1855, Chicago was the first city to install a sewer plan in the United States, and by 1905, all U.S. towns with population over 4,000 had city sewers.
9 As the City Beautiful gave way to the Sanitary City, the modern age of sewage systems and civil engineering was born. The planning of the Park and Parkway system in Buffalo (New York) by Frederick Law Olmsted and George E. Waring Jr. in the nineteenth century is one of the best examples of open-space planning in conjunction with sanitary engineering and transportation networks.
10 According to the 1930 U.S. Census.
11 With voltages increasing rapidly between 1900 and 1920, more power could be transmitted across longer distances. In addition to better roads and faster vehicles, an array of technologies

made decentralization possible and convenient, including electrical energy distribution, telecommunications including broadcasting (radio, television) and narrowcasting (telephone). See Alan S. Berger, *The City: Urban Communities and Their Problems* (Dubuque, IA: William C. Brown Company, 1978).

12 By the 1930s, 60 percent of households owned an automobile. The clamor and smell of horses and buggies were being replaced with the fumes of cars and trucks, and their attendant services (fuel stations, mechanical garages, and parking lots), naturally leading to the next challenge: traffic and congestion. Self-appointed traffic engineer William Phelps Eno came to the rescue of the ruleless road with inventions like the one-way street and the roundabout, in addition to countless rule books and recommended behavior changes. The theory of continuous, uniform traffic flow through control was central to Eno's view and is a respected tenet of transportation today. Road engineering became synonymous with urban planning, while speed and mobility became unquestioned drivers of urban form across North America. See William Phelps Eno, *The Story of Highway Traffic Control, 1899–1939* (Saugatuck, CT: The Eno Foundation for Highway Traffic Control, 1939), and *The Science of Highway Traffic Regulation, 1899 and 1920* (Washington, DC: Brentano's, 1920).

13 The most comprehensive account of landscape planning in America is Francesco Dal Co's "From Parks to the Region: Progressive Ideology and the Reform of the American City," in *The American City: From the Civil War and the New Deal*, edited by Giorgio Cucci, Francesco Dal Co, Mario Manieri-Elia, and Manfredo Tafuri (Cambridge, MA: MIT Press, 1979), 143–292.

14 Howard W. Odum's opus *Southern Regions of the United States* (1936) considerably influenced presidential policy in the early twentieth century. See William Edward Leuchtenburg, *The White House Looks South: Franklin D. Roosevelt, Harry S. Truman, Lyndon B. Johnson* (Baton Rouge, LA: Louisiana State Press, 2005).

15 See "New Deal City," by Sue Halpern, *Mother Jones* (May/June 2002).

16 Arguably, roads are the last and most important public space in North America.

17 See American Public Works Association, *Top Ten Public Works Projects of the Century Program, 1900–2000* (Washington, DC: APWA, 2000).

18 In total, 3.5 million people were employed in conservation projects, 2.5 billion trees planted, 40 million acres of farm land protected, 1 million acres of grassland reclaimed, and 800 state parks created

(along with 52,000 campgrounds) between 1933 and 1941. See Douglas Helms, "Hugh Hammond Bennett and the Creation of the Soil Erosion Service," *Historical Insights Number 8* (Washington, DC: Natural Resources Conservation Service, USDA, September 2008).

19 FDR was committed to electricity as an instrument of democracy: "But these cold figures do not measure the human importance of the electric power in our present social order. Electricity is no longer a luxury. It is a definite necessity. It lights our homes, our places of work and our streets. It turns the wheels of most of our transportation and our factories. In our homes it serves not only for light, but it can become the willing servant of the family in countless ways. It can relieve the drudgery of the housewife and lift the great burden off the shoulders of the hardworking farmer." See *The Public Papers and Addresses of Franklin D. Roosevelt*, vol. 1, 1928–32 (New York: Random House, 1938), 727.

20 FDR's epic vision of social progress was "a piece of social and physical engineering of a scale […] and profundity" that, according to historian Reyner Banham, was "difficult to match even in the Russian five-year plans." See "Valley of the Dams," in *A Critic Writes: Selected Essays by Reyner Banham*, edited by Mary Banham, Sutherland Lyall, Cedric Price, and Paul Barker (Berkeley: University of California Press, 1996), 204. See also Reyner Banham, "Tennesse Valley Authority: The Engineering of Utopia," in *Casabella* 542–543 (January–February 1988), 74.

21 Under Reagan, federal spending shifted from transportation and energy to the military sector. See John D. Donahue, *The Privatization Decision: Public Ends, Private Means* (New York: Basic Books, 1989).

22 Following Thatcher's Energy Policy of 1983, Reagan loosened the grip of government on the free-market economy. George H.W. Bush loosened the energy market in the early 1990s with Management Circular A-76. Clinton oversaw the deregulation the financial market in the late 1990s with the removal of New Deal-era anti-speculation laws (1933 Glass-Steagall Act) that kept banking, insurance, and brokerage separate. George W. Bush eased environmental standards for air and water pollution, sponsoring the growth of coal and petrochemicals. The compound effect of these deregulatory measures are considered the principal causes of the housing mortgage foreclosure crisis and credit crash in 2008–2009.

23 For an account of the benefits of the valuation of infrastructure as an asset,

see "Roads to Riches: Why Investors Are Clamoring to Take Over America's Highways, Bridges, and Airports—and Why the Public Should Be Nervous," by Emily Thornton in *Business Week (*May 7, 2007), and Amanda Witherell, "Who Owns Our Cities? Privatizing Public Services Imperils Cities," in *RP&E*, vol. 15, no. 1 (Spring 2008).

24 See Deborah Solomon, "The Builder: Interview with Felix Rohatyn," *New York Times* (February 18, 2009).

25 The underlying conflict in the privatization of public services is that it does not account for the spin-off benefits and synergies associated with public delivery of services that effectively equalizes the extremes between classes. See Jenny Anderson, "Cities Debate Privatizing Public Infrastructure," *New York Times* (August 26, 2008).

26 See ACSE, *Report Card for America's Infrastructure* (2008), and Pat Choate and Susan Walter, *America in Ruins: The Decaying Infrastructure* (Durham, NC: Duke Press Paperbacks, 1983).

27 Although the push for the federal-regional Land Use Policy was defeated in the 1970s, consolation prizes came in the form of notable environmental protection legislation (National Environmental Policy Act of 1969, the Clean Air Act Amendment of 1970, the Federal Water Pollution Act of 1970, the Federal Water Pollution Control Act Amendments of 1972, the Coastal Management Act of 1972), but these do not confront the larger challenge of long-range public planning.

28 "As long-predicted energy shortages appear, as questions about the interaction of energy and environment are raised in legislatures and parliaments, and as energy-related inflation dominates public concern, many are beginning to see that there is a unity of the single system of energy, ecology, and economics. The world's leadership, however, is mainly advised by specialists who study only a part of the system at a time." See Howard T. Odum, "Energy, Ecology, Economics" *Mother Earth News* (May 1974), 1.

29 This concept is borrowed from the work of Miho Mazereeuw, Arthur E. Wheelwright Traveling Fellow at the Harvard University Graduate School of Design, who is writing a book entitled *Preemptive Planning*, focusing on earthquake-prone regions around the world. See also János Bogárdi and Zbigniew Kundzewicz, *Risk, Reliability, Uncertainty, and Robustness of Water Resource Systems* (Cambridge: Cambridge University Press, 2002).

User-Generated Urbanism

Rebar

We believe that there are two broad constellations of processes of formation of urban systems. On the one hand, we have the technocratic planning establishment making use of capital-intensive strategic actions to shape space according to a circumscribed set of values. These values are made evident in familiar patterns of resource consumption and inform a discrete social ecology, cultivating what Indian physicist Vandana Shiva calls a "monoculture of the mind."[1]

In contrast to technocratic urbanism, there exists a set of people, processes, and places that we would characterize as user-generated urbanism. This is the urbanism of the tactician, those devising temporal and interim uses, and seeking voids, niches, and loopholes in the socio-spatial fabric. These processes are made evident in circular, hybridized, and overlapping patterns of resource consumption and tend to foster a diverse, resilient social ecology. Our work over the last few years has been a series of experiments devising tools for user-generated urbanism.

Our Park(ing) project transformed a metered parking spot into a temporary park. This simple two-hour intervention—made into an open-source meme with a free how-to manual—has catalyzed a global event called Park(ing) Day, where people worldwide claim the parking space as a site for creative social expression, activism, and participatory public art.

Our COMMONspace project exploited another niche space in San Francisco, the privately owned public open space (POPOS). Guided by Jerold Kayden's work in New York City,[2] we did a systematic exploration of POPOS in San Francisco, opening these sites as a space for creative intervention, exploring the legal boundary of public and private, and in so doing transforming the way that they are planned, built, and used.

Grass is not green. Last year we explored the productive potential of the San Francisco Civic Center by removing 10,000 square feet of lawn and transforming it into a food garden. With the help of hundreds of community volunteers, we grew 455 kilos of food for San Francisco's needy and catalyzed a national resurgence of the World War II-era Victory Garden program.

1 Vandana Shiva, *Monocultures of the Mind: Perspectives on Biodiversity and Biotechnology* (New York: Zed, 1993).
2 Jerold S. Kayden, *Privately Owned Public Space: The New York City Experience* (New York: Wiley, 2000).

With the help of CMG landscape architecture and the Finch Mob, we transformed 65 midsize car hoods, post-consumer-waste steel, 75 doors, and 3,000 half-liter plastic bottles into a community performance space. Anyone could sign up to use the space to perform music, dance, and theater.

Our latest project, Bushwaffle, is an effort at providing tools for urban inhabitants to shape space, to readapt existing static urban infrastructures to respond to the dynamic social ecology of metropolitan inhabitants.

We see two future scenarios for the ecological city. In one scenario, a global greening movement consolidates power in the hands of corporate multinationals, further eroding the public commons and civil liberties under the rubric of resource efficiency, resulting in SCAR(E)CITY. Another parallel greening movement, defined by dynamic, pluralistic, decentralized, and cooperative social ecology, results in a future of SUSTAINABLE ABUNDANCE.

A typical early Park(ing) Day intervention: a 10 x 20-foot temporary public open space in San Francisco

Nappening–a one-day free event held in one of San Francisco's privately owned public open spaces (POPOS)–provided space for anyone to take a 20-minute nap. Nappers were provided with a comfortable cot and blanket and a soothing sound-scape designed to induce rest. At the end of a 20-minute cycle, partici-pants were gently awoken with a bell, and the cots prepared for the next round of nappers. Part of Rebar's COMMONspace project, a one-year exploration of POPOS.

> The PARKcycle–a mobile, pedal-powered public open space. Built for PARK(ing) Day 2007 in collaboration with sculptor Reuben Margolin, the PARKcycle synchro-nizes with the automotive infrastruc-ture to deliver urban green space when and where it is needed.

The Civic Center Victory Garden transformed a 10,000-square-foot lawn into a productive garden, growing food for the San Francisco Food Bank.

Hundreds of volunteers participate in a community planting day.

Volunteers prepare organic soil contained in rice straw wattle planting beds.

Bushwaffle exhibition and public tour at the Harvard Graduate School of Design

Bushwaffles are individual inflatable cushions that tesselate together to create a variety of shapes, supporting numerous types of social interactions.

Bushwaffle provide impromptu outdoor seating at the Ecological Urbanism conference at the GSD

User-Generated Urbanism

INTERACT

Situating Urban Ecological Experiments in Public Space

Alexander J. Felson and Linda Pollak

Urban environments are poorly understood in ecological terms, in part because they are complex, but also because the discipline of ecology, since its inception as a field of knowledge in the early twentieth century, has avoided people.[1] Increasing the quantity and quality of urban ecological research is critical to developing strategies to address climate change, mitigate and reduce ecological degradation, increase the resilience of cities, and improve health. Such research requires innovative methods that extend beyond the discipline of ecology and suggests the reformulation of design approaches to relationships between nature and culture in cities.

Building a knowledge base for urban ecology requires establishing experiments in urban spaces, to enable scientists to analyze both visible and hidden ecological information—to study fluxes of energy and matter in urban ecosystems and how they change over the long term, and understand how the spatial structure of ecological, physical, and socioeconomic factors affects ecosystem function. The complexity of cities, however, limits the ability to conduct experiments. Further, engaging cultural, economic, and political factors is beyond the expertise of most ecologists.

For most of its history, the discipline of ecology has repressed the fact that all environments are the result of an intertwining of human decision-making and biological processes. The long-dominant ecological theory of the climax state did not attribute significant importance to landscape history, instead understanding succession as a trajectory toward a point of ultimate stability and viewing land-use changes as landscape artifacts. It is only recently that ecologists have broadly acknowledged that no site is untouched, and that changes in the environment brought about through human activity play a significant role in the definition of ecological systems. The recognition of disturbance as fundamental to ecological systems and supportive of biological diversity is part of a set of related shifts, including an understanding of ecosystems as more open and interconnected, in the context of new theories such as emergence, resilience, and patch dynamics.[2]

Yet the concept of disturbance has a different significance for an urban site.[3] Historical and present-day management and movement of energy and resources create unique patterns and dynamics at regional, continental, and global scales, which cannot be understood on the basis of research carried out in other places. Even adjacent sites may share few material characteristics; most urban soils are the result of fill, often including concrete or other debris, and building elements are as likely to come from other continents as from regional locations.[4]

The degradation of ecosystem processes in urban areas reflects the fact that the design of cities has tended to prioritize human activities—including vehicular circulation, public use, and safety—over other living systems. The dominance of impervious surfaces reduces habitat and connectivity, blocking soil processes and increasing storm-water runoff, altering watersheds, and conveying contaminants into water bodies; lack of soil, leaf matter, vegetation, and subsequent food webs hinders biological processes.

Although there is significant investment in making cities more sustainable, there is comparatively little knowledge of how ecological processes in cities actually work. Much of what constitutes knowledge of urban ecological conditions has been derived from translation of research of nonhuman-dominated environments. Ecologists shifting to urban study sites have tended to focus on the occurrence of remnant ecological patterns and processes, such as extant wildlife and

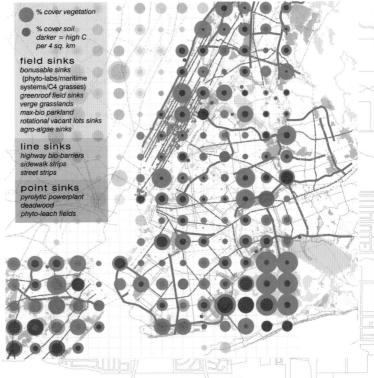

"Public Utility: CITY SINK," a proposal for the design and deployment of urban carbon sink infrastructure in New York City, Denise Hoffman Brandt, Van Alen Institute New York Prize Fellow, Spring 2009. CITY SINK investigates the physical, economic, and policy potential to catalyze urban carbon sequestration reservoirs, or sinks, and reframes urban planting practices as an ecologically operative program.

% cover vegetation

% cover soil
darker = high C
per 4 sq. km

field sinks
bonusable sinks
 (phyto-labs/maritime
systems/C4 grasses)
greenroof field sinks
verge grasslands
max-bio parkland
rotational vacant lots sinks
agro-algae sinks

line sinks
highway bio-barriers
sidewalk strips
street strips

point sinks
pyrolytic powerplant
deadwood
phyto-leach fields

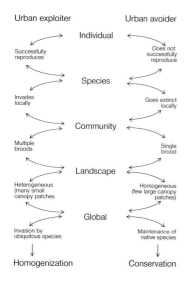

Urban exploiter   Urban avoider

Individual

Successfully reproduces   Does not successfully reproduce

Species

Invades locally   Goes extinct locally

Community

Multiple broods   Single brood

Landscape

Heterogeneous (many small canopy patches)   Homogeneous (few large canopy patches)

Global

Invasion by ubiquitous species   Maintenance of native species

Homogenization   Conservation

Identifying the traits that enable species to dominate highly urbanized surroundings may help to predict and possibly mitigate the biotic homogenization occurring in these areas.

As part of the NYC Reforestation project, researchers spray marking paint to communicate to the Parks Department and volunteers the desired location of high-diversity 10 m x 10 m plots, each containing six species. The Parks Department augered the holes in preparation for a day in which volunteers led by researchers arranged and planted more than 10,000 trees across New York City.

flora. However, the complex interactions in urban environments, the compromised biological integrity of urban sites, and the possible influence of social and cultural factors on biological patterns preclude typical ecological assumptions and research approaches, making it difficult or impossible to adhere to research practices such as replication and limitation to a single variable.

Undertaking ecological research in cities involves new challenges: dealing with regulatory constraints, political complexity, and project boundaries in terms of adjacent land uses, connectivity, setbacks, and other aspects of zoning and private property; persuading public and private entities of the value of research; and convincing stakeholders to accept the presence of experiments. Integrating human behavior into ecological experiments requires working within and across social boundaries, inventing strategies for grasping qualitative as well as quantitative data at a nexus of human, biological, and physical activities.

Designers can fruitfully collaborate with ecologists to integrate ecological experiments into urban spaces.[5] Collaboration can occur at multiple scales—from an individual building to neighborhood configurations and regional planning—to identify and develop experimental sites. Beyond helping to

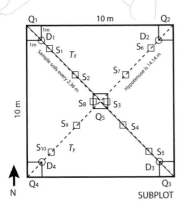

Q1 10 m Q2
D1
1m
1m S1 Tx
Sample soils every 2.36 m
D2
S6
S7 Hypotenuse is 14.14 m
S2
S8 S3
Q5
S9 S4
S10 Ty
S5
D4 D3
Q4 Q3
N
SUBPLOT

For the NYC Reforestation project, a typical sampling method is used to evaluate existing vegetation and soils on plots to be planted for long-term research. Trees are identified and caliper is recorded, shrubs are identified, and percent cover of herbaceous species sampled. Testing includes soil compaction and sampling (S1–S10), and readings of existing canopy cover (D1–D4). Additional baseline data where feasible include stem counts for herbaceous plants and seed-bank sampling.

navigate hurdles of property ownership, politics, and regulation, facilitating movement through review processes, and playing an advocacy role through different phases of a project to ensure its realization, designers can engage the social and cultural dimensions of an urban environment, making experimentation an integral part of urban life.

A critical aspect of situating an experiment in a populated environment is the interface between research and public space. The most common strategy of siting ecological research in nonhuman-dominated environments has been to keep it "below the radar," that is, to enable it to pass unnoticed. In an urban environment, however, not calling attention to something is not an adequate means of protecting it.

The boundaries of a site can be understood as a multifunctional dynamic zone serving the outside as well as the inside of the site: integrating as well as protecting an experiment, giving it a public surface, making a spatial and informational contribution to urban space, providing a culturally recognizable public identity to enhance an experiment's meaning and perceived value. It is not only that ecological experiments in public space may have an educational or demonstration component, but rather that this component is integral to the social/cultural program of situating experiments in cities. It is

RESEARCH METHODS

COMMUNITY VALUE

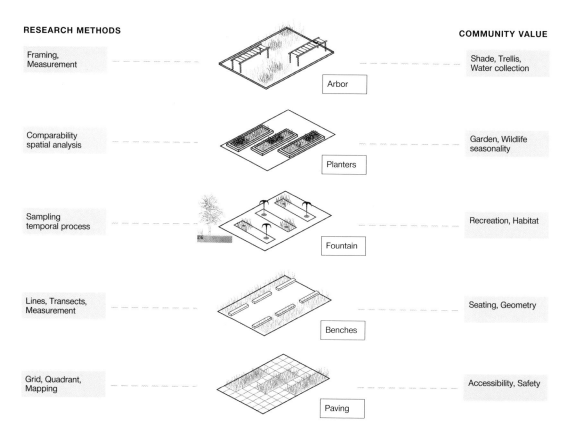

Framing, Measurement — Arbor — Shade, Trellis, Water collection

Comparability spatial analysis — Planters — Garden, Wildlife seasonality

Sampling temporal process — Fountain — Recreation, Habitat

Lines, Transects, Measurement — Benches — Seating, Geometry

Grid, Quadrant, Mapping — Paving — Accessibility, Safety

Interventions proposed for abandoned lots in Brooklyn introduced ecological research units as amenities for the community.

Ecologist Steven Handel's research at the Freshkills Park site has informed the planting of small, pioneer clusters of trees and shrubs that could attract bees and birds, which act as pollinators and seed spreaders.

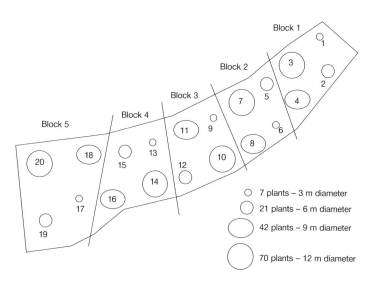

Block 1
Block 2
Block 3
Block 4
Block 5

○ 7 plants – 3 m diameter
◯ 21 plants – 6 m diameter
◯ 42 plants – 9 m diameter
◯ 70 plants – 12 m diameter

The Queens Plaza Bicycle and Pedestrian Improvement Project, by Marpillero Pollak Architects, extends from New York City's East River along a 1 1/3-mile length of heavily traveled wide roadways, coinciding with the exposed steel structure of the elevated subway. The "rooms" are like huge lanterns visible from near and far, their luminous presence revealing the hidden orders of the existing structure as they appear to float within it.

the connection—telling people what is going on—that would allow the existence of the experiment in the shared space of a city to make sense.

Collaboration may foster larger, more formative roles for ecology, creating new ecologically driven programs and form. By embracing design, ecologists can enable their research to become integral to the development of cities and public space. The design of public spaces as research environments may be understood as a hybrid practice, providing opportunities to influence cities in new ways, to monitor, evolve, and adapt to changing urban ecological conditions.

This essay is a prolegomenon to a longer work on collaboration between designers and ecologists in support of urban ecological research.

1 In the early twentieth century, F. E. Clements, the founder of modern ecology and the originator of the ecosystem concept, made a decision to study the natural world exclusively and therefore avoid human influence and human-dominated environments.
2 Until the 1970s, there was no major paradigm shift in ecology. Much of what was

ecology in the 1970s was built on theories that are now considered outdated.
3 There are questions about whether the concept of ecological disturbance is transferable to cities, which are catastrophically disturbed and do not have the same biological resilience as non-urban areas. Typically ecologists describe the threshold as the point at which an ecological system no longer functions the way it once did and does not return to a previous condition.
4 Unbuilt sites, from empty lots to urban wetlands, have often been used as dump-

ing grounds for material excavated to build tunnels, subways, and other infrastructure and buildings.
5 For the purpose of this essay, "urban" includes any intensively built environment. "Designers" include architects, landscape architects, urban designers, engineers, planners, artists, and others involved in the making of public spaces. Although this discussion focuses on public space, it is possible to consider private buildings, infrastructure, and landscapes as potential sites for situating ecological experiments.

The two matrixes of images belong to an issue-driven research by Linda Pollak on specific aspects of urban environment: they show traces of phenomena in which natural forces interact with urban infrastructure at a threshold between pedestrian and vehicular fields. Both address the role of water in relation to hard surfaces, which are part of pedestrian public space, and which belong to multiple groundplanes.

The matrix of images of historical cuts and patches documents a method of intervention, showing traces of human action on the surface in support of storm-water infrastructure.

The matrix of images of curbs is a registration of forces of disturbance, showing effects of storm-water runoff, including erosion, differential settlement of materials, and growth of vegetation.

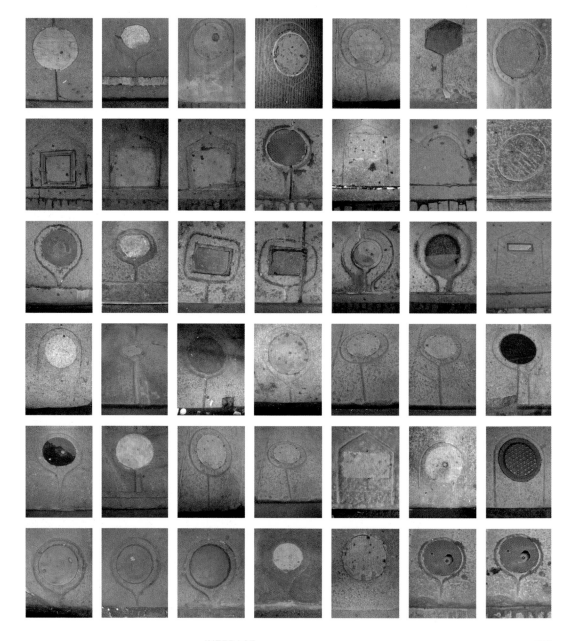

A Holistic View
of the Urban Phenomenon

Barcelona Urban Ecology Agency

Cities' dysfunctions have traditionally been approached from limited perspectives. They can be addressed successfully, however, with a holistic view that conceptualizes the city as an ecosystem with many interrelated variables. With this approach, competing strategies and management models could be developed to encourage more sustainable development. The work, organization, and methodology of the Barcelona Urban Ecology Agency makes use of this holistic vision. The Agency's aim is to rethink urban systems in specific areas such as mobility and public space, water management and energy, and waste treatment, using knowledge drawn from academic work on ecology and sustainability.

The Agency is a public consortium that employs forty professionals from all disciplines. It uses state-of-the-art tools and a teamwork approach. Each project is intended to analyze, diagnose, and propose an intentional model along four key axes: compactness, complexity, efficiency, and social cohesion. The Agency develops theory, conducts research, and promotes the convergence of advanced initiatives whether private, public, or from academia, in both Spain and the European Union. In short, the Agency could be described as an urban ecology lab with a desire to transform reality.

The contemporary city frequently expands beyond its limits, leading to greater use of private vehicles and resources. This process involves the permanent growth of the ecological footprint, which ultimately becomes a source of environmental, social, and economic imbalance. The pressure of the city on its external support systems exceeds carrying capacity in some cases. No city is self-sufficient, but the chosen urban management model can significantly reduce pressure on the environment. The same applies to the adoption of a competing strategy based on information rather than the consumption of material resources.

Three-Level Urban Planning

In this context, urban planning becomes an instrument of prime importance for sustainable development. Conventional urban planning works on a two-dimensional plane at ground level. This does not satisfactorily resolve the challenges that the city must face in the information age. Instead, new urban planning projects operate on three levels (underground, ground, and upper level), with the same detail and at the same scale that currently applies to the ground level. Three-level urban planning enables a set of interventions that represent decisive steps in the path toward sustainability.

– Biodiversity: A biodiversity layer at the upper level (green roofs) can connect to a layer below (trees and other urban greenery), restoring in part the biological capacity that the city has lost with buildings' preeminence.

– Urban metabolism: The integration of metabolic flows, minimizing consumption and its impact on buildings and public space, allows for the capture and storage of rainwater. It also makes possible sun, wind, and geothermal energy collection, and the installation of devices that act as passive systems for energy efficiency. The recycling of materials and the hierarchy of waste management (reduce, reuse, recycle) should be taken into account in the development of an urban area, its functioning, and eventually its deconstruction.

– Services and logistics: Underground planning includes the construction of accommodation for water and gas pipes, electricity, telecommunications, and platforms for merchandise distribution.

– Mobility and functionality: Implementing a network for every modality of transport and promoting public mass-transit networks in the underground and ground level minimizes friction among transport modalities.

Scheme section of three-level urban planning showing how metabolic flows and activity could be organized to enhance urban functionality

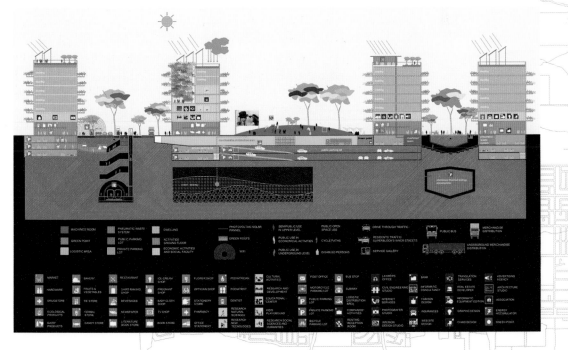

– Public space: The multiplication of the uses and functions of public space on the ground level lets people once again feel that they own the city and raises their status from pedestrians to citizens. To achieve this goal, some areas committed to parking and traffic must be liberated from these uses, without disturbing the functionality of the urban system.
– Urban complexity and the knowledge society: Three-level urban planning aligns with a compact, complex, efficient, and socially cohesive city model, as it makes possible greater proximity between uses and functions. At the same time it encourages mixture, multiplying organizational complexity. The information and knowledge society is articulated primarily within the framework of urban complexity.

An Indicator Plan to Measure Urban Sustainability

The Barcelona Urban Ecology Agency has developed, as part of its concept of new urban planning, a Special Plan of Urban Sustainability Indicators for the city of Seville, which can be used in other cities or urban contexts. Indeed, it has been tested in different neighborhoods, and urban area samples confirm the suitability of the established parameters. The usefulness of the indicators is twofold: first, they are a new tool for planning, and second, they can be used for quantitative analysis of a specific urban reality and its degree of accommodation to the four-axes city model.

Thirty-five indicators are divided into thematic groups: morphology, urban public space and comfort, mobility services,

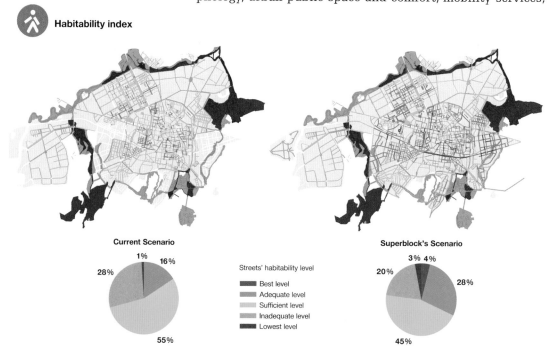

Habitability index

Current Scenario

1%
16%
28%
55%

Streets' habitability level

■ Best level
■ Adequate level
□ Sufficient level
■ Inadequate level
■ Lowest level

Superblock's Scenario

3% 4%
20%
28%
45%

urban organization and complexity, urban metabolism, urban biodiversity, social cohesion. A specific sustainability guide indicator takes into account some of the most strategic indicators from the groups and tells if the right steps toward a more sustainable model are being taken.

For example, urban metabolism includes the following indicators: energy self-sufficiency in households (a minimum of 35 percent of demand should be satisfied with local capture of renewable energy); water self-sufficiency (at least 35 percent of urban demand must come from rainwater harvesting and reuse of wastewater or other sources); and recycling of materials and closing of the organic matter cycle (fostering widespread use of composting and urban gardens).

As an exercise, the Barcelona Urban Ecology Agency tested all indicators on a new urban development project in the city of Seville (El Cortijo de Cuarto) to prove, theoretically, that compliance at 100 percent of the indicators in a given area is possible.

Two cases of the application of Agency analysis and work methods are described below.

Vitoria-Gasteiz Public Space and Mobility Plan

In Spanish cities, motor-vehicle traffic is the major source of dysfunction: noise, pollution, accidents, visual intrusion, congestion, loss of work time, and imbalance between the space devoted to vehicles and that dedicated to pedestrians. A basic network structured in superblocks liberates the inner area from drive-through traffic so that the pedestrian can recover his or her natural condition, using public space for parties, business, strolling, play, etc. The Barcelona Urban Ecology Agency has developed a Public Space and Mobility Plan based on the superblock concept for the city of Vitoria-Gasteiz (the Basque capital, with 236,000 inhabitants and a surface area of 275 square kilometers), through a commission from the City Council.

Networks have been planned to give formal continuity to private vehicle flow, public transport, and cycling. Seventy percent of public space is fully available for pedestrians (currently the road surface directly or indirectly used by cars is 71 percent). The plan reduces air pollution by 10 percent, the area exposed to noise is limited to the motor-vehicle lanes, and universal accessibility for disabled people becomes a reality throughout the city. One important aspect of this plan is an analysis of public space focused on how use improves as the new mode gets implemented. A specific methodology, including ergonomic, physiological, and psychological variables, assesses the conditions of the street from the perspective of human perception.

Social cohesion diagram

The Vitoria-Gasteiz Public Space and Mobility Plan has been developed with the support of the City Council and citizens' associations. After the plan was endorsed in 2007, the Municipal Council, with the support of the Agency, promoted implementation phases that will extend over twenty years. During 2009, new bus and bicycle networks will be developed.

Sustainability Strategy for Donostia-San Sebastián

The sustainability strategy of the Barcelona Urban Ecology Agency offers new courses of action in less explored areas that nevertheless are key to the future of the city. The aim is to increase the degree of organization of the territory and its potential for exchanging information, while reducing resource consumption. The proposed strategy for the Basque city of Donostia-San Sebastián unfolds along the four main axes proposed in the Agency city model: compactness, complexity, efficiency, and social cohesion.

Donostia-San Sebastián has an area of about 60 square kilometers, of which 18 are urbanized, and a population of 184,248. It is one of the municipalities with higher income in Spain, with much commercial and tourist activity. The city needs to renew its functional structures, to build a more sustainable model and foster information- and knowledge-based development. Although historically it has evolved as a compact city, in recent years urban growth has been more loose and the city has expanded outside of the traditional city limits in a less cohesive way, in a process largely influenced by a complicated topography and the presence of numerous transport infrastructures.

A new mobility model based on superblocks is proposed. Thus, as in Vitoria-Gasteiz, the public-space area for pedestrian use increases from 47 percent to 73 percent. The projected

**Donostia–San Sebastiàn.
Diversity index map and location
of new centrality areas**

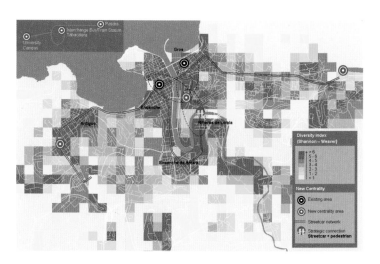

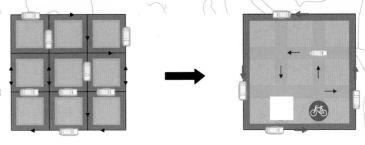

Graphic representation of open-space transformation based on a new mobility concept: the superblock

tram lines are aimed at connecting existing and new central areas. These transportation axes, along with the rail service, would provide service to 79 percent of the population that would have a station 300 meters or less from home. To preserve the urban continuum, new developments should be kept as compact as possible.

Concerning metabolic fluxes, the proposals are aimed at decreasing dependence on external resources, to reduce the ecological footprint. The purpose is to ensure the future by: increasing the local supply of renewable energy (wave, solar, wind) to meet 100 percent of city demand; finding alternative sources of water (rain, regenerated water) to meet 25 percent of total future water demand—making self-sufficiency possible with local water under a climate-change scenario; and reducing waste generation. The potential production of certain foods on municipal land has been considered (possibly supplying 100 percent of the city's beef, 29 percent of its milk, and 8 percent of its vegetables), using environmentally friendly techniques. Wave-power production is compatible with mollusc harvesting (100 percent self-sufficiency is the goal in this sector) and the regeneration of fishing grounds.

The creation of new central areas is suggested, supported by pedestrian axes. In new developments, a mix of residences and workplaces is recommended. In terms of biodiversity (complexity of the natural environment), the implementation of the superblocks is an opportunity to increase urban greenery. The ecological restoration of the Urumea River as a biological corridor could enhance vegetation on adjacent land.

An overarching urban planning objective is to ensure universal access to public space, social facilities, and services and housing, encouraging a mixture of different citizens in each area. It is therefore essential to increase the provision of public facilities and public space, taking into account current gaps and keeping as main criteria accessibility, proximity, function, and service. Housing policy should be based on rehabilitation, and public housing provided in an equitable way throughout town, creating mixed areas.

Optimal future scenario with local renewable energy supply in Donostia-San Sebastián

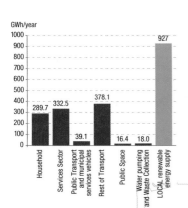

Gwanggyo New City Park System

Yoonjin Park and Jungyoon Kim (PARKKIM)

In the Gangnam area of Seoul, high-density residential developments occupy all of the level ground. In the absence of parks, citizens climb mountains on weekends in search of *yak-soo-teo* (natural springs). But mountain parks are too steep, too far away, and too unprogrammed to be a real substitute for an urban park. An urban park has to be accessible during lunchtime and not require changing clothes and shoes.

Seventy percent of Korea is mountainous, and it is hard to deny that the most economical and least destructive manner of development is to build on flat land. We can observe this pattern in Gangnam. So how can we create the culture of an urban park in Gwanggyo, south of Seoul, that is missing in Gangnam? PARKKIM proposes a system of "mountain parks" in Gwanggyo, where women in high heels—representing the group of people who cannot climb mountains—can walk to the top during their everyday lives. After diagnosing Gangnam's mountainous parks as too hard to reach and limited in their program offerings, we suggest, first, that promenades with an 8 percent maximum incline reach the tops of all twelve parks and, second, that openings in the forest with various programs be found along the promenades and other walkways. Third, we propose simple ecological strategies that can keep the mountains healthier than before the park programs were inserted.

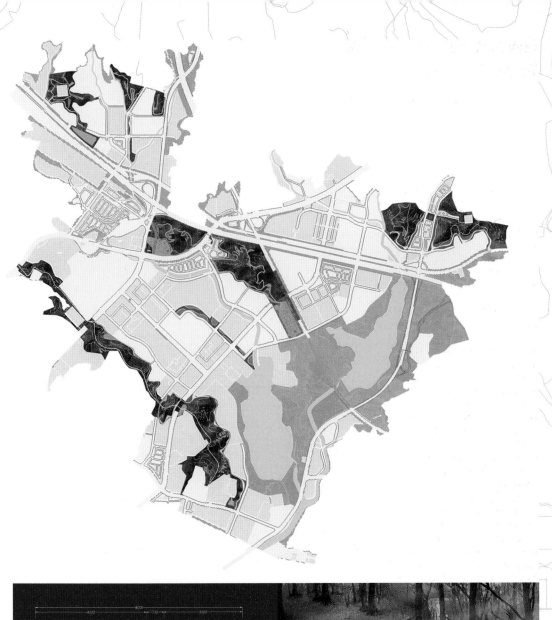

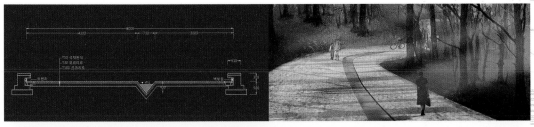

A Methodology
for Urban Innovation

Alfonso Vegara, Mark Dwyer, and Aaron Kelley

Fundación Metrópoli, based in Madrid, Spain, belongs to the emerging generation of "intellectual capital institutions" dedicated to creating and sharing knowledge toward building a sustainable future. It is the mission of Fundación Metrópoli to be a catalyst for the lasting and positive transformation of the cities and landscapes of the twenty-first century.

Fundación Metrópoli approaches its research and project development within a holistic framework, unique to the organization. Rather than approach the challenges of global sustainability from a problematic perspective, the Fundación bases its development concepts on the identification and effective use of a place's strategic advantages or, more appropriately, its components of excellence.

The basic aim of this methodology is to identify the competitive advantages of cities and reveal the quality and performance of their urban realm, together with their policies of innovation and creativity. This research methodology consists of two main parts: 1) Urban Profiles are made up of urban indicators (data on physical, socioeconomic, and environmental aspects) and critical cartography, highlighting the most prominent among these aspects; 2) City Forum consists of city experts—local stakeholders who have a deep-rooted understanding of the city based on their personal expertise in various urban roles; they are invited to give weighted responses to a questionnaire about 186 urban factors, to identify the components of excellence and derive clusters of excellence specific to each city. Moreover, they express open-ended expert opinions with an emphasis on critical deficits and basic priorities requiring action, which they consider critical to improving the city's competitiveness.

The methodology is thus made up of factual/objective as well as informed subjective elements, which together assist in drawing up the unique profile of each city—its DNA—that is crucial to its innovation capacity, creativity, and survival in the knowledge society. In particular, the Urban Profiles provide objective measurements that substantiate the urban reality of each city. They include data and trend extrapolations that quantify the physical, economic, demographic, social, cultural, and environmental factors of a city.

In addition, Fundación Metrópoli hosts a number of ongoing investigatory "laboratories" that contribute to the global discourse of urban innovation.
These include:
1. Proyecto CITIES: a continuing series of case studies through the FM framework, conducted on twenty cities from five continents.
2. Design LAAB: Laboratory of Advanced Architecture and Bioclimatism.
3. CITIES Lab: the metro-specific arm of Fundación Metrópoli, defining the strategic projects of the future.
4. CITIES Art: a program dedicated to the recovery of art as the motor of creativity and innovation in the design of human habitat.

Metropolitan mapping of Pamplona, Spain, showing its basic urban structure, including the historic core, urban growth patterns, natural features, park areas, and primary transit connections. The realized project for the eco-city of Sarriguren is also shown on the periphery of Pamplona.

The physical form and structure of cities have implications for their economic competitiveness, sociocultural cohesion, and environmental sustainability. For this reason, a set of interpretative graphics produced with critical cartography is a useful tool to understand the underlying structure of cities and their metropolitan regions. It reveals structural and spatial relations between different parts of the city and the distribution of urban activities. The diagrammatic nature of these graphics is able to project a synthetic perception of essential urban features, highlighting both assets and constraints. Critical cartography can also illustrate nonphysical factors, such as demographic, social, and economic characteristics and identify their spatial distribution, cohesion, inequalities, and fragmentation at a glance.

Seven graphic representations—scale, intensity, morphology, cohesion, nature, innovation, and connectivity—constitute the selected two-dimensional building blocks of the critical cartography method. These visual perceptions of urban characteristics assist in identifying the unique profile of cities.

Fundación Metrópoli engages this methodology through three internal processes that direct the evolution of each new project: investigation, innovation, and incubation.

Greenmetropolis

Henri Bava, Erik Behrens, Steven Craig, and Alex Wall

The Greenmetropolis is a pioneering European project for an extensive tri-national collaboration between the Dutch and Belgian Limburg regions and Germany's Aachen metropolitan region. Its starting point is a challenging economic, political, and spatial redevelopment of a postindustrial urban agglomeration with more than thirty-seven communities and 1.7 million inhabitants. In the context of the EuRegionale2008, the Greenmetropolis becomes a test bed for a new approach to shaping the future of this region by seeking to fuse communal and national commitment with regional thinking and action. The planning, design and implementation of the first twenty-two high-profile projects is well under way. They include the Indeland transformation of the immense opencast mine at Düren, a cross-border countryside park and valley between Germany and the Netherlands, the Horse Park at Aachen, and several mining dump landscape interventions for recreational and culture uses.

In spring 2003, based on the initiative of the province of North-Rhine Westphalia, the EuRegionale2008 agency was commissioned to mobilize individual stakeholders of the region around the idea of a tri-national development process. In an initial phase, several local project plans and ideas were collected across national borders. At the beginning of 2004, Henri Bava, Erik Behrens, Steven Craig, and Alex Wall delivered their competition entry, called Greenmetropolis– a flexible framework tying together the various local project ideas and a convincing regional development concept. In various workshops, ideas were refined and developed further as complementary building blocks set within the regional framework. The high level of communication associated with this planning process helped to overcome physical and mental borders, enabling new initiatives and jump-starting new processes. In autumn 2005, the Greenmetropolis successfully gained Interreg support by the European Union.

The Greenmetropolis is a unique mixture of urban culture and nature situated at the crossroads of the most important European development corridors. It stands between the large natural spaces of the Eifel/Ardennen and Kempten/Zeeland and is a region emerging from the process of modern industrialization. Defined by the perimeter of a coal field, the land has been shaped by the process of extraction, with mines sunk deep into the rich coal seams, leaving behind an amorphous field of settlements, perforations, and deterioration. The Greenmetropolis is an active reclamation process. It sets out to discover and reveal the existing qualities of this urban agglomeration and to express its future shape as a shared living space by introducing conceptual and creative interventions. It strives to synthesize its urban, postindustrial, agricultural, and natural attributes into a new kind of city region.

The area's identity can be read as a sequence of familiar elements:

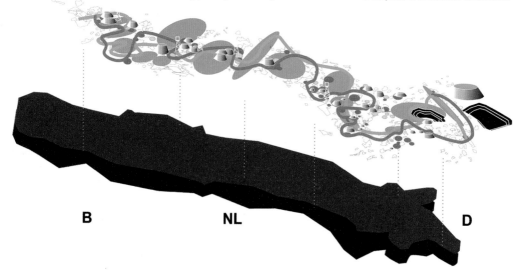

B   NL   D

city centers, open spaces and parks, abandoned collieries, historic mineworker settlements, opencast mining pits, and mining dumps, which are the dominant topographical features in this area. In combination with new uses and future-oriented developments, these elements could form new versatile centers of activity within the existing urban agglomeration and throw into relief the rich diversity of the region. Likewise, in the immediate vicinity of the cities, various design and accessibility measures will be carried out to make the mining dumps more attractive for the population. Visitors will enjoy stunning panoramas from the viewing platforms on top of the mining dumps. The brownfields of the former mine sites provide unique

development platforms for housing and employment spaces around the retained architectural monuments.

Providing legibility and accessibility, a Green Route and a Metropole Route will connect the new centers of activity and natural landscapes. The routes are intertwined like the strands of a double helix and connect the elements into a code of regional culture and urban identity (urban DNA). The Metropole Route establishes a regional main street that gives orientation and becomes the communication artery for residents and visitors alike. The Green Route acts as a pedestrian path/bikeway and follows the riverine structure that leads from the Eifel Mountains to the North Sea and offers the potential to establish

a continuous ecological structure that connects the various parks of the region.

A regional management structure along with a communications and branding strategy will support the ongoing development process. A charter currently being developed will summarize the strategic goals. Thus the Greenmetropolis will be a way of combining existing initiatives and creating a new identity for the region. At the same time, it will function as a platform for regional discussions across the borders of the three nations and a framework for additional projects centered on economic regeneration and tourism. It represents the start of a long-term process of negotiating its own future.

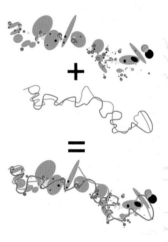

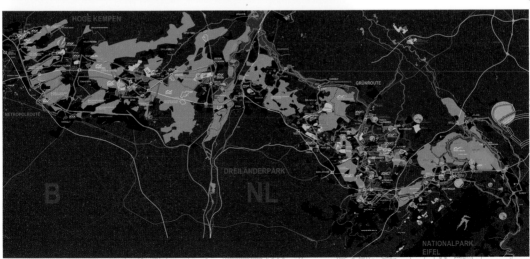

INTERACT

MOBILIZE

Mobility, Infrastructure, and Society
Richard Sommer

Sustainable Urban Mobility through Light Electric Vehicles
William J. Mitchell

Sustainable Mobility in Action
Federico Parolotto

Sustaining the City in the Face of Advanced Marginality
Loïc Wacquant

A General Theory of Sustainable Urbanism
Andrés Duany

The Political Ecology of Ecological Urbanism
Paul Robbins

The SynCity Urban Energy System Model
Niels Schulz, Nilay Shah, David Fisk, James Keirstead, Nouri Samsatli,
Aruna Sivakumar, Celine Weber, and Ellin Saunders

Oil City: Petro-landscapes and Sustainable Futures
Michael Watts

Niger Delta Oil Fields
Ed Kashi

The Upway
Rafael Viñoly

GSD RESEARCH
Nairobi Studio
Jacques Herzog and Pierre de Meuron

Mobility, Infrastructure, and Society

Richard Sommer

Freedom Train rolling past Monuments of Washington, D.C., 1947

Technologies exist or are emerging that will enable us to design and construct buildings in ways that will use far fewer natural resources. Engaging architecture and urbanism from a fully ecological perspective, however, means measuring environmental impacts, including carbon emissions and non-renewable resource usage, in an expanded context of social justice, economic opportunity, and human nature.

In societies aspiring toward modern forms of democracy, increasing mobility—in both geographic and socioeconomic terms—has become as critical to human emancipation as the more traditional liberal touchstones of civil liberty and equal representation. Concepts such as freedom and liberty have taken on competing meanings that pivot around Enlightenment-inspired ideals of civil society and more individualistic, romantic notions of unlimited human potential. Breaking from their bonds, their heritage, and their communities to improve their station in life, modern people have almost always needed to move: across a city, from one city to another, or from one continent to another.

The quintessential American figures of the pilgrim, the pioneer, and the beatnik all defined themselves by moving. Myth or no, this quest has been central to an understanding of "America" as a land of opportunity. This striking out is also related to a desire to own property—a mindset that has literally and figuratively driven the physical formation of modern societies such as the United States.

This phenomenon has been accelerated by mechanical forms of locomotion and digital telecommunication. Against this background, how are we to assess the ideas that most environmentalists, planners, and architects are proposing to achieve more sustainable, ecologically balanced forms of urbanity? There appears to be a remarkable degree of consensus among professionals, activists, and politicians that creating more compact and integrated urban agglomerations, with more efficient and public forms of transport to serve them, is the best bulwark against the coming environmental Armageddon. The experts agree that such reforms would both reduce environmental impacts and increase the potential for human collaboration and sociability.

Yet do we all agree that a more compact and ultimately less mobile city should be our goal? Almost half a century ago, Melvin Webber, in his essay "The Urban Place and the Non-Place Urban Realm," argued that modern expressions of urbanity depend less on traditional places than on forms of mobility facilitated by modern technologies of communication and physical transport; the most successful individuals in advanced economies were those who could take most advantage of travel and communication technologies to create the most expansive social and economic networks.[1] By virtue of the worldwide web, cell phones, cheap air travel, and (until recently) ever-increasing levels of "automobility," hasn't the relation between human community and place been undergoing a constant and in many ways emancipating transformation for many of us?

Most simply put, how do our current thoughts about how to create a more ecological urbanism jibe with entrenched and deeply held cultural proclivities toward freedom of movement and association? Moreover, even if we can agree that a wholesale change in the organization and pattern of urban development is a worthy ecological and social goal, do we really think we can put the industrial genie that is the modern city (i.e., a highly disaggregated system of infrastructure provision and land development) back into a tidy green bottle? Are there other ways of understanding what it might mean to design a more mobile, democratic, and ecologically sound city?

1 Melvin Webber, "The Urban Place and the Non-Place Urban Realm," in *Explorations into Urban Structure,* edited by Melvin Webber, John Dyckman, Donald Foley, Albert Guttenberg, William Wheaton, and Catherine Bauer Whurster (Philadelphia: University of Pennsylvania Press, 1964).

Congress of Racial Equality "Freedom Riders" after being forced from a bus by a Caucasian mob who stoned the bus, slashed the tires, and set it on fire (Anniston, Alabama, 1961)

Sustainable Urban Mobility through Light Electric Vehicles

William J. Mitchell

A typical American automobile weighs twenty times as much as its driver. A comfortable chair occupies only about 10 square feet, while a parked car generally uses up 200 square feet of valuable urban real estate. Furthermore, it is parked about 80 percent of the time—not only taking up space that could be put to better use but also costing money, consuming materials, and embodying energy. Although urban speed limits are usually set at 25 to 35 miles per hour, it is engineered for a top speed of more than 100 miles per hour. Urban trips are measured in miles or tens of miles, yet it has a 300-mile range. And of course, it is powered by gasoline—a rapidly diminishing, nonrenewable resource that arrives through increasingly problematic supply chains and emits greenhouse gases from the tailpipe.

It is not my purpose here to demonize automobile designers or car companies for foisting this massive over-engineering upon us. We have arrived at this point through a century-long evolutionary process involving diverse protagonists and complex social, political, and economic roots. But I do want to argue that it is time for a radical change. We should take this moment of economic crisis—one that is particularly strongly felt in Detroit—as an opportunity to reinvent urban personal mobility from the ground up. We can and should create systems that provide very high levels of mobility service while minimizing energy consumption and supporting a large-scale shift to clean, renewable, and more local energy sources.

Lightweight, smart, battery-electric vehicles are one obvious and essential part of such systems. Recharging infrastructure is a second part. The integration of electric vehicles and their recharging infrastructure with smart electric grids—to enhance the efficiency of grids and to make them friendlier to clean, renewable, but intermittent energy sources—constitutes a third part. The organization of electric vehicles into highly efficient mobility-on-demand systems is a fourth part. Finally, a powerful computational back-end—one that senses and meters the current state of the system, processes large amounts of information in real time, computes optimum responses to evolving demands and conditions, and controls overall system operation—is necessary for effective operation of these systems.

Integrating these five elements provides the foundation for creating smart, sustainable cities. These cities achieve high levels of operational efficiency—and, in particular, energy efficiency and carbon minimization—through optimized real-time response to the dynamically varying demands created by the daily activities of their citizens and by variation in the climate and other exogenous factors.

The GreenWheel Electric Bicycle

The most obvious starting point for the creation of such systems is the bicycle. This is an extraordinarily elegant and efficient vehicle type with a tiny footprint. (Compare a bicycle lane to a car lane, and a bicycle rack to a carpark.) However, it suffers from some obvious shortcomings. It is unattractive in bad weather. In many urban contexts the streets and roads don't accommodate it gracefully and safely. It works beautifully for the fittest among us, but not so well—particularly where it is hilly or hot—for those with physical limitations.

But all of these issues can be overcome. First, it is a very inexpensive vehicle type, so it does not have to be used in all weather. Where it is not expected to be the exclusive means of personal mobility and forms part of an ecosystem of energy-efficient vehicles, it can be used only when and where it makes sense.

The problem with bicycles on urban streets and roads exists because these thoroughfares are predominantly occupied by much larger, heavier, faster vehicles. But this isn't a given. Under the strategy that I shall develop here, vehicles generally become smaller and lighter, making most streets and roads much friendlier to both pedestrians and bicycles. This will not happen instantly, but eventually we will reach a tipping point.

The GreenWheel modular electric bicycle wheel

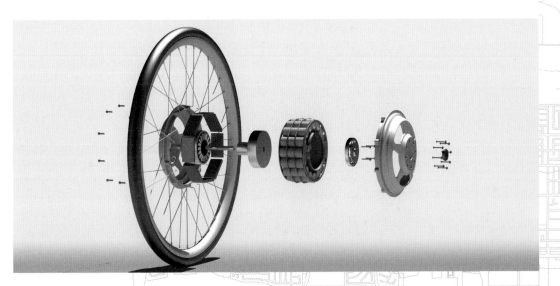

Finally, it is now possible to equip bicycles with sophisticated electric assist, thus making them useful and attractive to many more people. Electric-assist bicycles are not a new idea; tens of millions of them are sold in China every year. But the development and convergence of several new technologies has recently opened up some powerful new design approaches.

The GreenWheel, for example, has been developed by the MIT Media Laboratory's Smart Cities group. The GreenWheel is a compact, modular hub unit that provides electric assist and regenerative braking, and also contains lithium-ion batteries. Its gearing is arranged to minimize spinning mass, so that it does not affect the ride dynamics.

GreenWheels are mechanically and electrically self-contained and can be fitted to any standard bicycle. They do not require bicycle redesign, the purchase and installation of complex kits, or purchase of new bicycles. You just remove the back wheel of your bike and replace it with a GreenWheel. Thus GreenWheels provide a quick, easy, and inexpensive way of upgrading the world's vast existing bicycle fleet, and an opportunity to enhance the functionality of existing bicycle models.

The electric motor of a GreenWheel is digitally controlled, which enables precise management of torque. This is usually provided from a wireless controller on the handlebars (much like a motorcycle throttle), which allows the rider to control the motor with one hand and eliminates the need for a wire running to the hub. Where local regulations require it, a wire can of course be added. It is also possible to provide control from the pedals.

In combination with GPS and sensors, GreenWheel digital controllers can also manage entire trips. They can, for example, be programmed to require a constant level of physical exertion throughout the trip—whether going uphill, downhill, or on the flat. The level of effort may be set to zero (full electric assist, no pedaling), to some intermediate level that is comfortable for the particular rider, or to serious exercise level (the motor functions as a generator, providing resistance like an exercise machine and charging the batteries).

GreenWheels do not consume much electricity, and can easily be recharged overnight, from a standard 110-volt outlet, for the following day's riding. They can also be charged inductively from specially designed bike racks. When these racks are widely deployed, GreenWheel bicycles become like electric toothbrushes in their holders: whenever they are not in use, they are replenishing their chargers.

Introducing GreenWheels is an easy first step toward creating electric vehicle fleets for urban personal mobility. The technology is simple, and the costs and risks are low. Individuals can purchase GreenWheels for their own use, and employers, merchants, and government agencies can encourage consumer acceptance by deploying recharging racks at convenient locations.

The RoboScooter Folding Electric Scooter

In many cities throughout the world, motor scooters provide the least expensive form of powered personal mobility. They are inexpensive to acquire and operate, and they provide higher speeds and greater carrying capacity than bicycles. Their road and parking space demands are minimal since they have footprints not much larger than bicycles; they are not constrained to wide lanes like automobiles; and they can park in very small spaces that could not accommodate automobiles.

One downside of scooters is that, unlike enclosed powered vehicles, they do not provide weather protection—making them most suitable for use in temperate climates. They provide a little more crash protection than bicycles, but not nearly as much as automobiles. And gasoline-powered motor scooters are a major source of urban noise, local air pollution, and carbon emissions.

The trade-off points that scooters represent make them particularly popular in the developing world. They are also popular in European cities, where narrow streets and crowded conditions are inhospitable to automobiles. In the United States they have a limited use as primary personal transportation; they have recreational uses, and in cities with severe winters their use is mostly seasonal.

The RoboScooter folding electric motor scooter

The RoboScooter folding electric scooter, developed by the Smart Cities group, maximizes the advantages of the scooter

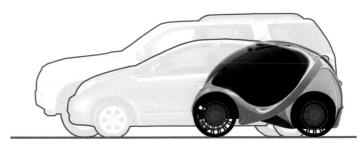

The CityCar compared to traditional automobiles

while minimizing some of its disadvantages. It features in-wheel electric motors, lithium-ion batteries, and a cast aluminum frame. To minimize the parking footprint—a key consideration in many contexts where scooters are popular—it folds up into a very compact configuration. For contexts where this is not necessary, the RoboScooter can also be produced in nonfolding models.

RoboScooters are designed to serve as approximate functional equivalents of 50cc gasoline-powered scooters. They are, however, clean, silent, and occupy less parking space. They are also much simpler—consisting of about 150 parts, compared to the 1,000 to 1,500 of an equivalent gasoline-powered scooter—which simplifies supply chains and assembly processes, reduces vehicle costs, and eases maintenance.

Like GreenWheels, RoboScooters can be recharged in their racks. Their battery packs are also small enough to be conveniently removable, which opens up the possibilities of charging spare batteries at home, and of battery vending machines that accept discharged batteries and provide fully charged ones.

The CityCar Electric Automobile

The CityCar electric automobile, developed and prototyped by Smart Cities, is designed to meet the demand for enclosed personal mobility—with weather protection, climate control and comfort, secure storage, and crash protection—in the cleanest and most economical way possible. It weighs less

The features of the CityCar

Early prototypes of the CityCar

than 1,000 pounds, parks in much less space than a Smart Car, and is expected to get the equivalent of 150 to 200 miles per gallon of gasoline. Since it is battery-electric, it produces no tailpipe emissions.

The architecture of the CityCar is radical. It does not have a central engine and traditional power train, but is powered by four in-wheel electric motors. Each wheel unit contains a drive motor (which also enables regenerative braking), steering, and suspension, and is independently digitally controlled. This enables maneuvers like spinning on its own axis (an O-turn instead of a U-turn), moving sideways into parallel parking spaces, and lane changes while facing straight ahead.

Shifting drive to the corners in this way enables the CityCar to fold to minimize parking footprint, and to provide front ingress and egress (since there is no engine in the way). This dramatically changes its relationship to streets and cities. It can park nose-in to the curb in far less than the width of a traditional parking bay, and it can park at very high densities. It is possible to park three or four CityCars in the length of a traditional parking bay.

The front compartment of a CityCar accommodates passengers, and the rear compartment provides generous storage for baggage, groceries, and so on. When a CityCar folds, the baggage compartment remains level and low for easy access.

CityCars accommodate two passengers, which suits them to meeting the requirements of the vast majority of urban trips without excess capacity. They are designed for intraurban trips, which are fairly short between recharge opportunities. This fits them gracefully to the capabilities of battery technologies that are presently available or likely to be available in the near future. They are not designed for intercity travel, for which different technologies are more appropriate.

Overall, CityCars are smaller and simpler than traditional automobiles, and in principle much more economical to manufacture. Most of the mechanical complexity is encapsulated in the wheel units. These can be designed to have a standard interface to the chassis, and their cost can be driven down through competition and innovation—much as with disk drives for personal computers.

Lithium-ion batteries are housed in the floor of the CityCar, which provides a large amount of space, keeps the center of mass low, and facilitates cooling. Recharging can be accomplished with inexpensive home charging units, and with units installed at workplace parking structures. More interestingly, it seems feasible to provide automatic recharging in parking spaces. This extends the principle of rack recharging as employed with the GreenWheel and the RoboScooter.

Recharging Infrastructure

Obviously battery-electric vehicles have finite ranges, and due to the relatively low energy density of batteries, these ranges tend to be significantly less than those of gasoline-powered vehicles. Furthermore, it generally takes longer to recharge batteries than to fill tanks with gasoline. An associated problem is that of "range anxiety"—the worry of drivers that they will run out of charge and be stranded by the side of the road. Recharging infrastructure must be designed to deal with these issues. Strategies will vary with vehicle type.

The difficulties are minimal with GreenWheels and other electric-assist bicycles. Electricity consumption is not high, and bicycle trips are usually quite short, so it is not necessary to carry large quantities of batteries that take a long time to charge. Range anxiety is not a big problem, since you can always pedal if you run out of charge. Overnight recharging at home from safe, inexpensive 110-volt chargers, combined with recharging in bike racks, should suffice to meet the needs of GreenWheel riders. GreenWheels thus provide an inexpensive, low-risk way for cities and electric utilities to begin experimenting with the deployment and management of electric vehicle recharging infrastructure.

Since RoboScooters are heavier and used for longer trips, they make more demands on recharging infrastructure. However, the combination of home and workplace charging units, combined with recharging racks, still seems workable. You cannot pedal a scooter if you run out of charge, and you cannot push it very far, but removable battery packs provide emergency backup and alleviate range anxiety.

Battery-electric automobiles, such as the CityCar, provide the greatest recharging infrastructure challenge since they are larger and heavier, require better acceleration and higher speeds, and travel longer distances. And traditional approaches to sizing batteries and providing recharging infrastructure have some severe disadvantages.

One traditional approach, as exemplified by the Tesla electric sports car, is to design electric automobiles for something like the 300-mile range of gasoline-powered automobiles. This results in battery-heavy, extremely expensive automobiles that cannot effectively meet the requirements of inexpensive, daily personal mobility on a large scale. It puts large numbers of batteries, which eventually have to be recycled, into circulation. And it means that either recharging times are long or extremely expensive high-speed chargers must be used.

Another approach is battery swapping—a very old idea that has recently been revived. A major problem with swapping large, heavy batteries into and out of automobiles is that it requires complex and potentially unreliable mechanical equipment to accomplish the task. (It is not like swapping a small battery pack in and out of a RoboScooter by hand.) It does little to minimize the number of batteries in circulation. It relies—probably unrealistically—on most drivers following good battery management practices, so that poorly managed, bad batteries do not get swapped into the vehicles of unsuspecting motorists. And it introduces product liability issues.

A third approach is to employ plug-in hybrids, extended-range electric vehicles such as GM's Volt, and other vehicle types that reduce the need for recharging infrastructure by augmenting vehicle batteries with gasoline engines. But these vehicles are heavy and expensive by comparison with City-Cars. Furthermore, to the extent that they still rely on combustion of gasoline, they continue to depend on petroleum and emit greenhouse gases.

A more attractive approach, I believe, is to provide ubiquitous, automatic recharging in parking spaces. Assuming that urban trips are relatively short, and that vehicles are typically parked long enough between trips to transfer sufficient energy, this provides an effectively infinite range within urban areas. It means that drivers never have to worry about filling up,

Parking CityCars

plugging in, or running out of energy. And it shifts as much hardware as possible out of the moving vehicle and into the fixed infrastructure, where it does not have to be carried around. Recharging infrastructure can be deployed incrementally, beginning with locations where demand is highest and proceeding over time to locations where demand is lower.

This raises the total cost of recharging infrastructure, since it requires more recharging stations, and perhaps expensive high-speed stations. And unlike home recharging at night, it shifts responsibility for investing in recharging infrastructure to the public sector, to employers and merchants, and to private parking facility operators. Or, under appropriate business models, the responsibility could be shouldered by electric utilities.

This shift does not seem unreasonable. Public investment in recharging infrastructure is analogous to the massive investments in roads, bridges, interstate highways, and so on that was an essential enabler of the large-scale adoption of gasoline-powered automobiles in the early decades of the twentieth century. It provides an avenue for public-sector investment to encourage a shift to a clean, green economy. At the municipal level, investment in recharging infrastructure can provide a town or city with a competitive advantage. For merchants, it is a way to attract customers. And for parking facility operators, it enables a valuable additional service. From the perspective of electric utilities, ubiquitous automatic recharging enables the integration of a large amount of battery storage capacity with the grid.

Integrating Electric Vehicles and Smart Electric Grids

Because demand for electricity fluctuates, electricity supply must always meet demand, and grids generally do not have storage capacity that could be used to buffer shortfalls in supply, balancing loads in electric grids presents a well-known difficulty. Generally there is a component of base load, which generators running continuously can efficiently meet, but above that there is fluctuating load that can only be met through the expensive expedient of maintaining reserve capacity and bringing it online and offline as required.

Clean, renewable, but intermittent energy sources such as solar cells and wind turbines exacerbate this problem by introducing uncontrolled fluctuations on the supply side as well. The sun does not necessarily shine when there is demand for electricity, nor does the wind blow.

However, large-scale use of battery-electric vehicles (particularly automobiles), combined with ubiquitous automatic recharging, introduces a large amount of battery storage capacity into the grid. In principle, this can be used to keep supply and demand in balance. When load on the grid is low and vehicles require recharging, they can transfer electricity from the grid to recharge. Conversely, when load on the grid is high and vehicles have excess stored energy, they can transfer electricity back to the grid. This is not the only advantage to the grid. This battery capacity can also be utilized to provide voltage and frequency regulation—thus enhancing the quality of the electrical supply.

This sort of system can be managed optimally through dynamic pricing. When overall electricity demand is high, electricity prices rise and price signals motivate vehicles to sell. Conversely, when overall demand is low, prices drop and price signals motivate vehicles to buy. Intelligent vehicles can be programmed with optimal electricity trading strategies that take account of their use patterns and attempt to minimize overall energy costs over some time horizon.

This is not possible with old-fashioned electric grids, of the kind that still operate in most parts of the world, but it becomes feasible with emerging smart grids. In smart grids there is an overlay of information networking on the electric supply network. This enables much more sophisticated metering at buildings and vehicle-charging stations, two-way flow of electricity (since buildings and vehicles now may not only be electricity consumption points, but also production and storage points), and the dynamic pricing that is necessary for effective management.

This also enables a grid that relies less upon large, centralized generation plants and makes more use of decentralized sources. Buildings can begin to effectively integrate solar panels, wind turbines, micro-CHP (combined heat and power) systems, and so on. Potentially large efficiencies can be achieved through the clever combination of smart grids, decentralized sustainable sources, and the battery capacity of electric vehicles.

It is sometimes objected that lightweight, efficient electric vehicles consume so little electricity, and therefore have such low operating costs, that price signals might provide insufficient motivation to sell electricity back to the utility. Why not simply hoard it to provide maximum available range at any moment? With ubiquitous automatic recharging, however, there will be little motivation to hoard. Furthermore, small price differences multiplied over large numbers of electric vehicles do add up to significant amounts of money. This means that fleet operators, such as those operating the mobility-on-demand systems, will be motivated to develop optimal recharging strategies that respond to price signals.

Mobility-on-Demand Systems

Smart electric vehicles—GreenWheels, RoboScooters, or City-Cars—can simply be marketed as appealing consumer products. But they can also be employed to launch new kinds of mobility services—mobility-on-demand systems that enable convenient point-to-point travel within urban areas, enable very high vehicle utilization rates, and extend availability to those who cannot or do not want to own their own vehicles. This category of users includes visitors to a city who generally don't bring their own vehicles with them, occasional riders and drivers who cannot justify the cost of ownership, those who don't have anywhere to store a vehicle, and those who don't want the responsibility and bother of ownership and maintenance.

Large-scale systems employing traditional, non-electric bicycles—for example, Vélib in Paris, Vélov in Lyon, Bicing in Barcelona, and Bixi in Montreal—have already demonstrated the feasibility of mobility-on-demand. In these systems, racks of bicycles are spaced around the city such that potential users are rarely more than a short walk away from a rack. To make a trip, a user walks to a nearby rack, swipes a card to provide identification and unlock a bicycle, rides to a rack near the trip destination, drops off the bicycle, and walks the rest of the way.

Substitution of lightweight electric vehicles bicycles increases the range and utility of these systems, and makes them useable by more people. Where this begins with GreenWheel bicycles it requires little additional infrastructure, since racks for traditional mobility-on-demand bicycle fleets require power supply and data connection in any case. It is straightforward to upgrade them to provide battery charging as well.

Automatically recharging CityCars in their parking spaces

Since acquiring real estate for vehicle pickup and dropoff points, and providing power supply at these points, are key issues in the implementation of mobility-on-demand systems, starting with a relatively simple, low-investment, GreenWheel-based system makes sense. This establishes the foundation for later expanding the system to scooters or automobiles.

Retail location theory suggests that, where pickup and dropoff points are of equal capacity, they should serve equal population catchments. This means that they will be closely spaced in areas of high population density. Alternatively, pickup and dropoff points might be evenly spaced, at intervals determined by comfortable walking distance, and varied in size according to surrounding population density.

Once pickup and dropoff points have been deployed and stocked, the fundamental management challenge with mobility-on-demand systems is to keep the system balanced. Across the system's service area, demand for vehicles—as expressed by customers showing up and wanting to pick up vehicles—varies dynamically from location to location and over time. Similarly, the supply of vehicles and parking spaces—as expressed by stocks available at access locations—varies dynamically. The task is to keep supply and demand in balance, such that customers never have to wait for unacceptable lengths of time for vehicles or parking spaces, and the numbers of vehicles and parking spaces required to achieve this balance are minimized.

The difficulty of the balancing task depends upon the skewness of the distribution of demand in space and time. Where desired trip origins and destinations are randomly distributed, the system can be expected to self-organize—keeping vehicles distributed fairly evenly throughout the service area. But where demand is highly skewed—for example, when it is dominated by morning and evening commutes—keeping the system balanced requires effort and costs money.

One way to balance the system is to move riderless vehicles to where they are needed, for example by loading bikes on trucks. This can be done by setting up the system in the small hours of the morning, letting it become gradually less balanced during the day, and then resetting it the following evening. Alternatively, vehicles can be moved continually—in effect, resetting it less sweepingly but at shorter time intervals. In either case, balancing is easier when there are buffers of excess vehicles and parking spaces in the system to absorb minor imbalances.

A more elegant approach is to exploit elasticities in times and locations of trips, and to manage demand through dynamic

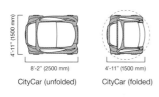

CityCar (unfolded) CityCar (folded)

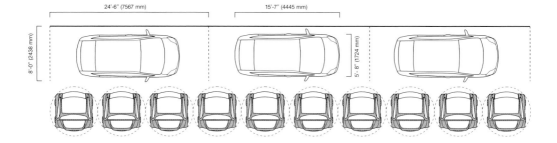

Parking density for CityCars compared to traditional automobiles

pricing. Under this strategy, it becomes more expensive for customers to pick up vehicles from locations where demand for them is currently high; similarly, it becomes more expensive to drop off vehicles at locations where parking spaces are currently heavily in demand. Price signals thus motivate customer behavior patterns that keep supply and demand in equilibrium. Here the cost of system balancing is not that of moving riderless vehicles, but of providing the necessary price incentives.

All of these strategies require the support of a sophisticated networked information technology. For both billing customers and monitoring the distribution of vehicles and parking spaces in the system, it is necessary to track vehicle pickups and dropoffs in real time. The system must also compute optimum balancing strategies, and either make price adjustments or send instructions to redistribution truck operators.

Mobility-on-demand systems can and should coexist with privately owned vehicles. Through appropriate standards, and use of appropriate information technology, they can share parking spaces and recharging infrastructure. Such a joint system is likely to be more effective in meeting all aspects of demand, and it facilitates economies of scale in both vehicle supply and infrastructure development.

The Computational Back-End—A Real-Time Urban Nervous System

A fundamental task of the computational back-end behind electric vehicle mobility-on-demand systems integrated with smart grids is to track the use of resources—that is, electricity, vehicles, and parking spaces—in real time. Smart meters can monitor electricity consumption by buildings and vehicle

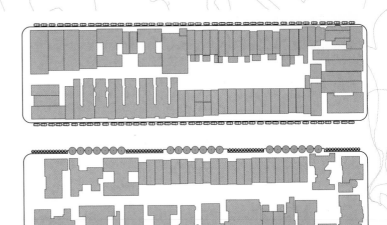

**Streetscape opportunities
created by the CityCar's lower
parking density**

recharging stations, and electricity supply back to the grid from these locations. Loads on the mobility system can be monitored by electronically tracking vehicle pickups and dropoffs, and the fluctuating stocks of vehicles and parking spaces at mobility-on-demand stations.

The high-level management task is one of organizing electricity, vehicle, and parking space supply so that supplies meet demands that are unevenly distributed in space and fluctuate over time. It is a large-scale, complex stock-and-flow management problem. At any moment there are stocks of electricity stored in vehicle batteries, of available vehicles at pickup points, and of available parking spaces at dropoff points. There are transfers of electricity into and out of batteries, and of vehicles among access points. The directions, magnitudes, and rates of these transfers are controlled by price signals that establish real-time feedback loops. The idea is to regulate the system optimally by means of these feedback loops.

For a mobility system user, the system should make an adequately charged vehicle available at a pickup station truly "on demand"—wherever and whenever the user needs it. For the electric utility, the system should accomplish this in the most cost-effective way possible, and with minimum carbon emissions. And for the mobility-on-demand system operator, the system operate with the minimum number of vehicles and parking spaces.

The first computational challenge in this is one of data-processing scale. The system must harvest data on a very large scale, organize it into databases, and query those databases to extract useful management information—all under very tight time constraints. The second challenge is one of optimization. Based on these inputs from the field, the system

**Potential distribution of different
types of charging stations in the
Boston area**

**Potential distribution of mobility-
on-demand access points in the
Taipei area**

must compute optimal pricing strategies for electricity and vehicle trips over some time horizon. And the third challenge is one of achieving dispersed control. The system must send price signals to tens of thousands (at least) of buildings and vehicles dispersed across the system's service area.

These challenges are not insurmountable, but they are formidable. And there is very little practical experience of building and operating large-scale systems of this type.

Conclusion: Smart Sustainable Cities for the Twenty-first Century

The strategies that I have described achieve efficiently integrated operation of major urban mobility and energy systems through use of lightweight energy-efficient hardware, ubiquitous intelligence, digital networking, and real-time control. They are technologically feasible and provide major sustainability benefits. They initiate the process of transforming cities into systems that are closely analogous to modern aircraft and spacecraft, racecars, and chemical process plants—that is, responsive, high-performance systems that rely on advanced real-time control capabilities.

Proposal for a mobility-on-demand system serving the historic center of Florence

Sustainable Mobility in Action

Federico Parolotto

The seemingly unstoppable growth of car usage around the world is affecting the urban fabric. Driving on the outskirts of cities such as Boston, Milan, Tripoli, Muscat, and Beijing is a similar experience, with buildings spread over vast areas— too far apart to foster pedestrian connectivity and too low in density to allow public transport to be effective.

The informal growth of cities determined by car accessibly, so clearly described by Stefano Boeri in *Il territorio che cambia* in relation to northern Italy, is a common element of the vast majority of developments around the world, especially in so-called emerging countries.[1] Driving from central Tripoli toward Tunisia, for instance, is a striking experience: you witness intense traffic determined by the continuous strip of buildings scattered along each side of the road to Tunis, buildings adjacent to the street accessible only by car, buildings that were not there just ten years ago. It is a growing phenomenon due to the steep rise in car ownership in that country.

What was described as a rather grim potential scenario in the visionary book by John Whitelegg, *Transport for a Sustainable Future: The Case for Europe* (1993), is becoming reality only sixteen years later. Whitelegg maintains that the car is a problem well beyond CO_2 emissions:

> It [the car] consumes vast amounts of energy in its manufacture, is used only 5% of the time and when in use is occupied by an average of 1.2 people. It creates enormous problems in waste disposal which is particularly serious for tyres, exhaust systems and batteries, is manufactured and sold on the basis that cities move much slower than 30 mph, and initiates environmental damage on an enormous scale to provide itself with roads, car parks and artifacts that generate even more cars … motorized transport has a serious

Road connecting Tripoli with Tunis

effect on human health including traffic accidents, loss of
dence for children and destruction of communities as a
road construction.[2]

He argues that private transport culture is activating an unsustainable process; the way we move and the way we have
shaped our territory determines trip patterns and energy consumption that is not sustainable:

> There is (as yet) no such thing as a green car…. Vehicles with zero
> emissions, zero fuel consumption and virtually zero impact on pe-
> destrians, cyclists, and urban population densities might be green
> but then we might as well rediscover bicycles and feet.[3]

My work has always focused on sustainable mobility, from
the more traditional approaches to the most radical ones.
I believe that the pattern of land use and the density and
distribution of buildings have embedded a pattern of mobility.

Section through Masdar

Travel distance to different destinations within Masdar

PRT prototype

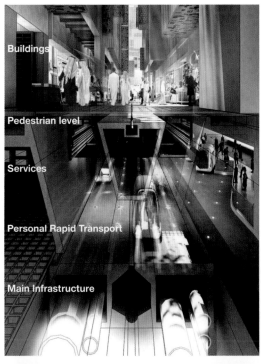

Buildings

Pedestrian level

Services

Personal Rapid Transport

Main Infrastructure

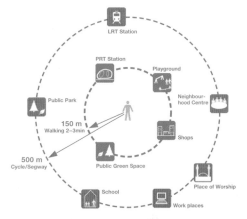

LRT Station

PRT Station

Playground

Public Park

Neighbour-
hood Centre

150 m
Walking 2–3min

Shops

500 m
Cycle/Segway

Public Green Space

Place of Worship

School

Work places

399

Therefore my approach emphasizes trying to prevent master plans from determining car-oriented development or, at least, to minimize the impact of private transport. But it is often a frustrating experience to try to shift developers and local authorities from a car-based culture that asks for fluidly in traffic and rarely takes into account the need to minimize emissions and produce safe and pleasant environments for pedestrians and cyclists.

Yet a new way of thinking is emerging from more enlightened developers, those inclined to produce more sustainable urban development, where the urban land-use mix, connection with public transport, and restriction of car use tends to generate a "better place" and therefore possible higher returns on investment. In recent years, I have worked on several projects strongly focused on sustainability, such as Burnby in Prague, designed by Asymptote and CMA; Canal City in Dubai, designed by KPF; and the most radical, the Masdar Initiative in Abu Dhabi, designed by Foster + Partners.

Masdar, currently under construction, is an attempt to create the first carbon-neutral, zero-waste development. The project was conceived as a car-free development from the outset. This makes Masdar the first effort to develop an urban fabric—accommodating about 70,000 people during the day—without allowing cars to circulate. The solution was to concentrate land use in a dense area of 1.5 square kilometers. Access to the site is granted by private transport—Abu Dhabi has virtually no public transport at the moment, although it is planning a different future—from a light-rail transit (LRT) system connecting the development with the more residential area of the Al Raha development to, in the long term, an underground connection as well as a fleet of buses and other high-occupancy vehicles. The ambitious aim is to achieve 40 percent of access to the site by private transport and the remaining 60 percent via public transport.

Masdar car park location, LRT stops within Masdar, and PRT routes below the parking deck

On reaching the development using private transport, you park at one of the nine car parks located on the perimeter.

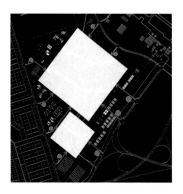 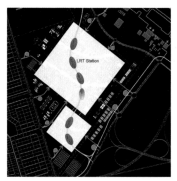 

1 Stefano Boeri, Arturo Lanzani, and Edoardo Martini, *Il territorio che cambia: ambienti, paesaggi e immagini della regione milanese* (Milan: Editrice Abitare Segesta, 1993).
2 John Whitelegg, *Transport for a Sustainable Future: The Case for Europe* (London: Wiley, 1993), 3.
3 Ibid.
4 Luca Guala conceived and developed the PRT system.

If you live in the development, you will be allowed to drive to the "walled" part of the city. If coming by bus or other high-occupancy vehicle, you will be dropped off at the ground floor of the car park. If accessing the city with the LRT system, you will be able to directly enter the heart of the citadel.

The most innovative element of Masdar is the personal rapid transit (PRT) system of fully automated vehicles that will allow access to the city from the car park and movement within the city itself.[4] The system represents a breakthrough in the transport world. The 38-kilometer network will accommodate 1,800 vehicles at about 87 stations for passengers; the PRT will also stop at about 120 freight stations, allowing for widespread distribution of goods. The PRT technology is relatively simple, based on electrical engines operated by lithium batteries. The complexity is constituted by the supervisory control system, which the vehicle fleet will have underneath, governing berths, paths, recharging, and so on.

The Masdar transport strategy is the first attempt to move away from a traditional transport system to an on-demand system that allows almost door-to-door service—an innovation in the world of transport. And maybe a first step to a better future.

Sustaining the City in the Face of Advanced Marginality

Loïc Wacquant

In their effort to tackle emergent forms of urban relegation, if only to contain their disruptive social effects and negative political repercussions, nation-states face a policy choice with a three-pronged alternative. Which branch of this alternative becomes the dominant path followed by the members of the European Union will largely determine the kind of supranational society they are to become.

The first option, representing a sort of immobile middle ground, consists in *patching up and redeploying the existing programs of the welfare state* aimed at supporting or rearming marginalized populations. This can be done, for instance, by extending medical coverage, reinforcing emergency programs such as the SAMU Social (France's "crisis social work" teams for street derelicts, patterned after medical emergency squads), by "activating" assistance programs to make them over into springboards toward training and employment, or by authorizing recipients of public aid packages to combine work and aid for a preset period (to close "poverty traps"), not to mention mobilizing the networks of the nonprofit sector.

It is clear that this is not getting the job done, or the problems posed by advanced marginality would not be so pressing today, and their accumulation in the dispossessed redoubts of the city would have been thwarted if not inverted. One might even argue that, shorn of a clear philosophy and operating increasingly on the subnational scale (at the level of the region, municipality, or neighborhood) and in part subcontracted to the nonprofit sector, these piecemeal, short-term responses to the recurrent disruptions caused by urban polarization from below can contribute to perpetuating them insofar as they increase the bureaucratic cacophony and inefficiency of the state, which cannot but sap the legitimacy of the social treatment of poverty in the long run.

The second, regressive and repressive, solution is to *criminalize poverty via the punitive containment of the poor* in the increasingly isolated and stigmatized neighborhoods in which they are confined, on the one hand, and in jails and prisons that operate as their spillway, on the other. This is the route taken by the United States in the aftermath of the ghetto uprisings of the 1960s and in reaction to the generalization of social insecurity over the ensuing two decades.[1] It is not by happenstance that the stupendous expansion of the carceral sector of the American state—the population behind bars has quadrupled in twenty-five years, and departments of correction have risen to the rank of third-largest employer in the country, even as crime levels remained grosso modo constant and then declined sharply over that period—was started just when unemployment and casual (under)employment were spreading, public assistance was fast shrinking before being "reformed" into a system of forced employment (called "workfare"), and when the ghetto was imploding as the result of the combined pressure of black mobilization, deindustrialization, and public policies of urban abandonment. Indeed, the atrophy of the social state and the hypertrophy of the penal state in the United States are two correlative and complementary transformations that partake of the institution of a new government of misery, whose function is precisely to impose desocialized wage labor as a norm of citizenship for the lower class while providing a functional substitute for the ghetto as a mechanism of racial control.

Although the United States is truly exceptional for the zeal with which it has embraced this "solution" to social polarization and for the scale on which it has implemented it,[2] the temptation to rely on the police, judicial, and carceral institutions to stem the effects of social insecurity generated by the spread of precarious work and the retrenchment of social welfare is present throughout Europe. This can be seen by noting four deep-seated features of penal evolution on the continent:

1. The spectacular rise of incarceration rates among most member countries of the European Union over the past two decades:[3] between 1983 and 2000, this rate jumped from 70 to 95 inmates per 100,000 in France, from 73 to 93 in Italy, from 87 to 124 in England, from 28 to 90 in the Netherlands, and from 37 to 114 in Spain.

2. The massive overrepresentation, within the carceral population, of non-European immigrants and of persons of color, as well as of drug retailers and users, the homeless, the mentally ill, and other rejects from the labor market. Thus, in 1997, foreigners comprised more than one-third of the population under lock and key in Germany, Belgium, and Holland, and nearly one-quarter in France, Italy, and Austria (although they only made up between 2 and 8 per cent of the population of those countries).

3. The overcrowding of custodial establishments, which reduces detention to its raw function of warehousing undesirable categories. In 1997, more than one-third of the jails and

prisons of France and Belgium and one-half of the prisons of Italy and Spain were in a situation of "critical overcrowding" (with an inmate count exceeding capacity by 20 percent). The congestion of confinement facilities translates into a shrinkage of living and private space, the deterioration of sanitary standards and medical conditions, the rise of violence and suicide, and penury in exercise as well as programs for education, training, and preparation for returning to society.

4. The generalized hardening of penal policies, more openly turned toward incapacitation at the expense of rehabilitation, and tacitly guided by the principle of "less eligibility,"[4] even when it grossly contravenes efforts to reduce recidivism after release.

Recent shifts in public discourse on urban disorder reveal a similar drift toward the penal treatment of poverty and the dislocations that, paradoxically, arise from having truncated the social and economic capacities of the state. One is thus impelled to predict that a downward convergence of Europe on the social front, entailing further deregulation of the labor market and the continued reduction of the collective safety net, will ineluctably result in an upward harmonization on the penal front, feeding a new burst of carceral inflation throughout the continent.[5]

Despite the colossal social and financial costs of the mass confinement of poor and disruptive populations, imprisonment remains a seductive diversion and tempting stopgap counter to mounting urban dislocations even in the most tolerant and egalitarian societies such as the Nordic countries.[6] But aside from the powerful political and cultural obstacles that stand in the way of the wholesale carceralization of misery embedded in the makeup of social-democratic or Christian-democratic states of Europe, as well as in the civic ethos of their population, punitive containment leaves untouched the root causes of the new marginality. This is to say that its implementation is bound to fail in the long run and eventually points to a third, progressive response to urban polarization from below: the *offensive reconstruction of the social state* that would put its structure and policies in accord with the emerging economic conditions, the transformation of family forms, and the remaking of gender relations as well as with new social aspirations to participation in collective life.[7]

Radical innovations such as the institution of a "citizen's wage" (or basic income grant provided to all without restrictions) that would decouple subsistence from work; free education and job training through the lifecourse; and an effective guarantee of universal access to the three essential

public goods of housing, health, and transportation are needed to expand the sphere of social rights and check the dele-
terious effects of the fragmentation of wage labor.[8] In the end,
this third option is the only viable response to the historic
challenge that advanced marginality poses to democratic
societies as they cross the threshold of the new millennium.

This text is excerpted and adapted from Loïc Wacquant, "Logics of Urban Polarisation from Below," in *Urban Outcasts: A Comparative Sociology of Advanced Marginality* (Cambridge, MA: Polity, 2008).

1 Michael Tonry, *Malign Neglect – Race, Crime, and Punishment in America* (New York: Oxford University Press, 1995); Loïc Wacquant, *Punishing the Poor: The Neoliberal Government of Social Insecurity* (Durham and London, Duke University Press, 2009).
2 With 710 inmates per 100,000 residents in 2000, the United States has become the world leader in incarceration. It confines five to twelve times as many people proportionately as do the EU countries (when the EU had fifteen members), although the latter have levels of crime (aside from homicide) similar to those of the United States.
3 The statistics that follow are drawn from the editions of the *Statistique pénale annuelle du Conseil de l'Europe* published by the Council of Europe in Strasbourg for the years covered.

4 Applied to the penal realm, the Benthamite criterion of "less eligibility" (initially formulated in 1796 and introduced during the Irish famine of 1840 for individuals asking for welfare support) stipulates that the situation of the most favored inmate should always be less desirable than that of the least favored "free" worker, so that wage earners are not incited to commit crimes to improve their condition by getting themselves imprisoned.
5 Loïc Wacquant, *Prisons of Poverty* (Minneapolis: University of Minnesota Press, 2009).
6 Nils Christie, "Eléments de géographie pénale," *Actes de la recherche en sciences sociales* 124 (September 1998): 68–74.
7 Gøsta Esping-Andersen, *Why We Need a New Welfare State* (Oxford: Oxford University Press, 2002).
8 Philippe Van Parijs, *Real Freedom for All: What (If Anything) Can Justify Capitalism?* (Oxford: Oxford University Press, 1995); Guy Standing, ed., *Promoting Income Security as a Right: Europe and North America* (London: Anthem, 2004).

A General Theory
of Sustainable Urbanism

Andrés Duany

The Crises

Three great crises are upon us, of such magnitude that they may be considered permanent: climate change, peak oil, and the evaporation of national wealth, otherwise known as the real estate bust. Because the crises are all downtrends, there is a general feeling that they are related, and there is in fact an objective linchpin: the lifestyle of the American middle class—the way we drive around for ordinary daily needs, dwell large on the land and in commoditized real estate products, and secure our food. It is that lifestyle, and now the worldwide export version, that is the cause of all the crises. If this lifestyle can be summarized, it is surely "suburban sprawl."

Designers have become engaged in reform, and while the first generation of responses has been restricted to buildings (LEED), the urban scale is now being deployed (LEED-ND). The name has been agreed to—"Sustainable Urbanism"—but confusion remains, as several paradigms are serious contenders for that title. Among these are the Old Urbanism, the now-mature New Urbanism, and the nascent Landscape Urbanism. There is another, but given the seriousness of the situation, Irresponsible Urbanism might finally be dismissed from the planning discourse.

The Contenders

The term Irresponsible Urbanism was derived from Rem Koolhaas's piece "Atlanta," which concludes, "The city is out of control, let us be irresponsible."[1] From its origins in Broadacre City, this paradigm has been gradually dumbed down through decades of inbreeding at the U.L.I., to a vegetative state in the care of today's libertarian fringe. But it is not yet dead. One of the tasks of Sustainable Urbanism is to retain what the Irresponsible Urbanism did well: being marketable, relatively inexpensive, and easy to administer. If this is not achieved, it may rise again. Remember that suburban sprawl is the idiot savant of urban planning, able to sucker the sympathy of Herbert Gans, Robert Venturi, and Denise Scott Brown—and quite recently the apologists of "unprecedented typologies," as if its problem were the absence of a suitable aesthetic.

The Old Urbanism was informally named by Alex Krieger when he asked, "But isn't the New Urbanism just the Old Urbanism?" It is not too flattering, but the term seems to be more acceptable than "Traditional Urbanism." The Old Urbanism is in resurgence as more people notice that living densely, walking, and taking transit is an environmentally responsible lifestyle. The word is that a Manhattanite has half the ecological footprint of the average American. Its predicament is that it is technically at odds with current environmental standards. The Manhattan we know is an unattainable ideal that could not be built today for a multitude of reasons—the first being the hundreds of streams buried in pipes that its urban pattern requires. While it is an environmental success in its secondary consequences, it is an environmental disaster in its technical premises. The Old Urbanism values nature not at all—and those days are over.

Despite Alex Krieger's question, the New Urbanism differs from the Old Urbanism in many ways—one being that in the past, cities used to compete with other cities on a level playing field, but today, cities compete with their own suburbs—which have a greater range of typological resources. It is technically pitted against Irresponsible Urbanism's polymorphic agility, which is enabled by cheap land and cheap oil. The New Urbanism mitigates the enormous physical impact of the car, but does not eliminate it. Its predicament as a hybrid is that it is capable of combining the best as well as the worst aspects of both city and suburb.

Landscape Urbanism is also a hybrid. Having its origins in the formal conceits of garden design, it is now updated with the "green" touchstones of native plant species, naturalistic hydrological systems, and corridor topology. This design innovation is now offering its services as a setting for buildings—and not just as their ornamental appendage—thereby reaching for the mantle of urbanism. But that is more than it can bear; with tools limited to the imitation of nature, Landscape Urbanism cannot avoid the ruralization of even high-density schemes (the other side of New Urbanism's urbanizing of low density). With rabid bias against spatial definition, there is no such thing in its repertoire as a "corridor street" or a "square." The public realm is primarily therapeutic: rustic walking, rooting about with edible planting, and communing with nature are surrogates for the social activity fostered by Old Urban places. Even Landscape Urbanism's vaunted engagement with "infrastructure" amounts to buffering arterials, improving the design of storm-water apparatus, and decorating parking lots with porous paving. But an urban paradigm cannot be based on the implantation of natural vignettes in the residual places between buildings. Besides, Landscape Urbanism is too adept at being compromised by providing a green camouflage for the so-called unprecedented typologies of big-box retailers and junkspace office parks.

The Challenge

How to assess these three contenders for Sustainable Urbanism, when there is not yet any consensus within this new discourse? One way is to establish an abstract theory that can provide the test while it is itself being qualified by the integrity and usefulness of its testing process. This protocol must manifest that mystique of technique that underpins credibility in the modern political forum. And its metrics must be based on recognizable forms of natural processes so that environmentalists may be conscripted among the informed assessors rather than remaining intransigent NIMBYs. Moreover, the theory must be simple enough to be administered by a bureaucracy that is accustomed to the robotic protocols of Euclidean zoning.

The Theory

Would the Rural-to-Urban Transect serve this rather abstract challenge as it has so many utilitarian ones?[2] The Transect is an environmental theory based on geography that ranges from wilderness to urban core. By integrating environmental methodology for habitat management with zoning methodology for urban design, the Transect breaks down the customary specialized assessment, enabling environmentalists to consider the design of the cultural habitats, and urbanists to protect the natural ones. It can analyze and project the mix of human and natural elements that symbiotically create functional habitats. Today it is a freeware operating system available for zoning codes and other technical standards intended to replace the current system of zoning.[3] It has proven to be a powerful taxonomic engine for the wildly disparate elements that must comprise a Sustainable Urbanism.

As the proposed General Theory of Sustainable Urbanism must mediate between worlds, it proposes as a common currency the concept of diversity, which both the natural sciences and the social sciences employ as an index. Both biological and economic activity is based on transaction (of chemicals, of heat, of goods or services). A currency is designed to clarify the evaluation of what is given in exchange for what is gained. A transaction is physically, economically, or politically sustainable so long as it is a fair trade. For instance, the NIMBY regime arose with the consciousness that suburban sprawl was not a fair trade—that a housing subdivision or shopping center was an exchange downward for the loss of a field or wood-land. Before suburban sprawl, development was generally considere d an upward trade: a woodland or farm might be lost, but the village or town gained was considered good value. For example, the wetlands of the Charles Town Peninsula were lost, but the City of Charleston was considered to be a fair

Intensity of elements along the transect

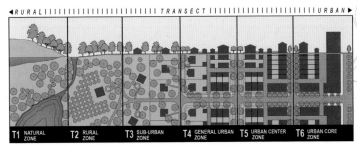

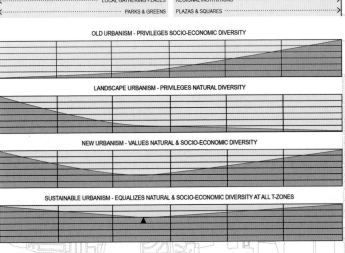

gain. It would not have been acceptable if what had replaced them was a suburban resort like nearby Hilton Head.

The Transect could elucidate a General Theory of Sustainable Urbanism with an equation:
At any point on the Rural-to-Urban Transect, the aggregate density of the social and natural diversity after urbanization must be approximately equal to or greater than the density of the natural diversity prior to urbanization.[4]

$$N: \Sigma \, [Ds + Dn]post \approx > N: [DN]pre$$

where:
   N = a constant number
   Ds = the diverse socioeconomic activities per unit of land, after urbanization
   Dn = the diverse natural habitats per unit of land, after urbanization
   DN = the diverse natural habitats per unit of land before urbanization

The graphs show the paradigms contending for Sustainable Urbanism in terms of this equation as an illustration of the General Theory. With the Old Urbanism, the social diversity of the T6 Urban Core correctly rates higher than T3 Suburban. But there is a conceptual problem, as this lopsided measure assigns an even lesser value to T2 Rural—and T1 Natural has no value at all. The Old Urbanism created value by creating jobs, housing, shops, and entertainment. The diversity was achieved by their organic proximity in pedestrian sheds when cars were rare. The positive environmental consequences of the Old Urbanism are compactness, complexity, walkability, and transit viability. The negative is that land must be denatured by network continuity into a commodity suitable for compact building. The Old Urbanism manifests an excellent environmental performance, but it cannot be inaugurated or extended without the elimination of nature.

Landscape Urbanism's problem is that the T3 Suburban rates higher than the T6 Urban Core, which has the worst performance. This is the result of the absolute privileging of natural diversity, revealing the serious conceptual flaw of this paradigm. Landscape Urbanism has no metrics to assess the urban side of the Transect. With only half the tools, the Urban Core's social diversity does not register except as impervious pavement and denatured heat island. Places like London and Manhattan are rated as enormously negative ecological footprints. Such urban patterns are considered part of the problem and not part of the solution.

1 Rem Koolhaas, "Atlanta: A Reading," in *Atlanta*, edited by Ramon Prat (Barcelona: Actar, 1996).

2 See www.transect.org and "Regulating as if Humans Matter," Andrés Duany and David Brain, *Regulating Place: Standards and the Shaping of Urban America*, edited by Eran Ben-Joseph and Terry S. Szold (New York: Routledge, 2005), 293–332.

3 See SmartCode, www.transect.org. There are some thirty Transect-based modules.

4 This type of equation contains both immeasurables (indices of diversity) and incommensurables (the natural and the social). Unlike the hard sciences, approximate metrics may constitute equations in the social and environmental sciences, as they serve to elucidate a trend. A discussion of this appears in *It Must Be Beautiful: Great Equations of Modern Science* (London: Granta, 2002) by Graham Farmelo.

The New Urbanism assigns T3 Suburban the lowest value, as it has the lowest index in both social and natural diversity, thus correcting the assessment of the other two paradigms. With an array of tools ranging from the urban boundary for the preservation of nature at T1–T2, and a transit orientation enabling density and social diversity at T5–T6, the New Urbanism is capable of selectively accepting or rejecting nature depending on the relative urbanity of the T-zone. However, it is unable to justify the persistence of the suburban single-family house, except as driven by market preference—a regrettable necessity to implement its larger agenda elsewhere along the Transect. This flaw precludes the New Urbanism from becoming the paradigm for Sustainable Urbanism.

Sustainable Urbanism retains the "correct" high points of social and natural diversity of the New Urbanism, but it improves the performance of T3 Suburban by integrating it technically to a green regime. T3 is redesigned by definition to compensate for its higher land occupation and transportation impact with requirements for energy generation, water reuse, recycling/composting, and food production. The ability to do this happens to coincide with its higher allocation of land per capita. These mitigating techniques are better handled by a freestanding house than by the urban building types of T5 and T6. The suburban thus becomes T-3 Sub-Urban, with no opprobrium attached. A general theory of Sustainable Urbanism thus equalizes the environmental performance all along the Transect, retaining the choice that is integral to the politics of a market economy.

Summary

Both natural and social diversity are combined in various ratios along the rural-to-urban transect. The high natural diversity of T1 Natural establishes the ideal for Landscape Urbanism, while the high social diversity of T6 Urban Core establishes the ideal for the Old Urbanism. But these two monovalent paradigms undervalue the positive consequences of the other, in the process assigning an unwarranted high value to T3 Suburban. The New Urbanism values both natural and social diversity at T1 and T6, while correctly devaluing the suburban point of T3, which has the lowest indices of both. Sustainable Urbanism, according to the General Theory, equalizes the combined level of diversity of all T-zones, creating the Sub-Urban, so that all are justified environmentally, and the market can exercise its preferences. The equation of the General Theory can determine if a transaction to the urban can fairly justify the loss of nature.

The Political Ecology
of Ecological Urbanism

Paul Robbins

During the summer of 1995, almost 500 people died in the Chicago heat wave that had the city in its locked embrace for a week. By all reasonable, apolitical, and traditional accounts, this is an urban natural disaster, amenable perhaps to better design of buildings and more investment in cooling infrastructure. On closer examination, as Eric Klinenberg reveals in his "social autopsy" of the disaster, the bodies that filled the morgue did not fully resemble the city's population at large, and were disproportionately elderly, poor, and African American.[1] Is this an aberration, or does it represent a structured pattern?

The city of Milwaukee has urban forest cover that is nationally celebrated and historically rooted in explicit policies to create and distribute trees around the landscape. Careful analysis of the actual distribution of trees in the city through air photography, however, suggests a less-than-fully even pattern. Specifically, there is a strongly positive relationship between dense canopy cover and high household income, and a negative relationship between tree canopy cover and the percentage of renters and African-American and Hispanic residents.[2] Are these uneven benefits of green urbanism an unfortunate accident, or instead a habit of the way cities work?

In the conurbation of Rawalpindi/Islamabad in Pakistan, flooding presents a large and growing hazard, as the streams that lace through the city overflow their banks as a result of urban growth, encroachments, and garbage disposal in the drainages. As Daanish Mustafa has observed, however, despite an enormous range of perceptions, solutions, and ideas professed by residents in the flood zone—ranging from solid waste control to park construction to diversions—the local experts who are charged and empowered to manage and control flooding actually perceive a much smaller range of choice than do residents.[3] The ideas and ecological knowledges of people living in and along these complex ecologies have come to count far less than the views of experts trained in hydrology in faraway places. Is this an incidental irony, or a more deeply entrenched relationship of authority surrounding what counts as true?

To answer these questions, or critically address any of these events or conditions, it is essential to take seriously the proposition that the immediate effects observed in urban environments may be the product of more deeply structured relationships, ones that often produce recurrent and even repellent outcomes. The loosely confederated field of research and activism that surrounds this proposition is usually referred to as *political ecology*, that body of action-knowledge that "combines the concerns of ecology and a broadly defined political economy."[4] This field, though long-rooted in agrarian politics and the conflicts that arise around forests, fields, and fisheries, has increasingly been brought to bear to explain how urban forms and transformations impinge on both the ecological systems operating within cities and the social and political configurations that are entangled with these. In this sense, urban political ecology is essentially an empirical effort to assess the social and political forces that regulate and direct the simultaneous flows of ecological elements (i.e., nutrients, water, shade, pollutants, information) and the flows of value and cost (i.e., profit, labor, amenities, suffering) that emanate from the changing configuration of cities.

The approach is necessarily disparate and eclectic, but it generally shares a few assumptions, rooted in the principles of ecology, but extended to their political implications. Following the well-known ecological principle that *everything is connected*, political ecology asks: how does ecological change empower or disempower those involved, both near at hand and connected across time and space? Taking seriously the observation that *everything must go somewhere*, political ecology explores the spatial and material patterns of creative destruction, accumulation, and flowing transfer that accompany all economic or political activity. Following the ecological principle that *there is no such thing as a free lunch*, political ecology asks: Who's buying? Quite in parallel, as Eric Swyngedouw puts it, "there is no such thing as an unsustainable city in general, but rather there are a series of urban and environmental processes that negatively affect some social groups while benefitting others."[5]

In working to achieve a sustainable city—one that produces less carbon, nurtures more biodiversity, or creates a more healthy citizenry—it is essential to acknowledge that the possibility of those outcomes rests on sorting through the messy implications that all ecology possesses. Put simply, urban political ecology encourages us to think about the greening of the city, not simply as a social good but as one with potentially uneven effects on differing populations, based on the deeply conditioned relationships.[6] As value is created and destroyed in reworking and reimagining the city, there are rare opportunities to reconfigure urban labor, power, and property relations. Conversely, deeply entrenched interests can seize any such moments of "creative destruction" to capture value in motion[7] or to seize control of collective property and exclude, marginalize, or remove diverse and "inconvenient" populations.[8] For political ecologists then, problems in city garbage management may contain within them struggles over development,[9] and cultural norms surrounding home landscaping may contain within them patterns of accumulation set in motion by global petrochemical producers.[10] The questions that can be put to ecological urbanism, with this in mind, are at least threefold.

First, it must be imagined that from the multitude of options available in reimagining or greening cities, some will carry more or fewer costs and benefits from different kinds of residents, any of which may be unforeseen without careful scrutiny. Consider the green park spaces of Philadelphia, a city designed with an explicit concern for a chain of greenery to flow throughout in its Fairmount Park System. As Alec Browlow demonstrates, however, the dwindling of resources dedicated to maintaining these parks over time created very unevenly distributed trends in care and management, ultimately resulting in dangerous, overgrown, and neglected spaces, fraught with real and perceived danger, especially by the disproportionately poor and minority residents in neighborhoods nearby.[11]

Question 1: Precisely what will constitute the criteria of a greener city, and where will the value from specific design choices and changes accrue, at the expense of whose labor and investment?

Much of the answer to this rests, urban political ecology suggests, on exactly which institutions and imaginaries are utilized in envisioning and executing ecological urbanism. The greening of Milwaukee, described above, for example, was overseen by the city's much-vaunted Bureau of Forestry. But this organization has a management core that is historically white (despite a heavily African-American labor force in its ranks) and is overseen by a governing philosophy directed toward homeowners and private property relative to renters and public spaces.[12] Despite its best efforts, therefore, it proved incapable of imagining and executing urban forest outcomes that were more socially just.

Question 2: Precisely who will green the city, and for whom?

Much of this, in turn, is an extension of the power wielded through expertise in defining what is and is not true about urban ecology. When people organizing against urban hazards draw attention to dumping sites and smokestacks, the legitimacy of their claims is often filtered, most obviously, through raced and gendered lenses. Women urban environmental activists, for example, have consistently been sidelined as "hysterical housewives," whose claims can be shunted aside, especially where their emotional and experiential knowledge is disbarred by calls to science.[13] Though often vindicated long after the fact, immediate, local, and experiential knowledge in urban ecology faces potentially immovable obstacles in an ecological urbanism founded on engineering, planning, and associated forms of expertise.

Question 3: Precisely what forms of environmental knowledge will count in creating new green cities? How will competing ideas be weighed and privileged?

The value of political ecology for producing green cities therefore lies in its cautious insistence that "alternative and sustainable forms of urbanism" may well exist, but they necessarily require the ongoing investigation of how new urban forms present both opportunities and problems rooted in the tangled and sometimes divisive social and political contradictions already inherent in cities. Put simply: ecological urbanism is inevitably political; facing this head-on is the key to sustainability.

1 E. Klinenberg, *Heat Wave: A Social Autopsy of Disaster in Chicago* (Chicago: University of Chicago Press, 2002).
2 N. Heynen, H. A. Perkins, and P. Roy, "The Political Ecology of Uneven Urban Green Space—The Impact of Political Economy on Race and Ethnicity in Producing Environmental Inequality in Milwaukee, *Urban Affairs Review* 42 (1), 2006: 3–25.
3 D. Mustafa, "The Production of an Urban Hazardscape in Pakistan: Modernity, Vulnerability, and the Range of Choice," *Annals of the Association of American Geographers* 95 (3), 2005: 566–586.
4 P. Blaikie and H. Brookfield, *Land Degradation and Society* (London and New York: Methuen, 1987).
5 E. Swyngedouw, *Social Power and the Urbanization of Water: Flows of Power* (Oxford: Oxford University Press, 2004).
6 N. Heynen, M. Kaika, and E. Swyngedouw, eds., *In the Nature of Cities* (New York: Routledge, 2006).
7 D. Harvey, *The Limits to Capital* (Oxford: Basil Blackwell, 1982).

8 D. Mitchell, *The Right to the City: Social Justice and the Fight for Public Space* (New York: Guilford Press, 2003).
9 S. Moore, "The Politics of Garbage in Oaxaca, Mexico," *Society and Natural Resources* 21 (7), 2008: 596–610.
10 P. Robbins, *Lawn People: How Grasses, Weeds, and Chemicals Make Us Who We Are* (Philadelphia: Temple University Press. 2007).
11 A. Brownlow, "An Archaeology of Fear and Environmental Change in Philadelphia," *Geoforum* 37 (2), 2006: 227–245.
12 N. Heynen, H.A. Perkins, and P. Roy, "Failing to Grow 'Their' Own Justice? The Co- production of Racial/Gendered Labor and Milwaukee's Urban Forest," *Urban Geography* 28 (8), 2007: 732–754.
13 J. Seager, "'Hysterical Housewives' and Other Mad Women: Grassroots Environmental Organizing in the United States," in *Feminist Political Ecology: Global Issues and Local Experiences*, edited by D. Rocheleau, B. Thomas-Slayter, and E. Wangari (New York: Routledge, 1996), 271–283.

The SynCity Urban Energy System Model

Niels Schulz, Nilay Shah, David Fisk, James Keirstead, Nouri Samsatli,
Aruna Sivakumar, Celine Weber, Ellin Saunders

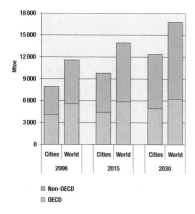

Urban and global trends in primary energy demand

Urbanization plays a central role in the heterogeneity of global energy-use patterns. In 2009, for the first time in history, more than half of the world's population is living in urban settlements, according to United Nations statistics. Urban areas all together used more than two-thirds (67 percent) of the technical primary energy in 2006, while covering less than 2 percent of the terrestrial planetary surface. The International Energy Agency projects that total primary energy demand will grow by 45 percent between 2006 and 2030 to more than 17 billion tonnes of oil equivalent annually. Moreover, the share of energy used in cities will have grown to 73 percent by 2030.[1] Providing this amount of energy in a sustainable way represents a major technical and environmental challenge.

The choice of infrastructure and the layout of settlement patterns for the current wave of urbanization has major implications for global energy demand and greenhouse gas emissions beyond the coming decades. Also the retrofitting of existing energy-inefficient cities will play a major role in achieving this goal. The BP-sponsored Urban Energy Systems Project at Imperial College London is addressing this challenge through work on improved models of urban energy infrastructure. It works to identify energy saving potentials through system integration at the level of entire urban settlements, with the aim of at least halving the energy intensity of cities. Since cities represent extreme density of energy-demand patterns as well as profound heterogeneity in energy-use patterns, they offer great opportunities for cross-sectoral and temporal integration of energy systems to achieve savings on the demand as well as the supply side.

Traditionally much of the urban energy infrastructures and functions (like heating, lighting, transport, etc.) were designed and operated in relative isolation. Most energy models, for example, focus either on individual buildings or functions within buildings (lighting, air conditioning, hot-water supply, other building services, etc.). The interaction of those functions and other buildings or even different urban activities is rarely reflected. Existing citywide models on processes between buildings typically focus on individual network functions such as transport systems or distribution grids for electricity, gas, and water; networks for information and telecommunication; or the logistics of commodities and waste collection and treatment. The systemic interaction of those subsystems is rarely addressed. Better understanding of the interconnectedness of such infrastructure could not only help improve the resilience of urban resource systems but could be used to better integrate demand and supply patterns across energy carriers.

The Urban Energy Systems Project was initiated in 2005 and developed an integrated modeling platform named SynCity to be able to rapidly prototype many alternative (synthetic) urban designs and layout configurations, and optimize those against various possible objective functions. The model provides spatially and temporally dynamic representations of energy-consumption activities and their effect on supply systems and overall urban energy and resource demand.

The SynCity model is constructed in a layered topography with three major submodels: 1) the layout model, 2) the agent-based land-use/transport model, and 3) the resource technology and service network model.

Layered structure of the SynCity urban energy systems model

Scope of interactions between the submodels and socioeconomic agents

Two alternative (high- and low-density) solutions of the land-use/layout submodel: Hi–high-density residential; Low–low-density residential; Li–light industry; C–commercial; PE–primary education; SE–secondary education; H–hospital; L–leisure

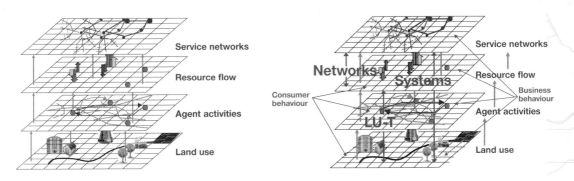

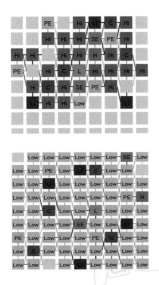

1. The land-use and layout model is aiming at a transport-flow-dominated representation of alternative spatial layout configurations. Typical land-use categories include high- or low-density residential, primary or secondary education, commercial, light industry, leisure, hospital, etc. Based on information on geographic features and context, and relatively simple assumptions on typical transport demand and compatibility of different urban land-use functions, it calculates an optimized spatial configuration of urban layouts that ensures the connectedness of each function and access to all activities. This submodel can include a wealth of constraints, such as preexisting geography and layout components, zoning and other planning regulations, and objective functions such as maximizing equal access to all urban functions or reducing overall transport energy demand.

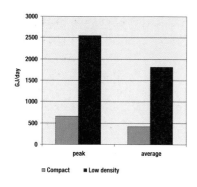

Difference in peak and average
transport fuel demand in
high- and low-density solutions

2. The transport model uses agent-based modeling to simulate how citizens are using the layout as provided either by the previous submodel or external data. While the previous submodel provides an optimization of the functional layout, this submodel aims to prescribe necessary capacity dimensions of transport systems and most likely spatial activity patterns. In high temporal resolution, it simulates where citizens are at specific points in time, what they are doing, and how they are moving between those activities. Activity patterns and mobility demand are then translated into specific resource demands.

3. The resource technology and service network model uses outputs from the submodels to model processes of resource use to satisfy the demand for energy services. Practically all material and energy flows, including waste streams, are considered as potential resource in this model. Three principal processes that are modeled for each cell include the production of resources (for example, the generation of electricity from specific fuel types), the transmission (import/export) of resources from adjacent cells, and the storage of resources in each cell. The model calculates a complete spatially disaggregated resource balance for the entire system at each time step. A resource-conversion technology database describes alternative installations that vary in resource-conversion capability and efficiency; storage and transmission capacity; investment, operating, and maintenance costs; and many other attributes. A heat pump, for example, can use low-grade heat and convert it (using electricity or mechanical energy) into medium-grade heat. The same resource could be generated by a combined heat and power plant, which would depend on gas or other

Optimal solution for a district
heating grid in the high-density
layout; result from the resource
technology and service network
submodel

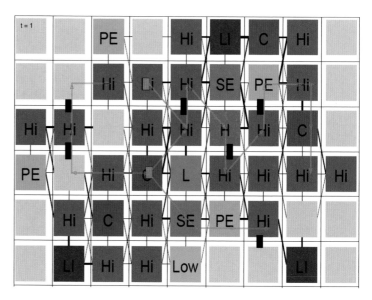

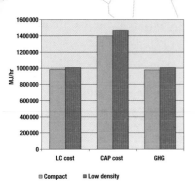

Variation in natural gas consumption for high- and low-density developments resulting from minimizing either life-cycle costs (LC), capital investment costs (CAP), or greenhouse gas emissions (GHG)

fuels, but generate electricity as a by-product of heat generation. District heating networks are typical distribution and storage media defining heat-flow capabilities between cells. Alternative objective functions can be applied such as minimizing investment costs, life-cycle costs, or overall greenhouse gas emissions, and the resource technology and service submodel will derive alternative configurations of energy-conversion infrastructure.

The SynCity model is currently being tested on a number of use cases. Examples included an application to the master plan of a proposed eco-town for the United Kingdom and ongoing case studies include settlements in the United States, China, India, and the Middle East.[2] We think this new and integrated planning tool is most useful for rapid prototyping studies in various contexts such as green- and brownfield developments, themed city assessments, and "what-if" scenarios about the introduction of innovative resource-conversion technology like plug-in electrical vehicles, distributed generation through renewable or hybrid sources including small-scale fuel cells, or combined heat and power plants.

1 International Energy Agency, *World Energy Outlook* (Paris: OECD, 2008).
2 J. Keirstead, N. Samsatli, and N. Shah, "Syncity: An Integrated Toolkit for Urban Energy Systems Modelling," in *Proceedings of the Fifth Urban Research Symposium: Cities and Climate Change– Responding to an Urgent Agenda*, Marseille, France, June 28–30, 2009. The World Bank online publication: http://www.urs2009.net/papers.html.

Oil City: Petro-landscapes and Sustainable Futures

Michael Watts

The secret of great wealth with no obvious source is some forgotten crime, forgotten because it was done neatly.
—Honoré de Balzac

Houston is popularly known as "the oil city." It has siblings bearing the same name in the great oil-producing regions of the world: Baku, Kirkuk, Luanda, Fort McMurray, Midland-Odessa, and Murmansk. Some cities carry the appellation because they are the hubs of corporate power in the universe of Big Oil (San Ramon, California, and Irving, Texas, come to mind). Others, like Dubai, are the products of vast oil wealth, spectacular excretions of a particular sort of financial and consumerist excess: as Mike Davis says, Dubai is the Miami of the Persian Gulf sutured to a "monstrous caricature of the future."[1] Virtually all American cities in their morphology and geographical dispersion—what John Urry has insightfully called the unbundling of home, leisure and work[2] to produce a "splintered" urbanism—are the products of hydrocarbon capitalism: a culture of automobility predicated on the availability of cheap gasoline to fuel the particular form of the internal combustion engine known as the car. Much of what is modern in the modern city is, in other words, the by-product of oil.

I want reflect upon a particular iteration of the oil city, and upon its future, namely cities standing at the epicenter of African oil and gas production, metropolises that house the fundamental oil infrastructure (refineries, gas plants, petrochemical plants, export terminals) and also serve as barracks for the armies of workers employed on the rigs and platforms and accommodate the corporate enclaves of the likes of Shell, Agip, and ExxonMobil. These cities stand as hubs within a vast regional (and ultimately global) network of oil "hardware." The global oil and gas infrastructure—the arteries and organs of the oil and gas global value-chain (this is the industry term of art)—is nothing short of gargantuan. To say that the value of the industry now totals over $40 trillion says everything and nothing. Close to 1 million producing oil wells puncture the surface of the earth (77,000 were drilled in 2008, 4,000 offshore); 3,300 are subsea, puncturing the earth's crust on the continental shelf, in some cases thousands of meters below the sea's surface. More than 2 million kilometers of pipeline cover the globe in a massive trunk-network. Seventy-five thousand kilometers of lines transport oil and gas along the sea floor. Another 156,000 kilometers of pipeline will be completed between now and 2012. There are 6,000 fixed platforms, and 635 offshore drillings rigs (the international rig total for 2009 is over 3,000, according to Baker Hughes, a global oilfield service company). Meanwhile, 4,295 oil tankers (vessels greater than 1,000 long tons or more deadweight) move 2.42 billion tons of oil and oil products every year, a figure that represents more than one-third of global seaborne trade. Worldwide, more than 700 refineries process crude oil; over 80 massive floating, production, and storage vessels have been installed in the last five years.

Overlaid on the oil and gas network is an astonishing patchwork of territorial concessions—the oil blocks acquired under long-term lease by the international and national oil companies—within which exploration and production are conducted. Spatial technologies and spatial representations are foundational to the oil industry: seismic devices to map the contours of reservoirs, geographic information systems to monitor and meter the flows of products within pipelines, and of course the map to determine subterranean property rights. Hard-rock geology is a science of the vertical, but when harnessed to the marketplace and profitability it is the map, detailing the spaces of oil, that becomes the instrument of surveillance, control, and rule. The oil and gas industry is a landscape of lines, axes, nodes, points, blocks, and flows.

These industrial landscapes—let's call them petrolic surfaces—become, over time, relics and ruins, or residual and abandoned landscapes, as photographer Edward Burtynsky calls them:

> You have an industrial process that has transformed a primal landscape, and then once forgotten, it begins to turn into something between the natural landscape and a man-imprinted landscape. They become the leftovers after the banquet, residual territories; not quite dead, as they regenerate, they begin to generate a new life, but it is a compromised life.[3]

The transformative powers of oil, that is, the human ecology of hydrocarbon capitalism, dwarfs virtually every other sector (with perhaps the exception of the specter of nuclear winter). The collateral damage associated with producing and moving vast quantities of oil—the nightmare of *Exxon Valdes*, the massive scarification of the Canadian tar sands—is hard to calculate. In any inventory of the most polluted spots on the face of the earth, the oilfield figures prominently. Virtually none of these costs ("externalities," as economists quaintly put it) show up in the price we pay at the gas pump. When deployed as a target of war or insurgency, oil infrastructure becomes a weapon all its own. The stunning aerial images of Kuwait's incendiary oilfields, detonated by Saddam's retreating forces, have become part of the iconography of war.

This oil hardware is fed by a seemingly unstoppable rush to discover more of a resource that everyone agrees is finite. The appetite for oil is insatiable, and the lengths to which the industry will go to obtain more is, well, to the ends of the earth, or more properly a mad gallop to the bottom of the ocean. Deepwater exploration is the new mantra (deepwater offshore production is expected to grow by 78 percent between 2007 and 2011). On August 2, 2007, a Russian submarine planted a titanium flag two miles down under the North Pole. At stake were the lucrative new oil and gas fields—by some estimations 10 billion tons of oil equivalent—on the Artic sea floor. In late 2006, a consortium of oil companies discovered oil at a staggering depth 150 miles in the Gulf of Mexico. The test well, Jack-2, delves through 7,000 feet of water and 20,000 feet of sea floor to tap oil in tertiary rock laid down 60 million years ago. The drill ships and production platforms required to undertake such work are massive floating structures, much larger than the largest aircraft carriers and much more expensive, costing well over a half-billion dollars (and close to $1 million a day to rent). In 2007 the vast new Tupi field in Brazilian coastal waters was discovered below a massive layer of salt in hugely inhospitable geological conditions. One test well cost more than $250 million. What is on offer is a great deepwater land grab at 700 meters.

We might say that oil cities are centers of political and economic calculation (I take the language from Bruno Latour) within a vast but only partially visible network of flows and connectivity. If oil has its onshore and aboveground pipelines, rigs, platforms, flowstations, floating production and storage vessels, and export terminals, it also encompasses an invisible underworld of reservoirs, subsea pipelines, submersibles, and risers.

These petro-networks, what I have called an oil complex, are extensive in their connectivity yet unevenly visible in their operations. As a space of flows and connectivity, the oil and gas universe is one of geostrategic operation, saturated by considerations of power, calculation, security, and threat.[4] This global oil network is reminiscent of Mark Lombardi's extraordinary atlas of the "uses and abuses of power in the global political economy."[5] Like the drug and money-laundering networks that so intrigued Lombardi in his attempts to map the black sites and blank spaces of the map of the global illicit economy, the world of Big Oil is, in spite of its formal market character, an industry shrouded in secrecy. It is a world in which even the most basic statistics can be meaningless, and a zone of economic and political calculation that can only be understood as a form of what Marx called primitive accumulation—that is, violent dispossession and appropriation. Oil cities, and oil regions generally, are epicenters of extraordinary violence and conflict. For Werner Herzog, they are landscapes of the apocalypse.

The hubs, spokes, flows, and nodes that make up the oil-military-construction-drug-finance network (the defining qualities of the oil complex) led David Campbell to see the oil and gas system as capsular: "capsules are enclaves and envelopes that function as nodes, hubs, and termini in the various networks and contain a multitude of spaces and scales."[6] Oil rigs, floating storage vessels, flow stations, refineries, gas stations, and of course cars are all capsules within the global oil and gas network. In turn, oil cities might also be read as particular capsules, composed of other capsules, which emerge from and are given shape by a network in which the visible and the invisible, secrecy and duplicity, spaces of flow and immobility, forces of power and security all operate to produce a perfect storm of violence, inequality, militarism, and corruption.

When located on this dark canvas, what makes African oil cities—Port Harcourt or Warri in Nigeria, Luanda or Cabinda in Angola—different? Oil states awash in petro-dollars embark on ambitious state-led modernization programs: gigantism and corruption are their hallmarks. Explosive rates of urbanization—driven by the prospect of urban employment amid a sea of rural poverty and typically by the collapse of agrarian employment (what economists call "the Dutch disease")—compound the problems of weak urban infrastructure and service provision. The slum world of the global south so vividly captured by Mike Davis in his *Planet of the Slums* assumes a new hypertrophied form.[7] Millions are barracked in the most terrifying squalor with few job opportunities conferred by a notoriously labor-extensive industry. At the same time, for the lucky few—those able to benefit from oil rents, political patronage, and massive corruption—the city becomes a personal enclave (the heavily walled and fortified compound is its urban form) of unimaginable wealth and conspicuous consumption. Inequality of the starkest sort becomes the stamp of the oil city.

Unprecedented rates of urban migration coupled with stupendous wealth among a class of oil oligarchs and state functionaries (whether military or civilian) makes for a peculiar dynamic in real estate markets. One the one hand, property prices in oil cities (Luanda is a striking case in point) may be among the highest in the world (driven by a search by oil, engineering, and construction companies desperate for scarce property in the city center). On the other, armies of the poor occupy illegally settled lands on the periphery of the city (or are displaced there by violent government-enforced slum clearance in the city center to make way for the latest oil recruits). Many ultimately fall under the sway of slumlords and local government officials eager to exploit their "illegal" status. The oil city is where the hypermodern (Luanda's sparkling corporate sea-front offices) meets the hyperpoor (Luanda's *musseques* [slums], where 85 percent of the population ekes out a miserable existence).

The oil city appears as a peculiar sort of parcellized sovereignty: capsules within the oil infrastructural grid. The corporate enclaves of Chevron and Shell resemble nothing more than militarized encampments. The upscale residences (and elite government residential areas) are gated communities with their own fully privatized water, electricity, and service provision. Those without such means build their own walled compounds with their generator, well, and guard. Capsules within capsules, enclaves within enclaves. In this sort of petrolic-cityscape, it is not at all clear what urban citizenship might possibly mean.

The slum world is held together ideologically by the call of evangelical churches or radical Islam, the oil elites by the siren call of the global economy and of neoliberalism. All of this exists cheek-by-jowl. Both groups fear the threat of crime, rebellion, and the shadow world of political violence and corruption. Oil cities are combustible, unstable, and ultimately unsustainable in human and ecological terms. Oil is, of course, finite. It will be exhausted. In this sense oil cities must confront their future, and their fate, from the moment the first oil begins to flow. They have in this regard built-in obsolescence. This is both an opportunity and a burden.

1 Mike Davis, "Sand, Fear, and Money in Dubai," in *Evil Paradises*, edited by Mike Davis et al. (London: Verso, 2007).
2 John Urry, "The System of Automobility," *Theory, Culture, and Society* 21/4 (2004).
3 Edward Burtynsky, "Residual Landscapes and the Everyday," *Space and Culture* 11/1 (2008): 39–50.
4 David Campbell, "The Biopolitics of Security," *American Quarterly* (2005): 950.
5 Mark Lombardi, *Mark Lombardi: Global Networks* (New York: Independent Curators, 2003), 19.
6 Campbell, "Biopolitics of Security," 951.
7 Mike Davis, *Planet of the Slums* (London: Verso, 2005).

Niger Delta
Oil Fields

Ed Kashi

Children playing among the oil
pipelines in their village.

Daily life scenes in Finima, a com-
munity of displaced people on
Bonny Island, with the Mobil Exxon
Gas plant close behind.

Views of the Trans-Amadi
Slaughter, the main abbatoir of
Port Harcourt. With a lack of
infrustructure and hygiene, animals
are killed in the open, their blood
spilled into the waterways below,
and their skin burned by the flames
of old tires, forming the thick
clouds of black smoke that hang
over the scene.

Trans-Amadi Slaughter is the largest abattior in the delta. They kill thousands of animals a day, roast them, cut them up and prepare the meat for sale throughout Rivers State and the rest of the delta. Nearly all of the workers here, especially the meat handlers, are Hausa and Yoruba, mostly Muslim too. In the delta fish was traditionally the main source of protein, but as fish stocks have dwindled due to pollution from oil and overfishing, meat is becoming more common.

Old Bonny Town on Bonny Island is a historical place, where the slave trade and palm-oil trade previously were based. It is stuck in poverty and underdevelopment, while the oil and gas companies expand. None of the locals are given work within the gas and oil facilities, which has caused widespread resentment. Brother John of the Assemblies of God Pentacostal Church preaches in the middle of the market.

Scenes of daily life in the oil city of Warri, in the Niger Delta. Warri is a troubled town, with rampant poverty, unemployment, angry and violent youth, and a crumbling infrastructure. Yet oil wealth is created in and around this area.

Scenes in the poor Niger Delta village of Imiringi.

A sign of the poor infrastructure in this oil-rich city of the Niger Delta. The congestion in Port Harcourt is a significant problem, and there seems to be no solution in sight.

Residents of Aker Camp, a slum of Port Harcourt, pick through the remains of their lives. One week earlier this neighborhood was burned down by the Nigerian military after one of their soldiers was killed while trying to foil a kidnapping of an Italian expat at a local bar. This kind of attack on civilians by the military is a constant reminder of the lack of human rights in the Niger Delta. Residents, who are all poor, try to salvage anything they can find. Preye Godswill, 27, was the owner of the destroyed Booze bar and restaurant. Here she looks at photographs of happier times in her bar, which attracted expats as well as Nigerians.

The Upway

Rafael Viñoly

The street systems of highly populated urban centers are functioning
far beyond their capacity. Regardless of their form of propulsion, cars
and service vehicles will continue
to overwhelm the streets, and
the policy of reducing the number
of lanes open to motor vehicles
to encourage the use of green forms
of transportation only increases
congestion. The street grid requires
an expansion comparable to the
introduction of the subway system
at the turn of the twentieth century.
That expansion can now occur only
above grade, through the "upway."

An upper track dedicated to electrically powered vessels circulating
at low to moderate speeds can
increase the capacity of the street
system by 40 percent. A system
of loops throughout the city serves
zones where density is highest.
The vehicles, accommodating one
or two passengers, can be accessed at parking stations located
between subway and bus stops,
using a prepaid magnetic card.
The total number of passengers
moved by the combination of all
modes of transportation, including
the subway, can be increased by
approximately 18 percent.

Total carbon emissions of the transit
system can be reduced by as much
as 30 percent from current levels.
The street becomes a kind of pergola
that incorporates all other public
services—lighting, communication,
cabling, information, and filters to
improve air quality—in an organized
structure. Driving to desired destinations along a silent and decon-
gested platform allows the public to
enjoy the views of the city from
a secure, efficient, and environmentally sustainable environment.

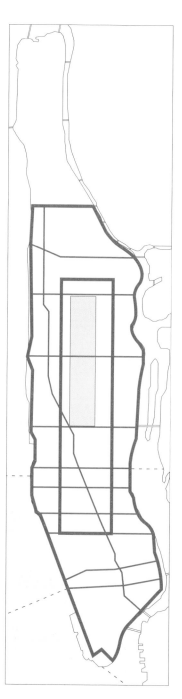

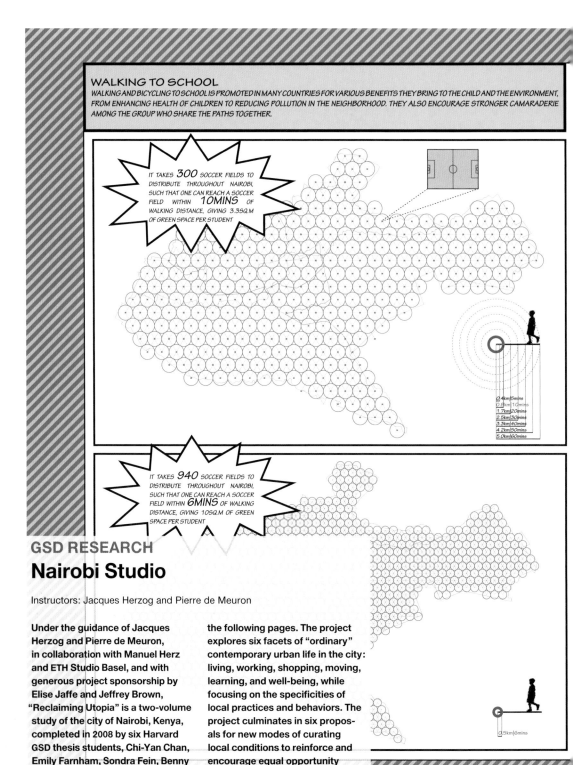

WALKING TO SCHOOL

WALKING AND BICYCLING TO SCHOOL IS PROMOTED IN MANY COUNTRIES FOR VARIOUS BENEFITS THEY BRING TO THE CHILD AND THE ENVIRONMENT, FROM ENHANCING HEALTH OF CHILDREN TO REDUCING POLLUTION IN THE NEIGHBORHOOD. THEY ALSO ENCOURAGE STRONGER CAMARADERIE AMONG THE GROUP WHO SHARE THE PATHS TOGETHER.

IT TAKES *300* SOCCER FIELDS TO DISTRIBUTE THROUGHOUT NAIROBI, SUCH THAT ONE CAN REACH A SOCCER FIELD WITHIN **10MINS** OF WALKING DISTANCE, GIVING 3.3SQ.M OF GREEN SPACE PER STUDENT

0.4km|5mins
0.8km|10mins
1.7km|20mins
2.5km|30mins
3.3km|40mins
4.2km|50mins
5.0km|60mins

IT TAKES *940* SOCCER FIELDS TO DISTRIBUTE THROUGHOUT NAIROBI, SUCH THAT ONE CAN REACH A SOCCER FIELD WITHIN **6MINS** OF WALKING DISTANCE, GIVING 10SQ.M OF GREEN SPACE PER STUDENT

0.5km|6mins

GSD RESEARCH
Nairobi Studio

Instructors: Jacques Herzog and Pierre de Meuron

Under the guidance of Jacques Herzog and Pierre de Meuron, in collaboration with Manuel Herz and ETH Studio Basel, and with generous project sponsorship by Elise Jaffe and Jeffrey Brown, "Reclaiming Utopia" is a two-volume study of the city of Nairobi, Kenya, completed in 2008 by six Harvard GSD thesis students, Chi-Yan Chan, Emily Farnham, Sondra Fein, Benny Ho, Meehae Kwon, and Yusun Kwon; extracts are presented on the following pages. The project explores six facets of "ordinary" contemporary urban life in the city: living, working, shopping, moving, learning, and well-being, while focusing on the specificities of local practices and behaviors. The project culminates in six proposals for new modes of curating local conditions to reinforce and encourage equal opportunity and self-initiative within a dynamic new urban framework.

THE STRUCTURE OF SCHOOL IN ASSOCIATION WITH A RELIGIOUS GROUP DATES BACK TO THE FIRST MISSIONARY SCHOOL IN 1836 MOMBASA. MISSIONARIES SET UP SCHOOLS IN HOPES TO SPREAD THEIR GOSPEL AND ONCE THEIR STRUCTURES ARE SET UP, THEY ARE OFTEN PASSED ON TO THE GOVERNMENT WHO THEN SUBSIDIZES NECESSARY FUNDINGS FROM TEACHER'S SALARIES TO TEXTBOOKS. OCCASIONALLY, THE PARENTS OR THE RELIGIOUS GROUPS SPONSOR TEACHERS FOR THE RESPECTIVE RELIGIOUS STUDIES. THE HOLY BASILLICA CATHEDRAL CHURCH IN THE CENTRAL BUSINESS DISTRICT SHARE THE COMMON OPEN SPACE WITH THE CATHOLIC PAROCHIAL SCHOOL. THEIR SYMBOLIC PRESENCE IS MORE EVIDENT IN THE NEIGHBORHOOD WITH THEIR PROVISION OF BYPASS TO THE PEDESTRIANS.

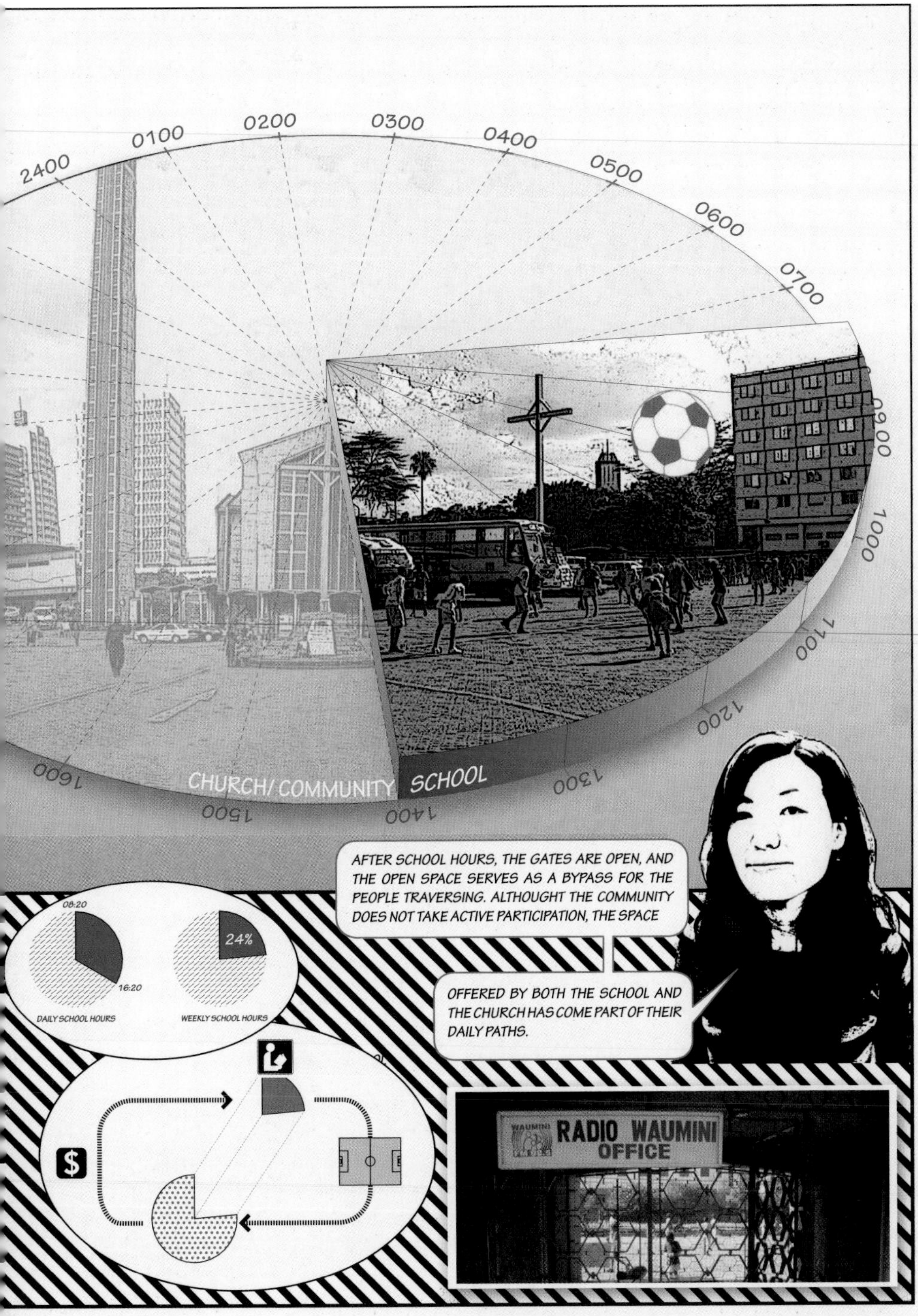

CHURCH/ COMMUNITY SCHOOL

AFTER SCHOOL HOURS, THE GATES ARE OPEN, AND THE OPEN SPACE SERVES AS A BYPASS FOR THE PEOPLE TRAVERSING. ALTHOUGH THE COMMUNITY DOES NOT TAKE ACTIVE PARTICIPATION, THE SPACE

OFFERED BY BOTH THE SCHOOL AND THE CHURCH HAS COME PART OF THEIR DAILY PATHS.

08:20
16:20
DAILY SCHOOL HOURS

24%
WEEKLY SCHOOL HOURS

RADIO WAUMINI OFFICE

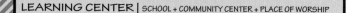

LEARNING CENTER | SCHOOL + COMMUNITY CENTER + PLACE OF WORSHIP

TRIAD RELATIONSHIP? INVOLVING THE COMMUNITY BUT HAVING THE SUB-DIVISION GROUPS UNDER THE BIG UMBRELLA WILL ALLOW THE SYSTEM TO REACH OUT TO MORE PEOPLE. THE CLARITY OF YOUR DIAGRAMMATIC IDEA IS GOOD. WE LIKE THE SIMPLE EXTRUSION OF YOUR DIAGRAM INTO A BUILDING. DOES THIS SYSTEM ALLOW SCALE OR COMPOSOTIONAL VARIATIONS TO ADJUST TO THE COMMUNITIES?

SCHOOL

COMMUNITY CENTER

PLACE OF WORSHIP

I BELIEVE THIS ASSOCIATION BETWEEN THE CHURCH AND SCHOOL LONG EXISTED SINCE THE INDEPENDENCE. IF WE SUSTAIN THE INVOLVEMENT OF THE COMMUNITY BY OPENING UP THE SCHOOL WITH WIDER RANGE OF LEARNING OPPORTUNITIES, IT WILL CREATE SYMBIOTIC RELATIONSHIP BETWEEN THE PARTIES THAT ARE INVOLVED! I AM AWARE OF THE SCALE OF THESE LEARNING CENTERS, HOW THEY HAVE TO BE MORE TANGIBLE AT THE COMMUNITY LEVEL. NOT THAT I AM TOTALLY TAKEN BY THIS SCHEME, BUT WHY NOT CREATE THESE MEGA "LEARNING-MALLS," JUST LIKE THE SHOPPING MALLS?

I LIKE THE IDEA OF SUSTAINING RELATIONSHIP WITH THE COMMUNITY. HAVING THEM INVOLVED BEYOND ESTABLISHING THE SCHOOLS..IS WHAT WE WOULD IDEALLY ANTICIPATE.

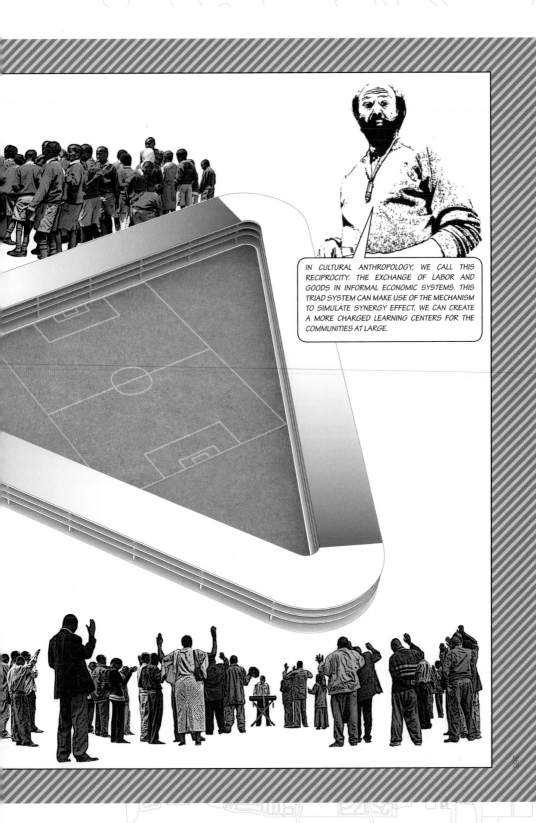

IN CULTURAL ANTHROPOLOGY, WE CALL THIS RECIPROCITY. THE EXCHANGE OF LABOR AND GOODS IN INFORMAL ECONOMIC SYSTEMS. THIS TRIAD SYSTEM CAN MAKE USE OF THE MECHANISM TO SIMULATE SYNERGY EFFECT, WE CAN CREATE A MORE CHARGED LEARNING CENTERS FOR THE COMMUNITIES AT LARGE.

LINKAGE TO OTHER NATIONAL DEVELOPMENT PROGRAMS

THE ACCELERATING PACE OF GLOBALISATION IS HAVING A PROFOUND EFFECT ON LIFE IN RICH AND POOR COUNTRIES ALIKE, TRANSFORMING REGIONS SUCH AS DETROIT OR BANGALORE FROM BOOM TO BUST IN A GENERATION. THE IT SERVICES BOOM HAS HELPED TO TRANSFORM THE INDIAN ECONOMY, WHICH IS NOW GROWING AT MORE THAN 9% PER YEAR, THE SAME RATE AS CHINA. HOWEVER, WITH THE BLOOMING ECONOMY, LABOUR COST IN INDIA AS RISEN, AND THUS GLOBAL COMPANIES ARE SEARCHING FOR OTHER POTENTIAL BUSINESS PROCESS OUTSOURCING (BPO) LABOUR POOL. WHEN KENYA'S HUMAN RESOURCES ARE EQUIPED WITH SKILLS TO PROVIDE COMPETENCE IN THE MARKET, THROUGH EDUCATION, KENYA CAN ANTICIPATE TO PLAY A ROLE IN THE OFFSHORE MARKET.

BANGALORE IN INDIA IS HOME TO SOME OF THE WELL RECOGNIZED COLLEGES, INSTITUTIONS, AND REASEARCH CENTERS. IT IS ALSO HOME TO NUMEROUS PUBLIC SECTORS SUCH AS HEAVY INDUSTRIES, SOFTWARE COMPANIES, AEROSPACE, TELECOMMUNICATIONS, MACHINE TOOLS, HEAVY EQUIPMENT, AND DEFENCE ESTABLISHMENTS.

WITH THE ESTABLISHMENT OF A PRIVATE COMPANY IN THE 60S, SHORT FOLLOWED BY THE TEXAS INSTRUMENTS, IN 1985, THE FIRST MULTINATIONAL COMPANY TO BE IMPLANTED, BANGALORE SOON TOOK OFF AS THE SILICON VALLY OF INDIA.

HINGING ON THAT IDEA, WHY NOT CREATE THIS RESEARCH AND DEVELOPMENT CORRIDOR ALONG THIKA ROAD, IN CLOSE PROXIMITY TO THE INDUSTRIAL ZONES.

'SINGLE-ZONING' AND COMMUTING LONG DISTANCES ARE THE INEFFECIENCIES CREATED BY THE URBAN SPRAWL. THE HYBRID MIX OF WORK, EDUCATION AND LIVING IS ACKNOWLEDGING THESE ISSUES.

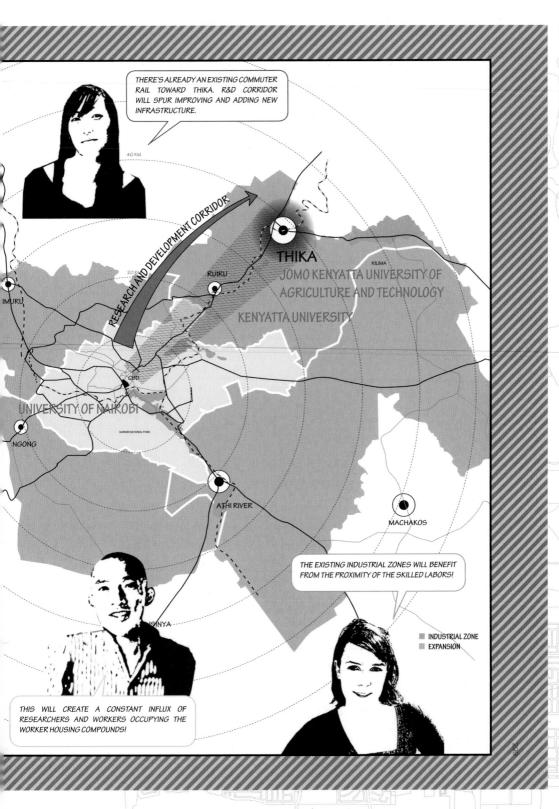

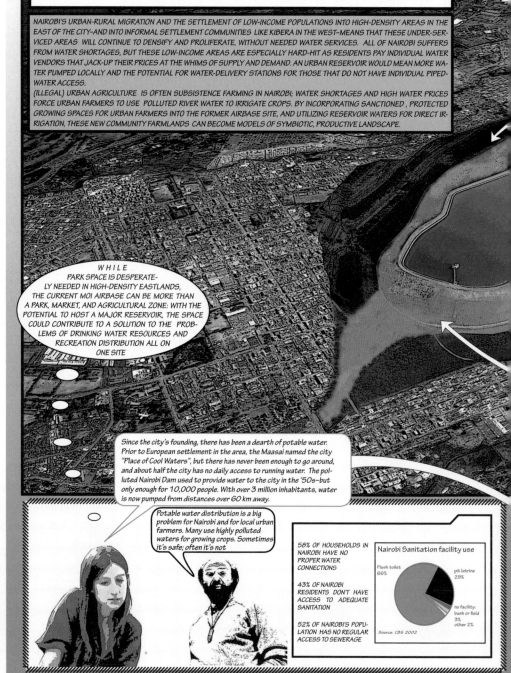

RETHINKING THE PRODUCTIVE LANDSCAPE   A RESERVOIR AS URBAN PARK

NAIROBI'S URBAN-RURAL MIGRATION AND THE SETTLEMENT OF LOW-INCOME POPULATIONS INTO HIGH-DENSITY AREAS IN THE EAST OF THE CITY–AND INTO INFORMAL SETTLEMENT COMMUNITIES LIKE KIBERA IN THE WEST–MEANS THAT THESE UNDER-SERVICED AREAS WILL CONTINUE TO DENSIFY AND PROLIFERATE, WITHOUT NEEDED WATER SERVICES. ALL OF NAIROBI SUFFERS FROM WATER SHORTAGES, BUT THESE LOW-INCOME AREAS ARE ESPECIALLY HARD-HIT AS RESIDENTS PAY INDIVIDUAL WATER VENDORS THAT JACK-UP THEIR PRICES AT THE WHIMS OF SUPPLY AND DEMAND. AN URBAN RESERVOIR WOULD MEAN MORE WATER PUMPED LOCALLY AND THE POTENTIAL FOR WATER-DELIVERY STATIONS FOR THOSE THAT DO NOT HAVE INDIVIDUAL PIPED-WATER ACCESS.
(ILLEGAL) URBAN AGRICULTURE IS OFTEN SUBSISTENCE FARMING IN NAIROBI; WATER SHORTAGES AND HIGH WATER PRICES FORCE URBAN FARMERS TO USE POLLUTED RIVER WATER TO IRRIGATE CROPS. BY INCORPORATING SANCTIONED , PROTECTED GROWING SPACES FOR URBAN FARMERS INTO THE FORMER AIRBASE SITE, AND UTILIZING RESERVOIR WATERS FOR DIRECT IRRIGATION, THESE NEW COMMUNITY FARMLANDS CAN BECOME MODELS OF SYMBIOTIC, PRODUCTIVE LANDSCAPE.

WHILE PARK SPACE IS DESPERATELY NEEDED IN HIGH-DENSITY EASTLANDS, THE CURRENT MOI AIRBASE CAN BE MORE THAN A PARK, MARKET, AND AGRICULTURAL ZONE: WITH THE POTENTIAL TO HOST A MAJOR RESERVOIR, THE SPACE COULD CONTRIBUTE TO A SOLUTION TO THE PROBLEMS OF DRINKING WATER RESOURCES AND RECREATION DISTRIBUTION ALL ON ONE SITE

Since the city's founding, there has been a dearth of potable water. Prior to European settlement in the area, the Maasai named the city "Place of Cool Waters", but there has never been enough to go around, and about half the city has no daily access to running water. The polluted Nairobi Dam used to provide water to the city in the '50s–but only enough for 10,000 people. With over 3 million inhabitants, water is now pumped from distances over 60 km away.

Potable water distribution is a big problem for Nairobi and for local urban farmers. Many use highly polluted waters for growing crops. Sometimes it's safe; often it's not

58% OF HOUSEHOLDS IN NAIROBI HAVE NO PROPER WATER CONNECTIONS

43% OF NAIROBI RESIDENTS DON'T HAVE ACCESS TO ADEQUATE SANITATION

52% OF NAIROBI'S POPULATION HAS NO REGULAR ACCESS TO SEWERAGE

Nairobi Sanitation facility use

Flush toilet 66%

pit latrine 29%

no facility: bush or field 3%

other 2%

Source: CBS 2002

1948 MASTERPLAN

JACQUES, DID YOU KNOW THE NAME FOR THE CITY LIKE-
LY CAME FROM THE TERM 'ENKARE NYROBI' WHICH MEANS
"PLACE OF COOL WATERS"? IT REALLY IS APPROPRIATE T
EXPLORE SOMETHING LIKE THE RIVERS AS THEY ARE S
FUNDAMENTAL TO THE CITY'S HISTORY AND CONTEXT...

LITTER BIN
KALONZ
CITY COUNCIL OF NAIROBI

60 YEARS AFTER THE 1948 MASTERPLAN

← 30 M →

1948 MASTERPLAN

...ASIDE FROM THE LARGE OPEN AREAS IN THE CITY LIKE THE MOI AIRBASE AND THE RAILWAY LANDS THAT I SHOWED YOU THE FIRST TIME WE TALKED ABOUT THE '48 MASTERPLAN, THE OTHER AREA OF OPPORTUNITY IS THE RIPARIAN LANDS ALONG THE RIVER BASIN. THE '48 MASTERPLAN LAID OUT STRICT GUIDELINES ENSURING THAT 30 METERS TO EITHER SIDE OF THE RIVER WOULD REMAIN FREE FROM BUILDING...

...IN ORDER TO CREATE A BUFFER ZONE AGAINST MOS-QUITOES. THESE LANDS, FOR THE MOST PART, REMAIN UNBUILT RIVERSIDE CORRIDORS. MOSQUITOES CAN BE CONTROLLED, SO THE REAL OBSTACLE WITH CONCEPTU-ALIZING THESE SPACES AS PUBLIC GREEN AREAS IS THE WATER POLLUTION AND RIVERSIDE DUMPING....

MEASURE

Five Ecological Challenges for the Contemporary City
Stefano Boeri

Revolutionizing Architecture
Jeremy Rifkin

The Canary Project
Susannah Sayler

"Performalism": Environmental Metrics and Urban Design
Susannah Hagan

Nature Culture
Kathryn Moore

**Investigating the Importance of Customized Energy Model Inputs:
A Case Study of Gund Hall**
Holly A. Wasilowski and Christoph F. Reinhart

Perception of Urban Density
Vicky Cheng and Koen Steemers

London's Estuary Region
Sir Terry Farrell

Urban Earth: London
Daniel Raven-Ellison

Sustainability Initiatives in London
Camilla Ween

Moving beyond LEED: Evaluating Green at the Urban Scale
Thomas Schroepfer

Landscapes of Specialization
Bill Rankin

**GSD RESEARCH
Half a Million Trees: Prototyping Sites
and Systems for Sustainable Cities**
Kristin Frederickson and Gary Hilderbrand

SlaveCity
Atelier Van Lieshout

EcoBox/Self-Managed Eco-urban Network
atelier d'architecture autogérée

Temporary Urban Scene: Beach on the Moon
Ecosistema Urbano

Five Ecological Challenges
for the Contemporary City

Stefano Boeri

When imagining the future city, one that stops exploiting the earth indiscriminately and enters into harmony with nature, the problem of contemporary urban policy is ineludible. Starting from a dialectic confrontation between different issues, the following notes—a preview of the strategies proposed for Expo 2015—suggest five large-scale urban policies that not only propose a new idea of urban ecology but also present an innovative model of urban economic development.[1]

1. Sustainability and Democracy

Today's environmental emergency is so pervasive and severe in our cities that the problem is irresolvable if left to top-down centralized policies. When thinking about pollution, consumption of oxygen, and CO_2 production, we must face the fact that it is not only large buildings, institutions, factories, and commercial centers that are to blame; heavy responsibility lies with the hundred of thousands of small, solitary, and amassed constructions that compose the connective tissue of our contemporary urban and suburban areas: millions of small cement, stone, and steel organisms that consume clean water, electricity, and oil while producing carbon and grime.

Jeremy Rifkin's call for architects and builders to commit to the realization of buildings that—in addition to consuming less energy—are able to collect and produce more energy than they need, thereby contributing to local energy networks, seems to offer a new perspective. In his view, the environmental emergency must necessarily be confronted by a molecular and democratic revolution that lies within the endless processes of construction and renovation of our cities.

Of course the idea of collector-buildings that gather solar and wind energy is not new. New, however, are the technical possibilities (made feasible by the latest developments in hydrogen storage) of actually realizing a more "generous" architecture that absorbs and conserves more energy than it needs and is therefore able to supply its surroundings. And also new is the individual responsibility of inverting the relation between nature and city, by designing and building a new generation of architecture.

It is an architecture that in addition to being loaded with technological devices (photovoltaic panels, wind blades, hydrogen batteries, heat pumps) uses vegetable surfaces—meadows, cultivated fields, trees—to envelop its roofs and vertical walls, thus diminishing energy consumption for internal conditioning; an architecture that hosts small energy-control centers; an architecture that designs these service spaces, transforming them into spaces of encounter and proximity for citizens and neighborhoods.

In Europe, the United States, and many Asian countries, some companies and institutions have understood the need for this democratic environmental policy and have likewise understood the economic advantage that it may bring. Rome, San Antonio, and Madrid are about to begin projects of diffused sustainability that, born from the hypothesis put forward by Rifkin, include businesses, institutions, professionals, and technicians of different skills.

2. Agriculture and Ground Consumption

A comparative study of data relating the extensive growth of Italian cities to other European models clearly shows how Italy, during the last three decades, has incorporated double the amount of land into its urban areas than have comparable French or German cities. It is evident that something is not working, particularly when the expansion is compared with the country's negative demographic trends.

It is necessary to find a development model no longer linked to perpetual horizontal expansion, which has not only devoured vast areas of agricultural land but also swept aside the living space of animals and plants. The alternative is a city that grows on itself—a model that is in fact typical of European cities and that has, in other historical moments (such as the Middle Ages), developed through processes of densification, stratification, or the replacement of old parts with new ones. The model is an integral aspect of European history, yet one that we should still consider for our contemporary cities.

If this is to actually take place, however, it must be linked with the future of periurban agriculture. Cultivated terrain around and between cities can once more become a crucial resource for our urban economies if we are willing to defend it from extensive urbanization and give it a new and strong economic value and use. We need to show that periurban agricultural spaces can become active and liveable spaces; that agriculture does not correspond to the biological desert of corn and cereals, but to an articulated landscape that is capable of hosting many crops, promoting biodiversity. It is also important to demonstrate that activity in agriculture can

445

once again become a significant source of work for young people and a unique resource for a healthier and more controlled food supply.

In the context of the Milan 2015 Expo—whose theme is in fact *Feeding the Planet, Energy for Life*—a project to work with fifty or so municipal farms is now under way. The project involves revitalizing the existing structures by turning them into places where urban agriculture is practiced and young people are offered the chance to become part of the agricultural labor market. But the topic also engages an urban aspect, involving the possibility of introducing biological and organic areas throughout the city (as in urban gardens), an idea that fits into policies that promote a demineralization of urban environments through the realization, especially within denser portions of the city, of both horizontal and vertical green surfaces.

3. Nature and Control

Yet even within the perspective of a different relation between nature and city, policies of agricultural proximity and urban demineralization are not enough. We must think of accepting a relationship with nature on equal terms in cities, ensuring that it has its own autonomy and is not unendingly influenced

by the needs of man. We must begin to foresee spaces for a nature that is close to us and yet is not controlled, toned down, or made artificial. In other words, we must begin to conceive the possibility of territories, at times even in proximity to inhabited areas, where we are no longer in control.

This is not a visionary project but one that already takes place around us. The French landscape designer Gilles Clément has asserted for years the need to acknowledge the diffusion of a "third landscape"—areas in which nature has gradually reconquered abandoned buildings or infrastructure. In a certain sense it is inevitable: our cities have extended to the point of enclosing zones traditionally belonging to other species. Deer that roam into the center of Bolzano, foxes appearing in the London underground, wild boar that populate the periphery of Florence are nothing but symptoms of a new type of proximity with the animal kingdom that we must learn to govern, knowing that often the best form of governance is the relinquishment of all control, the self-suspension of any type of planning.

In the next decades we will have to face the challenge of an urban ethic that is no longer completely anthropocentric—an ethic that, subtracting our species from its pedestal, reasons with notions of cohabitation of different species on the same territory, even if these are not domesticated.

There are already cities well along this route, such as Mumbai and Delhi, where ancient traditions of respect for other species is manifest in the contemporary presence of humans and animals in public space. But also in cities such as Vancouver and Boston, where urban policy is aimed at making the most of all natural and naturalistic systems, foreseeing green corridors and parks that are inaccessible to humans. Or in cities like Munich, Madrid, or Milan, where large forests that surround the city and vast surfaces of metropolitan reforestation have been imagined as places where biodiversity, both animal and vegetable, can find its own space.

4. Compact and Discard

There is a constant risk, both in Europe and the United States, that large portions of areas built during the last decades that present a diffused type of urbanization have entered an irreversible crisis. Vast expanses of low-density developments have begun to show growing signs of decay, insecurity, and limited inhabitability. Endless extensions of single-family housing, low-rise apartments, shopping centers, and warehouses present conditions in which there is no longer the possibility of creating public infrastructure, whether because the low density of population does not make it worthwhile

Metrobosco, multiplicity.lab
(Stefano Boeri with Isa Inti,
Giovanni La Varra, and Camilla
Ponzano), promoted by Province
of Milano, 2007

or simply because the space no longer exists within the never-ending carpet and diffused multitude of small objects and private enclosures. To think about how to face this crisis means also to imagine alternatives that within the compact inner city offer the living conditions, comfort, and equivalent costs to those offered by the suburbs.

Urban densification that incorporates compact and high-rise growth in determined parts of the city and therefore demographic development circumscribed to particular spaces is a possible answer to the dramatic housing crisis of territories marked by a diffused type of urbanization. We must think

of a limited, governed, and selective densification in nodes in which public transport is a deterrent for car use and consequently does not imply an increase in private traffic. Equally important is the fact that this densification—that can also include processes of reuse, substitution, or implantation of existing buildings—translates into an affordable and qualitative alternative to the traditional single-family house.

The idea to propose high-rise buildings laden with common green surfaces and spaces, as in the Bosco Verticale (Vertical Forest) project under development in Milan, is inserted in policies of demineralization of the city that combines ideally with projects of demographic densification and urban reforestation. It is by no means a proposal to substitute the presence of forests and parks in cities, but instead is based on the possibility of bringing into the city the equivalent in plants and trees (there are more than 2,100 plants in the forty-three floors of the two towers combined) of almost 4 hectares of forest. And to offer in terms of compact inhabitable surface (the two towers of the Bosco Verticale account for about 18,000 square meters of interior space and 6,000 square meters of tree-shaded terraces) an alternative to a diffused-model neighborhood equivalent to more than 45,000 square meters in a building footprint of only 1,200 square meters.

To associate, through fiscal and credit incentives, projects of urban densification with policies of discarding abandoned periurban territories is today a brave choice, yet a fundamental one if we are to effectively reduce excessive urban extension and build a new relation between the vegetable and anthropocentric spheres within the heart of our cities.

5. Desertification and Subsidiarity

All of the above does not make sense if we do not immediately activate policies to drastically reduce the existing urban "desertification." Although we live in empty cities, we are still obstinate in our desire to make them sprawl ever further. We are surrounded by thousands of empty apartments, yet we think only of building and rebuilding new houses—of how to expand, make higher, replicate. We can no longer afford to overlook this self-evident paradox.

It should be enough just to look around: notice the "for rent" and "for sale" signs on building façades and the vast number of closed-up houses, apartments, and offices along our daily routes. In Rome, of 1,715,000 homes, 245,000—one in seven—are uninhabited. In Milan, of 1,640,000 apartments, more than 80,000 are empty, and almost 900,000 square meters of office space, the equivalent of thirty Pirelli skyscrapers, is vacant.

The lack of concern about the causes of this desertification is indeed worrying. With regard to Italy, the reasons are three: a mistrust in a real estate system that does not guarantee certain rules; a fear of losing a valuable property to indebted or immobile tenants; and finally (and specifically related to office buildings), the exhaustion of rigid norms that do not permit diversified and mixed use (living and working, for example).

Urban desertification is not only an urban problem but a pervasive phenomenon that, if faced, could meet the needs of millions of families, small construction businesses, and professionals, thereby constituting a large laboratory of urban policies. Our city's empty spaces are in this sense a physical reflection of the void that separates public institutions from the vital energy of today's civil society. And it is not by chance that a series of "private social" agencies have appeared to fill this void through subsidiary programs and public action: nonprofit real estate companies—like those in Barcelona, Turin, and Milan—that guarantee income to owners and provide low-cost rentable spaces (about 30 percent lower than the market price) for those in need (not only immigrants and people in uncertain situations but also students, temporary workers, and young families).

For these experiences to become a diffused reality, melting away fears and lethargy while promoting a formidable market for interventions of recovery and restructuring of our built stock, it is necessary to create public policies that compel local authorities to offer guarantee funds that back social real estate interventions.

Yet it is, generally speaking, all the more essential to create urban policies that are able to trigger a creative recovery of our cities' territories. Cities must cease to grow by devouring nature and agricultural land and instead pay attention to their environment, regenerating and recovering the urban deserts that represent the real measure of today's political shortsightedness.

1 Established in March 2009 by the mayor of Milan, the Expo 2015 international architectural consultancy is formed by Stefano Boeri, Joan Busquets, Richard Burdett, Jacques Herzog, and William McDonough and has the scope of establishing guidelines for the Expo 2015 master plan.

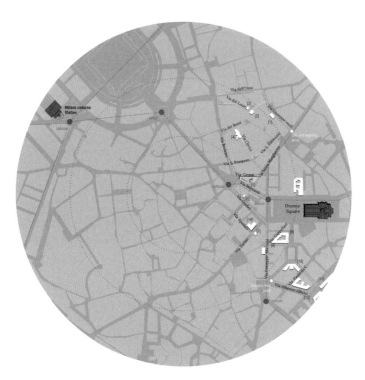

Revolutionizing Architecture

Jeremy Rifkin

This declaration, presented at the 11ᵗʰ International Architecture Exhibition of the Venice Biennale, asserts that architecture should develop new design and construction strategies that take account of future energy crises and global warming. It is the outcome of intense debate with four architects actively committed to incorporating sustainable solutions in their designs: Enric Ruiz-Geli (Cloud 9), José Luis Vallejo (Ecosistema Urbano), Jan Jongert (2012 Architekten), and Stefano Boeri (Boeri Studio).[1]

WE, the architects of the world, recognize that the increase in energy costs is leading to a slowdown in the global economy, creating hardships for families everywhere.

WE further recognize that the dramatic rise in carbon dioxide emissions from the burning of fossil fuels is raising the earth's temperature, threatening an unprecedented change in the chemistry of the plant and global climate, with ominous consequences for the future of human civilization and the ecosystems of the earth.

WE further recognize that buildings are the leading consumer of energy and the major contributor to human-induced global warming, consuming 30 to 40 percent of all the energy produced and contributing equal percentages of all CO_2 emissions.

WE further recognize that the world community needs a powerful new economic narrative that will push the discussion and agenda around the global energy crisis and climate change from fear to hope, and from economic constraints to economic possibilities.

WE further recognize that new technological breakthroughs make it possible, for the first time, to reconfigure existing buildings and design and construct new ones that create all of their own energy from locally available renewable energy sources, allowing us to reconceptualize buildings as "power plants."

WE further recognize that the same design principles and smart technologies that made possible the internet and vast "distributed" global communication networks are just beginning to be used to reconfigure the world's power grids, so that people can produce renewable energy with their buildings and share it peer-to-peer across regions and continents, just like they now produce and share information, creating a new, decentralized form of energy use.

WE further recognize that reconceptualizing buildings as power plants and transforming the world's power grids into intelligent utility networks to distribute that power will open the door to a Third Industrial Revolution that should have as powerful an economic multiplier effect in the twenty-first century as the first and second Industrial Revolutions of the nineteenth and twentieth centuries.

THEREFORE BE IT RESOLVED THAT we are committed to a revolutionary new concept of architecture in which homes, offices, shopping malls, factories, and industrial and technology parks will be renovated or constructed to serve as both power plants and habitats.

BE IT RESOLVED THAT these buildings will collect and generate energy locally from the sun, wind, garbage, agricultural and forestry waste, hydro and geothermal sources, and ocean waves and tides—enough energy to provide for their own power needs as well as surplus energy that can be shared.

BE IT RESOLVED THAT we will collaborate with the chemical and engineering industries to develop methods—including hydrogen, flow batteries, pump storage, etc.—that allow intermittent forms of renewable energy to be stored to assure twenty-four/seven continuous access to electricity.

BE IT RESOLVED THAT we will collaborate with the transportation and logistics industries to establish the appropriate interfaces so that buildings can provide renewable energy to power electric and hydrogen fuel-cell vehicles.

BE IT RESOLVED THAT this radical transformation of the role of architecture will be supported by confining urban growth entirely within the current boundaries of our cities, and undertaking the reforestation of extensive urban fringe areas that have not yet been built on.

WE therefore call on our fellow architects around the world to join us in revolutionizing architecture, with the goal of empowering millions of people in their businesses, public institutions, and homes to produce their own clean and renewable energy, and share their surpluses with others across intelligent utility networks, helping usher in a Third Industrial Revolution and a new post-carbon era dedicated to the democratization of energy and sustainable economic development.

1 *The Reader* #11 (supplement to *Abitare* 485, September 2008).

The Canary Project

Susannah Sayler

Peru's terrain and population distribution make it extremely vulnerable to the impacts of climate change. More than 70 percent of its population lives on the desert coast where there are almost no natural sources of water. The water for these people (8 million in Lima alone) comes from Andean glaciers in the central part of the country and from rainwater during the rainy season. Scientists, including the Intergovernmental Panel on Climate Change, predict that Peru's glaciers will be gone in fifteen years. Peru has already started to prepare with large-scale engineering projects, efforts to conserve water, and reconsideration of technologies used by ancient societies to conserve and store water.

In and around Lima, communities are being built into the dry foothills and dunes near the ocean. There is no running water in many of these areas, so it is supplied daily by water trucks that fill plastic barrels in front of homes. People buy and use water according to their budgets. The water here is more expensive than in the wealthiest parts of the city center, where water is supplied through pipes by the municipality. As water becomes scarcer, prices will go up and the people least able to pay for it will feel the greatest impact. Lake Paron in the Peruvian Andes, in which rainwater is collected during the rainy season and siphoned off during the dry season, is an example of the kind of projects needed to secure water resources in the future.

Water storage, Lake Paron, Peru, 2008

"Performalism": Environmental Metrics and Urban Design

Susannah Hagan

When environmental design threatened to go mainstream in European architecture ten years ago—not least because of European Union directives intent on making it do so—there were dark prophecies of the death of architecture, the strangling of aesthetics, and the laying waste of theoretical discourse by people who wore socks and sandals and whose motivation was only ethical. What we're getting instead is a range of architectures, emerging from a variety of positions on technology, architecture, and nature; a minority are highly engineered and determined by their environmental function, but the majority are mixtures of convention and invention.

Environmental design at the urban scale is now provoking the same alarm and caricature: the new city will be either informal, anticorporatist, and antidesign, or a mass of overplanned, overdesigned "natural" ecosystems disrupting the city's geometry and materiality. If "eco-architecture" is anything to go by, then both of these versions will appear at the scale of "ecological urbanism," but the majority of designs will be a mixture of the emergent and the planned, the biotic and the geometric, and this synthesis has yet to evolve. The ecological narrative and its modes of practice are embryonic. The narrative of urbanism is old and its modes of practice varied and embedded. The two haven't even begun to negotiate with each other, and it's not a marriage that can instantly be arranged. Different relationships will evolve between them, dependent on the different cultures, climates, politics, and economics of the cities where these interventions are made. So that although I address the design potential of environmental metrics, I also address their limitations.

Those trained in environmental design take the term "ecological urbanism" quite literally. With so many cities suffering from environmental pathologies, albeit pathologies that have social and economic causes and effects, such literalism is necessary. Besides, for those with a reflective turn of mind, it presents an interesting take on the idea of "urban metabolism"—a metaphor that is no longer a metaphor. At the urban scale, the environmental goal now is to create "artificial ecosystems"—cities that achieve the same interdependent efficiencies as natural ecosystems:

A heretofore neglected aspect of cities: the city as a metabolism, a metabolism that needs modeling on the ecosystem rather than on a 1950s Cadillac

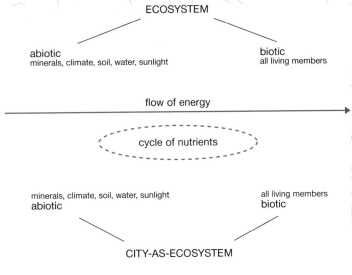

An ecosystem can be characterized by its abiotic constituents, including minerals, climate, soil, water, sunlight, etc., and its biotic constituents, consisting of all of its living members. Linking these constituent elements are two major forces: the flow of energy through the ecosystem and the cycle of nutrients within the ecosystem.[1]

Cities can be viewed in exactly the same way. There are few actual built examples on an urban scale, but Kalundborg in Denmark is one such, its existing flows and cycles of resources and wastes reconfigured into a more integrated and still-evolving metabolism.[2] Turning a city into an artificial ecosystem is a far more complex—and more interesting—process than covering all available urban surfaces in generic greenery.

While many in architecture are celebrating this glorious overthrow of the nature/culture binary, not enough are prepared to accept all of the consequences. In addition to theorizing and aestheticizing the relationships of architecture and cities to nature, there is the performance of nature compromised by the environmental performance of built culture to consider. In both cases, this performance is best understood—and improved—by metrics. The process is unashamedly utilitarian, empirical, quantifying, and politically charged. To this degree, the qualitative is quantified, in that the quantified built environment indicates basic quality of life, or its absence.[3] Ask any slum dweller.

If the nature/culture binary can be endlessly parsed, then the quantity/quality binary can be too. If nature is culture, then it's high time culture became nature. It now needs to cut both ways. The environmental concept of a "performative" or "productive" scape, for biomass, urban agriculture, water

The former *favela* of Paraisópolis,
São Paulo, now incorporated into
the city

The 70-hectare site in Barra Funda,
São Paulo, divided by a regional
railway, with the Tiete River to the
north

management, etc., posits a very different way of conceiving of city and non-city, and as such carries cultural implications. Land empty of built development is no longer viewed as empty, simply full of something else. The unbuilt is potentially a condition of equal intensity to the built. With a nod to Patrick Geddes, within a regional continuum one can now slide conceptually between areas of greater ecosystemic intensity (suburbs, countryside) and areas of greater constructed intensity (towns, cities).[4] In the future, one aims to be sliding between natural ecosystems (however much reconfigured by us) and artificial ecosystems (however much of nature we include). Meanwhile a growing number of cities can't keep up with the rate of their own urbanization. In such cases, where economic, social, and environmental problems are inseparable, there is a case for starting not with causes (governance) but with environmental effects. It could be argued that you need good governance to be able to start on any effective scale. Although this is indisputable, in actuality one might be arguing with one city department for good governance on one site, which makes the task less daunting. One could argue with a planning department, for example, that low-income families living in a subtropical climate that is chilly enough in winter to require electric heaters and hot enough in summer to need air conditioners are spending money and energy on machines they wouldn't need if they lived in well-insulated passive-solar housing. Their city's government would have more resources to spend on such housing if it didn't have to clean up after toxic floods every year, the result of an inability to enforce a minimum percentage of porosity in the urban surface and to clean up polluted urban rivers. The energy costs, like the economic costs, are quantifiable. The social costs are unaccountable.

In environmental design, therefore, one's choice as a designer is how far, rather than whether, to push metrics: they can be used simply to assess resource and waste input and output on a site, or to assess input and output at the beginning of the design process and then measure the design's success in minimizing these at the end. Or, controversially, they can be used as part of the design process itself. The metric analysis of a site will produce environmental priorities particular to that site, and among those there will be some that can generate the first level of a design, a continuous performative surface in the horizontal plane championed by Kenneth Frampton and developed by landscape urbanism.[5] Everywhere else, particularized environmental performance can be injected: buildings, infrastructure, the biotic, the abiotic, the dense, the empty. After that, negotiations have to

The unhierarchical morphology of São Paulo, with high and low rise, high and low density spread across the city

Barra Funda–typical brownfield urban fabric

take place between the city's history of incarnations, its current lives, and this environmental datascape.

Environmental metrics can be used to generate parametrics. Parametrics are now firmly embedded in experimental design, especially in the digital avant-garde. Here interest is divided between form-finding and the relationship between form and performance in the interests of a new and elegant economy of means. As Haresh Lalvani observes: "This approach… is deeply connected with sustainability, as limited resources require us to maximise performance."[6] Where digital innovators have tended to invent their own electronic ecologies, environmental innovators have engaged with actual ones, looping back out of cyberspace to apply their parametric work materially. Much experimental digital design is years ahead of any materialization. The "embodiment of artificial life and

intelligent systems... through biomachinic mutation of organic and inorganic substances,"[7] as described by Karl Chu, is a long way off, as are buildings that would find and adapt their forms in response to internal (genetic) pressures, and external (environmental) ones.

Within an environmental context, this performative parametric approach is easier to see and do at the architectural scale.[8] At the urban scale, where the environmental has incomparably more cultural and economic baggage, there is no similarly direct relationship possible between environmental cause and design effect. A roof can simply shelter. A city simply can't. Nevertheless, it can be useful to start with environmental parametrics at the urban scale, because the reaction to that environmental data can heavily influence the building of the site. The choice of environmental strategy—and it is a choice—will lead toward one among many possible relationships between buildings and site, site and city.

In São Paulo, in collaboration with Joana Goncalves and Denise Duarte of the University of São Paulo, and Swen Geiss of R/E/D, we examined the interrelationship of environmental metrics and socially beneficial outcomes.[9] In London, R/E/D is concentrating on relationships between environmental metrics and urban design to develop a transferable design process that leads with environmental performance, however difficult environmentally led urban design is to implement in a global governance culture of short-termism. The 70-hectare test site in Barra Funda, São Paulo, was chosen by the Laboratorio de Conforto Ambiental e Efficiencia Energetica (LCAEE)[10] because it typifies many of the conditions found in the city: near the old center, losing population, subject to annual flooding, marooned by road and/or rail infrastructure, with patches of brownfield emptiness. To the south is a park and middle-income apartment blocks. To the north, literally on the other side of the tracks—a regional railway bisects the site—are *favelas*, nineteenth-century working-class housing, and a polluted river. A large rail/bus station straddles the tracks in the center of the site, and to the east of the station is a culture park by Oscar Niemeyer, a collection of pavilions with no park.

The previous city government of São Paulo classified Barra Funda as one of its "urban operations," but the area's difficult conditions have made it resistant to regeneration. As so many of the difficulties are environmental, with social and economic causes and effects, it seemed appropriate to suggest an environmentally led approach. Though we began with the same kind of land-use, typology, and density analyses as anyone else, we then identified the environmental resources and

The environmental context
of the site: the metrics of on-site
water resources

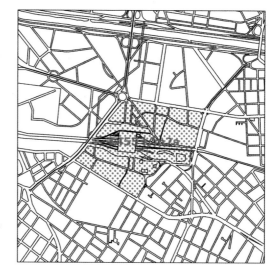

annual rainfall
1.455 l/m² a
14.550 m³/hec a
1.047.600 m³/a on site

annual drinking water demand
43,80 m³/pp a
17.520 m³/hec a
919.800 m³/a on site

potential annual drinking water reduction
25%
4.380 m³/hec a
229.950 m³/a on site

problems on and around the site to concentrate on first-level environmental scenarios. The Barra Funda site enjoys a large amount of sun and rainfall, though the rain is seasonal. The polluted river to the north floods annually, and there are very high levels of noise and air pollution from the railway bisecting the site and the arterial roads surrounding it. The sunfall suggests passive solar (free heating) at the very least for low-income housing, solar hot-water panels, and, if the money is there, photovoltaic panels for electricity. The seasonal rainfall suggests rainwater harvesting, to get through dry periods without costly imports of water from outside the city, and the flooding requires flood management and greatly increased site porosity.

Of these environmental parameters, passive solar and flood management have a direct effect on site design. Passive solar affects the layout of buildings, and flood management, the layout of buildings and the building of the site. Aiming for a specific density of dwellings per hectare and using different combinations of an agreed catalog of building typologies, we generate a series of diagrams to understand the initial spatial consequences of a range of environmental strategies—initial because although one or more of the resulting scenarios may achieve our metric targets, they may be less acceptable, or totally unacceptable, as urban places. This is the point at which these two narratives, ecological and urban, must negotiate, working equally important priorities into a design.

Such an environmentally led approach can mitigate the worst environmental problems on a site and bring generic social benefits, but may not reflect the particular social conditions of a particular city. Barra Funda has many small enterprises eking out an existence in an area of cheap rents.

The environmental context of the site: diagram of acoustic conditions

- 50 m distance to main roads
- 100 m distance to main roads
- 50 m distance to rail tracks
- 100 m distance to rail tracks

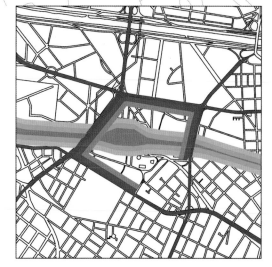

The environmental context of the site: diagram of flooding from Tiete River

- flooding buffer zone
- ° ° porous areas
- lower ground
- higher ground

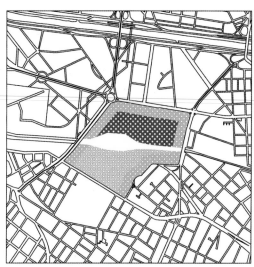

Flooding strategy: increase site porosity by 48 percent

- flood risk from nearby toxic river
- → flood risk from downhill roads

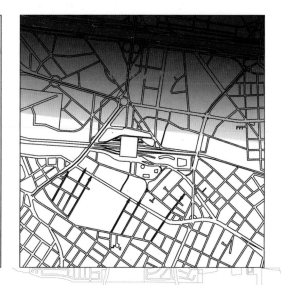

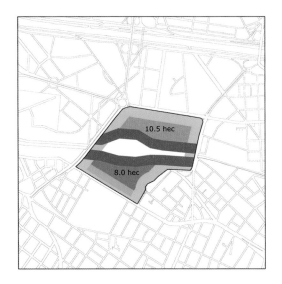

To the north are *favelas*—settlements made by the people who live in them. This bottom-up activity doesn't sit well with the creation of artificial ecosystems, which requires specialist expertise to be effective, and government intervention to clear a space in the market economy for such experiments to happen at all. This is not therefore about corporations creating new markets for themselves. It's about environmental reformation on a large scale in cities where there are large environmental problems. The intention of the LCAEE and R/E/D was to keep part of the site for self-build, work/live units, the kits of parts made to environmental standards. While this may safeguard a tradition of self-help, however, it can only guarantee sufficient environmental performance by at least partially regulating layout. The self-build units would have to be deployed at a certain distance from each other to ensure sufficient daylight levels and benefit from passive solar design. The cramming that characterizes *favelas* would not be reproduced in a new development. In other words, in many cities another synthesis is needed from ecological urban design—between bottom-up self-help and top-down management—to protect environmental performance. This should be acceptable to all but the most romantic about slums, as long as the managing is done in consultation with the managed, so such spatial changes are debated and understood.

R/E/D's EnLUDe project (Environmentally Led Urban Design) differs from current environmentally emphatic work such as Arup's Dongtan or Foster's Masdar in that it doesn't begin with a tabula rasa; it addresses existing cities, where the problems lie. The benefits of the new so-called eco-cities include knowledge transfer, but no direct mitigation of the pathologies of existing cities. R/E/D is investigating whether

Scenario 1: target porosity met, target mixed housing (60 percent social, 40 percent higher income) met, large roof area for water harvesting met, density targets not quite met. Density hasn't been met because environmental performance is privileged over density. Another scenario could reverse these priorities, producing a different site configuration.

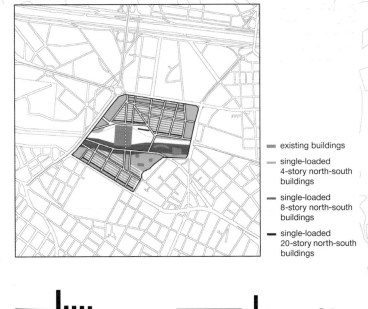

target density	21.000 p	
	400 p/hec	
gross floor area	740.000 m²	
gross build volume	2.190.000 m³	
target building footprint	170.000 m²	
	< 33,0 %	
target infrastructure	100.000 m²	
	< 19,2 %	
target green space/porosity	250.000 m²	
	< 48,0 %	
current density	18.500 p	
	356 p/hec	
gross floor area	649.500 m²	
gross build volume	1.495.300 m³	
current building footprint	115.700 m²	
	< 22,2 %	
current infrastructure	118.000 m²	
	< 22,6 %	
current green space/porosity	248.000 m²	
	< 47,7 %	

- existing buildings
- single-loaded 4-story north-south buildings
- single-loaded 8-story north-south buildings
- single-loaded 20-story north-south buildings

a kind of "performalism"—an initially direct relationship between environmental performance and urban form—can knit up culturally uninformed environmental design, and environmentally uninformed urban design, particularly in cities that are growing too rapidly.

1 *Encyclopaedia Britannica,* vol. 4 (Chicago: Encyclopaedia Britannica, 1985), 358–359.

2 See http://www.symbiosis.dk/industrial-symbiosis.aspx.

3 See Randall Thomas, ed., *Sustainable Urban Design* (London and New York: Spon, 2003).

4 Patrick Geddes, *Cities in Evolution* (London: Routledge, 1997).

5 Kenneth Frampton, "Toward an Urban Landscape," *Columbia Documents* no. 4 (1994), 83–93.

6 Haresh Lalvani, "The Milgo Experiment: An Interview with Haresh Lalvani," John

Lobell in *Programming Cultures, Architectural Design* 76(4), 2006, 53.

7 Karl Chu, "Metaphysics of Genetic Architecture and Computation," in *Programming Cultures, Architectural Design* 76(4), 2006, 39.

8 See www.ecologicstudio.com.

9 See Susannah Hagan, *Digitalia: Architecture and the Digital, the Environmental, and the Avant-Garde* (London and New York: Routledge, 2008), 115–124.

10 Laboratorio de Conforto Ambiental e Efficiencia Energetica (LCAEE), Faculdade de Arquitectura e Urbanismo, University of São Paulo.

Nature Culture

Kathryn Moore

Landscape is not only the physical context, the constructed public realm, the national parks, coastlines, squares, promenades and streets, places to walk or sit and watch the world go by; it also reflects our memories and values, the experiences we have of a place—as citizens, employers, visitors, students, tourists. It is the material, cultural, and social context of our lives.

This perspective demands that we redefine nature and overcome the dichotomy that has traditionally severed it from culture. This damaging duality lends it an almost mystical status and is one of the foremost reasons why the landscape continues to be associated with technology rather than ideas. But what exactly do we mean by nature? Why do we think "nature" is good for us, if by nature we mean the green stuff, the things that grow? Ask your average urbanite what is meant by nature in the city, for example, and he will mention trees, urban foxes, and rats, not necessarily in that order and not all inherently good for our souls. Is our supposed fondness for nature something we share culturally or even universally, as many would have us believe, its efficacy and value a matter of fact, beyond question or debate? To save the planet, is it a matter of scientific necessity to find out all there is to know about it? Should it be left to itself or tweaked and tampered with to suit our purpose? Neglect a garden and you get weeds; allow woodland to develop and you get biodiversity. Nature is what we make of it. The problem is that in the city, nature (landscape, "the green stuff"—call it what you will) is an afterthought, the trees and shrubs to be imported and manicured once the architects have left the building.

To be coldly objective and scientific or airily metaphysical about nature does considerable disservice to the very concept. Both views isolate it from the broader perspective, dislocating it from culture, cost, value, and profit. Reducing nature to natural systems and the like gives the impression that it can simply be detached from strategic and spatial decision-making. Easy to marginalize, it is left out of the frame, hard to justify, difficult to substantiate, compromised on after the event rather than considered from the start. And we've all seen the results. Relegated to hard-won square meters of grass, trees,

The master plan for the gardens evolved from an initial study of the organization and physiology of the orchid to a highly sophisticated and integrated 3D network of horticulture, art engineering, and architecture.

hedgerows, and ditches, "nature" is sandwiched in after the important objective economic decisions have been made, fitted neatly between settlements and roads, usually along the streams, rivers, or corners of parks or "informal green spaces"—nothing more than living embroidery. Nature seen like this is often cynically assumed to be enough to address matters of quality, and green space is justified in terms of its benefit for wildlife. Never mind the spatial structure of the constructed public realm, the ease of movement, the sense of belonging, the cultural identity of the place or the social and physical experience of the people who live and work in the places we design. No matter how much spirituality hovers around the concept of nature, in reality we find it difficult not to associate it with technology. It is critical in the wider arena to stop dividing things into bite-sized pieces, be they

MARINA CHANNEL

26 Water Taxi Landing
1 Cool Dry Conservatory (Discovery Terraces)
2 Cool Moist Conservatory (Cloudy Mountain)

14 Languid Lake
11 Lion Grove & Superficies

Bayfront MRT
6 Flower Market/ Exhibition Hall
9 Pride of Singapore

8 Water Taxi Landing
Barrage Visitor Centre
Barrage

Global Common Event Space

Culvert Road

BOULEVARD

biological or cultural, of scientific or artistic concern. This means ditching both narrowly scientific and wildly subjective approaches to nature.

Rather than ideas versus nature, we have ideas of nature. Instead of seeing nature as something separate from culture, from ourselves, we must recognize that in the way we live our lives, with every intervention we make, we are expressing (consciously or not) an attitude toward the physical world. The choice is not whether we work with art or ecology, with nature or culture, but how considerately, imaginatively, and responsibly we go about our business, because for every one of our actions there is a reaction in the physical world. Where we decide to build new cities or expand old ones, and place streets, squares, parks, and gardens, reflects the value we place on the quality of our physical environment. Working with natural processes, given the global challenges we face, is an ecological imperative. We have no choice in the matter. But it is the whole thing, the ideas and values we hold and their expression in physical form, be it green, gray, or blue, that defines us. This is what frames the experience we all have of the places we live in, and it is this experience that is a properly relevant definition of nature. After all, natural systems don't stop where the buildings start.

The Lovers' Wood, British Pavilion Garden, Japan Expo 2005. An illuminated, changing woodland flora garden enclosed by lime, sequentially planted with foxgloves, ferns, and grasses beneath the changing canopy.

The ideas we have about the landscape are a talking point as well as an explanation that empowers the clients, the community, and the various professions. Ideas can be cohesive; they bind all manner of things—argument, opinion, values. There can be no better way to capture the hearts and minds of everyone involved than a great idea.

What we are examining today are ways to provide a sustainable and lasting blueprint for the landscape—to give a fresh perspective, not simply reinforce existing practices. We must connect spatial strategies to real places and develop ways of working that encourage and demand the expression of the ideas that are fundamental to achieving design excellence, the ability to create good-looking places, because the quality of our environment is directly proportional to the quality of our lives. It's an equation as simple as it is compelling.

At the heart of the gardens are the Supertrees–a fusion of nature, art, and technology. The spectacular vertical tropical gardens feature ferns, orchids, and climbers as well as environmental engines for the gardens, equipped with photovoltaics, solar thermal collectors, rainwater harvesting devices, and venting ducts.

Investigating the Importance of Customized Energy Model Inputs: A Case Study of Gund Hall

Holly A. Wasilowski and Christoph F. Reinhart

Across the North American building design industry, there is growing interest in computer-based building energy simulation, or "energy modeling," which is used to make design decisions such as which energy-conservation measure provides the best return on investment. Until now, energy modeling has generally been performed by mechanical engineers or specialized consultants. However, the most recent generation of commercial, high-end graphical user interface (GUI) seems to cater to the needs of architectural firms, with the developers suggesting that these tools have become so intuitive that they can be used by "everyone, even architects." This project investigates the question, "How successfully can a group of architecture students learn to build an energy model of a complex commercial building?"

A key feature of these high-end GUIs is that they offer libraries of default values for internal energy loads. For example, if one were to model a classroom and did not know how many watts per square meter of plug-in appliances to expect, the modeler could look up the default values, embedded in the software, for a typical university classroom. This provokes the question, "In which situation are these defaults an acceptable shortcut, and in which situation is it worth the effort to generate custom inputs?"

Besides these internal load inputs, energy models require weather inputs. In many areas of the world, "Typical Meteorological Year" (TMY) weather files are available and used in energy modeling. This data, however, is usually not specific to the building site or the time period in question. This invites the question, "What impact do these weather files have on the accuracy of the energy model, and what should a modeler do in geographies where this data is unavailable?"

Each of these questions was addressed as part of a research seminar on "Building Performance Simulation—Energy" at the Harvard Graduate School of Design (GSD). The case-study building was the GSD's own Gund Hall, a near ideal "worst case" for this research because of its nonstandard occupant schedules and variety of occupant activity. Eleven graduate students surveyed and modeled Gund Hall using the DesignBuilder GUI for the U.S. Department of Energy's EnergyPlus simulation engine.[1]

The students issued occupant questionnaires, conducted walk-through observations, interviewed the facilities manager, and installed watt-meters to create custom model inputs.[2] These inputs included operation schedules for HVAC equipment as well as densities (such as people/m² or watts/m²) and time schedules for occupants, plug-loads, and lighting. The authors then ran an energy simulation using all-custom inputs, followed by a series of simulations replacing the custom inputs with DesignBuilder default values.

The students also created two custom weather files: one from a weather station the students installed themselves on the roof of Gund Hall,[3] and one from weather data collected from other local weather stations.[4] The authors then ran multiple energy simulations using these weather files and the default TMY weather file.[5] Finally, the simulated results were compared to each other and to measured utility data.

Measured monthly electricity use for Gund Hall was compared to simulations using different combinations of custom and default internal loads. Not surprisingly, the fully customized loads followed the metered electricity use more closely than simulations based on default assumptions. For the fully customized loads, the annual error was 0.2 percent, versus 18 percent for the all-default simulation (see first graph).

Gund Hall, Harvard Graduate School of Design

In addition to electricity, heating and cooling loads were investigated and, again, the customized simulation results surpassed the default results. Furthermore, each type of input (occupancy, plug-load, lighting, and HVAC schedule) made a significant impact on the accuracy of the simulation results.

Measured monthly heating loads for Gund Hall were compared to simulations using different weather files (see second graph). Each weather file produces similar accuracy. The same was true for cooling consumption.

Following the experience of modeling Gund Hall, the students were asked how comfortable they felt with their modeling skills and whether they would use the software again. They seemed to be reasonably satisfied with the simulation results, and there was a general expectation that with minor adjustments of the settings, the simulation results could be brought into even better alignment with the measured data. The students expressed their discomfort, however, with working on too complex a model, indicating that there remains a need for specialists, especially in the later design stages.

In Gund Hall, each of the internal load inputs studied made a significant impact on the simulation accuracy. This is only one building, but it suggests that collecting reliable internal load inputs is a very useful exercise for retrofitting projects, and that for new design projects, these simulation assumptions should be carefully reviewed with the building owner. Finally, this project indicates that making custom weather files is unnecessary where appropriate default files exist, which includes most major North American cities. In other locales, however, making one's own weather files is feasible and relatively inexpensive.[6]

Monthly electricity loads: measured versus simulations

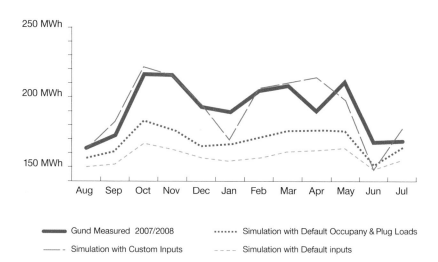

Gund Measured 2007/2008
Simulation with Custom Inputs
Simulation with Default Occupany & Plug Loads
Simulation with Default inputs

The authors would like to thank the following students for their dedication to this project:
Diego Ibarra, James Kallaos, Anthony Kane, Cynthia Kwan, David Lewis, Elli Lobach, Jeff Laboskey, Sydney Mainster, Rohit Manudhane, Natalie Pohlman, and Jennifer Sze. We further express our gratitude to the Harvard Graduate School of Design as well as the Real Estate Academic Initiative at Harvard University for supporting this effort.

1 This software package was chosen for its extensive library of default templates. DesignBuilder version 1.9.0.003BETA, last accessed February 2009, www.designbuildersoftware.com. U.S. Department of Energy, EnergyPlus Version 2.2.0.025, last accessed February 2009. DLL default version embedded in DesignBuilder, http://apps1.eere.energy.gov/buildings/energyplus/.

2 Watt meters used: watts up? Pro ES by Electronic Education Devices, www.wattsupmeters.com, and Kill A Watt EZ P4460 by P3 International Corporation, www.p3international.com.

3 Weather station used: HOBO weather station, Onset Computer Corporation, Bourne, Massachusetts, www.onsetcomp.com. Includes: weather station starter kit, HOBO software, solar radiation sensor, light sensor level, and tripod kit.

4 Weather station locations: Massachusetts Institute of Technology Green Building, location: 2.6 kilometers from Gund Hall. Weather station hardware: Davis Vantage Pro 2; software: VWS V12.08. University of Massachusetts-Boston, location: 9.4 kilometers from Gund Hall. Weather station hardware: Davis Vantage Pro Plus; software: unavailable.

5 U.S. Department of Energy, EnergyPlus Climate File Database, last accessed February 2009, http://apps1.eere.energy.gov/buildings/energyplus/cfm/weather_data.

6 The Gund weather station cost less than $2,500, produced adequate results, and could provide weather data for many building projects.

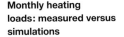

Monthly heating loads: measured versus simulations

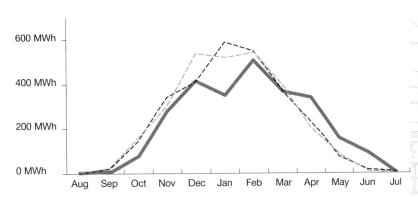

——— Gund Measured 2007/2008

- - - - Simulation with EPW1, MIT & UMass Weather 2007/2008

– – – – Simulation with EPW2, Gund Weather (Nov 2008) & Boston TMY Weather

Perception of Urban Density

Vicky Cheng and Koen Steemers

Urban density has been a controversial topic in recent decades, as global societies become increasingly urban. In the United Kingdom, for example, the presumed benefits of urban compaction—more efficient urban land use, transport, and infrastructure—have underpinned a number of planning initiatives including the Urban Task Force in 1999[1] and the subsequent Greater London Authority London Plan.[2] Densification seems to be inevitable. When planners talk about increasing plot ratio,[3] however, how does it affect us—our perceptual comfort? In other words, is it possible to increase physical density while limiting the perception of density?

Unlike matters such as land value, housing price, and the demand for utility services that can all be reasonably modeled with respect to density, the effect on our perceptual comfort is not well understood. Our perception does not merely correspond to physical density; other factors in the environment come into play. If we were able to manipulate these factors, we would open up opportunities for the integration of urban analysis in future developments and urban regeneration,

Plot ratio, site coverage, and sky view factor

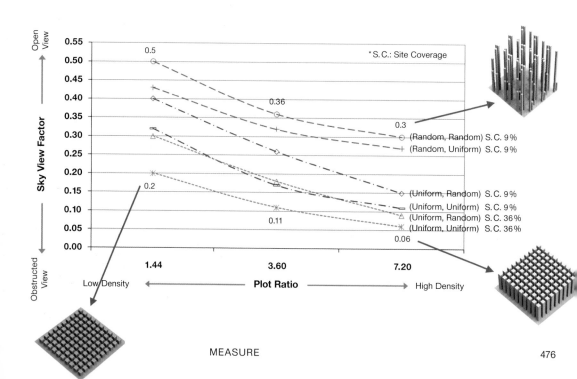

Looking down at Hong Kong, one of the densest urban fabrics in the world

Sky view factor map of the eight case-study sites in Hong Kong. The map shows the distribution of average sky view factor throughout the urban environments.

Sky View Factor

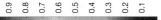

0.9 0.8 0.7 0.6 0.5 0.4 0.3 0.2 0.1

such that the perceptual discomfort arising from densification could be alleviated.

Using Hong Kong as an urban laboratory, we studied the main determinants of perceived urban density, exploring alternative parameters to those commonly used to define density. In this high-density context, we examined people's perception and satisfaction with regard to urban density. We deployed two methods to obtain feedback from subjects: (1) responses to photographs of real urban scenes; and (2) responses in actual urban locations. Both methods were administered by questionnaire. We selected eight sites, all located in the urban district of Hong Kong, as the context for the study. These sites manifest different densities and layouts that capture a wide range of urban built-form characteristics.[4]

The findings show a strong negative correlation of satisfaction with perceived density.[5] This suggests that high perceived density is seen as a negative aspect of urban life in Hong Kong. Hence, creating a satisfactory urban environment means reducing the perception of density. We then investigated a number of candidate urban parameters and gauged their effects on the perception of density.

Plot ratio, one of the most commonly used density measures in planning practice, has a significant but weak correlation with perceived density, suggesting that actual physical density has minor influence on the perception of urban density. Urban developments with similar plot ratios can exhibit different urban forms and are thus likely to be perceived

S1	S2	S3	S4
Battery Street	Parklane	Wai Ching Street	Southwall Road

S5	S6	S7	S8
TST East	Granville Road	Hillwood Road	Man Wah Estate

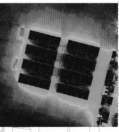

differently. Two study sites, Southwall Road and TST East, have similar plot ratios of about 5, but manifest very different urban forms. Southwall Road represents a typical example of low-rise buildings and high site coverage, while TST East exhibits the contrary. TST East was consistently perceived as having lower density and rated more satisfactorily than Southwall Road by study subjects. What makes TST East perceptually a more desirable place than Southwall Road is spatial openness.

We used the sky view factor as a measure of spatial openness: a sky view factor of 1 means an unobstructed view of the sky (i.e., open land), and a sky view factor of 0 means a complete lack of a sky view. According to our findings, the perception of density decreases with increasing sky view. TST East has a much higher sky view factor than Southwall Road[6] due to the low site coverage layout that results in ample open space.

It has to be emphasized that the quantity as well as the quality of open space is important. Although the relationship between the quality of open space and the perception of

Eight case-study sites. VOS is visible open space, the ratio of the total visible open-space area to the area of a 100-meter-radius reference circle; SVF point is the sky view factor, the proportion of visible sky to the total sky dome, from a single point.

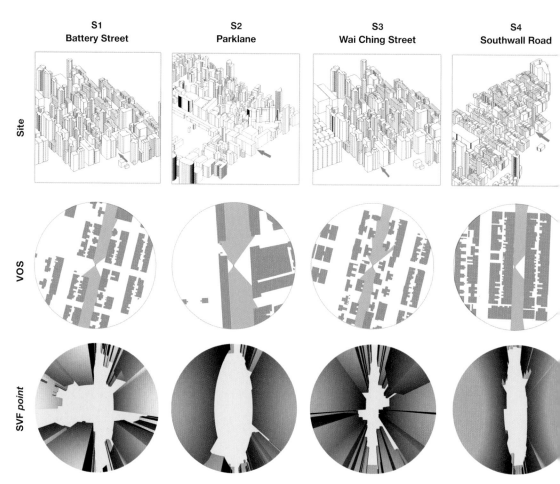

	S1	S2	S3	S4
	Battery Street	**Parklane**	**Wai Ching Street**	**Southwall Road**

Site

VOS

SVF *point*

density was not researched in detail in this study, the findings concerning a number of non-morphological properties on perceived density may shed light on this matter.

In the study, vehicular traffic, pedestrian intensity, and signage were consistently acknowledged as features of increasing perceived density. The effect of vegetation was ambiguous, although vegetation appears to reduce the sense of density. Nonetheless, some participants expressed the concern that vegetation may take up more of the already scarce urban pedestrian spaces and make the streets even denser. Similarly, the effect of public urban art, such as sculptures, is not clearly shown in the findings. The results in general show that public art is not widely appreciated, with many commenting that the streets in Hong Kong are too narrow and congested.

The sky view factor is a parameter that has been extensively used to define sky openness in urban microclimatic studies and is easy to compute.[7] It has been associated with environmental issues such as urban daylight performance and the urban heat island phenomenon.

| S5 | S6 | S7 | S8 |
| TST East | Granville Road | Hillwood Road | Man Wah Estate |

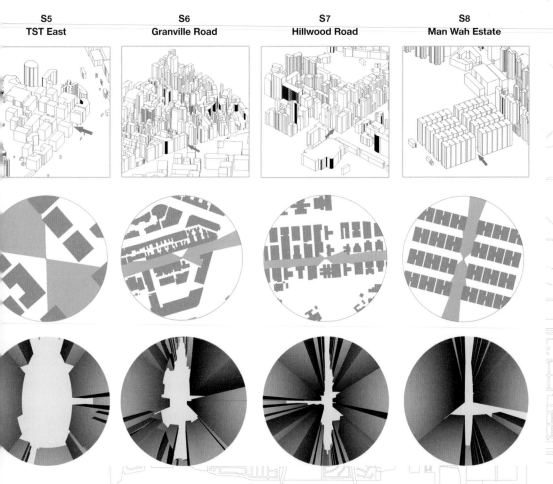

Theoretical studies of urban arrays show, as one would expect, that the average sky view factor reduces as physical densities increase. However, the same studies also reveal that for a given density (plot ratio), the sky view factor varies much more strongly as a function of site coverage. This demonstrates that one can create physically dense urban arrays—with, for example, a plot ratio of 7.2—where the sky view factor can range from as little as 0.06 to a more acceptable 0.3. As a result, an urban density with a plot ratio of 7.2 can theoretically have a lower perceived density than a development with a plot ratio of 1.44.

This study brings a new dimension—human perceptual comfort—to the application of the sky view factor. It reveals the potential for a holistic and synergetic integration of human perception and urban microclimatic knowledge into urban design, especially in a high-density context. The sky view factor can be an indicator for assessing the performances of urban design in terms of both human perception and urban microclimate. This work can shed light on the making of new urban planning policy.

1 R.G. Rogers, *Towards an Urban Renaissance: Final Report of the Urban Task Force* (London: Department of the Environment, Transport, and the Regions, 1999).
2 Greater London Authority, *The London Plan: Spatial Development Strategy for Greater London* (London: GLA, 2004).
3 Plot ratio (or floor area ratio) is the ratio of total gross floor area to site area. For the sake of comparison, the extent of the site area in this study is defined as the land area within a radius of 100 meters from a predefined reference point.
4 Plot ratio ranged from 2.9 to 7.8; site coverage ranged from approximately 29 percent to 49 percent.
5 Perceived density was rated on a 7-point scale, with 1 and 7 representing low and high densities respectively.
6 The average sky view factors of TST East and Southwall Road are 0.40 and 0.23 respectively.
7 V. Cheng, K. Steemers, M. Montavon, and R. Compagnon, "Urban Form, Density, and Solar Potential," *PLEA 2006: Twenty-third International Conference on Passive and Low Energy Architecture*, Geneva, Switzerland, September 6–8, 2006, 701–706; C. Ratti, N. Baker, and K. Steemers, "Energy Consumption and Urban Texture," *Energy and Buildings*, vol. 37, no. 7 (2005), 762–776.

**Street views from each of
the case-study sites in Hong Kong**

London's Estuary Region

Sir Terry Farrell

I have spent much time recently thinking about and working on the interrelationships of urban London and its suburban and rural hinterland. Seven million people live within the metropolitan boundary of this major world city, yet in this "urban realm" there are astonishingly 500 active farms as well as large parks and many rivers and lakes. This interrelationship is partly physical, including water supply, drainage, food production; it is also partly sociocultural (access to open space is measured by a government agency as a quality-of-life issue, and anyone—though invariably the poorer people—more than 300 meters away is categorized as "open space deprived").

The Thames Estuary, a natural subregion of the metropolis, has gradually become the engine room of London, handling its waste, power generation, and ports as well as being the

frontline flood defense against rising sea levels. Human experience tells us that hardship leads to invention; the potential of London's estuary to be an innovator for green industries has been recognized by various agencies and leading environmental thinkers such as Lord Nick Stern of the London School of Economics, who has helped us quantify the economic effects of reskilling an impoverished, marginalized labor force and regenerating the agriculture parkland and ecology of a postindustrial landscape. Waste management and recycling, new forms of power generation, water supply management, and so on are all a solid basis for twenty-first-century economic regeneration. It is also the basis for the area now being declared by the government as the United Kingdom's first eco-region. The aim is not to seek the ideal in short order but to use this government-designated "largest regeneration project in Europe" as part exemplar and part test bed for future U.K. regional and urban planning. The key to the relevance of this eco-region is that it is not about utopian new buildings but about retrofit and improving on what is already there (1.5 million people live in London's estuary region).

But the other and equally important aim is to connect urban dwellers back to nature and expand through education and demonstration a firmer foundation for the culture of the

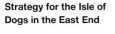

**Strategy for the Isle of
Dogs in the East End**

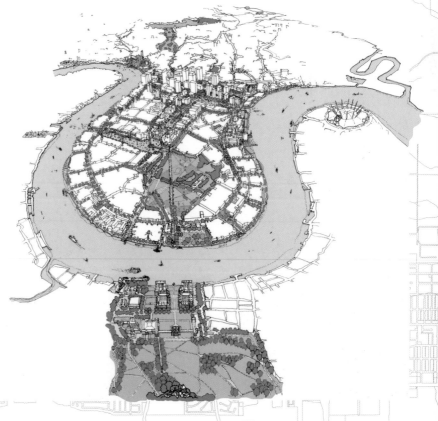

countryside. Once upon a time, London's estuary played a significant role in industrial workers' primary access to landscape. Paddle steamers and ferries brought the masses to summer work in hop fields in Kent and strawberry fields in Essex, and working people went on holiday here on the piers and water-edged promenades all along the Thames. All hard to believe now that it has been overwhelmed by oil depots, industrial sheds and wharves, car assembly plants, large-scale twentieth-century oil, gas, and coal-fired power stations, and most of the sewage treatment works for metropolitan London that pollutes the Thames.

When working for the city of Shanghai on its parkland project at Chongming Island eight years ago, I was impressed by how the emerging new urban cultures were thinking about the rural/urban balance. In Europe, parks like Germany's

Thames Gateway Parklands Plan

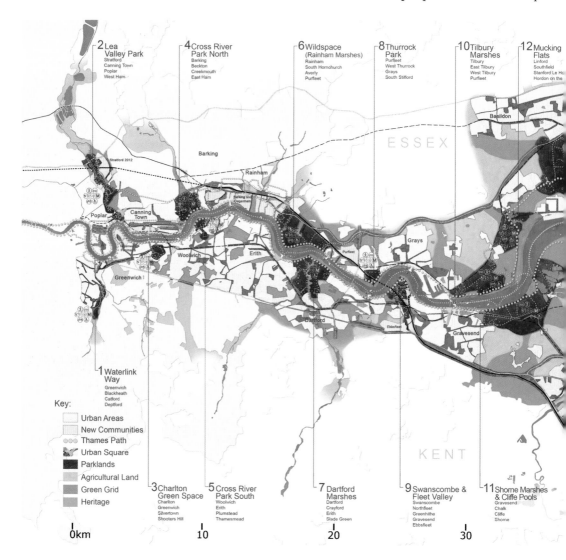

Emscher have been an object lesson in how to plan postindustrial landscapes. London, the great capital city and the United Kingdom's largest metropolis, has easily the worst public access to wilderness and parkland in the whole of the country. In the Midlands and North are once industrial cities now surrounded by great national parks, all based on conserving the open countryside landscape to the benefit of everyone. Now the need is even greater to reconnect landscape and wilderness, not only for agriculture and food production but also for community identity and widening of life's experience of the balance of people and nature.

So the idea emerged for London's Estuary to be the nation's first purpose-planned and -built national park, unique in that it would be an urban and rural park combined with its primary raison d'etre, anticipation of future global warming.

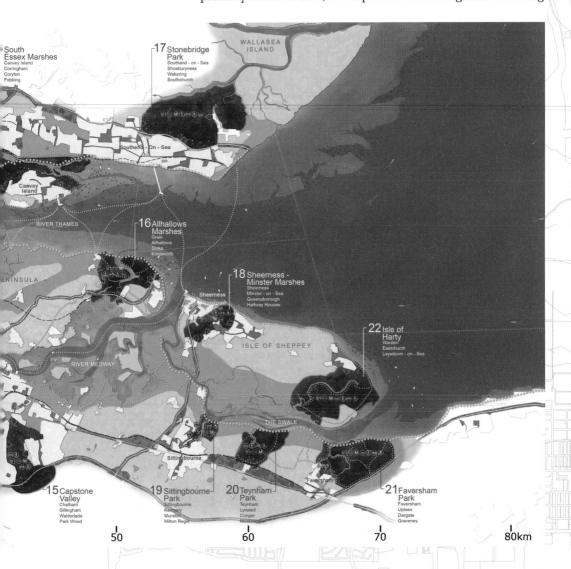

It has been inspiring to learn from so many scientists, naturalists, and volunteers in organizations such as the Royal Society for the Protection of Birds, English Nature, and the London Zoo (who are involved in fish breeding conservation in the Estuary, as it is the primary breeding ground for North Sea fish). This scientific community possesses the best grasp of the big picture—the regional, continental, and global natural world relationships that urban life depends on.

We began our study with the Campaign to Protect Rural England group. I admire their advocacy in establishing that the quality of urban life is a key to the quality of rural life and the protection of the natural world. It is critical to make all of London more liveable, healthier and greener, and less polluted, as this is the surest way to stop mindless expansion of the metropolis, with its resultant trashing of landscape and the

Thames Gateway Water Parklands Plan

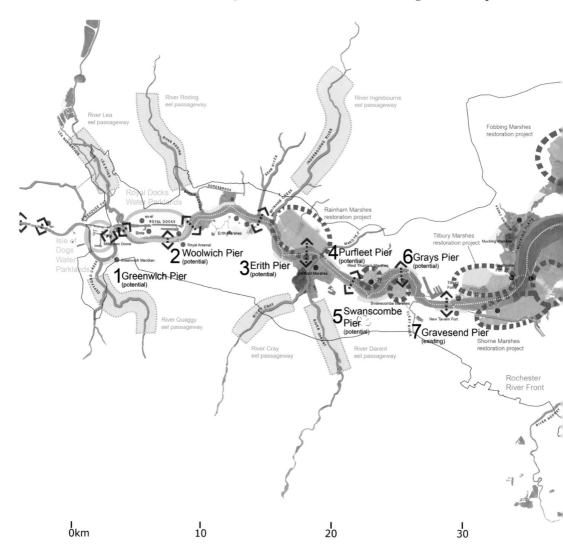

creation of unsustainable commuter communities. The surest way to conserve nature, landscape, agriculture, and rural communities is to improve the quality of urban life itself—to make its lifestyle "offer" completely irresistible.

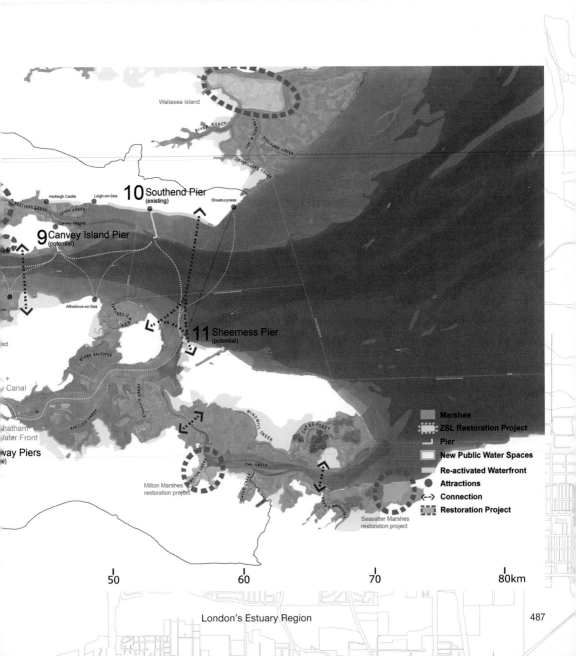

MEASURE

MEASURE

Urban Earth London

MEASURE

Sustainability Initiatives in London

Camilla Ween

How we will sustain ourselves in the future is a growing concern as access diminishes to resources beyond our own boundaries. Already in the mid-1990s, sustainability expert Herbert Girardet estimated that London's ecological footprint (the area of land required to sustain all of its activities) was 125 times the size of the city itself. A footprint study in 2000 called City Limits[1] found that London's ecological footprint was in fact 293 times its geographical area. The London Plan, a spatial development strategy, set out to change this relationship and establish London as a sustainable city. London's sustainability agenda is being driven by this tough policy as well as many experimental initiatives that explore how to change the way the city sustains itself.

A draft Climate Change Action Plan was published in 2008, ahead of the production of a binding Adaptation Strategy. The Action Plan set the ambitious target of reducing London's CO_2 emissions by 60 percent from a 1990 baseline by 2025. The emphasis is on changing the way we live, not our quality of life. London has been looking at a number of ways to tackle sustainability and is developing new ways of doing things.

Decentralized Energy

To meet the CO_2 reduction targets, the priority is to move 25 percent of London's energy supply to local decentralized energy systems. London has been exploring the development of decentralized energy supply, such as capturing surplus industrial process heat to deliver carbon savings at very low cost.

The London Development Agency is developing a pilot district heating project with the London Thames Gateway Heat Network, a hot-water transmission network that will connect sources of low- or zero-carbon heat to existing and new developments. Heat from the production of electricity at Barking Power Station (previously wasted) will be captured in hot water and distributed via underground pipes to properties where it will be used for domestic hot water and central heating, replacing conventional boilers. Up to 120,000 homes and properties, including schools, could have their heat requirements met by the 23-kilometer network, saving almost 100,000 tonnes of CO_2 output each year. The first customers could be supplied by early 2011. The ultimate vision is to have multiple local district heating networks across London, using low- or zero-carbon heat from a number of differing sources.

Transportation

Catering to ever-growing transport demand is one of London's greatest challenges. Transport for London (TFL) is exploring a wide range of sustainable initiatives, with a strong emphasis on shifting more journeys away from cars and toward public transport, walking, and cycling. Personal car travel is being restrained partly through having very restrictive parking standards in new development. Central London has introduced the London Congestion Charging Scheme, which aimed to reduce congestion by charging for the privilege of driving. In 2003 a zone was created within which all vehicles (with a few exceptions including public transport, taxis, police, and ambulances) would have to pay a daily charge of £5. In the first year there was a 21 percent reduction in traffic, a 30 percent reduction in congestion, and a 43 percent increase in cycling, as well as a reduction in accidents and £125 million raised in revenue for public transport improvements.

In 2000, Mayor Ken Livingstone set out to make London the most walkable city in the world. Much has been invested in public realm projects and improving the walking environment. Walking and cycling are central to TFL's integrated transport, as a shift to these modes will release capacity across the transport network. TFL is developing a sophisticated walking tool, Legible London, to encourage walking and support wayfinding. Based on the theory of "mental mapping," it helps people connect areas, regions, and transport systems. Distinctive "totems" will show the direction to walk, walk time, notable landmarks, and "heads up" maps that provide information to mobile phones.[2]

Waste Treatment and Recycling

The way we deal with waste is an urgent priority. The London Plan requires a reduction of the amount of waste sent to landfill; by 2020, 85 percent of waste will have to be processed within London. There is also a requirement to reduce the amount of waste generated, particularly in the construction industry, and to increase reuse, recycling, and composting of waste. The production of renewable energy from waste is being encouraged using new and emerging technologies, especially where the products of waste treatment could be used as fuels (e.g., biofuels and hydrogen).

The perception of what "waste" is has changed and led to a new approach: reduce, reuse, and recycle—with disposal as the last resort. LondonWaste, London's largest recycling and sustainable waste management facility, aims to send "Zero Waste to Landfill." Its EcoPark looks for closed-loop solutions: organic waste is turned into compost within twelve weeks; and untreated wood is shredded into chips, new wood-based products, or fuel. Waste that cannot be recycled is incinerated in the Energy Centre, where the heat generated is used to create electricity, currently sufficient to provide power for 66,000 homes annually.

The transport and energy implications of waste collection are also being considered. A new development at Wembley City of 4,200 homes will collect waste using a network of underground vacuum tunnels. The system will reduce refuse truck miles by up to 90 percent and CO_2 emissions by 400 tonnes a year compared with conventional refuse collection. The waste is automatically transported through a fully enclosed system of underground vacuum pipes, at 50 miles per hour, to a central collection station.

Open Space and Biodiversity

Fundamental to people's well-being is an understanding of the natural world and being connected to our planet. London has therefore set out to protect and restore urban ecosystems, to ensure no overall loss of wildlife habitats and create more open space. Every opportunity is taken, through the development process, to design places that will attract diverse species and restore eroded habitats, such as regenerating degraded open land, creating new eco-habitats, and promoting green roofs. The 104-acre WWT London Wetland Centre, for example, was created on the site of disused concrete water reservoirs and transformed into the best urban site in Europe for observing wildlife, including migrating birds.

Sustainable Housing

Part of London's green strategy has been the exploration of more sustainable approaches to housing. BioRegional developed London's first experimental low-carbon housing development, BedZED, which led to the One Planet Living concept, developed by BioRegional and the International World Wildlife Fund. This global initiative is based on ten principles of sustainability: zero carbon; zero waste; sustainable transport; local and sustainable materials; local and sustainable food; sustainable water; natural habitats and wildlife; culture and heritage; equity and fair trade; health and happiness. It sets out the choices and challenges humanity faces if it is to enjoy a high quality of life within the means of the planet's resources.

1 By consultants Best Foot Forward.
2 For more information, see:
tfl.gov.uk/legiblelondon.

An early coherent example of sustainable living was BedZED, designed in 2002 by Bill Dunster Architects. One of the key objectives was to show that eco-development and green life-styles could be accessible and affordable. The principles of sustainability in housing are now being developed and embraced in a number of developments across London.

Greenwich Millennium Village was designed to be an exemplar sustainable twenty-first-century community, transforming an uninhabitable brownfield. The master plan, created by Ralph Erskine, set out to create a place for people to have priority over cars. The 2,700-home mixed-tenure project includes community and commercial uses, a school and health center, open space and an ecology park. The project set high targets for environmentally sustainable development over its lifetime (from 2000 average): 80 percent reduction in primary energy consumption; 50 percent reduction in embodied energy; 50 percent reduction in construction waste; 30 percent reduction in water use; 30 percent reduction in construction costs; and 25 percent reduction in project construction time. A key design strategy was that social rented housing should be seamlessly mixed in with the private-market housing, to ensure social mix and integration.

Another example is One Gallions, designed by Feilden Clegg Bradley Studios based on the principles of One Planet Living. It aims to reduce the carbon impact of construction. The development will have a combined heat and power unit to achieve net zero CO_2 emissions. The buildings are designed to be highly energy and water efficient, and sustainable transport and waste management are core to the design.

Moving beyond LEED:
Evaluating Green at the Urban Scale

Thomas Schroepfer

To evaluate the success of sustainable projects at an urban scale and make useful comparisons of various efforts, it is necessary to develop more sophisticated measurement tools and methodologies. At present, tools such as LEED measure only individual building performance against a standard, and ways of assessing sustainable design within a comprehensive framework are still emerging. With "eco-cities" being built around the world—including Masdar, UAE, currently under construction, and Sarriguren, Spain, almost completed—how can the critical role that design plays in the creation of sustainable urban environments be brought to the foreground through an evaluation process? Two established eco-cities suggest new approaches:

– *Vauban*, a 38-hectare former barracks site near the center of Freiburg, Germany, was purchased by the city in 1994 with the goal of converting it into a flagship environmental and social project. Vauban comprises 2,000 homes to house 5,000 people, and business units to provide more than 500 jobs. The project is nearing completion and is widely seen as one of the most positive examples in Europe of environmental thinking in relation to urban design. Vauban displays a complex network of environmentally friendly planning measures that work synergistically within its lively social and community framework. The development presents itself as a viable and real alternative to preconceived models of architectural typology or urbanism, bringing back qualities of the city into neighborhood development and yet at the same time seeking environmental alternatives to car-reliant development.

– *solarCity Linz* comprises about 1,300 homes and 3,000 inhabitants. It was designed as a flagship development for renewable energies in urban design and includes projects by architects including Foster and Partners, Richard Rogers, and Thomas Herzog. Construction of the nucleus of solarCity took place from 1995 to 2005. This experimental project aims to be a model for ecological living at the beginning of the twenty-first century while being at the forefront of architectural and landscape design. The development as a whole,

including the aspects of design and environmenta̶ ̶
ogy, interact in providing an integrated sustainable
nity that reveals new possibilities in aesthetic expr

An evaluative system for assessing sustainable projects at an urban scale must be capable of highlighting the role of architectural and urban design in creating integrated environmental technology systems, so that these projects form part of the larger inhabitable environment rather than remain limited showcases of environmental science. A comprehensive framework for evaluation cannot be based primarily on technical and ecological terms, as projects will be successful only when they exceed the sum of their environmental technologies, such as photovoltaic and waste disposal systems, and consider aesthetic, economic, and social dimensions. Designers can create urban environments that address multiple variables— quality of life, diversity of population, alternative modes of transportation, and ecologies of site. By becoming part of a comprehensive framework for evaluation, such variables could foster new trajectories in the development of future sustainable cities. Establishing a design framework for evaluating sustainable projects would serve as an invaluable tool for designers in creating innovative architecture and urbanism.

Center of solarCity, designed by Auer + Weber

Landscapes of Specialization

Bill Rankin

One of the recurring themes of the green movement is the virtue of localism. Even though we know that tracking food-miles is not always a simple affair—it's actually greener for London to import its apples from New Zealand than to get them from England—the assumption persists that "local" and "sustainable" are kindred concepts. But analyzing the geography of agriculture suggests that our ideas of localism are seriously flawed. The geography of U.S. agriculture, for example, is not a smooth space of overlapping local conditions; it is instead a disjointed and lumpy space of specialization. With the exception of some crops in the Midwest, there are few areas where different commodities are grown side by side, and while cattle are distributed relatively evenly throughout the country, the production of all other animals is quite concentrated. No major city could source all of its food from local farms—not even those close to major agricultural areas. These patterns should not surprise us,

since American agriculture has always been dominated by the logic of global comparative advantage. And with organic production accounting for less than 0.3 percent of agricultural land (and farm subsidies accounting for less than 3 percent of the total value of U.S. agricultural output), this seems likely to be the case for the foreseeable future.[1]

Agriculture is lumpy in time as well as space. The global spread of cropland over the last 300 years has been a dance of intensification and expansion. Nearly every area of the world has seen agriculture become more locally dense: agricultural land has become more and more agricultural, even in areas where it has been long established and where population density has increased as well. Since 1850, this steady-state of intensification has been punctuated by several episodes of rapid expansion into previously untapped areas: the Great Plains in the late nineteenth century, Argentina in the early twentieth century, and in last

few decades, Brazil and central India. Decline is relatively rare, but it has happened, such as in the central Amazon, northern Patagonia, or the Appalachian Piedmont after World War II.[2]

What are the implications here for ecological urbanism? First, for the idea of the local to make any sense at all, it needs to be seriously modified. Instead of being defined in terms of simple geographic distance, the local should be seen in terms of the kinds of transportation and distribution efficiencies that define modern markets. This in turn means that many of the ecologies of future urbanism will have to be global. Designers should not reject the reality of global commodity markets, pitting the local (the province of design) against the global (the province of the market).

Percent of land used for growing crops

0%   20%   40%   60%   80%   100%

1700

1870

1930

1990

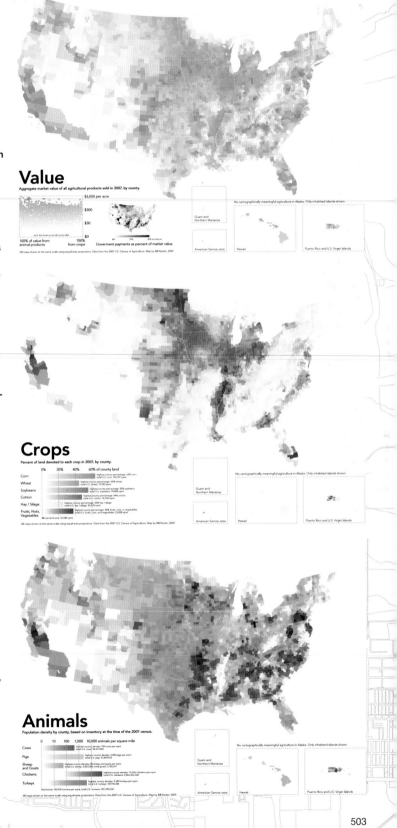

Second, the transportation revolution that began in the mid-nineteenth century is far from over: vast stretches of Africa, South America, and Southeast Asia could still be opened up to agricultural uses. Preserving these rainforest areas will require further intensification elsewhere. With many agricultural areas at close to 100 percent exploitation, it would seem that much of the logic of density and densification usually applied to the urban condition could apply equally well to agricultural areas. Simple divisions between "local" and "global" or "urban" and "rural" are perhaps less instructive than an analysis of different kinds of adjacencies and intensifications. How can the strategies of urban design be adapted to deal with these new conditions of proximity and density?[3]

1 Data from the U.S. Census of Agriculture, 2007.
2 Data from Navin Ramankutty (McGill) and Jonathan Foley (University of Minnesota), 1999.
3 See www.radicalcartography.net.

The spread of agriculture has not been uniformly distributed in either space or time. High-density agriculture is a relatively recent phenomenon, confined to a few major areas. Maps by Bill Rankin, 2009; data published 1999.

The lumpy geography of agriculture is a challenge to our understanding of localism. Should we protest distant food production, or search for new efficiencies of transport? Maps by Bill Rankin, 2005/2009; data from 2007.

Value

Aggregate market value of all agricultural products sold in 2007, by county.

Crops

Percent of land devoted to each crop in 2007, by county.

Animals

Population density by county, based on inventory at the time of the 2007 census.

Half a Million Trees: Prototyping Sites and Systems for Sustainable Cities

Instructors: Kristin Frederickson and Gary Hilderbrand

The performance value of mature urban trees has long been proven, and its translation to economic benefit well known. However, any real measure of value should take account of the embodied energy and operations costs on the path to performance, especially in the face of the chronically high mortality rate of urban tree planting. If carefully considered, these factors may make a compelling case for locally grown nursery stock to produce the most efficient ecological footprint for urban tree production. Can we produce trees locally?

This text is from the Fall 2007 studio at the Harvard Graduate School of Design and the forthcoming book, *Half a Million Trees: Prototyping Sites and Systems for Sustainable Cities,* by Kristin Frederickson and Gary Hilderbrand.
Urban Tree Production and Performance: Is It Really Green? Research by Charlotte Barrows, Christopher Doerr, and Simón Martínez.

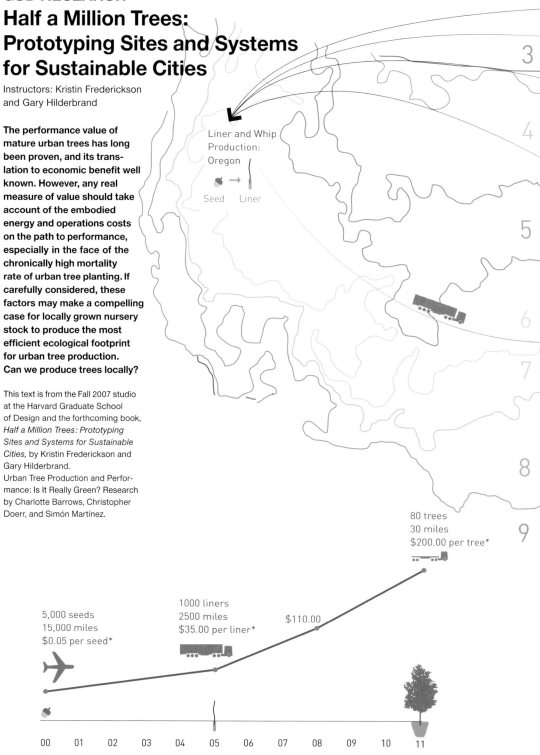

Liner and Whip Production: Oregon

Seed Liner

80 trees
30 miles
$200.00 per tree*

1000 liners
2500 miles
$35.00 per liner*

$110.00

5,000 seeds
15,000 miles
$0.05 per seed*

00   01   02   03   04   05   06   07   08   09   10   11

1. "From Seed to Tree" mapping. Producer and Grower Interviews, 2006.
2. "Quantity, Transport and Dollar Value" diagram. Compiled Price Lists, 2006.
3. Median Street Tree in New York City. STRATUM Study 2005 - 2006. "Trees Count," New York City Department of Parks and Recreation.

* Dollar value of item at purchase.

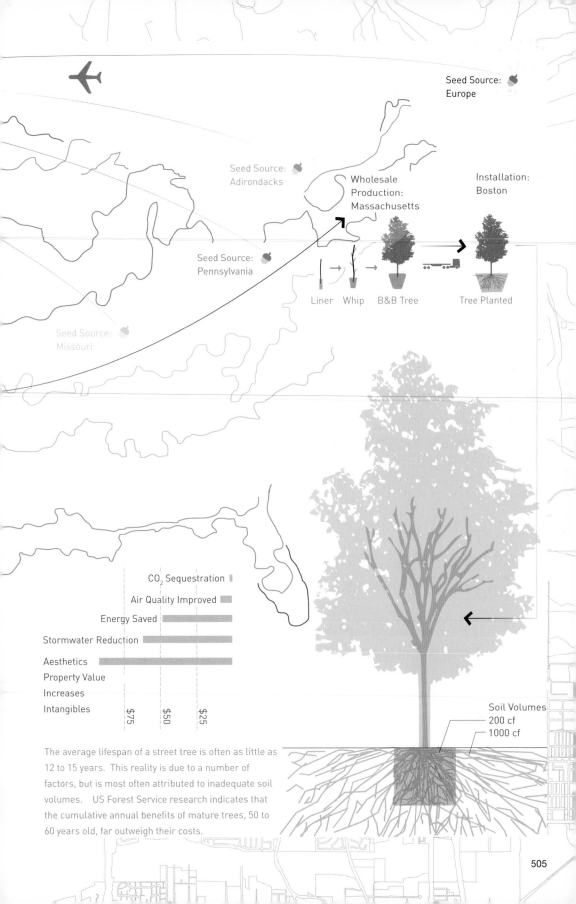

Seed Source:
Europe

Seed Source:
Adirondacks

Wholesale
Production:
Massachusetts

Installation:
Boston

Seed Source:
Pennsylvania

Seed Source:
Missouri

Liner   Whip   B&B Tree   Tree Planted

CO$_2$ Sequestration

Air Quality Improved

Energy Saved

Stormwater Reduction

Aesthetics

Property Value
Increases

Intangibles

$75 $50 $25

Soil Volumes
200 cf
1000 cf

The average lifespan of a street tree is often as little as
12 to 15 years. This reality is due to a number of
factors, but is most often attributed to inadequate soil
volumes. US Forest Service research indicates that
the cumulative annual benefits of mature trees, 50 to
60 years old, far outweigh their costs.

SlaveCity

Atelier Van Lieshout

SlaveCity can be described as a sinister utopian project that is very rational, efficient, and profitable (2.8 billion euro net profit per year). Values, ethics, aesthetics, morals, food, energy, economics, organization, management, and market are turned upside-down, mixed and reformulated for a town of 200,000 inhabitants.

SlaveCity is built with the latest technology and management insights. The inhabitants (called "participants") work seven hours a day on tele-services such as customer service, telemarketing, and computer programming. After that, they work seven hours in the fields or in workshops. The efficiency of participants is monitored and measures taken if it drops below a set level.

SlaveCity is the first "zero energy" town of this size in the world and functions without imported fossil fuel or electricity; energy needs are met by biogas, solar and wind energy, and biodiesel. Everything is majestically recycled, even the participants. No waste products are created: SlaveCity is a green town that is not wasting the world's resources.

In addition to the many necessary infrastructure and service buildings, there is a sumptuous head office, a safe and cozy village for higher-level employees, education facilities, a health center, a brothel, and an art center.

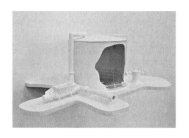

Facts:

Built surface	900,000 m²
Total surface	60,000,000 m²
Participants	200,000
Employees	3,500
Total investment	€ 860 million
Annual profit	€ 2.8 billion
Arts budget	€ 28 million

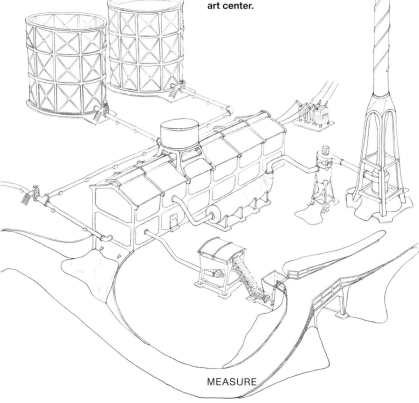

...aveCity

PER...

PERSO...

GENERAL INFORMATION

WHAT

WHO

WHERE

WHEN

WHY

WHICH MEANS

ABSTRACT

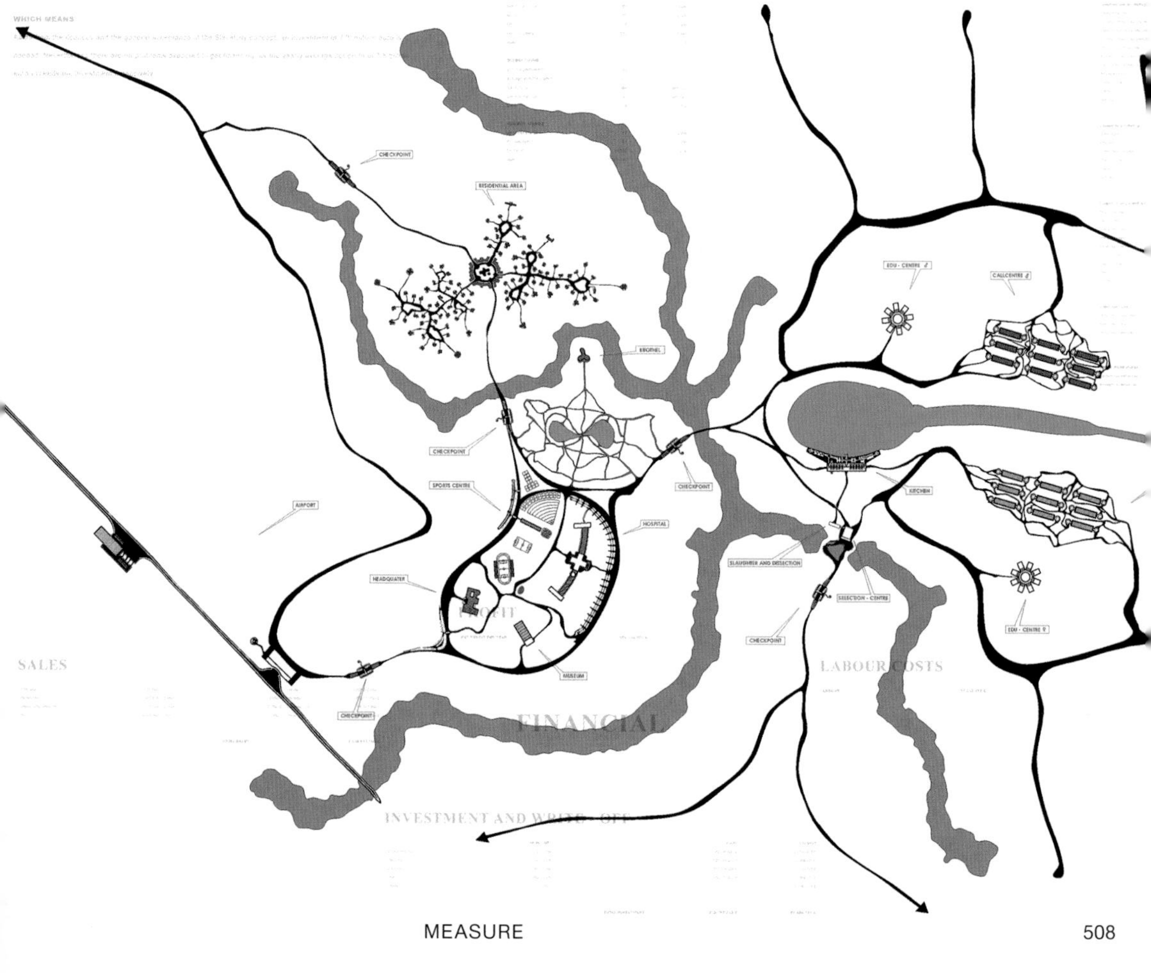

CHECKPOINT
RESIDENTIAL AREA
BROTHEL
CHECKPOINT
SPORTS CENTRE
CHECKPOINT
AIRPORT
HOSPITAL
HEADQUATER
MUSEUM
CHECKPOINT
EDU - CENTRE ♂
CALLCENTRE ♂
KITCHEN
SLAUGHTER AND DISSECTION
SELECTION - CENTRE
CHECKPOINT
EDU - CENTRE ♀

SALES

PROFIT

FINANCIAL

LABOUR COSTS

INVESTMENT AND WRITE-OFF

PARTICIPANTS

INVENTORY

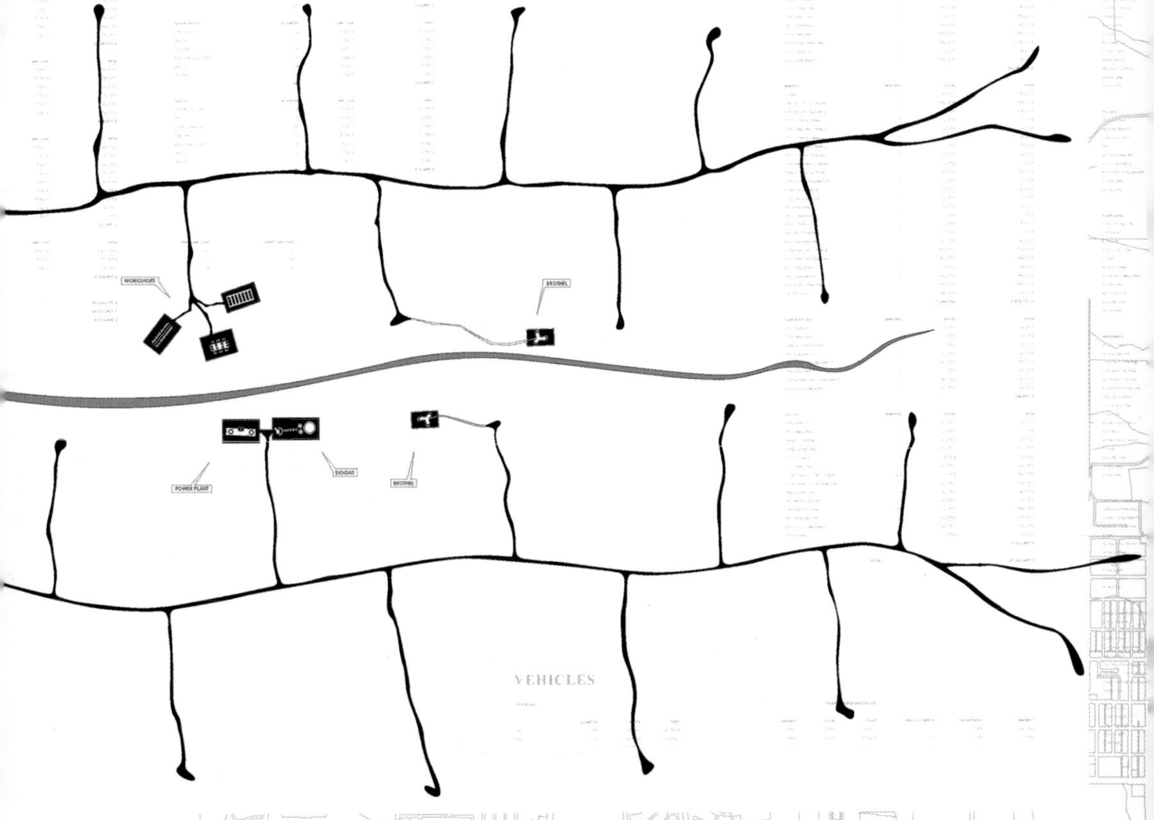
WORKSHOPS
BROTHEL
POWER PLANT
BIOGAS
BROTHEL

VEHICLES

ECObox/Self-Managed Eco-urban Network

atelier d'architecture autogérée (AAA)

In 2001, AAA initiated a network of self-managed projects in the La Chapelle area of northern Paris, encouraging residents to get access to and critically transform temporary underused spaces. This approach valorizes a flexible and reversible use of space and aims to preserve urban "biodiversity" by allowing the coexistence of a wide range of lifestyles and living practices. ECObox, the catalyzer of this "rhizomatic agency," has progressively emerged as a platform for urban criticism and creativity, initially curated by the AAA members and then by local residents.

ECObox started with a demountable and transportable garden of pallets located on a temporary available site belonging to the French railway company, comprising 3,000 square meters of indoor and outdoor spaces in a derelict railyard. Mobile modules such as a toolbox, a kitchen, a library, and a media lab were conceived to accompany gardening and other collective activities: cooking, debating, radio broadcasting, reading, chatting. These mobile modules moved through different spaces, activating encounters between people from diverse social and cultural backgrounds and challenging everyday life practices.

After four years, ECObox was threatened with eviction by city authorities. The users, however, demonstrated their attachment to the project and its values and negotiated with the city for a new location. ECObox's demountable and transportable architecture allowed for a quick reinstallation in a new location and preserved the continuity of the social networks created by the project. Recently the garden has moved for the third time.

ECObox was a politically emancipatory experience for the city residents involved in the project, who learned how to negotiate space for collective use. It was emancipatory for the AAA too, who learned that architects don't need a client, a budget, and a site to practice architecture but can rely on their status as citizens to create nomadic space through urban tactics.

ECObox "rhizomatic" mobility: progressive construction (2002–2004), dismantling and move (2005), temporary reinstallation on a new plot (2005–2007), destruction and research for new location (2007–2008), reinstallation (2009)

"Participative peepholes" in the
concrete fence of the existing courtyard
that allow visibility of the palette garden
from the street, ECObox 2003

The mobile kitchen and the palette
garden, ECObox 2004

Temporary Urban Scene: Beach on the Moon

Ecosistema Urbano

In contrast to traditional problem-solving methods for reactivating degraded public spaces in historic urban centers, we believe that another form of intervention is possible—without spending vast amounts of money, time, and energy. We focus on low-cost actions capable of generating responses from residents, in effect obtaining a system of self-produced revitalization where the citizen plays an active role in the creation of public space. This proposal demonstrates new notions of neighborhood connectivity, developed to positively affect the existing way of life through the creation of a new, temporary urban scene (Beach on the Moon).

This proposal aims to aid a neighborhood united by the need to improve a degraded area near the Gran Vía, in downtown Madrid. It was necessary to act in a short period of time, support residents' ideas and wishes, and garner the media attention required to force those responsible to negotiate with residents for substantial improvements in a neighborhood with many needs.

A new, temporary urban environment called Moon Beach provided an activity zone for neighborhood residents while offering an amenity for users of the Gran Vía. During the months of the urban installation (summer 2006), many unexpected connections were generated, multiplying the effects of the project. In this period of time, the idea emerged that it is possible for citizens to make decisions about their city and feel part of the urban space.

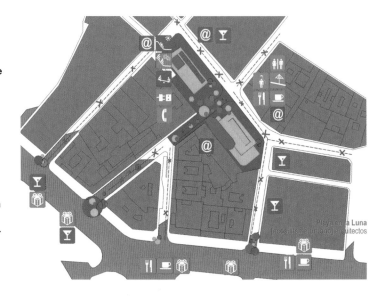

100 m

PLAZA LUNA - PLAYA LUNA
Service Area *****

500 M3- ARENA   30 LITROS DE
8 DUCHAS   PINTURA
50 SOMBRILLAS   4 CARTELES
200 SILLAS   1 CHIRINGUITO

ESTE VERANO, CON 12.000 €,
LLEVAMOS LA PLAYA A MADRID.

****

L A   P L A Y A   D E   L U N A

COLLABORAT

Comfort and Carbon Footprint
Alex Krieger

**Ecological Urbanism and Health Equity:
An Ecosocial Perspective**
Nancy Krieger

Nature, Infrastructures, and the Urban Condition
Antoine Picon

Sustainability and Lifestyle
Spiro Pollalis

Ecological Urbanism and the Landscape
Martha Schwartz

Old Dark
John Stilgoe

Religious Studies and Ecological Urbanism
Donald K. Swearer

Ecological Urbanism and East Asian Literatures
Karen Thornber

Comfort and Carbon Footprint

Alex Krieger

To become a conservation-minded planet still requires much correlating of society's responsibilities, such as devising more sustainable patterns of settlement, with individual awareness of how daily actions affect the environment. Although the *rhetoric of green* is upon us, habits are slower to change, as are gains in environmental insight beyond the sound bite.

For example, "Cities are less consumptive then suburbs" may be an effective new slogan against our sprawling instincts, but may not be the best way to make individuals appreciate how their actions burden resources wherever they may live. Urban advocates are convinced that the carbon footprint of city dwellers, on average, is substantially lower per capita then that of suburbanites–Manhattanites presumably being better stewards of our environment than Long Islanders. Considerable research supports this, yet it seems counterintuitive to many citizens who, for example, see few lights on past midnight in their suburban subdivisions while Manhattan, as satellite imagery shows, tends to glow all night long. People in the city no doubt buy fewer lawnmowers, but it is not clear that city dwellers overall consume fewer material goods then others at the same economic level. Urban density is more efficient then sprawl, though at its extreme–say in the *favelas* of Rio de Janeiro or in Mumbai's Dharavi slum–density is not an indicator of a high quality of life despite vastly reduced carbon footprints. Our growing expectations of wiser stewardship of the environment still lead still to varying intuitions about the consequences of our habits, dwelling choices, and hope in technological ingenuity.

Replacing incandescent light bulbs with compact fluorescent lights is a good idea, so is turning out lights more frequently or turning them on more reluctantly. Replacement is made possible by technological ingenuity, society having devised more energy-efficient lights. Turning these lights on and off more responsibly requires modifying habits. In combination, such a "one-two punch" is essential for an ecologically minded future. By contrast is the not uncommon logic of purchasing a more fuel-efficient vehicle in order to drive more miles, or at least drive as much as before at less cost. A fuel-efficient vehicle (a social priority) that spends more time in the garage (an individual's decision) would be better still for the environment.

Some intellectual circles are ready to proclaim the gap between conservation and indulgence to be narrowing, that environmental sustainability and material consumption are no longer at odds. The evidence for this is slim. Affluence still seems to produce an abundance of effluence. Can an affluent culture become less consumptive or learn to consume only "green" things? This is not a trivial question. More stuff generally requires more energy to produce and then produces more waste. Society will mandate energy conservation and recycling innovations, but less consumption at the household scale would be helpful too. Again, greater reciprocity between individual action and cumulative societal impact would assist sustainability.

An image from a public awareness
campaign by the Ministry for
the Environment/Manatū Mō Te Taiao,
New Zealand, 2007

Have a shower
and clean your
conscience too.

Which brings me to an alternative title for this essay: *What does my morning's extra-long hot shower have to do with ecological urbanism?* One carbon footprint-lowering initiative for both city folks and suburbanites would be to shut off hot-water heaters regularly. An unlikely occurrence to be sure, but consider the impact of 100 million American households each maintaining 60–100 gallons (or more) of hot water constantly. How many of us even think of turning the switch off prior to a weekend's escape? Do we take comfort in those gallons of hot water waiting for us, or are we mostly oblivious, just welcoming the hot water at the turn of the tap.

Society will demand and produce more efficient hot-water heaters, maybe even equipped to turn on and off like our TV's remote-recording features. But quicker showers using less hot water on occasion would also help the environment. This is neither a call for sloppier personal hygiene or for denial of the pleasures of a hot shower. It is another reminder that individual decisions are important to ecological urbanism.

I've enumerated trivial examples of accustomed comforts. There are many others, trivial and less so, steadily increasing society's overall carbon footprint. There may yet come a time when conservation and restraint, not accumulation, will yield personal and universal pleasure. Some work toward such a future remains to be done.

What does my morning's extra-long hot shower have to do with ecological urbanism?

Ecological Urbanism and Health Equity: An Ecosocial Perspective

Nancy Krieger

Ecological urbanism. This suggestive phrase locates—literally—issues of health equity in the nexus of people, places, and the polis. As context, in August 2008 the World Health Organization's first Commission on the Social Determinants of Health came to the honest—even if not new—conclusion that "Social injustice is killing people on a grand scale."[1]

A map we recently produced at the Harvard School of Public Health—the first for any such analyses of urban health inequities in the United States—depicts the proportion of premature deaths in Boston (that is, deaths before age seventy-five) that would not have occurred if all residents experienced the same age-specific mortality rates as residents of the city's least impoverished census tracts.[2] Shockingly, this excess fraction exceeded 20 percent for eight of Boston's sixteen neighborhoods and 68 percent of Boston's 156 census tracts. Moreover, within two of Boston's poorest and predominantly black neighborhoods, Roxbury and Dorchester, this excess fraction reached 25–30 percent in more than half of their census tracts. In other words, for every 100 deaths among people under age seventy-five, twenty-five to thirty of those deaths would not have happened if the residents in these census tracts had the same mortality experience as residents in Boston's least impoverished census tracts.

How can we make sense of—and rectify—these social and spatial health inequities? Theory can help, and my vantage is that of ecosocial theory, which I first proposed in 1994 and have elaborated since.[3] Paying heed to societal and ecologic context, to lifecourse and historical generation, to levels of analysis, and to interrelationships between—and accountability for—diverse forms of social inequality, including racism, class, and gender, a central focus is on "embodiment," clarifying how we literally embody, biologically, our lived experience, thereby creating population patterns of health and disease. Translated to ecological urbanism, this theory asks: how do city design and policy priorities promote or hinder people's ability to lead healthy lives and magnify or reduce the extent of health inequities? Answers will arise through the joint engagement of public health workers with the people who design cities, who live and work in them, and who govern them.

Encouragingly, many in public health—in the United States and globally—are stepping forward to do this work, bringing to the proverbial table, in solidarity, not as technocrats, our knowledge on the extent and causes of health inequities. One useful example is the High Point project in Seattle,[4] featured in the recent award-winning U.S. television series, "Unnatural Causes: Is Inequality Making Us Sick?"[5] Exemplifying the new public health work concerned with ecology, walkability, transportation, trees and parks and gardens, safety, food accessibility, and economic equity, this project is revamping a decrepit old housing project and creating a new mixed-income community

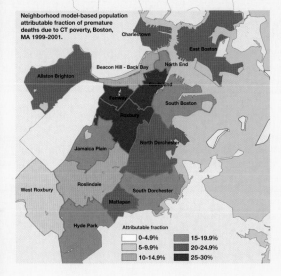

Neighborhood model-based population attributable fraction of premature deaths due to CT poverty, Boston, MA 1999-2001.

Charlestown, East Boston, Beacon Hill - Back Bay, North End, Allston Brighton, South End, Fenway, South Boston, Roxbury, Jamaica Plain, North Dorchester, Jamaica Plain, Roslindale, South Dorchester, West Roxbury, Mattapan, Hyde Park

Attributable fraction
0-4.9% 15-19.9%
5-9.9% 20-24.9%
10-14.9% 25-30%

Census tract model-based population attributable fraction of premature deaths due to CT poverty, Boston, MA 1999-2001.

Charlestown, East Boston, Beacon Hill - Back Bay, North End, Allston Brighton, South End, Fenway, South Boston, Roxbury, Jamaica Plain, North Dorchester, Roslindale, South Dorchester, West Roxbury, Mattapan, Hyde Park

Attributable fraction
0-4.9% 15-19.9%
5-9.9% 20-24.9%
10-14.9% 25-30%

that pays attention simultaneously to the social as well as physical environments of the residents, including the construction of "healthy homes" for low-income families afflicted by asthma.[6]

In summary, issues of ecological urbanism and health equity are inherently intertwined. To achieve both, we must act, as the WHO Commission pointedly concluded, on the social determinants of health: "(1) improve daily living conditions; (2) tackle the inequitable distribution of power, money, and resources; and (3) measure and understand the problem and assess the impact of action."[7] Doing so requires us to address the profound connections between social justice and public health, between our bodily truths and the body politic, and to work with myriad others to further the goal of embodying equity—in an ecologically sustainable world.

1 WHO Commission on Social Determinants of Health, *Closing the Gap in a Generation: Health Equity through Action on the Social Determinants of Health. Final Report of the Commission on Social Determinants of Health* (Geneva: WHO, 2008). Available at http://www.who.int/social_determinants/final_report/en/index.html; accessed on April 20, 2009; G. Davey Smith and N. Krieger, "Tackling Health Inequities," *British Medical Journal* 2008; 337: a1526, doi: 10.1136/bmj.a1526

2 J.T. Chen, D.H. Rehkopf, P.D. Waterman, S.V. Subramanian, B.A. Coull, B. Cohen, M. Ostrem, and N. Krieger, "Mapping and Measuring Social Disparities in Premature Mortality: The Impact of Census Tract Poverty within and across Boston Neighborhoods, 1999–2001," *Journal of Urban Health* 2006; 83: 1063–1085.

3 N. Krieger, "Epidemiology and the Web of Causation: Has Anyone Seen the Spider?" *Social Science and Medicine* 1994; 39: 887–903; "Theories for Social Epidemiology in the 21st Century: An Ecosocial Perspective," *International Journal of Epidemiology* 2001; 30: 668–677, "Ecosocial Theory," in N. Anderson, ed., *Encyclopedia of Health and Behavior* (Thousand Oaks, CA: Sage, 2004), pp. 292–294; "Proximal, Distal, and the Politics of Causation: What's Level Got to Do with It?" *American Journal of Public Health* 2008; 98: 221–230.

4 Seattle Housing Authority, High Point. Available at http://www.seattlehousing.org/redevelopment/high-point/; accessed on April 20, 2009. J. Krieger, C. Allen, A. Cheadle, S. Ciske, J.K. Schier, K. Senturia, and M. Sullivan, "Using Community-Based Participatory Research to Address Social Determinants of Health: Lessons Learned from Seattle Partners for Healthy Communities," *Heath Education and Behavior* 2002; 29: 361–382; J. Krieger, "Healthy Homes and Early Learning: Addressing Social Determinants of Health in Seattle and King County," presentation for Moving Upstream: Working Together to Create Healthier Communities, a conference sponsored by the Blue Cross and Blue Shield Foundation of Minnesota, Minneapolis, November 13, 2006. Available at at http://www.bcbsmnfoundation.org/objects/Tier_3/krieger.pdf; accessed on April 20, 2009.

5 "Unnatural Causes: Is Inequality Making Us Sick?" Available at http://www.unnaturalcauses.org/; accessed on April 20, 2009.

6 See note 4.

7 See note 1.

ECOSOCIAL THEORY:
LEVELS, PATHWAYS, & POWER

embodiment
pathways of embodiment
cumulative interplay of exposure, susceptibility & resistance
accountability
agency

POLITICAL ECONOMY & ECOLOGY

racial/ethnic inequality

class inequality

Population distribution of health

historical context + generation

gender inequality

Levels: societal & ecosystem
global
national
regional
area
household
individual

Processes:
production
exchange
consumption
reproduction

Lifecourse:
in utero infancy childhood adulthood

Source: Krieger, Soc Sci Med 1994; Krieger, Epidemiol Review 2000; Krieger, Int J Epidemiol 2001; Krieger (ed), *Embodying Inequality*, 2004; Krieger, JECH 2005; Krieger, AJPH 2008

Nature, Infrastructures, and the Urban Condition

Antoine Picon

We are probably on the eve of a spectacular inversion of the relations between urban infrastructure and the natural milieu. For centuries, the city was perceived as an enclave with a very specific environment that did not follow the usual rules of nature. Urban infrastructures played a decisive role in this perception. In the case of many cities of northern France, two types of infrastructures were especially instrumental in isolating and differentiating the city from the countryside. Fortification was the first of the two. With the evolution leading from the medieval masonry wall to the bastioned earthworks of the Renaissance and seventeenth century, fortification became larger and larger, thus contributing to separating the city from the countryside by a no-man's-land of glacis and moats that would often span a few hundred yards. The dense network of waterways that was vital for industries such as drapery and tanning represented another characteristic of northern France's urban environments. As historian André Guillerme has shown, from the late middle age to the eighteenth century, many major northern French cities such as Amiens, Rouen, and Beauvais were organized along a system of rivers and canals that make them comparable to "little Venices"–that is, artificial environments without equivalent in the countryside.[1] Throughout that period, Paris remained an exception. While the city remained fortified until the mid-seventeenth century, the waterway system was less developed than in other major urban centers. Nonetheless, the capital city was also perceived as a special environment following different rules than its surroundings.

Despite eighteenth- and nineteenth-century attempts to open the city to natural elements, the fragments of nature that were integrated in the urban fabric appeared generally as somewhat artificial. Often presented after Walter Benjamin as the "capital of the nineteenth century," Paris was also the place where this artificial character reached its climax with its Haussmannian parks planted with exotic flowers grown in municipal glasshouses, and its rows of trees conceived as an integral part of the technological equipment of the city.[2]

Why are we now reaching a turning point? In recent decades, cities have grown in a dramatic way. The urban condition has become the norm. But this pervasive character has cast new light on the presence of nature in urban settings. In the extremely large contemporary urban territories, natural elements can no longer be considered as artifacts. From parks to empty lots gradually reclaimed by vegetation, from water management to urban agriculture, nature represents, to the contrary, a fundamental dimension of urbanization. In addition, urban infrastructures that once were perceived as adverse to natural life now appear sometimes as wildlife preserves. In Europe, uncultivated land alongside freeways has become, for instance, the dwelling place of various endangered species. Leaving aside this type of extreme situation, one cannot but be struck by the new partnership

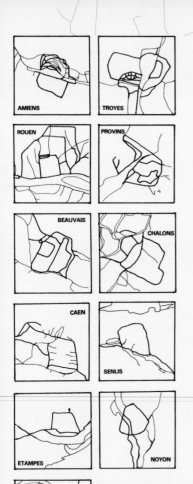

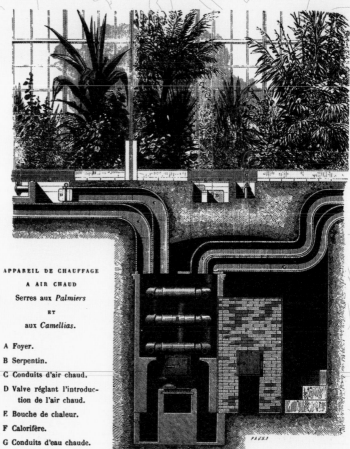

APPAREIL DE CHAUFFAGE

A AIR CHAUD

Serres aux *Palmiers*

ET

aux *Camellias*.

A Foyer.

B Serpentin.

C Conduits d'air chaud.

D Valve réglant l'introduction de l'air chaud.

E. Bouche de chaleur.

F Calorifère.

G Conduits d'eau chaude.

Fig. 154. Coupe sur le calorifère
Échelle de 0ᵐ,02 p. m.

dérivation ou aménagement
cours d'eau non aménagé

that is emerging between the infrastructural approach and the affirmation of the new role of nature in cities.

In the case of the French capital, this new relation represents a common background to the various proposals that have been made by the team of architects engaged in reflections on "Grand Paris"–greater Paris. From Richard Rogers to Christian de Portzamparc, infrastructures are extremely present, not only as supports for circulation but as platforms enabling a reconsideration of the role of nature in the city.

Urban waterways of northern French cities in comparison with the Venetian system (from Guillerme, 1983)

Charles Adolphe Alphand's Promenades Calorifère

1 André Guillerme, *Les Temps de l'Eau: La Cité, l'Eau et les Techniques* (Seyssel: Champ Vallon, 1983).
2 See, for instance, Christine Blancot and Bernard Landau, "La Direction des Travaux de Paris au XIXe Siècle," in *Le Paris des Polytechniciens: Des Ingénieurs dans la Ville,* edited by Bruno Belhoste, Francine Masson, and Antoine Picon (Paris: Délégation à l'Action Artistique de la Ville de Paris, 1994), 155–173.

Sustainability and Lifestyle

Spiro Pollalis

Gerhard Schmitt–architect, professor of information technology, and senior vice president of ETH-Zurich–had a vision: to make the second campus of ETH, about 8 kilometers from the city center, a vibrant community, to link it with the downtown ETH campus and create a new model for the integration of virtual and physical space. After more than ten years, he has succeeded. The Hoenggberg campus of a little more than 100 hectares, now called "Science City," is filled with new buildings and renewable energy sources and is an example of sustainable development at a larger scale. It represents a remarkable achievement in an educational environment, where leadership is elected by senior professors–or perhaps because of that, as it was based on both vision and consensus.

Information technology, in the form of the "ETH World" project, which I led during my 2001 Harvard sabbatical, was the beginning of Science City, its first and fundamental building block. Environmental sustainability was its second building block; urban planning and design were next, and architecture provided interesting buildings and spaces. Everything is planned, everything is designed, everything is measured. Buildings produce about 46 percent of the CO_2. Transportation to and from homes and the main campus are responsible for another 8 percent. Knowing the residential addresses of students, which courses they take and their research activities, and even whether they buy public transportation passes, makes this

calculation rather accurate. Then what accounts for the missing 46 percent of CO_2 production?

According to Professor Schmitt, that 46 percent is travel of the faculty, and 94 percent of that is travel by plane. ETH faculty, like faculty everywhere, regularly travel the world to lecture, attend meetings and conferences, conduct research, and advise. Researchers report that planes produce only 3 percent of the total CO_2. However, just our panel traveled 42,600 miles to be here and produced an estimated 21 tons of CO_2; 103 trees would have to be planted in the tropics to absorb the CO_2 that we produced, equivalent to burning 2,000 gallons of heating oil.[1] So, unless we can demonstrate that international meetings and conferences save the world a multiple of their CO_2 expense, I wonder if we are just hypocrites, like the bankers who caused the current economic crisis.

This data also supports that CO_2 production is stratified by social class. Ecological sustainability is not about urbanity, it is about today's global economy and lifestyle. Furthermore, we all know that sustainable activities in excess can be more energy consuming than fewer nonsustainable activities. It is also known that affluence has propelled modern societies to excess. I will not line up statistics on urbanity, on people living in cities, on energy consumption. I will just say that as we are planning and building new cities, especially in the developing world, as we intervene in old cities, we should focus on lifestyle, on scale, as well as on design and technology. And we should lead by example, as the entire world wants to live the "American dream."

1 This text is an extract of remarks delivered during the Ecological Urbanism conference held at the Harvard Graduate School of Design, April 3–5, 2009.

This data also supports that CO_2 production is stratified by social class. Ecological sustainability is not about urbanity, it is about today's global economy and lifestyle.

Ecological Urbanism and the Landscape

Martha Schwartz

It is always a bit of a dilemma to write about the landscape's role in sustainability. How do we sound relevant when our basic training and ethos have been conjoined to the ideal of sustainability even before the word "sustainable" became common parlance? At school we learn and teach how to site buildings to sit softly on the landscape and operate passively to conserve and generate heat; to shelter buildings from winds; to control and harness water and protect a site's permeability; to create and preserve habitat and encourage biodiversity; to use plants to remediate and modify climate conditions; and to create beauty. As landscape architects, learning to design with "green" in mind is core to what we do as a profession.

"Ecological urbanism" through the eyes of a landscape architect pushes the focus of building cities to the forefront of the discussion. The topic of the landscape and even ecology is much broader than architecture, but most people do not put landscape and city together, nor ecology with urbanism. The word "landscape" is often mistakenly thought of as "nature," not something to be found anywhere near the city. It exists outside of the built environment, somewhere out there in "the wilderness." It is precisely the friction between the words landscape and city, and ecology and urban, that generates the power and radicalism of "landscape (ecological) urbanism."

The more robust role of landscape architecture in sustainability does not materialize unless we start to think about cities—the much larger aggregation of resources found in the habitats we create for ourselves. It is when cities are thought of as living organisms, rather than collections of buildings, that the landscape becomes a major player in discussions about sustainability.

"Ecological urbanism" forces us, as landscape architects, to not only consider the workings of the landscape—the geology, topography, soil structures, phenomenology, and plant and animal ecologies—but to understand more specifically how the landscape functions within the city. We start to better comprehend the interrelated systems that influence the use, governance, economy, and social structure of a society that is underpinned by a specific urban landscape. As with the study of ecology, unless we truly embrace all of these systems—human and natural—we will not be able to design optimal cities for people. Ecological urbanism shifts the focus of the profession from the suburbs to the city, to include human systems as part of ecology.

Collectivization is the best means we have to conserve natural resources and slow global warming, so a vital role of ecological urbanism is to encourage people to live, and help them thrive, in cities. The highest and best use of our training as landscape architects lies in our ability to create dense population centers that people will choose over living in our vast and wasteful suburbs. Landscape architects must now learn to pay attention not only to natural systems but to human systems if we are to build sustainable cities that will both be light on the land and create conditions that offer good quality of life across socioeconomic boundaries. The goal is to achieve true balance—socially, economically, and environmentally. I embrace the term "landscape urbanism," because, finally, these two often diametrically opposed terms stand side-by-side. It is my belief that our profession is more surely rooted in society and culture than in technology and science. If we are to deliver a sustainable built environment, we must create places that people will value and to which they can connect emotionally. Without human connection to a site or a city, even our best efforts at creating sustainable environments will not succeed. We must build constituencies of users devoted to the places we build, and recognize that the public landscape is one of the most fragile components of our cities, but perhaps the most critical; without it, natural and social systems cannot function.

The urban landscape that we humans share with ecological systems and plant and animal habitat forms our identity as individuals and becomes the image of the city. It can be degraded and ugly, or glorious in its diversity and beauty. It can determine the health of the earth itself, establish the liveability of a city, support a city's economy, and help to create health and happiness for its citizens. This is what "ecological urbanism" can be.

If we are to deliver a sustainable built environment, we must create places that people will value and to which they can connect emotionally.

Old Dark

John Stilgoe

Darkness confuses and dispirits. The nighttime artificial illumination that enraptured nineteenth-century urban dwellers now fluoresces as mere utility.[1] City dwellers rarely ponder the illumination, let alone displaced dark. They fear shadows, avoiding them so deftly and so quickly that their eyes never adjust to seeing in places lit by ambient urban glow. Illumination empowers. When the generating plant or transmission line fails, urbanites speak of power failure: they hover around the dim glow of standby generator or battery-pack bulb and wait for standard light. Only rarely do they use cell-phone screens as flashlights, but they know how. They expect illumination after sundown, straight on until morning. They crave light, forgetting that darkness figures fundamentally in the diurnal-nocturnal rhythm ordering natural systems, especially biosystems. Ecological urbanism means throwing the switch, letting there be dark.

Nighttime ecology figures solidly if subtly in American suburbanization. After the Civil War, some meditative, well-educated city dwellers moved countryward in part to enjoy nature at night. As electricity supplanted flaring gaslight, their numbers increased and their observations grew more sophisticated: in the first years of the twentieth century they remarked on the rapidly decreasing severity of New England winters, which transformed robins and blue jays from migratory to in-place species. In an era of ten-hour workdays framed by long railroad commutes, they valued the night as prime

outdoor recreational time in dark environments. "Any student of birds who has paid much attention to these voices of the night, in the migrating season, must have noticed how very much alike in general character they are," observed James Buckham in his 1903 *Where Town and Country Meet.* Waterfowl excepted, the passing birds tend to make "the same tremulous, thin, clear, rather melancholy whistle, with that transcendent unearthly quality" in both spring and fall. In the not-yet-suburbanized borderlands of northeast cities, newcomers valued dark nights free from artificial noise: they delighted in the dark ecosystem.

Buckham cataloged dark sounds: the eldritch screech of the tree toad on a hot summer night, the whimpering of skunks stalking roosting hens, the hollow booming made by the wings of the deep-diving nighthawk, "the bittern's ah-unk, ah-unk" that so resembled the sound made by an ax driving stakes in a swamp, many Americans still call the bird "stake-driver."[2] Anyone listening at night beyond the inner suburban residential ring still hears the yelping bark of the fox, the scream of the saw-whet owl (named because its screech mimics the whetting of a handsaw), and sometimes the cry of the loon. The last sound draws city people to wilderness vacation spots: summering near loons proves very upscale nowadays: loons tend to laugh well after sunset, pleasing vacationers relaxing in dark, open-window cabins free of air-conditioning noise, drinks in hand. Roaming the dark on moonlit, starlit, and dark-as-a-pocket nights let the attentive hear and sometimes see what the illumined miss, often in the purlieus of cities, in down-scale space.[3]

"That such things are not seen oftener is simply because people are dull and go to bed instead of sitting out under the witch-hazel at midnight of a full moon," averred Winthrop Packard in his 1909 *Wild Pastures.*[4] The cognoscenti luxuriated in the nocturnal ecosystem and vanished from urban attention. Then the energy-efficiency ideology of the 1970s snared sanctimonious apartment residents in a calculus factoring in all-night corridor, entrance, and parking-lot lighting, all variables the large-lot suburbanites might eliminate. Ecological urbanism lays the same snare. Nature retakes anything humans build, its green circle strangling the unwary city.[5] At night it advances stealthily, the green growing dark at every sundown.[6] The surest and fastest way to snuggle nature around an exurban house and deep into every city is to switch off the lights. Farmers and ranchers know what it means to be acquainted with the night, to see the owl cross beneath the Milky Way, to hear the whirr of the bat, to merge with darkness itself.[7] Now city people must welcome old dark.

1 Chris Otter, *The Victorian Eye: A Political History of Light and Vision in Britain, 1800–1910* (Chicago: University of Chicago Press, 2008).

2 James Buckham, *Where Town and Country Meet* (New York: Eaton, 1903), 55–61.

3 Vinson Brown, *Knowing the Outdoors in the Dark* (New York: Collier, 1972), remains a useful introduction.

4 Winthrop Packard, *Wild Pastures* (Boston: Small, Maynard, 1909), 115.

5 Douglas W. Rae, *City: Urbanism and Its End* (New Haven: Yale University Press, 2003), esp. 361–392.

6 Herman Hesse, "The City" [1919], *Fairy Tales,* translated by Jack Zipes (New York: Doubleday, 1995), 43–49.

7 Robert Frost, "Acquainted with the Night" [1928], *Poetry,* edited by Edward Connery Lathem (New York: Holt, Rinehart and Winston, 1969), 255.

Religious Studies and Ecological Urbanism

Donald K. Swearer

The Summer 1996 issue of *Daedalus*, the Journal of the American Academy of Arts and Sciences, was dedicated to the theme, "The Liberation of the Environment." Although the volume cautioned that the quality of life on the planet will depend on what conventions and habits will eventually come to dominate in individual societies, the general trajectory of the eleven essays in this issue reflected the sentiment expressed in the epigraph at the U.S. National Academy of Sciences in Washington, D.C.: "To science, pilot of industry, conqueror of disease, multiplier of harvest, explorer of the universe, revealer of nature's laws, eternal guide to truth"—and concluded, "We have liberated ourselves from the environment. Now it is time to liberate the environment itself."

Believing that the humanities should have a voice in environmental discourse, five years later the Academy published a collection of essays from a conference on religion and ecology sponsored by the Forum on Religion and Ecology that was founded in 1998. Subtitled "Religion and Ecology: Can the Climate Change," Mary Evelyn Tucker and John Grimm, the cofounders of the Forum and editors of this issue of *Daedalus*, observed in their introduction, "As key repositories of enduring civilizational values and as indispensable motivators in moral transformation, religions have an important role to play in projecting persuasive visions of a more sustainable future." Tucker and Grimm then cited Lynn White's 1967 essay, "The Historical Roots of Our Ecological Crisis," published in the journal

Science, in which White opined, "What people do about their ecology depends on what they think about themselves in relation to things around them. Human ecology is deeply conditioned by beliefs about our nature and destiny—that is, by religion."

As a religious studies scholar and a board member of the Forum on Religion and Ecology, I strongly believe that the humanities can and should play a constructive role in ecological discourse in regard to what Larry Buell characterizes as "the arts of imagination in appreciating and valuing the environment," and the normative ethical values necessitated by sustainable lifestyles. To that end the Center for the Study of World Religions and the Center for the Environment cosponsored a conference in March 2006 that resulted in the book *Ecology and the Environment: Perspectives from the Humanities*.

Religion, in the sense suggested by Tucker, Grimm, and White, challenges "ecological urbanism" to include broadly humanistic questions of value and meaning, justice and community, care and compassion, and the well-being of the biotic community as a whole. Religion challenges ecological urbanism to be about much more than "sustainable cities," unless sustainability is understood in unconventionally broad terms. I note, for example, that the hundred or so categories on the urbanism.org website include graffiti, vandalism, and tall buildings but not religion or even education.

The description of this conference states, "Ecological urbanism represents a more holistic approach than is generally the case with urbanism today, demanding alternative ways of thinking and designing."[1] This sounds good, but what will actually be included in this "holistic approach"? The field of religion and ecology has much to contribute to this discussion. It brings to the table appreciably more than whether reconceptualizing urban spaces includes the preservation of places of worship. It shares much in common with Ken Wilbur's philosophy of "integral ecology," and the ecosophy of Félix Guattari and Arne Naess that posits the intimate interconnectedness of human subjectivity, the environment, and social relations. Religion conceives of human flourishing in broad, interconnected terms that includes the spirit as well as the body, spaces as well as forms, and not only green but all the colors of the rainbow—a symbol of hope, expectation, aspiration, and promise.

Religion conceives of human flourishing in broad, interconnected terms that includes the spirit as well as the body, spaces as well as forms, and not only green but all the colors of the rainbow—a symbol of hope, expectation, aspiration, and promise.

1 This text is an extract of remarks delivered during the Ecological Urbanism conference held at the Harvard Graduate School of Design, April 3–5, 2009.

Ecological Urbanism and East Asian Literatures

Karen Thornber

Developing more sustainable cities is vital to the future of East Asia: a majority of Japanese, Koreans, and Taiwanese live in urban areas, while the percentage of Chinese in such spaces has doubled in the past three decades. The region is home to some of the world's most populous cityscapes: Tokyo-Yokohama ranks highest, with Seoul-Incheon, Osaka-Kobe-Kyoto, Shanghai, Shenzhen, Beijing, and Guangzhou-Foshan all in the top twenty. Its urban areas also have considerable footprints, with Tokyo-Yokohama again ranking first, and Nagoya, Osaka-Kobe-Kyoto, Beijing, and Guangzhou-Foshan all in the top twenty. East Asia's urban areas likewise are among the densest in the world.

Ecologies—social, cultural, economic, political, as well as environmental—vary greatly among and within East Asia's many cities. So too does commitment to strategies of ecological urbanism aimed at improving conditions of human beings and the biotic and abiotic nonhuman both in cityscapes themselves and in the many nonurban spaces on whose resources cityscapes depend. To be sure, East Asian literary works (texts with aesthetic ambitions; imaginative writing) addressing urban environmental problems generally offer more reflection, description, critique, and warning than they do comprehensive solutions, much less official policy. But the drafting of policies promoting ecological urbanism, not to mention their implementation, requires changes in consciousness (i.e., changes in perceptions, understandings, and expectations).

East Asian literatures have the potential to play vital roles in this endeavor. A substantial subset of Chinese, Japanese, Korean, and Taiwanese creative works exposes the unsustainability of many urban practices, pointing to the dangers to human beings and the biotic and abiotic nonhuman of everything from unchecked pollution to efforts to "green" East Asia's cities.

East Asian creative exposés of ecologically unsustainable urban practices date to the region's earliest literary production. But the decades after World War II have witnessed the greatest outpouring of such discourse. The Chinese writer Chen Jingrong's (1917–1989) poem "Dushi huanghun jijing" (City Scene at Dusk, 1946) declares that the noises of the city have "drowned dusk," while voices on the radio "tear apart the city's nerves." Although many texts, like the Chinese writer Gao Xingjian's (1940–) *Lingshan* (Soul Mountain, 1989), contrast human survival with nonhuman demise in the face of overwhelming urban pollution, many others depict the future as boding poorly for human and nonhuman alike. The Korean writer Ch'oe Süngho's (1954–) poem "Mul wi e mul arae" (Below the Water That's Above the Water, 1983) speaks not only of pond snails "poisoned by poison in the wastewater," but also of "civilizations born on the waterfront/ festering together with all kinds of untreated excrement." In "Women de cheng bu zai fei hua" (Flowers No Longer Fly in Our City, 1965), the Taiwanese poet Rongzi (Wang Rongzhi, 1928–) comments that "life increasingly fades" among the "rain of soot" and the "thunder of urban noise."

Similarly, disturbed by the sight of a lone chicken strutting on a paved road, "pecking" at cars, sulfurous acid gas, and noise, the poet in Korean writer Chŏng Hyŏnjong's (1939–) "Munmyŏng ŭi sasin" (Death God of Civilization, 1991) describes his city as "blanketed in the black asphalt of development headed toward death." Just as disturbing are works such as the Japanese writer Tsutsui Yasutaka's (1934–) short story "Tatazumu hito" (Standing Woman, 1974) that point to the superficiality and lethality of efforts to "green" the city. Also sobering are creative works like the Japanese writer Hayashi Fumiko's (1903–1951) novel *Ukigumo* (Floating Clouds, 1951) that highlight the degree to which life in urban areas depends on death in non-urban, often overseas sites. Exposing the dangers of unsustainable urban environments, these and numerous other East Asian creative texts demonstrate the importance of changing consciousness, and ultimately behaviors.

… the drafting of policies promoting ecological urbanism, not to mention their implementation, requires changes in consciousness (i.e., changes in percep-tions, understandings, and expectations). East Asian literatures have the potential to play vital roles in this endeavor.

Flowers no longer fly in our city   in March
Crouching everywhere, those colossal beasts of buildings - - -
Sphinxes in the desert   spy on you with mocking eyes
And packs of urban tigers roar
From morning until dusk

From morning until dusk
Rain of soot   thunder of urban noise
Discord among gears
Jostling among machines
Time broken into fragments   life increasingly fades…

Night falls, our city like a large poisonous spider
Spreads its flashing, rippling, seductive net
Trapping the steps of pedestrians
Trapping the loneliness of hearts
The void of the night

I often sit quietly on the dreamless night field
And watch the city at the bottom of the night   like
A gigantic diamond brooch
Displayed in the glass showcase of the commission house
Waiting for a high price

–Translated by Karen Thornber

Rongzi (Wang Rongzhi), "Flowers No Longer Fly in Our City"
(Women de cheng bu zai fei hua), in *Rongzi shi chao*
(Taipei: Lanxing Shishe, 1965), pp. 84–85.

I turned my feet toward the park. In the morning no children came to that small space of less than 70 square meters in the middle of a cramped residential area. It was quiet there, so I made it part of my morning walk. These days in the small city even the limited green of the park's ten or so trees is priceless ... I went out onto the main thoroughfare, where there were too many passing cars and few pedestrians. A cat-tree about 30–40 centimeters high had been planted by the sidewalk. Sometimes I catch sight of a cat-pillar that has just been planted and hasn't yet become a cat-tree ... Perhaps, I thought, it's better to turn dogs into dog-pillars. They become vicious and harm people when there's no food. But why did they have to turn cats into cat-pillars? Had the number of strays grown too large? Were they trying to improve the food situation just a bit? Or were they doing this to green the city? ... [I overheard three students chatting about a progressive critic who had just been arrested and turned into a man-pillar] "There are students who protested his arrest and tried to use force in the Diet. People say they've all been arrested and will be turned into man-pillars" ... "People say they'll be planted like rows of trees on both sides of Student Street, the street in front of their university."

–Translated by Karen Thornber

Selection from Tsutsui Yasutaka's short story "Tatazumu hito" (Standing Woman), in *Tsutsui Yasutaka zenshū*, vol. 16 (Tokyo: Shinchōsha, 1984), pp. 184–193.

ADAPT

Insurgent Ecologies:
(Re)Claiming Ground in Landscape and Urbanism
Nina-Marie Lister

Performative Wood:
Integral Computational Design for a Climate-Responsive
Timber Surface Structure
Achim Menges

Shrinking Gotham's Footprint
Laurie Kerr

Adaptivity in Architecture
Hoberman Associates, Ziggy Drozdowski and Shawn Gupta

GSD RESEARCH
Climate Change, Water, Land Development, and Adaptation:
Planning with Uncertainty (Almere, the Netherlands)
Armando Carbonell, Martin Zogran, and Dirk Sijmons

Insurgent Ecologies: (Re)Claiming Ground in Landscape and Urbanism

Nina-Marie Lister

Ecology has come of age. In the past two decades, designers of landscape projects have become increasingly fascinated with the science of living systems as both instrument and metaphor. From the large, performative, operational landscape designs for brownfield and derelict sites to the "designer ecologies"[1] being deployed in smaller city parks, ecology is now central to the vocabulary and language of the contemporary landscape.

In the strict sense, ecology is a branch of the biological sciences; it is the study of the complex relations between organisms and their environment.[2] More broadly, ecology is often used in a metaphorical context for the relationship between humans and their various constructed environments, from social-cultural to political-economic.[3] In the realm of critical social science, ecology is used in the vernacular plural to describe human relationships with everything from urbanism, culture, and religion, to food, fear, and pizza.[4] Yet as the shape and form of our physical, constructed environment changes with the political-economic and social-cultural forces of globalization, decentralization, and post-industrialization, the ground plane of the contemporary metropolitan region has reshaped the paradigm of ecology. This coupled and reinforcing relationship between ecology and landscape hinges around design: All of our ecologies—multiple, layered, complex, and insurgent—collectively inform the design of our urban and urbanizing landscapes. And these emergent landscapes, in turn, continue to shape the ecologies that define us.

In the context of the rise of ecology as science, strategy, and speculation within the growing confluence of landscape and urbanism, two case studies in Toronto highlight the changing role(s) of ecology in design: River + City + Life, a proposition to remediate and transform the Lower Don Lands on Toronto's waterfront, and Evergreen Brick Works, a master plan to reclaim and reinterpret an abandoned quarry and brickmaking industry on the Don River. These cases are testimony to the prominence of not one but several distinct ecologies of design, each of which is relevant to the challenge of postindustrial landscape design, and more broadly, to an "ecological urbanism."

Landscape and Urbanism

Given the multifaceted evolution of our built environments, design for the bounded and bifurcated notion of "city" and "landscape" is now both outmoded and insufficient. Rather, design for the contemporary metropolitan landscape is the challenge ahead. This blurred continuum from urban, suburban, and exurban to rural demands both a fundamental and contextual reengagement of culture and nature.

The emerging theory of landscape urbanism[5] is evidence of this broader trend toward a confluence—or if we consider the historical evolution of the disciplines, a rapprochement—between ecology, planning, and landscape architecture, in the context of contemporary urbanism. Prior to industrialism, "city" and "landscape" were neither dualistic nor opposing forces. It is only through the industrial era that city, country, and landscape (and their attendant disciplines of practice) became isolated, discrete zones of practice. It is widely accepted that this separation was driven by Cartesian, deterministic planning and design, underwritten by a Newtonian mechanistic worldview, and rooted firmly in the ideals of order, prediction, and control. However, new understandings in ecology[6] have fundamentally challenged the assumptions of predictability and control of living systems. This evolved understanding of ecology, coupled with the increasing forces of globalization and decentralization, has leveraged the opening of the post-industrial landscape to the deployment of a new breed of urbanism—one that is characterized by multiplicity, plurality, diversity, and complexity.

A variety of recent projects for post-industrial sites[7] bear witness to the primacy of landscape as a new medium of urban order, and a number of these involve a progressively more sophisticated reading and use of ecology in design. As various designers have observed, post-industrial reclamation and remediation projects involve a trajectory of strategies in repurposing, transforming, and eventually recalibrating the site. Each of these progressively complex strategies is defined by the use of ecology, both grounded in science and inferred in speculation and representation. As Jane Amidon notes, "These designers remarried the *idea* of nature with the real thing—working ecologies—mending centuries of divorce."[8]

The implications of landscape urbanism are principally concerned with engaging processes that facilitate design in the context of complex and dynamic cultural-natural systems. In this respect, landscape urbanism is necessarily more than just another "new" urbanism; it is concerned with more than merely urban form, and centers on a more complex problematic; it is a multiscaled and multilayered urbanism involving cultural, social, political, economic, infrastructural, and eco-logical conditions that are layered, tangled, and mutually de-pendent. The dynamic metropolitan landscape is no longer a tabula rasa; it is a living field that has been and will con-tinue to be reinvented many times over, from pastoral green-fields to post-industrial brownfields, at times engaging and other times ignoring the history and context implicit in Sola-Morales Rubió's notion of the "terrain vague": those places characterized by "void, absence, and yet also promise, the space of the possible, of expectation."[9] These are the voids that Georgia Daskalakis and Omar Perez have called the "post-urban residual spaces of the abandoned industrial city."[10] In these spaces—whether made, remade, created and recreated, or remediated and reclaimed—each unfolding emerges with new ecologies yet to be identified and validated. Indeed the potential for *synecologies*, or synthetic, integrated cultural-natural ecologies that emerge from forgotten landscapes, is an impetus to fundamentally reconsider the notions of both landscape and urbanism.

James Corner has offered "landscraping" as another tactic for post-industrial landscape design.[11] These sites are often contaminated and can accept no new construction until they are cleared, remediated, and literally scraped clean. In so do-ing, the post-industrial landscape represents a new palette for designers: one characterized by landscapes of potential, awaiting the recognition of insurgent ecologies that, despite degraded environments, have emerged or may yet emerge in the interstitial spaces of past uses and current conditions. These too are apertures for the creation of new hybrid ecolo-gies, open to multiple interpretations in the evolving context of the future city.

Similarly, Charles Waldheim has observed that landscape is more than just the lens of representation; it is a medium of construction.[12] In this context, landscape is a layered, synthetic phenomenon, encompassing more than a two-dimensional surface. If our collective analyses of site and context shift beyond the ground plane and embrace the social-cultural and political-economic dynamics of landscape, new typologies of infrastructure necessarily emerge.[13] Indeed, contemporary urbanism requires a multifocal perspective, one that encom-passes the notions of *form, function, field,* and *flows*[14] across and between the dynamic layers. In this sensibility, aspects of "culture" and "nature" are neither separate nor confused, but woven together throughout the metropolitan landscape.

Adaptive Design for an Ecological Urbanism

But how do we design effectively, meaningfully, and responsibly in the dynamic context of an *ecological* urbanism? Clearly, the complexity inherent in post-industrial metropolitan sites demands strategies that move past the static notions of restoration and rehabilitation to some pristine state. Underscoring contemporary strategies in recent landscape projects that span a spectrum of interventions, from remediation, reclamation, and restoration to transformation and recalibration, is a progressively more sophisticated notion of *adaptive design*.

Adaptive design is a term[15] coined by me, and evolved through research based on the work of C.S. Holling,[16] to refer to an integrated, whole-system, learning-based approach to the management of human-ecological interactions, with explicit implications for planning interventions and resulting design forms. These interventions and their forms must be both adaptive and resilient to sudden, discontinuous environmental change—change that is normal, but cannot be predicted with certainty or controlled completely.

Long-term sustainability and health of landscape systems demands the capacity for *resilience*—the ability to recover from disturbance, to accommodate change, and to function in a state of health—and therefore, for adaptation to environmental change that, while normal, is often limited in predictability and "surprising" in effect.[17] Adaptive design (or properly, adaptive ecological design) draws on current ecological science and is a response to urbanizing landscapes that are under pressure from competing resource demands and land uses. Adaptive design is, by definition, sustainable design; the long-term survival of human and other species demands adaptability, which is predicated on resilience. But resilience and therefore sustainability must not be limited to merely "surviving" in an ecological context. Indeed, resilient, adaptive, and thus sustainable design means "thriving," and therefore must necessarily include economic and ecological health and cultural vitality as planning and design goals.

Recent insights from the ecological and complex systems sciences have challenged decision makers, planners, and designers to become less concerned with prediction and control and to move toward more organic, adaptive, and flexible planning, design, and management strategies.[18] In the absence of ecological certainty and predictability, the implications for decision making and ultimately, design, are that an integrated and whole-systems approach to landscape is necessary: a single discipline or expertise cannot solve complex ecological problems that occur at multiple scales. Where the notion of expertise is challenged in the face of ecological uncertainty, meaningful community engagement in the planning and design process is therefore necessary—decisions must be discussed, debated, negotiated, and ultimately *learned* rather than predetermined by rational choice. Adaptive design thus constitutes decision making that is inclusive of multiple perspectives, adaptive to regular but unpredictable environmental change, and both resilient and responsive to these changes, responding, for example, to new ecological information in a timely way, before critical and irreversible thresholds are crossed. In this way, adaptive design emerges from a deliberative, integrative, cyclic, and continuous—rather than deterministic and discrete—approach to planning, design, and management. The adaptive context is one where learning is a collaborative and conscious activity, derived from empirically monitored or experientially acquired information, which in turn is transformed into knowledge through adapted behavior. This tactic relies on continuous learning through scale-appropriate experiments in community-appropriate design—experiments that are responsive, responsible, and ultimately "safe-to-fail" (rather than "fail-safe").

What then might adaptive ecological design look like, in the context of an ecological urbanism? The following two project examples depict early efforts at adaptive ecological designs in practice, applied to post-industrial sites in Toronto, Canada.

River + City + Life: A Design for Toronto's Lower Don Lands

Located in the Great Lakes Basin, on the north shore of Lake Ontario in the industrialized heart of North America, Toronto is a city-region of 5 million and is one of the five fastest-growing metropolitan areas in North America.[19] It is also one of the world's most ethno-culturally diverse cities,[20] and its social ecology is as complex as the native riparian ecologies of the lakeshore and the ecologies of the Great-Lakes/St. Lawrence-Lowland forest that characterize its landscape. At the intersection of these ecologies, on the Toronto

Graffiti at Toronto's Brick Works (2007) prior to the plan for its adaptive reuse as an environmental learning center

waterfront, the design emphasized resilience, weaving these ecologies through-out the plan.

River + City + Life is a design proposal led by Stoss Landscape Urbanism, a finalist in an international design competition to remediate and revitalize 40 hectares of post-industrial Toronto waterfront, at the mouth of the Don River.[21] A key part of the city's multibillion-dollar waterfront revitalization plans, the site is potentially prime real estate, yet suffers from a legacy of contamination and a complex pattern of land tenure, shared between private and public sector holdings, further complicated by multi-agency oversight.

The Don River flows from its headwaters in a glacial moraine north of Toronto through the heart of Canada's largest city, bisecting the region into a series of forested ravines before reaching Lake Ontario. The Don River watershed is the largest urbanized watershed in Canada, draining an area of 227 square miles. At its outflow, the Don is significantly degraded, having been channeled for the final one-and-a-half miles of its journey to the lake. Suffering from oxygen depletion, high turbidity, poor flow, and seasonal contamination by sewage effluent, the river is effectively stagnant, polluted, and choked with debris. As such, the Don is characteristic of many post-industrial waterfront sites: derelict and forgotten as the armature of the city has all but subsumed it.

Post-industrial decay and displacement on the Toronto waterfront: The squatter community of Tent City was evicted and the site bulldozed while awaiting the revitalization promised by WATERFRONToronto with the new "Lower Donlands" community.

Awaiting realignment into a new estuary as part of the Lower Donlands master plan, the mouth of Toronto's Don River and Canada's largest urban watershed "drains" into Lake Ontario through a cumbersome 90-degree turn.

As a response to the challenge to remediate and revitalize the lower Don Lands, River + City + Life is a radical and bold exploration of the creative tension between "nature" and "culture" in the urban condition. This complex urban project challenged design teams to renaturalize the mouth of the Don River, while simultaneously reengineering the floodplain and creating a new urban edge to the city's downtown. Working at the confluence of the urban core and the derelict Port Lands on the city's waterfront, the Stoss team explicitly adopted an adaptive design concept, based on the primacy of the river and its dynamics. Centered on the notion of resilience, the

River + City + Life: The Stoss master plan and competition finalist scheme for Toronto's Lower Donlands community on the city's east-central waterfront

plan recalibrates the mouth of the river and its floodplain, resulting in a new estuary. Importantly, this is not a restored estuary but a landscape transformed through the creation of a new river channel, supported by several secondary channels to accommodate seasonal inundation, and defined by the "river spits"—sculpted landforms, able to withstand changing lake levels, seasonal flooding, and multiple recreational, educational, and residential uses.

The Stoss plan effectively proposes a new set of integrated cultural and natural ecologies for the site, organized principally by the river and its own self-organizing hydrology. The engagement of a complex ecological, social-cultural, and economic system rests squarely on "putting the river first," reversing the convention of the last century and a half. In hinging the design on "renewal" rather than "restoration," the Stoss team made explicit and central the bold (but essential) notions of adaptation to occasional flooding, mediation between "natural" and "alien" species, and a thick layering of habitats and ecotones—some cultural, others natural; some seasonal and others permanent. The result is a design that weaves a resilient waterfront: an urban tapestry of public amenity, urban edge, and ecological performance. This proposal reconceives the city as a hybrid cultural-natural space—a signature step for landscape urbanism and its operational ecologies.

Evergreen Brick Works

Some 4 miles upstream of the Lower Don Lands, on the Don River, is a different emerging example of the intersection of ecology, landscape, and urbanism. This 40-acre site is located in the geographic core of downtown Toronto, on an arterial road off a major expressway, and is a designated cultural and natural heritage site. Evergreen, a Canadian national charity,

Bird's-eye view of the proposed River + City + Life master plan for Toronto's Lower Don and the waterfront: Engineered river spits and braided channels provide the armature for a flood-adapted waterscape that fluctuates with the seasons, changing lake levels, and storm events.

commissioned a master plan to transform this post-industrial site into an international showcase for urban sustainability and ecological design, centered on the reclamation and reinterpretation of the abandoned quarry and former brick works.

The project is an innovative public and nonprofit development partnership in which the city and the regional conservation authority own the land and manage the restored quarry (now a 28-acre wetland), while Evergreen has proposed and won a long-term lease for the 12-acre industrial pad and heritage buildings. Adjacent to the historic Todmorden Mills (ca. 1790), the site was home to the Don Valley Brick Works, a brick-making facility that produced, at its peak, 43 million bricks per year—the majority of brick used in urban construction across Canada for almost a century, from 1889 to 1984.[22] Over the years, the quarry exposed layers of extraordinary quaternary geology, resulting in a UNESCO World Heritage designation for the site. The quarry was filled in and restored as a wetland during the 1990s and is currently managed by the city as a recreational park and by the regional Conservation Authority as a natural heritage conservation site. To redevelop the industrial buildings and remediate the site, Evergreen is raising the $55 million (Canadian) project budget, of which $32 million has been invested to date.

Evergreen's mandate—to deepen the connection between people and nature by bringing nature, culture, and community together in the city[23]—is central to the site plan and design scheme. At its core, Evergreen Brick Works is a year-round learning center for citizens. The master plan proposes Canada's first large-scale environmental discovery center integrating cultural and natural heritage, and ecological and social services, through a wide range of features. These include sustainable "green" buildings; a native plant nursery; a demonstration kitchen and children's gardens; a local farmers' market; an organic restaurant; conference and event facilities; children's camps; and family, youth leadership, and youth-at-risk programming.

The Brick Works project departs from other urban ecology endeavors in that it is not principally about restoration. Rather, in recognizing Evergreen's urban constituency and its place at the heart of the urban landscape, the project centers on establishing a relationship between nature and culture. Interestingly, at its inception in 1991, Evergreen's core mission was to "bring nature back to the city," achieved primarily through naturalization and restoration efforts. The past decade has seen Evergreen's mission evolve to a more sophisticated reading of urban ecologies and the means by which these are expressed in the urban landscape. This shift in thinking mirrors the evolution of other post-industrial remediation projects. The brick works master plan reflects this paradigm shift, as is evident in the four themes underpinning the project: Innovation & Discovery, showcasing innovative technologies and programming to help citizens integrate sustainability into their lives; Food & Community, focusing on nutrition programs for family and youth-at-risk, and the promotion and support of local, sustainable food sources; Natural & Cultural Heritage, conserving and protecting archaeological, industrial, and natural heritage through adaptive reuse of heritage buildings and landscape resources; and Gardening & Greening, providing opportunities for learning about local foods and cooking, native plant recognition and gardening, green design, and local habitats.[24]

As a learning center explicitly geared toward the integration of culture, nature, and community, situated in the heart of Canada's largest city, Evergreen Brick Works is an innovative plan for the deployment of several ecologies within a complex urban landscape. Although juxtaposing elements of wild nature with groomed gardens, and arts and cultural activities with the old industrial buildings, the Brick Works does not suffer from conflicting land-use goals, as one might expect. Instead, the site is engaging creative ecological design as a manifestation of both cultural and natural heritage within the urban context. Not unlike Latz + Partner's Duisberg Nord Park in Germany, the Brick Works site moves past the convention of ecology-as-nature preservation and into the realm of cultural and political ecologies, both as metaphor and program for learning and teaching ecological literacy. Yet the project still manages to give traction to operational ecologies of remediation and reclamation, both in its landscape plan for native habitats and in its adaptive reuse and "green" building. In all its complexity, the site offers a wide array

Garden in the city: Adaptive reuse of the Evergreen Brick Works turns a post-industrial brick-making plant into a native plant nursery, farmer's market, and environmental learning center.

of contemporary interpretations of ecologies in the context of landscape and urbanism—from the artful juxtaposition of creative performance in an abandoned factory to urging the community to "rethink space."

Reflections

The last decade of large-scale post-industrial urban projects has seen landscape and ecology become primary vectors in contemporary urbanism, and indeed, in city building writ large. In a "coming of age" moment, ecology has gone from subservient science to design partner in shaping global cities. From the vantage point of ecology, this is no small achievement, especially as it originates through the practice of landscape architecture, and to a lesser degree, through urban planning. As such, this new role for landscape offers concomitant fresh perspectives on, and roles for, its related and supporting disciplines, in particular, ecology. The (re)engagement of these disciplines signals a timely reinvigoration of both landscape architecture and planning, underscoring their centrality in the making of contemporary cities.

In this context, the Toronto examples are only two of a growing number of projects across North America that reflect a catalytic moment in the evolution of the metropolis. In these and other similar cases, the post-industrial landscape is less concerned with restoration than remediation: casting back to a precolonial ideal of nature is neither feasible nor desirable. Rather, a new synthesis has emerged, seizing the niche between culture and nature, manifest in the insurgent ecologies of our time.

Yet that quintessentially human act of intentional manipulation[25]—the design of space and place—is nothing if not intimately connected with other species and the context in which we dwell. In the dynamic landscapes that characterize the modern urban region, the act of designing and thus

Winter city: Adaptive reuse shifts with the seasons—summer greenhouses become winter ice pads and outdoor snowscapes, with the exposed steel structure open to the sky and the elements.

Evergreen Brick Works, Toronto, begins the process of adaptive reuse with a simple paint job, urging passersby to "Rethink Space."

affecting and ultimately shaping both new and existing ecologies must therefore be born of an intimate understanding of place—of scale, context, and history. This is not a manifestation of ecological modernism, but rather, an evolution into an *ecological urbanism*. To design ecologies that sustain vibrant, healthy, and self-organizing urban landscapes, our interventions must necessarily be contextual and deliberative. To do so demands both fundamental renegotiation of our relationship with what we perceive as "nature" and our place with/in it, and a consequent reengagement with culture. Good (and thus necessarily ecological) design that results from this context, as I have articulated here and elsewhere,[26] is adaptive, resilient, and reflective; it is born of place, and it honors the land that sustains us.

1 I have used the term "designer ecologies" to refer to the largely symbolic gestures designers use to recall or represent a relationship to nature, often out of necessity at relatively small scales or in conditions that are constrained. See Nina-Marie Lister, "Sustainable Large Parks: Ecological Design or Designer Ecology?" in Julia Czerniak and George Hargreaves, eds., *Large Parks* (New York: Princeton Architectural Press, 2007), 31–51. In a similar but more pejorative context, William Thompson uses the term "boutique ecology" to refer to the often superficial ecological representation in landscape projects in which designers brand their projects "ecological" but avoid the challenges of dealing fundamentally with ecological complexity. See William Thompson, "Boutique Ecologies" *Landscape Architecture*, April 10, 2006,

2 As defined by Eugene P. Odum and Howard T. Odum in the classic text *Fundamentals of Ecology* (third edition) (Philadelphia: Saunders, 1953 [1971]).

3 As used in this broader context, for example, by Gregory Bateson, *Steps to an Ecology of Mind* (Chicago: University of Chicago Press, 1972). Similar examples can be found in the scholarship of John Dryzek, Tim Forsyth, Roger Keil, Sian Sullivan, Adam Swift, and Paul Robbins (and others) in political ecology, and Murray Bookchin, Ramchandra Guha, and David Pepper (and others) in social ecology.

4 Among many examples are: Harvard University Graduate School of Design's new seminar in *Ecology as Urbanism* (see: http://www.gsd.harvard.edu/academic/upd/maudmlaudrequirements.htm); York University's Faculty of Environmental Studies curriculum stream in political and cultural ecologies (http://www.yorku.ca/fes/about/WhatIsEnvironmentalStudies.

htm); the new research journal, *Ecology of Food & Nutrition* (published by Taylor & Francis); SAFE–*Society for Agriculture and Food Ecology*, a U.C.-Berkeley students' group (http://agrariana.org/safe-s-mission); Mike Davis's *The Ecology of Fear* (New York: Vintage Books, 1998); and Sandra Steingraber's *The Ecology of Pizza* (http://www.motherearthnews.com/Real-Food/2006-06-01/The-Ecology-of-Pizza-Or-Why-Organic-Food-is-a-Bargain.aspx).

5 See Charles Waldheim, ed., *The Landscape Urbanism Reader* (New York: Princeton Architectural Press, 2006).

6 The evolution of ecological science in relation to planning has been traced by N.M. Lister, in "A Systems Approach to Biodiversity Conservation Planning," *Environmental Monitoring and Assessment* 49, no. 2/3 (1998): 123–155. See also Brad Bass, R. Edward Byers, and Nina-Marie Lister, "Integrating Research on Ecohydrology and Land Use Change with Land Use Management," *Hydrological Processes* 12 (1998): 2217–2233.

7 For example, Field Operations' design for Fresh Kills, New York; OMA, Bruce Mau, and Inside Outside's design for Parc Downsview, Toronto; Latz + Partner's design for Landschaftspark Duisburg Nord; and Stoss's design for the Lower Don Lands, Toronto.

8 Jane Amidon, "Big Nature," in Lisa Tilder and Beth Bloustein, eds., *Designing Ecologies* (New York: Princeton Architectural Press, 2009).

9 Ignasi de Sola-Morales Rubió, "Terrain Vague," in Cynthia C. Davidson, ed., *Anyplace* (Cambridge, MA: MIT Press, 1995), 120.

10 Georgia Daskalakis and Omar Perez, "Things to Do in Detroit," in Georgia Daskalakis, Charles Waldheim, and Jason Young, eds., *Stalking Detroit* (Barcelona: ACTAR, 2001).

11 James Corner, "Landscape Urbanism," in Mohsen Mostafavi, ed., *Landscape Urbanism: A Manual for the Machinic Landscape* (London: Architectural Association, 2003), 58–63.

12 Charles Waldheim, "Landscape as Urbanism," in Waldheim, ed., *The Landscape Urbanism Reader*, 37–53.

13 The infrastructures of ecology, transportation, fuel, waste, water, and food are but a few of the extensions of surface conditions into the realm of urbanism. This concept was explored by a variety of landscape scholars at the symposium "Landscape and Infrastructure," convened by Pierre Bélanger, Associate Professor in Landscape Architecture at the University of Toronto, October 25, 2008 (publication forthcoming).

14 With thanks to Professor Brian Orland, who offered the addition of "flows" to this line of logic, following my Bracken Lecture on September 23, 2008, at Pennsylvania State University, Department of Landscape Architecture.

15 For a detailed development of adaptive ecological design, see Nina-Marie Lister, "Sustainable Large Parks," and "Ecological Design for Industrial Ecology: Opportunities for (Re) Discovery" in Ray Coté, James Tansey, and Ann Dale, eds., *Linking Industry and Ecology: A Question of Design* (Vancouver: UBC Press, 2005), 15–28. For a broader socio-ecological systems context, see David Waltner-Toews, James Kay, and Nina-Marie Lister, *The Ecosystem Approach: Complexity, Uncertainty, and Managing for Sustainability* (New York: Columbia University Press, 2008).

16 C.S. "Buzz" Holling, "The Resilience of Terrestrial Ecosystems: Local Surprise and Global Change," in W. C. Clark and R. Edward Munn, eds., *Sustainable Development of the Biosphere* (Cambridge: Cambridge University Press, 1986), 292–320.

17 Ibid.

18 Lister, "Sustainable Large Parks," and Waltner-Toews, Kay, and Lister, eds., *The Ecosystem Approach*.

19 City Mayors' Statistics, "The World's Largest Cities and Urban Areas in 2006," http://www.citymayors.com/statistics/urban_2006_1.html (accessed October 27, 2008).

20 See Statistics Canada, *Annual Demographic Report 2005*, catalog no. 91-213-XIB (Ottawa: Ministry of Industry, 2006); and Elizabeth McIsaac, "Immigrants in Canadian Cities: Census 2001 – What Do the Data Tell Us?" *Policy Options* (May 2003), 58–63.

21 The international design competition was sponsored in 2007 by WATERFRON-Toronto, a government agency charged with overseeing the revitalization of the Toronto waterfront. See: http://www.waterfrontoronto.ca. The Stoss-led team was comprised of Stoss Landscape Urbanism (Boston), Brown & Storey Architects Inc. (Toronto), and ZAS Architects (Toronto) with Nina-Marie Lister, *pLandform*, and Jackie Brookner, Brookner Studio NYC.

22 Evergreen, http://evergreen.ca/rethinkspace/?page_id=12 (accessed October 30, 2008).

23 Evergreen, http://www.evergreen.ca/en/about/about.html (accessed October 30, 2008) and http://www.evergreen.ca/en/brickworks/pdf/EBWCampaign_2008.pdf (page 3) (accessed October 30, 2008).

24 Evergreen, http://evergreen.ca/rethinkspace/?page_id=12 (accessed October 30, 2008).

25 While it may be argued that other species (social mammals in particular) also shape their habitats, it is generally accepted that only humans and the higher-order primates do so with intention – not merely instinct.

26 Lister, "Sustainable Large Parks," 35–57.

Hands-on experiential learning at the Children's Discovery Centre, Evergreen Brick Works, Toronto

Performative Wood: Integral Computational Design for a Climate-Responsive Timber Surface Structure

Achim Menges

Wood differs from most building materials in that it is a naturally grown biological tissue. Thus wood displays significant differentiation in its material makeup and structure as compared to most industrially produced, isotropic materials.[1] Upon closer examination, wood can be described as an anisotropic natural fiber system with varied material characteristics and related behavior in different directions relative to the main grain orientation.[2] Because of its differentiated internal capillary structure, wood is also hygroscopic: it absorbs and releases moisture in exchange with the environment, and these fluctuations cause differential dimensional changes.

Spruce cones can open and close, time and again, due to changes in moisture content of the material and in reaction to the relative humidity of the environment.

The change of moisture content in a composite veneer plate triggers a dimensional change that results in a rapid shape change.

In architectural history, the inherent heterogeneity of wood and the related more complex material characteristics have been mainly understood as a major deficiency by the timber industry, engineers, and architects. This project investigates an alternative design approach that aims to understand wood's differentiated makeup as its leading capacity rather than viewing it as a shortcoming. Utilizing wood's intrinsic characteristics, a surface structure that responds to changes in relative humidity with no need for additional electronic or mechanical control was developed. This suggests an alternative approach to architectural design, one that unfolds the complex performative capacity of relatively simple material systems from an in-depth investigation of their inherent characteristics, and an integral computational design process based on the system's exchange with environmental influences. The resultant performative material systems investigate the ecological potential of meso-structures that form the natural yet unexplored link between the micro-structure of materials and the macro-structure of the built environment.

The Responsive Surface Structure research project, conducted at my Department for Form Generation and Materialization at HFG Offenbach by Steffen Reichert, sought to develop a skin structure capable of adapting its porosity in response to changes in ambient humidity. Thus the project instrumentalizes the hygroscopic properties of wood and the related surface expansion as a means to embed climate sensor, actuator, and regulating element all in one very simple component. One typical example of various biological systems operating on this principle is the spruce cone. The initially moist, closed cone gradually dries, and during this process the cone opens and seeds are released. What is particularly interesting is that, because the behavioral response is latent in the material, this system works without any contact with the tree, and the opening and closure can be repeated over a large number of cycles without any material fatigue.

With regard to timber, the fiber saturation point describes the state in which the cell walls are fully saturated with bound water, whereas the cell cavities are emptied of free water. How much of the bound water evaporates, and therefore how much shrinkage will occur, mainly depends on the relative humidity level of the atmosphere; for example, at 100 percent relative humidity, no bound water is lost, while all bound water would be removed at zero relative humidity.

The long axis of the cells is more or less parallel to the orientation of the long-chain cellulosic structure in the cell walls. Consequently, as water molecules leave and enter the cell walls due to changes in relative humidity, the resulting

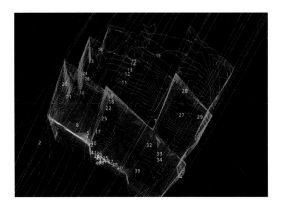
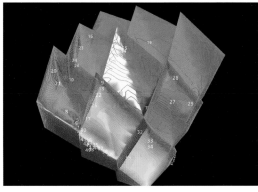

Through iterative computational and physical test models, the element is derived as an associative geometric component based on investigations of the thermodynamic behavior of the element's open and closed state.

The reciprocal effects between macro- and micro-thermodynamic modulations registered in iterative CFD analysis drive the evolutionary form-generation process of the overall surface articulation.

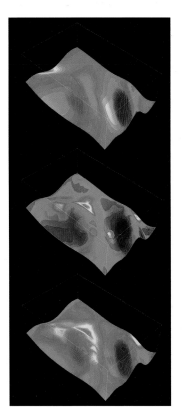

shrinkage or swelling is mainly perpendicular to the cell walls and does not influence their length. Thus the main effect of changing bound-water content in wood occurs in tangential shrinkage and swelling and the correlated dimensional changes. The anatomical structure of wood causes the main difference between tangential and radial shrinkage and swelling, the latter having a considerably lower value due to the restraining effect of wood rays, whose long axes are radially oriented.[3]

Rather than employing complicated electro-mechanical control devices, the project seeks to employ the shape change of simple veneer elements triggered by changing bound-water content. The gaps opening up between the deformed veneer elements and the substructure locally regulate the structure's degree of porosity. The development process commenced with a series of physical experiments investigating a simple composite veneer element. Critical variables of the key element's parameters—for example, the length-width-thickness ratio in relation to main fiber directionality—were tested for their influence on the element's shape change and response time in changing humidity conditions. Initially rotary-cut beech veneer was selected on the basis of its high swelling and shrinkage value in the tangential plane. However, a number of comparative empirical tests proved that sycamore maple veneer was more suitable due to its considerably lower elastic modulus.

Following the first series of empirical tests, the development of a surface element as the basic constituent of the system commenced. Through iterative computational and physical test models, the element is derived as an associative geometric component based on the manufacturing and assembly logics of a larger, multicomponent system as well as investigations of the thermodynamic behavior of the element's open and closed state. The resulting surface component consists of a load-bearing substructure on which two triangular veneer

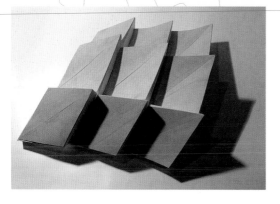

A test assembly of nine veneer composite components indicates the change of surface shape and related surface porosity in response to an increasing level of relative humidity. Key design parameters, such as fiber orientation or the ratio of thickness, length, and width, were tested in relation to the element's response time to changes in moisture content and resultant shape change.

elements are mounted along their long edge. The substructure to which the moisture-sensitive elements are attached is developed as a parametrically defined folded structure with planar component-to-component attachment faces. The cut pattern of each component to be constructed from sheet material is automatically generated through the parametric computational model. Similarly, the associative model defines the main fiber direction of the element as being parallel to the fixed edge, which is also reflected in the automatically derived cut pattern of each element. The veneer element's shape change perpendicular to the main fiber direction, caused by changes in relative humidity, results in local surface openings.

An increase of moisture content triggered by a rising level of relative humidity causes the swelling of the veneer elements. Due to the fibrous restrictions of wood anatomy, the elements expand primarily in the tangential plane orthogonal to the grain. This dimensional change causes a shape change, and the veneer elements curl up, creating an opening for ventilation. A large number of test cycles verified that the movement induced by moisture absorption is fully reversible. Furthermore, the response time is surprisingly short. The shift from closed to fully open state takes less than 20 seconds with a substantial increase in relative humidity. The developed component enables the construction of a locally controlled, humidity-responsive surface structure, in which each sublocation independently senses changes of local humidity concentrations and reacts by changing the local level of system porosity. The emergent thermodynamic modulation along and across the surface is directly influenced by both the local component geometry and the overall system morphology.

To account for the complex reciprocity of individual component and overall system behavior and related macro- and micro-thermodynamic modulations, a feedback-based evolutionary computational process is used to prototypically

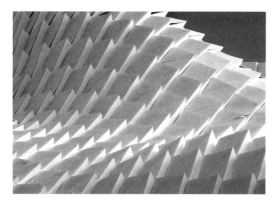
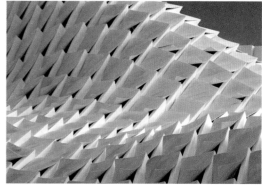

The functional full-scale prototype demonstrates the performance capacity of the system. In response to changes in relative humidity and related changes to the bound water content of the veneer composite patches, they facilitate the opening and closure of each local component, resulting in different degrees of porosity across the surface.

> The full-scale prototype is both structure and responsive skin that integrates distributed sensors, actuators, and climate-regulation device in the simple veneer composite elements.

develop a global surface articulation. For this process, the surface geometry is mathematically controlled through an equation with a number of variables. Iterative changes to these variables provide a robust yet simple base for the hygromorphic evolution of the surface geometry. This process is driven by the stochastic alteration of the mathematical surface, the subsequent associative component generation, and the related computer fluid dynamics analysis of each system instance's behavior. The relevant data is continuously fed back and informs the next system generation. The evolving load-bearing structure's overall curvature orients the responsive veneer elements either toward or away from local airstreams and humidity concentrations. The resultant calibration of overall curvature and local component morphology in different opening states enables a highly specific modulation of airflow and related humidity levels across and along the system.

To verify and further inform the developed integral design approach, a full-scale, functional surface prototype was built from 600 geometrically different components. Subsequent test cycles confirmed the performative capacity of the responsive surface structure. Once exposed to changes in relative humidity, the veneer composite elements respond by opening or closing components, resulting in different degrees of porosity over time and across the surface. Thus the material system is directly responsive to environmental influences with no need for any additional electronic or mechanical control. This demonstrates the high level of integration of form, structure, and material capacity enabled by the computational design process.

1 J. R. Barnett and G. Jeronimides, eds., *Wood Quality and Its Biological Basis* (Oxford: Blackwell CRC Press, 2003).

2 J. M. Dinwoodie, *Timber: Its Nature and Behaviour* (London: Spon, 2000).
3 C. Skaar, *Wood Water Relations* (Berlin: Springer, 1988).

Shrinking Gotham's Footprint

Laurie Kerr

PlaNYC, New York City's plan for sustainable growth through 2030, grew out of pragmatic needs. In 2005, after several decades of renewal and reinvestment, the city had recovered from the suburban exodus and population loss of the 1950s through 1970s, with the city's demographers projecting almost 1 million more people by 2030. Where would an already dense archipelago, with no possibility for lateral expansion, house an additional population the size of San Francisco? And how could it provide them with basic services—transportation, sewage treatment, energy, etc.—when it had essentially outgrown the infrastructure built for the midcentury city of roughly 8 million?

Clearly, New York would have to do more with less, and thus sustainability was married to an effort that began as a long-range land-use plan. It was not an end in itself, but the conceptual structure necessary to maintain and improve the quality of life for New Yorkers by addressing complex interrelationships between the city's looming challenges. Land use could not be separated from transportation, which is part of the city's overall infrastructure, which includes aging, inefficient power plants, which impact air quality—all of which ultimately contribute to climate change. And of course, if climate change is not stabilized, none of the other issues will matter—particularly in New York City, with more than 580 miles of coastline.

Most far-reaching of the plan's ten goals is a 30 percent reduction in greenhouse gas emissions citywide by 2030. To begin, the city needed to create a Greenhouse Gas Emissions Inventory to see where its emissions come from. The results were quite surprising. Almost 80 percent of the city's emissions—more than twice the national average—results from energy used in buildings: the gas and oil that power the boilers, the electricity for lights and appliances. This is largely because most New Yorkers walk and use public transportation rather than drive; also the city has a small industrial base, and a smaller agricultural one. What's left is the buildings.

Another surprise was that New York City, that old symbol of profligacy and waste, that antithesis of the natural, provides a remarkably efficient lifestyle, with a per capita carbon footprint less than one-third the national average. Again, public transportation plays a role, but the city's buildings factor in too. New Yorkers generally live and work in compact spaces—New York apartments seem impossibly small to visitors—and the buildings abut each other, providing less surface for heat loss or gain. Still, efficient though it is, the city's sheer size results in emissions comparable to those of a small country—somewhere between Norway and Ireland—which means that reducing New York's emissions would have a measurable global impact, while also improving things locally by producing cleaner air and less costly, more reliable power—two other goals of PlaNYC. But how could the city reduce its emissions, and by how much?

The underlying trends are sobering. The city's carbon emissions aren't shrinking, they're growing at roughly 1 percent per year, which translates into a 28 percent increase by 2030 over a 2005 baseline. Projections show every energy indicator outpacing population growth, especially electricity consumption, with an expected 44 percent growth by 2030, due to increased air conditioning and electronic equipment. Unfortunately, this growth rate mirrors the national and global situation, where even California, with its sustained, aggressive efforts at efficiency over thirty years, has not managed to completely curtail per capita electricity growth. Reversing these trends to achieve significant CO_2 reductions represents a tremendous, perhaps unprecedented challenge.

A granular, bottom-up analysis of available strategies revealed that New York could achieve a 30 percent reduction cost effectively if it targeted all the opportunities in every sector. The most economic solution is the most diverse one: if any one area is ignored, the others need to be pushed harder to compensate, which is more costly. Roughly half of the reductions would result from efficiency improvements in buildings, another 30 percent from improvements in electrical power production, with the remaining 20 percent from transportation.

New York is projected to grow by almost a million people in the first three decades of this century.

PlaNYC's ten goals

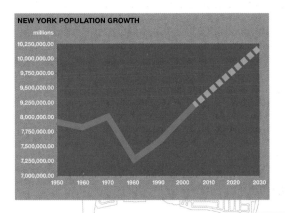

NEW YORK POPULATION GROWTH

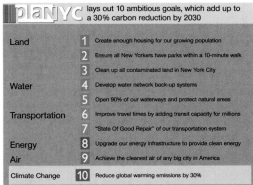

planYC lays out 10 ambitious goals, which add up to a 30% carbon reduction by 2030

Land	1	Create enough housing for our growing population
	2	Ensure all New Yorkers have parks within a 10-minute walk
	3	Clean up all contaminated land in New York City
Water	4	Develop water network back-up systems
	5	Open 90% of our waterways and protect natural areas
Transportation	6	Improve travel times by adding transit capacity for millions
	7	"State Of Good Repair" of our transportation system
Energy	8	Upgrade our energy infrastructure to provide clean energy
Air	9	Achieve the cleanest air of any big city in America
Climate Change	10	Reduce global warming emissions by 30%

How New York will reduce its emissions

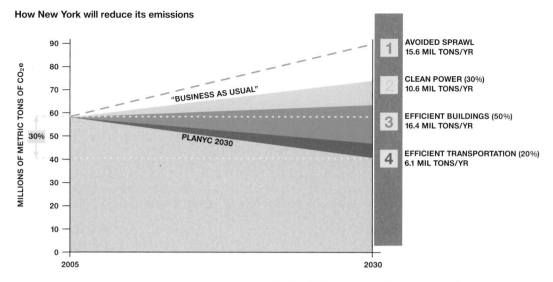

In the "business as usual" scenario, New York's greenhouse gas emissions are projected to grow by 28 percent over a 2005 baseline by 2030. Instead, the city has committed to reducing its emissions by 30 percent in that timeframe.

Focusing on the building sector, it became clear that green building, while necessary, would be insufficient. Each new building creates a new emissions source, so making new buildings more efficient can only slow the rate of increase. To actually reduce emissions, the city must tackle the existing buildings, and aggressively so, because an estimated 85 percent of New York's buildings in 2030 will be the buildings that are already here today. There are almost 1 million of them, ranging from eighteenth-century townhouses to ultramodern skyscrapers, with museums, schools, and Broadway theaters thrown in. How to address such complexity?

First, know thyself. To begin, the city analyzed how much of its emissions come from each building sector, and within each sector, how energy is used; it studied how space is distributed in buildings of various types and sizes; and it considered the cycles of renewal and renovation in its old buildings. From this survey emerged the idea that the city should start by focusing on four promising areas.

The governmental and institutional sectors, which produce 18 percent of the city's building-based emissions, constitute the first focus area. These entities own and operate their buildings over the long haul, so they stand to benefit from deep, long-term reduction strategies that reduce operating costs. The city has led with its own buildings and operations, committing itself to an accelerated 30 percent greenhouse gas reduction target in ten years, and it has challenged the institutional sector to match it, with sixteen universities and thirty-three hospitals having committed thus far. Collectively, these accelerated efforts affect almost 10 percent of New York's footprint.

Breakdown of NYC greenhouse gas emissions

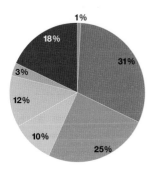

2005 Adjusted Citywide CO$_2$e Emissions by Sector

Total = 63.1 MMT

Buildings = 78%
- Residential
- Commercial
- Industrial
- Institutional

Transportation = 21%
- Transit
- On-Road Vehicles

Other = 1%
- Methane

Seventy-eight percent of New York's greenhouse gas emissions come from energy used to power its buildings.

The other three areas address the residential and commercial sectors, where shorter ownership cycles and tenant-owner contracts make things more complicated, necessitating regulatory requirements to spur action. The first area is renovations because the building stock is constantly being renewed, and the most cost-effective efficiency increases are the incremental improvements to projects being undertaken anyway. The second is lighting, which contributes some 19 percent of building-based carbon emissions and can yield significant reductions due to extremely rapid technological improvements. And the third is the city's largest buildings, since roughly 2 percent of the city's buildings produce almost 50 percent of its emissions—making a vast problem much simpler.

The city's Greener, Greater Buildings Plan, announced on Earth Day and currently being considered by City Council, addresses these three focus areas. The plan removes a loophole from the current energy code that exempts small renovations, and it requires the city's largest buildings to be annually benchmarked for energy performance, to upgrade their lighting to meet code, and to be audited and perform those energy upgrades that are cost-effective. Supporting the regulatory package is a green jobs training effort and a revolving loan fund. All together, this plan forms the most comprehensive effort by any American city to reduce emissions from existing buildings—an effort that should collectively reduce emissions by 5 percent—equivalent to making the city of Oakland carbon-neutral.

So how well is New York doing? A local law requires the city to track its efforts, and in April 2009, PlaNYC released its second annual progress report. The report totals the CO$_2$ emissions reductions that are complete, under way, or planned. It itemizes state and federal policies as well as city ones because the jurisdictions form a complex patchwork, with the federal government setting appliance and automotive efficiency standards, the state historically controlling the building energy code and most energy efficiency funding, and the city controlling its own large building portfolio, taxis and limousines, and perhaps soon its own energy code. Added up, an estimated 56 percent of the greenhouse gas emissions reductions necessary to achieve the 30 percent target are complete, under way, or planned. This may be cause for cautious celebration: cautious because most of the work for these pieces has yet to be done, and there's the remaining 44 percent to deal with, along with the even more radical reductions required by 2050, but still heartening because these numbers demonstrate that perhaps this unprecedented challenge can be systematically addressed by cities at the large scale.

Almost half of New York City's square footage is housed in buildings of more than 50,000 square feet–the size of a fifty-unit Manhattan apartment building. Yet these buildings represent only about 2 percent of its 1 million buildings.

ADAPT

THE NEW YORK CITY
GREENER, GREATER
BUILDINGS PLAN

New York is a city of buildings. They are where we live, work, and play; they make up the skyline that identifies our city to the world.

The electricity, heating, and hot water we consume in buildings accounts for almost 80% of our greenhouse gas footprint, and $15 billion per year in energy costs. The city's largest buildings – over 50,000 square feet – comprise nearly half of our total space.

Making these existing buildings energy efficient is the biggest step we can take towards a greener, greater New York.

Working together, Mayor Bloomberg and City Council Speaker Quinn and her colleagues have proposed a six-part plan to make our existing large buildings energy efficient. Buildings will have to make certain improvements – but only those that pay for themselves. The plan relies on existing technology only, and low-cost measures that have proven track records.

This plan will save New Yorkers $750 million in energy costs, improve conditions for tenants, create 19,000 construction jobs, and reduce our greenhouse gas emissions by 5% – the largest single advance towards our 30% goal.

Adaptivity in Architecture

Hoberman Associates (text by Ziggy Drozdowski and Shawn Gupta)

The notion that a building can move or reconfigure itself is not novel. The premise of modularity and dynamic control in combination with unique mechanisms has permeated architectural practice at many points and through a diverse range of projects. But often the large scale and custom nature of these systems, with consideration given to structure, mechanism, and control, result in a cost that can only be justified by a project's high profile (Milwaukee Art Museum, by Santiago Calatrava) or commercial benefit (the Arizona Cardinals' stadium, by Peter Eisenman and HOK Sport).

Yet the built environment is inherently adaptive. Environmental forces beyond gravity and pressure are constantly causing building materials to deflect, expand, contract, rupture, and deform all around us. Standard design guides us to limit movement in favor of stability. However, if stability can be maintained while incorporating movement, new design opportunities are suddenly possible.

New material systems in architecture have always produced such opportunities. For example, reinforced concrete was born through combining a metal lattice with liquid concrete. This technical advance enabled many of the innovative structures we see today. Adaptive Fritting, an installation by Hoberman Associates for the Harvard Graduate School of Design, is a first embodiment of a new material

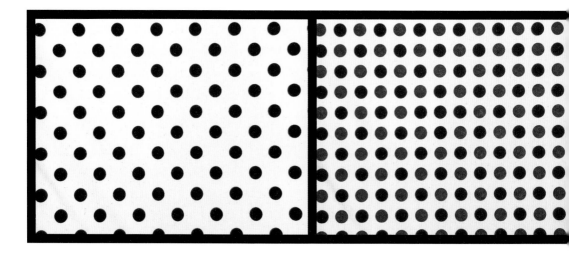

system that allows the designer micro-control of the user experience.

Inherent to the development of Adaptive Fritting was the desire to take an established architectural treatment and imbue it with expanded functionality. Such a development would provide architects with both a new design element that is already a familiar part of their vocabulary and a performance increase that expands on current interest in using fritted glass (to easily customize shading while preserving transparency where desired).

Solar control in building-envelope design is full of conflicting requirements. For example, maximizing view often increases solar gain. While all-glass façades give occupants a connection to the outside environment, even high-performance glazing cannot insulate as well as solid mass construction. Furthermore, unshaded glass allows profuse amounts of direct daylight into a space, creating areas of high contrast between light and dark (glare) that often force occupants to close the blinds completely. Counterproductively, the darkness requires additional lighting, which consumes electricity and generates heat.

An effective shading system allows view, blocks solar radiation, and scatters diffuse daylight deep into the space. More specifically, a shading system's effectiveness is based on the percentage of opaque material, thickness, opacity, reflectance, and position within the façade. Adjustable blinds and exterior louvers can be effective at reducing solar exposure of glazing, but they add complexity and expense through additional hardware installation. Spectrally selective solar coatings are the most cost-effective methods of blocking solar radiation. The best coatings available today can allow more than twice as much visible light as solar heat gain through a window pane.

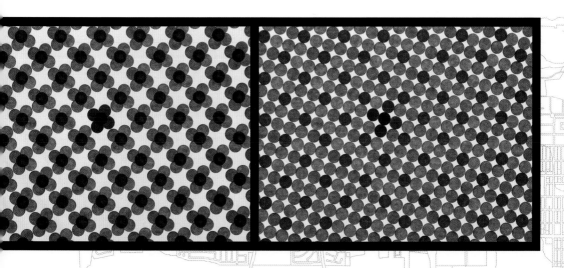

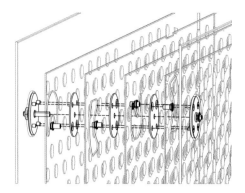

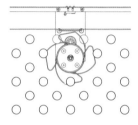

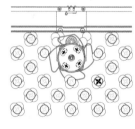

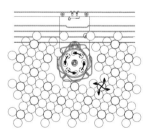

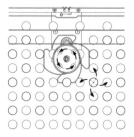

However, as better-performing coatings selectively block more of the visible spectrum, the color distribution does not always remain neutral. Therefore many designers have chosen fritting as an additional shading component, allowing a lesser-performing solar coating and a more neutral-color glass.

The solar coating is effective because the shading technology is concentrated in a very thin layer within the façade. This consolidation of hardware and complexity makes Adaptive Fritting simpler to install than external blinds and louvers. Architecturally, the façade can become thinner and higher performing. The building envelope designer is really designing porosity and energy flow through a series of material surfaces. As an abstraction, Adaptive Fritting is concerned with modulating the parameters of pattern, porosity, and movement at a micro scale. In contrast, special solar and electrochromic coatings are applied to glass homogeneously. Thus their effectiveness is not optimized as to where the sun is located in the sky. Adaptive Fritting's multilayer solution could potentially block solar radiation based on hemispherical angles of incidence, tracking the sun's movements above while allowing view for the occupants.

Because complexity increases exponentially with moving parts, finding economies is vital to an effective design. The maximum benefit must be extracted from every inch of motion. Adaptive Fritting is just one example, and infinite variants can be explored through altering any parameter—motion, usage, material, or configuration. What if Adaptive Fritting utilized rotational motion instead of translational motion? What if the acrylic sheet was punctured with holes instead of fritted with dots? This modulated porosity could control air flow instead of sunlight.

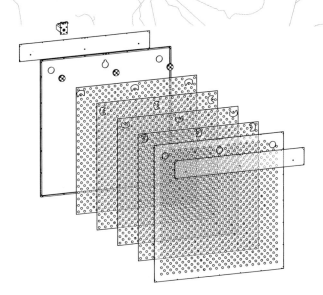

Reference
Lee, E., S. Selkowitz, V. Bazjanac, V. Inkarojrit, and C. Kohler. *High-Performance Commercial Building Facades.* Berkeley: Lawrence Berkeley National Laboratories, 2002.

Adaptive techniques in building design will ultimately be adopted in a multitude of ways. Designers will integrate this thinking early in the design process and will be able to create more dynamic buildings that they can tune. Adaptive components will be able to interface with building management systems and become an active part of central control to achieve regulatory benefits. Ultimately, adaptive architectural design will free people from having to make choices based on a building's location and will allow a building to tune itself to work within its surroundings.

My interest is in the behavior, rather than in the appearance, of natural systems. In the case of Adaptive Fritting, I am exploring how small movements lead to macroscopic changes. A shift in relative position between the glass layers causes the panel to go from transparent to opaque. Ultimately, physical transformations in organisms occur through the aggregation of many such small movements. –Chuck Hoberman

This 2009 installation at the Harvard Graduate School of Design is based on Chuck Hoberman's invention of "Adaptive Fritting." As with standard fritted glass, this invention utilizes a graphic pattern to control heat gain and modulate light, while allowing sufficient transparency for viewing. But where conventional fritting relies on a fixed pattern, Adaptive Fritting provides a surface-controllable transparency that can modulate between opaque and transparent states. This performance is achieved by shifting a series of fritted glass layers such that the graphic pattern alternately aligns and diverges. The installation consisted of six motorized panels comprising a 24-foot by 4-foot window, housed within a curved wall. These panels were programmed to form a dynamic field where light transmission, views, and enclosure would continuously adapt and change.

The project won the Wyss Prize for Bioinspired Adaptive Architecture from Harvard University's Wyss Institute for Biologically Inspired Engineering. The Institute was launched in 2009 with philanthropic support from Hansjörg Wyss, with the mission of exploring how the principles nature uses to build living things can be applied in the creation of new devices and materials to benefit medicine and the environment.

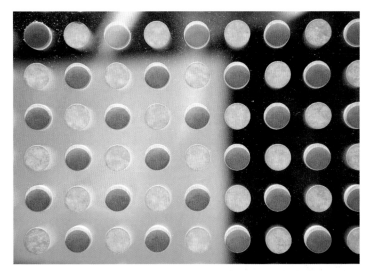

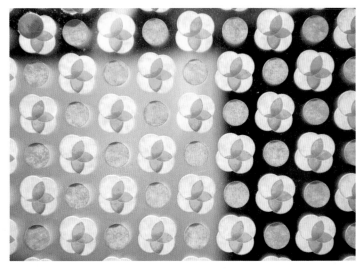

Climate Change, Water, Land Development, and Adaptation: Planning with Uncertainty (Almere, the Netherlands)

Instructors: Armando Carbonell, Martin Zogran, and Dirk Sijmons

Adaptation responses to climate change have been categorized by the Intergovernmental Panel on Climate Change of the United Nations along three modes of action: protect, accommodate, and retreat. These modes are also known by the three "R's" of resistance, resilience, and retreat—terms we have adopted in this studio.[1] Throughout history, and especially following deadly floods in 1953, the Netherlands has taken a near absolutist position on protecting its population from flooding. This is reflected in a level of financial commitment for hard structural defenses against floods that has been compared to the proportion of GDP spent on national defense in the United States, and in recent statements from the Ministry of Transport, Public Works, and Water Management that "The Netherlands is continuing its age-old fight against water." Retreat, in the sense of abandoning built-up areas, is not easily seen as a viable proposition in the Netherlands,

although "Room for the River," a program adopted by the government in 2006, reflects attitudes consistent with resilience that move away from absolute resistance. One might say the Netherlands is poised between two policy impulses, captured by Professor Jerold Kayden in the slogan: "Water is Our Enemy, Water is Our Friend." The research studio explored this shifting policy context for spatial thinking and planning, as climate change raises the stakes for decision makers.

The studio considered the following measures as part of a resilient adaptation strategy in the context of Almere, a rapidly expanding Dutch new town: [2]

1. Work with natural hydrology and propensity for flooding whenever possible and encourage a) building at higher ground with increased residential densities in these areas, and b) promoting

decreased residential densities in lower ground and/or floodable structures in these areas.

2. Restore natural landscapes (e.g., gradual boundaries/ topography between deepwater systems and uplands) with natural processes, whenever possible, for maximum provision of ecosystem services.

3. Implement flood-control disaster preparedness and landscape interventions on a neighborhood scale in existing urbanized areas and primary transportation corridors.

1 This study was sponsored by The Netherlands Ministry of Transport, Public Works, and Water Management and the Ministry of Housing, Spatial Planning, and Environment through Deltares.
2 Adapted from Armando Carbonell and Douglas Meffert, "Climate Change and the Resilience of New Orleans: The Adaptation of Deltaic Urban Form," World Bank, 2009.

Project: Bouchot Mussel Filters, by Jean-Paul Charboneau

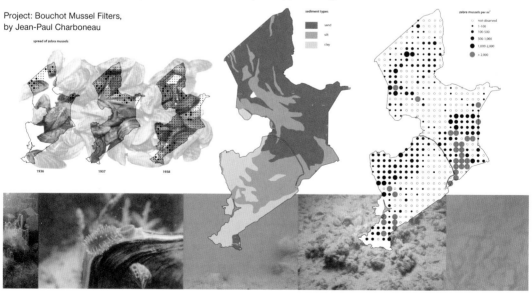

INCUBATE

Balances and Challenges of Integrated Practice
Toshiko Mori

The Luxury of Reduction:
On the Role of Architecture in Ecological Urbanism
Matthias Sauerbruch

Bank of America
Cook+Fox Architects

GSD RESEARCH
A Place in Heaven, A Place in Hell:
Tactical Operations in São Paulo
Christian Werthmann, Fernando de Mello Franco, and Byron Stigge

In Situ: Site Specificity in Sustainable Architecture
Anja Thierfelder and Matthias Schuler

Progetto Bioclimatico
Mario Cucinella

Wangzhuang Eco-city of Agriculture
Arup

Ecosystemic Master Planning, DISEZ Region, Senegal
ecoLogicStudio

Vegetal City: Dreaming the Green Utopia
Luc Schuiten

Verticalism (The Future of the Skyscraper)
Iñaki Ábalos

Urban Prototypes
Raoul Bunschoten

Taiwan Strait Climate Change Incubator
Chora Architecture and Urbanism

Balances and Challenges
of Integrated Practice

Toshiko Mori

Architects must confront the ecological impact of building construction and use when discussing ecological urbanism. In dense urban environments, building construction has become the largest contributor to greenhouse gases. Eighty percent of greenhouse gas emissions in New York and Boston are attributed to building construction, as compared to 20 percent for automobiles.[1] Buildings are responsible for one-third of total energy consumption and two-thirds of electricity use. Up to 40 percent of American landfills are taken up by construction waste.[2] These negative performance statistics have spurred architects and engineers to find integrated and interdisciplinary approaches. I would like to cite examples of my current work that deal with three strategies for integrating ecology and urbanism: optimizing building performance; assessing and improving the quality of the indoor building environment to increase comfort and productivity; and proposing education as infrastructure for the future development of ecological urbanism.

Nature as a lab continually tests and improves its own systems through optimization. Optimization occurs organically in nature, but it is achievable in design only through intense disciplinary integration. We recently completed the Visitor Center for Frank Lloyd Wright's Darwin Martin House, built

View of east façade of Visitor Center for Frank Lloyd Wright's Darwin D. Martin House

in 1905 in Buffalo, New York. The design of the Visitor Center reinterprets Wright's manifesto of principles of organic architecture by optimizing the building performance using highly engineered and integrated technologies. The building is geothermally conditioned through a radiant heating and cooling floor slab, and the air is circulated by natural convection through displacement ventilation. CO_2 sensors monitor building occupancy and adjust air supply accordingly, while solar sensors monitor heat gain and control automatic shades. This optimization was only possible because of the close collaboration with a team of engineers and consultants who were involved in the project from the beginning of the design process.

In discussions of ecology and urbanism, too little consideration is given to the effect of environmental quality. The Syracuse Center of Excellence in Energy and Environmental Systems is an interdisciplinary federation dedicated to proving that better indoor environmental quality improves the health and therefore the productivity of its occupants. Our design for their new headquarters in Syracuse, New York, acts as a living lab for the sustainable technologies being tested at the Center. Through detailed analysis of local climate data, the design proves that it is possible for a building to generate enough energy, electricity, and water for its own use through renewable and alternative sources available on site. The building also tests microclimate control systems, such as individual lighting control, which can increase productivity by 7.1 percent. Likewise, according to current data, ventilation control improves productivity by 1.8 percent, and thermal control by 1.2 percent.[3] Translating improved environmental quality into productivity metrics provides a powerful financial argument

Interior view of Visitor Center

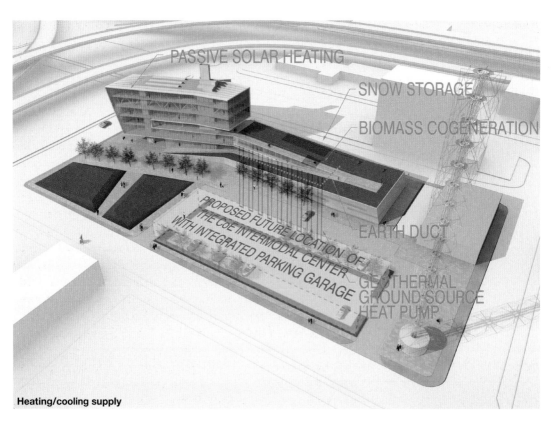

PASSIVE SOLAR HEATING

SNOW STORAGE

BIOMASS COGENERATION

EARTH DUCT

GEOTHERMAL GROUND-SOURCE HEAT PUMP

PROPOSED FUTURE LOCATION OF THE CoE INTERMODAL CENTER WITH INTEGRATED PARKING GARAGE

Heating/cooling supply

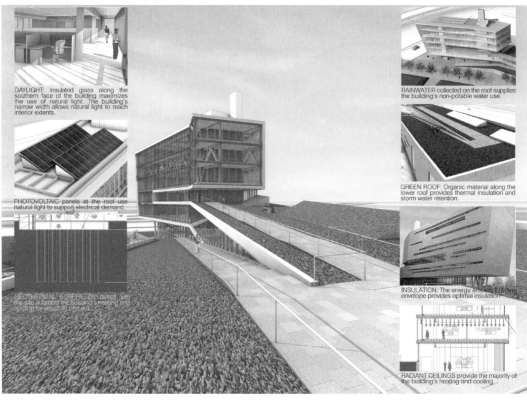

DAYLIGHT: Insulated glass along the southern face of the building maximizes the use of natural light. The building's narrow width allows natural light to reach interior extents.

PHOTOVOLTAIC panels at the roof use natural light to support electrical demand.

GEOTHERMAL BOREFIELDS drilled into the site augment the building's heating and cooling by about 40 percent.

RAINWATER collected on the roof supplies the building's non-potable water use.

GREEN ROOF: Organic material along the lower roof provides thermal insulation and storm water retention.

INSULATION: The energy efficient building envelope provides optimal insulation.

RADIANT CEILINGS provide the majority of the building's heating and cooling.

The Syracuse Center of Excellence in Environmental and Energy Systems Headquarters. The building acts as a living lab for sustainable technologies being tested at the center.

for investing in sustainable and integrated good design, especially in the face of slow policy implementation and lack of adequate financial incentives and fair evaluation methods to measure the long-term value of buildings based on their performance metrics.

I advocate education as the infrastructure for the future development and propagation of sustainable practices. One example of a project that combines social, educational, and ecological missions is our design for a proposed corporate educational campus in Lima, Peru. To support the Peruvian educational system, a private corporation is proposing to provide education for a broad spectrum of the population. This includes basic education for a large number of people from underserved rural areas, vocational training for various trades, continuing education for white-collar workers, and advanced global education for executives. Our design for this corporate education campus consists of vertically stacked, mat-type buildings arranged around courtyards that act as social spaces. Within the campus, the different groups mix and separate within the compound to accommodate the diverse demography while assuring security for a free exchange of ideas. The project maximizes the use of sunlight and takes advantage of the mild weather and prevailing winds

Aerial view of Interbank Corporate University Complex site

View of courtyard

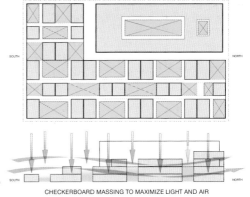

CHECKERBOARD MASSING TO MAXIMIZE LIGHT AND AIR

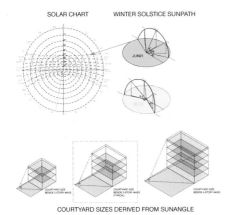

SOLAR CHART   WINTER SOLSTICE SUNPATH

JUN 21

COURTYARD SIZE BESIDE 2-STORY MASS   COURTYARD SIZE BESIDE 3-STORY MASS (TYPICAL)   COURTYARD SIZE BESIDE 4-STORY MASS

COURTYARD SIZES DERIVED FROM SUNANGLE

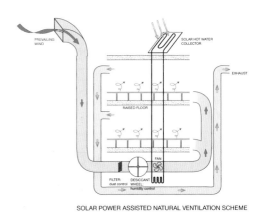

PREVAILING WIND   SOLAR HOT WATER COLLECTOR

EXHAUST

RAISED FLOOR

FAN

FILTER: dust control   DESICCANT WHEEL: humidity control

SOLAR POWER ASSISTED NATURAL VENTILATION SCHEME

OFFICE BUILDING
GROUND TO SEVENTH FLOOR

ADMINISTRATION
THIRD FLOOR

LEADERSHIP CENTER
SECOND & THIRD FLOOR

CLASSROOMS
FIRST FLOOR

TECHNICAL TRAINING
GROUND FLOOR

COMPLEMENTARY FACILITIES
GROUND & B1 FLOOR

RECRUITING CENTER
MEZZANINE FLOOR

COMPUTER CENTER
MEZZANINE FLOOR

PARKING
B5 TO MEZZANINE FLOOR

INCUBATE

Daylighting and natural ventilation is maximized through strategic siting and massing.

The educational complex integrates a range of programs for a diverse population.

for passive ventilation. It uses local climate and natural resources to create a prototype for a large educational infrastructure and a system for integrating a diverse population and program.

Often behavioral change has a much greater impact than expensive technological development, as individual behavior modification compounds over an entire population, cumulating in an exponential wave of change. No matter how much research is devoted to developing sustainable technologies, our natural resources will no longer be able to accommodate our consumer-oriented lifestyles unless people of both developed and developing countries are educated in the benefits and the necessity of sustainable practices and conservation measures. Developed nations need to be educated to accept a more sustainable lifestyle, while developing nations need basic education to empower them with knowledge of health care, social justice, and human rights as a foundation for an approach to ecological urbanism. As each community exists as a unique set of economic, cultural, and ecological circumstances, it is impossible to give a universal "total design" solution, which tends to lead to controlling, totalitarian agendas that endanger human rights. To maintain the unique vibrancy of each urban environment, it is necessary to develop an adaptive and flexible strategy, instead of a uniform and prescriptive solution, for precinct-oriented urban ecology that can operate across multiple scales of events demography. This bottom-up approach at an individual level, coupled with top-down decision making and policy implementation, will create a viable overall balance for a socially sustainable urban environment. It is our ultimate challenge to find an intelligent, sensitive, and sensible ecological solution for future urban environments.

1 *Inventory of New York City Greenhouse Gas Emissions*, Mayor's Office of Long-Term Planning and Sustainability, April 2007; *City of Boston Climate Action Plan Summary*, City of Boston, April 2007.

2 Paul Hawken, Amory Lovins, and L. Hunger Lovins, *Natural Capitalism: Creating the Next Industrial Revolution* (New York: Little Brown, 1999), 94.
3 Gregory H. Kats, "Green Building Costs and Financial Benefits," *Massachusetts Technology Collaborative*, 2003, 6.

The Luxury of Reduction: On the Role of Architecture in Ecological Urbanism

Matthias Sauerbruch

Ecological urbanism is meant to respond to the growing global awareness of limited resources, expanding ecological footprints, and climate change caused by excessive carbon emissions. It is intended to provide a discipline in which a new green paradigm can find its application and physical manifestation in the body of the city. It aims to provide answers to the question of how the global population will match consumption with available resources and how our urban systems will operate in the future, given that, at the beginning of the twenty-first century, a majority of the planet's population lives in cities.

From the perspective of the rich industrialized countries, the task at hand will have to be the drastic reduction of resource and energy consumption as well as carbon emissions. In this way, the first- and the second-world countries (largely responsible for the current situation) might not only repay some of their ecological debt but also demonstrate how to avoid the unnecessary repetition of mistakes. To achieve this, huge changes have to be made; almost every Western government has already committed itself to some kind of reaction, mostly major carbon reductions in the not-too-distant future.

Generally speaking, there are two ways to achieve these ambitious targets: reduce demand and increase efficiency in use—of all resources, but fossil fuels in particular. And in pursuit of these strategies, there are again two theoretical routes: behavioral or instrumental change. In other words, we

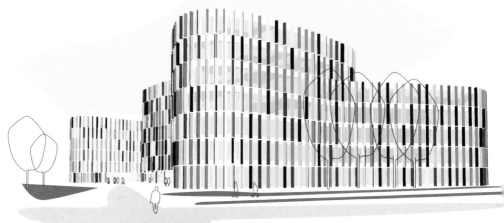

could leave our cities more or less as they are if we were ready to live less carbon-intensive lifestyles—that is, if we would forego unnecessary air travel, feed ourselves on locally grown food, use a bicycle and our feet to move within our cities, accept high summer temperatures in our offices, etc. If we were ready to prioritize the reduction of energy demand in our lives, not much else would have to be done. This would no doubt be the cheapest, most effective, and fastest way to achieve our targets; it would, however, probably bring our economies to a halt. In addition, it would require a cultural revolution, which at present seems difficult to imagine. We have grown accustomed to the amazing amount of choice that has become part of our everyday lives, and we would undoubtedly read such behavioral reform as a reduction in our cherished personal liberties.

The second-best route is to let technology do the job for us. German car manufacturers, for example, are working to develop a carbon-neutral car capable of a speed of 300 kilometers per hour. This is a vision in which technological progress will present us with the best of both worlds: increased personal freedom and an ecologically balanced environment, along with a stable business plan for the foreseeable future.

Many aspects of the city could be addressed by this way of thinking. Almost all infrastructural systems of cities are capable of significant improvement. Traffic can be rationalized, energy generation can (at least partially) be switched to renewable sources. Every urban process can be optimized and every component made more economical. And at best, all of these should be controlled by automated systems. Human intervention ends up being the only factor that prevents the systems from performing to specification.

Such a total systemization of our lives, however, is not what cities are about. Historically the city has been associated with liberation from the yoke of feudal oppression. In modern times, it has provided an increase in choice and a certain political, economic, social, and cultural intensity. The city always offered more things to do and people to meet; it beckoned with the potential of a place where the confluence of ambition and ingenuity with power and mass develop its own unforeseeable dynamic.

Today some of these myths are still alive. The city is still the favorite place to live, partly because of its economic pull, but partly—and this is particularly true for Western countries—because it is a desirable place to be. Both the social and cultural potential are strong attractors for people who are looking for opportunity and inspiration. And given that most cities do not depend on major industries these days, they have

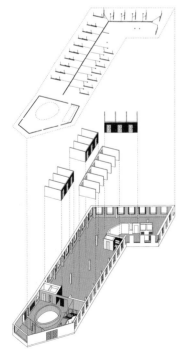

become more of a total habitat than ever before. That is, the traditional distinction of city versus country, work versus leisure, civilization versus nature, or even the modern trisection of work, leisure, and living have merged into one place where everything is potentially happening at the same time.

If anything, the city is about maximization of mental and sensual stimuli rather than the spirit of reduction. The city is about liberation rather than control of people's behavior and hence may not be the most likely venue for ecological correctness. Or to reverse the argument: too much ecological goodwill could easily destroy the essential qualities that make cities so attractive.

To implement change in the city is realistically going to be a question of multiple strategies that might even be contradictory at times. A combination of legislation and incentive might bring about new behavioral patterns (as in the congestion charge in London), and updated technologies (such as wind and solar power) will help to reduce carbon emissions. At the same time, the city will have to perform as a habitat, developing a combination of ecological efficiency and the qualities of a place one might want to call home.

In all of this, architecture has to work like some kind of user interface. Cities are made of houses, which determine physical contact with visitors and inhabitants alike. So if you want to change the city, you may as well start by changing its architecture. In this, a house can act like a microcosm, as it can certainly subscribe to the double agenda of reduce and improve. There is a lot of potential efficiency in the way buildings are designed, in terms of both their layout and their construction. And as far as the improvement of service technology is concerned, a whole industry is banking on the increase in energy efficiency it can offer with every generation of equipment it puts on the market.

Most of all, though, buildings must act as the manifestations of the transformation of which they are meant to be part.

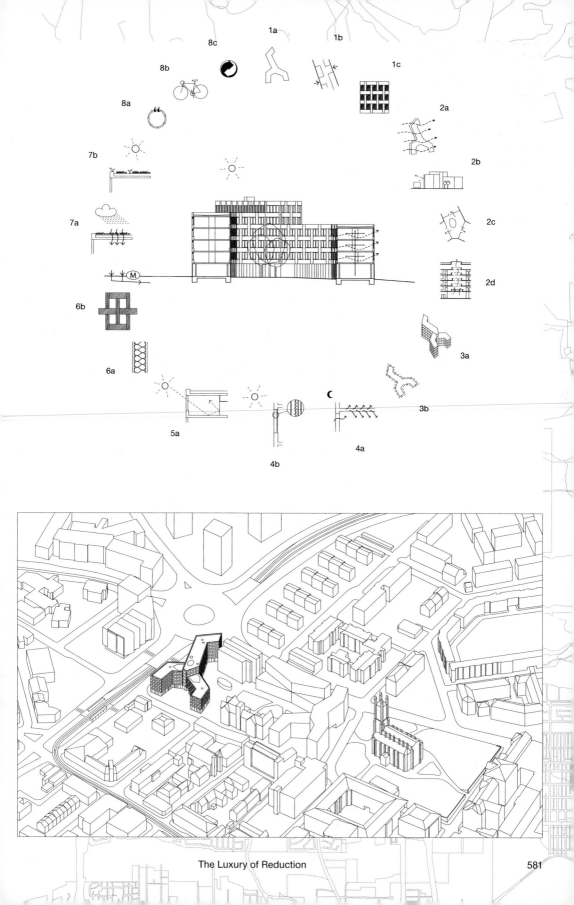

The Luxury of Reduction

The building repairs the urban fabric by reinforcing the existing street system. As a perimeter building that defines these street edges, it forms a strongly delineated exterior and a protected inner area. Supporting pedestrianization, Jessop West creates a generous entrance area off the main campus route as well as from the west.

Sheffield University—existing

Proposal for a public space at the heart of the university campus

In terms of general massing, Jessop West has been conceived to fit in the existing context.

Main Branch of the Municipal Savings Bank Oberhausen, 2004–2007. The interior of this space is oriented along the idea of a "green city" where vegetation is as important as the built form: the space of the branch is made up of a sequence of "floating" rectangular planes and volumes; six large glass "vases" planted with bamboo bring daylight into the depth of the space.

They are to communicate the big shift in paradigm that will (it is hoped) be the hallmark of this century. They have to convince, seduce, and enthuse people to become the willing protagonists of change, and they have to demonstrate a certain can-do mentality through their own credibility. If they are reliable performers, this will be the best propaganda for ecological reform. In this, technology is probably the weakest part—despite its iconographic popularity. For one thing, most mechanical and electronic components in houses have a tendency to go wrong. They are made by humans and are just as

fallible. Second, complex maintenance is necessary, which is often forgotten in the equation. Third and most important, the promise of technology offers the end-user the opportunity to delegate his or her responsibilities to the machine. Buying a hybrid car or putting solar panels on your roof mostly relieves a bad conscience, but does not necessarily make a significant contribution. Instead the problem is literally instrumentalized, put into a seemingly quantifiable logic and considered apart from one's own being.

For buildings to become agents of change, they have to engage the user with their whole physicality. They have to demonstrate a respectful relationship to the natural environment and a certain economy in their use of resources, but at the same time they have to celebrate the joy of being. Sustainable architecture has to be considered as the sensual environment in which one wants to spend most of one's life, while it also has to demonstrate the economy mentioned above. To me, the oxymoron of simultaneous moderation and delight seems to suggest a quasi-Epicurean approach of an intelligent modesty that is the natural consequence of a total embrace of life.

Buildings unquestionably have a crucial role, but it is also clear that they are only one of the tools required to achieve the desired goals. The key to success has to remain with the city as a whole and its many infrastructures. It is the city that offers the economies of scale and thus the more significant energy reductions. It is also the city that provides the social environment so attractive to so many. Buildings cannot be conceived without considering a constructive role in the community, yet cities will only be the locations of great sensual and aesthetic pleasure and therefore sustainability if buildings play their appropriate part.

The Municipal Savings Bank is part of the overall plan for the metamorphosis of Oberhausen to a "Park City."

Bank of America

Cook+Fox Architects

Located across from Bryant Park in midtown Manhattan, the Bank of America Tower combines innovative design and advanced technologies to create a high-performance work environment that uses energy intelligently, consumes far less water, and, it is hoped, raises the profile of green design in the United States. The building is expected to receive LEED Platinum certification from the U.S. Green Building Council, making it the first high-rise office building to earn this honor and one of the most environmentally responsible buildings in the world.

The design of the tower was guided by a vision of creating a healthy, daylit work environment that would help the Bank attract and retain the best employees. A highly transparent floor-to-ceiling glass façade fills offices with daylight and connects occupants with the urban and natural context, reinforcing a concept known as biophilia. Behind the scenes, state-of-the art technologies including an under-floor ventilation system, a 4.6-megawatt cogeneration plant, a thermal storage system, and graywater recycling combine to conserve energy and reduce water usage by nearly 50 percent. As a project that explores new ways of thinking about high-rise design, the Bank of America Tower demonstrates how buildings can make a difference in New York City and beyond.

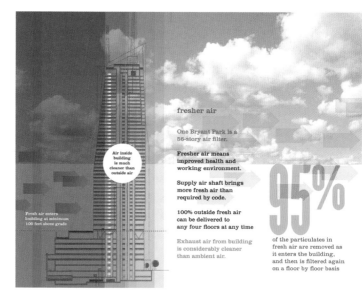

fresher air

One Bryant Park is a 56-story air filter.

Fresher air means improved health and working environment.

Supply air shaft brings more fresh air than required by code.

100% outside fresh air can be delivered to any four floors at any time

Exhaust air from building is considerably cleaner than ambient air.

Air inside building is much cleaner than outside air

Fresh air enters building at minimum 100 feet above grade

95%

of the particulates in fresh air are removed as it enters the building, and then is filtered again on a floor by floor basis

© Doyle Partners for Cook + Fox Architects LLP

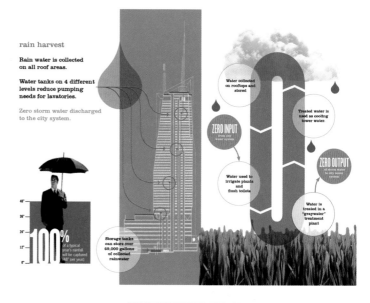

rain harvest

Rain water is collected on all roof areas.

Water tanks on 4 different levels reduce pumping needs for lavatories.

Zero storm water discharged to the city system.

Water collected on rooftops and stored

ZERO INPUT
from city water system

Treated water is used as cooling tower water.

Water used to irrigate plants and flush toilets

Water is treated in a "graywater" treatment plant

ZERO OUTPUT
of storm water to city sewer system

100%
of a typical year's rainfall will be captured ("48" per year)

Storage tanks can store over 69,000 gallons of collected rainwater

EXAMPLES OF REGIONALLY SOURCED MATERIALS

● MANUFACTURING LOCATION
● HARVESTING/EXTRACTION LOCATION

1 STRUCTURAL STEEL (Columbia, SC)
2 CURTAIN WALL (Montreal, CA/Windsor, CT)
3 CONCRETE (Port Chester, NY)
4 BATHROOM COUNTERTOPS (Brooklyn, NY)
5 QUARRIED STONE: JET MIST, IMPERIAL DANBY, CHAMPLAIN MIST (various locations in Vermont)
6 STONE FABRICATION (PARTIAL) (Patterson, NJ/Bronx, NY)
7 MILLWORK (Jamaica, NY)
8 ACCESS FLOORING (Red Lion, PA)
9 GYPSUM WALLBOARD (Shippingport, PA)

INCUBATE

Bank of America

A Place in Heaven/A Place in Hell: Tactical Operations in São Paulo

Instructors: Christian Werthmann, Fernando de Mello Franco, and Byron Stigge

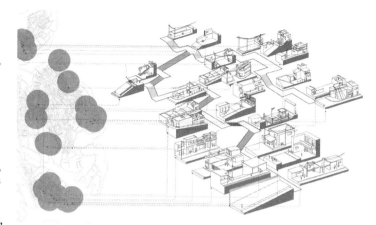

A new type of infrastructure will unfold in the public space of favelas, challenging landscape architects to develop socially and environmentally effective spaces in extremely dense conditions.[1] Leapfrogging informal cities to a more environmentally sound position will require rethinking the design process: knowledge will have to be expanded, new technologies tested, prototypes built; an intense collaborative process among a new generation of environmentally literate engineers, social workers, and design professionals must be fostered. The test site at hand was chosen because it is one of the most striking examples of complex environmental and infrastructural conditions. The 30,000-person favela of Cantinho do Céu in the far south of São Paulo, Brazil, was built on a large, illegally clear-cut area of intact rainforest in a no-build zone directly adjacent to the largest reservoir serving the metropolis. It is a case where the interest of the city in maintaining clean drinking water is diametrically opposed to the interests of the population of Cantinho do Céu, who need a place to live and would like to stay in the homes they have built. Can these two conflicting uses be reconciled? Can Cantinho do Céu be developed as a healthy city next to a biologically intact lake?

1 This text is adapted from the essay "The Challenge," from the studio publication *A Place in Heaven. A Place in Hell. Tactical Operations in São Paulo's Informal Sector*, edited by Christian Werthmann (São Paulo: São Paulo Housing Agency, 2009).

Peer-to-Peer Open Spaces: Playscapes in São Paulo's Informal Sector, by Andrew tenBrink

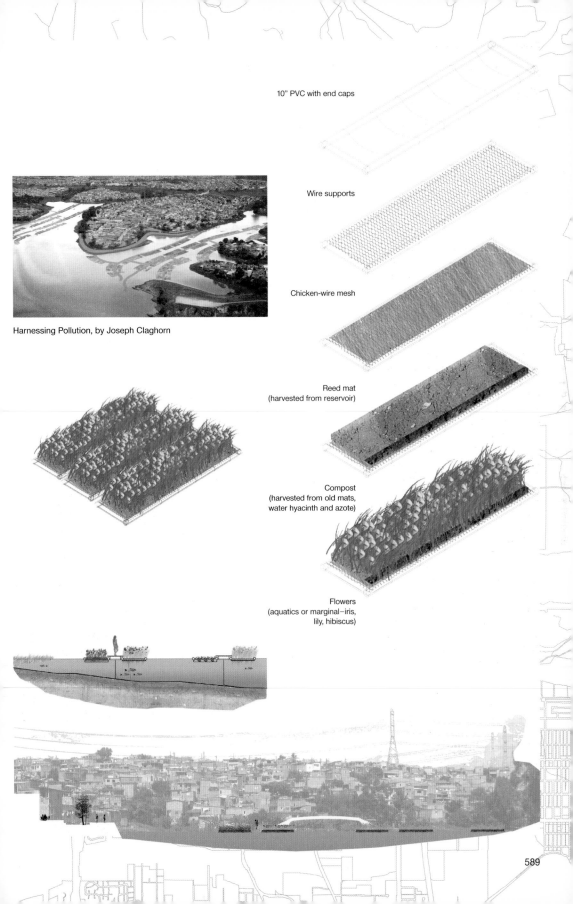

10" PVC with end caps

Wire supports

Chicken-wire mesh

Reed mat
(harvested from reservoir)

Compost
(harvested from old mats,
water hyacinth and azote)

Flowers
(aquatics or marginal–iris,
lily, hibiscus)

Harnessing Pollution, by Joseph Claghorn

In Situ: Site Specificity in Sustainable Architecture

Anja Thierfelder and Matthias Schuler

Genius Loci

Architecture doesn't exist in a vacuum. It comes into being in sites with unique characteristics. The Norwegian architect and architectural critic Christian Norberg-Schulz, convinced of the inadequacy of using analytical, scholarly terms to describe architecture, published his phenomenology of architecture, *Genius Loci,* in 1980.[1] For him, a place is always a whole consisting of concrete things with material substance, form, surface, and color—a qualitative overall phenomenon with its own atmosphere and character. Understanding this is the precondition for finding a foothold for design in a given space.

In the 1980s and 1990s, there was little mention of genius loci, but now, with people gradually becoming jaded by globalization and the international uniformity following it, the term is surfacing in international architectural discourse along with words like *identity* and *rootedness.* In 2005, for example, Jean Nouvel complained, in his *Louisiana Manifesto,* that architecture, more than ever, is annihilating places, banalizing them, violating them. The global economy is accentuating the effects of the dominant architecture, which claims, "We don't need context." Nouvel talks about a struggle between the partisans of situational architecture and the profiteers of decontextualized architecture.

> We must establish sensitive, poetic rules, approaches, that will speak of colors, essences, characters, ... the specificities of the rain, wind, sea and mountain.... The ideology of the specific aspires to autonomy, to the use of the resources of the place and the time, to the privileging of the non-material. How can we use what is here and nowhere else? How can we differentiate without caricaturing? How can we achieve depth? ... Architecture means transformation, organizing the mutations of what is already there.... Architecture should be seen as the modification of a physical, atomic, biological continuum.... Architecture means the adaption of the condition of a place to a given time by the willpower, desire, and knowledge of certain human beings. We never do this alone.[2]

Norberg-Schulz and Nouvel agree; both refer to the genius loci, the spirit of a place, as the point of departure for meaningful, independent, site-specific architecture.

As climate engineers, we start each project with measurements of the unique climate data for each site. Determining and analyzing site characteristics is the prerequisite for all subsequent decisions. Our site analysis, however, does not end here. We are also trying to determine the *genius* of the place. What potentials do the site and its surroundings hold? How can they be used to the advantage of the building project in the most creative and effective ways? What special features do they suggest? What features of the site need to be preserved? What improvements would be worthwhile? What interventions are likely to produce what consequences?

Projects

Mining Water:
Zollverein School, Essen, Germany, SANAA

From 1851 until 1986, hard coal was mined at the Zeche Zollverein to provide energy for steel production in the Ruhr Valley. Today, even twenty-two years after the mining has stopped, water continues to be pumped out of its galleries (which can extend to depths of 1,000 meters) to keep the mine accessible for possible later reuse. The mine water, pumped at a flow rate of 600 m³/h, has a year-round temperature of approximately 29 °C/82 °F. The climate in Essen is moderate, with temperatures seldom dropping below freezing or rising above 30 °C/86 °F.

As part of extensive reorganization efforts in the Ruhr region, the Zollverein School was created at the edge of the Zeche Zollverein. SANAA won the international architectural competition with a simple concrete cube featuring distinctive window openings. By using mining water, the area's unique energy source, it was possible to realize the architectural idea of thin monolithic concrete walls with a thickness of only 30 centimeters/12 inches. This was the beginning of a totally new concept: "active insulation." Inside the concrete

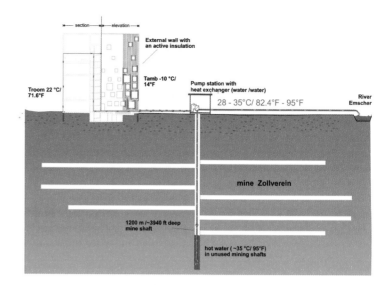

wall, plastic pipes conduct the warm mining water, thus heating the wall. This "active" insulation has to ensure that its inner surface temperature is above 18 °C/64 °F, within the comfort range for a heated environment. The design took into consideration the fact that the system is losing approximately 80 percent of its heat to the environment through the uninsulated external surface, but because the energy source was free and CO_2 neutral, this "waste" did not matter. The monolithic wall construction, even with the integrated piping system, was much cheaper than a double-shell concrete wall and would save more money than was paid for the mining water system. Thus it was possible to realize a geothermal system for the Zollverein School, whereas a similar system was rejected for a neighboring building where there were no savings to cover the high investment costs.

Based on the idea of using the free renewable-energy potential of the mining water, the concept proposes to add a heat exchanger at the surface point of the mining shaft, using part of the water flow to heat up a secondary water circuit that then delivers heat as a district heat source to the Zollverein School. This separation is necessary due to the low water quality of the mining water. The heat exchanger has to be easy to maintain to ensure proper functioning and prevent clogging. Water analysis and material tests have to be conducted before building starts to ensure that the system works. This project, responsive to local mining traditions, has a strong connection to its site. Its unique energy solution is only possible at this school. Its concept has already created ideas for the further use of the mining water as a local CO_2-free energy source.

Urban Island:
Masdar City Master Plan, Abu Dhabi, Foster and Partners

Abu Dhabi, the capital of the United Arab Emirates, is located on the Persian Gulf, which due to its shallowness heats up along the shore to around 35 °C/95 °F in the summer; daytime sea breezes push warm and humid winds into the city from the northwest. Therefore the city has a very hot—up to 47 °C/116 °F—and humid climate in summer. Prior to air conditioning, the location was used only during late fall, winter, and spring for the pearl diving business. During the summer, people moved to Al Ain in the mountains to escape the humidity (but not the heat). Nevertheless, during six months of the year, outdoor conditions are comfortable and allow inhabitants to leave their windows open.

Masdar Development, the vision of the UAE government to build the world's first carbon-neutral city, sited here at one of the sunniest places on the planet, had to take into consideration these conditions as well as the high solar gains (2,000–2,200 kWh/m²a). Although outdoor comfort has been ignored in the rest of contemporary Abu Dhabi, with its wide avenues on which pedestrians almost faint before they reach the other side of a street, good urban development requires it.

The master plan, based on several analytical computer evaluations and wind-tunnel models, proposes narrow streets to protect against the sweltering heat and to keep the street spaces cooler than those outside the city. In limiting street length and influencing street orientation, the "cold island" of Masdar reinterprets traditional local wind towers, ventilating street spaces at night and protecting them against the hot summer winds during the day. "Green fingers" reach through the city from northwest to east to allow for basic ventilation and to catch the cooler east winds. All these efforts ensure that the thermal and visual comfort of the city spaces have a positive direct impact on building loads.

Lake and Soil:
Linked Hybrid Building, Beijing, Steven Holl Architects

China needs many new high-quality apartments in its city centers. Environmental damage, as a price of economic growth and limited energy resources, has pushed the country to initiate strong efforts to construct energy-efficient buildings. The site for the Linked Hybrid project is the northeast corner of the third ring in Beijing. In the immediate neighborhood, project developer Modern Group has already built and sold two sustainable residential towers that set the ecological standard in the area.

The project has 750 apartments for 2,500 people in eight residential towers built around a central public land/waterscape with a large pond. Residents can access semiprivate spaces (spa, pool, health club, art gallery, and café) in bridges connecting the towers on their twenty-third floors. Thus the security demands of the inhabitants are met without building a "gated city." The pond, symbolizing the element of water,

an important resource in Beijing, uses gray water from the apartments to minimize water consumption.

Beijing's mean outdoor temperature of 12 °C/53.6 °F allows the ground to be used as a natural heating and cooling source. For this purpose, 600 boreholes will be drilled, each 300 feet deep, to serve as heat sinks or heat sources, and sometimes as direct cooling sources. To make this work, the external loads had to be minimized by increasing the insulation level in walls and windows, employing external shading devices for exposed façades, and installing operable windows and a central ventilation unit. To take advantage of the natural ground temperature range of 59° to 63 °F, a slab cooling system with embedded pipes in the exposed concrete ceilings was installed for basic air conditioning. Because cooling demand is greater than heating demand in Beijing, the geothermal heating and cooling system would lead to an increase of soil temperatures over several years. To allow for an energy balance, the soil is naturally cooled in the spring through the boreholes, using the 7,800-square-meter lake surface as a natural recooling unit.

Ornament and Light Filter:
Louvre Abu Dhabi, Abu Dhabi, Atelier Jean Nouvel

On Saadiyat Island off of Abu Dhabi, the rulers of the United Arab Emirates decided to build a cultural city with four museums and a complex for the performing arts. The special demands of a project in Abu Dhabi, with its hot and humid summer, are described in the description of the Masdar project. The strong summer solar gains with high sun positions demand shading and light filtering, which have a long tradition in Middle Eastern building history. At the oasis, the

center of life in a desert region, palm trees always formed the first shading and filtering layer below which other plants and outdoor life gathered.

Atelier Jean Nouvel was contracted to design the Louvre Abu Dhabi, with strong connections to thirteen French museums including the Louvre, Centre Pompidou, and Quai Branly, on a site along the seashore.

The project design creates an artificial island with single cubes for the museum and connected programs. All of these, along with large outdoor piazzas, are covered by a large flat dome that floats roughly 9 meters above the street and even extends out over the sea. An ornamental perforation of the dome allows it to limit the solar gains on the whole project, creating "a rain of light" that changes its pattern depending on the position of the sun. The intention is to create a microclimate below the dome where the outdoor piazza is not mechanically conditioned but uses natural cooling sources such as the ground, the sea, or nighttime radiation in combination with thermal mass to improve outdoor conditions. During hot periods, airflow through the dome must be controlled. This is strongly influenced by the suction effect of the wind passing over the dome and the placement of temporary windbreaks outside or below the dome. The aim is to allow visitors to enjoy the space below the dome as an environment that contrasts sharply with the bright and hot outside space.

Outlook

Sustainability in architecture becomes more effective the more closely it is tied to a place. What else can be inferred? Starting out decades ago as the ideological concern of a small group in Central Europe, sustainability is now a worldwide focus. Former Vice President Al Gore received the Nobel Peace Prize for his eye-opening film on climate change. Many prominent American actors are promoting environmental projects ranging from saving the rainforests to creating eco-cosmetics. Hundreds of products—including gas-efficient cars, plant-based household detergents, fair-trade designer cotton clothing made in Africa, eco fast-food meals using only local produce, briefcases made from recycled tractor inner tubes, biodegradable slippers made in India from coconut fiber and natural latex—advertise their sustainability. Ecological awareness and action are increasingly part of corporate identities.

In 2000, Paul H. Ray and Ruth Anderson coined the term LOHAS (people with Lifestyles of Health and Sustainability) in their *Cultural Creatives*.[3] According to the *New York Times*, eco-buyers constitute the world's fastest growing consumer group. A study on consumer ethics conducted in 2007 by Trend-büro Hamburg reveals that this group tends to pamper itself rather than trying to improve the world; its approach to ethics derives more from aesthetics.[4] LOHAS do not regard pleasure and environmentalism as mutually exclusive. For LOVOS (people with Lifestyles of Voluntary Simplicity), in contrast, these poles are irreconcilable. They believe that the integration of ecological goals with "lifestyle" preoccupations is contradictory, halfhearted, and inconsistent; they believe that it is better to reduce consumption, renounce all that is unnecessary, and live life in a new way. Peter Sloterdijk, currently the most popular philosopher in the German-speaking world, shares this stance in his newest book, *Du mußt dein Leben ändern. Über Religion, Artistik und Anthropotechnik* (You Must Change Your Life [echoing poet Rainer Maria Rilke's "Archaic Torso of Apollo"]: On Anthropotechnology).[5]

What is the future of sustainability? Is it just a phase, another trend that will prompt a backlash? One thing is certain: attention to the subjects introduced by the green movement— climate change, overpopulation, limited resources, pollution, disappearance of species, and more—isn't just a passing fad; these concerns are driven by hard facts that we cannot avoid dealing with in the future.

1 Christian Norberg-Schulz, *Genius Loci: Towards a Phenomenology of Architecture* (New York: Rizzoli, 1991).
2 Jean Nouvel, *Jean Nouvel: Louisiana Manifeste,* edited by Michael Juul Holm (Øresund, Denmark: Louisiana Museum of Modern Art, 2006).

3 *Cultural Creatives: How 50 Million People Are Changing the World* (New York: Harmony Books, 2000).
4 Trendbüro Hamburg, www.trendbuero. de/index.php?f_categoryId=166&f_page=1, OTTO Trendstudie Konsum-ethik 2007.
5 *Du mußt dein Leben ändern: Über Religion, Artistik und Anthropotechnik* (Frankfurt: Suhrkamp, 2009).

Progetto Bioclimatico

Mario Cucinella

| | ENVIRONMENTAL ANALYSIS | STRATEGIES_ |

SUN

SOLAR RADIATION
Significant potential, especially in summer.

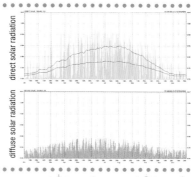

direct solar radiation

diffuse solar radiation

PASSIVE SOLAR DESIGN
Optimum orientation of the building façade according to the sun path diagram and shadow analysis. Maximization of winter solar gains. Minimization of summer solar gains with shading system.

AIR

WIND ENERGY POTENTIAL
The prevailing wind direction is NE-SW. The average wind speed on the ground level is approximately 3–4 meters/second.

HUMIDITY
In the summer months, during the day the relative humidity is quite high, on average 60%–70%.

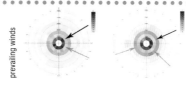

prevailing winds

relative humidity

VENTILATION
The orientation of the building and surrounding vegetation encourages the channeling summer nighttime breezes.

WIND ENERGY
Insertion of vertical-axis wind turbines on the building roof to take advantage of the wind energy at a high point above ground level.

WATER

WATER RESOURCES
The water resources in the project area are notable. There is the Foglia river and other canals for agricultural cultivation, while the ground water is at a depth of 10 meters.

RAINWATER
There is modest rainfall in the project area.

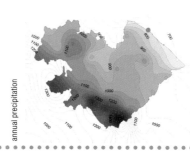

annual precipitation

RAINWATER COLLECTION
Water can be reused after process of filtration.
CONSTRUCTED WETLAND
A subsurface filtration system integrating vegetation for the recuperation of used water from the sanitary system.
MICROCLIMATE CONTROL
Humidification of the air in external spaces during summer to reduce the temperature of the outside air.

GROUND

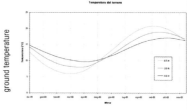

POOR AIR QUALITY
The project area is densely populated and is compromised by the industries and agricultural cultivation in the immediate vicinity.

THERMAL INERTIA
In order to maximize energy efficiency and reduce energy demand, the plant takes advantage of the huge thermal inertia of the ground.

ground temperature

BIODIVERSITY
Renaturalization of the outdoor spaces with the insertion of new plant species and diversification of the green layout.
Creation of green barriers excludes visual and sound pollution while ensuring continuity of green corridors.
COMBINED HEAT AND POWER PLANT
Eventual definition of a zone for a central biomass energy plant.

STRATEGIES_architectonic scale

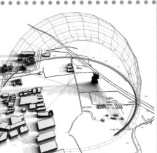

SOLAR SHADING
Reduction of incident solar gains on external transparent surfaces in the summer period and maximization of solar gains in winter. Natural light is taken advantage of as far as possible for illumination of the internal environment.

ACTIVE SOLAR SYSTEMS
Photovoltaic Solar Panels_production of electrical energy.
Solar Thermal_production of hot water for sanitary use and winter heating.
Solar cooling_production of cold air for summer cooling.

NIGHT COOLING
Passive nighttime ventilation mediates the internal environment with fresh cool air.

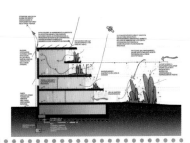

RECUPERATION OF USED WATER
Water from toilets and w.c is collected for successive purification and filtration through a constructed wetland filtration system.

MICROCLIMATE CONTROL
Minimization of the overheating risk of the interiors by humidification of external inlet air. It lowers the temperature of inlet air using water vapor.

recuperation of rainwater

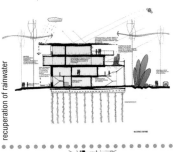

GROUND SOURCE HEAT PUMP WITH GEOTHERMAL LOOPS AND/OR WATER SOURCE HEAT PUMP
In winter a ground source heat pump extracts heat from the ground outside to provide heat energy for the interior. In summer the heat transfer is inverted, and the plant removes hot air from the interior to the ground outside.

GROUND COOLING
Potential system of a heat exchanger for pre-heating/cooling of the air. It takes advantage of the thermal inertia of the ground.

ground source heat pump

Wanzhuang Eco-city of Agriculture

Arup

The proposed new eco-city of Wanzhuang, China, is located on an 80-kilometer-square site to the west of Langfang, halfway between Beijing and the port city of Tianjin. The eco-city is expected to accommodate a resident population of more than 330,000 by 2025. Wanzhuang offers a vision of a thriving sustainable community, combining robust economic growth, social inclusion, and culturally rich, healthy living.

Essential to the future success of Wanzhuang is a low-carbon infrastructure and an ecologically sound platform for clean industrial development and economic growth. Wanzhuang will be positioned as an attractive business location with opportunities in clean manufacturing, information technology, and agriculture. The aim is that the unique cultural character and heritage, agricultural base, and fifteen existing villages of Wanzhuang (with 30,000 current residents) will not be eroded or lost, but rather enhanced through sympathetic development. By mixing agriculture with the city, the developers hope that the successful development of Wanzhuang will offer a new way to address China's urban-rural gap and provide a model for harmonious urbanization.

常规案例用地（现有规划）
BUSINESS-AS-USUAL DEVELOPMENT
(EXISTING PLAN)

生态城占地
ECO-CITY DEVELOPMENT

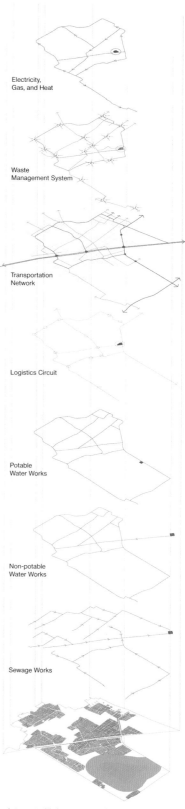

Electricity,
Gas, and Heat

Waste
Management System

Transportation
Network

Logistics Circuit

Potable
Water Works

Non-potable
Water Works

Sewage Works

Integrated Infrastructural System

INCUBATE

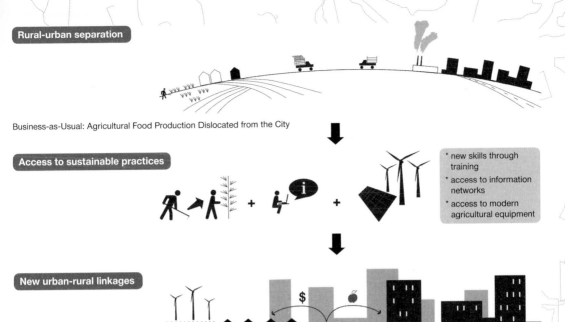

Business-as-Usual: Agricultural Food Production Dislocated from the City

Access to sustainable practices

* new skills through training
* access to information networks
* access to modern agricultural equipment

New urban-rural linkages

Eco-city Configuration: Sustainable Rural-Urban Linkage

Wanzhuang Eco-city of Agriculture

Sustainable Industries

95% of the jobs created and/or offered will be associated with low-impact or sustainable industries

Energy Production and Use

Electricity demand

Wanzhuang is designed to source **100%** of its electricity from renewable sources

North China electricity grid network obtains **7%** of its electricity from renewable sources

Typical baseline building energy demand

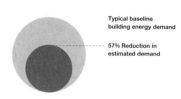

Typical baseline building energy demand

57% Reduction in estimated demand

Water Management

Expected potable water consumption
(for industrial, residential and commercial purposes / excluding agricultural)

water consumption

100% B.a.U. expected demand

69% Expected eco-city demand

Agricultural water consumption
(percentage of agricultural water demand met by non-potable sources)

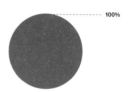

100%

Waste Management

Waste recovery
(Recycled, reused, composted, or turned into energy)

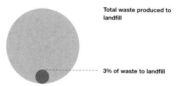

Total waste produced to landfill

3% of waste to landfill

Local waste recovery
(within project area)

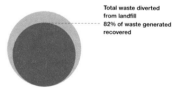

Total waste diverted from landfill
82% of waste generated recovered

Transport and Accessibility

Modal share
(Car, public transport, cycle, walking)

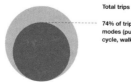

Total trips

74% of trips using non-car modes (public transport, cycle, walking)

Dwellings within 3 to 5 minutes of cycle paths or bus stops

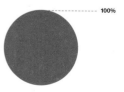

100%

INCUBATE

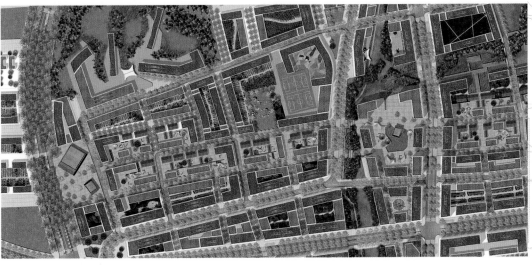

Wanzhuang Eco-city of Agriculture

Ecosystemic Master Planning, DISEZ Region, Senegal

ecoLogicStudio

Responding to the brief of a long-term urbanization plan for this rural region of Senegal, this work has focused on the exploration of systemic planning strategies and urban development methods. The Dakar Integrated Special Economic Zone (DISEZ) region has been framed through managerial regions differentiated by topographic condition and ecologic potential. The main aim has been to develop a series of strategic pilot projects or catalytic prototypes within these frameworks, turning the sites into models for the generation of a larger urban co-action plan. The project of the regional eco-plan is generated through the interaction of three main components, addressing different levels of complexity:

– strategic diagramming (definition of specific territorial relationships that will set up the intentions of the projects)
– mapping (identification of environmental and social dynamics on site)
– prototyping (development of a toolbox of specific prototypes or pilot projects responding to the identified dynamics)

Pilot projects can be identified for each topographic region; the collective of prototypes has interacted at different levels, tracing the lines of a single systematically defined eco-plan.

[AF] Algae Farm is a new type of energy plant that synthesizes landscape qualities with sociocultural training and renewable energy production. The prototype integrates a research center focused on bio-energies and training facilities for locals.

[AR] African Roundabout is a prototype roundabout that integrates the local tradition of organizing villages and paths in concentric circles around baobab trees. It will allow a more intense dialogue between the new fabric and the strong element in the landscape.

[GB] Green Belts have been adopted in London to frame urbanization in areas of flat land. Here the type is hybridized with functions of waste processing and energy generation (bio-digesters will process organic waste while paper, plastic, metals, and glass will be collected and recycled separately).

Water-flow patterns simulation: rain basins and water channels are mapped across the landscape using a particle flow technique.

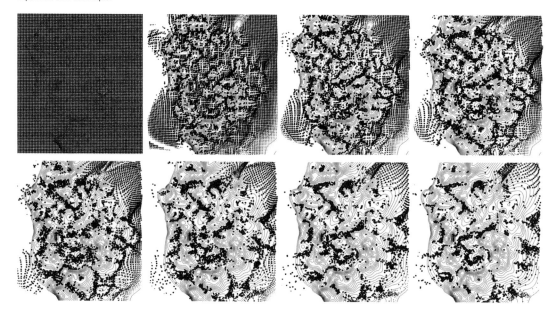

Senegalese village from satellite

Schematic of layout logic

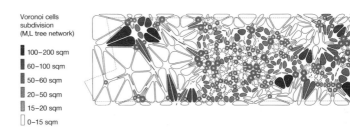

Voronoi cells
subdivision
(M,L tree network)

■ 100–200 sqm
■ 60–100 sqm
■ 50–60 sqm
■ 20–50 sqm
■ 15–20 sqm
□ 0–15 sqm

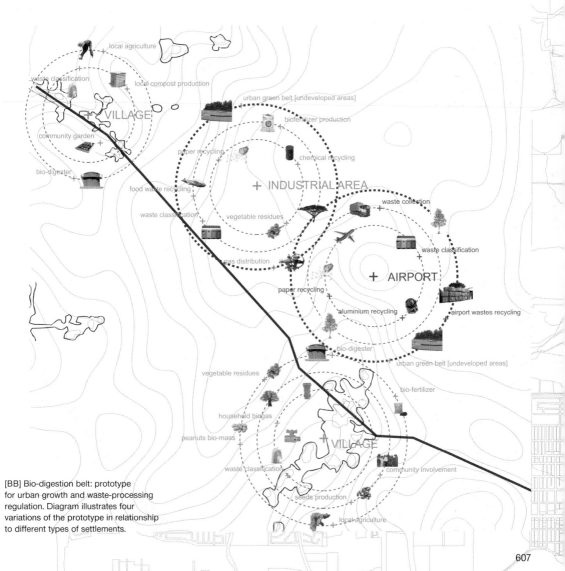

local agriculture

waste classification

local compost production

VILLAGE

urban green belt [undeveloped areas]

biofertilizer production

community garden

paper recycling

chemical recycling

bio-digester

INDUSTRIAL AREA

food waste recycling

waste collection

waste classification

vegetable residues

waste classification

gas distribution

AIRPORT

waste classification

paper recycling

aluminium recycling

airport wastes recycling

bio-digester

urban green belt [undeveloped areas]

vegetable residues

bio-fertilizer

household biogas

peanuts bio-mass

VILLAGE

community involvement

waste classification

seeds production

local agriculture

[BB] Bio-digestion belt: prototype
for urban growth and waste-processing
regulation. Diagram illustrates four
variations of the prototype in relationship
to different types of settlements.

Vegetal City: Dreaming the Green Utopia

Luc Schuiten

1900

1950

Since the late 1970s, Luc Schuiten (b. Brussels, 1944) has developed a body of work based on his personal understanding of architecture as a living system where the logics of the element (the cell) are translated, in a net of growing complexity, to the design of the house and the city. For over thirty years, starting with his idea of the *habitarbre* ("inhabi-tree"), Schuiten has explored new ways to reformulate the relationship between man and dwelling, building and environment, city and landscape. Through his concept of *archiborescence* (architecture + arborescence), his early projects for *maisons biosolaires* (bio-solar houses) and *habitarbres* evolved into the design of "archiborescent cities," visionary projects where the vegetalistic style of his houses became a reflection on the possibilities of the fusion between city and natural ecosystems.

As a counterpart to the increasingly technified approach to the design of the architecture and the city of the future, *Vegetal City* offers a biological vision of the organization, form, and materiality of the future city that introduces the utopian twist of the 1960s in the ecologically concerned panorama of the new millennium.

Excerpted from a Spring 2009 exhibition at the Harvard Graduate School of Design, curated by Aude-Line Duliere and Luis Miguel Lus Arana; text by Luis Miguel Lus Arana.

1800

1900

vegetal city
a vision by Luc Schuiten

vege
a vis

2050

2100

2150

2150

Evolution of a Street, 1900–2150

As a counterpart to the overall architectural view offered by the evolution of Laeken, these images illustrate the point of view of the pedestrian, witness to the progressive changes on the urban scene, in a resolutely optimistic perspective of a long-lasting future.

2100

2200

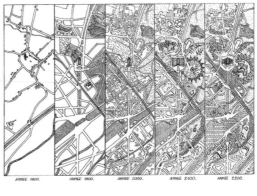

ANNÉE 1800.   ANNÉE 1900.   ANNÉE 2000.   ANNÉE 2100.   ANNÉE 2200.

vegetal city
a vision by Luc Schuiten

vegetal city
a vision by Luc Schuiten

Verticalism
(The Future of the Skyscraper)

Iñaki Abalos

Modern architects thought of the skyscraper in terms of the organization of work, as offices. The prototypical skyscraper of modernity is the pure expression of this organization—the optimized form to archive and connect workers who archive and connect data. This reification of bureaucracy, beyond any pejorative connotation, was symbolically interpreted by the most skilled architects, such as Mies van der Rohe, through rectilinear prisms of glass and steel, artificially climatized, and organized in rings around a communication core. Projects such as the Seagram Building in New York and the fabulous BBV Building by Sáenz de Oiza in Spain gave definitive and undying form to this concept. But they did not include (or the moment had yet to arrive for) many of the possibilities that vertical construction opens, which we have seen multiply over past decades with the growth of the global economy and demographic expansion in Southeast Asia.

Today the vast majority of skyscrapers are located in the tropics (particularly in Asia), are residential, with concrete structures, and are naturally ventilated. Lacking any monumental semblance, they are a product for consumption. Without overdramatizing, we can say that all contemporary metropoli are doomed for densification, and even the most recalcitrant mayors begin to understand that the densification process is an instrument with which they need to become familiar. Meanwhile, many European and American architects, who until recently monopolized the skyscraper typology, still seem to be seduced by the skyscraper's iconic character. Their discourse is enclosed in a self-referential verticality—representing capital and its surplus—as if we were witness to a final, mannered phase of this typology's history.

Nevertheless, we are merely observing the infancy of the skyscraper. Today, "verticalism," the conceptualization of space and the contemporary city in vertical terms, has only just begun. We are witnessing a fascinating process of transformation. We have begun to think about the city—and historic cities—from positions that effectively substitute the bidimensionality of urbanism with a new verticalism. It has yet to be seen whether this is a complementary or alternative way of thinking about the city (in plan or in three dimensions, urbanism or verticalism). In the professional work of the generation of architects in their forties and fifties, and in younger generations, we see vertical university campuses flourish, vertical museums, vertical libraries, vertical laboratories, vertical fashion buildings, vertical parks, vertical convention centers, vertical sports facilities, along with combinations of all of these mixed with residential, hotel, and office typologies. Together, these mixed-use buildings can become authentic cities in which the building section has become what the city plan represented until now. Other examples mix towers with different uses, but with the same formal logic, creating a group or cluster of towers (the so-called bundle of towers). These examples serve as an opportune and effective alternative to the grand vertical mixed-use building, and in many contexts virtually displace interest from the objects to the air that surrounds the buildings, to the space that they create, and to the form in which the new constructions interact with one another. As such, these buildings transfer the iconic emphasis of the autobiographical object to the public space, and to the city that they generate.

This strategy of urban infiltration with small towers—a strategy of "acupuncture"—also offers multiple solutions for historic cities. In comparison with Haussman's Parisian boulevard approach, this strategy has the benefit of a minimal footprint with the maximum capacity for transformation.

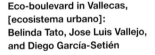
**Eco-boulevard in Vallecas,
[ecosistema urbano]:
Belinda Tato, Jose Luis Vallejo,
and Diego García-Setién**

European cities such as Rotterdam, Paris, and Turin are looking to increase their density this way.

The Metropolitan Detention Center, Harry Weese's skyscraper built in 1975 on the Chicago Loop, whose image resembles a large punchcard, includes a jail for those who have committed misdemeanors, public spaces, and superimposed offices in a coherent ensemble. Weese's building is one of the first references to propose new possibilities for mixed use, beyond the clichéd image, produced by developers, that mixes a shopping mall, a hotel, offices, and apartments. Hugh Stubbins's Citicorp building in New York, also proposed in 1975, includes a church, exterior and interior plazas, various pieces of public art, and one of New York's best subway accesses. The building is crowned with the city's first large solar collectors, which were never put to use, strictly for commercial reasons.

Today many wonder why we continue to build industrial parks on the plains, with only a single story to extensively occupy the best available land. It is absurd to advocate for urban densification without questioning these surfaces, whose sole raison d'être is for the investor economy. In contrast, the industrial skyscraper is a serious proposal that is urgently needed in places like the Basque Country, with scarce horizontal land for urban development.

The productive skyscraper is also proposed to redefine some difficult uses, such as the *abattoir*. After finishing the "Pig City" theoretical project, MVRDV is building a less ambitious (but probably more important) version in the port of Rotterdam. Along with *abattoirs*, cemeteries are another typology that can be easily integrated into the idea of the skyscraper. Each helps to resolve a growing spatial problem, offering imaginative solutions for cities lacking in land.

Pig City, MVRDV

Netherlands Pavilion, MVRDV

Verticalism (The Future of the Skyscraper)

Orange County Museum of Art,
Abalos + Sentkiewicz arquitectos

Madrid International Convention
Center (CICCM), Mansilla + Tuñón

Politicians and architects need to focus their attention on this burgeoning of skyscrapers because of the new qualities and enormous degrees of liberty that they add to cities when used in support of public objectives. The exploration of these emerging forms of beauty will be one of the central challenges for architecture schools in the coming years. The successful experience of the modern skyscraper, centered essentially on private business, should be reverted and conceptualized for the public benefit (or on behalf of both), exploring new modalities of urban management that anticipate the future.

The public space that makes contemporary verticalism more strategically possible, its small footprint on places, and the obvious sustainability it offers by synergistically utilizing the various activities of its section—all are factors that increasingly add to verticalism's acceptance. The public space generated historically by the skyscraper—that mix of commercial streets and picturesque parks inaugurated by Central Park in New York, with its capacity to transform Eighth Avenue, and later, Midtown—likely contains the genetic code of contemporary public space. Trees and skyscrapers nourish one another, generating in their amalgam one of the true leitmotivs of contemporary architecture. Thinking about vertical constructions means, necessarily, thinking about new modalities of the public sphere that satisfy the demands that arise from social, cultural, and demographic changes produced by global metropoli. Verticalism is also the strategy that can allow historic European cities to continue to remain relevant in a highly competitive future that is already here.

Tour La Chapelle, Paris,
Abalos + Sentkiewicz arquitectos

Translated by Stephen Ramos

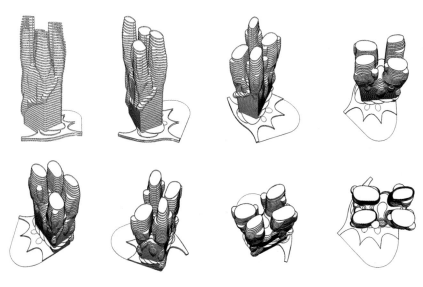

Urban Prototypes

Raoul Bunschoten

An urban prototype is something we need to change the overall dynamics of a city. It is a form that specifically belongs to urban complexity, which links processes within this complexity to create a new connection, a new network, a new function. An urban prototype is an organizational form; it is a test, an experiment, a trial of a new technology, design, or behavioral pattern, as well as a model, a demonstration, a showcase. Prototypes are used in the manufacturing industry, in design processes, and sometimes in construction, such as a prototype house. It is used in software development and in medical science; the cloned sheep Dolly was a prototype—a new phenomenon, an original organism, and a demonstration that cloning is possible. She also became a famous showcase.

Prototypes are both machines and models, they connect processes and create pilot projects. They contain systems that create an output that changes an environment, and they enable us to study the effect of that output; they are engines of change as well as didactic tools about the benchmarks of that change. Prototypes are usually specially manufactured objects, using materials that are not necessarily meant to be the final ones used for production. They are not always complete and can remain a fragment or a simplified version of a design. They are usually more costly than the final product once it goes into production. But they are unique, original, and can lead to radical change through their eventual application.

We need urban prototypes in cities to alter the whole flux of processes, to form new relationships between these processes, to change the inherent structure of a city. Urban prototypes are like singularities placed in the dynamic flux of a city, singularities that connect existing flows with something new, a process coming from elsewhere, from top down, a global process, and from inside out, coming from the heart of a community. The design of an urban prototype is its organizational form; the material substance (its shape) is a secondary thing in many cases. The Bilbao Guggenheim Museum became a prototype because of its radical curvy shape, placed in a deteriorated harbor environment. It attracted tourists, but did not change radically the mesh of the city. Still, it became a prototype in that afterward, every city with problems wanted a Bilbao. Brunel's Thames Tunnel was invisible but did change radically the infrastructure of London. It was a prototype because it pioneered new tunnelling techniques and became a model for other tunnel projects.

The Hagia Sophia was a radical new design for a dome; there was nothing like it in the world when it was built. But it remained unique, a one-off creation until after the conquest of Constantinople by the Ottoman Empire. The architect Sinan used it as a prototype for his mosques, and it reappeared in many versions and adaptations that shape the skyline of modern-day central Istanbul. The Hagia Sophia was an early Christian building that used the geometry of square and sphere to interpret early Christian cosmology and its mosaic decoration to form a neoplatonic model: light reflecting inside the volume of the church was a manifestation of the body of God. Sinan took the geometry and turned it into a toolbox, a typology, and simplified the condition of light. The toolbox allowed him and those coming after him to build many versions of the typology, and to adapt it to different sites and functional requirements. The internal surface became an ornamented skin, partly written on, rather than the magic skin of a neoplatonic volume. A basic rule of urban prototypes is that they can adapt and proliferate. They are not static one-offs but react to their contexts and multiply. We can design and employ a limited range of prototypes and yet aim at changing an entire city's dynamics eventually.

We need urban prototypes because the relationship between cities and energy has changed. Energy will become the primary driver of the form and structure of cities, new and old alike. But we cannot test the way we need to design energy into existing or new city fabric in models only, through 3-D graphics, statistics, scientific laboratories. We need to gather everything we know about the new technologies available for renewable energy generation and energy efficiency, link them to new building technologies, social and cultural patterns, and economic mechanisms, and try to initiate pilot projects that act alone or in clusters, within the context of an overall choreography—the new urban energy master plan. The city is the laboratory, the test bed, and only in the live city can we monitor the output of technical devices, the effects of new passive designs, the new behavior of a population that becomes engaged in the task of overall energy efficiency increase. Unlike the examples above, many urban prototypes will not be buildings but combinations of buildings and technologies, infrastructure and energy systems, policies combined with pilot projects, media attention linked to behavioral patterns.

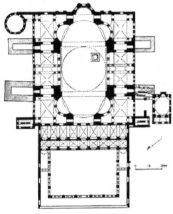

Photo and ground plan of the Hagia Sofia

Airlift into the future: Berlin Tempelhof as a communal space and alternative power plant.
In May 2009, the Berlin Senate announced three equal prizes for an international urban ideas competition for the Columbia Quartier and the former Tempelhof airfield. Chora Architecture and Urbanism, in partnership with Buro Happold, Gross Max, and Joost Grootens, was one of the three winners.

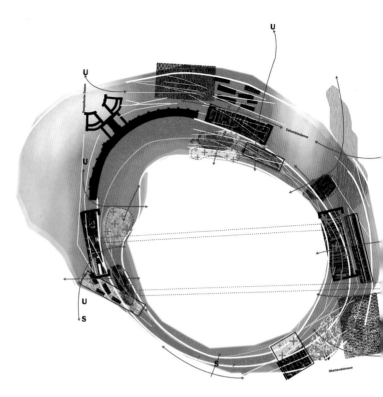

Within the image:
[53]

IGA   IBA   KREUZBERG

LUFTBRÜCKEPARK

SEI

TEMPELHOF

NEU KOLLN

At the core of the proposal is a participatory instrument enabling inhabitants and other stakeholders to creatively negotiate a processed-based development. The result is radical: an economic, social, cultural, and political context to turn the whole area into an alternative power plant. Tempelhof becomes a communal space connecting people, supplying renewable energy, and implementing the goal of the German government to lower CO$_2$ emissions—an energy incubator.

We use urban prototypes as a tool, a technique, within a larger methodological framework: the Urban Gallery. This is a management tool and support system for a complex planning mechanism such as an overall urban energy master plan. The urban gallery links the urban prototype to basic information of processes, stakeholders and scenarios, and action frameworks. It is a tool that enables the choreography of dynamics relating to climate change, and to the role that cities can play in tackling this issue: searching for mitigating factors; and adapting to this new and frightening reality of rising temperatures, increased unsettledness of weather patterns, and of course the depletion of fossil-fuel sources and growing tensions over who owns them. The urban planner or other specialist working with the Urban Gallery is an urban curator. Urban prototypes are the instruments with which they instigate change or choreograph the new dynamics of energy-producing cities. Technically this is all possible; culturally we have to be curators and artists, and treat urban planning like an art form, creating new realities, shaping visions of the future that people can be involved in with their hearts and souls.

The Tempelhof proposal follows the   Database, Prototype, Scenario Game,
four stages of Chora's Urban Gallery: and Action Plan

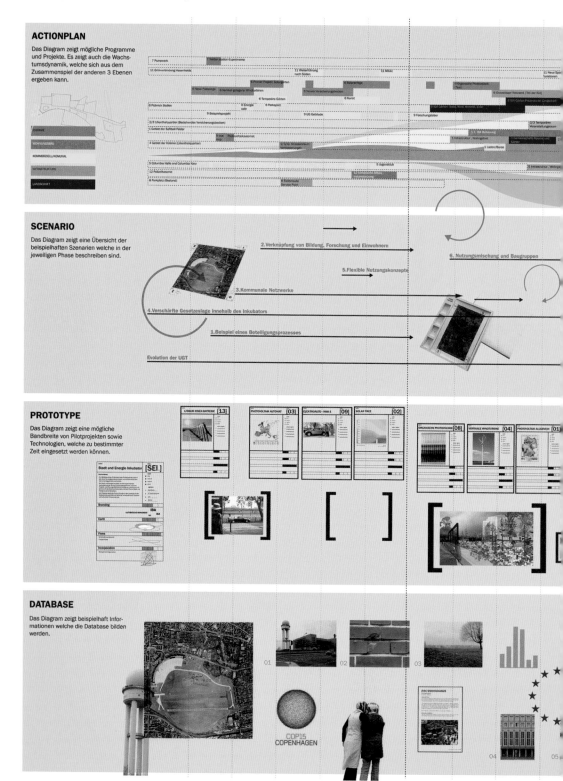

ACTIONPLAN

Das Diagram zeigt mögliche Programme
und Projekte. Es zeigt auch die Wachs-
tumsdynamik, welche sich aus dem
Zusammenspiel der anderen 3 Ebenen
ergeben kann.

SCENARIO

Das Diagram zeigt eine Übersicht der
beispielhaften Szenarien welche in der
jeweiligen Phase beschrieben sind.

PROTOTYPE

Das Diagram zeigt eine mögliche
Bandbreite von Pilotprojekten sowie
Technologien, welche zu bestimmter
Zeit eingesetzt werden können.

DATABASE

Das Diagram zeigt beispielhaft Infor-
mationen welche die Database bilden
werden.

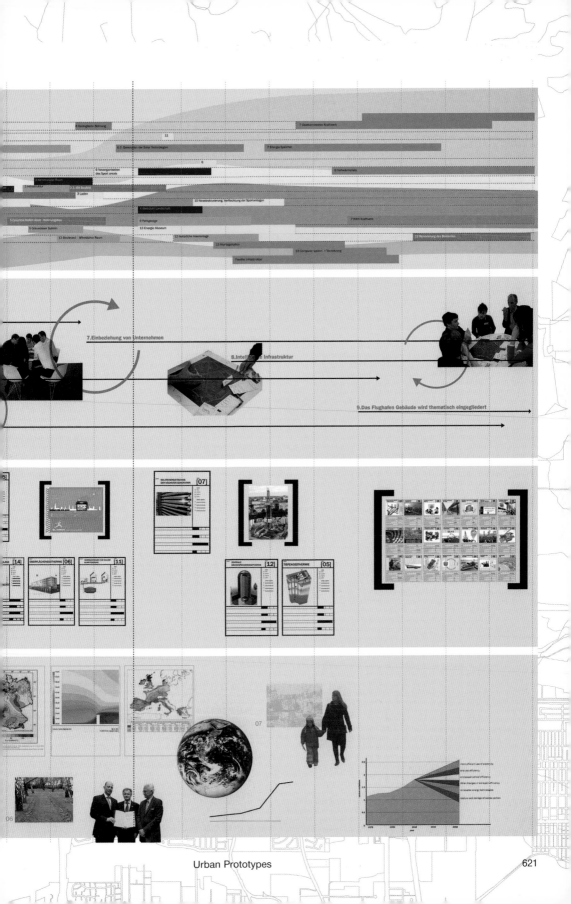

Taiwan Strait Climate Change Incubator

Chora Architecture and Urbanism

Chora's inventory of prototype projects, arranged according to scale and cost, provides an overview of available technologies for adapting the existing city toward more ecological futures. Geothermal heating is joined by Trombe walls, plug-in energy farms, urban carbon sinks, hydrogen vehicle networks, and carbon trading. The catalog of sixty-five prototypes is organized according to scale and cost, and each prototype according to the criteria of branding, construction costs, project costs, and carbon reduction efficiency.

The *Taiwan Strait Atlas,* initiated by Raoul Bunschoten and Joost Grootens, mapped emergent urban conditions in the Taiwan Strait, a region that Chora calls a "Liminal Body." The process of mapping the Taiwan Strait led to the idea that the Liminal Body can be an incubator for urban prototype projects related to climate change, energy production, and energy efficiency. Incorporating a cross-strait renewable energy management plan for the cities of Xiamen and Taichung, the Taiwan Strait Climate Change Incubator maps the complex web of economic, cultural, and ecological connections across the Taiwan Strait and exploits these ecologies in developing sustainable prototypes at the urban scale.

The economics of global carbon trading are used to finance a series of urban prototypes, using the Clean Development Mechanism (CDM). The CDM is a policy under the Kyoto Protocol that allows industrialized countries to gain emission reduction credits for engaging developing countries with sustainability. The Incubator, the organizational device for the prototypes, presents new standards for architectural design, urbanism, and creative financial management.

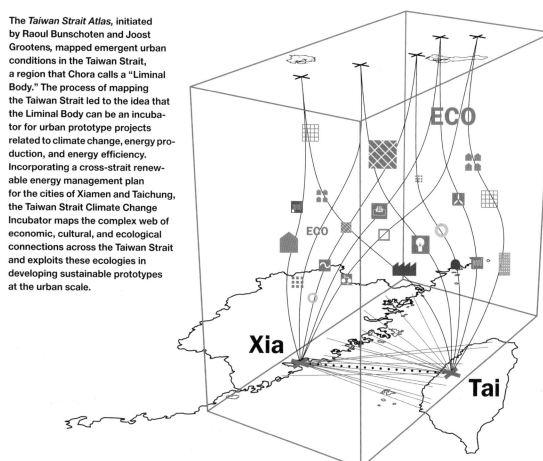

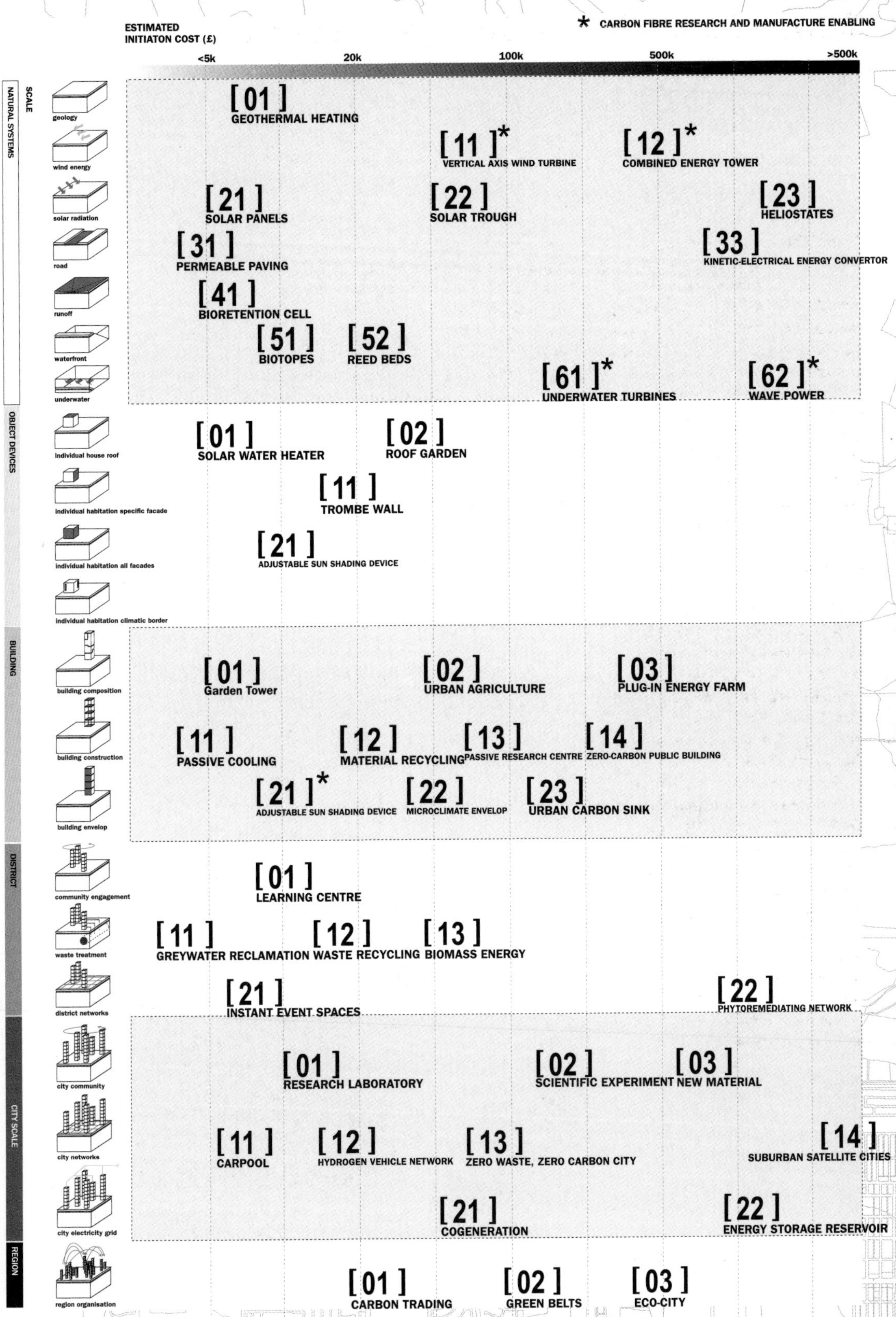

* CARBON FIBRE RESEARCH AND MANUFACTURE ENABLING
ESTIMATED INITIATON COST (£)
<5k
20k
100k
500k
>500k
SCALE
NATURAL SYSTEMS
geology
wind energy
solar radiation
road
runoff
waterfront
underwater
[01] GEOTHERMAL HEATING
[11]* VERTICAL AXIS WIND TURBINE
[12]* COMBINED ENERGY TOWER
[21] SOLAR PANELS
[22] SOLAR TROUGH
[23] HELIOSTATES
[31] PERMEABLE PAVING
[33] KINETIC-ELECTRICAL ENERGY CONVERTOR
[41] BIORETENTION CELL
[51] BIOTOPES
[52] REED BEDS
[61]* UNDERWATER TURBINES
[62]* WAVE POWER
OBJECT DEVICES
individual house roof
individual habitation specific facade
individual habitation all facades
individual habitation climatic border
[01] SOLAR WATER HEATER
[02] ROOF GARDEN
[11] TROMBE WALL
[21] ADJUSTABLE SUN SHADING DEVICE
BUILDING
building composition
building construction
building envelop
[01] Garden Tower
[02] URBAN AGRICULTURE
[03] PLUG-IN ENERGY FARM
[11] PASSIVE COOLING
[12] MATERIAL RECYCLING
[13] PASSIVE RESEARCH CENTRE
[14] ZERO-CARBON PUBLIC BUILDING
[21]* ADJUSTABLE SUN SHADING DEVICE
[22] MICROCLIMATE ENVELOP
[23] URBAN CARBON SINK
DISTRICT
community engagement
waste treatment
district networks
[01] LEARNING CENTRE
[11] GREYWATER RECLAMATION
[12] WASTE RECYCLING
[13] BIOMASS ENERGY
[21] INSTANT EVENT SPACES
[22] PHYTOREMEDIATING NETWORK
CITY SCALE
city community
city networks
city electricity grid
[01] RESEARCH LABORATORY
[02] SCIENTIFIC EXPERIMENT
[03] NEW MATERIAL
[11] CARPOOL
[12] HYDROGEN VEHICLE NETWORK
[13] ZERO WASTE, ZERO CARBON CITY
[14] SUBURBAN SATELLITE CITIES
[21] COGENERATION
[22] ENERGY STORAGE RESERVOIR
REGION
region organisation
[01] CARBON TRADING
[02] GREEN BELTS
[03] ECO-CITY

INCUBATOR FLOW

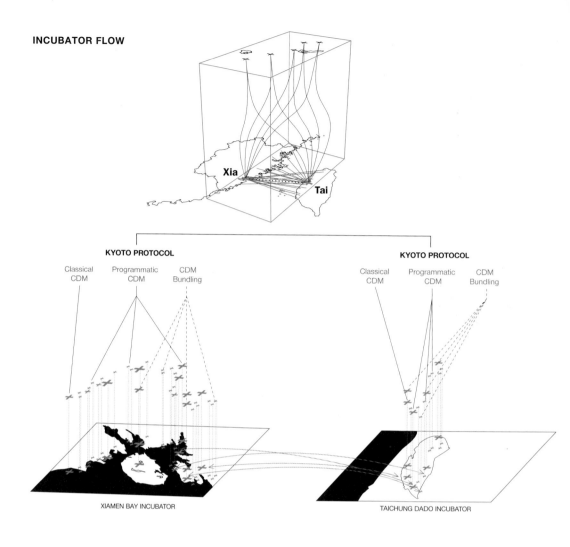

KYOTO PROTOCOL

Classical CDM   Programmatic CDM   CDM Bundling

KYOTO PROTOCOL

Classical CDM   Programmatic CDM   CDM Bundling

XIAMEN BAY INCUBATOR

TAICHUNG DADO INCUBATOR

XIAMEN- PROGRAMMATIC CDM

actors

emission reduction projects
Architects
masterplanners
Structural Engineers
developers and manufacturers
financial investors

carbon credit investors
Annex 1 Country Gov't
financial investors
World Bank
International Banks

host country
implementing organisations
local government officials

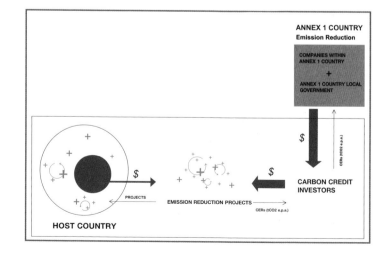

PROGRAMMATIC CDM-FINANCIAL PLAN

FINANCING AND PREPAYING MECHANISM

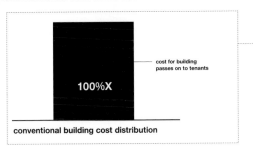

100%X

cost for building
passes on to tenants

conventional building cost distribution

conventional building costs = **US$ 210-250** per sq. m

for 20-storey commercial/ residential building
center of Xiamen City.

(land cost and cost for interior design not included)

20%X

P-CDM capital input for
fuel switch, EE and RE devices

80%X

cost for building
pass onto tenants

P-CDM building cost distributions

individual
project
CER   x   number of
bundled projects   = total CER

for certain project programmes
approximately 8 buildings under such
operational principles could generate CER
equivalent to a small hydroelectric plant.

P-CDM additionality

The programme needs the CDM because:
1. other funds cover only 80% of the costs and without the programme the households cannot afford the EE or RE programme;
2. implementing body's perspectives: Government would not proceed without CDM support;
3. Prototype Function: developing model projects for other prototype development in other cities through project multiplication.

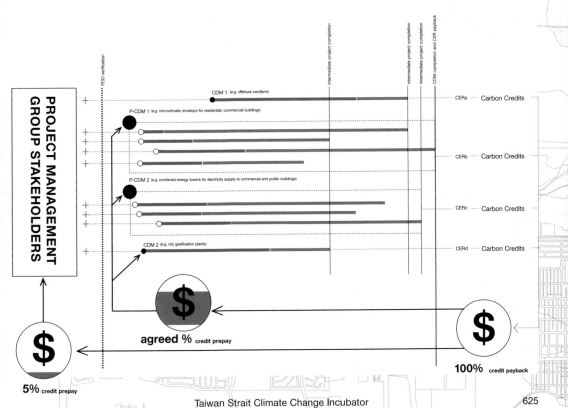

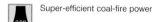	Super-efficient coal-fire power		Energy façade
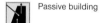	Passive building		Solar power plant
	Graywater recycling		Energy island
	Home-improvement kit		Biomass
	Low-impact construction	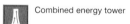	Combined energy tower
	District cooling	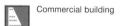	Commercial building
	Localsmart grid	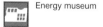	Energy museum
	Green technology	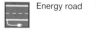	Energy road
	Intelligent infrastructure		Industrial headquarters
	Clean transportation	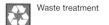	Waste treatment

INCUBATE

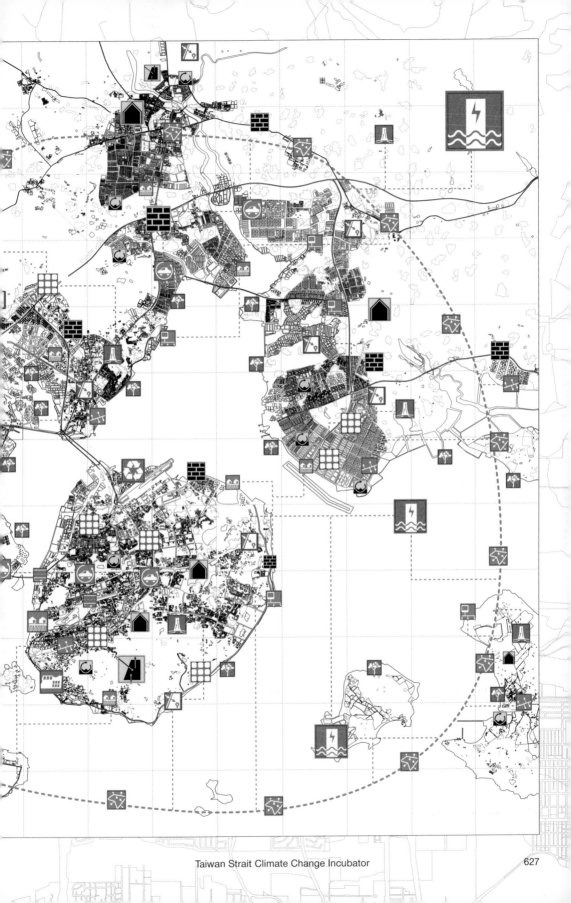

Taiwan Strait Climate Change Incubator

THE CITY

An apparition
seen on a mountain
by shepherd boys
founds a cathedral
rectory and convent
a huddle of hovels
some whores and usurers
seeking sanctuary.
A road, bridge, some houses
School, hospital, served by pious rich ladies;
Blacksmith, forge, farrier, some
Day labourers at Whitsun
And Michelmas
A jester, goldsmith, coffin maker
chimney sweep, tavern
viaduct, amphitheatre, cemetery, and more
set between field and forest,
urbs, civitas, polis, metropolis
megalopolis, necropolis
A large consequence from an apparition
or was it a spectre?

Ian McHarg
(from *Some Songs to the Stars,* Knossus Publishers, 2001)

GSD:ecologicalurbanism

GSD:ecologicalurbanism is an online platform created by students at the Harvard Graduate School of Design (GSD) to accompany the Ecological Urbanism conference and exhibition that took place on April 3–5, 2009. This platform was meant to document, react, criticize, and debate the panels and discussions that occurred during the conference.

Elaborating and reflecting on the issues raised at the event, students from the various departments used GSD:ecologicalurbanism as an informal platform for building their agenda toward ecological urbanism: what is it now and what it might turn out to be. Some extracts follow, in reverse chronological order.

For more critical reflections on ecological urbanism, see: http://gsd-ecologicalurbanism. blogspot.com/

The GSD Blogging Team:
Matthew Allen, MArch I
Ilana Cohen, MLA
Yonatan Cohen, MAUD
Dan Handel, MArch II
Zakcq Lockrem, MUP
Quilian Riano, MArch I AP

Guest Bloggers:
Kazys Varnelis
Orhan Ayyuce
Javier Arbona

SUNDAY, APRIL 5, 2009

Boeri on Autonomy

Stefano Boeri, in his morning lecture, gave an efficient presentation that seemed to me to be echoing Branzi's lecture from yesterday in the sense that he was trying to shake the environmentalist notion of nature as exterior to human activity (e.g., the city). He went through three main trajectories for reconciliation: mimesis (that is, copying natural forms by technological means), confinement (which he interprets as increased control over nature), and autonomy, for him the more promising trajectory. Boeri described autonomy as nature reinhabiting cities, creating a curious, essentially ecological condition of shared spaces between humans, animals, and plants without moral or evolutionary hierarchies. For me this notion of autonomy plays a dual role: on the one hand it is presented as a positive, pragmatic way out of current failures in sustainable thinking, while on the other it maintains the dystopian imagery ever present. In this sense Boeri collapsed the two lines of human history: the apocalyptic and the progressive, presented by Koolhaas on Friday, into a single, perversely irrational, post-technocratic view on the future of cities.

POSTED BY DAN HANDEL AT 8:57 PM

REDUNDANCY!
I was just talking to a Leslie, a California-based landscape architect visiting for the conference, about my thesis when REDUNDANCY came up. She was saying that since I can never be 100 percent sure of how water flows and other ecologies will work, I need to build in redundant systems to make sure it works. I liked that idea a lot because redundancy is another "humble" design tactic. It makes us accept that we cannot control it all, we can just try to mediate it. I like it because in systems that are predetermined and completely engineered, there is little to no room for design. Redundancy allows design to come in and mediate indeterminacy. In short, redundancy can make sure that ecological urbanism is not about top-down efficiency.

POSTED BY QUILIAN RIANO AT 3:03 PM

On ethics:
"I don't believe in good intentions."

On infrastructure:
"Infrastructure is the catalyzer
of a new architecture."

On Informality

By Guest Blogger Kazys Varnelis

On aesthetics:
"To reach a new idea of beauty,
we have to pass through ugliness."

Kazys Varnelis is the Director of the Network Architecture Lab at the Columbia University Graduate School of Architecture, Planning, and Preservation. With Robert Sumrell, he runs the nonprofit architectural collective AUDC.

–Iñaki Ábalos

POSTED BY ILANA COHEN AT 1:01 PM

Quilian Riano asked me to participate in the blogging revolving around the GSD event on Ecological Urbanism. Although Quilian is live-blogging the event (like the live blogging for Postopolis going on simultaneously), I think it makes much more sense to the participants than to those of us listening in at a remove, observing highly compressed fragments of the conversation. Even if I take my knowledge of the event secondhand, I thought I'd offer a response, prematurely broaching a topic that I've been engulfed in for the first part of this year. I'll begin with the event's statement of purpose, the core of which reads as follows:
"The conference is organized around the premise that an ecological approach is urgently needed both as a remedial device for the contemporary city and an organizing principle for new cities. An ecological urbanism represents a more holistic approach than is generally the case with urbanism today, demanding alternative ways of thinking and designing." In ecological urbanism, the informal seems to crop up repeatedly. Instead of "green architecture" and its outworn advocacy of LEED to design our way out of a global ecological crisis, the conference proposes an urbanism produced bottom-up, in a natural way, like an ecosystem.
Sanford Kwinter's keen observation that New York's culture has come to a crashing halt under the weight of capital, overdevelopment, and hipsterdom serves as a setup to ecological urbanism. Instead of a vital urban realm, we have a stuffed animal (to use a phrase Peter Eisenman once applied to European cities…and let's just be clear that today cities anywhere in the developing world don't fare any better than Manhattan does). In the face of this collapsing formal urbanism, then, Quilian observes, informality is thriving.
We've heard this before, in the recent fascination with favelas and their capacity for self-organization. When Rem Koolhaas spoke, he brought out Lagos, his exemplar of such a self-organizing city, a nightmare condition that nevertheless he feels somehow works. In doing so, he replays Venturi, Scott Brown, and Izenour's *Learning from Las Vegas* as well as Reyner Banham's *Los Angeles: The Architecture of Four Ecologies,* but in going to Africa, Koolhaas is not so much flipping the valence on a "low," pop phenomenon as replaying the modernist obsession with the primitive (to be fair, in the East, the West is often seen in terms of the primitive). The modern obsession with the primitive suggested that in such contexts we would identify the next modernity. So Koolhaas hopes to do in Lagos…

POSTED BY GSD: ECOLOGICAL URBANISM AT 10:20 AM

Andrea Branzi Videos
If you were not there for Branzi's lecture, you can catch up by watching the videos on his site. The following are my favorites:
No-Stop City
Concorso
Agronica
Vertical
Home
I had not seen the videos before Branzi presented them last night. The music, editing, and collage gave me new insights into his work. I now see clearly the connections to minimalist music and biological processes, and he even gave hints at these being set within real landscapes.
The hints of real landscapes bring up some questions I have always had for Branzi:
First, what is your site, your landscape? From *No-Stop City* to my personal favorite, *Agronica,* the site seems like an abstraction and a real place at the same time. In *Agronica* the video is edited with images of a real landscape organized in perfect rows. Where is that? Is that "the site?" Does it matter?
Second, why has the "language" developed in *No-Stop City* never been deployed in a mountainous site? The language looks like it wants to be universal, yet as deployed right now it would work in very few places in the world. Does it matter? Would it be a fruitful exercise?
Third, the projects with their extreme horizontality seem very American. More specifically, midwestern. *Agronica* reminds me of the agroindustrial fields from Missouri to Iowa. Is that intentional?

POSTED BY QUILIAN RIANO AT 8:55 AM

Defining Moment

Andrea Branzi's lecture was probably the highlight of the conference. After severely attacking environmentalism and environmentalists for creating problems as much as offering solutions and for simply making ugly things, Branzi was challenged by Matthias Schuler, an environmentalist himself, as to whether humanity should not prioritize, at this stage, survival over aesthetics. Branzi's simple "no" contrasted a progressive positive worldview, characterizing much of sustainable thinking, with an utter negation of both technology and rationality as means of improving the human condition and offered a crisp, pristine moment of reflection saved for rare occasions of great intellectual clarity.

MS A question as an environmentalist: You said environmentalists are missing the point. Don't you think that to find a way of sustainable living is a question of survival in our society?
AB Till now the solution proposed can ... impoverish the society and the environment.
CW You made a very pointed critique of environmentalism ...
AB Environmentalism has of course the chances but it has to deal with also the aesthetical qualities ... So environmentalism doesn't work if the projects are worse, uglier, than what there was before ... It is a big problem. This *is* the problem!
MS If it's a question of survival, isn't environmentalism better?
AB Not so sure! Not so sure! Maybe better to die.

MS – Matthias Schuler
AB – Andrea Branzi
CW – Charles Waldheim, moderator

–Ecological Urbanism conference, Saturday, April 4, 2009

POSTED BY DAN HANDEL AT 12:04 AM

Architecture Imagined as Ecological

by Guest Blogger Javier Arbona

Javier Arbona is a University of California, Berkeley, PhD candidate in geography with a background in architecture and urbanism.

The all-encompassing discourse of sustainability is tangled up with global geopolitics at every turn, but that discourse hides its tail. What's worse is that "sustainable architecture" can be the proverbial "greenwash," as I think has become more than evident. We would only have to do a roll-call of all the eco-resorts done in years

Velib!
A question from the audience during the "mobility, infrastructure, and society" panel brought up the bicycle. The panelists hadn't really mentioned its role in mobility and infrastructure. The Velib program in Paris is a great example of how the bicycle can become an integral part of urban transportation infrastructure. All cities should have this sort of program and at this scale. It's brilliant: twenty-four hours a day, seven days a week you have access to a free bicycle, available at stations spaced approximately every 300 meters throughout the city.

POSTED BY ILANA COHEN AT 6:11 PM

of economic fluidity. Thinking about a sustainable practice is (still) supposed to arouse in us a moral instinct of how to satisfy our needs without "compromising the needs of future generations." The small-house movement serves as a good example of an architecture informed by notions of what is said to be "basic." Our "needs," however, are a mirage. We know that they are essentially malleable. They're subject to crass marketing manipulation. They evolve through the sieves of culture and desire. They're hard to pin down and it's no accident that capitalism pulls the rug out from under us as soon as we try. Besides, unless the global economic crisis ends up destroying capitalism, we satisfy our so-called needs through an increasingly global economy, despite the localist and nationalist fantasies some may have. Even if we didn't have capitalism, we'd still have trade, and subscribers to notions of Malthusian natural limits fail to adequately take this into account. Sometimes the sustainability talk sounds to me even xenophobic in its suggestions that a certain number of citizens will have a right to the city (blurring further the notion of what is natural: Numerical limits? Naturalization, as in citizenship?). The ideologues of sustainability might deny that it is an issue of power and not morals, but it is. It has to do with who determines how much is a reasonable need for some and not others, both at a local and global level. By the way, I'm sorry for even using these terms like "local" and "global" because they pertain to imprecise scales, especially when ecological processes are involved. But none of this has slowed down the field of architecture. As oftentimes is clear in the works of architects like Michael Sorkin and other adherents to the "ecological footprint," design indexes how much nature is judged to be fair and balanced according to some metric of consumption.

POSTED BY GSD: ECOLOGICAL URBANISM AT 5:43 PM

Ruralization of Urbanism?
According to Andres Duany, the environmental movement is
elevating the value of greenspace and is ruralizing cities.
And when you ruralize a city, it becomes a suburb. And suburbs,
as we all know, are the root of all evil.
I am skeptical. McHargian environmentalism, while still alive
and relevant, is not the only strain of environmentalism. Those
that emphasize environmental health and/or environmental
justice tend to be more encompassing and less critical of the
fundamental value of the city. While Sustainable South Bronx
and Youth Ministries for Peace and Justice might be advocating
for the "greening" of the Bronx, I don't think they fully embrace
the McHargian disdain for the city. These environmentalists
love their neighborhoods and want to make them healthy and
sustainable. They understand that their neighborhoods cannot
promote public health or support healthy economies without
being ecologically sustainable. They are making the Bronx more
"ecological" and the suburbs have nothing to do with it.

POSTED BY ILANA COHEN AT 5:42 PM

Why Informal?
Informality seems to be coming up more than I anticipated. We have heard it from Koolhaas, Bhabha, Kwinter, Mostafavi, Kirkwood, and others in different contexts. In fact I think it is being used as often, and with more focus, than ecology. I want to share my first impressions as I try to find reasons for the focus on the informal in a conference about ecology.

A Way In
Designers seem to have a hard time getting into ecology as a way of working. The informal allows us a way into the discussion. The word "informal" seems to stand in for the larger economic, political, environmental, and social contexts that designers cannot fully account for and thus control. This condition then produces many products, including built environments.
We can strategically choose some of the systems to act upon and be flexible to account for the rest. This is what I think Koolhaas means when he talks about the formal and informal growing together. Koolhaas says that he learned that lesson after going to Lagos. However, his design for La Villette was already trying to design such a condition. The design provides the minimum infrastructure required while allowing major sections of the park to change as economy, community, and political will allow.

Western Anxiety
Kwinter officially declared New York City dead last night. He says that it is a boring place now. Such a strong statement has to have a cause larger than a few porn shops turning into Disney stores. Maybe the statement has to more to do with anxiety around the failure of the formal structures in the West. Populations are dropping, immigration increasing, manufacturing and economic strength shifting to other nations. Western nations are facing a changing culture at home and a shifting power structure abroad. As formal structures fail, informal systems take over.
This anxiety was partially on display last night. Koolhaas, Bhabha, and Kwinter talked about Lagos and Mumbai with excitement and interest, about New York and Europe with a measure of pessimism. Studies in the informal are a way to then anticipate and mediate changes in Western cities as well as in developing nations.

Preempting Top-Down Ecological Solutions
I think that all the talk about informality is partly about the humility by designers that Koolhaas and Kwinter called for last night. They are telling designers that they will really never know everything about a condition, there is no reason design as if you do … there are intelligences out there as great as your own.

POSTED BY QUILIAN RIANO AT 3:52 PM

Farming the Horizontal Plane
I was delighted to hear members of the panel on productive
urban environments seriously discuss urban agriculture
in the context of a design conference without obsessing over
the potentials of vertical gardens and mega farm towers in
the city. It was an exciting discussion, which mentioned the
work of brilliant community-based organizations such as
Growing Power and New York City's Council on the Environ-
ment's New Farmer Development Project. Vibrant community-
based organizations are not designing tower farms in the
sky. They are BUILDING them on the ground. While designers
are fantasizing about pigs floating high above us, community
organizers and educators at East New York Farms!, Added
Value, The Food Project, the People's Grocery, and many other
organizations are making food-system change happen
right now.
What is the role that designers can play in this bottom-up
movement? As my interviews with Deborah Greig and Owen
Taylor, two urban farmers, educators, and local food advocates,
about the Work AC installation at PS1 illustrate, there is wary
enthusiasm among the local food community around designer
input into urban agriculture. This morning Nina-Marie Lister
outlined for us some opportunities for designers and planners.
We can map interstitial spaces in cities and facilitate growth
of these community-based, bottom-up systems. But is that all?
Can't we do more?

POSTED BY ILANA COHEN AT 2:00 PM

I have to disagree with Ilana on the first panel and with Matthew's characterization that "ecology is approached ... as a matter of existential praxis." I felt that the first panel, in fact, tended to reinforce what Kwinter later called the "false dichotomy," negating much of its value in my opinion and showing just how deep the diametrically opposed Thoreauvian conceptions of nature and city run. During the keynote, on the other hand, many of the issues that I hoped would be raised during this conference were, from the role of capital to showing alternatives to the nature/ city dualism.

As the sole planner writing about the conference, I have to admit that I was a little concerned about having an architect and a literary critic delivering the keynote at a conference that is specifically urban. For someone who studies the city full time, architects' presentations on urbanism can, at times, seem woefully naive. Setting aside the (admitted) irony of Rem Koolhaas declaring an end to starchitecture, I was extremely impressed by the nuance and depth of his presentation, as well as the ease of his movement between the architectural and urban scales with clarity.

I especially enjoyed the short look at the California Academy of Sciences building as well as the characterization that we have too often "equated literal greening" with ecological sustainability. I recently saw a project that included significant introduction of northern American foliage to a park in Albuquerque with the goal of "greening" the city. Yes, perhaps the color green will abound, but only at a huge environmental cost to create the necessary ecosystem for it to exist in that climate. This, as Koolhaas said, is the "artificiality to which we've become accustomed."

POSTED BY ZAKCQ LOCKREM AT 1:30 PM

Excluded Thirds

We continuously bring up the city-nature dyad only to lament the exclusion of a third term. Practically anything can be framed as the excluded third of a dialectic pair. This is how post-Enlightenment thought works. Sanford Kwinter, in his opening address to the keynote, argued that what is excluded by the "false dichotomy" of technology and nature is nothing less than the "social and cultural dimension" itself. I would argue, to the contrary, that ecology is typically approached today as a matter of existential praxis even by those technocrats and hippies that in the end address ecological problems within the narrow means of the technology-nature dyad. The problem is one of feasibility: a technological or naturalist scope each yield results that are implementable in our liberal/capitalist world, while an "existential ecology" yields unbuilt utopia. I would argue that the blind spot Sanford points out does not in fact exist; scratch a technocratic or hippie environmentalist and you will find the sensibility of a deep ecologist.

Rem Koolhaas thankfully presented a resolutely hybrid interpretation of ecology. His argument incorporated a narrative of "reasonable progress" and a narrative of "disasters," each of which contained a social/cultural dimension. Rem's excluded third was the pairing of knowledge with ambition: he lamented the "devastating effect on knowledge" of ways of working with informal architecture that occurred during the growth of the market economy post-1970.

The ways of quantifying ecology developed during the 1960s were not advanced beyond a touchingly naive stage. The ambition to carry out large-scale projects with serious ecological impact exemplified by Buckminster Fuller imploded during the same period. Both Sanford and Rem argued in a way that carved out a niche for themselves, one as a practitioner of the formal where it intersects with the informal, the other as a theorist working on the specific social and cultural dimensions of the science of ecology.

POSTED BY MATTHEW ALLEN AT 11:20 AM

Good Quotes from the Day
Here are two quotes from the day's proceedings,
entirely out of context and intended to perhaps provoke
and certainly amuse:

"Sustainable urbanism should not mean green cities for wealthy white people."

–Lizabeth Cohen

"Good cities are like French cheeses. The worse they smell, the better they are."

–Homi Bhabha

I thought it was interesting how in the opening panel of this weekend's conference, the terms sustainable, green, and ecology were used so interchangeably. Different panelists latched on to different terms for their own purposes, and in this smashingly interdisciplinary panel there were a multitude of agendas and positions. Are these terms identical in meaning? If not, what is the difference between them? Is one more inclusive than another? And is this disparate conversation useful for defining a clear agenda for a new sort of urbanism? Or is it impossible to have a single agenda for something as abstractly defined as ecological urbanism?

As for the French cheese comment, it certainly elicits visceral reaction, though it strikes me as a rather romantic notion of the city. Smelly cities may be more complex and implicitly more exciting than the sterile or "dead" city (Sanford Kwinter just killed New York tonight, by the way), but isn't this just the sort of excitement that lends itself to a touristic voyeurism and encourages a view of the city as place exclusively of voyeurism and vice? Maybe New York was more "alive" in the 1970s than it is today, and we can have a nostalgia about that time, with some very good reason, but I must say that the quality of life can be much higher in a city with a more refreshing and neutral smell. Personally, my parents (longstanding NYC residents) are much happier that the neighborhood whorehouse has been converted to condos and that the subways are safe at all hours. Maybe the city is more sterile, but we shouldn't forget that sterility too has its charms.

POSTED BY ILANA COHEN AT 1:42 AM

Landscape Provocations

While it was not technically part of the conference, I thought it appropriate that the first dialogue in the Landscape Provocations series was today, leading up to the conference. Contemporary issues of practice, research, and representation in landscape architecture must confront ecology at all levels, and the event was an exciting prequel to the weekend.

The conversation between Gary Hilderbrand and Chris Reed touched on the economic value of ecology in the urban environment, addressing the ever-increasing value of defining eco- system services and the potential for urban ecology to provide an infrastructural role in the city. As Gary hinted at this afternoon, a street tree is not just a tree, but a critical element of our city, cleaning air, sequestering carbon, diminishing the urban heat-island effect, and providing countless other environmental and economic benefits to the city. Indeed, a city of trees there- fore would be a more livable city ecological or otherwise. Chris spoke of the potential of landscape to function as a water-filtration mechanism, and to be both more cost-effective and attractive than traditional systems of civil engineering. In the examples they raised, landscape functions as infrastructure—an idea that fits nicely into the more abstract ecological urbanism. A landscape always contains ecology. So it would follow that the more landscape you have, the more ecology. Landscape infrastructure should therefore be a fundamental component of the Ecological City.

The thing that I like about the exhibition, and what I hope to discover through the conference, is the notion that ecological urbanism includes not only this infrastructural landscape approach but that it goes beyond the landscape. If more plural- istic and encompassing of multiple disciplines, it says that it isn't just us landscape folks who can green the city, and you don't have to pretend to be a landscape designer to be a part of this movement. What I can ascertain from the exhibition is that ecological urbanism is design that impacts the city at all its scales, and attempts to do so in a way that learns from nature and/or is harmonious with its principles. That's exciting.

POSTED BY ILANA COHEN AT 6:24 PM

I just picked up the exhibition guide and found myself reading the line, "Urbanism is clearly no longer the sole domain of cities …" What does that mean? Is it what Roman Polan- ski said about Chinatown? Is that why, as Ilana pointed out, a chair and a coffin belong in an exhibition on Ecological Urbanism?

POSTED BY ZAKCQ LOCKREM AT 3:43 PM

When Ecological Optimism Gives Way to Fear

The discussion around ecology and how it can influence design often turns into a discussion of efficiency and economy of resources. We seek to use the latest in technology to design more efficient buildings and cities. We hope that by saving resources, we will be able to maintain our lifestyle and produce more things for a longer period of time. In other words, cut costs to eventually make more profits. A city designed for efficiency requires "rational" systems, where everything and everyone does something beneficial according to some standard. In the exhibition, Atelier Van Lieshout takes this premise and gives us Slave City. What at first may have been a beneficial system takes on a sinister tone, utopia giving way to dystopia. I was amazed to see this project in the exhibition. It is there as a preindictment of designs that may have the impulse to go too far. Though we know that no one would intentionally go this far, dystopia comes in small steps.

That is why I was even more amazed to see the work of Senseable City lab just in front of Slave City. Don't get me wrong, I like their work, but have to admit that I am afraid of it. I am not sure, for example, if I am comfortable with a government office having the technology to track my bike or cell phone. Today's cool tool of urban study is tomorrow's way to track dissent.

As the discussion of ecological design (whatever that turns out to mean) continues, it seems that issues of privacy, appropriate use of technology, and even freedom will have to join the discussion of efficiency. Furthermore, ecological design should include a larger social agenda that does not allow it to be coopted as a mere marketing and political tool. Or as the "Trays" zine editorial put it, Ecology, INC.

POSTED BY QUILIAN RIANO
AT 11:55 AM

TUESDAY, MARCH 31, 2009

Two questions: How is Ecological Urbanism different from Landscape Urbanism?
And what is Urbanism, anyway?
I thought that urbanism implied an urban (i.e., large scale). That doesn't implicitly mean a giant intervention into the city—tactical insertions into the city are urbanism as well— but it does imply an approach that examines design at a city scale.
The exhibition is provocative in that it suggests that the design of a chair is urbanism. The design of a coffin is as well. Landscape urbanism doesn't address chairs and coffins. Is that the difference?

POSTED BY ILANA COHEN AT 10:01 PM

APPENDIX

Contributors

Acknowledgments

Index

Illustration Credits

Contributors

Since 2006, **Iñaki Ábalos** has managed his own office based in Madrid–Ábalos arquitectos–and collaborates with Renata Sentkiewicz (Ábalos + Sentkiewicz arquitectos). Iñaki Ábalos was the Kenzo Tange Professor at Harvard University Graduate School of Design in 2008.

The **atelier d'architecture autogérée** (Studio for Self-managed Architecture, **AAA**) was founded in 2001 by Constantin Petcou and Doina Petrescu to conduct explorations, actions, and research on urban mutations and emerging cultural, social, and political practices in the contemporary city. The collective includes architects, artists, urban planners, landscape designers, sociologists, students, and residents.

D. Michelle Addington is an Associate Professor of Architecture at Yale University. She previously worked as a research engineer with NASA and in the chemical industry with Dupont. She holds degrees from Harvard GSD, Temple University, and Tulane University. She recently co-authored *Smart Materials and Technologies for the Architecture and Design Professions*.

Founded in 1946, **Arup** became world-renowned for its design of the Sydney Opera House, followed by its work on the Centre Pompidou in Paris. Arup's most recent work for the 2008 Olympics in Beijing has reaffirmed its reputation for delivering innovative and sustainable designs that reinvent the built environment.

Kye Askins is an accidental geographer, currently teaching, researching, and campaigning via Northumbria University. She is passionate about issues of social and environmental justice.

Atelier Van Lieshout (AVL), Rotterdam, founded by artist Joep van Lieshout, is a multidisciplinary art practice encompassing installation, design, furniture, and architecture. The name Atelier Van Lieshout emphasizes that the works of art do not stem solely from Joep van Lieshout, but are produced by a creative team of artists, designers, and architects.

The **Barcelona Urban Ecology Agency (BCN Ecologia)**, created in 2000, is a government consortium made up of the Barcelona City Council, The Metropolitan Water Services and Waste Treatment Body, and the Provincial Council of Barcelona. The Agency was created to rethink the cities and bring urban management as close to sustainable development as possible.

Henri Bava founded Agence Ter with Michel Hoessler and Olivier Philippe in 1986. Since 1998, he has been Titular Professor at the University of Karlsruhe, where he heads the landscape institute of the architecture faculty. In 2000, he started the German bureau of Agence Ter in Karlsruhe; he currently directs projects from the French and German offices.

Ulrich Beck is Professor of Sociology at the University of Munich, and the British Journal of Sociology Visiting Centennial Professor at the London School of Economics and Political Science since 1997. He is editor of *Soziale Welt*, and of the *Second Modernity* series published by Suhrkamp. His interests focus on risk society, globalization, individualization, reflexive modernization, and cosmopolitanism.

Pierre Bélanger is an Associate Professor at Harvard GSD. His academic research and public work focus on the convergence of landscape and infrastructure in the interrelated fields of planning, design, and engineering. Bélanger's recent publications include *Landscape as Infrastructure* (2009), *Landscapes of Disassembly* (2007), and *Synthetic Surfaces* (2007).

Josh Bers is a Senior Engineer in the Advanced Networking Business Unit of BBN Technologies. His professional experience and interests are in the areas of distributed systems and multimodal human-computer interfaces. Specific application areas include: embedded spoken-language interfaces, mobile robot teams, wireless ad hoc networking, sensor networks, and network management systems.

Homi K. Bhabha is Anne F. Rothenberg Professor of the Humanities, Department of English, Harvard University; Director of the Humanities Center at Harvard; and Distinguished Visiting Professor in the Humanities at University College, London. His *Location of Culture* is a Routledge Classic, and forthcoming titles include "A Measure of Dwelling" and "The Right to Narrate."

Assaf Biderman teaches at MIT, where he is the Associate Director of the SENSEable City Laboratory. He has a background in physics and human-computer interaction, and focuses on working in partnership with city administrations and industry members worldwide to explore how miniaturized and distributed technologies can be used to create more sustainable future cities.

Stefano Boeri is Editor-in-Chief of the international magazine *Abitare* and was formerly Editor-in-Chief of *Domus* magazine. He is Professor of Urban Design at the Milan Polytechnic, and has taught as visiting professor at Harvard GSD, MIT, and the Berlage Institute. His Milan-based Boeri Studio is active in urban design and architecture.

Andrea Branzi is Professor in the Third Faculty of Architecture and Industrial Design at the Politecnico di Milano. From 1964 to 1974 he was a partner of Archizoom Associati.

Since 1967, he has worked in the fields of industrial and research design, architecture, urban planning, education, and cultural promotion.

Giuliana Bruno is a film and visual culture scholar and Professor of Visual and Environmental Studies at Harvard University. She explores what film shares with the design of space and the visual arts. Her book, *Jane and Louise Wilson: A Free and Anonymous Monument*, examines the multi-screen art installation of the Turner Prize nominees.

Lawrence Buell is Powell M. Cabot Professor of American Literature at Harvard University. He is the author of *The Future of Environmental Criticism* and is co-editor, with Wai Chee Dimock, of *Shades of the Planet: American Literature as World Literature*.

Raoul Bunschoten, principal of CHORA architecture and urbanism, is Professor of Urban Systematics at the University of Applied Science in Düsseldorf, Germany, and is advisor to the German Ministry of urbanism and construction on issues related to sustainable city planning and energy efficiency in city design.

Armando Carbonell is a Design Critic at the GSD and Chairman of the Department of Planning and Urban Form at the Lincoln Institute of Land Policy in Cambridge. He is co-editor of the volume *Smart Growth: Form and Consequences*, and a member of the Forum for Urban Design in New York and the Loeb Fellowship Council at Harvard.

Vicky Cheng has been researching in the field of environmental architecture and urban design over the last seven years, having obtained a degree in building services engineering. She currently works at the University of Cambridge and Cambridge Architectural Research Limited on a range of research and consultancy projects.

Lizabeth Cohen is Howard Mumford Jones Professor of American Studies and Chair of the History Department at Harvard. She authored *Making a New Deal: Industrial Workers in Chicago, 1919–1939*, winner of the Bancroft Prize and finalist for the Pulitzer. She is currently writing *Saving America's Cities: Ed Logue and the Struggle to Renew Urban America in the Suburban Age*.

Preston Scott Cohen is Gerald M. McCue Professor in Architecture and Chair of the Department of Architecture at Harvard GSD. His firm, Preston Scott Cohen, Inc. in Cambridge, MA, engages in projects ranging from houses to educational and cultural institutions. Recent commissions include a Student Center for Nanjing University in Xianlin, China (2007–2009).

Verena Andermatt Conley teaches in Romance Languages and Literatures and Literature and Comparative Literature at Harvard. Her publications include *Hélène Cixous: Writing the Feminine;* and *Eco-politics: The Environment in Poststructuralist Thought*. She is currently finishing a manuscript entitled *Spatial Fictions: Subjectivity, the City and the Nation-State in post-68 French Cultural Theory*.

Cook+Fox Architects is an award-winning New York City studio focused on exploring the aesthetics of sustainability and integrated, high-performance design. The firm works on projects of all scales, seeking out work that fundamentally rethinks how buildings interact with people and the natural environment.

Leland Cott FAIA is Adjunct Professor of Urban Design at Harvard GSD. He is a founding principal of Bruner/Cott & Associates, whose designs have been widely published and have received over 50 local and national awards. He is a former president of the Boston Society of Architects.

Margaret Crawford is Professor of Architecture at the University of California, Berkeley, and was previously Professor of Urban Design and Planning Theory at the Harvard Graduate School of Design. Her books include, *Building the Workingman's Paradise: The Design of American Company Towns* and *Everyday Urbanism*.

Born in Italy, **Mario Cucinella** graduated from the Genoa University Architecture Faculty in 1987 and founded Mario Cucinella Architects in Paris in 1992, and in Bologna in 1999. His work focuses on themes connected with environmental planning and sustainability in architecture. Mario Cucinella also devotes himself to the research and development of industrial design products, and to teaching.

Dilip da Cunha is an architect and city planner, and visiting faculty at the University of Pennsylvania and at Parsons School of Design. Dilip, with Anuradha Mathur, is author of *Mississippi Floods: Designing a Shifting Landscape, Deccan Traverses: the Making of Bangalore's Terrain;* and *SOAK: Mumbai in an Estuary*.

Fernando de Mello Franco cofounded MMBB Architects in 1990, and is currently a professor at São Judas Tadeu University. He received the "Best Entry Award" at the Rotterdam International Biennale (2007), and has participated as a Member of the Deutsche Bank Award Jury at Urban Age São Paulo (2008). He has co-curated exhibitions including "São Paulo: Networks and Places" at the Venice Biennale in 2006.

Pierre de Meuron is Arthur Rotch Design Critic in Architecture at the GSD and co-founder of Herzog & de Meuron. He is also co-founder of ETH Studio Basel–Contemporary City Institute. Herzog & de Meuron has received awards including The Pritzker Architecture Prize and the RIBA Royal Gold Medal. Recent projects include the National Stadium Beijing for the 2008 Olympic Games.

Gareth Doherty is a Doctor of Design candidate at Harvard University Graduate School of Design, where his dissertation is an ethnographic study of contemporary landscape and urbanism in Bahrain. He spent 2007–2008 in Bahrain on a Sheldon Traveling Fellowship. He has received a Harvard University Certificate of Distinction in Teaching, and is a founding editor of *New Geographies*.

Herbert Dreiseitl trained as an artist in England, Norway, and Germany. In 1980, inspired by a vision for water, architecture, environment, and art, Herbert founded the Atelier. Herbert continues to delight in collaborating with a diverse array of partners, from local craftsmen to renowned architects such as Foster and Partners.

Ziggy Drozdowski has been with Hoberman Associates since 2004 and currently holds the position of Technical Director. His work ranges from computational design and modeling to motion control system specification and implementation. He received his Bachelor's degree in Engineering from The Cooper Union, with concentrations in electrical engineering and acoustics.

Andrés Duany is a founding principal at Duany Plater-Zyberk & Company (DPZ). A leader of the New Urbanism, DPZ has completed designs for almost 300 new towns, regional plans, and community revitalization projects. Duany's publications include *The New Civic Art* and *Suburban Nation: The Rise of Sprawl and the Decline of the American Dream*.

Before forming BDa, **Bill Dunster** worked at Michael Hopkins and Partners (MHP); his final MHP project–Nottingham University New Campus unit–was awarded the Stirling Prize, Sustainability Award 2001. Bill developed the environmental strategy and detailed façade design for Portcullis House. In 1995 he built Hope House–a prototype low energy live/work unit.

Mark Dwyer is an architect and urban designer; he holds a Master of Architecture in Urban Design from Harvard GSD, and has taught at the GSD and the University of Pennsylvania. Before joining the Fundación Metrópoli (2009), Mark was an Associate in the New York office of Enrique Norten.

Claudia Pasquero and Marco Poletto are Directors of the experimental design practice **ecoLogicStudio** and Unit Masters at the Architectural Association in London. EcoLogic-Studio has recently completed a shopping mall eco-roof in Carugate, Milan, a large-scale systemic master-planning work in Senegal, the Lightwall house in Turin, and a library interior in Cirie.

[ecosistema urbano] focuses on the research of new projects that understand sustainable development as a resource for innovation and enthusiasm. They have received several international awards and their work has been widely published and exhibited. Currently, they are working on URBAN INTERFACE, an urban proposal for Shanghai Expo 2010.

Amy C. Edmondson is the Novartis Professor of Leadership and Management and Co-Unit Head of the Technology and Operations Management Unit at Harvard Business School. In the 1980s, she was Chief Engineer for architect/inventor Buckminster Fuller; her book, *A Fuller Explanation*, clarifies Fuller's mathematical contributions for a non-technical audience.

David Edwards is a Professor of biomedical engineering at Harvard University and founder of Le Laboratoire, an art and design center in Paris. He is a member of the national academies of engineering in the U.S.A. and France, and a French chevalier de l'ordre des arts et des lettres.

Susan Fainstein is Professor of Urban Planning at Harvard GSD. Her research and teaching focus on the politics and economics of urban redevelopment, tourism, comparative urban and social policy, planning theory, and issues of gender and planning. Among her books are *Readings in Planning Theory*, and *Cities and Visitors*.

Sir Terry Farrell CBE is the U.K. Government's lead advisor on the Planning and Vision for its Thames Gateway project, and also the London Mayor's Architect Planning Advisor for the Outer London Commission. He is Visiting Professor of Planning at the Bartlett School of Planning, University College London.

Alexander Felson holds a joint faculty position between the schools of Forestry and Architecture at Yale University. His research and practice combine ecological experiments with urban design to analyze and shape urban ecosystems. His implemented "designed experiments" include a long-term ecological research project across N.Y.C. through the Million Trees Project.

Richard T.T. Forman is PAES Professor of Advanced Environmental Studies in Landscape Ecology at Harvard University and a faculty member at the Graduate School of Design. Considered a "father" of landscape ecology and of road ecology, he plays a key scholarly role in the emergence of urban-region ecology and planning.

Kristin Frederickson practices with Reed Hilderbrand Associates in Watertown, Massachusetts. She received her Bachelor of Arts (cum laude) in English and Studio Art from Williams College, and a Master of Landscape Architecture (with distinction) from the Harvard University Graduate School of Design, where she was awarded the Charles Eliot Traveling Fellowship.

Gerald Frug is the Louis D. Brandeis Professor of Law at Harvard Law School. His specialty is local government law. He is the author of *City Bound: How States Stifle Urban Innovation* (2008, with David Barron) and *City Making: Building Communities without Building Walls* (1999).

Peter Galison is Joseph Pellegrino University Professor of the History of Science and of Physics at Harvard University. His books include: *How Experiments End, Image and Logic*, and *Einstein's Clocks*. He co-produced two documentary films: "Ultimate Weapon: The H-bomb Dilemma" and "Secrecy," which premiered at the Sundance Film Festival (2008).

Edward Glaeser is Fred and Eleanor Glimp Professor of Economics at Harvard and Director of the Taubman Center for State and Local Government and the Rappaport Institute for Greater Boston. He studies the economics of cities and the role that geographic proximity can play in creating knowledge and innovation.

Shawn Gupta currently works within the Buro Happold Façade Engineering group in London. He holds a Bachelor's degree in Materials Science Engineering from the University of Pennsylvania and a Master's degree in Architecture from the University of California, Los Angeles.

Susannah Hagan is Director of R/E/D (Research into Environment + Design) and Professor of Architecture at the University of Brighton. She is a Fellow of the Royal Society of Arts and the Forum for Urban Design. Her books include *Taking Shape: The New Contract between Architecture and Nature.*

Jacques Herzog is Arthur Rotch Design Critic in Architecture at the GSD and co-founder of Herzog & de Meuron. He is also co-founder of ETH Studio Basel–Contemporary City Institute. Herzog & de Meuron has received awards including The Pritzker Architecture Prize and the RIBA Royal Gold Medal. Recent projects include the National Stadium Beijing for the 2008 Olympic Games.

Sandi Hilal graduated in architecture and is Head of UNRWA's Camp Improvement Unit in the West Bank. She is a Visiting Professor at the International Academy of Art Palestine,

and co-curator of the project Decolonizing Architecture. In 2006 she obtained the title of research doctorate in transborder policies for daily life at the University of Trieste.

Gary Hilderbrand is Adjunct Professor of Landscape Architecture at the GSD and Principal of Reed Hilderbrand Associates, Inc. Hilderbrand served on the editorial advisory board of *Harvard Design Magazine* and the advisory board of the former Spacemaker Press. He was elected as a Fellow of ASLA in 2001 and is a Fellow of the American Academy in Rome.

Chuck Hoberman is founder of Hoberman Associates, currently engaged in architectural projects to create the next generation of adaptive buildings. His work has been exhibited at the Museum of Modern Art, New York, and in 2009 Hoberman was the recipient of the Wyss Prize for Bioinspired Adaptive Architecture at Harvard University.

Mike Hodson joined The Centre for Sustainable Urban and Regional Futures at the University of Salford, U.K. in 2003 as a Research Fellow. His research interests focus on city-regional transitions to low-carbon economies, the ways in which this may or may not happen, and understandings of the lessons to be learned from such processes.

Walter Hood is Professor and former Chair of the Landscape Architecture Department at the University of California, Berkeley, and Principal of Hood Design in Oakland, CA. He has worked in architecture, urban design, community planning, environmental art, and research. He is currently researching and writing a book entitled "Urban Landscapes; American Landscape Typologies."

Zhang Huan lives and works in Shanghai and New York. Recent solo shows include PaceWildenstein NY; White Cube London, Haunch of Venison London, Berlin, and Zurich; and the Asia Society. As Director and Set Designer, his first opera, Semele, is now at the Theatre Royal de La Monnaie in Brussels.

Dorothée Imbert is an Associate Professor in the Department of Landscape Architecture at Harvard University's Graduate School of Design. She is the author of *Between Garden and City: Jean Canneel-Claes and Landscape Modernism*, as well as numerous essays.

Donald Ingber is the Director of the Wyss Institute for Biologically Inspired Engineering at Harvard University. His pioneering work, demonstrating that tensegrity architecture is a fundamental principle that governs how living cells and tissues are structured at the nanometer scale, has inspired a new generation of biologists, engineers, and nanotechnologists.

Founded and directed by Julien de Smedt, JDS Architects has offices in Copenhagen, Brussels, and Oslo. Recently awarded the Rotterdam Maaskant Prize, JDS Architects focuses on architecture and design–from large scale planning to furniture–turning intense research and analysis of practical and theoretical issues into the driving forces behind the design.

As well as presenting "Play Me, I'm Yours" in cities around the globe, Luke Jerram creates sculptures and installation artworks. He is currently an artist and research fellow at the University of Southampton, where he is designing Aeolus–an acoustic wind pavilion.

Mitchell Joachim is a faculty member at Columbia University and Parsons The New School of Design. He was selected by *Wired* magazine for "The 2008 Smart List: 15 People the Next President Should Listen To" and, most recently, made the *Rolling Stone* list of "100 People Who Are Changing America."

Ed Kashi is a photojournalist, filmmaker, and educator dedicated to documenting the social and political issues that define our times. A sensitive eye and an intimate relationship to his subjects are the signatures of his work. Kashi's complex imagery has been recognized for its compelling rendering of the human condition.

Aaron Kelley is a master's degree candidate in City and Regional Planning at the University of Pennsylvania, School of Design; he has a bachelor's degree in geography. Aaron is collaborator with Fundación Metrópoli on a range of ongoing projects and publications.

Sheila Kennedy is Professor of the Practice of Architecture at MIT, Principal of Kennedy & Violich Architecture Ltd. (KVA), and Director of Design at MATx. Kennedy has appeared in *The Economist, The Wall Street Journal*, and *The New York Times*; her work has been featured on BBC World News and CNN Principal Voices.

Laurie Kerr works in the New York City Mayor's Office of Long Term Planning and Sustainability; she is developing the city's greenhouse gas emissions policy related to buildings and the greening of the building codes. Her architectural criticism has appeared in *The Wall Street Journal, Slate*, and *Architectural Record*.

Niall G. Kirkwood is Professor of Landscape Architecture and Technology at the Harvard Graduate School of Design, where he has taught since 1992, and was Chair of the Department of Landscape Architecture from 2003 to 2009. Recent publications include, *Manufactured Sites: Rethinking the Post-Industrial Landscape.*

Rem Koolhaas co-founded the Office for Metropolitan Architecture (OMA) and is a Professor at Harvard University, where he conducts the Project on the City research program. Koolhaas and OMA have received awards including the Pritzker Architecture Prize and the RIBA Gold Medal. Koolhaas is a member of the European Council of Foreign Relations and the EU Reflection Group.

Alex Krieger FAIA is a Professor at Harvard GSD and Interim Chair of the Department of Urban Planning and Design. His publications include editing *Urban Design* and co-editing two volumes of *Harvard Design Magazine*. He is founding principal of Chan Krieger Sieniewicz, an architecture and urban design firm in Cambridge, Massachusetts.

Nancy Krieger is Professor of Society, Human Development, and Health at the Harvard School of Public Health, and Co-Director of the HSPH Interdisciplinary Concentration on Women, Gender, and Health. Dr. Krieger is editor of *Embodying Inequality: Epidemiologic Perspectives*.

Sanford Kwinter is Professor of Architectural Theory and Criticism at Harvard GSD. His articles and books include *Far From Equilibrium: Essays on Technology and Design Culture* and *Requiem: For the City at the Turn of the Millennium*. He is currently writing a book on Africa and the origin of form.

Bruno Latour is a professor at Sciences Po, Paris, associated with the Centre de sociologie des organisations (CSO), where he is also Vice-President for Research. He is author of *Politics of Nature: How to Bring the Sciences into Democracy* and *The Making of Law: An Ethnography of the Conseil d'Etat*.

Mathieu Lehanneur, designer, lives and works in Paris. He graduated from ENSCI-Les Ateliers in 2001 and opened a studio dedicated to industrial design and interior architecture. His projects are part of several permanent museum collections, including MoMA in New York, FRAC in Paris, and the Musee des Art Decoratifs (Paris).

Nina-Marie Lister is Associate Professor of Urban and Regional Planning at Ryerson University in Toronto, Canada. She is founding principal of *planform*, a creative studio practice exploring the relationship between landscape, ecology, and urbanism. Lister is co-editor of *The Ecosystem Approach: Complexity, Uncertainty, and Managing for Sustainability*.

Simon Marvin is Professor and Co-Director of The Centre for Sustainable Urban and Regional Futures at the University of Salford, U.K. Recently, he has been working on comparative urban responses to economic and ecological pressures–in particular in London, New York, and San Francisco.

Anuradha Mathur is an architect and landscape architect. She is Associate Professor at the School of Design, University of Pennsylvania. Mathur, with Dilip da Cunha, is author of *Mississippi Floods: Designing a Shifting Landscape*; *Deccan Traverses: the Making of Bangalore's Terrain*; and *SOAK: Mumbai in an Estuary*.

Fernando de Mello Franco co-founded MMBB Architects in 1990, and is currently a professor at Sao Judas Tadeu University. He received the "Best Entry Award" at the Rotterdam International Biennale (2007), and has participated as a Member of the Deutsche Bank Award Jury at Urban Age Sao Paulo (2008). He has co-curated exhibitions including "Sao Paulo: networks and places" at the Venice Biennale in 2006.

Achim Menges is Professor and Director of the Institute for Computational Design at Stuttgart University. Currently, he is also Visiting Professor in Architecture at Harvard University's Graduate School of Design, and Visiting Professor for the Emergent Technologies and Design MArch/MSc Program at the Architectural Association in London.

William J. Mitchell is the Alexander Dreyfoos Professor of Architecture and Media Arts and Sciences at MIT, where he directs the Smart Cities group in the MIT Media Laboratory and heads the MIT Design Laboratory. His recent books include *Imagining MIT*, *World's Greatest Architect*, and the forthcoming "Reinventing the Automobile."

Kathryn Moore is Professor at Birmingham Institute of Art and Design, Birmingham City University, and a former president of the Landscape Institute. Moore's book entitled "Overlooking the Visual" proposes a radical reappraisal of the relationship between senses and intelligence.

Toshiko Mori is Robert P. Hubbard Professor in the Practice of Architecture at Harvard GSD, and was Chair of the Department of Architecture (2002–2008). She is Principal of Toshiko Mori Architect; current work includes houses in Connecticut, New York, and Taiwan, and institutional projects in Syracuse, Providence, Buffalo, and New York City.

Mohsen Mostafavi is Dean of the Harvard Graduate School of Design and Alexander and Victoria Wiley Professor of Design. He has served on the steering committee of the Aga Khan Award for Architecture and the juries of the Holcim Foundation for Sustainable Construction and the RIBA Gold Medal. His books include *Surface Architecture* (2002), *Approximations* (2002), *Landscape Urbanism* (2004), and *Structure as Space* (2006).

MVRDV–based in Rotterdam–works in the fields of architecture, urbanism, and city planning. Founders are Winy Maas, Jacob van Rijs, and Nathalie de Vries. Recent projects include an urban masterplan in Oslo (Norway), Gwang Gyo (Korea), Greater Paris (France), Tianjin and Chengdu (China), and an eco-city in Logroño (Spain).

Erika Naginski is Associate Professor of Architectural History at Harvard GSD. She is a historian of European art and architecture interested in Enlightenment aesthetics, theories of public space, cultural memory and historic preservation, and the critical traditions of art history. Her forthcoming book is entitled "Sculpture and Enlightenment."

Christoph Niemann's illustrations have appeared on the covers of *The New Yorker*, *Atlantic Monthly*, *The New York Times Magazine* and *American Illustration*. Niemann is author of two children's books, *The Pet Dragon* and *The Police Cloud*.

An architect and urban designer, **Christine Outram** is currently a Research Fellow at the SENSEable City Laboratory, where she focuses on harnessing emerging technologies to tackle problems of sustainability and livability in inner urban areas. She is leading the Copencycle project that will be displayed at the COP15 United Nations Climate Summit.

PARKKIM, Yoonjin Park and Jungyoon Kim received Master in Landscape Architecture degrees from Harvard GSD in 2000. They both worked at West 8 (Rotterdam, the Netherlands) and taught at Wageningen University before they founded PARKKIM in 2004, upon winning the Chichi Earthquake Memorial International Competition.

Federico Parolotto graduated in architecture from the Polytechnic of Milan. He joined Systematica in 1998 and worked as transport consultant on international projects including Burnby Masterplan, Prague with Asymptote; Tour Phare, Paris with Morphosis; and Masdar with Foster+Partners. In 2009, he founded MIC Mobility in Chain with Federico Cassani and Davide Boazzi.

Alessandro Petti, architect, is a Research Fellow at Centre for Research Architecture, Goldsmiths College, University of London. He co-curated research projects including Borderdevices and Stateless Nation, and has written works including *Dubai Offshore Urbanism in Heterotopia and the City*, Routledge 2008. He is currently working on a research project entitled "Atlas of Decolonization."

Antoine Picon is Professor of the History of Architecture and Technology and Co-Director of Doctoral Programs at Harvard GSD. He has published books including *French Architects and Engineers in the Age of Enlightenment*, and has received awards including the Medaille de la Ville de Paris. Picon has degrees in engineering, architecture, and history.

Linda Pollak is a principal of Marpillero Pollak Architects. She has received grants from the American Academy in Rome and National Endowment for the Arts. Co-author of *Inside Outside: Between Architecture and Landscape*, Linda is also on the Board of Directors of the Storefront for Art and Architecture and Design Trust for Public Space.

Spiro N. Pollalis is Professor of Design, Technology and Management at Harvard GSD. In 2007, he founded the 5-year RMJM Program for Integrated Design, and in 1997, he founded the Center for Design Informatics at Harvard. His recent books include, *Understanding the Outsourcing of Architectural Services* (2007), and *Computer-Aided Collaboration in Managing Construction* (2006).

Bill Rankin is a PhD candidate at Harvard University, dually enrolled in the architecture and history of science programs. His dissertation research focuses on international mapping and navigation technology in the twentieth century.

Professor **Carlo Ratti** practices architecture in Turin and teaches at MIT, where he directs the SENSEable City Laboratory. He has co-authored over 100 scientific publications and holds several patents. At the World Expo 2008, his Digital Water Pavilion was hailed by *TIME* magazine as one of the "Best Inventions of the Year."

Daniel Raven-Ellison is the founder of the URBAN EARTH project. A geographer, teacher, activist, and adventurer, Daniel works to find ways to encourage people to see the world in new ways.

Rebar is an art and design collective based in San Francisco. Rebar's work varies broadly in scale, scope and context, and therefore belies discrete categorization. It is, at minimum, situated in the domains of environmental installation, urbanism, and absurdity. Rebar is directed by Matthew Passmore, John Bela, Blaine Merker, and Teresa Aguilera.

Chris Reed is the founder and Principal of Stoss Landscape Urbanism, a Boston-based strategic design and planning practice. Reed is a Design Critic at the Harvard Graduate School of Design, and an Adjunct Associate Professor at the University of Pennsylvania School of Design. He is a registered landscape architect.

Christoph Reinhart is an Associate Professor of Architectural Technology and area coordinator for the "Sustainable Design" concentration at Harvard GSD. He works on daylighting, user-building interactions as well as enhanced design workflows and performance metrics. He serves on several editorial boards and has contributed to over 75 scientific publications.

Jeremy Rifkin is founder and President of the Foundation on Economic Trends, Bethesda, MD. He is author of seventeen bestselling books on the impact of scientific and technological changes on the economy, society, and the environment. He currently advises the European Commission, the European Parliament, and several EU heads of state.

Paul Robbins is Professor in the School of Geography and Development, University of Arizona. His research centers on the relationships between individuals (homeowners, hunters, professional foresters), environmental actors (lawns, elk, mesquite trees), and the institutions that connect them. His current concern is management of the common mosquito in cities of the U.S. Southwest.

Matthias Sauerbruch is a partner at Sauerbruch Hutton in Berlin, whose prize-winning projects are known for their serious engagement with issues of sustainability and have been the subject of many exhibitions and monographs. Sauerbruch has taught at the GSD since 2008 and is a member of the Academy of the Arts Berlin.

Susannah Sayler, a 2009 Loeb Fellow at Harvard GSD, is a photographer and Co-Founder of the Canary Project with Edward Morris. The Canary Project produces visual media, events, and artwork that build public understanding of human-induced climate change and energize commitment to solutions.

Thomas Schroepfer is Associate Professor of Architecture at Harvard GSD. He has worked for Studio Daniel Libeskind and was previously an editor of *FuE Forum*. His work has been recognized by the Union Internationale des Architectes (UIA). Schroepfer has degrees from The Cooper Union, University of the Arts Berlin, and the GSD.

Luc Schuiten applies concepts of biomimicry at the urban scale. Since 1995, the Atelier Luc Schuiten has developed a series of projects for "vertical gardens" that introduce vegetation in the residual spaces of Brussels, as well as other projects for "green" infrastructures. Schuiten has published three books on this topic: *Archiborescence* (2006), *Habitarbre* (2007), and *Vegetal City* (2009).

Matthias Schüler is Adjunct Professor of Environmental Technology at the GSD. He is founder of Transsolar, Stuttgart, Germany, consultants on sustainable building and collaborators with Herzog & de Meuron, Stephen Holl, Behnisch and Partners, Jean Nouvel, Gehry Partners, Murphy/Jahn, OMA, and Foster + Partners. He is author of, *Transsolar Climate Engineering*, and co-author of *Glazing Atlas*, Detail 1999.

Niels Schulz led the Urban Energy Systems (UES) project team at Imperial College until

March 2008, when he moved to a position as Research Scholar at the International Institute of Applied Systems Analysis (IIASA). He is also a research analyst for the German advisory council on global change to the federal government (WBGU).

Martha Schwartz is Professor in Practice of Landscape Architecture at Harvard GSD; she teaches design studios focusing on artistic expression in the landscape. Her firm, Martha Schwartz, Inc. in Cambridge, Massachusetts and Martha Schwartz Partners in London, U.K., specializes in landscape design and site-specific public art commissions.

Jesse Shapins is an urban media historian, artist, and theorist. His work has been exhibited at MoMA and many other venues internationally. His research toward a PhD at the Harvard GSD is focused on György Kepes and Kevin Lynch's 1955–59 urban research experiment, "The Perceptual Form of the City."

Dirk Sijmons is a co-founder of H+N+S Landscape Architects, recipient of the National Prince Bernard Culture Award (2001). He is currently Professor of Environmental Design at TU–Delft; his most recent publication is *Greetings from Europe* (2008). Sijmons was State Landscape Architect of the Netherlands (2004–2008) and received the Edgar Doncker Award (2007).

soa architectes was founded in Paris in 2001 by Pierre Sartoux and Augustin Rosenstiehl. soa's architecture is defined by a collective working method reinforced with a strong aesthetic, theoretical, and sociological background. soa aspires to an architecture of poetry, dreams, and *joie de vivre*.

Richard Sommer, formerly a member of Harvard GSD's faculty and Director of its Urban Design Programs, has recently been appointed as Dean and Professor of Architecture and Urbanism at the Daniels Faculty of Architecture, Landscape and Design, University of Toronto.

Koen Steemers is Professor of Sustainable Design and Head of the Department of Architecture, University of Cambridge. His research team is concerned with sustainable architecture and urban design, with a particular emphasis on the role of human perception and behavior.

Byron Stigge leads the Sustainability Consulting group for the North America region of Buro Happold. He has worked on projects around the world, from city-scale sustainable master-planning projects, to LEED Platinum buildings, to detailed systems and façade-analysis projects. Recent projects include: Orange County Great Park in Irvine, California; Tellapur City, Hyderabad, India; CSOB Bank, Prague; and Governors Island Strategic Plan, New York City.

John R. Stilgoe is the Robert and Lois Orchard Professor in the History of Landscape Development at Harvard University. Most recently author of *Train Time: Railroads and Imminent Landscape Change* and *Landscape and Images*, Stilgoe conducts research on subjects including national critical infrastructure, steganography, catoptropmancy, catoptrics, energy-independent housing, and old-field landscape.

Donald Swearer is Director of the Center for the Study of World Religions and Distinguished Visiting Professor of Buddhist Studies at the Harvard Divinity School. His recent books include *The Buddhist World of Southeast Asia*, and *Becoming the Buddha: The Ritual of Image Consecration in Thailand*.

Anja Thierfelder, Architect, lectures on "introduction into design" at Technische Universität Stuttgart, Germany, and at the University of Limerick, Ireland. She was an editor and photographer for *Transsolar Climate Engineering* (2002), and has since been conducting background research in collaboration with Transsolar, mainly about bionics and sustainability in urban planning.

Karen Thornber is Assistant Professor of Comparative Literature in the Department of Literature and Comparative Literature at Harvard. Author of *Empire of Texts in Motion: Chinese, Korean, and Taiwanese Transculturations of Japanese Literature* (Harvard 2009), her current book project is titled *Ecoambivalence, Ecoambiguity, and Ecodegradation: Changing Environments of East Asian and World Literatures*.

Sissel Tolaas studied mathematics, chemical science, linguistics and languages, and visual art. Her focus is on smell/smell and language communication within different sciences, fields of art, and other disciplines. Tolaas established the RE_searchLab Berlin for smell and communication in 2004, supported by IFF (International Flavors & Fragrances Inc., New York).

Triptyque, made up of architects Greg Bousquet, Carolina Bueno, Guillaume Sibaud, and Olivier Raffaelli, have been working in São Paulo since 2000 and in Paris since 2008. Triptyque is based on the idea of an exchange platform, where the different repertoires, cultures, and references of participants blend and strive to obtain one cohesive work.

Michael R. Van Valkenburgh is Charles Eliot Professor in Practice of Landscape Architecture at Harvard GSD. As lead principal of Michael Van Valkenburgh Associates Inc., with offices in New York City and Cambridge, Van Valkenburgh has designed a wide range of project types including public parks and civic and institutional landscapes.

Vector Architects, based in Beijing, was established by Gong Dong and Hongyu Zhang in 2008. With combined experience in architecture design practice and real estate development, the firm pursues simplicity and clarity through considering the social, cultural, historic, climate, and urban context of each project.

Alfonso Vegara is an architect, economist, and sociologist, with a PhD in City and Regional Planning. He is founder and President of the Fundación Metrópoli, and fellow and trustee of the Eisenhower Foundation. He has taught at the Universities of Madrid, Navarra and Pennsylvania School of Design. Vegara co-authored the book *Territorios Inteligentes*.

Rafael Viñoly is Principal of Rafael Viñoly Architects PC (founded 1983 in New York). He has completed many critically and publicly praised buildings throughout the United States, Europe, Latin America, and Asia. He is known as an architect of imagination and rigor with a proven capacity to create beloved civic and cultural spaces.

Marije Vogelzang is an eating designer and founder of Proef, a place to eat in Rotterdam and a design studio/restaurant in Amsterdam. The basis for Proef's work is the verb "to eat," designing and advising for, among others, hospitals, museums, and restaurants. Vogelzang's recent book is called *EAT LOVE*.

Loïc Wacquant is Professor of Sociology at the University of California, Berkeley, and Researcher at the Centre de sociologie européenne, Paris. His interests span urban marginality, the penal state, incarnation, ethnoracial domination, and social theory. His books include *Punishing the Poor: The Neoliberal Government of Social Insecurity* (2009).

Charles Waldheim is Professor and Chair of Landscape Architecture at Harvard GSD. He has edited *The Landscape Urbanism Reader*, *CASE: Lafayette Park Detroit*, and is co-editor of *Stalking Detroit*. He is currently writing the first book-length history of Chicago's O'Hare International Airport, entitled "Chicago O'Hare: A Natural and Cultural History."

Holly Wasilowski earned a Master of Design Studies in Sustainable Design and is pursuing a Doctor of Design degree at Harvard GSD. Her research focuses on building performance simulation and occupant impact on building energy consumption. She is a registered architect and LEED accredited professional.

Michael J. Watts is Professor of Geography and Director of Development Studies at the University of California, Berkeley. He was Director of the Institute of International Studies there from 1994 to 2004. He has written extensively on the oil industry, and his most recent book is *The Curse of the Black Gold: Fifty Years of Oil in the Niger Delta*.

Camilla Ween, RIBA, MIHT, FRSA, Loeb Fellow 2008, is an architect/urban planner working on the development of strategic master plans in London. Her interest is in developments that are sustainable with high quality public transport infrastructure, public realm, and have innovative solutions to water, waste, and energy supply.

Eyal Weizman is Director of the Centre for Research Architecture at Goldsmiths College, London. A member of the architectural collective "decolonizing architecture," his books include *A Civilian Occupation*, *Hollow Land*, and *The Lesser Evil*, the series *Territories 1, 2* and *3*, *Yellow Rhythms*, and articles in journals, magazines, and edited books.

Matt Welsh is an Associate Professor of Computer Science at Harvard. His research interests span aspects of complex systems, including internet services, distributed systems, and sensor networks. Current projects involve the development of novel programming languages and operating systems for sensor networks, resource management abstractions, and building open sensor network test beds supporting experimental research.

Christian Werthmann is Associate Professor of Landscape Architecture at Harvard GSD. He won the 2000 San Francisco Prize for his Harvey Milk Memorial proposal. He authored *Green Roof: A Case Study* (Princeton Architectural Press, 2007), and is co-founder of the interdisciplinary research group TransUrban. His latest research initiative is called *Dirty Work*.

Kongjian Yu received his Doctor of Design degree from Harvard GSD. He is founder and Dean of the Graduate School of Landscape Architecture at Peking University, and founder and President of Turenscape. His recent book is *The Art Of Survival–Recovering Landscape Architecture*, and he is Chief Editor of *Landscape Architecture China*.

Martin Zogran is Assistant Professor of Urban Design at the Harvard GSD. He previously worked at Chan Krieger & Associates, managing urban design and planning projects for cities including Washington DC and New York. He has worked in the offices of Rafael Viñoly and Margaret Helfand, and his work has been in *Domus*, *Interior Design*, and *Places* magazines.

Acknowledgments

The making of any serious publication requires the engagement and support of numerous people, including but invariably exceeding the list of names on the contents page. The deliberate interdisciplinary scope and wide intended reach of *Ecological Urbanism* makes this especially so; we are indebted to the encouragement, participation, and vision of so many in the Harvard community and beyond. With their help, we hope that we've begun a conversation that will continue to resonate across multiple fields of research and action.

We must begin by thanking Drew Gilpin Faust, President of Harvard University, for sponsoring the Ecological Urbanism conference in spring 2009 at the Harvard Graduate School of Design, which provided an opportunity, with the accompanying exhibition, to explore many of the ideas represented in this volume. We are grateful to Boston Mayor Thomas M. Menino for presenting opening remarks.

This ambitious publication would not have been possible without the financial support of John K. F. Irving, AB '83, MBA '89, and Anne C. Irving Oxley, MLA; we thank them for their great generosity and commitment to the advancement of new modes of thinking about complex issues.

The conference was held in collaboration with the Harvard University Office of the President, the Harvard Center for the Environment, and the Harvard Kennedy School of Government's Taubman Center for State and Local Government, and Rappaport Institute for Greater Boston. We appreciate this critical participation, with special thanks to Daniel Schrag, the Sturgis Hooper Professor of Geology and Professor of Earth and Planetary Sciences at Harvard University, and Director of the Harvard Center for the Environment; Edward Glaeser, the Fred and Eleanor Glimp Professor of Economics at Harvard University, Director of the Taubman Center, and Director of the Rappaport Institute; and David Luberoff, Executive Director of the Rappaport Institute. We also gratefully acknowledge Donald E. Ingber, Director of Harvard's Wyss Institute for Biologically Inspired Engineering, for cosponsoring the Wyss Prize for Bioinspired Adaptive Architecture at the GSD; this award allowed us to feature the work of Chuck Hoberman in the exhibition and publication. The Rouse Visiting Artist Fund at the GSD likewise sponsored Sissel Tolaas as the Rouse Visiting Artist, 2009.

In putting together this multifaceted volume, we were most fortunate to have Lars Müller, who over the past twenty-five years has established a worldwide reputation for producing serious and beautifully designed volumes on art and architecture, as our publisher and graphic designer. In addition to his inspiring collaboration, we benefited from the bookmaking expertise of Esther Butterworth, Milana Herendi, Ellen Mey, and Martina Mullis from his team in Baden, Switzerland.

At the GSD, we recognize Executive Dean Patricia Roberts and Associate Dean Hannah Peters, Melissa Vaughn and Amanda Heighes of the Publications Department, Dan Borelli and Shannon Stecher of the Exhibitions Department, Leslie Burke and Jane Acheson of the Dean's Office, and conference organizer Brooke Lynn King. Jared James May developed and managed the system for storing thousands of images from which the book's visual material would be drawn.

Students had a vital role to play in developing some of the themes that would be investigated in the conference, exhibition, and book. In particular, we thank the participants in the Fall 2008 cross-departmental seminar "Curating Ecological Urbanism": Abdulatif Almishari, Adi Assif, Peter Christensen, Elizabeth Christoforetti,

Suzanne Ernst, Anna Font, Melissa Guerrero,
Caitlin Swaim, and Aylin Brigitte Yildrim. Lindsay
Jonker, Dan Handel, Almin Prsic, Ryan Shubin,
and Quilian Riano deserve thanks for their help
with the conference, including the student blog,
excerpts of which are featured here. Shelby
Doyle provided key graphics assistance in the
development of the book.

During the conference, the following faculty,
fellows, and doctoral students led discussion
groups whose conversations informed the
content of this volume: Julia Africa, Rania Ghosn,
Brian Goldstein, Jock Herron, Li Hou, Har-Ye
Kan, Shelagh McCartney, Alexios Nicolaos Mono-
polis, Edward Morris, Masayoshi Oka, Antonio
Petrov, Ivan Rupnik, Fallon Samuels, Susannah
Sayler, Thomas Schroepfer, Zenovia Toloudi,
Heather Tremain, Dido Tsigaridi, Lin Wang, and
Christian Werthmann.

Finally, the many leading thinkers from the
worlds of science and art, academia and
practice, who contributed texts and images
to this book deserve our sincere thanks.
Their belief in the ability of varied perspectives
to contribute to a more powerful yet nuanced
understanding of the relationship of the urban
and the ecological animates this volume.

Index

Aachen, 374
Ábalos, Inaki, 610, 631, 642
Ábalos and Herreros, 28
Abu Dhabi, 70, 244, 400, 593, 595–596
adaptive design, 539–541, 560
Adaptive Fritting (Hoberman), 309, 327, 560–564
Africa, 40, 51, 61–62, 231, 257, 345, 412, 414, 420, 423, 503, 596, 606, 631, 644, 649
agriculture, urban, 9, 30, 107, 111–112, 118, 142–143, 175–176, 182, 256–257, 259, 262, *262,* 263, *264,* 266, 267, 247–276, 287, 292, *315,* 316, 318, 334, 337, *338–339,* 374, 445–446, 452, 455, 459, 483, 485, 487, 502–503, 520, 546, 554, *598,* 600, *603,* 635
Agronica, 118–1*20,* 632
air pollution, 283, 298–299, 367, 385, 464
airports, 204, 332, 344, 349
Alberta, 17–18, 340
allotment gardens, 19, 39, 260–261, 263–264
Almere, 568
Ambani, Mukesh, 18–19
Amidon, Jane, 537, *546*
Amsterdam, 262
Angola, 19, 423
animals, 113, 146, 166, 200, 235, 267, 285, 312, 317, 328, *425–426,* 445, 447, 502, 524–525, 630–631
Appadurai, Arjun, 133
architects, 12–13, 17, 28, 47, 68–69, 122, 127, 133, 137–139, 191, *238,* 254, 259, 261, 301–302, 309, 348, 361, *361,* 380, 444, 454–455, 468, 472, 499–500, 510, 521, 524–525, 547, 549, 561, 572, 584, 588, 594, 610–611, 614, 633, 635, 642–646
Archizoom, *116–*117, 120, *120*
arts, 30, 51, 58, 69, 130, 136–137, 184, 219, 224, 256, 276, 282, 284, *286,* 290, 299, 313, 330, 350, 364, 373, 420, 469–*471,* 479, 506, 528, 544, 560, 584, 594–595, 597, 612, *614,* 619
Arup, 208, 210, 600
Asia, 191, 257, 503, 530, 610
Asymptote, 400
automobiles, 104, 143, 224, 385–390, *386, 394,* 572

Baghdad, 18
Bahrain, 175–176, *176,* 177, 181–183
Baltic Coast, 238
Baltimore, 33, 135, 313, 348
Banham, Reyner, 33, 51, 349
Bank of America, 584
Barra Funda, *460, 462*–464
Bateson, Gregory, 44, 51, 546
batteries, 382, 384, 386–392, 395, 398, 401, 445, 455, *477–478*
Beach on the Moon, 512
BedZED, 277, *277,* 498, 499
Beijing, 222, *222,* 254, 283, 398, 530, 594, 595, 600
Bel-Air, 299
Belgium, 70, 403–404
Benjamin, Walter, 520
Berkeley, California, 51, 131, 183, 240, 349, 546, *633*
Berlin Biennale, *148*
Berlin, Brent, 147, 183
Bhabha, Homi, 115, 120, 637

bicycles, 100, 171, 173, *361,* 368, *383,* 383–385, 388, 392, 399, 579, 633
Bilbao, 616–617
biodiversity, 29, 32, 111, 115, 136, 212, 263, 317, 318, 329, *351,* 365, 367, 369, 413, 445, 447, 468, 498, 510, 524, 546, *598*
bioinspired adaptive architecture, 308–309, 564
biology, 228, 312
biotechnology, 224, 351
birds, 80, *231,* 235, *360,* 486, 498, 526
Birmingham, 184
Bloch, Maurice, 183
Boeri, Stefano, 398, 401, 444, *447, 448, 450, 452,* 452, 454, 630
Bordeaux, 263
Bosco Verticale, 449, *450*
Boston, *135, 169,* 297, 307, *396,* 398, 447, 475, 518–519, 527, 547, 572, 577
Branzi, Andrea, 30, 110, 112, *115,* 116, 118, *119,* 120, *120,* 632
Brazil, 67, 99, *262,* 502, 588
Bristol, 184
Broadacre City, 28, 406
Bronx, 300, 634
Browlow, Alec, 414
brownfields, *462*
Brundtland Report, 12
Buffalo, 259, 348, 573
Bunschoten, Raoul, 616, 622
Burnby, 400

Calatrava, Santiago, 560
Calgary, 18
California, 51, 69, 183, 240, 259, 306, 349, 420, 555, 633, 635
Calvino, Italo, 168
Cambridge, Massachusetts, 135, 164, 165, *165,* 183, 215, 316, 318, 329, 348–349, 405, 546–547
Campbell, Scott, 300, 301
Canada, 12, 18, *339, 347,* 540–541, 543, 547
canal, 219, *219–221,* 317
Canal City, 400
Canary Project, 456
carbon dioxide (CO_2), 66, 125, 173, 224, 276, 280, 398, 444, 454, 496, 498, 499, 522–523, 555, 557, 573, 580, 592, 619
carbon emissions, 140–141, 238, 306, 380, 385, 395, 428, 555, 557, 578, 580
carbon footprint, 140, 142, 190, 256, 270, 277, 307, 516–517
carbon neutrality, 209
carbon trading, 278, 622
Carter, Jimmy, 341
Casa Burguesa, *270,* 272–273, *273*
census, 135, *135,* 306, 335, 348, 503, 518, 519, 547
Chicago, 51, 83, 120, 134, *135,* 137, 183, 348, 412, 415, 467, 527, 546, 612
China, 68, 99, 208–209, 215, *222,* 222, 279, 283–*285,* 287, 288, 384, 419, 594, 600
Chongming Island, 484
Chu, Karl, 463, 467
Citicorp building, 612
CityCar, *386–387,* 388
CitySense, 164–165, *165*
Clément, Gilles, 447
Cleveland, 134–1*35*

climate change, 67, 106–109, 171, 208–209, 213–215, 218, 224, 245, 274, 302, 313, 317, 318, 356, 369, 406, 419, 454, 456, 496, 528, 554, 568, 578, 596, 597, 619, 622
CMA, 400
collaboration, 32, 51, 219, 267, 280, 296–297, 299, 325, *352,* 358, 361, 374, 380, 430, 463, 573
colonialism, 107
Columbia, *124–126,* 476, 547, *618,* 631
COMMONspace project, 350, *352*
computational design, 548–549, 552
computer science, 173, 228
cooling, 215, 388, 412, 474, 573, 574, 595–596, *599, 626*
CopenCycle, *171*
Copenhagen, 12, 171–1*72, 260–*261
Copenhagen Summit, 12
Corner, James, 120, 325, 329, 538, 547
Cuba, 263, 267

Daedalus, 528
Dakar Integrated Special Economic Zone, 606
Dalby, Simon, 212, 215
dams, 218
Darwin Martin House, 572
date palms, 176–177, 182
Davis, Mike, 420, 423–424
Deleuze, Gilles, 138
Delhi, 99, 201, 447
democracy, 48, 50, 65, 274, 339, 349, 380, 444
Denmark, 70, 261, 459, 597
deregulation, 341, 344–345, 349, 404
Design and the Elastic Mind, 299
Desvigne, Michel, 263, *264,* 267
Detroit, 39, *135,* 382, 546
Dharavi, *98–*102, 105, 516
Dissimiliarity Index, 135
Dongtan, 208–210, 466
Donostia-San Sebastián, 368–*369*
Downsview Park competition, 325
Dubai, 33, 283, 400, 420, 424
Dublin, 132
Duisberg Nord, 544
Dunster, Bill, 274, 278, 499
Dust Bowl, 339, *339*
Dyson, Freeman, 66, 224, 228

East Asia, 530
ECObox, 510, *510–511*
eco-city, 208, 209, 243, 280, *373,* 600
Ecojustice, 18
ecological infrastructure, 284, 285, *285,* 286
ecological resources, 212–213
ecological security, 208, 211, 212–215
ecologists, 312, 329, 356–358, 361, 414
ecology, 13, 17, 26, 29, 44, 48, 51, 57, 62, 78–79, 94, 102–104, 117, 137–139, 186, 191–192, 209–210, 225, 228, 231, 238, 263, 286, 290, 300–301, 312–313, 316–318, 324–325, 328–329, 344, *346,* 347, 349–351, 356, 366–368, 412–415, 421, 444, 470, 483, 499, 518, 524, 528–529, 536–537, 540, 542–547, 572–573, 577, 634–639
economic activity, 30, 213, 408
eco-region, 208, 483

ecosystem, 26, 51, 72, 212, 238, 268, 284, 286, 288, 312, 314–316, 325, 356–357, 361, 364, 383, 454, 458–459, 459, 461, 466, 498, 526–527, 547, 568, 606, 608, 631, 635, 638
education, 60, 106–107, 122, 135, 147, 288, 315, 359, 404, 417, 417, 475, 483, 506, 519, 522, 528, 542, 572, 575, 577, 577
Eisenman, Peter, 560, 631
electric automobile, 386, 388
electric scooter, 385
electricity, 66, 211, 245–246, 248–249, 249, 272, 275, 277, 306, 308, 337, 338, 340, 349, 365, 384, 388, 390–391, 394–395, 397, 417–419, 424, 444, 455, 464, 473–474, 474, 496, 498, 506, 526, 554–555, 561, 572–573, 602
Emscher Park, 485
energy conservation, 215, 472, 516
energy modeling, 472
engineering, 17, 61, 64, 66, 70, 71, 164, 168, 170, 173, 208, 210, 219, 228, 238, 270, 273–277, 286, 287, 296, 298, 308–309, 312, 325, 328, 328, 330, 335, 337, 345, 347, 348–349, 382, 415, 424, 455–456, 469, 541, 564, 638
EnLUDe project, 466
equity, 102, 136, 300–301, 498, 518–519
Erskine, Ralph, 499
Esposito, Roberto, 136–137
Essen, 591
ETH-Zurich, 430, 522
Euclidean zoning, 334, 348, 408
European Union, 364, 374, 402–403, 458
Evergreen Brick Works, 536, 542–544, 544, 546, 547

Fab Tree Hab (Joachim), 143
favelas, 40, 463, 466, 516, 588, 631
Feilden Clegg Bradley Studios, 499
Finnegans Wake (Joyce), 132
Flesh and Stone (Sennett), 132
floods, 286, 286, 332, 342, 568
Florence, 116, 397, 447
food, 166–167, 256–267
Forum on Religion and Ecology, 528
fossil fuels, 67, 107, 245, 454, 578
Foster and Partners, 70, 500, 593
Frampton, Kenneth, 461, 467
France, 44, 51, 66, 256, 349, 402–404, 419, 520
Fuller, Buckminster, 62–64, 70–71, 257, 636

garbage, 36, 147, 168, 290, 300, 335, 412, 414–415, 455
Geddes, Patrick, 39, 461, 467
Geertz, Clifford, 198, 200–201
General Electric, 210
Genius Loci (Norberg-Schulz), 590–591, 597
geothermal, 248, 265, 455, 573, 592, 595, 599, 622
Germany, 297, 304, 312, 374, 403, 484, 500, 544, 591
Girardet, Herbert, 208, 215, 496
global warming, 12, 65, 106, 215, 238, 454, 485, 524
Gore, Al, 12, 105, 596
governance, 30, 213, 215, 302–303, 341, 447, 461, 463, 524
Grand Paris, 266, 521
Great Depression, 337, 339
Great Flood, 333, 333

Great Lakes, 540
green design, 244, 544, 584
Green Grass of Home (Sigurdardóttir), 130
green roof, 69, 218, 254, 365, 498
greenhouse gases, 18, 212, 315, 382, 389, 572
Greenmetropolis, 374, 375, 377
GreenWheel, 383, 383, 384–385, 388, 392–393
Greenwich Millennium Village, 499
Grootens, Joost, 618, 622
Grow Your Own, 19
Guardian, 17, 51, 67, 69
Guattari, Félix, 22, 26, 29, 50–51, 79–80, 83, 95, 104, 138–139, 529
Guillerme, André, 520–521, 521
Gulf, 12, 40, 42, 174–175, 183, 333, 420, 422, 593, 631
Gund Hall, 472–475, 473

Hagia Sophia, 617, 617
Harvard Graduate School of Design, 109, 120, 146, 183, 352, 472–473, 475, 504, 523, 529, 560, 564, 608, 630
Harvard School of Public Health, 518
Helsinki, 238
High Line, 26
Hilberseimer, Ludwig, 118, 118, 120
Hilbert, David, 174, 183
Hoberman Associates, 560
Hoberman, Chuck, 297, 309, 327, 563–564
Hong Kong, 477, 477, 479, 481
Houston, 125, 127, 134, 135, 306–307, 420
Hurricane Katrina, 39, 344
HVAC systems, 248, 250

Il territorio che cambia (Boeri), 398, 401
Imperial College London, 416
In Vitro Meat Habitat (Joachim), 226
incarceration, 403, 405
India, 18–19, 68, 80–83, 99, 100, 111, 194, 197, 198, 200–201, 283, 350, 419, 502, 596
inequality, 106, 108–109, 135, 415, 423, 518–519
Infinite in All Directions (Dyson), 228
Intergovernmental Panel on Climate Change, 456, 568
Invisible Cities (Calvino), 168
Ireland, 555, 646
Islamabad, 412
Israel, 181, 230–231, 234–235
Italy, 256, 398, 403–404, 445, 450

jet packs, 225
jobs, 142, 213, 296, 300, 402, 404, 410, 412, 500, 546, 557, 579
Johnson, Mark, 133

Kahn, Matthew, 306–307
Kalundborg, 459
Kay, Paul, 174, 183
Kayden, Jerold, 350, 351, 568
Khuri, Fuad, 176, 183
Klein, Naomi, 17–18
Klinenberg, Eric, 412, 415
Koolhaas, Rem, 56, 120, 406, 411, 630–631, 634–636
Korea, 370, 530–531
KPF, 400
Krieger, Alex, 255, 228, 407, 516
Kyoto Protocol, 12, 622

La Tour Vivante, 292
Lagos, 39, 61, 215, 631, 634
Lake Ontario, 325, 540–541, 541
Lakoff, George, 133
Lalvani, Haresh, 462, 467
landscape architecture, 29, 130, 190–191, 259, 262, 266, 329, 351, 524, 537, 545–547, 638
landscape urbanism, 62, 114, 119, 324, 406–407, 410–411, 461, 525, 537, 541–542, 546–547, 639
landscraping, 538
Latin America, 257
Latour, Bruno, 124, 138, 422
Latz + Partner, 544, 546
Le Laboratoire, 299
Le Roy, Charles-Georges, 136–137
learning, 146, 296–297, 316, 342, 430, 519, 524, 539–540, 540, 543–544, 544, 547, 631
LEED, 13, 122, 135, 406, 500, 584, 631
Lefebvre, Henri, 23, 26, 51, 138–139
light, 23, 51, 118–119, 190, 237, 246–247, 261, 272, 273, 304, 309, 349, 382, 417, 417, 475, 479–480, 516, 520, 525–527, 561, 564, 595–596, 599, 617
light electric vehicles, 382
Lima, 456, 575
Limburg, 374
Lister, Nina-Marie, 325–326, 329, 536, 546–547, 635
literature, 102, 106, 136, 302, 530–531
Liverpool, 19, 39
Livingstone, Ken, 497
Local River, 268
locavores, 168, 268
Logroño, 280, 645
London Congestion Charging Scheme, 497
London Development Agency, 496
London Plan, 476, 480, 496–497
London School of Economics, 83, 483
London Thames Gateway Heat Network, 496
Loos, Adolf, 259
Los Angeles, 33, 51, 134, 135, 186, 306, 631
Los Angeles: The Architecture of Four Ecologies (Banham), 33, 51, 631
Louisiana Manifesto (Nouvel), 590
Louvre Abu Dhabi, 595–596
Lower Don Lands, 328, 536, 540–542, 546
Luanda, 420, 423–424
Luke, Tim, 211

Mackaye, Benton, 340
Madrid, 317, 372, 445, 447, 512, 614
Mahim Creek, 197, 201–202
Mali, 107
Manama, 177, 180–182
Manhattan, 28, 132, 259, 407, 410, 516, 558, 584, 631
Mapping Main Street, 186
maps, 142, 194, 196–198, 201, 318, 322, 497, 503, 622
marginality, 402, 404–405
Masdar, 70, 209–210, 244, 399–401, 399, 466, 500, 593–594
Mazzolini, Donatella, 133
McHarg, Ian, 62, 324, 329, 629, 634
megacities, 133, 139
Melbourne, 215, 313

metaphor, 132–133, 143, 458, 536, 544
metrics, 190, 337, 408, 410–411, 458–459, 461–464, 573, 575
metropolis, 114, 117, 120, 132–133, 215, 228, 337, 374–377, 420, 482, 485–486, 545, 588, 629
Mexico, 304, 333, 347, 415, 422
Mexico City, 84–85, 151, 153, *154*
microelectromechanical systems (MEMS), 169
microgeneration, 275, 279
Middle East, 70, 183, 337, 345, 419, 595
Midwest (U.S.), 134–135, 142, 186, 312, 335, 337, 339, 502, 632
Migge, Leberecht, 259, 261, 267
Milan 2015 Expo, 446
military, 63, 230–231, *232*, 334–335, 337, 341, 348–349, 423–424, *427*
Milwaukee, 267, 412, 414–415, 560
MIT Energy Initiative, 272–273
MIT Media Laboratory, 384
Mithi River, 192, *197*, 201
mobility, 33, 47, 104–105, 117, 143, 171, 214–215, 228, 238, 273, 339, 348–349, 364–369, 380–389, 392, 395, 397–399, 418, 510, 633
mobility-on-demand, 382, 392–397
monsoon, 194, 196–207
Morgan, Arthur, 340
Mostafavi, Mohsen, 12, 79–80, 114, 547, 634
Mouffe, Chantal, 48, 51
multinational corporations, 191
Mumbai, 18–19, 78, 80–85, *95*, 99–101, 190–198
Munich, 219, 329, 447
Museum of Modern Art, New York, 299
music, 82, 95, 184, 351, 632
MVRDV, 280, 612, *612*

Naess, Arne, 529
Nairobi, 430
NASA, 67, 125, *154*, 247, 298–299, 348
Nasalo (Tolaas), *154*
National Science Foundation, 164
Netherlands, *47*, 374, 403, 568, *612*
New Athens Charter, 110, 119
New Deal, 337–339, 349
New Orleans, 30, 39, 333, 568
New Urbanism, 48, 225, 406–407, 411, 537
New Waterscapes (Singapore), 218–219
New York City, 26, 32, 36, 134, 186, 300, 302–303, 330, 348, 350–351, *357–358, 361,* 554, *558,* 577, 584, 634–635, 643–646
Niger Delta, 425, *426–427*
Nigeria, 423, *427*
NIMBY, 300, 408
noise, 164, 190, 318, 367, 385, 464, 526, 530–531, 532
Norberg-Schulz, Christian, 590, 597
North East Coastal Park, 28
Norway, 70, 555
No-Stop City, *116–117*, 117–118, 120, 632
Nouvel, Jean, *264*, 266, 590, 595–597
NYC Green Initiative, 169

Obama administration, 300
Obama, Michelle, *257*
Oklahoma City, 306
Old Urbanism, 406–407, 410–411

Olmsted, Frederick Law, *336*, 348
OMA, 28–29, 51, 72, 546
One Gallions, 499
One Planet Living, 12, 498–499
Oush Grab, 231, *232, 234*

Pakistan, 412, 415
Palestine, *231*, 235
Parc de La Villette, 28, 51
Paris, 26, 44, 47, 51, 59, 124, 139, 259, 263, *264*, 266–267, 299, 392, 419, 510, 520–521, 612, *614*, 633
Park(ing) project, 28, 286, *286*
Payne, Andrew, 136–137
peak oil, 274–275, 278, 406
Pembina Institute, 18
Persian Gulf, 72, 174, 183, 420, 593
personal rapid transit, 401
Peru, 456, 575
Phoenix, 134, 135, 313
photovoltaics, 69, 245–246, 248, 270, 272, 276–277, 280, 292, 309, 445, 464, *471*, 501, 599
Pig City, 612, *612*
Planet of the Slums (Davis), 423–424
plants, 66–67, 136, 142, 218, 268, 276, 288, 298–299, 309, 312, 314, 316, 326, 332, 341, 344, 347, *359*, 391, 397, 419–420, 445, 449, 454–455, 484, 524, 554, 596, 630
PlaNYC, 554–555, *555*, 557
Play Me, I'm Yours (Jerram), 184
poetry, 177, 527
political ecology, 412–415, 546
Pollan, Michael, 256
population growth, 39, 555
Porto, 270, 272–273, *273*
Portugal, 270, 272–273
Portzamparc, Christian de, 521
Potager du roi, 256, 257, 267
poverty, 61, 108–109, 116, 402, 404–405, 423, 426, 519
Prague, 226, 400
Promenade Plantée, 26
public health, 29, 51, 142, 164, 312, 335, 518–519, 634
public space, 28, 39, 51, 79, 288, 301, 302, 349, 351, 356, 359, 361–362, 364–369, 414–415, 447, 512, *582,* 588, 611–612, 614
public transportation, 306, 522, 554–555

Qiaoyuan Park, 288, *290*
Qinhuangdao City, 290

R/E/D, 463, 466
racial segregation, 135
rainwater, 139, 218, 292, 365, 367, 456, 464, *471,* 598–599
Rancière, Jacques, 49, 50, 51
Reagan, Ronald, 341, 349
real estate, 140, 382, 393, 406, 424, 450, 452, 475, 541
recycling, 28, 36, 99, 169, 209, 218, 266, 288, 300, 365, 367, 411, 483, 497–498, 516, 584, *626*
Renaissance, 57, 267, 480, 520
Renaudie, Jean, 44, 47
reservoirs, 72, *197,* 218–219, *237,* 287, 317, *318, 326, 357,* 421–422, 498, 588, *589*
retrofits, 140

Rifkin, Jeremy, 444–445, 454
rivers, 64, 94, 132, 186, *192, 194, 196,* 197, *197,* 201, 218–219, *221,* 268, *286, 287,* 290, 304, 313, 316–317, *318, 325, 328,* 333, *333–334,* 340, *341, 344, 347,* 361, 369, 375, *426, 460,* 461, *463–464, 465,* 469, 482, 520, 536, 540–542, *541, 542,* 568, 598
RoboScooters, 386, 388, 392
Rogers, Richard, 480, 500, 521
Rome, 33, 51, 65, 67, 95, 445, 449
Rongzhi, Wang, 530, 532
Roosevelt, Franklin, 337, *338,* 349
Ruegg, Margrit, 19
Russia, 107

Sahara, 59, 109
San Diego, 134, *135,* 306
San Francisco, 33, 69, 131, 268, 306–307, 350, *351–352,* 554, 644–645, 647
São Paulo, 184, *184,* 236, *262, 460, 462,* 463, 467, 588
Sarkozy, Nicolas, 47, 266
Saudi Arabia, 18, 175
Schmitt, Gerhard, 522
Science City, 522
sea, 70, 72, 73, 82,106, 175, *180,* 183, 194, 196–198, *196–198,* 200–201, *204,* 230, 309, 326, 375, 421–424, 483, 486, 590, 593, 596
Seattle, *169,* 313, 518–519
self-sufficiency, 238
Senegal, 606, 643
Sennett, Richard, 132
Senseable City Lab, *168,* 171, *171,* 173, 639
sensors, 164–165, 170–171, 384, *552,* 573
Seoul, 69, 370, 530
Shanghai, 209, *282,* 283, 484, 530
Shenyang Architectural University, 287, *288*
Shenzhen, 530
Shenzhen Logistic City, *123*
Siberia, 64, 107
Sigurdardóttir, Katrin, 130–131
Silent Spring (Carson), 313
Simone AbdouMaliq, 40, 51
Sinan, 617
Singapore, 36, 69, 174, 218–219
skyscrapers, 449, 556, 610, 614
Slave City, 639
Sloterdijk, Peter, 597
slums, 47, 81, 83, 423–424, 466
Smart Cities Group, 384–385
smart electric grids, 382, 390
smell, 39, 146–147, *147,* 150–151, 153, *153–154,* 349, 637
social justice, 51, 107, 115, 300–301, 380, 415, 519, 528, 577, 634
Soft Cities, 270, *270,* 272–273
Sola de Morales Rubio, Ignasi, 546
solar energy, 62, 249
solarCity Linz, 500
Sørensen, C.Th., *260,* 261
Southeast Asia, 503, 610
Spain, 364, 368, 372, *373,* 403–404, 500, 610
St. Louis, 134, *135*
Stern, Lord Nick, 483
Steven Holl Architects, 594
storm water, 218, *221,* 254, 263, 282, 286–287, *287,* 290, 357, *362,* 407
Stoss Landscape Urbanism, 541, 547

Strawberry Creek, 240
Stubbins, Hugh, 612
subways, 147, 361, *361*, 428, 612, 637
sustainable design, 13, 122, 500, 539
Swyngedouw, Eric, 413, 415
Sydney, 36, 184, 475
SynCity model, 417, 419
Syracuse, 299, 573, *575*
Syracuse Center of Excellence in Energy and
Environmental Systems, 573

Taiwan Strait Climate Change Incubator, 622
Talking Nose_Mexico City (Tolaas), 151, *153*
Tanghe River Park, 290
tax credits, 140
Tennessee Valley Authority, 340, 348
Thames Estuary, 482
Thames Gateway, 209–210, *484*, *486*, 496
Thatcher, Margaret, 341, 349
The Three Ecologies (Guattari), 22, 51, 79, 83,
138–139
The Social Life of Trees (Bloch), 183
"The Urban Place and the Non-Place Urban
Realm" (Webber), 381
Thoreau, Henry David, 306–307
Toronto, 28, 325, *328*, 329, 348, 536, 540–542,
540–542, 545–547, *546–547*
Transport for a Sustainable Future (Whitelegg),
401
Trash|Track project, 169, *169*, 173
Tschumi, Bernard, 29
Tunis, 398, *398*

U.S. Army Corps of Engineers, 333, 335, 348
zoning, 72, 201, 316, 334–335, *335*, 348, 358,
408, 417
U.S. Green Building Council, 584
United Arab Emirates, 593, 595
United Kingdom, 17, 209, 276–277, 419, 476,
483, 485
United Nations, 171, 416, 568
United States, 32, 63, 67–68, 95, 105, 132,
134–136, 200, 212, 214, 218, 227, 256–257,
267–268, 283, 301, 306–307, 332–335, 337,
345, *347–349*, 380, 382, 403, 405–407, 411,
412, 414–415, 420, 424, 472, 474, 502–503,
517, 519, 523, 526, 528, 540, 545, 557, 572,
584, 596, 610, 632, 635
urban agriculture, 142, 256–257, 259,
262–263, 266–267, *315*, 316, 445–446, 459,
520, 635
urban density, 134, 335, 476–477, 480, 516
urban design, 29, 116, 132, 153, 208, 224, 225,
228, 286, 313, 329, 361, 408, 417, 458, 463,
466–467, 480, 500–501, *503*
urban heat island effect, 638
urban infrastructure, 214, 341, 348, 351, 362,
423, 520
urban migration, 51, 348, 423
urban planning, 26, 40, 47, 118, 130, 133, 183,
285, 301, 316, *318*, 337, 347, 349, 364–366,
365, 369, 406, 480, 483, 522, 545, 619
urban regions, 142, 312–313, *314*, 315–318,
322, 345, 347
Urban Revolution (Lefebvre), 138–139
urban scale, 164–165, 192, 213, 273, 406, 458,
459, 463, 500–501, 622, 635

Van Eesteren, Cornelis, 262
Van Eyck, Aldo, 262
Vancouver, 447, 547
Vauban, 500
Vegetal City, 608
Venice, 120, 454, 520
Vico, Giambattista, 137
Virilio, Paul, 138
Vitoria-Gasteiz, 367–368

Wagner, Martin, 259
Waldheim, Charles, 114, 538, 546–547, 632
walking 32, 84, 85, 166, 181, 317, 393, 407, 497
Wall-E, 168, 227
Wanzhuang, 600
Waring, George E., 335, *336*, 348
Waste Isolation Pilot Plant, 304
Waters, Alice, 256
wave power, 252, 369
wealth, 33, 94, 105, 108, 135, 177, 301, 406,
417, 420, 423, 426, 637
Webber, Melvin, 381
Weese, Harry, 612
White House, 256, *257*, 263, 349
Whitelegg, John, 398, 401
Whitman, Walt, 132
Whole Earth Catalog, 257, 267
wind energy, 70, 444, 506, 598
without Borders – NOSOEAWE (Tolaas), 148
World Health Organization, 518
World War II, 134, 138, 304, 337, 339, 350, 502,
530
Wright, Frank Lloyd, 28, 572–573, *572*
Wyss Institute for Biologically Inspired Engi-
neering, 309, 564
Wyss Prize for Bioinspired Adaptive Architec-
ture, 309, 564

Yasutaka, Tsutsui, 531, 533
Yew, Lee Kuan, 218
Yongning Park, 286
You Must Change Your Life (Sloterdijk), 597
Yunus, Muhammad, 110

zero-carbon, 70, 276, 278, *279*, 496–497
Zhongshan Shipyard Park, 288, *288*
Žižek, Slavoj, 50, 51
Zollverein School, 591–592
zoning, 26, 201, 316, 334, 335, *335*, 345, 348,
358, 408, 417

Illustration Credits

10–11, Susannah Sayler, The Canary Project
14–15, The Pembina Institute
20–21, Agnes Denes
24–25, Patrick Blanc
27, Atelier Parisien d'Urbanisme – Apur
31, Andrea Branzi, et al.
34–35, Magnum Photographer: Ferdinando Scianna
37, Image by Ciro Fusco/epa/Corbis
38, REUTERS/Lucas Jackson (United States)
41, Ed Kashi
42, 43, Charlie Koolhaas
45, Gabriele Basilico
52–53, Olafur Eliasson, The New York City Waterfalls (Brooklyn Piers), 2008, Commissioned by Public Art Fund, © Olafur Eliasson, 2008. Photo: © Bernstein Associates, Photographers, courtesy of Public Art Fund
56–77, images by OMA except the following:
57 (second from top), http://en.wikipedia.org/wiki/File:Vitruvius.jpg (from *Vitruvius on Architecture* by Thomas Gordon Smith)
57 (middle), http://www.finebooksmagazine.com/issue/0602/graphics/topten/10-vitruvius.jpg
58 (second from top), from Johann Wolfgang von Goethe, 1749-1832: Goethe's Color Theory. Arranged and edited by Rupprecht Matthaei. New York: Van Nostrand Reinhold, 1971
58 (middle), 59 (top) and 59 (middle), Bildarchiv Preussischer Kulturbesitz/Art Resource, NY
59 (bottom), 60, and 61, from E. Maxwell Fry and Jane Drew, *Tropical Architecture in the Humid Zone* (London: Batsford, 1956)
63 (top), The Estate of R. Buckminster Fuller and Lars Müller Publishers
63 (bottom), The Estate of R. Buckminster Fuller
66 (top), http://www.worldmapper.org/
66 (bottom), US Department of Energy, Lawrence Livermore National Laboratory
71 (bottom), The Estate of R. Buckminster Fuller
72, http://www.zeekracht.nl/
85–93, Urban Earth
96–103, all photos by Noorie Sadarangani
115–121, all images by Andrea Branzi, et al., and Archizoom Associati, except:
117 (top two images), P. V. Aureli
118 (left), Reprinted from Ludwig Hilberseimer, The New City (Chicago: Paul Theobald, 1944) p. 121, ill. 92, Ludwig Hilberseimer Papers, Ryerson & Burnham Library Archives, The Art Institute of Chicago
118 (right), Reprinted from Ludwig Hilberseimer, The New City (Chicago: Paul Theobald, 1944) p. 55, ill. 33, Ludwig Hilberseimer Papers, Ryerson & Burnham Library Archives, The Art Institute of Chicago
122–123, JDS Architects
124, 125, 126, NASA
130–131, Katrín Sigurdardóttir
141, The Boston Globe. Illustration by Shelby Murphy first appeared in an article by Michael Fitzgerald, "Urban retrofits: How to make a city green–without tearing it down" June 28, 2009
143, Arup
148–149, Sissel Tolaas

152 (top four), Justin Knight
152 (bottom), Mary Kocol
154–155, Sissel Tolaas
156–163, Urban Earth
165, Josh Bers, BBN (both images)
166–167, Proef, Marije Vogelzang
168–173, SENSEable City Laboratory
175, Miracle Publishing
176, from Historic Maps of Bahrain 1817–1970, Archive Editions Ltd.
178–179, Gareth Doherty
180, 181, Ministry of Municipalities and Agriculture Affairs, Manama
184, 185, Luke Jerram and on page 185 (top, middle) Caio Buni
186, 187, Jesse Shapins, Kara Oehler and Ann Moss
190–193, Leena Sangyun Cho, and on page 193 (bottom) Niall Kirkwood
194–207, all images by Anuradha Mathur and Dilip da Cunha, except, 196, William A. Tate, Plan of the Islands of Bombay and Salsette, detail, by permission of the British Library
209, *The New Scientist*
210, 211, Arup
213, Vincent Callebaut Architectures
214, GSA Today
216–217, City Limits London
219, 220, 221, Atelier Dreiseitl
222, 223, Zhang Huan
224, Michael Hickman
225, Mitchell Joachim
226, 227, Mitchell Joachim, Eric Tan, Oliver Medvedik, Maria Aiolova
228, 229, Mitchell Joachim, Lara Greden, Javier Arbona
231–235, Sara Pellegrini
236, 237, Triptique
238, 239, MVVA
240, 241, Hood Design
245, Michelle Addington
246, 247, NASA/Goddard Space Flight Center, Scientific Visualization Studio
249, US Department of Energy, Lawrence Livermore National Laboratory
250, University Operations Service, Harvard University
252–253, Pelamis Wave Power Ltd.
254–255, Vector Architects
257 (left), The White House/Joyce N. Boghosian
257 (right), Dorothée Imbert
258-259, The Sunday Times
260 (top), C.Th. Sørensen collection, Royal Danish Academy of Fine Arts
260 (bottom), Dorothée Imbert
261, from *Jedermann Selbstversorger* (1918) by Leberecht Migge
262 (top), Christian Werthmann
262 (bottom), Dorothée Imbert
263, Lukas Schweingruber
264, 265, Michel Desvigne
266, Dorothée Imbert and Scheri Fultineer with Megumi Aihara, Tzufen Liao, and Takuma Ono
267, Tzufen Liao
268, 269, Mathieu Lehanneur
271, Photo credit, Hans Georg Roth
272, 273, Photo credit, KVA MATx

275, from a presentation by Colin Campbell to the House of Commons, London
277–279, ZEDfactory
280–281, © MVRDV
282, both images from Baidu.com
283 (left), Baidu.com, (middle) Painting by Ou Yang, (right) Kongjian Yu
284 (top right), Photos: a and c from Xinhua.net, b and d by Kongjian Yu
272 (bottom), Painting by Li Yansheng
285 (top and bottom), Kongjian Yu and Peking University Graduate School of Landscape Architecture
286–291, all images by Kongjian Yu/Turenscape
292–293, soa architectes
297, image courtesy of Hoberman Associates, New York
299, Mathieu Lehanneur, David Edwards
305 (left), concept Michael Brill, illustration Safdar Abidi; (right) concept and illustration by Michael Brill. From: K. M. Trauth et al., "Expert Judgment on Markers to Deter Inadvertent Human Intrusion into the Waste Isolation Pilot Plant," SAND92-1382 UC-721, November 1993)
308, Donald E. Ingber
314, 315, Richard T. T. Forman
319–321, maps reproduced by permission of Cambridge University Press and Richard T. T. Forman. Illustrations by Taco Iwashima Matthews
322–323, Adi Assif
325–329, Stoss Landscape Urbanism
330–331, Christoph Niemann
333, National Weather Service – National Oceanic & Atmospheric Administration
334, Coast and Geodetic Survey, RG 23 – National Archives and Records Administration
335, © 2009 Open Systems
336 (top), National Park Service, Frederick Law Olmsted National Historic Site
336 (bottom), University of Washington Library, George E. Waring Jr. Papers
338 (top), Bureau of Public Roads, Historical Division, courtesy of Federal Highway Administration, Office of Infrastructure
338 (middle), Library of Congress – National Archives, 1937
338 (bottom), U.S. DOT – Federal Highway Administration – Office of Infrastructure
339 (top), Forest History Society, courtesy of Alvin J. Huss Archives
339 (bottom), National Weather Service – National Oceanic & Atmospheric Administration, George E. Marsh Album Collection
340, United States Farm Security Administration – Office of War Information (Overseas Picture Division, Washington Division) courtesy of the Library of Congress
341, Minnesota Department of Transport, courtesy of Homeland Security Digital Library, 2007
342–343, © 2009 Open Systems
343, Tennessee Valley Authority, 2008
345, © 2009 Open Systems
346 (top), *Ecological & General Systems Theory*, 1971

Ecological Urbanism

Edited by Mohsen Mostafavi, with Gareth Doherty
Harvard University, Graduate School of Design

Design: Integral Lars Müller, Lars Müller and Martina Mullis
Production: Amelie Solbrig
Lithography: connova GmbH, Appenweier, Germany
Printing and binding: E&B Engelhardt und Bauer, Karlsruhe, Germany

© Mixed Sources
Product group from well-managed
forests, controlled sources and
recycled wood or fiber
www.fsc.org Cert no. SGS-COC-003186
© 1996 Forest Stewardship Council
FSC

Print compensated
Ident-No. 103460

Lars Müller Publishers
Baden, Switzerland
www.lars-mueller-publishers.com

ISBN 978-3-03778-189-0

Printed in Germany

9 8 7 6 5 4 3 2 1

Related titles in our program:

R. Buckminster Fuller
Operating Manual for Spaceship Earth
Reprint, edited by Jaime Snyder
Lars Müller Publishers, 2008, 2010
ISBN 978-3-03778-126-5 English
ISBN 978-3-03778-188-3 French

Petra Kempf
**You Are the City: Observation, Organization
and Transformation of Urban Settings**
Lars Müller Publishers, 2009
ISBN 978-3-03778-159-3 English

**Sense of the City
An Alternate Approach to Urbanism**
Edited by Mirko Zardini and the Canadian
Centre for Architecture CCA
Lars Müller Publishers, 2005
ISBN 978-3-03778-060-2 English
ISBN 978-3-03778-061-9 French